The Cambridge Handb

The Cambridge Handbook of Creativity is a comprehe⌐ ⌐…andbook on creativity from the most respected psychologists, researchers, an⌐ ⌐ducators. This handbook serves as a thorough introduction to the field of creativity and as an invaluable reference and current source of important information. It covers such diverse topics as the brain, education, business, and world cultures. The first section, "Basic Concepts," is designed to introduce readers to the history of and key concepts in the field of creativity. The next section, "Diverse Perspectives on Creativity," contains chapters on the many ways to approach creativity. Several of these approaches, such as the functional, evolutionary, and neuroscientific approaches, have been invented or greatly reconceptualized in the last decade. The third section, "Contemporary Debates," highlights ongoing topics that still inspire discussion. Finally, the editors summarize and discuss important concepts from the book and look at what lies ahead.

James C. Kaufman, PhD, is an Associate Professor of Psychology at the California State University at San Bernardino, where he directs the Learning Research Institute. Dr. Kaufman's research focuses on the nurturance, structure, and assessment of creativity. He is the author or editor of more than 150 publications, including seventeen books either published or in press. These books include *Creativity 101* (2009), *Essentials of Creativity Assessment* (with Jonathan Plucker and John Baer, 2008), and *The International Handbook of Creativity* (with Robert J. Sternberg, 2006). His research has been featured on CNN, NPR, and the BBC and in the *New York Times*, *Los Angeles Times*, and *New Yorker*. Kaufman is a founding coeditor of the official journal for the American Psychological Association's Division 10, *Psychology of Aesthetics, Creativity, and the Arts*. He also is the associate editor of *Psychological Assessment* and *Journal of Creative Behavior*, the editor of *International Journal of Creativity and Problem Solving*, and the series editor of the Psych 101 series. He received the 2003 Daniel E. Berlyne Award from APA's Division 10, the 2008 E. Paul Torrance Award from the National Association for Gifted Children, and the 2009 Early Career Research Award from the Western Psychological Association.

Robert J. Sternberg, PhD, is Provost and Senior Vice President of Oklahoma State University. Until 2010, he was Dean of the School of Arts and Sciences and Professor of Psychology and Education at Tufts University. He is also Honorary Professor of Psychology at the University of Heidelberg. He was previously IBM Professor of Psychology and Education in the Department of Psychology; Professor of Management in the School of Management; and Director of the Center for the Psychology of Abilities, Competencies, and Expertise at Yale. His PhD is from Stanford, and he holds 11 honorary doctorates. Sternberg was the 2003 President of the American Psychological Association and is the past President of the Eastern Psychological Association. He is currently President of the International Association for Cognitive Education and Psychology and President-Elect of the Federation of Associations of Behavioral and Brain Sciences. The central focus of his research is on intelligence, creativity, and wisdom, and he also has studied love and close relationships as well as hate. He is the author of approximately 1,200 journal articles, book chapters, and books, and he has received more than $20 million in government and other grants and contracts for his research, conducted on five different continents. He has won more than two dozen awards for his research. Sternberg has been listed in the *APA Monitor on Psychology* as one of the top 100 psychologists of the twentieth century and is listed by the ISI as one of its most highly cited authors in psychology and psychiatry.

The Cambridge Handbook of Creativity

Edited by

JAMES C. KAUFMAN

California State University, San Bernardino

ROBERT J. STERNBERG

Oklahoma State University

CAMBRIDGE
UNIVERSITY PRESS

CAMBRIDGE UNIVERSITY PRESS
Cambridge, New York, Melbourne, Madrid, Cape Town, Singapore,
São Paulo, Delhi, Dubai, Tokyo, Mexico City

Cambridge University Press
32 Avenue of the Americas, New York, NY 10013-2473, USA

www.cambridge.org
Information on this title: www.cambridge.org/9780521730259

First published 2010

Printed in the United States of America

A catalog record for this publication is available from the British Library.

Library of Congress Cataloging in Publication data

The Cambridge handbook of creativity / edited by James C. Kaufman, Robert J. Sternberg.
  p.   cm. – (Cambridge handbooks in psychology)
Includes bibliographical references and index.
ISBN 978-0-521-51366-1 – ISBN 978-0-521-73025-9 (pbk.)
1. Creative ability.   I. Kaufman, James C.   II. Sternberg, Robert J.   III. Title.   IV. Series.
BF408.173   2010
153.3'5 – dc22   2010000993

ISBN 978-0-521-51366-1 Hardback
ISBN 978-0-521-73025-9 Paperback

We would like to dedicate this book to the memory of Colin Martindale – a brilliant and prescient scholar, supportive mentor, and valued friend.

Contents

List of Tables and Figures

Tables

Figures

Contributors

ROBERT S. ALBERT
Pitzer College

JOHN BAER
Rider University

RONALD A. BEGHETTO
University of Oregon

ADAM S. BRISTOL
Aquilo Partners, San Francisco

JOHN F. CABRA
Buffalo State University of New York

BONNIE CRAMOND
University of Georgia

ARTHUR CROPLEY
University of Hamburg

DAVID CROPLEY
University of South Australia

GREGORY J. FEIST
San Jose State University

JULIE A. FIORELLI
Case Western Reserve University

LIANE GABORA
University of British Columbia

ELENA L. GRIGORENKO
Yale University and Moscow State
University, Russia

KYUNG HEE KIM
The College of William and Mary

BETH A. HENNESSEY
Wellesley College

ALLISON B. KAUFMAN
University of California, Riverside

JAMES C. KAUFMAN
California State University, San Bernardino

SCOTT BARRY KAUFMAN
Yale University

YULIYA KOLOMYTS
University of Alabama

SERGEY A. KORNILOV
Moscow State University, Russia

AARON KOZBELT
Brooklyn College

PAUL J. LOCHER
Montclair State University

TODD LUBART
Université Paris Descartes

MATTHEW C. MAKEL
Duke University

SEANA MORAN
Stanford University

JONATHAN A. PLUCKER
Indiana University

GERARD J. PUCCIO
Buffalo State University of New York

RUTH RICHARDS
Saybrook Graduate School, McLean
Hospital, and Harvard Medical School

MARK A. RUNCO
University of Georgia

SANDRA W. RUSS
Case Western Reserve University

R. KEITH SAWYER
Washington University

PAUL J. SILVIA
University of North Carolina at
Greensboro

DEAN KEITH SIMONTON
University of California, Davis

JEFFREY K. SMITH
University of Otago, New Zealand

LISA F. SMITH
University of Otago, New Zealand

ROBERT J. STERNBERG
Oklahoma State University

MEI TAN
Yale University

JOYCE VANTASSEL-BASKA
The College of William and Mary

THOMAS B. WARD
University of Alabama

Preface

With the world changing more rapidly than ever before, creativity is at a historical premium. As many investors have discovered, yesterday's investment strategies do not necessarily work anymore. As many politicians and citizens alike have discovered, yesterday's ideas about ethical behavior and propriety do not necessarily apply today. As many CEOs have discovered, the competition today is quite different from at any time in history. Printed newspapers, for example, have to compete not only with each other, but with their own online versions. We live in a society where those who do not creatively innovate risk failure in any of several domains of life.

Just what is creativity? It can refer to a person, process, place, or product. It can be found in geniuses and in small children. It has been studied by psychologists, educators, neuroscientists, historians, sociologists, economists, engineers, and scholars of all types. Legendary thinkers throughout time, from Aristotle to Einstein, have pondered what it means to be creative. There are still debates, after more than six decades of

intensive research, on how to measure, utilize, and improve it.

The first step to understanding creativity is to define it. Most definitions of creative ideas comprise three components (Kaufman & Sternberg, 2007). First, creative ideas must represent something different, new, or innovative. Second, creative ideas are of high quality. Third, creative ideas must also be appropriate to the task at hand or some redefinition of that task. Thus, a creative response is novel, good, and relevant.

It has been more than a decade since Robert J. Sternberg, one of the editors of this volume, edited Cambridge's last *Handbook of Creativity*. Since it was published in 1999, there have been more than 10,000 published papers concerning creativity, along with hundreds of books. More than ever, there is a flourishing community of scholars focusing on creativity. The American Psychological Association's Division 10, the Society for the Psychology of Aesthetics, Creativity, and the Arts, now sponsors an official APA journal on this topic (*Psychology of Aesthetics, Creativity, and the Arts*).

Established journals such as the *Creativity Research Journal, Journal of Creative Behavior, Empirical Studies of the Arts*, and *Imagination, Creativity, and Personality* continue to publish exciting new papers. New journals have emerged (e.g., *Thinking Skills and Creativity, International Journal of Creativity and Problem Solving*). Other journals feature work on creativity in different areas, such as gifted education (*Roeper Review* and *Gifted Child Quarterly*) and business (*Innovation and Creativity Management, Leadership Quarterly*). Several major written and edited works by leading scholars have appeared in the last decade. A few examples of such works include Dorfman, Locher, and Martindale (2006); Piirto (2004); Puccio, Murdock, and Mance (2006); Runco (2007), Sawyer (2006), Simonton (2004); and Weisberg (2006). Kaufman (2009) provides a detailed overview of these recent works.

Structure of This Handbook

We have structured *The Cambridge Handbook of Creativity* into four parts. The first part, which we call "Basic Concepts," is designed to introduce readers to the history and key concepts in the field of creativity. This section begins with a history of creativity research by Mark A. Runco and Robert S. Alpert. It is followed by a thorough review of major theories of creativity written by Aaron Kozbelt, Ronald A. Beghetto, and Mark A. Runco. Next, Jonathan A. Plucker and Matthew C. Makel review creativity assessment, followed by Seana Moran's discussion of the role of creativity in today's society.

The next section is titled "Diverse Perspectives on Creativity." This section contains chapters on the many ways to approach creativity. Several of these approaches, such as functional, evolutionary, and neuroscientific approaches, have been invented or greatly reconceptualized in the last decade. We begin with Thomas B. Ward and Yuliya Kolomyts describing the cognitive approach to creativity, then shift to Gregory J. Feist's chapter on the creative personality. Paul

J. Locher writes about creativity and aesthetics, and Gerard J. Puccio and John F. Cabra cover organizational approaches. Dean Keith Simonton then discusses major (or "Big C") creativity, followed by Ruth Richards on everyday (or "little c") creativity. Neurobiological foundations of creativity are discussed by Allison B. Kaufman, Sergey A. Kornilov, Adam S. Bristol, Mei Tan, and Elena L. Grigorenko, while Sandra W. Russ and Julie A. Fiorelli write about developmental approaches to creativity. Jeffrey K. Smith and Lisa F. Smith discuss educational perspectives on creativity, and Todd Lubart analyzes cross-cultural research and theory. Next, Liane Gabora and Scott Barry Kaufman highlight evolutionary theories of creativity. Finally, David Cropley and Arthur Cropley write about functional creativity.

The third section of the book offers essays that cover "Contemporary Debates" in creativity – ongoing debates that still inspire discussion. John Baer addresses the question of whether creativity is one thing (domain-general) or many things (domain-specific). Beth A. Hennessey analyzes how intrinsic motivation may affect creativity. R. Keith Sawyer discusses the comparatively new area of group (as opposed to individual) creativity. Paul J. Silvia and James C. Kaufman highlight the controversial topic of creativity and mental illness, and Kyung Hee Kim, Bonnie Cramond, and Joyce VanTassel-Baska outline the often-conflicting literature on how creativity relates to intelligence. Mark A. Runco distinguishes between the idea of divergent thinking and creativity, and Ronald A. Beghetto concludes the section with a discussion of creativity in the classroom.

Finally, in the last section, we both summarize and highlight important concepts from the book and look to the future at what lies ahead.

The chapters in this book discuss research and theories from all aspects of creativity. The authors tackle such diverse topics as the brain, education, business, and world cultures. We hope that this handbook not only can serve as an introduction to the study of creativity but also can represent a launching pad for more debates, discussions, and future research.

References

Dorfman, L., Locher, P., & Martindale, C. (Eds.). (2006). *New directions in aesthetics, creativity, and the arts (Foundations and Frontiers in Aesthetics)*. Amityville, NY: Baywood Press.

Kaufman, J. C. (2009). *Creativity 101*. New York: Springer.

Kaufman, J. C., & Sternberg, R. J. (2007). Resource review: Creativity. *Change, 39*, 55–58.

Piirto, J. A. (2004). *Understanding creativity*. Scottsdale, AZ: Great Potential Press.

Puccio, G. J., Murdock, M. C., & Mance, M. (2006). *Creative leadership: Skills that drive change*. Thousand Oaks, CA: Sage.

Runco, M. A. (2007). *Creativity: Theories and themes: Research, development, and practice*. San Diego, CA: Elsevier Academic Press.

Sawyer, R. K. (2006). *Explaining creativity: The science of human innovation*. Oxford: Oxford University Press.

Simonton, D. K. (2004). *Creativity in science: Chance, logic, genius, and zeitgeist*. New York: Cambridge University Press.

Weisberg, R. (2006). *Creativity: Understanding innovation in problem solving, science, invention and the arts*. Hoboken, NJ: John Wiley.

Acknowledgments

Editing this book has been a labor of love, and it has been an honor to work with such a distinguished and noteworthy group of authors. We would like to thank Maria Avitia, Candice Davis, Ryan Holt, Amber Lytle, Tessy Pumaccahua, Amanda Roos, Lauren Skidmore, Roberta Sullivan, Oshin Vartanian, Arielle White, and Vanessa Zarate for their assistance in preparing the manuscript; Simina Calin and Jeanie Lee from Cambridge University Press and Phil Laughlin and Eric Schwartz, formerly of Cambridge University Press; and our departments and universities for their support. James would like to thank Allison, Jacob, Mom and Dad, and everyone else in his family for their support and love. Bob would like to thank Karin for her love, support, and patience while he read and edited chapter after chapter after chapter.

Section I

BASIC CONCEPTS

CHAPTER 1

Creativity Research

A Historical View

Mark A. Runco and Robert S. Albert

Creativity Research: A Historical View

The growth of creativity studies continues to accelerate. This makes perfect sense given the applications of creative studies to education, innovation and business, the arts and sciences, and society as a whole (Florida, 2002; Runco, 2007; Simonton, 1997). Ironically, there is much to be learned about creativity, both by moving ahead with new research and theories and by looking back at what has been explored before. An examination of the history of research on creativity suggests that many ideas and issues have been discussed literally for hundreds of years. This chapter presents one history of research on creativity. There are other perspectives on the topic. Some of these focus on one era or compare two periods of time. Bullough, Bullough, and Mauro (1980), for instance, compared eighteenth-century Scotland with fifteenth-century Italy. Kroeber (1944), Lamb and Easton (1984), Martindale (1990), Murphy (1958), and Naroll and colleagues (1971) also compared specific historical eras in terms of various indices of creativity. Many others have inferred something about creativity and history via biography and autobiography (see Gardner, 1993). Our own perspective directed us to the work of eminent individuals (e.g., Francis Bacon, Darwin, Galton, Malthus, Adam Smith) who had a particular impact on the clarification and eventual meeting of the concepts of research and creativity. The present chapter is unique in that instead of focusing on one era or person, it takes a broad view and examines extended historical changes in the concept of creativity.

Our assumption is that history is the medium in which ideas and events build up and arrive, with some significant effects rarely going away. (This is history seen as a slow boil.) In this chapter we take the position that the early conceptualizations of creativity and research were in themselves exceptional creative acts, as was the eventual bridging of these concepts through deliberately applying research methods. These methods were essential not only to the meaning and significance of creativity in human experience, but to how and why historical events were set in motion. Understanding this should help us appreciate the following three aspects of creativity within history.

The first is that the significance of historical processes lies as much in their timing as in their content. "When" determines "what" will be important. This has been recognized in reports that Rembrandt was not all that well known in his own time, Van Gogh died a pauper, and no one gave much credence to Mendel's theories for 50 years. Yet the impact of "when" applies well beyond the recognition of individual creativity. It applies to the concepts related to creativity and to the methods used to study it. Second, institutions and identifiable groups are critical in selecting and giving coherence to the important strands of possibilities from those already in the work and minds of interested persons. Third, the relevance of ideas becomes apparent only when there is a group of engaged articulate persons deeply concerned with the same question, problem, or set of possibilities. This implies that (a) a critical mass of information and interest must coexist and be in place and (b) significance and meaning not only are abstract but, as William James pointed out, come from consequences, not all of which are predictable. Seen in this light, history is experimental.

Some of the most evident creativity in Western history can therefore be found by tracing evolving concepts of research and creativity through the past 2,000 years, and by examining their eventual linkage in the late nineteenth century after centuries of being apart. The necessary first step in doing research was to have the concept of research in mind, which more or less required the invention of research. The next step was nearly as difficult but no less important. This was to believe that doing research on human nature – rather than merely speculating about it – was as important and as feasible as doing research on physical nature. The history of research on creativity began with the recognition that research constitutes an effective and practical way of learning about and understanding the world around us. Aristotle, Kant, and many other luminaries had much to say about creativity (see Rothenberg & Hausman, 1976), but they often included it in genius and other expressions of exceptionality, and they did not base their ideas about it on rigorous empirical evidence.

The concept of creativity has its own history, taking an intellectual path that was for two centuries independent of the institutionalization and conceptualization of research. At their beginnings and during most of their histories of development, research and creativity were not viewed as related to one another; therefore, if there were to be creativity research, the pairing of creativity and research had to go through several major intellectual transformations, and a deliberate extension in how scientific research was defined and could be applied needed to be undertaken. As it was, it took another 150 years after research was a recognized and widely encouraged institutional undertaking before the concept of creativity was sufficiently sculpted out of the many debates regarding the meaning and eventual separation of such competing ideas as imagination, originality, genius, talent, freedom, and individuality (Engell, 1981; Gruber, 1996; Kaufman, 1926; Martindale, 2007; Runco, 2007, chapter 13; Singer, 1981–1982). As we will show in detail, the invention of research was the outgrowth of long-standing questions about the nature of physical laws and the belief that it was possible for men and women to understand the physical world without divine intervention. The conceptualization of creativity, on the other hand, grew out of discussions and arguments regarding the basic nature of the human being when released from institutional doctrine. Early on, these debates involved only a slight interest in how this could be investigated. The main issue was freedom, a topic taken up later by Barron (1968) and Maslow (1973).

Creativity research is booming. Yet not long ago there were few empirical articles and scholarly books specifically on the subject (Albert, 1969; Feist & Runco, 1993; Guilford, 1950). In the words of Feist and Runco (1993), "One of the most widely cited

statements from Guilford's arti...
of the 121,000 titles listed in ...
Abstracts from the late 1920s ...
186 dealt with creativity. This ...
2 articles out of 1,000. We rec...
ered that the figure for more re...
ity research is roughly five time...
percentage of articles dealing ...
ity in the *Psychological Abstract*...
from .002% in the 1920s to ap...
.01% in the 1980s. From the late...
1991, almost 9,000 creativity refe...
been added to the literature" (p. ...
ally every major twentieth-centu...
ogist (e.g., Freud, Piaget, Rogers...
has taken creativity seriously and...
what it means to be creative, and...
the field can be described only as ...

[handwritten marginal note overlapping text:] Pre-Christian Views: — Genius → mystical source of protection + good fortune — Greeks — Daimon [guardian spirit] ↳ Creative = indiv. appetites — Aristotle — Creative + imaginative + madness — Romans — deliuotuum malero; Creative power passed to children (women only creative is childbirth)

It has been noted that the maturing of a professional interest can be seen in the growth
of its journals. Creativity research now has
its own scholarly journals (e.g., *Creativity
Research Journal*, and *Psychology of Art, Creativity, and Aesthetics*), and "creativity" is
attracting increasing attention in the media
and popular press.

Conceptions of Creativity

Pre-Christian Views of Creativity

Long before the Christian view of creativity had begun to emerge, there were efforts
to grasp the meaning for humankind of what
we now recognize as creativity for humanity.
In general, the pre-Christian understanding,
a view that has had influence on our thinking throughout the centuries, is the concept
of genius that was originally associated with
mystical powers of protection and good fortune. It is when the Greeks placed emphasis
on an individual's daimon (guardian spirit)
that the idea of genius became mundane and
was progressively associated with an individual's abilities and appetites, both destructive and constructive. Creativeness took on
a social value, and by the time of Aristotle an
association with madness and frenzied inspiration arose, a view that reappeared during
most of the nineteenth and the first half
of the twentieth centuries. The succeeding

... additional
... as seen as
... wer, and it
... en. At this
... ity. Giving
...
...ivity
...f creativ-
...n given in
...lea of the
...Boorstin,
...ribed it
...city to
...*um was a landmark. It
declared that a people become a community through their belief in a Creator and
His Creation. They confirmed their creative powers through their kinship, their
sharing qualities of God, their intimate
and voluntary relationship to a Creator –
God. Christianity, [by] turning our eyes
to the future, played a leading role in the
discovery of our power to create. (1992,
pp. 42, 55)*

This belief reflects a significant difference
between Western and Eastern thinking
about the goal of creativity and the participants' role in the process. For the Hin-
dus (1500–900 BC), Confucius (c. 551–479
BC), and the Taoists and Buddhists, creation
was at most a kind of discovery or mimicry.
Apparently the early Buddhists emphasized
natural cycles, and thus "the idea of the creation of something ex nihilo (from nothing) had no place in a universe of the yin
and yang" (Boorstin, 1992, p. 17). Plato felt
that nothing new was possible, and art in
his time was an effort to match or mimic
ideal forms. Originality, which has become
the critical contemporary marker of creativity (Runco, 1988), was not an early attribute
of creativity (Child, 1972; Dudek, in press;
Pratt, 1961). Incidentally, evidence of parallel
differences between the East and the West
can still be found (Kwang, 2001; Runco, 2001,
2004). More often they are today explained
in terms of collectivism and individuality,

but these lead to the same conclusions, with the East tending to relegate creativity and the West giving individuals the option for it.

These assumptions were not seriously challenged for nearly 1,200 years. Then, during the Middle Ages, a new Western perspective arose, with special talent or unusual ability manifested by an individual (almost always a male) viewed as a manifestation of an outside "spirit" for which this individual was a conduit. Early in the Renaissance, a significant change in this view took place. At this historical moment the divine attribute of great artists and artisans was recognized and often emphasized as their own abilities and perspective. This change in perspective was not isolated, but rather part of a broad set of social transformations. Winston-Given (1996) identified the spread of the English language, the growth within the medical and judicial professions, a rise in religious diversity and even nonconformity, and the dramatic reduction of serfdom as the major influences on these transformations.

These changes were quite subtle until the Renaissance was clearly underway (approximately in the fourteenth through seventeenth centuries). Even though Chaucer used the word "create" as early as 1393, the conceptual outline of creativity remained relatively faint and even at times was lost sight of until most of the major philosophers (e.g., Hobbes [1588–1679] and Locke [1632–1704]) of the Enlightenment were able to move beyond a concern with imagination, individual freedom, and society's authority in human affairs.

The Invention of Research

Throughout most of the years and the many philosophical discussions that took place, scientific works were known for their power of discovery and cultural and religious disruption. Three of the Western world's greatest scientists – Copernicus (1473–1543), Galileo (1564–1642), and Newton (1642–1727) – had given proof of this. Yet it took more than their example. It required a widespread change in perceiving the laws of the physical world working in the here and now as well as

a recognition of how this lawfulness related to human existence, how science produced knowledge about that relationship, and – just as important – the social purposes scientific knowledge could serve (Shapin, 1996).

In the eighteenth century, two profound intellectual perspectives concerning reason and individualism shaped Western thought: The Enlightenment became an identifiable and coherent intellectual philosophy, the clearest expression of which was the intellectual attacks on what was believed to be unwarranted authority emanating from a variety of (dogmatic) nonscientific sources. While the Enlightenment was reaching its own critical mass, natural science as an institutionalized philosophy and methodology was taking shape (Bronowski & Mazlish, 1960). What made this primarily an English intellectual movement was that although parts of the Enlightenment did occur in continental Europe, they did so primarily among poets and artists. Those scientists who were interested were "speculative." Evidence of this growing interest in science is that the word "research," meaning deliberate scientific inquiry, entered English in 1639, soon after the appearance of the word "researcher" in 1615.

Just how profound these changes were for Western culture can be gauged by the transformed status of the Bible. For hundreds of years it had been a divine source of wisdom and morality, but by the late eighteenth century it had become a secular model of literature. Prickett (1996) put it this way:

> During the late 18th century the Bible underwent a shift in interpretation so radical as to make it virtually a different book from what it had been 100 years earlier. Even as historical criticism suggested that, far from being divinely inspired or even a rock of certainty in a world of flux, its text was neither stable nor original, the new notion of the Bible as a cultural artifact became a paradigm of all literature. While formal religion declined, the prestige of the Bible as a literary and aesthetic model rose to new heights. (p. ii)

Knowing the depth, power, and range of the Enlightenment's resistance to divine authority and religion's "wisdom," we should not be at all surprised that another kind of freedom would become a part of the paradigmatic shift. This was the individual's right to explore his world without institutional permission and divine guidelines or intervention.

Although ideas related to creativity had been relatively unchanged between the years 1500 and 1700, the other changes taking place were exceptionally fertile grounds for the idea of research. It is around this time that "science" and scientific thinking took form as the preeminent instrument of discovery and models for thinking about the physical world. The changes that evolved from this merger of scientific model and technique were so complete that many writers believe this was the beginning of a distinctive, modern Western civilization, "from a world of things ordered according to their ideal nature to a world of events running in a steady mechanism of before and after" (Bronowski, 1951).

Institutional and Philosophical Antecedents to Research on Creativity

At the same time that a more far-reaching intellectual revolution, known as the English Enlightenment, was gathering persuasive force and an increasing coherence of new attitudes and concerns was emerging, Francis Bacon's (1605/1974) *Advancement of Learning* became an accepted argument for the importance of empirical investigation. The Enlightenment's widespread philosophical and social opposition to authority (e.g., religion, monarchies, and political oppression) grew in parallel to science's own opposition to the ideas of these authorities. These arguments included an ever-increasing belief in the necessity of freedom of speech, the press, and the life of the individual. Freedom, so it was argued, was essential because of the individual's basic rationality, which daily – so it seems – was being confirmed by and in science. The conclusion from all this was that people had no need for artificial authority and social restraint.

As these ideas were being openly championed, the institution that was to embody them and drive the argument home through the seventeenth and eighteenth centuries rapidly took shape. Science and scientific research were institutionalized when the Royal Society was chartered by Charles II in 1662, with John Locke (1632–1704) one of its early members. Two similar academies already existed in France and Italy, but these organizations had little influence on their host societies. Such societal influence distinguished the Royal Society and demonstrates how good a fit there was between science and English society.

At this point research had acquired the purpose of discovery. It is not simply that the Royal Society quickly became a meeting place for otherwise scattered (and often rancorous) scientists and mathematicians of historical eminence, but that the Royal Society institutionalized recognition of their work. The Royal Society formally required that each scientist was to present his work to all the other members. Not only were members expected to publish their scientific work, but to do so only in the Society's Philosophical Transactions. Private papers were no longer to be circulated.

Furthermore, if others were to understand and be able to use an individual scientist's work, then other rules would have to be followed. Personal idiosyncratic language was to be avoided, or at least minimized (Bronowski & Mazlish, 1960). The form of presentation, the symbolism, and the system of notation used by a member would have to be made comprehensible to other scientists.

Of all its requirements, probably the most influential was the obligation to publish one's results in the Society's Transactions, which soon gave the Royal Society a great influence over the reputations of the members. Just how important this influence on reputation became was illustrated in the Society's mediation of the prolonged and bitter debate between Robert Hooke and Isaac Newton. The expectation to "publish for merit," although driven primarily by each individual's motivation for recognition,

at least early on, was itself institutionalized by the Society in two ways: by sense
of responsibility to science as an institution, and by its emphasis on publication of scientific results. This requirement
accompanied a second goal, which was to
make evident the power and practicality of
science.

There were two notable consequences
of these institutional requirements (vestiges
of which remain). One was the reduced
individuality shown in published papers.
While encouraging individual originality and
genius, as they were understood at the time,
the Royal Society had installed a set of
requirements that effectively stripped scientific communication of signs of individuality. (These expectations operate to this
day in scientific journals, although in somewhat modified form.) The second consequence was to shift the Society's early concern with individuality – which ironically
some seventeenth- and eighteenth-century
writers believed was the sine qua non of
creativity – to the Royal Society's explicit
emphasis on the lawfulness of nature and
the discovery of the practical benefits from
science. These benefits, so it was thought,
underscored the validity of natural laws and
the importance of scientific experimentation in the physical world (i.e., nature).
Early debates and speculation on the question about where "ideas" for this program
came from were soon overshadowed by a
growing confidence in the inventive power
of empirical methods and natural science's
apparent infinite capacity to produce practical benefits. Yet although physical nature
was accepted as science's prime source of
knowledge, and man was accepted as a
part of nature, the scientific investigation of
human nature was not seriously considered
during the seventeenth and early eighteenth
centuries.

The Great and Nearly Endless Debate

Several further intellectual developments
took place before a concept of creativity really developed. One was during the
last half of the eighteenth century when
science's premise of natural law became
widely accepted. Everyday justification for
an unshakable confidence was seen all
around in the practical inventions natural
science was credited for putting into the
English economy – the spinning machine
and the steam engine – inventions that were
accelerating the Industrial Revolution and
England's own lead in manufacturing and
business over foreign competition.

On a somewhat more speculative level,
for English and European artists, poets, writers, and philosophers there remained two
questions that had been endlessly discussed
throughout the eighteenth century: What
were the limits to freedom of thought? What
was the social and political significance of
such freedom? These questions reflected the
abiding issues throughout the eighteenth
century. As we know now, until they were
answered, there could be no clear understanding of what creativity was, much less
what it can do.

The most significant distinctions made in
the mid-1700s have to be the separations
of the idea of "creativity" from "genius,"
"originality," "talent," and formal education.
At the heart of these debates were efforts
to clarify the legitimate sphere of individual freedom as distinguished from social
and political restraints. Society's laws and
the somewhat arbitrary limitations imposed
by authority were naturally in opposition
against "original" genius and constituted a
pernicious barrier to men's freedom and
originality (Addison, 1711/1983). But perhaps
there was nothing as influential in propelling the history of creativity than the
concerted efforts to understand the differences between talent and "original genius."
By the end of the eighteenth century it was
concluded that although many persons may
have talent of one sort or another, and that
this talent would be responsive to education, "original genius" was truly exceptional
and by definition was to be exempt from
the rules, the customs, and the obligations
that applied to the talented. This was not
an abstract argument. As Kaufman (1926)
and Engell (1981) made clear, these prolonged debates regarding the relationships

and differences among "genius," "originality," "exceptionality," "innate ability," and "freedom" eventually came together in the eighteenth century doctrine of individualism (with the American and French Revolutions just around the corner). But still no concept of "creativity" existed at this time.

Hobbes (1588–1679) was the first major figure to recognize how important imagination was in human thought and planning, and how constructive it could be, an idea that reappeared as a starting point of discussions during the Enlightenment (Braun, 1991; Singer, 1981–1982). To appreciate how difficult it was to develop the concept of creativity, remember it had taken several generations of writers, philosophers, and artists to come close to the concept. Their difficulty can be seen in the fact that their discussions of "imagination" led as early as the 1730s to the phrase, "the creative imagination." By the late 1700s, "imagination itself" was accepted as governing artistic creativity (Engell, 1981, pp. VII–VIII).

Tedious and tangential as they were at times, nevertheless the debates through the eighteenth century eventually came to four important acceptable distinctions, which were to become the bedrock of our present-day ideas about creativity: (a) genius was divorced from the supernatural; (b) genius, although exceptional, was a potential in every individual; (c) talent and genius were to be distinguished from one another; and (d) their potential and exercise depend on the political atmosphere at the time. (For the reader who believes these matters are settled, in our own times similar issues of separation and distinctions [i.e., discriminant validity] can be seen in the research on domain specificity [Albert, 1980; Baer, 1995; Bloom, 1985; Gardner, 1994; Runco, 1986]).

By the end of the eighteenth century it was accepted that neither genius nor talent could survive in repressive societies. When freedom did exist, according to Duff, one of the most prolific and convincing eighteenth-century writers on genius and talent (Kaufman, 1926), spontaneity and genius would be "irresistible" because it reflected an innate predisposition and needed no education, a belief soon shared by Rousseau and later Romantics. On a practical level, the arguments over these distinctions were important in helping define the differences between the exceptional and unpredictable force of genius and the less extraordinary, more predictable talent seen everyday. By the end of the century it was concluded that whereas many people had talent that could respond to education, genius was "original." It was manifested in someone or something that seems to come out of nowhere, out of reach or need of education, and immune from the rules and obligations appropriate for talent. (It is interesting and politically significant that Rousseau saw "genius" in every man with the same exemptions.)

The Influence of Unintended and Unanticipated Consequences

There were two models that incorporated many of the important arguments and practical observations related to research and creativity. One of the models – that of rational science – bears on science's power and the practical use of research, which has been pretty much covered. The other model can be called the "ideology of creativity." It had to do with the social significance and potential dangers of originality and individualism in the context of compliance to authority and maintenance of social order.

The rational-science model has always been formal in its arguments and can appear moderately removed from the day-to-day consequences of research. On the other hand, although there have been much older discussions about the religious and secular significance of creativity, creativity acquired an ideology because of its relevance in defining human nature and social-political conditions.

Although natural science and practical inventors such as Arkwright and Watt were busy demonstrating what human reason and English inventiveness could do, it was the ever-increasing power and numerous practical inventions that eventually led to unforeseen and unintended dire consequences. Rapid population shifts of farmers and laborers out of their farms and villages and into increasingly dirty sprawling cities, out of cottages and into regimented impersonal factories, led to surges in population shifts and growth, which soon alarmed many persons. Interestingly, while science was still busy demonstrating what rational human reason could do, there now was growing a parallel concern regarding the ultimate effect of these results, especially in terms of social and political stability.

It was not long before increasing numbers of people, especially among the upper-middle class and gentry, were having second thoughts about "individualism," its alleged "irresistible" spontaneity, and the unrestricted use of science. What they were witnessing was clearly not the efficient machine-driven society envisioned early in the Industrial Revolution. The rapidity and threat that characterized this change became one of the most important influences in the development of social sciences. The unpredicted widespread dislocations resulting from natural sciences were too obvious to overlook in spite of natural science's century-old belief that physical nature was governed by rational and intelligible laws. More and more threatening, poorly understood "unintended and unanticipated consequences" were entering the social world and with them calls for political movements and social action. The spreading doctrine of individualism, which motivated the unrest, quickly became the accepted explanation for and source of fear over these "unintended and unanticipated" consequences. In order to understand one of these consequences, we need to recognize that such consequences were not new; they had been an intractable concern during most of Adam Smith's lifetime (1723–1790). He knew they often happened (as did his Swiss contemporary, Jean-Jacques Rousseau).

From the mid-1700s there was an almost constant turmoil in England and Europe. The many dislocations from the Industrial Revolution led to two very diverse but equally influential responses. One was Adam Smith's (1723–1790) rational argument, and the other was Jean-Jacques

Rousseau's (1712–1778) Romanticism, which, among other social consequences, became the source of an artistic counterthrust to scientific rationalism. This part of Romanticism's response to the Industrialization of Europe was expressed in artists' emphases on inner feelings as natural and therefore democratic sources of wisdom and artistic inspiration. The conflict soon was identified as between science and feeling, which in turn was personified as between the overly rational scientist and the artist as the misunderstood genius. In 100 years this new identity, which marked artists' sense of deviance and their deliberate defiance of middle-class society, would be used by charlatans such as Lombroso as justification to denigrate artists in general and genius and creativity specifically. Although both reactions occurred at the same time, their consequences for research and creativity had different timetables. These were not coordinated until the end of the nineteenth century through the achievements of Galton and Freud.

Romanticism influenced conceptions of creativity in various ways. It may, for instance, support the associations between creativity and psychopathology. Sass (2000) wrote, "whereas romanticism views creative inspiration as a highly emotional, Dionysian, or primitive state, modernism and postmodernism emphasize processes involving hyper-self-consciousness and alienation (hyperreflexivity). Although manic–depressive or cyclothymic tendencies seem especially suited to creativity of the romantic sort, schizoid, schizotypal, schizophreniform, and schizophrenic tendencies have more in common with the (in many respects, antiromantic) sensibilities of modernism and postmodernism" (p. 55). He defined modernism as "the formally innovative, often avant-gardist, art and literature of approximately the first half of the 20th century" and postmodernism as the "cultural and artistic developments largely occurring after World War II" (p. 56).

More concretely, Romanticism may have direct impact on the stereotypes held by artists, other creators, and audiences. Becker (1995, p. 224) described how, in an effort to differentiate themselves from those less gifted and their artistic predecessors, intellectuals and artists during the Romantic period adopted idiosyncratic behaviors. These behaviors supported the stereotypical labels of those who wanted to see pathology in genius – those who were defending the cultural or societal status quo. She quoted Coser on this point: "Many a Romantic genius may have assisted in a labeling process "in which others took him more seriously than he perhaps wished, and assigned him to the status of a madman" (from Becker, 1995, p. 224). The significance of such thinking, and of stereotypes about creative persons, are not just theoretical. The short life expectancy of writers (Kaun, 1991) might, for example, be explained in part by the tendency of writers to conform to the eccentric and unhealthful lifestyle that is a part of a stereotype (think of the personality and life of an F. Scott Fitzgerald).

Adam Smith was one of the first to recognize the need for a science of human behavior. His *The Wealth of Nations* (1776) was a deliberate effort to bring together the many reasons for a social science; it is "almost an encyclopedia of the effects of unintended consequences in human affairs . . . the consequences of action are often different from the intentions which motivate the actors" (from Muller, 1995, p. 85). His argument was free of blame and pontifications. His point was that not all consequences were either good or bad, but they were often "unintended" and "unanticipated." One undeniable unanticipated consequence he pointed to was the dramatic and frightening population and industrial upheaval, and one of its consequences he believed was the American Revolution, to which Smith devoted extensive attention. Because of such consequences Smith and others argued that it was imperative to develop a science based on systematic, political, and social knowledge. It was thought such a social science would help anticipate social change before it got out of hand.

Eight years after Smith's death there occurred a major intellectual and empirical development that contributed to the establishment of a social science – the publication of Malthus's *Essay on Population* (1798). It was not simply an argument (there were enough of them) but documentation with exhaustive empirical evidence (rudimentary statistics) detailing the apparent uncontrollable growth and social disorganization in the English population, predicting unanticipated consequences if social and political action were not taken.

The importance of Malthus's work is twofold. His research was as empirical as nonphysical science research would be until Galton. And 40 years later a phrase he had used to explain the social disruptions he described in his *Essay on Population*, "the struggle for existence," provided Darwin (1859) with the explanation for natural selection he was trying to articulate. This particular idea helped organize Darwin's efforts, and the *Origin of Species* added new evidence that human existence was indeed precarious, subject to unintended and unanticipated shifts and demands of natural selection. It did not move according to any individual's wishes or plans, nor embody any morality or purpose. Natural selection was blind.

The intellectual breakthrough for understanding of creativity in the late nineteenth and early twentieth centuries was implied in the role Darwin gave to adaptation in survival. (Freud, who read Darwin and met Galton, was later to incorporate this idea in his psychodynamic theory of defenses and creativity; Albert, 1996; Ellenberger, 1970; Freud, 1900/1953, 1908/1958.)

Adaptation, Diversity, and Natural Selection: Darwin's Empirical Formula for Creativity

From the time it was first discussed, creativity has been enclosed in abstract questions and connected to issues larger than itself (e.g., what is individualism and why do we need individual freedom?). It is only after Darwin worked out the processes underlying natural selection that several basic characteristics of creativity were brought into sharp focus, especially its value in adaptation. One role of importance that creativity has had since Darwin was in solving problems and "successful" adaptations, "individual" in character.

We can understand this by recognizing that evolutionary theory's basic principles are diversity and adaptation and the relationship they have with each other and to natural selection: "The generation of adaptations and the generation of diversity . . . [are] different aspects of a single complex phenomenon, and the unifying insight, [Darwin] claimed, was not the idea of evolution, but 'the principle of natural selection.' Furthermore, Darwin argued, 'natural selection would inevitably produce adaptation'" (Dennett, 1995, pp. 42–43). The idea most difficult for many persons to accept was the most counterintuitive of all. Because evolution occurs without foresight, "adaptations get their start as fortuitous" – unintended – "effects that get opportunistically picked up by selective forces in the environment" (Dennett, 1995, p. 248).

Something akin to this takes place in creative compositions and breakthroughs (Campbell, 1960). What was laid before us is the possibility of research on creativity if we try to observe adaptations in controlled everyday conditions.

The Transfer From Darwin to Galton

The intellectual bridge from Darwin to Galton was built early in Galton's career through a steady correspondence and visits between Darwin and Galton up to Darwin's death. The content of their exchanges more often than not was about evolution. Early in their relationship Galton proposed his own version of heredity and evolution, but soon became convinced of the validity and greater explanatory power of Darwin's model as it centered on natural selection, and the necessity of diversity and the role of adaptation in natural selection. However, it was natural that in Galton's hands, diversity would become a problem of measurement. In order for him to solve it, he operationalized diversity as individual differences within an environment of known dimen-

sions (Galton, 1874, 1883). This environment consisted of measuring instruments, most of Galton's design. Thus one of Galton's significant contributions to psychological research, and indirectly to research on creativity, was the operational definition of broad evolutionary diversity as manifested in specific individual differences that could be measured.

Galton had two compelling interests that tied together much of his career. One was the study of individual differences. The second was what he believed was the need for eugenics as a deliberate program to scientifically increase British talent. Whether or not he was aware of it, Galton was following in the footsteps of Adam Smith and Malthus in his wish to protect society from unintended social consequences. Eugenics was Galton's program meant to minimize the uncertainty in natural selection as it might specifically affect Britain. These two research interests led to Galton's most direct contribution to research on creativity – his choice of eminent-achieving families as examples of hereditary ability. Out of this came the selection of eminent persons as subjects of obvious creativity (although some researchers will argue the point), and the practical use of statistics, some of which Galton developed.

It is here that we see another of Galton's lasting contributions. Earlier we described "The Great and Nearly Endless Debate" moving through the eighteenth century, out of which came four important distinctions. It seems to us that, intentionally or not, what Galton gave us evidence for was that "Genius was divorced from the supernatural" and that "Genius, although exceptional, was a potential in every individual," because ability is distributed throughout populations.

From Galton to the Present

The reader might wonder if Galton was the only person interested in creativity at this time. The answer is absolutely not. But he was the strongest force in applying empirical methods in the selection of subjects and the measurement of their individual differences. Sternberg and Lubart (1996) have suggested that one impediment to research on creativity over the years was the tie between creativity and mysticism, in the sense that creativity was thought perhaps to have mystical origins. This mistake could no longer be made after Galton. The magnitude of Galton's achievement is apparent when we learn of other persons who were interested in the same problems around the same time.

After her review of the nineteenth-century research, Becker (1995) concluded that, in spite of the differences in the characteristics of the authors and articles, the themes of the nineteenth century are not dissimilar to the themes of the twentieth century. She stated that a number of nineteenth-century authors concentrated on five basic questions: (a) What is creativity? (b) Who has creativity? (c) What are the characteristics of creative people? (d) Who should benefit from creativity? And (e) Can creativity be increased through conscious effort? No one doubts that these questions are important questions for understanding creativity, but at the time only Galton made real progress in suggesting how they could be answered. It is not so much asking these questions, all with some merit, but asking how one goes about answering them that matters the most in science. We have two illustrations of this.

As early as 1827 Bethune was interested in the ability for "originating new combinations of thought" and felt creative genius could "store away ideas for future combinations" (see Becker, 1995). According to Becker (1995), Bethune foresaw some of Freud's thinking, arguing that those future combinations would be conscious only "when the chain of association is regained." Actually, quite a few writers anticipated bits of Freud without putting them together as Freud did. Becker also quoted Jevons (1877), who defined genius as "essentially creative" and who foresaw many ideas later used in Guilford's (1968) distinction of convergent and divergent thinking. Jevons referred to a "divergence from the ordinary grooves of

thought and action" (Becker, 1995, p. 576), for instance, and went on to describe a process that clearly resembles various associative theories of creativity (e.g., Mednick, 1962).

The idea of divergent thinking, or at least the possibility of complex ideation, was also formulated by William James (1880), who understood the rarity of ideational complexity. "Instead of thoughts of concrete things patiently following one another in a beaten track of habitual suggestion, we have the most abrupt cross-cuts and transitions from one idea to another... the most unheard-of combinations of elements, the subtlest associations of analogy; in a word, we seem suddenly introduced into a seething caldron of ideas... where partnerships can be joined or loosened in an instant, treadmill routine is unknown, and the unexpected seems the only law" (Becker, 1995, p. 456) Like Galton, James appreciated empirical research. This was especially clear in James's public lectures during 1896 in which he demolished the "wild" assertions then being made by untrained self-appointed social critics and medical experts regarding exceptional mental states (James, 1896/1992).

It is not easy to know just when and where Galton's influence ends. Most of it seems to have been assimilated in the ongoing interests and research of a period. We know that by 1879 Galton had developed the earliest laboratory in which to measure individual differences in sensory functioning, and that this research was related to the assumption that sensory discrimination was positively associated with intelligence. And by 1883 he had concluded that "creative products" came largely from "general ability," which in *Hereditary Genius* (1869) he stated was one of the essential capacities for genius (Albert, 1975; Cropley, 1966). But by the 1900s measuring individual differences in intelligence had become a research interest of many psychologists. In fact, by 1904 Binet and Spearman were doing their empirical investigations on intelligence tests with Binet's test, including items he believed required imagination and what is now called divergent thinking (Brody, 1992; Willerman, 1986). Terman was among this group, revising the Binet-Simon test; although the IQ test was his research instrument of choice, the conceptual framework came from Galton (Terman, 1924).

Even though Galton's work no longer stood out, his influence continued. Terman was the earliest American psychologist to take a research interest in genius. How profound and deep in his career (and twentieth-century research) this interest ran can be seen in the titles and dates of his work (Terman, 1906, 1917, 1924; Terman & Chase, 1920) and in the five-volume *Genetic Studies of Genius*. This research was important in two ways, not only for its methodological challenge but also for its educational and social implications. Both Galton and Terman worried about their nations' futures and how to safeguard them. (We hope the reader sees the concern connecting Adam Smith, Malthus, Galton, and Terman.) Terman has been criticized at times because of what we sometimes see as his narrow focus on IQ as giftedness, to the exclusion of creativity and nonacademic achievement. True as it is, the course Terman's research always took was guided by his wish to help make "an American society based on the principles of meritocracy" (Minton, 1988, p. 139). To do this required identifying individual differences in ability and bestowing on children with high native ability (IQ) appropriate educational opportunities. What is significant is that Terman's research program ran counter to the intellectual changes taking place in Europe, which were to some degree a return of Rousseauian philosophy. These changes were antimaterialism, antielitism, antipositivism, and antirationality. With them came a rediscovery of the power and validity of the subjective, intuition, and preconscious thought by Bergson, Freud, and Marx (Barron, 1995; Hughes, 1953).

Guilford (1967) astutely observed that, over the years, Terman's project was directed toward being able to scale people along a dimension (much as Galton and some German experimentalists had done with mixed success). His method was relatively simple, whereas creativity was too complex, mentalistic, and removed from educational performances for the same treatment. Catherine Cox's dissertation (directed by Terman) was a study that was planned as an extension of Terman's (1917) own method of estimating Galton's IQ to a sample of individuals achieving eminence between 1450 and 1850. But more important than its methodology was its developmental goal, which was to determine if Galton's conclusions concerning genius (Galton, 1869, p. 43) would apply to these children who would later achieve eminence. A subtext to Cox's research, which is not usually recognized, is that Terman and Cox were aware of Lombroso's dubious methods (e.g., craniometry) and conclusions and wished to test their validity empirically (Cox, 1926, pp. 14–15).

Although there were limits to its perspective and emphasis on "practical" results, it is through Terman's interest in Galton that the latter had so much influence on Cox's research (1926). Galton's (1869) research was both a stimulus and the model for her monumental study of 300 historically eminent men. Like Galton, Cox never questioned what she too assumed was the high positive correlation between eminent achievement and "very high abilities." In fact, all three – Galton, Terman, and Cox – took for granted that achievement was a valid measure of "mental capacity," which helps explain why Terman and Cox start their research where Galton's ended – believing creativity to be an integral part of intelligence. Both Galton's and Cox's subjects were no longer alive and were selected from archives, but Cox improved on Galton's work in several important ways. Her sample was much broader, larger, and objectively selected. Cox used experts' ratings for her criteria of eminence. (Expert judgment has been used ever since. It was used extensively at the Institute of Personality Assessment and Research, for example, by Barron [1953, 1955, 1968], Helson [1999], and MacKinnon [1963, 1970].) Another of Cox's and Terman's improvements over Galton was in her deliberate use of biographical, autobiographical, and sociocultural information – all exhaustively coded – from which she and several other psychologists estimated subjects' IQs and their childhood traits. This made her subjects more alive and their "stories" plausible, not mere numbers, and this made clearer the personal relevance and acceptance of her conclusions much easier. Other than an average IQ of 154 for her sample, the most quoted conclusion from Cox (1926) is her most consequential findings as far as research on creativity goes: "Youths who achieved eminence are characterized not only by high intellectual traits, but also by persistence of motive and effort, confidence in their abilities, and great strength or force of character" (p. 218). Note that this is a configuration of particular traits, which she carefully documented (pp. 177–213), varied according to her subjects' areas of achievement, indicating domain-specificity. It is no accident that these traits figure in Cox's conclusions. Like other similarities between Galton and Cox, there is the recognition of intrinsic motivation described earlier by Galton (1869) as "one of the vital 'qualities of intellect and disposition' acting as an inherent stimulus" (from Runco, 1993, p. 62). Just how valid Cox's conclusions are is attested to by the contemporary emphasis and evidence on persistence, intrinsic motivation, and autonomy (Albert & Runco, 1989; Amabile, 1990; MacKinnon, 1963, 1983).

It is difficult to think of any other research up to World War II that makes contributions equal to Cox's (1926) research on creativity. Nor should we overlook the fact that the method of investigation she chose, the historiometric, was selected because she understood that her project concerned a problem common to psychology and history. This was "the application to historical data of the criteria of standardized measures of the mental ability of children" (Cox 1926, p. 21). This methodology is still being used (e.g., Albert, 1996; Simonton, 1999). Another aspect of Cox's contribution derives from the timing of her work.

Cox's research in the mid-1920s coincided with the development of ego psychology.

The configuration of childhood traits characteristic of some of her eminent individuals fit the new ego psychology's growing interest in mastery, confidence, persistence – the basic ego drives. This suggested that creativity was not primarily unconsciously driven. Moreover, the small differences in the subjects' IQs and the diversity of traits Cox described argued for caution in overemphasizing the influence of IQ on creativity. The combination of Cox's work and ego psychology's orientation demonstrated that creativity is not simply one type of behavior (psychopathology), nor does it originate only on one level of dynamics (the unconscious), nor does it express just one (or a dominant) trait of the individual (antisocial), nor has it just one adaptive purpose. This view of creativity fit the psychoanalytic proposition that creativity, like all behavior, was overdetermined (i.e., multivariate), and this has led to recent definitions of creativity as a complex (Albert & Runco, 1989) or syndrome (MacKinnon, 1975; Mumford & Gustafson, 1988). Her results reinforced the importance that ego psychology saw in the interdependence of personal identity and conscious processes of adaptation (Erikson, 1958; Kubie, 1961; Vaillant, 1977). Soon after World War II the focus of research would increasingly center on the personalities, the values, the talents, and the IQs of exceptionally creative men and women, and compare them to their more average counterparts (e.g., Barron, 1953, 1955; Helson, 1987, 1990; MacKinnon, 1962, 1963, 1983; Roe, 1952). This body of work confirmed that, for all their differences, the most influential factors were developmental and family differences. A difference in IQ was not one of the more significant differences. At IQs greater than 115, creativity and intelligence function as two more or less independent sets of abilities from late childhood on (e.g., Albert & Runco, 1989; MacKinnon, 1983; Wallach, 1983).

Helson (1996) looked back at the 1950s and the research on the creative personality then going on. She reminded us that during the 1950s and 1960s the "creative" personality was the hot new topic. Whether they knew it or not, researchers on creativity were in the avant-garde of a new version of individualism. Creative people of all types became our culture's heroes. What Helson described reflected a change but not a paradigmatic shift, such as those that we have attempted to track in this history of research on creativity.

Soon afterward interests widened even more. Other researchers shifted the emphasis to creative types or styles, and still other researchers, such as Dudek and Hall (1991), described comparison participants with as much respect as their creative counterparts, achieving a depth of portrayal at times absent from early studies, which would exaggerate less-creative persons' deficiencies. Over the last 50 years research on creativity has merged an interest in creative persons with empirical methods and a feeling for the humanity and dignity of subjects, out of which has come respect for the unambiguously creative, as well as everyday creativity (e.g., Runco & Richards, 1997).

MacKinnon (1963) noted that the history of the concepts of ego and self has been a long and confused one, but there is today rather general agreement on the sense in which each is to be used in psychological theory. In a functionalist psychology of personality, the ego is conceived to be a system of regulating functions – reality testing, decision making, and so on – which serve to integrate the subsystems of personality. On the other hand, it permits the individual to express himself in creative actions, which change the environment and contribute to the actualization of himself through the development and expression of his potentialities. (pp. 252–253).

When we look back at Darwin and think over MacKinnon's (1963) observation we can only marvel at how historical questions and efforts to make sense of them may work themselves together with profound implications for research. Over its history that research on creativity has been able to progress as science, when at times blind to the next step; it is empirical, as Bacon (1605/1974) told us science should be.

References

Addison, J. (1983). On genius. In R. S. Albert (Ed.), *Genius and eminence* (pp. 3–5). Oxford: Penguins Press. (Original work published 1711)

Albert, R. S. (1969). The concept of genius and its implications for the study of creativity and giftedness. *American Psychologist*, 24, 743–753.

Albert, R. S. (1975). Toward a behavioral definition of genius. *American Psychologist*, 30, 140–151.

Albert, R. S. (1980). Genius. In R. H. Woody (Ed.), *Encyclopedia of clinical assessment* (Vol. 2). San Francisco, CA: Josey-Bass.

Albert, R. S. (1996, Fall). Some reasons why creativity often fails to make it past puberty and into the real world. *New Directions in Child Development*, 72, 43–56.

Albert, R. S., & Runco, M. A. (1989). Independence and cognitive ability in gifted and exceptionally gifted boys. *Journal of Youth and Adolescence*, 18, 221–230.

Amabile, T. M. (1990). In M. A. Runco & R. S. Albert (Eds.), *Theories of creativity* (Rev. ed.). Cresskill, NJ: Hampton Press.

Bacon, F. (1974). *Advancement of learning*. Oxford: Oxford University Press. (Original work published 1605)

Baer, J. (1995). Generality of creativity across performance domains. *Creativity Research Journal*, 4, 23–39.

Barron F. (1953). Complexity-simplicity as a personality dimension. *Journal of Abnormal and Social Psychology*, 48, 163–172.

Barron, F. (1955). The disposition toward originality. *Journal of Abnormal and Social Psychology*, 51, 478–485.

Barron, F. (1968). *Creativity and personal freedom*. New York: Van Nostrand.

Barron, F. (1995). *No rootless flower: An ecology of creativity*. Cresskill, NJ: Hampton Press.

Becker, M. (1995). 19th century foundations of creativity research. *Creativity Research Journal*, 8, 219–229.

Bloom, B. J. (1985). *Developing talent in young people*. New York: Ballantine.

Boorstin, D. J. (1992). *The creators: A history of heroes of the imagination*. New York: Random House.

Braun, E. T. H. (1991). *The world of imagination*. Savage, MD: Rowman & Littlefield.

Brody, N. (1992). *Intelligence* (2nd ed.). New York: Academic Press.

Bronowski, J. (1951). *The common sense of science.* London: Methuen.

Bronowski, J., & Mazlish, B. (1960). *The Western intellectual tradition.* London: Hutchinson.

Bullough, V., Bullough, B., & Mauro, M. (1980). History and creativity: Research problems and some possible solutions. *Journal of Creative Behavior,* 15, 102–116.

Campbell, D. T. (1960). Blind variation and selective retention in creative thought as in other knowledge processes. *Psychological Review,* 67, 380–400.

Child, I. L. (1972). Aesthetics. In P. H. Mussen & M. R. Rosenzweig (Eds.), *Annual review of psychology.* Palo Alto, CA: Annual Review.

Cox, C. M. (1926). *Genetic studies of genius: Vol. 2. The early mental traits of three hundred geniuses.* Stanford: Stanford University Press.

Cropley, A. J. (1966). Creativity and intelligence. *British Journal of Educational Psychology,* 36, 259–266.

Darwin, C. (1859). *On the origin of species by means of natural selection.* London: Murray.

Dennett, D. C. (1995). *Darwin's dangerous idea.* New York: Touchstone.

Dudek, S. Z. (in press). Art and aesthetics. In M. A. Runco (Ed.), *Creativity research handbook* (Vol. 2). Cresskill, NJ: Hampton Press.

Dudek, S. Z., & Hall, W. (1991). Personality consistency: Eminent architects 25 years later. *Creativity Research Journal,* 4, 213–232.

Ellenberger, H. F. (1970). *The discovery of the unconscious.* New York: Basic Books.

Engell, J. (1981). *The creative imagination: Enlightenment to romanticism.* Cambridge, MA: Harvard University Press.

Erikson, E. H. (1958). *Young man Luther: A study in psychoanalysis.* New York, London: Norton.

Feist, G. J., & Runco, M. A. (1993). Trends in the creativity literature: An analysis of research in the *Journal of Creativity Behavior* (1967–1989). *Creativity Research Journal,* 6, 271–286.

Florida, R. (2002). *The rise of the creative class: And how it's transforming work, leisure, community and everyday life.* New York: Basic Books.

Freud, S. (1953). The interpretation of dreams. In J. Strachey (Ed. & Trans.), *The standard edition of the complete psychological works of Sigmund Freud* (Vols. 4–5). London: Hogarth Press. (Original work published 1900)

Freud, S. (1958). The relation of the poet to day-dreaming. In B. Nelson (Ed.), *On creativity and the unconscious.* New York: Harper & Row. (Original work published 1908)

Galton, F. (1869). *Hereditary genius.* New York: MacMillan

Galton, F. (1874). *English men of science: Their nature and nurture.* London: MacMillan.

Galton, F. (1883). *Inquiries into human faculty.* London: Macmillan.

Gardner, H. (1993). *Creating minds: An anatomy of creativity seen though the lives of Freud, Einstein, Picasso, Stravinsky, Eliot, Graham, and Gandhi.* New York: Basic Books.

Gardner, H. (1994). More on private intuitions and public symbol systems. *Creativity Research Journal,* 7, 265–275.

Gruber, H. E. (1996). The life space of a scientist: The visionary function and other aspects of Jean Piaget's thinking. *Creativity Research Journal,* 9, 251–265.

Guilford, J. P. (1950). Creativity. *American Psychologist,* 5, 444–454.

Guilford, J. P. (1967). *The nature of human intelligence.* New York: McGraw-Hill.

Guilford, J. P. (1968). *Creativity, intelligence, and their educational implications.* San Diego, CA: Knapp/EDITS.

Helson, R. (1987). Which of those women with creative potential became creative? In R. Hogan & W. H. Jones (Eds.), *Perspectives in personality* (Vol. 2, pp. 51–92). Greenwich, CT: JAI.

Helson, R. (1990). Creativity in women: Inner and outer views over time. In M. A. Runco & R. S. Albert (Eds.), *Theories of creativity* (pp. 46–58). Newbury Park, CA: Sage.

Helson, R. (1996). In search of the creative personality. *Creativity Research Journal,* 9, 295–306.

Helson, R. (1999). Institute of Personality Assessment and Research. In M. A. Runco & S. Pritzker (Eds.), *Encyclopedia of creativity* (pp. 71–79). San Diego, CA: Academic Press.

Hughes, H. S. (1953). *Consciousness and society.* New York: Vintage Press.

James, W. (1880). Great Men, Great Thoughts, and the Environment. Lecture delivered before the Harvard Natural History Society. Published in the *Atlantic Monthly,* October, 1880.

James, W. (1992). William James on exceptional mental states: The 1896 Lowell lecture. In R. S. Albert (Ed.), *Genius and eminence* (2nd ed., pp. 41–52). Oxford: Pergamon.

Jevons, W. S. (1877). *The principles of science: A treatise on logic and scientific method.* New York: Macmillan.

Kaufman, P. (1926). *Essays in memory of Barrett Wendell* (pp. 191–217). Cambridge, MA: Harvard University Press.

Kaun, D. E. (1991). Writers die young: The impact of work and leisure on longevity. *Journal of Economic Psychology*, 12, 381–399.

Kroeber, A. (1944). *Configurations of cultural growth*. Berkeley: University of California Press.

Kubie, L. S. (1961). *Neurotic distortion of the creative process*. New York: Noonday Press.

Kwang, N. (2001). *Why Asians are less creative than Westerners*. Singapore: Prentice-Hall.

Lamb, D., & Easton, S. M. (1984). *Multiple discovery: The pattern of scientific progress*. Abebury, UK: Abebury.

MacKinnon, D. W. (1962). The nature and nurture of creative talent. *American Psychologist*, 17, 484–495.

MacKinnon, D. W. (1963). Creativity and images of the self. In R. W. White (Ed.), *The study of lives* (pp. 251–278). New York: Atherton Press.

MacKinnon, D. W. (1970). The personality correlates of creativity: A study of American architects. In P. E. Vernon (Ed.), *Creativity*. Harmondsworth: Penguin.

MacKinnon, D. W. (1975). IPAR's contribution to the conceptualization and study of creativity. In I. A. Taylor & J. W. Getzels (Eds.), *Perspectives in creativity*. Chicago: Adaline.

MacKinnon, D. W. (1983). The highly effective individual. In R. S. Albert (Ed.), *Genius and eminence: A social psychology of creativity and exceptional achievement* (pp. 114–127). Oxford: Pergamon. (Original work published 1960)

Malthus, R. (1798). *Essay on the principle of population*. London: J. Johnson.

Martindale, C. (1990). *The clockwork muse. The predictability of artistic change*. New York: Basic Books.

Martindale, C. (2007). The foundation and future of the Society for the Psychology of Aesthetics, Creativity, and the Arts. *Psychology of Aesthetics, Creativity, and the Arts*, 1, 121–132.

Maslow, A. H. (1973). Creativity in self-actualizing people. In A. Rothenberg & C. R. Hausman (Eds.), *The creative question* (pp. 86–92). Durham, NC: Duke University Press.

Mednick, S. A. (1962). The associative basis of the creative process. *Psychological Review*, 69, 220–232.

Minton, H. L. (1988). Charting life history: Lewis M. Terman's study of the gifted. In J. G. Morawski (Ed.), *The rise of experimentation in American psychology* (pp. 138–160). New Haven, CT: Yale University Press.

Muller, J. Z. (1995). *Adam Smith in his time and ours*. Princeton, NJ: Princeton University Press.

Mumford, M. D., & Gustafson, S. G. (1988). Creativity syndrome: Integration, application, and innovation. *Psychological Bulletin*, 103, 27–43.

Murphy, G. (1958). The creative eras. In *Human potentialities* (pp. 142–157). New York: Basic Books.

Nahm, M. (1957). *The artists as creator*. Baltimore, MD: Johns Hopkins University Press.

Naroll, R., Benjamin, E. C., Fohl, F. K., Fried, R. E., Hildreth, R. E., & Schaefer, J. M. (1971). Creativity: Cross-historical pilot study. *Journal of Cross-Cultural Psychology*, 2, 181–188.

Pratt, C. (1961). Aesthetics. In P. H. Mussen & M. R. Rosenzweig (Eds.), *Annual review of psychology*. Palo Alto, CA: Annual Reviews.

Prickett, S. (1996). *Origins of narrative: The Romantic appropriation of the Bible*. Cambridge: Cambridge University Press.

Roe, A. (1952). *The making of a scientist*. New York: Dodd, Mead.

Rothenberg, A., & Hausman, C. R. (1976). *The creativity question*. Durham, NC: Duke University Press.

Runco, M. A. (1986). Divergent thinking and creative performance in gifted and nongifted children. *Educational and Psychological Measurement*, 46, 375–384.

Runco, M. A. (1988). Creativity research: Originality, utility, and integration. *Creativity Research Journal*, 1, 1–7.

Runco, M. A. (1993). Operant theories of insight, originality, and creativity. *American Behavioral Scientist*, 37, 59–74.

Runco, M. A. (2001). Foreword: The intersection of creativity and culture. In N. A. Kwang, *Why Asians are less creative than Westerners*. Singapore: Prentice-Hall.

Runco, M. A. (2004). Personal creativity and culture. In L. Sing, A. N. N. Hui, & G. C. Ng (Eds.), *Creativity: When East meets West* (pp. 9–21). Singapore: World Scientific Publishing.

Runco, M. A. (2007). *Creativity: Theories, themes, and issues*. San Diego, CA: Academic Press.

Runco, M. A., & Richards, R. (1997). *Eminent creativity, everyday creativity, and health*. Norwood, NJ: Ablex.

Sass, L. A. (2000). Schizophrenia, modernism, and the "creative imagination": On creativity and psychopathology. *Creativity Research Journal*, 13, 55–74.

Shapin, S. (1996). *The scientific revolution.* Chicago, IL: University of Chicago Press.

Simonton, D. K. (1997). Political pathology and societal creativity. In M. A. Runco & R. Richards (Eds.), *Eminent creativity, everyday creativity, and health* (pp. 359–377). Greenwich, CT: Ablex.

Simonton, D. K. (1999). Historiometry. In M. A. Runco & S. Pritzker (Eds.), *Encyclopedia of creativity* (pp. 815–822). San Diego, CA: Academic Press.

Singer, J. L. (1981–1982). Towards the scientific study of imagination. *Imagination, Cognition and Personality*, 1, 5–28.

Sternberg, R. J., & Lubart, T. L. (1996). Investing in creativity. *American Psychologist*, 51, 677–688.

Terman, L. M. (1906). Genius and stupidity: A study of the intellectual processes of seven "bright" and seven "stupid" boys. *Pedagogical Seminary*, 13, 307–373.

Terman, L. M. (1917). The intelligence quotient of Francis Galton in childhood. *American Journal of Psychology*, 209–215.

Terman, L. M. (1924). The mental tests as a psychological method. *Psychological Review*, 31, 93–117.

Terman, L. M., & Chase, J. M. (1920). The psychology, biology, and pedagogy of genius. *Psychological Bulletin*, 17, 397–409.

Valliant, G. E. (1977). *Adaptation to life.* Boston, MA: Little, Brown.

Wallach, M. A. (1983). What do tests tell us about talent? In R. S. Albert (Ed.), *Genius and eminence* (pp. 99–113). Oxford: Pergamon.

Winston-Given, C. (1996). *An illustrated history of the late medieval England.* Manchester: Manchester University Press.

Willerman, L. (1986). *The psychology of individual and group differences.* San Francisco, CA: W. H. Freeman.

CHAPTER 2

Theories of Creativity

Aaron Kozbelt, Ronald A. Beghetto, and Mark A. Runco

Introduction: Moderation and Pluralism in Considering Theories of Creativity

The claim usually worded "moderation in all things" applies to many aspects of creativity. For instance, autonomy is good for creativity and its development, but too much autonomy, and there may be no direction, no focus (Albert & Runco, 1989). The same can be said about competition, challenges, constraints, attention, experience, and many other potential influences on creativity (Runco, 2001; Runco & Sakamoto, 1996). Moderation is also applicable to creative behavior. For example, creative ideas often result from divergent thinking, but too much divergence leads to irrelevant ideas that are not creative in the sense of being both original and useful. Moderation also plays a role in the tactic usually summarized as "shift your perspective," which can contribute to original insights. Changes in perspective can be useful, but not if they are so extreme that ideas and solutions have no connection to the problem at hand.

The notion of shifting one's perspective can also extend the idea of moderation to a higher level – that of the scientific enterprise, as applied to the study of creativity. To understand creativity in all of its richness, there is a need for moderation, where no one theoretical perspective is emphasized at the expense of others. Another way to consider moderation in this context is to emphasize *pluralism*, whereby a multitude of theoretical perspectives, with different assumptions and methods, and operating at different levels of analysis, all (ideally) contribute to a more robust – if at times, contestable – understanding of human creativity.

This chapter provides a comparative review of major contemporary theories of creativity. The chapter is organized into two major sections. The first section presents a discussion of how the theories will be classified and compared, highlighting key challenges, considerations, and limitations. The second presents an overview of ten categories of contemporary creativity theories, highlighting the underlying assertions, key concepts, major studies, and contemporary exemplars associated with each category. The chapter closes with a brief discussion of future directions and considerations for the future development of theories of creativity.

Section I: Classifying and Comparing Theories

When attempting to review something as diverse and complex as creativity theories, it is helpful to stake out points or elements of comparison. Of course, every classification system has limitations. The choice of comparative elements is open to debate, and the resulting categorizations run the risk of oversimplifying and obscuring some aspects of a theory, while overemphasizing and privileging others. In this chapter, we choose categories and comparative elements to highlight similarities and differences across the diverse array of major creativity theories. We believe that these categories and comparative elements provide a reasonable overview of the theoretical landscape of creativity studies, which researchers can use to guide subsequent inquiry and theory development. In the sections that follow, the classifications and comparative elements used in organizing this chapter are discussed.

Classifying Theory Types and Orientations

Not all creativity theories are alike. This quickly becomes evident when considering the panoply of perspectives on creativity. This variation is partly due to the richness of the topic itself, which encompasses the subjective experience of the moment of a private, minor insight by an ordinary individual as well as the greatest achievements of human genius throughout our history – what might be called "the mind's best work" (Perkins, 1981). The variation is compounded by the fact that creativity involves a multitude of definitions, conceptualizations, domains, disciplines that bear on its study, empirical methods, and levels of analysis, as

well as research orientations that are both basic and applied – and applied in varied contexts. When faced with such an array of perspectives, the need for some way to characterize commonalities among creativity theories – while still recognizing important differences – becomes paramount.

We have organized our review across ten major categories of theories: in order, *Developmental, Psychometric, Economic, Stage and Componential Process, Cognitive, Problem Solving and Expertise-Based, Problem Finding, Evolutionary, Typological*, and *Systems*. Each category is discussed in the second section of this chapter. Some, but not all, of the theoretical categories have their basis in prior categorization systems (e.g., Runco, 2004a, 2007a) and thus have some precedent in the creativity literature. Still, the categories are not monolithic; in some cases there is as much within-category variation in the type of theories as there is difference between categories. One such area of within-category variation pertains to the orientation – more scientific versus more metaphorical – of representative theories. Although we do not label each theory reviewed in this chapter in this way, we think it important to contrast these two orientations as a way of highlighting their relative strengths and weaknesses. In this way we hope to communicate the benefits and challenges that this aspect of theoretical plurality offers.

We define scientifically oriented theories as having an underlying goal of mapping the empirical reality of creative phenomena. In contrast, more metaphorically oriented theories attempt to provide alternative representations of creative phenomena. We describe theories as having an "orientation" to signal that these two basic types (scientific vs. metaphorical) are not mutually exclusive nor endpoints on a unidimensional continuum, but instead are better thought of in terms of two separate dimensions, empirical support and metaphoricity. For instance, metaphorically oriented theories are often underwritten by rigorous empirical study; likewise, more scientifically oriented theories often use metaphors (e.g., the mind as an information processor) to illustrate key principles.

Although the two orientations can share common ground, there are obviously also important differences. Scientifically oriented theories aspire to meet *traditional scientific standards*: a search for objective truth, generating empirically falsifiable hypotheses, and developing formal or computational models, along the lines of the harder sciences. Consider the observations of Nobel laureate Peter Medawar (1991, p. 85), potent and sobering food for thought for any creativity researcher:

> *We must study particulars and not abstractions. . . . The scientific student of creativity would accordingly investigate a number of different kinds of creative episodes to see what he could find in common between them. A scientist will shun an explanation which, while it outwardly has the form of an explanation, does no more in fact that interpret one unknown in terms of another. A scientist will take evidence from all quarters likely to be informative, not excluding introspection, for no good would come of self-righteously abjuring such an important source of evidence. A scientist must be resolutely critical, seeking reasons to disbelieve hypotheses, perhaps especially those which he has thought of himself and thinks rather brilliant.*

From such a hard-nosed perspective, many so-called "theories" of creativity are, to quote physicist Wolfgang Pauli, "not even wrong" – that is, they are not sufficiently well articulated or substantive to be informative one way or the other. Although not all approaches to creativity aim to meet traditional standards, noting these standards is useful not only for those who seek an unabashedly scientific understanding of creativity, but also for forming a basis of comparison for more metaphorically oriented theories.

Whereas scientifically oriented theories endeavor to provide an empirically accurate map of reality, often with the hope of growing into grand theories that have wide (if not universal) applicability, metaphorically oriented theories offer a more speculative stance on phenomena and focus on provoking new understandings and possibilities. Said another way, metaphorically oriented theories offer a moderating counterbalance to the sometimes stark empirical focus of scientific theories. This is important given the potential for more scientifically oriented theories to drift into conceptual and empirical extremes, in which researchers find themselves (inadvertently) shackled to the observable, failing (or perhaps refusing) to consider or conjecture beyond that which is directly observable. The problem with an extreme empiricist position is perhaps best captured in T. H. Huxley's admonition, "those who refuse to go beyond fact seldom get as far as fact" (cited in Smythe, 2005, p. 283). When extreme empiricism becomes the driving force in a field of study, the resulting research programs run the risk of drifting into a form of analytically rigorous journalism (chasing after and documenting phenomena), as opposed to mapping out potential, not yet experienced, possibilities. Einstein's breakthrough theoretical work on special relativity, for instance, would have been impossible if he had limited himself to the directly observable.

The promise of metaphorically oriented theories, then, is that they focus more on hypothetical or "as if" (Vaihinger, 1911/1952) modes of thinking, which can "provide entry into imaginative possibilities both for theorizing and for self-understanding in everyday life" (Smythe, 2005, p. 284). Such theories can spark new possibilities in thought and action, help people break free from overly restrictive and hegemonic beliefs about creativity, and – in some cases – carry more ontological traction and deliver more practical significance than more scientifically oriented frameworks. Of course, this doesn't mean that anything goes when it comes to more metaphorically oriented theories; otherwise they would run the risk of becoming nothing more than wild speculations and self-justifications. Metaphorically oriented theories are of maximal use when they balance speculation with agreed-upon methods of empirical exploration, peer review, and the postulation of theoretical propositions that are open to empirical inquiry, elaboration, and refinement.

*In sum, t*he phenomenon of creativity, richly considered, involves many nuances and interpretations; only rather narrow aspects of creativity are readily understandable in terms of empirically falsifiable hypotheses, with resulting verdicts that suggest definite winners or losers. Also, conclusions may depend strongly on how terms are defined; a conclusion that appears true by one definition of creativity may simply not apply when another is used. Since the empirical study of creativity is of fairly recent origin (Guilford, 1950), it is probably a healthy viewpoint that theories not be overly restrictive, lest researchers lose sight of important issues and potential connections.

Categories of Creative Magnitude

When comparing theories of creativity, it is also useful to differentiate between levels of creative magnitude – smaller c (often more subjective) versus Larger C (more objective) creativity (Csikszentmihalyi, 1996, 1998; Stein, 1953). This allows us to consider the scope and focus of theories, what may be missing, and what methods and measures might be most appropriate for empirically testing and exploring a theory's central propositions. Beyond being useful, some creativity researchers have argued that such distinctions are necessary, as they may allow for a more complete consideration and conceptualization of creativity. Stein (1953), for instance, asserted that the tendency for creativity researchers to focus on genius (or Larger C) levels of creativity "causes us to *overlook a necessary distinction* between the creative product and the creative experience" (p. 312, italics added).

The creative experience represents the more subjective forms of creativity, possibly never resulting in a tangible product, never undergoing external evaluation, or never traveling beyond an individual's own personal insights and interpretations (Beghetto & Kaufman, 2007; Runco, 1996; Vygotsky, 1967/2004). Overlooking these subjective

creative experiences in favor of objectively evaluated creative products can result in a partial conception of creative phenomena (Stein, 1953), runs the risk of excluding theoretical consideration of creative potential (Runco, 2004b, 2007b), and may reinforce myths and misconceptions about the nature of creativity (Beghetto, 2007; Plucker, Beghetto, & Dow, 2004).

When comparing theoretical conceptions of creativity, it therefore seems important and perhaps, as Stein (1953) argued, even "necessary to distinguish between internal and external frames of reference" (p. 312). Such distinctions allow for a clearer understanding of the scope, nature, and limitations of theories under consideration. The most common distinction has been the *Big C* (eminent) / *little-c* (everyday) dichotomy. Big-C Creativity refers to unambiguous examples of creative expression (e.g., Dickinson's poetry, Coltrane's jazz, Freud's psychology). In contrast, little-c creativity focuses on the creativity of everyday life (Richards, 2007) – experiences and expressions accessible to most anyone, for example, the novel way a home cook includes ingredients in a recipe, which is later praised by family and friends.

As with most dichotomies, however, the Big-C / little-c categories can lack nuance and, somewhat paradoxically, be too inclusive in some instances and not inclusive enough in others. For instance, compare a non-eminent artist (who makes her living selling watercolor paintings and teaching water-coloring at the local community college) with that of a weekend watercolorist (who dabbles in his free time, gives some of his creations away to friends, but doesn't care to sell a painting) with that of an elementary school student who loves to paint with watercolor (and every time she does, she has new and personally meaningful insights about how to combine shapes, shades, textures, and colors). Each represents qualitatively different levels of creativity; however, none qualify as Big-C Creativity (comparable to the watercolors of Cézanne, Dürer, or Kandinsky) – so should these non-eminent examples all be lumped together into the little-c category? Doing so obscures potentially important within-category differences. One way to resolve this limitation is to make the categories more restrictive (e.g., including only objective and clear-cut examples of creativity), but doing so runs the already mentioned risks of excluding consideration of creative potential and more subjective forms of creative experience.

In an effort to address this limitation in the traditional dichotomy, Kaufman and Beghetto (2009) argued for the use of two additional categories (*mini-c* and *Pro-c*). The mini-c category helps differentiate the subjective and objective forms of little-c creativity (Beghetto & Kaufman, 2007); making room for the more subjective or personal (Runco, 1996, 2004b), internal (Stein, 1953), or mental or emotional (Vygotsky, 1967/2004) forms of creativity. Adding the Pro-c category helps distinguish the grey area between little-c and Big-C Creativity. Pro-c makes room for professional-level creators (like professional artists) who have not yet attained (or may never attain) eminent status, but who are well beyond little-c creators (such as the weekend watercolorist who dabbles for relaxation and enjoyment) in knowledge, motivation, and performance.

Using these four categories in comparing theories can be helpful in highlighting the similarities and differences in the focus and scope of creativity theories. Such categories may also be helpful for considering future directions and potential connections, as well as highlighting the limitations of theories. However, the use of categories to classify creative phenomena (no matter how precise or flexible) is always limited, potentially obscuring as much as clarifying the nature of creativity. Keeping this in mind, we will attempt to judiciously use these categories as a comparative element when we critically consider the theories reviewed in this chapter.

The Four (or Six) P's of Creativity

Besides the previous comparative elements, theoretical approaches to creativity may also

be considered in terms of which aspect or facet of creativity they emphasize (Rhodes, 1961; Runco, 2004b). Traditionally, these aspects have been referred to as the "four P's of creativity": *process, product, person* (or personality), and *place* (or press). More recent versions of this framework (e.g., Runco, 2007a) have extended it to six P's, adding *persuasion* (Simonton, 1990) and *potential* (Runco, 2003). Since this alliterative framework nicely organizes many issues in the study of creativity, we will use it as another means of comparing the scope of different theoretical perspectives. First, we summarize each "P" in turn.

Theories that focus on the creative process aim to understand the nature of the mental mechanisms that occur when a person is engaged in creative thinking or creative activity. Process theories typically specify different stages of processing (e.g., Mace & Ward, 2002; Simonton, 1984; Wallas, 1926; Ward, Smith, & Finke, 1999) or particular mechanisms as the components of creative thought (e.g., Mumford, Baughman, Maher, Costanza, & Supinski, 1997; Mumford, Mobley, Uhlman, Reiter-Palmon, & Doares, 1991). Some key issues in the study of the creative process include the extent to which creative thinking involves the same basic cognitive mechanisms as non-creative thinking, the relative roles of conscious versus unconscious processes, the relative contributions of chance or stochastic processes versus more controlled and guided processes, and the nature and reliability of evaluative processes during the process of creation. A number of theories addressing these process-level themes are described in this chapter.

Probably the most objective approach to creativity focuses on products: works of art, inventions, publications, musical compositions, and so on. Products can usually be counted, thus permitting considerable quantitative objectivity, and they are often available for viewing or judging, so inter-rater reliability can be readily determined – two substantial advantages. A down side is that when studying a product, little can be directly said about the process leading to it or the creator's personality; inferences are thus necessary to inform the creative process or person. Moreover, unambiguously creative products are constructed by unambiguously creative persons. Thus, studies of products tell us about highly creative individuals but not about persons with as-yet-unfulfilled creative potential (Runco, 1996).

Another longstanding perspective on creativity has focused on the creative person (or personality). Much early research compared mathematicians, architects, writers, and other groups in terms of the traits that may be indicative or contraindicative of creative potential. Several traits cut across domains; these include intrinsic motivation, wide interests, openness to experience, and autonomy (Barron, 1995; Helson, 1972). A number of personality traits also appear to be more pervasive either among persons in artistic domains or in scientific domains (Feist, 1998, 1999). Personality is now usually viewed as one influence on creative behavior, rather than a complete explanation (Feist & Barron, 2003).

The expression of personality often depends on the setting or climate in which an individual resides. The research on places or "press" factors (press from pressures) is especially useful in defining such interactions between persons and environments. There are individual differences in terms of preferred environments, but again also general tendencies: Creativity tends to flourish when there are opportunities for exploration and independent work, and when originality is supported and valued (Amabile, 1990; Witt & Boerkem, 1989).

Simonton (1990) offered another perspective following the alliterative scheme by describing creativity as persuasion: Creative people change the way others think, so they must then be persuasive to be recognized as creative. The notion of creativity as persuasion shares assumptions with the social perspective (Amabile, 1990), the attributional theory of creativity (Kasof, 1995), and Csikszentmihalyi's (1988a) systems model. In the last of these, persuasive individuals are the ones who are likely to influence the direction taken by a domain. The emphasis on

persuasion implies that everyday originality (Runco & Richards, 1998) may not be deemed creative, since it is often largely personal.

The enterprise of the study of creativity can thus be categorized in terms of process, products, personality, places, and persuasion. Runco (2008) recently suggested that this might be further organized into a hierarchy that starts with theories of creative *performances* versus creative *potentials*. The former is divided into products and persuasion theories, and any other perspective that focuses on manifest, unambiguously creative behavior; the latter is divided into creative personality and places, and any other perspective that appreciates yet-unfulfilled possibilities and subjective processes. This hierarchical framework captures the earlier alliterative scheme but allows research on everyday creativity and the creative potentials of children and others who may have most of what it takes but require educational opportunities or other support before they can perform in a creative fashion.

Section II: Categories of Theories

We review 10 categories of theories. Space permits only a brief description of the distinguishing features of each category; readers are advised to consult the references for more detailed specifics on particular theories. Our goal is to provide a "big picture" (rather than exhaustive) overview of each type. Likewise, within each category, we highlight a sample of individual theories to illustrate (rather than enumerate) representative theories.

We draw on the comparative elements discussed in Section I to help facilitate this overview. Most of the theories we describe have been discussed in the literature for at least several decades, boast considerable research support, and typically span multiple P's, levels of analysis, and methodologies. We do not review theories that are limited to understanding a fairly narrow aspect or subtopic within creativity – such as creativity's relation to mental illness (Jamison, 1996), or to personality (Barron, 1995; Feist, 1998, 1999), its biological underpinnings (Martindale, 1999), applied techniques intended to enhance creativity (Nickerson, 1999), cultural differences in creativity (Lubart, 1999), and so on. The theories and comparative elements reviewed in Section II are also summarized in Table 2.1.

Developmental Theories

Developmental theories of creativity are among the most practical. Not only do they help us to understand the roots of creativity, as suggested by the background of unambiguously creative persons, but they also often suggest how to design environments so that the creative potentials of children will be fulfilled. Thus, developmental views mainly emphasize the person, place, and potential aspects of creativity, and range from mini-c to Pro-c. Although products are not the primary focus of developmental theories, they still play an important, but often tacit, role. This is because these theories imply a trajectory that starts with more subjective forms of creativity (mini-c) and develops into more tangible and mature forms of creative expression. Early developmental theories were devised by examining the lives and family backgrounds of eminent creative persons (Goertzel & Goertzel, 1976). These suggested that particular developmental experiences were correlated with creativity. For instance, parents of creative children seemed to expose their children to diverse experiences and most were themselves in some ways creative. These families were also characterized by a moderate amount of independence (Albert & Runco, 1989): Parents were aware of what their children were doing but were not overly restrictive. Note that this is not simply an observation without functional connection to creativity. Independence is logically tied to the creative process, as well as apparent in studies of families. Optimal independence allows children to develop autonomy that can then be used in their thinking and would allow them to devise original ideas.

Somewhat more controlled studies of development have focused on family structure. This is not surprising because family structure (e.g., birth order, ordinal position within the family, age interval between siblings, and sibsize – the term used to indicate the number of siblings in a family) have interested social and behavioral scientists, and natural philosophers whose work far predated the social sciences, for some time. To name one outstanding example, Galton (1869) had much to say about hereditary genius. He reported that firstborn children had a significant developmental advantage, and for that reason were often successful. Galton did not look specifically at creativity but instead focused on individuals with more conventional achievements.

Research on family structure has proven useful for constructing theories of creativity. For instance, consider the idea that middle children have certain developmental advantages. Sound evidence suggests that middle children are often rebellious and revolutionary (Gaynor & Runco, 1998; Sulloway, 1996), probably because they are raised in families where there are older, more capable siblings whose maturity earns them parental attention. Middle children therefore find alternative ways to get attention, often by rebelling against parental values and the status quo and finding a unique niche. Rebellion may be within the context of the family, in one's thinking, or, during adulthood, in artistic or scientific revolutions.

Another important area of research involves play and creativity (Ayman-Nolley, 1999; Pearson, Russ, & Cain Spannagel, 2008; Russ & Schafer, 2006). This line of work contributes to our understanding of how nurture and the environment may support creative efforts (e.g., permissive environments allow exploration and imaginative play) and to theories of the creative process itself (e.g., creative ideas may result from the relaxation and enjoyment of play).

The most powerful and trustworthy developmental research is longitudinal. Findings from longitudinal research should thus be very useful for the construction of theories of creativity, although such

Table 2.1: Summary of Theories of Creativity

Category	Primary Assertion	Key Concepts	Six P's Focus	Levels of Magnitude	Major Studies and Examples
Developmental	Creativity develops over time (from potential to achievement); mediated by an interaction of person and environment.	Place and family structures Role of play Support during transitions Longitudinal process Multivariate influences	Person, Place, Potential, & Product	Mini-c to Pro-c	Helson (1999) Subotnik & Arnold (1996) Albert & Runco (1989)
Psychometric	Creativity can be measured reliably and validly; differentiating it from related constructs (IQ) and highlighting its domain-specific nature.	Reliable and valid measurement Discriminant validity Thresholds Domain specificity	Primarily Product	Little-c to Big-C	Guilford (1968) Wallach & Kogan (1965)
Economic	Creative ideation and behavior is influenced by "market forces" and cost-benefit analyses.	Influence of macro-level factors Psychoeconomic perspective Markets of creativity Investment decisions	Person, Place, Product, & Persuasion	Little-c to Big-C	Rubenson & Runco (1992, 1995) Florida (2002) Sternberg & Lubart (1992, 1995)
Stage & Componential Process	Creative expression proceeds through a series of stages or components; the process can have linear and recursive elements.	Preparation stages Incubation and insight Verification and evaluation Component mechanisms	Primarily Process	Mini-c to Big-C	Wallas (1926) Runco & Chand (1995) Amabile (1999)
Cognitive	Ideational thought processes are foundational to creative persons and accomplishments.	Remote association Divergent/convergent thinking Conceptual combination, expansion Metaphorical thinking, imagery Metacognitive processes	Person & Process	Little-c to Big-C	Mednick (1962) Guilford (1968) Finke, Ward, & Smith (1992)

(continued)

Table 2.1 (*continued*)

Category	Primary Assertion	Key Concepts	Six P's Focus	Levels of Magnitude	Major Studies and Examples
Problem Solving & Expertise-Based	Creative solutions to ill-defined problems result from a rational process, which relies on general cognitive processes and domain expertise.	Ill-defined problems Cognitive, computational approach Expertise-based approaches Problem representation & heuristics	Person, Process, & Product	Little-c to Big-C	Ericsson (1999) Simon (1981, 1989) Weisberg (1999, 2006)
Problem Finding	Creative people proactively engage in a subjective and exploratory process of identifying problems to be solved.	Subjective creative processes Exploratory behaviors On-line discovery	Process, Person, & Potential	Primarily Mini-c	Getzels & Csikszentmihalyi (1976) Runco (1994)
Evolutionary (Darwinian)	Eminent creativity results from the evolutionary-like processes of blind generation and selective retention.	Chance-configuration Blind generation of ideas Selective retention of ideas Equal-odds rule Social judgment and chance	Person, Process, Place, & Product	Primarily Big-C	Campbell (1960) Simonton (1988, 1997)
Typological	Creators vary along key individual differences, which are related to both macro- and micro-level factors and can be classified via typologies.	Individual differences Categories of creators Seekers versus finders Integrate multiple levels of analysis	Primarily Person; but also Process, Product, & Place.	Little-c to Big-C	Galenson (2001, 2006) Kozbelt (2008c)
Systems	Creativity results from a complex system of interacting and interrelated factors.	Evolving systems Network of enterprises Domain and field Gatekeepers Collaborative Creativity Chaos and Complexity	Varying emphasis across all P's.	Little-c to Big-C	Gruber (1981a) Csikszentmihalyi (1988a) Sawyer (2006)

investigations are difficult and expensive. A number of very good longitudinal studies have been reported (e.g., Albert & Runco, 1999; Helson, 1999; Plucker, 1999; Subotnik & Arnold, 1996). Albert, for example, has followed a sample of exceptionally gifted boys for over 20 years. He found that during their childhoods, the truly gifted had the support and wherewithal to make cognitive and emotional transitions – one from general to creative talent, and the other from capability to a motivational state that leads directly to actual performance and achievement. Studies like these reinforce theories of creativity that take cognitive processes, motivation, affect, and personality each into account.

Psychometric Theories

Psychometric theories are not constructed to describe the developmental background of creative individuals, nor their thinking patterns or traits or motives. Rather, they are unique in focusing on measurement, and as such they inform all other theories of creativity. Thus, psychometric theories emphasize products over the other P's, and they range from little-c to Big-C Creativity. They do not have any particular dependence on any one model of creativity, nor are they tied to any particular theoretical framework (e.g., cognitive, social, clinical, etc.).

Psychometric theories are concerned, among other things, with the reliability and validity of assessment, which are issues in all scientific work on creativity. *Reliability* represents agreement or consistency of measurement. It includes inter-judge reliability and, within any particular test, inter-item reliability. *Validity* represents the accuracy of measurement. It is usually defined by asking, "are you measuring what you intend to measure?" One category of validity is *criterion-related*, which includes *predictive validity* and *discriminant validity*. Predictive validity indicates how much a measure of creativity offers information about some criterion of real creative behavior. Discriminant validity is especially important because it indicates the degree to which a measure of creativity is distinct from other indices of non-creative talents, like traditional intelligence, IQ, convergent thinking, and so on. This was the most important question in early research, which was motivated to establish creativity as an independent subject of study.

Several seminal studies have supported the discriminant validity of various creativity tests (Wallach & Kogan, 1965), although the exact relationship depends on the level of ability of the individuals being tested, the testing environment, and the tests administered. The first of these, level of ability, has come to be known as a threshold theory because it suggests that below a moderate level of general ability, IQ and the like are strongly related to creativity indices; above that threshold, they are largely independent (see Fuchs-Beauchamp, Karnes, & Johnson, 1993; Kim, 2005; Runco & Albert, 1986). The second item, considering the testing environment, is important for educational settings, as it suggests that permissive environments allow more divergent, original thinking than do typical testing environments.

The third item above, concerning the exact tests used to assess discriminant validity, is clearest in comparisons of *convergent* and *divergent thinking*. These are general labels given to tasks requiring that thinking converges on one correct or conventional answer or else is allowed to move in different directions. Guilford (1968) proposed these ideas as part of his Structure of Intellect (SOI) Theory. He used the terms convergent and divergent production, but what is important here is that the more a test allows divergent thinking, the more it will be independent from measures of convergent thinking. Also very relevant to theories of creativity is that original ideas are possible only when tests (and settings) allow divergent thinking. When it is allowed, a number of ideas can be generated and considered, some of which may be unique or novel. It has been argued that the more remote an idea is (i.e., the farther from the starting point), the more likely it is to be original and potentially creative.

Psychometric studies have also suggested that different domains of creative performance may be distinct from one another. This is another example of discriminant validity (e.g., measures of mathematical creativity differing from verbal creativity), but the implications are enormously important for theories of creativity. Indeed, the idea of domain-specific talents is now prevalent (Albert, 1980; Gardner, 1983; Runco, 1986). It has been around for many years (e.g., Patrick, 1935, 1937), but more recent psychometric studies make it hard to refute (Baer, 1998; Ludwig, 1995; Plucker, 1998). This theme is further taken up in our discussion of the impact of expertise on creativity (in "Problem Solving and Expertise-Based Theories").

Economic Theories

One of the more recent categories of creativity theory draws heavily from economics. This is arguably a fresh and useful perspective, partly because it takes into account very general macro-level processes and influences. Economic theories also offer testable hypotheses about creative efforts. They predict, for instance, that larger groups will inhibit brainstorming because the costs of being different, and therefore original, are higher when the audience is large. They also predict that individuals with high levels of expertise will be less flexible about alternatives, at least those that challenge their own views, than individuals who have invested less into their careers or into a particular theory or method. The macro-level quality of economic and investment theories encompasses all of the P's except process, and spans little-c to Big-C Creativity.

There are several different economic or investment theories of creativity. For instance, Rubenson (1990; Rubenson & Runco, 1992, 1995) offered a psychoeconomic perspective. Rubenson and Runco described the market for creativity, which illustrates macro-level processes and interactions involving the allocation of resources. Markets can provide benefits to certain behaviors, or impose costs on them. Just as in learning theory, benefits tend to literally reinforce and elicit certain behaviors, whereas costs inhibit them and make them less likely. This perspective is psychoeconomic in that benefits and costs may be defined in psychological terms. For example, there might be a stigma to being unconventional, which may inhibit the originality that is required for creativity.

Florida (2002) also examined the market for creative behaviors, going so far as to define a creative class or segment of society. This in turn allowed him to compare different cities and countries in terms of support for and manifestations of creativity. Here again the practicality of economic theory is clear, in that Florida proposed that a key component of the market for creative work is tolerance. Unconventional people sometimes need to be tolerated; and creative societies do a good job of that. Creativity is also, for Florida, dependent on talent and technology.

Sternberg and Lubart (1992, 1995) emphasized investments in creative behavior. Briefly stated, they advocated the idea that creativity sometimes results when an individual buys low (i.e., invests in an idea that is currently unpopular) and then sells high (i.e., the idea gains respect). Sternberg and Lubart also offered an economic metaphor for situations and contexts that influence creative effort, describing both bull and bear markets for creative action.

Stage and Componential Process Theories

As noted, a number of models of the creative process have been proposed that attempt to understand the structure and nature of the creative process in terms of stages, which can be sequential or recursive, or underlying componential cognitive processes. Obviously, such models emphasize process over the other P's; in terms of creative magnitude, they range from mini-c to Big-C Creativity.

One of the most popular and enduring stage theories is that of Wallas (1926; cf. Helmholtz, 1896). It begins with a *preparation* stage where the individual gathers information and defines a problem. Next comes *incubation*, which involves taking some time away from a problem, at least consciously. If incubation is effective, a third stage occurs: insight, or what Wallas called *illumination*. At this point, a solution or idea suddenly makes itself known. Importantly, although the insight may seem like an "a-ha!" moment and may feel like a very sudden inspiration (which is why insights are often symbolized with a light bulb turned on), Gruber (1981b) demonstrated that insights frequently have protracted histories. For Wallas, the final stage was *verification*. At that point, the individual tests the idea or applies the solution. The linearity of Wallas's model has been largely discredited; thus, more recent models have acknowledged the likelihood of recursion, whereby an individual may cycle through the stages multiple times, in various combinations. For example, the individual may attempt to verify an idea but find it only partially adequate, and return to the preparation stage and start over.

Many contemporary theories have delineated the preparation stage of the creative process. This has been called *problem finding* (Getzels & Csikszentmihalyi, 1976; Runco, 1994) or *problem construction* (Mumford, Baughman, Threlfall, Supinski, & Costanza, 1996; Mumford, Reiter-Palmon, & Redmond, 1994); sometimes models specify a sub-stage of *problem identification*, followed by *problem definition*. (See the section titled "Theories Based on Problem Solving and Expertise" for more on problem finding and problem construction.) Similar empirical specificity has been directed at incubation (Gruber, 1981b), insight (Epstein 1990; Epstein & Laptosky, 1999), and verification (Runco, 1989; Runco & Smith, 1991; Runco & Vega, 1992), the last of which is sometimes broken down into valuative and evaluative processes.

Some recent process theories have defined the creative process in terms of component mechanisms rather than stages (e.g., Mumford et al., 1991; Mumford, Supinski, Baughman, Costanza, & Threlfall, 1997). Runco and Chand (1995), for example, presented a two-tiered componential model of the creative process. This differs from the model of Wallas primarily in including a second tier that recognizes the influence of knowledge and information, both procedural and factual, and the influence of motivation, both intrinsic and extrinsic. Amabile's (1999) componential model includes three facets: domain-relevant skills (e.g., knowledge about the domain, technical skills), creativity-relevant skills (e.g., appropriate cognitive style, knowledge of heuristics for generating novel ideas), and task motivation (e.g., attitudes toward specific tasks, perceptions of one's motives). For Amabile, the first of these depends heavily on innate abilities and skills, whereas the second depends on training and experience. The third is a function of intrinsic motivation, absence of extrinsic constraints, and the individual's capacity to minimize the debilitating effects of constraints.

Cognitive Theories

It is difficult to think about creative achievements or performances without assuming that they have some basis in cognition. It is also difficult to think about creative people without assuming that they have some special cognitive abilities. Neither of these assumptions need be true, but there is some indication that differences in cognition can play a major role in creativity. Cognitive theories emphasize the creative process and person: process, in emphasizing the role of cognitive mechanisms as a basis for creative thought; and person, in considering individual differences in such mechanisms.

Cognitive theories of creativity are quite varied. Some focus on universal capacities, like attention or memory; others focus on individual differences, such as those indexed by divergent thinking tasks. Some focus on conscious operations (e.g., tactics), whereas others point to preconscious, implicit, or unintentional processes. Some posit that creativity is a kind of problem solving, and others include cognitive processes that are arguably relatively independent of problem solving, such as problem finding.

One venerable cognitive theory argues that creative insights can result from associative processes. Mednick (1962) described how ideas are chained together, one after another, and how *remote associates* tend to be original. Associations among ideas may be formed for various reasons, for instance, being functionally or even acoustically related. Apparently some individuals tend to move quickly from obvious associates to remote ones. In this view, more creative individuals tend to have flatter hierarchies of associations than less creative individuals; in other words, more creative people have many more relatively strong associates for a given concept, rather than only a few, which is thought to provide greater scope for the simultaneous activation of far-flung representations.

As noted earlier, another theory that relies on the idea as the unit of cognition is Guilford's (1968) SOI model, which originally contained 80 different kinds of cognition. Later, Guilford claimed that he had identified 120 different kinds, and not long before his death he proposed 180 "cells" in the SOI (Guilford, 1980). His statistical methods were questionable, however, and usually it is his distinction between *divergent* and *convergent thinking* that is used in studies of creative cognition. Divergent thinking occurs when ideas and associations move in varied directions, and as a result new and original ideas may be found (Mednick, 1962; Torrance, 1995). Convergent thinking, on the other hand, occurs when cognition is used to identify one correct or conventional answer. Divergent and convergent thinking can both be involved in creative efforts, which allows the generation of ideas that are both original and effective (Cropley, 2006).

There is good reason to believe that cognitive research can determine what occurs before creative ideas are conceived. One promising line of research focuses on concepts as the unit of analysis. Concepts may be viewed as rather flexible cognitive structures. Research in the past 10 years or so suggests that conceptual combination – bringing two different sets of information together – is often involved in creative problem solving and ideation (Estes & Ward, 2002; Mobley, Doares, & Mumford, 1992; Mumford, Baughman, et al., 1997; Sternberg & Lubart, 1995; Ward et al., 1999). Indeed, Estes and Ward (2002) argued that this is how emergent properties and insights arise. They described how original insights are more likely when two disparate features are brought together and how connections between these concepts might be seen only at a very high level of abstraction. This kind of thinking has been called metaphoric logical, the idea being that something like "angry weather" is only comprehensible in a non-literal fashion. Such metaphorical thinking and conceptual combination apparently suggest creative alternatives to trite or common lines of thought.

More generally, research in the "creative cognition approach" tradition (e.g., Finke et al., 1992; Ward et al., 1999), another important contemporary view of creativity, has likewise emphasized ideas drawn from cognitive psychology (e.g., conceptual combination, conceptual expansion, creative imagery, and metaphor) to understand how individuals generate ideas and explore their implications in lab-based invention and design tasks. Such processes are thought to play out in two fundamental regimes of thought: generating ideas and exploring their implications. In practice, the two are strongly interleaved and combined in the "geneplore" model of creative thought (from *gene*rate + ex*plore*).

Metacognitive processes are also frequently tied to creative thinking. These are entirely under conscious control. For instance, tactical thinking is metacognitive, and not surprisingly dozens of tactics for increasing the probability of creative problem solving have been proposed, including "think backwards," "turn the situation upside down," "shift your perspective," "put the problem aside," and "question assumptions." Tactical thinking is especially useful for programs designed to facilitate creative problem solving precisely because they are a function of conscious decisions and can be employed when the need arises (Davis, 1999).

Theories Based on Problem Solving and Expertise

A related major category of creativity theories, again drawn primarily from cognitive psychology, emphasizes problem-solving processes and expert knowledge (e.g., Ericsson, 1999; Newell, Shaw, & Simon, 1962; Simon, 1981, 1989; Weisberg, 1999, 2006). This perspective is largely a theory of the creative person and the creative process: person, in emphasizing domain-specific expertise as a necessary condition for significant creative achievements; and process, in emphasizing how traditional cognitive psychological concepts like problem representations and heuristic search through problem spaces explain how people generate creative solutions to problems. Like the creative cognition approach, the problem-solving/expertise view explicitly argues that creative thought ultimately stems from mundane cognitive processes (see also Perkins, 1981), although expertise-based theories often focus on Big-C Creativity, whereas the creative cognition approach more typically addresses little-c creativity.

Problem solving has usually been studied in puzzle-problems like cryptarithmetic (Newell & Simon, 1972), but its principles also apply to ill-defined problems, which are more relevant to creativity. Such problems, like writing a symphony or designing a house, have goals and operators that are not pre-specified and that admit multiple "good-enough" solutions, rather than one "correct" answer. Simon (1981) argued that ill-defined problems can often be broken into a set of well-defined problems, which can then be solved in familiar ways. Moreover, one can search not only for a solution to a problem, but also for a way to formulate or represent the problem (Simon, 1989).

In this view, Big-C instances of creativity typically emerge through the application of a domain-specific expert-knowledge base acquired over a decade or more of intensive study. Across domains, expertise profoundly affects performance and cognition: Experts remember domain-relevant patterns better, are more adept at generating effective problem representations, and typically engage in efficient forward reasoning in problem solving, rather than laborious backward reasoning (Ericsson & Charness, 1994). It has been argued that such advantages can facilitate performance even in more open-ended, "creative" domains, like art or music composition (Ericsson, 1999; Kozbelt, 2008c).

The problem-solving/expertise view boasts considerable support, from many lines of evidence. Many of the processes and structures described in the creative-cognition approach can be straightforwardly related to those of the problem-solving/expertise view (Kozbelt & Durmysheva, 2007b). Similarly, laboratory studies of insight problems (e.g., Kaplan & Simon, 1990; Weisberg & Alba, 1981) have demonstrated the importance of generating appropriate problem representations, using heuristics like noticing invariant characteristics of unsuccessful solution attempts, and have further demystified some of the cognitive processes leading to "a-ha!" moments.

Archival studies also show the key importance of expert knowledge for Big-C Creativity. For instance, Hayes (1989) found that for 73 of 76 great composers, at least 10 years of musical study were required before writing a masterwork; the exceptions occurred in years 8 and 9. The "ten-year rule" has been found in many domains (Bloom, 1985; Chase & Simon, 1973; Gardner, 1993; Kozbelt, 2005, 2008c; Simonton, 1991a). Likewise, Weisberg (1986, 1993, 1999, 2006) has repeatedly demonstrated the ubiquity of expert knowledge for Big-C Creativity, in detailed historical case studies of great creators, ranging from Mozart to the Beatles and from Watt to Watson and Crick. Similarly, the archival study of individual creative episodes, taken from the notebooks of eminent scientists, has generated a number of computational models of the creative process (e.g., Kulkarni & Simon, 1988; Langley, Simon, Bradshaw, & Zytkow, 1987), which have replicated many major scientific discoveries.

In sum, the problem-solving/expertise view regards creativity as an essentially rational phenomenon. At the level of the investigator, creativity is amenable to rigorous empirical study; at the level of the creator, it is amenable to meaningful strategic guidance and long-term learning. Thus, another advantage of this view is pragmatic and pedagogical: Its foci are strategic, knowledge-based factors that individuals can partly control, rather than factors that are linked to creativity but that are more fixed, like IQ or personality, or undesirable, such as early parental loss. At the same time, the problem-solving/expertise view acknowledges that Big-C problems are difficult; one simply cannot create a good symphony or theory of physics without enormous amounts of relevant background knowledge.

On the other hand, the problem-solving/ expertise view has some limitations. For instance, the explanatory power of expertise is limited in that it is a necessary but not sufficient condition for Big-C Creativity; in other words, it is only one of a number of factors that contribute to high-level creativity (Eysenck, 1995; Murray, 2003; Simonton, 2004). Moreover, some eminent creators appear to have violated the "ten-year rule" (Galenson, 2001, 2006). Along these lines, it has been argued that the expertise view overstates the role of cumulative deliberate practice, at the expense of talent (Simonton, 1991a, 1991b, 2000, 2007b; Sternberg, 1996; Winner, 1996, 2000). Finally, the computational approach to creativity championed by Simon and colleagues has been criticized as fundamentally misguided (e.g., Csikszentmihalyi, 1988b; Sawyer, 2006; Simonton, 2004), but this is too complex an issue to resolve here.

On balance, the problem-solving/expertise perspective has made major and provocative contributions to the scientific study of creativity. However, it has been starkly contrasted with other accounts – particularly the "problem-finding" and "Darwinian" views of creativity, which are now described in turn.

Problem-Finding Theories

"Problem finding," another influential view of creativity, can be seen as a reaction against the application of traditional problem-solving ideas to creativity (Runco, 1994). The problem-finding view holds that the traditional problem-solving view is inadequate to explain how creators come to realize that a problem exists in the first place, and how they are motivated to proactively bring their subjective experience to understand the problem. In this view, heuristic search through a problem space simply does not apply to situations like making a painting, since there is no pre-specified set of alternatives to comprise the problem space. Problem finding is widely regarded as independent of problem solving, and it is mainly a theory of the creative process; it can also be seen as a theory of the creative person, assuming that something like the propensity for identifying interesting problems represents a stable personality variable (Perkins, 1981). In terms of creative magnitude, the act of problem finding can often be construed as an instance of mini-c creativity (as problem finding involves the more subjective, novel insights and personally meaningful interpretations of creators), although there is room for higher levels of creative achievement as well (when, for instance, creators are able to share their process and others come to see it as a novel and meaningful way for identifying and exploring problems).

Getzels and Csikszentmihalyi (1976) most influentially articulated the concept of problem finding. They observed 31 college art students in an open-ended task in which they arranged and drew from a set of objects. The researchers were particularly interested in exploratory behaviors, that is, activities that were not pre-determined but that emerged in the course of the task – and that they saw as representing a kind of processing rooted strongly in motivational factors and existential concerns. Getzels and Csikszentmihalyi found that the more creative artists more often engaged in behaviors like handling more objects before drawing, manipulating them more, and introducing more changes to the emerging drawing. Notably, exploratory behaviors during one drawing session predicted success in the art world years later (Csikszentmihalyi & Getzels, 1989).

Perhaps because the problem-finding view is more subjectively oriented than the problem-solving/expertise view, it is more difficult to cite evidence directly and definitively bearing on problem finding, either pro or con. This is especially true because the precise nature of problem finding is unclear (Dudek & Côté, 1994). Although a number of studies have claimed to find evidence supporting the notion of problem finding (Moore, 1985; Runco, 1994), it may be possible to reinterpret such results via a more traditional problem-solving framework (Kozbelt, 2008b) or other conceptualizations, like "problem expression" (Dudek & Côté, 1994). The problem-finding view also arguably overemphasizes on-line discovery, at the expense of considering habitual patterns of behavior. For instance, Getzels and Csikszentmihalyi (1976) coded any unusual artistic behaviors as exploratory, although these could well be standard – if idiosyncratic – aspects of an artist's approach to art making; this distinction would not be evident unless multiple sessions were observed. More generally, as Simon (1988) observed, many problems in science, such as the nature of universal gravitation in Isaac Newton's time, were widely appreciated and did not have to be "discovered" in any meaningful sense; what counted as creative was solving the known problem.

In sum, the distinction between the problem-solving and problem-finding frameworks may be less a matter of substantive differences between the theories and more a matter of the emphases, goals, and tastes of individual researchers. If one is more interested in creators' subjective experience or their reasons for making art, problem finding is likely to be the more appealing framework; if one is more interested in the cognitive mechanisms by which new ideas arise and are given form, problem solving,

applied to ill-defined problems, is probably more appealing. Interestingly, more recent models examining the creative process have tended to focus less on such labels and more on the nature of the underlying processes. For instance, Mumford and colleagues (e.g., Mumford et al., 1994; Mumford et al., 1996) have typically used the label "problem construction" to encapsulate the constellation of processes involved in understanding, representing, strategizing to solve, and searching for a creative solution to an ill-defined problem.

Evolutionary Theories

Researchers have proposed a number of theories of creativity drawing on ideas from evolutionary biology, which can be Darwinian (e.g., Albert, in press; Lumsden, 1999; Lumsden & Findlay, 1988; Simonton, 1997, 1999) or Lamarckian (Johnson-Laird, 1993) in nature. Of these, a strong candidate for the most comprehensive theory of creativity – generally speaking – is the Darwinian (formerly "chance-configuration") model of Dean Keith Simonton (1984, 1988, 1997, 1999, 2003, 2004). To varying extents, Simonton's model covers all of the P's of creativity: person and potential, in identifying dispositional and developmental idiosyncrasies associated with the realization of initial creative potential into actual creative achievements; process, in laying out a two-step model of ideation and elaboration, in which chance combinations of ideas play a paramount role and whose complexities are hard to control; product, in noting sometimes unreliable initial assessments versus longer-term stable judgments of creative artifacts; place, in identifying social factors leading to outstanding creativity; and persuasion, in emphasizing how social dynamics establish verdicts of creative outcomes. More than any other theory of creativity, Simonton's Darwinian view aims to understand the nature of genius, eminence, and Big-C achievements.

The basis of Simonton's Darwinian model is a two-stage mental process, involving the blind generation and selective retention and elaboration of ideas (Campbell, 1960). In this view, ideas are combined in some blind fashion, typically below the threshold of awareness; the most interesting combinations are then consciously elaborated into finished creative products; these in turn are judged by other people. Simonton (1984, 1988, 1997, 2004) has developed Campbell's argument into a sophisticated quantitative model of how creative productivity unfolds over the life span, with broad implications for understanding the nature of eminence, the creative process, and creative environments. The model takes individual differences in "creative potential" as a starting point. Over time, a creator expends this potential through creation and recoups a smaller amount through learning. These assumptions permit modeling of the typical inverted, backwards J-shaped trajectory of career-wise creative productivity via a differential equation with only four parameters (initial creative potential, career age, ideation rate, and elaboration rate), which closely matches observed data (Simonton, 1997). In general, it is probably fair to say that the model's highly quantitative basis gives it a rigor that is unsurpassed by any other major theory of creativity.

Simonton has mustered substantial support for the Darwinian view by pioneering the analysis of archival data. These data detail variations in career trajectories and landmarks (e.g., first, best, and last hit) that are well explained via individual differences in creative potential and inter-domain differences in ideation and elaboration rates. For instance, age at best work is unrelated to eminence, at least after control for potential confounds, just as specified by Simonton's model (Murray, 2003; Oromaner, 1977; Over, 1982, 1988; Simonton, 1991b; but see Kozbelt & Durmysheva, 2007a). Moreover, domains like theoretical physics and lyric poetry, which have relatively fast ideation and elaboration rates, show sharper career-wise increases and declines – and earlier peaks – than, say, history or geology, which have slower rates (Simonton, 1997).

Another provocative claim is that creative ideation follows a constant probability of success: the "equal-odds rule" (Dennis, 1966). One implication of the rule is a hypothesized null relation between creators' lifetime hit ratios and total output, a result consistent with empirical findings (see Simonton, 2004). Another is its longitudinal aspect, which states that hit ratio – high-impact works divided by total works created in a particular age interval – should show no systematic relation with creator age (Simonton, 1977a, 1985). Simonton (1999) forcefully argued that hit ratio cannot be increased by any known learning mechanism. Thus, in considering careerwise creative productivity, the same basic curves would result if either all works or only high-impact works are analyzed. Indeed, positive correlations have been found between the major and minor work production over the lifespan, indicating that the zenith of a creator's career includes both the most masterworks and the most ephemera (Cole, 1979; Simonton, 1977a).

The Darwinian view has major psychological implications. First, because of the sheer complexity of the creative process, creators should have little control over guiding the progress of their works; thus, it has been claimed that the creative process is replete with false starts and wild experiments (Simonton, 1999; cf. Weisberg, 2004). Second, creators should not be particularly good judges of their ideas or works, and critical acumen should not improve with age (Simonton, 1977a, 1984; cf. Kozbelt, 2007). Once works are finished, creators have little control over their fates, because this is a social judgment (Csikszentmihalyi, 1988a; Sawyer, 2006). Thus, mass production is the optimal strategy for those seeking eminence, because producing more works is more likely to yield at least some hits than producing fewer works, all else being equal. Indeed, great creators are almost always very productive (Simonton, 1977b, 1984, 1988, 1997).

Despite its comprehensiveness, the Darwinian view can be critiqued along several lines. For instance, it arguably overemphasizes the role of chance factors in explaining creativity. Recent incarnations of the theory (e.g., Simonton, 2003, 2004, 2006) argue that chance is not the *only* factor in creative achievement, noting substantial though subsidiary roles for logical and evaluative thinking in creativity. However, some may find it unsatisfying to elevate chance to causal status and to define it to include simultaneously not only stochastic conceptual combination or search, but virtually any psychological or social factor that is not well understood presently (Simonton, 2004). Also, despite the convenience and parsimony of a two-step cognitive process for modeling how life-span creativity unfolds, process particulars are left unspecified (Simonton, 1997).

An array of theoretical arguments has also been offered that dispute fundamental premises of the Darwinian view (e.g., Dasgupta, 2004; Gabora, 2005, 2007; Sternberg, 1998). For instance, one objection is that ideas are not discrete, independent units that exist in some dormant state, waiting to be selected out from other alternatives in a Darwinian manner. An alternative emphasizes the context-driven actualization of potential, that is, simply a change of state in response to a context, which can propel creative thought via a non-Darwinian process (Gabora, 2005).

Similarly, empirical objections have been raised, particularly regarding the longitudinal aspect of the equal-odds rule and associated claims about the validity of creators' evaluations. Despite reports appearing to support the longitudinal aspect of the equal-odds rule, its empirical foundation is less secure than other aspects of Simonton's model, owing to conflicting results. For instance, in contrast to Simonton's (1977a) null findings, Kozbelt's (2008c) study of 65 eminent composers found large age effects on hit ratio, including a strong linear increase throughout much of their careers, consistent with an independent analysis by Weisberg and Sturdivant (2005, reported in Weisberg, 2006).

In sum, the Darwinian view is arguably the most ambitious account of Big-C Creativity. It has contributed a very rich repository of results and ideas and numerous specific quantitative predictions, and many (but not all) of its claims boast substantial support. Nonetheless, however well the Darwinian view works as a first approximation to many phenomena in the study of creativity, it explains little of the considerable error variance in relations between productivity and eminence, age and productivity, the production of masterworks versus minor works, or in the varied career trajectories of different creators (Simonton, 1988, 1997). Understanding thorny questions of individual differences, including why some creators appear to improve with age while others get worse, is a focus of the next category of theories.

Typological Theories

One approach to understanding individual variation in creators' personalities, working methods, career trajectories, and so on, has been to posit typologies of creators, who differ in systematic ways (e.g., Epstein, 1991; Epstein, Pacini, Denes-Raj, & Heier, 1996; Gombrich, 1984; Isaksen, Lauer, & Wilson, 2003; Kaufmann, 1979; Kirton, 1976, 1989; Martinsen, 1993, 1995; for a review, see Kozbelt, 2008a). Here we focus on a recent typology by Galenson (2001, 2006), whose theory can be conceptualized as bridging the problem-solving/expertise and Darwinian views. This model is a more or less unified theory of creativity, and it touches on aspects of all of the P's, in each case emphasizing individual differences rather than nomothetic trends. Galenson's emphasis has been on Big-C Creativity, though other typological theories encompass other levels of magnitude as well. Notably, his typology encompasses two very different levels of analysis: macro-level career trajectories and micro-level descriptions of creators' working methods.

Galenson argues that there are two fundamental types of creators: aesthetically motivated experimentalists, or "seekers," and conceptual innovators, or "finders." The two types differ in how they approach the creative process, as well as in their career trajectories and the basis of their reputations.

For seekers, the creative process is a frustrating struggle. Often eschewing preparatory work, they typically begin without a clear idea of their goals, proceed by trial and error, labor over their decisions, and have a difficult time declaring a work completed, using mainly perceptual criteria to do so. Over time, these creators show great continuity in their stylistic development, tend to improve steadily with age, and are ultimately known for a body of work of fairly even quality, rather than individual standout achievements. Because their approach relies on a large body of expert technical knowledge and perceptual skills that take time to acquire, seekers rarely produce outstanding works early in their careers. In contrast, finders frequently make detailed preparations and clearly know their goals at the outset. They thus typically work very efficiently and can easily decide when a project is finished. Often their careers are marked by abrupt changes of style, each marked by a few capstone works, which form the basis of their reputation. Because finders radically change a domain's rules, they can largely circumvent the normally laborious process of expertise acquisition and often make a noteworthy contribution quite early in their careers – although in principle, radical conceptual innovations can happen at any point in a creator's career.

Drawing from painters, sculptors, film directors, novelists, poets, architects, and others, Galenson has amassed considerable evidence relating differences in career trajectories to the working methods employed by creators. The archival evidence includes both subjective accounts of creators' working methods and rigorous quantitative analyses of citations and auction data. Others (e.g., Jensen, 2004; Kozbelt, 2008c; Kozbelt & Durmysheva, 2007a) have also obtained results consistent with Galenson's predictions.

Although Galenson's model is one of the few to bring together disparate levels of analysis into a common theoretical framework, it has some limitations. For instance, many of its aspects can be found in earlier creator typologies, including some referenced at the start of this section. Moreover, despite support from some quarters, other research has failed to support the theory's predictions (e.g., Ginsburgh & Weyers, 2006; Simonton, 2007a). More conceptual issues apply to any typology: specifically, a tendency to set up typologies as dichotomous categories or endpoints on a unidimensional continuum rather than in a potentially multidimensional space, and potentially unreliable classification, partly owing to the subjective interpretation of qualitative data.

However, such typologies represent a promising and ambitious future direction for creativity research. Not the least virtue of this approach is the potential rapprochement between historically opposed camps in the study of creativity, such as the problem-solving/expertise and Darwinian approaches, both of which can be at least partly absorbed into Galenson's model (Kozbelt, 2008c). It is debatable whether such a "unified" theory of creativity is possible, or even desirable, from the standpoint of moderation and pluralism raised at the outset of this chapter. In any case, any comprehensive account of creativity ultimately has to take into account the unique and highly varied characteristics of individual creators and the milieus in which they work. These higher-level themes are characteristic of the final category of models we will discuss: "systems" views of creativity.

Systems Theories

Some of the broadest and most ambitious theories of creativity take the view that creativity is best conceptualized not as a single entity, but as emerging from a complex system with interacting subcomponents – all of which must be taken into account for a rich, meaningful, and valid understanding of creativity. Thus, in contrast to most of the theories described earlier, "systems" theories take a very broad and often quite qualitative contextual view of creativity. A number of such theories have been proposed, almost all of which address each of the P's, although with different emphases, depending on the relevant level of creative magnitude.

One seminal theory is that of Gruber (1981a; Gruber & Wallace, 1999) and colleagues, who pioneered the *evolving systems* approach to creativity. This has mainly been applied to understanding the unique attributes of the creative person, via very detailed archival case studies of Darwin (Gruber, 1981a) and others (Gruber, 1996; Wallace & Gruber, 1989). Often such case studies are motivated by a particular question – for instance, how Darwin devised the idea of evolution by natural selection (Gruber, 1981a), or how it was possible for Herbert Simon to be a twentieth-century Renaissance man (Dasgupta, 2003). Unlike more cognitively oriented case-study methods (e.g., Weisberg, 1999), the evolving-systems approach focuses less on understanding the particulars of a specific creative act than on how those particulars fit into the context of an individual creator's goals, knowledge, and reasoning, as well as larger social forces and creative paradigms.

The evolving-systems approach is primarily an account of what creators *do* (Gruber & Wallace, 1999). Its emphasis is on dynamic, developmental processes that play out in complex ways and contexts, over very different timescales. To provide a structural framework for understanding creative individuals in the midst of such complexity, Gruber introduced a number of foundational concepts. One is the notion that great creators likely use an *ensemble of metaphors* in their thinking, which together characterize a developmental process leading to creative meaning making (Gruber, 1978), rather than relying exclusively on one dominant metaphor – as, sadly, many researchers have done when trying to understand these issues. Another key idea is that of a *network of enterprises*, a system of goals that describes how an eminent creator may work on seemingly disparate topics and projects, consecutively or concurrently, and continually evolve a sense of the relations between the topics. Note that the level of analysis of an enterprise is more general than that of single projects (cf. Weisberg, 1999). Such analyses put a great deal of interpretive pressure on researchers using an evolving systems approach, particularly in absorbing the details and global qualities of a large amount of material and in avoiding pat, hindsight-biased conclusions about a creator's entire career, which probably do not characterize the creator's thinking at any given point during that career. However, if used judiciously, the evolving-systems method has the potential to inform not only the big picture about a creator, but to inform it in a dynamic way with a qualitative richness and rigor that is probably unmatched by the methods of any other theoretical approach.

A different systems theory has been advocated by Csikszentmihalyi (1988a, 1999), whose model has influenced many researchers (e.g., Gardner, 1993; Sawyer, 2006; Simonton, 2004). His theory is less focused on the creative person than the evolving systems approach, but it likewise involves multiple factors and takes a broad view of the phenomenon of creativity – even more so than Gruber's model. Perhaps more than any other theory of creativity, Csikszentmihalyi's systems view emphasizes the ubiquitous role of place (or environment) among the P's, especially for Big-C achievements; it also elaborates the nature of the creative person by detailing how individuals other than the creator contribute to the emergence of creativity.

Csikszentmihalyi (1988a) introduced his systems view by reframing the basic question of "What is creativity?" to "Where is creativity?" Rather than regarding creativity as an intrinsic attribute of particular artifacts, Csikszentmihalyi argued that creativity judgments emerge via three interacting components: 1) the domain, or body of knowledge that exists in a particular discipline at a particular time; 2) the individual, who acquires domain knowledge and produces variations on the existing knowledge; and 3) the field, comprised of other experts and members of the discipline, who decide which novelties produced by all of the individuals working in that discipline are worth preserving for the next generation. Each has a say in what counts as creative.

This view deemphasizes intrapsychic processes and individual contributions and instead places much more emphasis on collaborative creativity – a theme taken up most notably in recent years by Sawyer (2006) – and the societal conditions that can best foster genius, for example, during such cultural peaks as Periclean Athens, Medicean Florence, and *fin-de-siècle* Paris and Vienna. Csikszentmihalyi's systems view also highlights issues like the importance of "gatekeepers" (e.g., journal editors, art gallery owners, etc.) who play a major practical role in determining which contributions will be given the opportunity to be judged as creative, but who had previously gone almost entirely undiscussed in the research literature.

Csikszentmihalyi's systems view has many advantages, particularly in its conceptual richness, but also potential limitations. First, it acknowledges the immense importance of extrapersonal, sociocultural factors in creativity; it can also be used to generate specific hypotheses about how the domain, field, and individual (and culture, society, and personal backgrounds more generally) impact creativity (Csikszentmihalyi, 1999). In principle, such questions are amenable to empirical study. However, the qualitative nature of many aspects of the model may make it more difficult to test hypotheses unambiguously. Moreover, the fact that Csikszentmihalyi's model ambitiously spans multiple levels of analysis can create problems in interdisciplinary crosstalk, particularly as his approach is less grounded in methodological particulars than, say, Gruber's (1981a). However, this seems a necessary risk; as Csikszentmihalyi (1994) argued, for a rich understanding of creativity, many more variables and levels of analysis need to be considered besides a quantitative, empirical approach to individual traits, which leads to a parochial understanding of the nature of creativity.

In another model, Albert (in press) pointed to families, schools, and cultures in his view of influential systems. Information is shared among the levels of the system and determines how behaviors, including creative behaviors, are interpreted. These interpretations determine what constraints are placed on behavior and, conversely, how much freedom there is for novelty and creativity. For Albert, the actual impact on action and development is apparent in person–environment interactions. Very significantly, the more complex the system, the more freedom there is for individuals. Here again, freedom is necessary for behavioral and ideational variation, originality, and creativity.

Conclusion: Future Directions for Creativity Theories

Where to go from here? At the outset of this chapter we suggested that the ancient dictum of "moderation in all things" might serve as a useful guide for considering the plurality of perspectives, assumptions, and purposes found in contemporary creativity theories. This dictum may also prove useful in guiding future directions for scholars as they endeavor to develop and refine existing and new theoretical perspectives and make connections between them. With respect to refining existing theoretical frameworks, scholars might ask, "What aspects of this theory seem out of balance or underdeveloped, particularly when viewed in the light of the broader landscape of creativity studies?" Such questions might, for instance, reveal a need to test key assumptions of a metaphorically oriented theory with more rigorous empirical work; or highlight the need for a more *Product* oriented theory to account for the moderating and mediating influences of *Person, Place, Process,* and *Persuasion;* or reveal the possibility of linking a Larger-c theory of creative achievement to smaller-c theories of creative potential.

In suggesting that scholars apply a "golden mean" to existing creativity theories, we are not necessarily advocating for the development of such models into grand unifying theories, although such efforts might be inspired by this suggestion. Rather, we are suggesting that scholars better situate their theories in the broader theoretical and empirical landscape of the domain, acknowledging and, when possible, incorporating the plurality of perspectives that have taken root and flourished. At the very least, this requires that scholars acknowledge the contested nature of their own theoretical assumptions and perspectives. By doing so, they may discover areas of overlap between seemingly contested positions, which not only advance the standing of their own theoretical perspectives, but also enrich our broader knowledge of creativity.

One example – highlighting how incorporating differing perspectives can advance knowledge in the field – can be seen in the work of two creativity scholars, John Baer and Jonathan Plucker, who held opposing positions on the issue of the domain-specific (creativity differs by discipline and domain) versus domain-general (creativity is trans-disciplinary) nature of creativity. Following a point–counterpoint debate on this topic (Baer, 1998; Plucker, 1998), these two scholars later put forth what might be considered more moderate positions, recognizing both the domain-general and domain-specific aspects of creativity (see Baer & Kaufman, 2005; Plucker & Beghetto, 2004).

With respect to the development of new theories, we encourage scholars to consider how they might actively acknowledge and (when appropriate) incorporate the plurality of the field in their models. Scholars might also specify the levels of creative magnitude that make the most sense for their models (without denying the existence of other levels of magnitude) and highlight which P's of creativity will be in the foreground (while still considering the P's in the background). Doing so would require scholars to balance a rigorous empirical approach with metaphorical aspects (which can help illuminate and communicate not-yet-experienced possibilities and insights) and to draw on and acknowledge the influences of prior theories and programs of research (so as to situate their new insights within the tradition of prior work on the topic).

In closing, we hope our overview of creativity theories has made clear that the study of creativity has no dearth of theoretical approaches and models. This plu-ralistic set of perspectives will continue to inform the phenomenon of creativity, whose study is still in its early phases (Guilford, 1950). Although it may not be possible to predict, with a high level of certainty, how this plurality will play out in the form of new, revised, or even more-unified theories of creativity, what is certain is that creativity scholars have much work ahead of them – be it focused on expanding existing theories or in developing new, more robust models, all of which hold the potential to yield ever-richer perspectives on this most fascinating and important topic.

References

Albert, R. S. (1980). Family position and the attainment of eminence: A study of special family positions and special family experiences. *Gifted Child Quarterly*, 24, 87–95.

Albert, R. S. (in press). The achievement of eminence as an evolutionary strategy. In M. A. Runco (Ed.), *Creativity research handbook* (Vol. 2). Cresskill, NJ: Hampton Press.

Albert, R. S., & Runco, M. A. (1989). Independence and cognitive ability in gifted and exceptionally gifted boys. *Journal of Youth and Adolescence*, 18, 221–230.

Albert, R. S., & Runco, M. A. (1999). A longitudinal study of exceptional giftedness and creativity. *Creativity Research Journal*, 12, 161–164.

Amabile, T. M. (1990). Within you, without you: The social psychology of creativity, and beyond. In M. A. Runco & R. S. Albert (Eds.), *Theories of creativity* (pp. 61–91). Newbury Park, CA: Sage.

Amabile, T. M. (1999). Consensual assessment. In M. A. Runco & S. Pritzker (Eds.), *Encyclopedia of creativity* (pp. 346–349). San Diego, CA: Academic Press.

Ayman-Nolley, S. (1999). A Piagetian perspective on the dialectic process of creativity. *Creativity Research Journal*, 12, 267–275.

Baer, J. (1998). The case for domain specificity in creativity. *Creativity Research Journal*, 11, 173–177.

Baer, J., & Kaufman, J. C. (2005). Bridging generality and specificity: The amusement park theoretical (APT) model of creativity. *Roeper Review*, 27, 158–163.

Barron, F. (1995). *No rootless flower*. Cresskill, NJ: Hampton Press.

Beghetto, R. A. (2007). Creativity research and the classroom: From pitfalls to potential. In A. G. Tan (Ed.), *Creativity: A handbook for teachers* (pp. 101–116). Singapore: World Scientific.

Beghetto, R. A., & Kaufman, J. C. (2007). Toward a broader conception of creativity: A case for mini-c creativity. *Psychology of Aesthetics, Creativity, and the Arts*, 1, 73–79.

Bloom, B. S. (Ed.). (1985). *Developing talent in young people*. New York: Ballantine.

Campbell, D. T. (1960). Blind generation and selective retention in creative thought as in other thought processes. *Psychological Review*, 67, 380–400.

Chase, W. G., & Simon, H. A. (1973). Perception in chess. *Cognitive Psychology*, 4, 55–81.

Cole, S. (1979). Age and scientific performance. *American Journal of Sociology*, 84, 958–977.

Cropley, A. (2006). In praise of convergent thinking. *Creativity Research Journal*, 18, 391–404.

Csikszentmihalyi, M. (1988a). Society, culture, and person: A systems view of creativity. In R. J. Sternberg (Ed.), *The nature of creativity: Contemporary psychological perspectives* (pp. 325–228). New York: Cambridge University Press.

Csikszentmihalyi, M. (1988b). Motivation and creativity: Towards a synthesis of structural and energistic approaches to cognition. *New Ideas in Psychology*, 6, 159–176.

Csikszentmihalyi, M. (1994). The domain of creativity. In D. H. Feldman, M. Csikszentmihalyi, & H. Gardner (Eds.), *Changing the world: A framework for the study of creativity* (pp. 135–158). Westport, CT: Praeger.

Csikszentmihalyi, M. (1996). *Creativity: Flow and the psychology of discovery and invention*. New York: HarperCollins.

Csikszentmihalyi, M. (1998). Reflections on the field. *Roeper Review*, 21, 80–81.

Csikszentmihalyi, M. (1999). Implications of a systems perspective for the study of creativity. In R. J. Sternberg (Ed.), *Handbook of creativity* (pp. 313–335). New York: Cambridge University Press.

Csikszentmihalyi, M., & Getzels, J. W. (1989). Creativity and problem finding. In F. H. Farley & R. W. Neperud (Eds.), *The foundations of aesthetics* (pp. 91–116). New York: Praeger.

Dasgupta, S. (2003). Multidisciplinary creativity: The case of Herbert A. Simon. *Cognitive Science*, 27, 683–707.

Dasgupta, S. (2004). Is creativity a Darwinian process? *Creativity Research Journal*, 16, 403–413.

Davis, G. (1999). Barriers to creativity and creative attitudes. In M. A. Runco & S. Pritzker (Eds.), *Encyclopedia of creativity* (pp. 165–174). San Diego, CA: Academic Press.

Dennis, W. (1966). Creative productivity between the ages of 20 and 80 years. *Journal of Gerontology*, 9, 175–178.

Dudek, S. Z., & Côté, R. (1994). Problem finding revisited. In M. A. Runco (Ed.), *Problem finding, problem solving, and creativity* (pp. 130–150). Norwood, NJ: Ablex.

Epstein, R. (1990). Generativity theory. In M. A. Runco & R. S. Albert (Eds.), *Theories of creativity* (pp. 116–140). Newbury Park, CA: Sage.

Epstein, S. (1991). Cognitive-experiential self-theory: An integrative theory of personality. In R. Curtis (Ed.), *The relational self: Convergences in psychoanalysis and social psychology* (pp. 111–137). New York: Guilford.

Epstein, R., & Laptosky, G. (1999). Behavioral approaches to creativity. In M. A. Runco & S. Pritzker (Eds.), *Encyclopedia of creativity* (pp. 175–183). San Diego, CA: Academic Press.

Epstein, S., Pacini, R., Denes-Raj, V., & Heier, H. (1996). Individual differences in intuitive-experiential and analytical-rational thinking styles. *Journal of Personality and Social Psychology*, 71, 390–405.

Ericsson, K. A. (1999). Creative expertise as superior reproducible performance: Innovative and flexible aspects of expert performance. *Psychological Inquiry*, 10, 329–333.

Ericsson, K. A., & Charness, N. (1994). Expert performance: Its structure and acquisition. *American Psychologist*, 49, 725–747.

Estes, Z., & Ward, T. (2002). The emergence of novel attributes in concept modification. *Creativity Research Journal*, 14, 149–156.

Eysenck, H. J. (1995). *Genius: The natural history of creativity*. New York: Cambridge University Press.

Feist, G. J. (1998). A meta-analysis of personality in scientific and artistic creativity. *Personality and Social Psychology Review*, 2, 290–309.

Feist, G. J. (1999). Personality in scientific and artistic creativity. In R. J. Sternberg (Ed.), *Handbook of creativity* (pp. 273–296). New York: Cambridge University Press.

Feist, G. J., & Barron, F. X. (2003). Predicting creativity from early to late adulthood: Intellect, potential, and personality. *Journal of Research in Personality*, 37, 62–88.

Finke, R. A., Ward, T. B., & Smith, S. M. (1992). *Creative cognition: Theory, research, and applications*. Cambridge, MA: MIT Press.

Florida, R. (2002). *The rise of the creative class: And how it's transforming work, leisure, community and everyday life.* New York: Basic Books.

Fuchs-Beauchamp, K. D., Karnes, M. B., & Johnson, L. J. (1993). Creativity and intelligence in preschoolers. *Gifted Child Quarterly, 37,* 113–117.

Gabora, L. (2005). Creative thought as a non-Darwinian evolutionary process. *Journal of Creative Behavior, 39,* 65–87.

Gabora, L. (2007). Why the creative process is not Darwinian. Commentary on "The creative imagination in Picasso's *Guernica* sketches: Monotonic improvements or nonmonotonic variants?" by Dean Keith Simonton. *Creativity Research Journal, 19,* 361–365.

Galenson, D. W. (2001). *Painting outside the lines: Patterns of creativity in modern art.* Cambridge, MA: Harvard University Press.

Galenson, D. W. (2006). *Old masters and young geniuses: The two life cycles of artistic creativity.* Princeton, NJ: Princeton University Press.

Galton, F. (1869). *Hereditary genius.* New York: Macmillan.

Gardner, H. (1983). *Frames of mind: The theory of multiple intelligences.* New York: Basic Books.

Gardner, H. (1993). *Creating minds.* New York: Basic Books.

Gaynor, J. L. R., & Runco, M. A. (1998). Family size, birth order, age-interval, and the creativity of children. *Journal of Creative Behavior, 26,* 108–118.

Getzels, J. W., & Csikszentmihalyi, M. (1976). *The creative vision: A longitudinal study of problem finding in art.* New York: Wiley.

Ginsburgh, V., & Weyers, S. (2006). Creation and life cycles of artists. *Journal of Cultural Economics, 30,* 91–107.

Goertzel, V., & Goertzel, M. G. (1976). *Cradles of eminence.* Boston, MA: Little, Brown.

Gombrich, E. H. (1984). *Tributes: Interpreters of our cultural tradition.* Oxford: Phaidon.

Gruber, H. E. (1978). Darwin's "Tree of Nature" and other images of wide scope. In J. Wechsler (Ed.), *On aesthetics in science* (pp. 121–143). Cambridge, MA: MIT Press.

Gruber, H. E. (1981a). *Darwin on man: A psychological study of scientific creativity* (Rev. ed.). Chicago: University of Chicago Press. (Original work published 1974)

Gruber, H. E. (1981b). On the relation between 'a ha' experiences and the construction of ideas. *History of Science, 19,* 41–59.

Gruber, H. E. (1996). Starting out: The early phases of four creative careers – Darwin,

van Gogh, Freud, and Shaw. *Journal of Adult Development, 3,* 1–6.

Gruber, H. E., & Wallace, D. B. (1999). The case study method and evolving systems approach for understanding unique creative people at work. In R. J. Sternberg (Ed.), *Handbook of creativity* (pp. 93–115). New York: Cambridge University Press.

Guilford, J. P. (1950). Creativity. *American Psychologist, 5,* 444–454.

Guilford, J. P. (1968). *Creativity, intelligence, and their educational implications.* San Diego, CA: Knapp.

Guilford, J. P. (1980). Some changes in the structure of intellect model. *Educational and Psychological Measurement, 48,* 1–4.

Hayes, J. R. (1989). Cognitive processes in creativity. In J. A. Glover, R. R. Roning, & C. R. Reynolds (Eds.), *Handbook of creativity* (pp. 202–219). New York: Plenum.

Helmholtz, H. von (1896). *Vorträge und Reden.* Brunswick, Germany: Friedrich Vieweg.

Helson, R. (1972). Personality of women with imaginative and artistic interests: The role of masculinity, originality, and other characteristics in their creativity. *Journal of Creative Behavior, 6,* 295–300.

Helson, R. (1999). A longitudinal study of creative personality in women. *Creativity Research Journal, 12,* 89–101.

Isaksen, S. G., Lauer, K. J., & Wilson, G. V. (2003). An examination of the relationship between personality type and cognitive style. *Creativity Research Journal, 15,* 343–354.

Jamison, K. R. (1996). *Touched with fire: Manic-depressive illness and the artistic temperament.* New York: Free Press.

Jensen, R. (2004). Anticipating artistic behavior: New research tools for art historians. *Historical Methods, 37,* 137–152.

Johnson-Laird, P. N. (1993). *Human and machine thinking.* Hillsdale, NJ: Erlbaum.

Kaplan, C. A., & Simon, H. A. (1990). In search of insight. *Cognitive Psychology, 22,* 374–419.

Kasof, J. (1995). Explaining creativity: The attributional perspective. *Creativity Research Journal, 8,* 311–366.

Kaufmann, G. (1979). The explorer and the assimilator: A cognitive style distinction and its potential implications for innovative problem solving. *Scandinavian Journal of Educational Research, 23,* 101–108.

Kaufman, J. C., & Beghetto, R. A. (2009). Beyond big and little: The four C model of creativity. *Review of General Psychology, 13,* 1–12.

Kim, K. H. (2005). Can only intelligent people be creative? A meta-analysis. *Journal of Secondary Gifted Education*, 16, 57–66.

Kirton, M. (1976). Adaptors and innovators: A description and measure. *Journal of Applied Psychology*, 61, 622–629.

Kirton, M. (1989). A theory of cognitive style. In M. Kirton (Ed.), *Adaptors and innovators: Styles of creativity and problem solving* (pp. 1–36). New York: Routledge.

Kozbelt, A. (2005). Factors affecting aesthetic success and improvement in creativity: A case study of the musical genres of Mozart. *Psychology of Music*, 33, 235–255.

Kozbelt, A. (2007). A quantitative analysis of Beethoven as self-critic: Implications for psychological theories of musical creativity. *Psychology of Music*, 35, 147–172.

Kozbelt, A. (2008a). Gombrich, Galenson, and beyond: Integrating case study and typological frameworks in the study of creative individuals. *Empirical Studies of the Arts*, 26, 51–68.

Kozbelt, A. (2008b). Hierarchical linear modeling of creative artists' problem solving behaviors. *Journal of Creative Behavior*, 42, 181–200.

Kozbelt, A. (2008c). Longitudinal hit ratios of classical composers: Reconciling "Darwinian" and expertise acquisition perspectives on life-span creativity. *Psychology of Aesthetics, Creativity, and the Arts*, 2, 221–235.

Kozbelt, A., & Durmysheva, Y. (2007a). Life-span creativity in a non-Western artistic tradition: A study of Japanese ukiyo-e printmakers. *International Journal of Aging and Human Development*, 65, 23–51.

Kozbelt, A., & Durmysheva, Y. (2007b). Understanding creativity judgments of invented alien creatures: The role of invariants and other predictors. *Journal of Creative Behavior*, 41, 223–248.

Kulkarni, D., & Simon, H. A. (1988). The processes of scientific discovery: The strategy of experimentation. *Cognitive Science*, 12, 139–175.

Langley, P., Simon, H. A., Bradshaw, G. L., & Zytkow, J. M. (1987). *Scientific discovery: Computational explorations of the creative process*. Cambridge, MA: MIT Press.

Lubart, T. I. (1999). Creativity across cultures. In R. J. Sternberg (Ed.), *Handbook of creativity* (pp. 339–350). New York: Cambridge University Press.

Ludwig, A. (1995). *The price of greatness*. New York: Guilford.

Lumsden, C. J. (1999). Evolving creative minds: Stories and mechanisms. In R. J. Sternberg (Ed.), *Handbook of creativity* (pp. 153–168). New York: Cambridge University Press.

Lumsden, C. J., & Findlay, S. C. (1988). Evolution of the creative mind. *Creativity Research Journal*, 1, 75–92.

Mace, M. A., & Ward, T. (2002). Modeling the creative process: A grounded theory analysis of creativity in the domain of art making. *Creativity Research Journal*, 14, 179–192.

Martindale, C. (1999). Biological bases of creativity. In R. J. Sternberg (Ed.), *Handbook of creativity* (pp. 137–152). New York: Cambridge University Press.

Martinsen, Ø. (1993). Insight problems revisited: The influence of cognitive style and experience on creative problem solving. *Creativity Research Journal*, 6, 435–447.

Martinsen, Ø. (1995). Cognitive styles and experience in solving insight problems: Replication and extension. *Creativity Research Journal*, 8, 291–298.

Medawar, P. B. (1991). *The threat and the glory: Reflections on science and scientists*. Oxford: Oxford University Press.

Mednick, S. A. (1962). The associative basis of the creative process. *Psychological Review*, 69, 220–232.

Mobley, M. I., Doares, L. M., & Mumford, M. D. (1992). Process analytic models of creative capacities: Evidence for the combination and reorganization process. *Creativity Research Journal*, 5, 125–155.

Moore, M. (1985). The relationship between the originality of essays and variables in the problem-discovery process: A study of creative and non-creative middle school students. *Research in the Teaching of English*, 19, 84–95.

Mumford, M. D., Baughman, W. A., Maher, M. A., Costanza, D. P., & Supinski, E. P. (1997). Process-based measures of creative problem-solving skills: IV. Category combination. *Creativity Research Journal*, 10, 59–71.

Mumford, M. D., Baughman, W. A., Threlfall, K. V., Supinski, E. P., & Costanza, D. P. (1996). Process-based measures of creative problem-solving skills: I. Problem construction. *Creativity Research Journal*, 9, 63–76.

Mumford, M. D., Mobley, M. I., Uhlman, C. E., Reiter-Palmon, R., & Doares, L. M. (1991). Process analytic models of creative capabilities. *Creativity Research Journal*, 4, 91–122.

Mumford, M. D., Reiter-Palmon, R., & Redmond, M. R. (1994). Problem construction and cognition: Applying problem representation tactics in ill-defined domains. In M. A. Runco

(Ed.), *Problem finding, problem solving, and creativity* (pp. 3–39). Norwood, NJ: Ablex.

Mumford, M. D., Supinski, E. P., Baughman, W. A., Costanza, D. P., & Threlfall, K. V. (1997). Process-based measures of creative problem-solving skills: V. Overall prediction. *Creativity Research Journal, 10,* 73–83.

Murray, C. (2003). *Human accomplishment: The pursuit of excellence in the arts and sciences, 800 B.C. to 1950.* New York: HarperCollins.

Newell, A., Shaw, J. C., & Simon, H. A. (1962). The processes of creative thinking. In H. E. Gruber, G. Terrell, & M. Wertheimer (Eds.), *Contemporary approaches to creative thinking* (pp. 63–119). New York: Atherton Press.

Newell, A., & Simon, H. A. (1972). *Human problem solving.* Englewood Cliffs, NJ: Prentice-Hall.

Nickerson, R. S. (1999). Enhancing creativity. In R. J. Sternberg (Ed.), *Handbook of creativity* (pp. 392–430). New York: Cambridge University Press.

Oromaner, M. (1977). Professional age and the reception of sociological publications: A test of the Zuckerman-Merton hypothesis. *Social Studies of Science, 7,* 381–388.

Over, R. (1982). Is age a good predictor of research productivity? *Australian Psychologist, 17,* 129–139.

Over, R. (1988). Does scholarly impact decline with age? *Scientometrics, 13,* 215–223.

Patrick, C. (1935). Creative thought in poets. *Archives of Psychology, 26* (178).

Patrick, C. (1937). Creative thought in artists. *Journal of Psychology, 4,* 35–73.

Pearson, B., Russ, S. W., Cain Spannagel, S. A. (2008). Pretend play and positive psychology: Natural companions. *Journal of Positive Psychology: Dedicated to furthering research and promoting good practice, 3,* 110–119.

Perkins, D. N. (1981). *The mind's best work.* Cambridge, MA: Harvard University Press.

Plucker, J. A. (1998). Beware of simple conclusions: The case for the content generality of creativity. *Creativity Research Journal, 11,* 179–182.

Plucker, J. A. (1999). Is the proof in the pudding? Reanalyses of Torrance's (1958 to present) longitudinal data. *Creativity Research Journal, 12,* 103–114.

Plucker, J. A., & Beghetto, R. A. (2004). Why creativity is domain general, why it looks domain specific, and why the distinction does not matter. In R. J. Sternberg, E. L. Grigorenko, &

J. L. Singer (Eds.), *Creativity: From potential to realization* (pp. 153–167). Washington, DC: American Psychological Association.

Plucker, J. A., Beghetto, R. A., & Dow, G. (2004). Why isn't creativity more important to educational psychologists? Potential, pitfalls, and future directions in creativity research. *Educational Psychologist, 39,* 83–96.

Rhodes, M. (1961). An analysis of creativity. *Phi Delta Kappan, 42,* 305–310.

Richards, R. (2007). Everyday creativity: Our hidden potential. In R. Richards (Ed.), *Everyday creativity and new views of human nature: Psychological, social, and spiritual perspectives* (pp. 25–53). Washington, DC: American Psychological Association.

Rubenson, D. L. (1990). The accidental economist. *Creativity Research Journal, 3,* 125–129.

Rubenson, D. L., & Runco, M. A. (1992). The psychoeconomic approach to creativity. *New Ideas in Psychology, 10,* 131–147.

Rubenson, D. L., & Runco, M. A. (1995). The psychoeconomic view of creative work in groups and organizations. *Creativity and Innovation Management, 4,* 232–241.

Runco, M. A. (1986). Divergent thinking and creative performance in gifted and nongifted children. *Educational and Psychological Measurement, 46,* 375–384.

Runco, M. A. (1989). Parents' and teachers' ratings of the creativity of children. *Journal of Social Behavior and Personality, 4,* 73–83.

Runco, M. A. (Ed.). (1994). *Problem finding, problem solving, and creativity.* Norwood, NJ: Ablex.

Runco, M. A. (1996). Personal creativity: Definition and developmental issues. *New Directions for Child Development, 72,* 3–30.

Runco, M. A. (2001). Creativity as optimal human functioning. In M. Bloom (Ed.), *Promoting creativity across the lifespan* (pp. 17–44). Washington, DC: Child Welfare League of America.

Runco, M. A. (2003). Education for creative potential. *Scandinavian Journal of Education, 47,* 317–324.

Runco, M. A. (2004a). Creativity. *Annual Review of Psychology, 55,* 657–687.

Runco, M. A. (2004b). Everyone has creative potential. In R. J. Sternberg, E. L. Grigorenko, & J. L. Singer (Eds.), *Creativity: From potential to realization* (pp. 21–30). Washington, DC: American Psychological Association.

Runco, M. A. (2007a). *Creativity: Theories and themes: Research, development, and practice.* New York: Academic Press.

Runco, M. A. (2007b). A hierarchical framework for the study of creativity. *New Horizons in Education*, 55, 1–9.

Runco, M. A. (2008). Creativity and education. *New Horizons in Education*, 56, 107–115.

Runco, M. A., & Albert, R. S. (1986). The threshold hypothesis regarding creativity and intelligence: An empirical test with gifted and nongifted children. *Creative Child and Adult Quarterly*, 11, 212–218.

Runco, M. A., & Chand, I. (1995). Cognition and creativity. *Educational Psychology Review*, 7, 243–267.

Runco, M. A., & Richards, R. (Eds.). (1998). *Eminent creativity, everyday creativity, and health*. Norwood, NJ: Ablex.

Runco, M. A., & Sakamoto, S. O. (1996). Optimization as a guiding principle in research on creative problem solving. In T. Helstrup, G. Kaufmann, & K. H. Teigen (Eds.), *Problem solving and cognitive processes: Essays in honor of Kjell Raaheim* (pp. 119–144). Bergen, Norway: Fagbokforlaget Vigmostad & Bjorke.

Runco, M. A., & Smith, W. R. (1991). Interpersonal and intrapersonal evaluations of creative ideas. *Personality and Individual Differences*, 13, 295–302.

Runco, M. A., & Vega, L. (1992). Evaluating the creativity of children's ideas. *Journal of Social Behavior and Personality*, 5, 439–452.

Russ, S. W., & Schafer, E. D. (2006). Affect in fantasy play, emotion in memories, and divergent thinking. *Creativity Research Journal*, 18, 347–354.

Sawyer, R. K. (2006). *Explaining creativity: The science of human innovation*. New York: Oxford University Press.

Simon, H. A. (1981). *The sciences of the artificial* (2nd ed.). Cambridge, MA: MIT Press.

Simon, H. A. (1988). Creativity and motivation: A response to Csikszentmihalyi. *New Ideas in Psychology*, 6, 177–181.

Simon, H. A. (1989). The scientist as problem solver. In D. Klahr & K. Kotovsky (Eds.), *Complex information processing: The impact of Herbert A. Simon* (pp. 375–398). Hillsdale, NJ: Erlbaum.

Simonton, D. K. (1977a). Creative productivity, age, and stress: A biographical time-series analysis of ten classical composers. *Journal of Personality and Social Psychology*, 35, 791–804.

Simonton, D. K. (1977b). Eminence, creativity, and geographic marginality: A recursive structural equation model. *Journal of Personality and Social Psychology*, 35, 805–816.

Simonton, D. K. (1984). *Genius, creativity, and leadership*. Cambridge, MA: Harvard University Press.

Simonton, D. K. (1985). Quality, quantity, and age: The careers of ten distinguished psychologists. *International Journal of Aging and Human Development*, 21, 241–254.

Simonton, D. K. (1988). *Scientific genius*. New York: Cambridge University Press.

Simonton, D. K. (1990). History, chemistry, psychology, and genius: An intellectual autobiography of historiometry. In M. A. Runco & R. S. Albert (Eds.), *Theories of creativity* (pp. 92–115). Newbury Park, CA: Sage.

Simonton, D. K. (1991a). Emergence and realization of genius: The lives and works of 120 classical composers. *Journal of Personality and Social Psychology*, 61, 829–840.

Simonton, D. K. (1991b). Career landmarks in science: Individual differences and interdisciplinary contrasts. *Developmental Psychology*, 27, 119–130.

Simonton, D. K. (1997). Creative productivity: A predictive and explanatory model of career landmarks and trajectories. *Psychological Review*, 104, 66–89.

Simonton, D. K. (1999). *Origins of genius: Darwinian perspectives on creativity*. New York: Oxford University Press.

Simonton, D. K. (2000). Creative development as acquired expertise: Theoretical issues and an empirical test. *Developmental Review*, 20, 283–318.

Simonton, D. K. (2003). Scientific creativity as constrained stochastic behavior: The integration of product, person, and process perspectives. *Psychological Bulletin*, 129, 475–494.

Simonton, D. K. (2004). *Creativity in science: Chance, logic, genius, and zeitgeist*. New York: Cambridge University Press.

Simonton, D. K. (2006). Creative genius, knowledge, and reason: The lives and works of eminent creators. In J. C. Kaufman & J. Baer (Eds.), *Creativity and reason in cognitive development* (pp. 43–59). New York: Cambridge University Press.

Simonton, D. K. (2007a). Creative life cycles in literature: Poets versus novelists or conceptualists versus experimentalists? *Psychology of Aesthetics, Creativity, and the Arts*, 1, 133–139.

Simonton, D. K. (2007b). Cinema composers: Career trajectories for creative productivity in film music. *Psychology of Aesthetics, Creativity, and the Arts*, 1, 160–169.

Smythe, W. E. (2005). On the psychology of "as if." *Theory & Psychology*, 15, 283–303.

Stein, M. I. (1953). Creativity and culture. *The Journal of Psychology*, 36, 311–322.

Sternberg, R. J. (1996). Costs of expertise. In K. A. Ericsson (Ed.), *The road to excellence: The acquisition of expert performance in the arts and sciences, sports and games* (pp. 347–354). Hillsdale, NJ: Erlbaum.

Sternberg, R. J. (1998). Cognitive mechanisms in creativity: Is variation blind or sighted? *Journal of Creative Behavior*, 32, 159–176.

Sternberg, R. J., & Lubart, T. I. (1992). Buy low and sell high: An investment approach to creativity. *Current Directions in Psychological Science*, 1, 1–5.

Sternberg, R. J., & Lubart, T. I. (1995). *Defying the crowd: Cultivating creativity in a culture of conformity*. New York: Free Press.

Subotnik, R. F., & Arnold, K. D. (1996). Success and sacrifice: The costs of talent fulfillment for women in science. In K. D. Arnold, K. D. Noble, & R. F. Subotnik (Eds.), *Remarkable women: Perspectives on female talent development* (pp. 263–280). Cresskill, NJ: Hampton Press.

Sulloway, F. (1996). *Born to rebel*. New York: Pantheon.

Torrance, E. P. (1995). *Why fly?* Norwood, NJ: Ablex.

Vaihinger, H. (1952). *The philosophy of 'as if': A system of the theoretical, practical and religious fictions of mankind*. London: Routledge. (Original work published 1911)

Vygotsky, L. S. (2004). Imagination and creativity in childhood. (M. E. Sharpe, Inc., Trans.) *Journal of Russian and East European Psychology*, 42, 7–97. (Original work published 1967)

Wallace, D. B., & Gruber, H. E. (Eds.). (1989). *Creative people at work*. New York: Oxford University Press.

Wallach, M. A., & Kogan, N. (1965). *Modes of thinking in young children*. New York: Holt, Reinhart, & Winston.

Wallas, G. (1926). *The art of thought*. New York: Harcourt Brace and World.

Ward, T. B., Smith, S. M., & Finke, R. A. (1999). Creative cognition. In R. J. Sternberg (Ed.), *Handbook of creativity* (pp. 189–212). New York: Cambridge University Press.

Weisberg, R. W. (1986). *Creativity: Genius and other myths*. New York: Freeman.

Weisberg, R. W. (1993). *Creativity: Beyond the myth of genius*. New York: Freeman.

Weisberg, R. W. (1999). Creativity and knowledge: A challenge to theories. In R. J. Sternberg (Ed.), *Handbook of creativity* (pp. 226–250). New York: Cambridge University Press.

Weisberg, R. W. (2004). On structure in the creative process: A quantitative case-study of the creation of Picasso's Guernica. *Empirical Studies of the Arts*, 22, 23–54.

Weisberg, R. W. (2006). *Creativity: Understanding innovation in problem solving, science, invention, and the arts*. Hoboken, NJ: Wiley.

Weisberg, R. W., & Alba, J. W. (1981). An examination of the alleged role of "fixation" in the solution of several "insight" problems. *Journal of Experimental Psychology*, 110, 169–192.

Weisberg, R. W., & Sturdivant, N. (2005). *An analysis of creative productivity in four classical composers*. Unpublished manuscript, Temple University.

Winner, E. (1996). The rage to master: The decisive role of talent in the visual arts. In K. A. Ericsson (Ed.), *The road to excellence: The acquisition of expert performance in the arts and sciences, sports and games* (pp. 271–301). Hillsdale, NJ: Erlbaum.

Winner, E. (2000). Giftedness: Current theory and research. *Current Directions in Psychological Science*, 9, 153–156.

Witt, L. A., & Boerkem, M. (1989). Climate for creative productivity as a predictor of research usefulness and organizational effectiveness in an R&D organization. *Creativity Research Journal*, 2, 30–40.

CHAPTER 3

Assessment of Creativity

Jonathan A. Plucker and Matthew C. Makel

Nearly 40 years ago, Torrance (1970) lamented that "Children are so accustomed to the one correct or best answer that they may be reluctant to think of other possibilities or to build up a pool of ideas to be evaluated later" (p. 86). Torrance was referring, of course, to the psychological hurdles that must be overcome when encouraging creativity in the classroom. A major aspect of education involves assessment, and anyone seeking to foster creativity inevitably is faced with questions about how to measure the success of intervention efforts.

The assessment of creativity has a long, rich history, and interest in psychometric approaches to the study of creativity has increased in recent years. This work provides a strong foundation for future research and evaluation efforts in creativity and innovation and bodes well for the potential contributions of psychometric methods to our understanding of creativity.

Defining Creativity

Any exploration of assessment in this context should begin with a definition of "creativity." The world is full of similar, overlapping, and possibly synonymous terms (e.g., imagination, ingenuity, innovation, inspiration, inventiveness, muse, novelty, originality, serendipity, talent, unique), and definitions of each term vary widely. Despite the abundance of definitions of creativity and related terms, few are widely used and many researchers simply avoid defining the relevant terms at all.

Williams (1999) observed that the clarity of definition of higher-order cognitive constructs is connected to the usefulness of those terms. Unfortunately, most creativity research does not include an explicit definition; this lack of definition partially accounts for the often-conflicting research on the topic (e.g., two studies on the exact same aspect of creativity may produce highly conflicting results, when in reality different definitions of creativity are being employed). As such, those in the field become estranged from each other by semantic issues and those outside the field become distanced because it appears no one in the field can even define creativity.

Plucker and Dow (in press) analyze this issue from the perspective of schema development, the creation of "interconnections of ideas that grow into complex, organized mental structures of information." Although schema development may be flexible, it is very difficult completely to change schemas, even in the light of contradictory evidence (Wheatley & Wegner, 2001). When schemas are based on inaccurate or incomplete information, a person's decision making may be seriously hampered. We believe that creativity, primarily owing to its lack of precise definition, appears to be plagued by schema problems.

Plucker, Beghetto, and Dow (2004) recommend that all examinations of creativity clearly define the authors' conception of creativity as used in that work. As a result, we use the following definition: Creativity is "the interaction among *aptitude, process, and environment* by which an individual or group produces a *perceptible product* that is both *novel and useful* as defined within a *social context*" (Plucker et al., 2004, p. 90, emphasis in original).

Getzels and Jackson (1962) point out that initial developers of intelligence tests considered creativity to either be a subset of intelligence or wholly independent from it. Sternberg and O'Hara (1999) suggested five potential ways in which creativity and intelligence could be related, "(1) Creativity is a subset of intelligence; (2) intelligence is a subset of creativity; (3) creativity and intelligence are overlapping sets; (4) creativity and intelligence are essentially the same things (coincident sets); and (5) creativity and intelligence bear no relation at all to each other (disjoint sets)" (p. 251). In a subsequent review of the research on the creativity–intelligence relationship, Sternberg, Kaufman, and Pretz (2002) concluded that the relationship between creativity and intelligence depends largely on how each is defined and measured.

With intelligence tests easily applied to identifying the needs of and grouping young students as well as successful adults, developing independent tests of creativity could easily have seemed either redundant or far less relevant than improving intelligence tests. Getzels and Jackson (1962) stated that

"we have most often behaved as if the intelligence test represented an adequate sampling of all mental abilities and cognitive processes. Despite the already substantial and increasing literature regarding the intellectual functions closely allied to creativity, we still treat the latter concept as applicable only to performance in one or more of the arts to the exclusion of other types of achievement requiring inventiveness, originality, and perfection" (p. 7). Sadly, little appears to have changed in the nearly 50 years since that time.

Others (e.g., Plucker et al., 2004; Sternberg, 2003) also note that the mystification of creativity has likely contributed to why so many researchers have shied away from studying it. If creativity is inspired by a muse, then it falls beyond the scope of scientific investigation.

Further, Sternberg (2003) posits that the push toward developing creativity in the business world by individuals such as de Bono (1971, 1985) and Osborn (1963) may have also hurt the reputation of creativity as a topic of scientific study.

The Assessment of Creativity

Few topics within the study of creativity and innovation incite as much passion as assessment or measurement. This appears to be especially true when the topic is discussed among nonacademics who work in creative fields: A colleague once shared a story concerning his speaking about creativity with designers at a major entertainment company. He off-handedly mentioned measurement and . . . suffice it to say that he did not find the kingdom to be so magical from that point forward. The conventional wisdom that creativity is too difficult to measure is a by-product of the definitional issues mentioned above, and many educators and researchers are surprised to learn that creativity assessment has a long, rich history; indeed, many appear to be surprised that the field is so advanced (Plucker & Runco, 1998).

The varying beliefs about the progress of the field may stem from disparate conceptions of creativity. For example, two questions that have been used in numerous research studies (both in and out of the field of creativity) are the classic radiation problem (Duncker, 1945) and the fortress-general problem (Gick & Holyoak, 1980). However, many individuals probably do not associate them with tests of creativity even though they (and questions like them) are commonly used as measures of creative problem solving.[1] Many probably equate only questions like "think of as many uses for a brick as possible" to measuring creativity.

The predominance of the psychometric approach likely stems from researchers who originally became interested in creativity only after having already investigated other cognitive phenomena using similar methods – they simply extended their methodological preferences to the study of creativity (see Cramond, 1993; Gardner, 1993). For example, in 1958, when the Minnesota Bureau of Education Research began studying the factors associated with variance in ability, aptitude, and intelligence test scores, its director at the time, E. Paul Torrance, chose to focus on creativity (Cramond, 1993).

J. P. Guilford's 1950 Presidential Address for the American Psychological Association is traditionally considered the formal starting date of scientific creativity research. But the psychometric tradition, and creativity research in general, dates from much earlier. For example, the 1883 publication of Galton's *Inquiries into Human Faculty* discussed the measurement of creativity (Taylor & Barron, 1963a), leading to several investigations into creativity and imagination in subsequent decades. Torrance

(1982) found evidence of significant efforts by Whipple around the turn of the century (i.e., tests of imagination and invention) and in the Human Engineering Laboratories during the 1930s and 1940s, and Barron and Harrington (1981) note that divergent thinking tests were developed by Binet and Henri before 1900. Maier (1945) also asked participants to perform tasks that are now considered creative problem solving. Several investigations into the creativity–intelligence relationship between 1898 and 1950 are also noted by Guilford (1967a). However, the rise of behaviorism dimmed the lasting influence of this work.

Unlike this largely forgotten early work, the ideas generated in the quarter century after Guilford's famous address have had a tremendous and continuing influence on the field (see Taylor & Barron, 1963a), and the vast majority of the creativity work from this era was conducted from a psychometric perspective. The collective proceedings from the National Science Foundation-sponsored Utah Conferences on the Identification of Creative Scientific Talent (Taylor, 1964; Taylor & Barron, 1963b; Taylor & Williams, 1966) serve as a comprehensive summary of much of the creativity research conducted in the late 1950s and early 1960s.

Summarizing the work of this period, Torrance (1979) noted that the psychometric study of creativity was essentially dichotomous.

> *Creativity tests tend to be of two types – those that involve cognitive-affective skills such as the* Torrance Tests of Creative Thinking *. . . and those that attempt to tap a personality syndrome such as the* Alpha Biological Inventory. *. . . Some educators and psychologists have tried to make an issue of whether creativity is essentially a personality syndrome that includes openness to experience, adventuresomeness, and self-confidence and whether the cognitive processes of rational and logical thinking in creative thinking are precisely the same as those used by high-IQ children.* (p. 360)

---

1 Duncker's (1945) radiation problem reads, "Imagine you are a doctor treating a patient with a malignant stomach tumor. You cannot operate but you must destroy the tumor. You could use high intensity X rays to destroy the tumor but unfortunately the intensity of the X rays needed to destroy the tumor also will destroy healthy tissue through which the X rays must pass. Less power full X rays will spare the healthy tissue but will not be strong enough to destroy the tumor. How can you destroy the tumor without damaging the healthy tissue?"

However, over the past 20 years, psychometric work has grown beyond the traditional cognitive and personality approaches. This expansion has been based largely on the work of Amabile (1983), Torrance (1979), and researchers and theorists who have promoted more-encompassing systems theories of creative development (e.g., Csikszentmihalyi, 1988; Kaufman & Baer, 2005; Sternberg & Lubart, 1995). For example, researchers have begun using psychometric methods to assess the creativity of products (Horn & Salvendy, 2006a, 2006b), investigate environmental characteristics associated with creativity and innovation (Amabile & Conti, 1999; Amabile, Schatzel, Moneta, & Kramer, 2004; Tighe, Picariello, & Amabile, 2003), and develop new measures of personality (Kelly, 2004). Indeed, the argument can be made that the field of creativity assessment has never been as active and dynamic as it currently is.

Traditional Areas of Psychometric Study

Psychometric methods in creativity research are typically grouped into four types of investigations: creative processes, personality and behavioral correlates of creativity, characteristics of creative products, and attributes of creativity-fostering environment (Rhodes, 1961). Unlike the more recent development of systems theories and the rise of multidisciplinary approaches, which consider varied perspectives and influences, the psychometric approach generally studied each of the four aspects in isolation. This section reviews seminal and recent work in each of these areas and concludes with a comparison among the specific areas of psychometric investigation. Readers will not find a detailed listing of the hundreds of creativity tests, instruments, and rating scales that have been developed in recent decades, and are referred elsewhere for these reviews (Hunsaker & Callahan, 1995; Kaufman, Plucker, & Baer 2008; Plucker & Renzulli, 1999; Runco, 1999).

Creative Processes

Researchers have used psychometric measures of creative process extensively for decades, and they remain a popular measure of creative process and potential. Assessing creative processes is also evident in our schools (Hunsaker & Callahan, 1995). Nevertheless, a majority of criticisms and adverse reactions directed at creativity measures are primarily (but not exclusively) directed at "creativity tests." These "tests," used to quantify the creative process, have often been divergent-thinking batteries and have been a lightning rod for the psychometric study of creativity. These divergent-thinking batteries ask participants to use "cognition that leads in various directions" (Runco, 1999, p. 577). In contrast to most standardized tests, of achievement or ability, divergent thinking tests require individuals to produce several responses to a specific prompt. Guilford (1968) emphasized the importance of, and distinction from, divergent thinking relative to convergent thinking:

> In convergent-thinking tests, the examinee must arrive at one right answer. The information given generally is sufficiently structured so that there is only one right answer. . . . [A]n example with verbal material would be: "What is the opposite of hard?" In divergent thinking, the thinker must do much searching around, and often a number of answers will do or are wanted. If you ask the examinee to name all the things he can think of that are hard, also edible, also white, he has a whole class of things that might do. It is in the divergent-thinking category that we find the abilities that are most significant in creative thinking and invention. (p. 8) emphasis in original

The emphasis on quantity of responses is often referred to as ideational fluency, or simply ideation. The idea that "more is better" is a key component of ideation, but is clearly not the sole component of the creative process. Divergent thinking (DT) is often contrasted with convergent thinking, in which cognitive processes are used to produce one or very few possible solutions to a given problem (such as on most standardized tests).

Kaufman et al. (2008) have noted that it is one of the great ironies of the study of creativity that so much time and energy have been devoted to the use of a single class of assessments. In fact, not only has the most energy been expended on DT tests; almost all of the earliest tests of DT remain in wide use in creativity research and education. These include Guilford's (1967b) Structure of the Intellect (SOI) divergent-production tests, Torrance's (1962, 1974) Tests of Creative Thinking (TTCT), and Wallach and Kogan's (1965) and Getzels and Jackson's (1962) DT tests. Although space does not permit a detailed description of each existing test and battery, a brief description of the most widely cited instruments is provided.

Although the content and instructions of DT tests vary, how responses are categorized remains largely consistent. In general, DT tests ask for multiple responses to either figural or verbal prompts, and responses are scored for fluency, flexibility, originality, and elaboration of ideas. Fluency is operationally defined as the number of responses to a given stimuli, "the total number of ideas given on any one divergent thinking exercise" (Runco, 1999, p. 577). Originality is operationalized as the uniqueness of responses to a given stimuli, "the unusualness . . . of an examinee's or respondent's ideas" (Runco, 1999, p. 577). Flexibility is operationalized as the number and/or uniqueness of categories of responses to a given stimuli, or more broadly, "a change in the meaning, use, or interpretation of something" (Guilford, 1968, p. 99). Elaboration is operationalized as the extension of ideas within a specific category of responses to a given stimuli, "to fill [ideas] out with details" (Guilford, 1967b, p. 138).

For example, if a person were trying to decide what to buy as a birthday present for her brother, she could come up with as many ideas for presents as she possibly could

(fluency), presents that no one else would think of (originality), a list of different types of presents he might like (flexibility), or a list of the different basketball-related presents he might like (elaboration). However, in this example, as in life, choices have to be made eventually and evaluative convergent thinking must be done to select the actual present to be purchased.

Major Approaches to DT Assessment

J. P. Guilford's (1967b) SOI Model proposed 24 distinct types of DT: one type for each combination of four kinds of content (Figural, Symbolic, Semantic, Behavioral) and six categories of product (Units, Classes, Relations, Systems, Transformations, Implications). For example, the SOI DT battery consists of several tests on which participants are asked to exhibit evidence of divergent production in several areas, including divergent production of semantic units (e.g., listing consequences of people no longer needing to sleep), of figural classes (finding as many classifications of sets of figures as is possible), and of figural units (taking a simple shape such as a circle and elaborating on it as often as possible).

Tasks on the SOI are characterized by the need for trial-and-error strategies and flexible thinking. One well-known example of an SOI task is the Match Problem (divergent production of figural transformations). There are several versions of the Match Problem but each is a variation on the basic theme of using 17 matches to create a grid of two rows and three columns (i.e., six squares). Participants are asked to remove three matches so that the remaining matches form four complete squares. By asking participants to transform objects visually and spatially, Guilford was assessing flexibility. Other examples include the Sketches task (fluency with figural units), in which participants draw as many pictures as possible given a specific shape, such as a circle; the Alternate Letter Groups task (flexibility with figural classes), which requires participants, given a set of letters, to form subgroups of letters according to the figural aspects of the letters; and the Associations I task (originality with semantic transformations), in which a person, given two words, finds a third word that links the two (e.g., movie and fishing are linked by reel). Guilford's entire SOI divergent production battery consists of several dozen tests of the various DT components of the SOI model.

Guilford and his colleagues gathered enormous amounts of assessment data in order to validate the SOI model. Results of these analyses are generally supportive of the SOI model (e.g., Chen, Shyuefee & Michael, 1993; Guilford & Hoepfner, 1966; Holly & Michael, 1972), although some researchers have suggested revisions to the model (Chen & Michael, 1993; Michael & Bachelor, 1992) or concluded that the model has serious weaknesses (Alliger, 1988; Horn, 1967; Horn & Knapp, 1973 Sternberg & Grigorenko, 2000–2001).

Torrance Tests of Creative Thinking

The TTCT, which are based on many aspects of the SOI battery, are by far the most commonly used test of DT. Over the course of several decades, Torrance (1974) refined the administration and scoring of the TTCT, which may account for its enduring popularity. The battery includes Verbal and Figural tests that each include a Form A and Form B that can be used alternately. There are seven Verbal subtests: Asking, Guessing Causes, Product Improvement, Unusual Uses[2], Unusual Questions, and Just Suppose.

The first three verbal subtests provide a picture to be used as a stimulus. For example, the image might be an elf gazing at its reflection in a pool of water. In this case, participants would have to ask as many questions as they could about the image; guess causes for what made the image come to be; and guess the consequences that will result from the image.

The other four verbal subtests are independent and do not rely on an external stimulus. For Product Improvement, participants are given a toy and asked for different ways it could be improved. The Unusual Uses test requires participants to list different uses for an everyday object such as a cardboard box. A slight variation on this is the Unusual Questions tasks, which asks participants to ask as many questions as possible about an object. The final verbal subtest, Just Suppose, calls for participants to imagine what would happen if an improbable situation took place, such as if people no longer had to sleep.

There are three Figural subtests consisting of Picture Construction, Picture Completion, and Lines/Circles. Picture Construction requires participants to make a picture out of a basic shape, whereas the Picture Completion subtest provides a partially complete picture and asks participants to finish and name the drawing. The Lines/Circles subtest provides participants with either a set of lines or circles to modify and shape.

Administration, scoring, and score reporting of the TTCT are standardized with detailed norms (see Torrance, 1972b, 1974; Torrance & Ball, 1984). Although Torrance recommended that scorers be trained, he found that cursory levels of training (i.e., reading and understanding the scoring manual) allowed novice raters to produce scores associated with acceptable reliability estimates. His one caveat was that untrained raters tend to deviate from the scoring system when assessing originality, injecting their own personal judgments on the scoring of individual responses.

The original test produced scores in the traditional four DT areas of fluency, flexibility, originality, and elaboration, but the streamlined scoring system introduced in the 1984 revision made significant changes. Under the streamlined system, the Figural tests can be scored for resistance to premature closure and abstractness of titles in addition to the familiar scores of fluency, elaboration, originality. Flexibility was

2 This subtest does not appear in later editions.

removed because those scores tended to be largely undifferentiated from fluency scores (Hébert, Cramond, Spiers-Neumeister, Millar, & Silvian, 2002).

Although the SOI and TTCT may be the best-known DT batteries, there are several others that have been used for decades. Getzels and Jackson (1962) and Wallach and Kogan (1965) developed DT batteries that are very similar to the SOI tests. For example, the Instances Test requires that students list as many things that move on wheels (things that make noise, etc.) as possible (Wallach & Kogan, 1965), and on variations of the Uses Test students provide responses to prompts such as "Tell me all the different ways you could use a chair" (newspaper, knife, tire) (Wallach & Kogan, 1965, p. 31) or use bricks, pencils, or toothpicks (Getzels & Jackson, 1962). The most appreciable difference between the batteries lies in the conditions in which students take the tests. Wallach and Kogan (1965) supported gamelike, untimed administration of DT tasks, which they believed allows creativity to be measured distinctly from intelligence as a result of the creation of "a frame of reference which is relatively free from the coercion of time limits and relatively free from the stress of knowing that one's behavior is under close evaluation" (p. 24). This constraint-free administration is in contrast to the testlike, timed procedures used with most other DT measures.

Psychometric Evidence

Evidence of reliability for the SOI, TTCT, Wallach and Kogan, Getzels and Jackson, and similar tests is fairly convincing (e.g., Cline, Richards, & Abe, 1962; Eisen, 1989; Hoepfner & Hemenway, 1973; Torrance, 1981c; Torrance, Khatena, & Cunnington, 1973; Williams, 1979, 1980), but the predictive and discriminant validity of DT tests enjoys mixed support (cf. Bachelor, 1989; Clapham, 1996; Cooper, 1991; Fox, 1985; Renzulli, 1985; Rosen, 1985; Thompson & Anderson, 1983). However, the perceived lack of predictive validity (Baer, 1993b, 1993c, 1994; Gardner, 1988,

1993; Kogan & Pankove, 1974; Weisberg, 1993) has led some researchers and educators to avoid the use of these tests and continues to serve as a lightning rod for criticisms of the psychometric study of creativity. Although psychometric tests of creativity may lack evidence of predictive validity, researchers have also suggested several possible reasons for DT tests' perceived weakness (see Kaufman et al., 2008). At the forefront of these hypotheses is the potential lack of methodological rigor of research, impugning the integrity of psychometric measures of creative processes. For example, Plucker and Renzulli (1999) note that score distributions are often nonnormally distributed, violating the assumptions of many statistical procedures.

However, one important caveat is that it is not universally accepted that psychometric measures of creative processes have poor predictive power. In fact, several studies provide at least limited evidence of discriminant and predictive validity for DT tests (Howieson, 1981; Milgram & Hong, 1994; Milgram & Milgram, 1976; Okuda, Runco, & Berger, 1991; Rotter, Langland, & Berger, 1971; Runco, 1986a; Torrance, 1969, 1972a, 1972b, 1981a, 1981b; Torrance & Safter, 1989; Torrance, Tan, & Allman, 1970; Torrance & Wu, 1981; Yamada & Tam, 1996). The evidence becomes more positive under certain sampling and assessment conditions recommended in the literature (e.g., samples of high IQ children, utilizing content specific DT measures; see Clapham, Cowdery, King, & Montang, 2005; Hocevar, 1981; Ignatz, 1982; Milgram & Milgram, 1976; Runco, 1986a, 1986b). Plucker (1999a), in a reanalysis of Torrance data using more sophisticated statistical techniques, found that DT test scores were three times better than IQ test scores at predicting adult creative achievement. In this study, adult creative achievement was operationalized in two different ways. First, as the number of publicly recognized creative achievements (e.g., inventions, publications, awards for creativity). Second, a panel of three judges rated the list of adult creative achievements to create an overall creative quality index.

The conditions under which tests are administered (e.g., gamelike vs. testlike, timed vs. untimed, individual vs. group, specific instructions to "be creative" vs. generic instructions) also influence originality and/or fluency scores (Chand & Runco, 1992; Harrington, 1975; Hattie, 1980; Renzulli, Owen, & Callahan, 1974; Runco, 1986c; Runco & Okuda, 1991; Torrance, 1971). Some have also noted that scores on divergent production tests are susceptible to training and intervention effects (see evidence presented by Clapham, 1996; Feldhusen & Clinkenbeard, 1986; Torrance, 1972a, 1988). Because many of these tests are frequently applied in educational settings or have variations found online, some concern over predictive validity has obvious merit.

A final concern with the psychometric measurement of creative processes involves how these batteries are typically scored. There is some evidence that alternatives to the traditional frequency tabulations of fluency, flexibility, originality, and elaboration should be considered (e.g., Torrance, 1972d). These alternatives include the calculation of summative scores (i.e., totaling fluency, flexibility, and originality scores), uncommon scores (answers given by less than five percent of participants), weighted fluency scores, percentage scores, and scores based on the entire body of each participant's answers as opposed to scoring individual responses in a list of ideas (Hocevar & Michaels, 1979; Runco & Mraz, 1992; Runco, Okuda, & Thurston, 1987).

Additionally, a measurement dilemma unique to DT tests is the possibility of fluency acting as a contaminating factor, especially on originality scores (Clark & Mirels, 1970; Hocevar, 1979c, 1979d; Runco & Albert, 1985; Seddon, 1983). Hocevar (1979a, 1979c), after partialing fluency effects out of other DT test scores, found little evidence of reliability for originality and flexibility scores. But this work has significant empirical (Runco & Albert, 1985) and theoretical limitations (e.g., the role of associative hierarchies in creative individuals, see Mednick, 1962; Milgram & Rabkin, 1980). A case in point is the effort by Runco and Albert

(1985) to utilize both verbal and nonverbal tasks, because Hocevar (1979a, 1979c) used only verbal tests. Runco and Albert (1985) found that originality scores produced evidence of reliability after removing fluency effects on the nonverbal tasks, with significant differences among groups based on achievement (i.e., gifted vs. nongifted students). Collectively, this work suggests that the role of fluency is more complex than originally thought.

Moreover, there is concern over the emphasis on the *quantity* of creative achievement over the *quality* of those achievements. As evidenced by the traditional scoring methods of the batteries discussed above, the quantity–quality imbalance is not surprising. Runco (1986) stressed that both quantity and quality of creative achievement should be included as outcome variables. Studies that have included both quantity and quality factors have provided support for the predictive validity of DT tests (e.g., Davidovitch & Milgram, 2006; Plucker, 1999a).

Although many other strategies have been suggested as ways to control for fluency effects, an especially intriguing technique has recently been created by Snyder, Mitchell, Bossomaier, and Pallier (2004). They proposed the calculation of a Creativity Quotient (CQ) to score DT test responses, a formula that rewards response pools that are highly fluent but also highly flexible. Although readers are referred to Snyder et al. (2004) or Kaufman et al. (2008) for a more detailed explanation of the CQ, Bossomaier, Harré, Knittel, and Snyder (2009) have recently extended and fine-tuned the technique, which appears to be a promising line of DT assessment research.

In summary, DT tests occupy nearly the entire spotlight on research of the creative process. Although the ability to generate ideas is only one aspect of creative process (cf., Runco, 2007b; Runco & Okuda, 1988), its predominance implicitly devalues the role of creativity in the solving of problems (Davis, 1973; Dombroski, 1979; Rickards, 1994; Speedie, Treffinger, & Houtz, 1976;

Sternberg & Davidson, 1992). Although old habits die hard (and slowly), the field is wending its way toward including both quantity and quality of outcome variables. Professing a viewpoint long held by many researchers (e.g., Basadur, Wakabayashi, & Graen, 1990; Osborn, 1963; Parnes, Noller, & Biondi, 1977; Simonton, 1988b; Torrance, 1976), Runco (1991) observed, "the evaluative component of the creative process has received very little attention. This is surprising because it is a vital constituent of the creative process, and is required whenever an individual selects or expresses a preference for an idea or set of ideas" (p. 312).

The Creative Person

A second major area of activity involves assessments of creative personality. Measures focusing on characteristics of the person are diverse, typically focusing on self-report or external ratings of past behavior or personality characteristics. In a meta-analysis on personality and creativity research, Feist (1998) categorized research on the creative person as either a between-group (e.g., comparing scientists with non-scientists) or within-group (e.g., creative versus less creative scientists) comparison.

Personality Scales

Instruments intended to measure personality correlates of creative behavior are generally designed by studying individuals already deemed creative and then determining their common characteristics. These traits are then used as a reference for other children and adults under the assumption that individuals who compare favorably are predisposed to creative accomplishment. Such measures are quite common in creativity research and include the Group Inventory for Finding Talent and Group Inventory for Finding Interests (see Davis, 1989), What Kind of Person Are You? (Torrance & Khatena, 1970), Big Five NEO-Five Factor Inventory (Costa & McCrae, 1992), work undertaken at the Institute of

Personality Assessment and Research (Hall & MacKinnon, 1969; Helson, 1971; MacKinnon, 1965, 1975, 1978), and specific scoring dimensions of the Adjective Check List (Domino, 1970, 1994; Gough, 1979; Smith & Schaefer, 1969) and the Sixteen Personality Factor Questionnaire (Cattell & Butcher, 1968; Cattell, Eber, & Tatsuoka, 1970). After analyzing the results of research in which these and several other related instruments were used, Davis (1992) concluded that personality characteristics of creative people include awareness of their creativity, originality, independence, risk taking, personal energy, curiosity, humor, attraction to complexity and novelty, artistic sense, open-mindedness, need for privacy, and heightened perception. Similarly, Feist (1998) found consistently that creative people tend to be "autonomous, introverted, open to new experiences, norm-doubting, self-confident, self-accepting, driven, ambitious, dominant, hostile, and impulsive" (p. 299), with the traits with the largest effect sizes being openness, conscientiousness, self-acceptance, hostility, and impulsivity. These studies mirror the results of other, recent studies and reviews of the literature (e.g., Batey & Furnham, 2006; Qian, Plucker, & Shen, in press; Treffinger, Young, Shelby, & Shepardson, 2002; Wang, 2003). However, it should be noted that mounting evidence suggests that creative personality characteristics are developmental in nature, with the potential for greatest change occurring during adolescence and young adulthood (Nie & Zheng, 2005; Soldz & Vaillant, 1999; Wang, 2003).

Activity Checklists

In addition to personality traits, past behavior of creative individuals is also often examined to determine whether experience is associated with creative production. As a result, self-reports are relied on for information about an individual's previous behaviors and accomplishments that may reflect creative potential and achievement. Based on the assumption that "the best predictor of future creative behavior may be past creative behavior" (Colangelo, Kerr, Huesman, Hallowell, & Gaeth, 1992, p. 158), several investigators have developed self-report biographical or activity inventories such as the Alpha Biological Inventory (Taylor & Ellison, 1966, 1967), Creative Behavior Inventory (Hocevar, 1979b), or other checklists (Anastasi & Schaefer, 1969; Holland & Nichols, 1964; Holland & Richards, 1965; James, Ellison, Fox, & Taylor, 1974; King, McKee, & Broyles, 1996; Milgram & Hong, 1994; Milgram & Milgram, 1976; Runco, 1986, 1987a; Runco, Noble, & Luptak, 1990; Runco & Okuda, 1988; Schaefer & Anastasi, 1968; Wallach & Wing, 1969). Hocevar (1981; Hocevar & Bachelor, 1989), Plucker (1998, 1999b), and Wallach (1976) believe self-reports of activities and attainments to be the preferable technique with which to measure creativity.

Two recent efforts to create this type of instrument include the Creativity Achievement Questionnaire (CAQ; Carson, Peterson, & Higgins, 2005) and the Runco Ideational Behavior Scale (RIBS; Runco, 2008). The CAQ (Carson et al., 2005) assesses creativity with 96 items across 10 domains that load onto an Arts (Drama, Writing, Humor, Music, Visual Arts, and Dance) and a Science factor (Invention, Science, and Culinary). A respondent indicates the extent to which given items describe her or his creative achievements in each area. For example, within the Humor scale, items range from "I do not have recognized talent in this area" to "I have created jokes that are now repeated by others" to "I have worked as a professional comedian" to "My humor has been recognized in a national publication." The CAQ is associated with high levels of evidence of reliability and with acceptable evidence of concurrent validity.

The RIBS was developed in response to Runco's (2007b) perceived need for a more appropriate criterion in studies of predictive validity for divergent thinking tests. Runco hypothesized that researchers were using DT tests to predict inappropriate criteria, such as those traditionally used in studies of the predictive validity of intelligence tests. Runco reasoned that a more appropriate criterion would be one that emphasizes ideation: the use of, appreciation of, and skill of generating ideas. Sample items include, "I think about ideas more often than most people," "Friends ask me to help them think of ideas and solutions," and "Sometimes I get so interested in a new idea that I forget about other things that I should be doing."

Runco, Plucker, and Lim (2000–2001) examined the psychometric integrity of the RIBS, with results suggesting adequate evidence of reliability and construct validity. Plucker, Runco, and Lim (2006) subsequently used the RIBS as a criterion measure in a study of divergent thinking and time-on-task, with positive conclusions about the ability of DT assessments to predict ideational behavior.

One weakness of this approach is that the administration of self-report scales may not be logistically feasible with all groups, such as very young children. In response to this need, several instruments have been developed to allow parents, teachers, other adults, and even peers to assess personality and past behavior correlates of creativity (Pearlman, 1983; Rimm, 1983; Runco, 1984, 1987b, 1989b; Torrance, 1962; Wasik, 1974). Perhaps the most popular instruments, at least within educational settings, are the Scales for Rating the Behavioral Characteristics of Superior Students (SRBCSS; Renzulli, Hartman, & Callahan, 1981; Renzulli et al., 2002). Teachers rate specific students on a six-point scale ranging from *never* to *occasionally* to *always*, with creativity scale items such as "The student demonstrates . . . imaginative thinking ability", " . . . an adventurous spirit or a willingness to take risks," and " . . . the ability to adapt, improve, or modify objects or ideas." The SRBCSS has been found to be the most frequently used measure of creativity in gifted-education screening procedures (Callahan, Hunsaker, Adams, Moore, & Bland, 1995; Hunsaker & Callahan, 1995).

Validity evidence of both self-reports and ratings by "familiar others" are inconclusive – with respect to creativity and to talent in general – with evidence supporting both the presence of validity (Burke, Haworth, & Ware, 1982; Gagné, 1994; Plucker, 1999b, 2004; Pyryt, 2004; Renzulli et al., 1981; Runco, 1984) and a lack thereof (Baer, 1998; Dollinger, Burke, & Gump, 2007; Hocevar & Bachelor, 1989; Holland, 1959; Lee, Day, Meara, & Maxwell, 2002; Pegnato & Birch, 1959; Priest, 2006).

Attitudes

The measurement of attitudes toward creativity is important because, as Basadur and Hausdorf (1996) describe in their attitude research within the business community, "Managers with more positive attitudes could be encouraged to participate in activities where these views can be optimized.... Alternatively, managers with less positive attitudes could participate in training to improve their attitudes and skills. Thus, the understanding and measurement of these attitudinal concepts provides a pathway to increasing managers' and companies' success." (p. 23) Additionally, theoretical and empirical support exists for a connection between ideational attitudes and ideational thinking (Basadur & Finkbeiner, 1985). Although attempts to measure creative attitudes have not been widespread, considerable effort has been expended on the creation of attitude measures for the purpose of evaluating attitude interventions in business across cultures (Basadur, Graen, & Scandura, 1986; Basadur, Pringle, & Kirkland, 2002; Basadur, Wakabayashi, & Takai, 1992) and identifying individuals who are predisposed to innovation or adaptation (Kirton, 2006).

For example, Basadur and colleagues (Basadur & Finkbeiner, 1985; Basadur & Hausdorf, 1996; Basadur, Taggar, & Pringle, 1999; Basadur et al., 1990; Runco & Basadur, 1993) have developed two scales that assess attitudes toward important aspects of DT, the six-item Preference for Active Divergence scale and the eight-item Preference for Premature Convergence (or premature closure) scale, with the former being indica-

tive of positive DT attitudes and the latter being counterindicative. Items on the Active Divergence scale include "One new idea is worth 10 old ones" and "I feel that all ideas should be given equal time and listened to with an open mind, regardless of how zany they seem to be." Items representing Premature Convergence include "Lots of time can be wasted on wild ideas," "Quality is a lot more important than quantity in generating ideas," and "I wish people would think about whether or not an idea is practical before they open their mouths."

A relatively new area of creative-attitude research is in the area of creative self-efficacy. Tierney and Farmer (2002), building on the work of Gist and Mitchell (1992), proposed the concept of creative self-efficacy as representing a person's beliefs about how creative he or she can be. These beliefs are often rooted in a situational or narrow context (e.g., Jaussi, Randel, & Dionne, 2007). A broader view of creative self-efficacy examines creative personal identity, which is also reflective of how much someone values creativity (e.g., Randel & Jaussi, 2003). Measures of creative self-efficacy are often brief; as an example, Beghetto (2006) used a three-item scale: I am good at coming up with new ideas, I have a lot of good ideas, and I have a good imagination. All of these researchers have gathered evidence of reliability and validity, although the theoretical and psychometric distinctions between measures of creative self-efficacy and instruments such as the RIBS, which have similar items but are intended to measure different constructs, have yet to be clarified.

Creative Products

Assessment of creative products receives much less attention in the literature than assessment of personality, process, or even environmental variables, yet a case can be made that the ability to measure a product's creativity is among the most important aspects of creativity assessment. For example, if a company designs a new digital music player or cell phone, being able to assess the degree of creativity in various designs may lead to substantial profit – and potential savings as resources are not wasted on non-creative designs. How does a teacher determine whether a student's product is truly creative? In a different vein, the creativity of artistic products is often hotly debated; those debates are almost always subjective in nature and perhaps need not be.

From a psychological and educational perspective, Runco (1989a) noted that analysis of creative products may address the measurement problems caused by the inconsistent psychometric quality of other forms of creativity measurement. More to the point, Baer and Kaufman (see Baer et al., 2004), among others, believe that product assessments are probably the most appropriate assessments of creativity. (Several researchers have referred to such assessments as the "gold standard" of creativity assessment.) This logic is compelling: If one goal of creativity psychometrics is to predict who is most likely to produce creative works in the future, being able to create such products in the past or present would appear to be a key indicator.

Advanced techniques for the assessment of creative products clearly have a wide range of potential applications, and after some stagnation in the mid- to late-1990s, a number of potentially fruitful efforts have emerged in recent years. Although a number of high-quality product assessments have been developed, including the Creative Product Semantic Scale (Besemer, 1998; Besemer & O'Quin, 1999) and Student Product Assessment Form (Reis & Renzulli, 1991), the most active area is that of the Consensual Assessment Technique (CAT; see Amabile, 1979, 1982, 1983, for information on the early development of the methodology).

The Consensual Assessment Technique

The CAT is a clever solution for the "criterion problem" in creativity research: How do we know we are using the correct criteria of creativity when we design assessments? The criterion problem is a direct result of

the field's difficulty defining its terms, which was discussed in the section on "Defining Creativity" at the beginning of the chapter. Amabile (1982) hypothesized that "a product or response is creative to the extent that appropriate observers independently agree it is creative" (p. 1001). In other words, people know creativity when they see it, and the use of expert judges to evaluate a product's creativity should, theoretically, avoid criterion problems. This view is partially validated by the studies of implicit creativity theories and definitions (e.g., Lim & Plucker, 2001; Runco & Johnson, 2002). Evidence of reliability is considerable across a wide range of applications (Amabile, 1983, 1996; Baer, 1993a; Baer, Kaufman, & Gentile, 2004; Conti, Coon, & Amabile, 1996; Hennessey, 1994; Runco, 1989a), and the technique has been applied to assess the creativity of a broad range of products across diverse research contexts (e.g., Baer, 1994, 2003; Baer et al., 2004; Fodor & Carver, 2000; Hickey, 2001; Myford, 1989; Niu & Sternberg, 2001; Ruscio, Whitney, & Amabile, 1998; Sternberg & Lubart, 1995).

However, the use of expert judges is not without some controversy. Early in the development of the CAT, evidence suggested that determining the necessary level of expertise for judges depends on a variety of factors, including the skill of the subjects, the target domain, and the purpose of the assessments (e.g., Amabile, 1996; Runco, McCarthy, & Svenson, 1994; Runco & Smith, 1992). Although Amabile (1996) recommends that experts have "at least some formal training and experience in the target domain" (p. 73), several researchers have examined the level of expertise that is necessary when using the CAT or similar assessment strategies. Indeed, over the past decade, researchers have learned a great deal about the use of expert judges to evaluate creative products. In general, expert and novice judges tend to produce quite different ratings of product creativity, although the domain in which the product is created impacts the degree to which the groups' ratings overlap. For example, Kaufman, Baer, Cole, and Sexton (2008) found that expert and novice (e.g., college student) ratings of poetry barely correlated, yet Kaufman, Baer, and Cole (2009) found a higher correlation between the similar groups when evaluating the creativity of short stories. When using artistic products, Dollinger, Urban, and James (2004) found rather large correlations between artists and psychologists.

Recent research suggests that expertise, at least in this context, should be conceptualized as a continuum. When Kaufman, Gentile, and Baer (2005) compared expert judges and quasi-experts (gifted high school writers), they found appreciably higher correlations between the two groups' ratings of creative writing products than previous research would have predicted. Similarly, Plucker, Kaufman, Temple, and Qian (2009) found that the movie ratings of professional movie critics (experts), film Web site users (novices), and college students (laypeople) fall on a continuum, with lowest ratings from critics and highest ratings from college students, with novices firmly in between the other two groups.

Three issues should be considered when evaluating the research on the CAT. First, the CAT, as it has been applied in various ways by researchers, is associated with very convincing evidence of reliability, and recent efforts to modify the technique show promise for further improvement (e.g., Dollinger & Shafran, 2005). However, evidence of validity is primarily found in the area of face validity, which is theoretically convincing but empirically limiting. This concern leads to the second issue, which involves questions about the appropriateness of using external judges to evaluate creativity. Runco and his colleagues (Runco & Chand, 1994; Runco et al., 1994; Runco & Smith, 1992; Runco & Vega, 1990) have long questioned why "expert" opinion would be more valid or useful than self-ratings or the evaluations of peers, teachers, and other groups that are not necessarily experts. This is not a trivial concern: Given the expense and difficulty often encountered when planning and implementing studies involving expert raters, determining the appropriate level of expertise (if any) required for valid

results when using CAT-like assessment strategies should continue to be a priority for researchers.

Consumer Product Design Models

As research on design has become more prevalent in the psychological and educational literature, the assessment of creative products from a design perspective has likewise become more common. As Christiaans (2002) has observed, "the result of a design activity is often expected to be original, adding value to the existing world of design. In the selection of designs for production in companies, for design awards, and in the field of design education, creativity assessment relies on human judgments" (p. 41). Although some researchers have used existing instruments and techniques (e.g., Christiaans used an approximation of the CAT and the Creative Product Semantic Scale), new models are also in development. A recent case in point is the research of Horn and Salvendy (2006a, 2006b), in which the researchers have questioned the applicability of existing product measures to the design context and propose an alternative model consisting of six components: novelty (the newness of the product), resolution (the ability of a product to resolve a problem), emotion (the pleasure or arousal induced by the product), centrality (ability to match consumer needs), importance (importance to consumer needs), and desire (how critical or desirable the product is). Although this work is relatively new, the increasing importance of design suggests this approach to creative product assessment could increase in importance.

Creative Environments and Environment–Person Interactions

Hunter, Bedell, and Mumford (2007), in their comprehensive review of research on situational influences on creativity, identified a number of environmental variables suspected to be related to creativity, including intra- and inter-group interactions, leadership, organizational structure, competition, and cohesion, among many others. A casual review of research literature in business and management shows many studies of how creativity and work environments are related (or not).

Much of this research examines the correlation between successful work and situational variables and does not focus on assessments of creative environments per se. For example, Forbes and Domm (2004), in an approach influenced by the work of Amabile and her colleagues, developed an environment survey that required participants to rate the importance of items related to a recent, successful, creative project on which they worked. Six factors emerged from the data: mental involvement, intrinsic motivation, time and resource constraints, extrinsic motivation, external control, and team management.

One exception to this trend is the work of Amabile and her colleagues. Based on extensive research on organizational creativity (e.g., see Amabile & Gryskiewicz, 1987, 1989; Amabile, Hill, Hennessey, & Tighe, 1994), Amabile, Conti, Coon, Lazenby, and Herron (1996) developed the *KEYS: Assessing the Climate for Creativity* instrument. Amabile et al. (1996) created the KEYS in order to examine employees' perceptions of aspects of their work environment that may influence creative work – especially creative work by teams. They note that the self-report instrument is designed to assess "individuals' perceptions and the influence of those perceptions on the creativity of their work" (p. 1157). This instrument is associated with evidence of reliability and validity and is widely used by researchers.

The value of this work is made obvious in studies such as that of Amabile and Conti (1999), who used KEYS to study changes in the work environment of a downsizing company. Their results suggest that creativity-enhancing variables in the work environment decreased during the downsizing (and rebounded partially over time), with creativity-inhibiting variables showing the opposite pattern. Their study concludes with recommendations for mediating the negative effects on creativity in similar, future contexts.

Nemiro (2001) is pursuing a similar line of work in her examination of the climate for creativity in virtual teams (i.e., teams working synchronously or asynchronously on tasks using technology such as the Internet). Nemiro developed the Virtual Team Creative Climate measure (VTCC) with 11 scales that represent dimensions that influence creativity of individual members of virtual teams: acceptance of ideas and constructive tension, challenge, collaboration, dedication/commitment, freedom, goal clarity, information sharing, management encouragement, personal bond, sufficient resources and time, and trust. The VTCC can also be scored in three broader scales of connection, raw materials, and management and team member skills. Although the VTCC is still early in its development, Nemiro deserves credit for applying psychometric methods to an important area of creative work.

Strengths and Weaknesses of Creativity Assessment

In reviewing the extensive literature on this topic, a number of clear strengths and weaknesses of creativity assessment become obvious. The sheer depth of psychometric work is impressive, with decades of studies and instrument development available to the interested researcher or practitioner. Indeed, a case can be made that many of the foundational ideas of the field are based on this voluminous psychometric research; this work appears to be particularly influential outside of the United States (e.g., Kaufman & Sternberg, 2006; Makel & Plucker, 2007). For example, psychometric methods provided the foundation for problem-solving programs in a variety of contexts (Basadur, Graen, & Green, 1982; Isaksen & Treffinger, 1985), school-based creativity training programs (Renzulli, 1976), remediation programs (Meeker, 1969; Meeker & Meeker, 1982), and whole-school talent-development models (Renzulli, 1994; Taylor, 1988). The work of Renzulli and Reis (1985; see also Reis & Renzulli, 1999), probably the most influential within the field of gifted education, is arguably based on creativity research that is psychometric in nature (see Renzulli, 1978).

Another strength is that, in certain contexts (e.g., samples of high-IQ children, using content-specific DT measures), evidence of validity – including predictive validity – is rather convincing. A related weakness, of course, is that many popular instruments are not associated with such convincing evidence or, more often, have been subjected to too little psychometric evaluation.

Third, criticisms of creativity assessment aimed at divergent thinking are probably overblown. Although the field's reliance on divergent thinking is a weakness, those researchers interested in creativity should consider Guilford's observation that "Most of our problem solving in everyday life involves divergent thinking. Yet in our educational practices, we tend to emphasize teaching students how to find conventional answers" (1968, p. 8). In this current age of increased education testing and "accountability," this comment is as salient today as when Guilford first wrote it. However, a better way forward almost certainly involves strategies that move well beyond DT, such as multifaceted, multimodal assessment systems involving many of the other strong measures discussed in this chapter.

With all of that said, many criticisms and concerns about creativity psychometrics appear to be valid. Some should be relatively straightforward to address, others more difficult. First and foremost, for nearly half a century, scholars have been calling for more research on the criterion problem. As Cattell and Butcher (1968) noted, "obtaining a criterion score on 'creativity' to check the predictive power of our tests is going to present formidable conceptual and practical problems" (pp. 285–286). Indeed it has over the past 40 years, but we are ready to go out on a limb and suggest that the use of expert ratings of creative products, such as the consensual assessment techniques reviewed above, are close to becoming that criterion. This is

the area that has received the most attention from researchers in recent years, and we know much more today about the evaluation of creative products than we did when Plucker and Renzulli (1999) last comprehensively reviewed the field.

The traditional criticisms about lack of predictive, discriminant, and construct validity evidence still hold true, although as noted above, there are many caveats and exceptions. But creativity assessment researchers still do not conduct evaluations of psychometric integrity very often, which adds to the problem by both failing to gather needed data and giving the impression that this type of work is unimportant. In many ways, it is the important psychometric evidence, and we need many more studies in this area. This research is needed for every type of assessment, from DT tests to the CAT. For example, critics have hypothesized that the lack of consistent construct validity evidence for the TTCT is due to response set bias (i.e., the use of the same participant responses to derive multiple scores, which can lead to high score intercorrelations; see Heausler & Thompson, 1988; Thorndike, 1972). Other DT tasks not scored in this way (e.g., much of Guilford's work) are associated with more positive evaluations of construct validity than the TTCT. A potential solution is obvious: Score the TTCT without response set bias and examine the resulting construct validity evidence. Yet we have not been able to find any such studies in the 20 to 30 years since this hypothesis was discussed in the published literature. In a completely different area, CAT research is marked by a distinct lack of predictive validity studies, which is surprising given that many CAT advocates have stridently criticized DT assessments for their purported lack of evidence of this type. Addressing these traditional criticisms should not be difficult, yet we are at a loss to explain why this research is so uncommon.

Another common criticism is that the field is living in the past, methodologically speaking: the almost exclusive reliance on classical test theory, the use of traditional assessment strategies, and so forth. These criticisms are not without warrant, and we would go further to call for explorations in the use of biometric and neurocognitive methods that are gaining popularity in other fields but have generally not been applied in the assessment of creativity. Applying many of these methods will be expensive and time-consuming, but the potential benefits could be tremendous.

The critique that creativity assessment has become stale, although increasingly inaccurate, should still give creativity assessment researchers pause. Even somewhat cutting-edge work in creativity measurement tends to be variations on traditional themes. Yet there are ample avenues for truly original approaches to creativity assessment. Take, for example, the propulsion theory of creativity offered by Sternberg, Kaufman, and Pretz (2001, 2002, 2003), in which eight qualitatively distinct kinds of creativity (or creative leadership) are posited. The idea of propulsion stems from the concept that creative ideas propel a field forward. The eight types are grouped into three categories: those that accept current paradigms (replication, redefinition, forward incrementation, advance forward incrementation), those that reject them (redirection, reconstruction/redirection, reinitiation), and those that synthesize them (integration). The distinctions are meant to differentiate type, not amount or quality of creativity. Such a unique approach to creativity appears to be a promising foundation on which to build a new series of creative product assessments, yet no one beyond Sternberg and his colleagues appears to be willing to take the bait.

Finally, Runco (2007a) recently observed that many creativity researchers are not comprehensively surveying the literature of the field when planning their studies, relying increasingly on only the latest, published work. This recency bias is present in every field, but Runco's broader point (i.e., the irony of creativity researchers continually

reinventing the wheel) should provoke some food for thought. This bias may be especially damaging with respect to creativity assessment, given that many criticisms of this research are mischaracterizations of previous work or are simply incorrect.

Runco's broader concern is also relevant to a researcher's tendency not to look outside of the field for previous and related work. For example, Mehta and Zhu (2009) recently found evidence that the colors of materials influence cognitive performance, including creative cognition. This would appear to have considerable implications for the design and administration of creativity assessments in a wide range of settings. A broad, interdisciplinary field such as creative studies should adopt a more inclusive view of which fields are doing relevant work; the alternative, which we currently experience, is that the field's impact is unnecessarily limited.

Looking Ahead

At the end of Plucker and Renzulli's (1999) survey of psychometric approaches to creativity, they concluded that

> psychometric conceptions of creativity have been far too narrow, focusing only within specific areas ... and on certain types of creative process and achievement. . . . While psychometric study of creativity will certainly have a lasting legacy, whether the legacy is one of activity or passivity is yet to be determined. After all, the Latin language has a lasting legacy but survives no more. Researchers electing to measure creativity must adapt their methods to address the serious and often accurate criticisms of psychometric approaches to avoid the creation of a dead methodology. (p. 51)

Roughly a decade later, we are pleased to observe that the assessment of creativity is a vibrant area of research, with little imminent danger of becoming a "dead methodology." There exists a healthy mix of distinguished and early scholars, and also of traditional and emerging lines of research.

However, this progress has been unevenly distributed across the field of creativity assessment, and although many areas of potential gain are relatively untouched, other well-developed areas have lingering questions that need to be answered. Creativity is becoming a popular topic in educational, economic, and political circles throughout the world – whether this popularity is just a passing fad or a lasting change in interest in creativity and innovation will probably depend, in large part, on whether creativity assessment keeps pace with the rest of the field.

References

Alliger, G. M. (1988). Do zero correlations really exist among measures of different intellectual abilities. *Educational and Psychological Measurement*, 48, 275–280.

Amabile, T. M. (1979). Effects of external evaluation on artistic creativity. *Journal of Personality and Social Psychology*, 37, 221–233.

Amabile, T. M. (1982). Social psychology of creativity: A consensual assessment technique. *Journal of Personality and Social Psychology*, 43, 997–1013.

Amabile, T. M. (1983). *The social psychology of creativity*. New York: Springer-Verlag.

Amabile, T. M. (1996). *Creativity in context: Update to the social psychology of creativity*. Boulder, CO: Westview.

Amabile, T. M., & Conti, R. (1999). Changes in the work environment for creativity during downsizing. *Academy of Management Journal*, 42, 630–640.

Amabile, T. M., Conti, R., Coon, H., Lazenby, J., & Herron, M. (1996). Assessing the work environment for creativity. *Academy of Management Journal*, 19, 1154–1184.

Amabile, T. M., & Gryskiewicz, N. D. (1987). *Creativity in the R and D laboratory* (Tech. Rep. No. 30). Greensboro, NC: Center for Creative Leadership.

Amabile, T. M., & Gryskiewicz, N. (1989). The Creative Environment Scales: The Work Environment Inventory. *Creativity Research Journal*, 2, 231–254.

Amabile, T. M., Hill, K. G., Hennessey, B. A., & Tighe, E. M. (1994). The work preference inventory: Assessing intrinsic and extrinsic motivational orientations. *Journal of Personality and Social Psychology*, 66, 950–967.

Amabile, T. M., Schatzel, E. A., Moneta, G. B., & Kramer, S. J. (2004). Leader behaviors and the work environment for creativity: Perceived leader support. *Leadership Quarterly*, 15, 5–32.

Anastasi, A., & Schaefer, C. E. (1969). Biographical correlates of artistic and literary creativity in adolescent girls. *Journal of Applied Psychology*, 53, 267–273.

Bachelor, P. (1989). Maximum likelihood confirmatory factor-analytic investigation of factors within Guilford's Structure-of-Intellect model. *Journal of Applied Psychology*, 74, 797–804.

Baer, J. (1993a). *Creativity and divergent thinking: A task-specific approach*. Hillsdale, NJ: Lawrence Erlbaum Associates.

Baer, J. (1993b). *Divergent thinking and creativity: A task-specific approach*. Hillsdale, NJ: Lawrence Erlbaum Associates.

Baer, J. (1993c, December/January). Why you shouldn't trust creativity tests. *Educational Leadership*, 51, 80–83.

Baer, J. (1994). Performance assessments of creativity: Do they have long-term stability? *Roeper Review*, 7, 7–11.

Baer, J. (1998). The case for domain specificity in creativity. *Creativity Research Journal*, 11, 173–177.

Baer, J. (2003). Impact of the Core Knowledge Curriculum on creativity. *Creativity Research Journal*, 15, 297–300.

Baer, J., Kaufman, J. C., & Gentile, C. A. (2004). Extension of the consensual assessment technique to nonparallel creative products. *Creativity Research Journal*, 16, 113–117.

Barron, F., & Harrington, D. M. (1981). Creativity, intelligence, and personality. *Annual Review of Psychology*, 32, 439–476.

Basadur, M. S., & Finkbeiner, C. T. (1985). Measuring preference for ideation in creative problem-solving training. *Journal of Applied Behavioral Science*, 21, 37–49.

Basadur, M. S., Graen, G. B., & Green, S. G. (1982). Training in creative problem solving: Effects on ideation and problem finding and solving in an industrial research organization. *Organizational Behavior & Human Performance*, 30, 41–70.

Basadur, M. S., Graen, G. B., & Scandura, T. A. (1986). Training effects on attitudes toward divergent thinking among manufacturing engineers. *Journal of Applied Psychology*, 71, 612–617.

Basadur, M., & Hausdorf, P. A. (1996). Measuring divergent thinking attitudes related to creative problem solving and innovation management. *Creativity Research Journal*, 9, 21–32.

Basadur, M., Pringle, P., & Kirkland, D. (2002). Crossing cultures: Training effects on the divergent thinking attitudes of Spanish-speaking South American managers. *Creativity Research Journal*, 14, 395–408.

Basadur, M., Taggar, S., & Pringle, P. (1999). Improving the measurement of divergent thinking attitudes in organizations. *Journal of Creative Behavior*, 33, 75–111.

Basadur, M. S., Wakabayashi, M., & Graen, G. B. (1990). Individual problem solving styles and attitudes toward divergent thinking before and after training. *Creativity Research Journal*, 3, 22–32.

Basadur, M. S., Wakabayashi, M., & Takai, J. (1992). Training effects on the divergent thinking attitudes of Japanese managers. *International Journal of Intercultural Relations*, 16, 329–345.

Batey, M., & Furnham, A. (2006). Creativity, intelligence, and personality: A critical review of the scattered literature. *Genetic, Social, and General Psychology Monographs*, 132, 355–429.

Beghetto, R. A. (2006). Creative self-efficacy: Correlates in middle and secondary students. *Creativity Research Journal*, 18, 447–457.

Besemer, S. P. (1998). Creative product analysis matrix: testing the model structure and a comparison among products – three novel chairs. *Creativity Research Journal*, 11, 333–346.

Besemer, S. P., & O'Quin, K. (1999). Confirming the three-factor creative product analysis matrix model in an American sample. *Creativity Research Journal*, 12, 287–296.

Bossomaier, T., Harré, M., Knittel, A., & Snyder, A. (2009). A semantic network approach to the creativity quotient (CQ). *Creativity Research Journal*, 21, 64–71.

Burke, J. P., Haworth, C. E., & Ware, W. B. (1982). Scale for Rating Behavioral Characteristics of Superior Students: An investigation of factor structure. *Journal of Special Education*, 16, 77–85.

Callahan, C. M., Hunsaker, S. L., Adams, C. M., Moore, S. D., & Bland, L. C. (1995). *Instruments used in the identification of gifted and talented students* (Rep. No. RM-95130). Charlottesville, VA: National Research Center on the Gifted and Talented.

Carson, S. H., Peterson, J. B., & Higgins, D. M. (2005). Reliability, validity, and factor structure of the creative achievement questionnaire. *Creativity Research Journal*, 17, 37–50.

Cattell, R. B., & Butcher, H. (1968). *The prediction of achievement and creativity*. Indianapolis, IN: Bobbs-Merrill.

Cattell, R. B., Eber, H. W., & Tatsuoka, M. M. (1970). *Handbook for the Sixteen Personality Questionnaire (16 PF)*. Champaign, IL: Institute for Personality and Ability Testing.

Chand, I., & Runco, M. A. (1992). Problem finding skills as components in the creative process. *Personality and Individual Differences*, 14, 155–162.

Chen Shyuefee, A., & Michael, W. B. (1993). First-order and higher-order factors of creative social intelligence within Guilford's Structure-of-Intellect Model: A reanalysis of a Guilford data base. *Educational and Psychological Measurement*, 53, 619–641.

Christiaans, H. H. C. M. (2002). Creativity as a design criterion. *Creativity Research Journal*, 14, 41–54.

Clapham, M. M. (1996). The construct validity of divergent scores in the Structure-of-Intellect Learning Abilities Test. *Educational and Psychological Measurement*, 56, 287–292.

Clapham, M. M., Cowdery, E. M., King, K. E., & Montang, M. A. (2005). Predicting work activities with divergent thinking tests: A longitudinal study. *Journal of Creative Behavior*, 39, 149–167.

Clark, P. M., & Mirels, H. L. (1970). Fluency as a pervasive element in the measurement of creativity. *Journal of Educational Measurement*, 7, 83–86.

Cline, V. B., Richards, J. M., Jr., & Abe, C. (1962). The validity of a battery of creativity tests in a high school sample. *Educational and Psychological Measurement*, 22, 781–784.

Colangelo, N., Kerr, B., Hallowell, K., Huesman, R., & Gaeth, J. (1992). The Iowa Inventiveness Inventory: Toward a measure of mechanical inventiveness. *Creativity Research Journal*, 5, 157–163

Conti, R., Coon, H., & Amabile, T. M. (1996). Evidence to support the componential model of creativity: Secondary analyses of three studies. *Creativity Research Journal*, 9, 385–389.

Cooper, E. (1991). A critique of six measures for assessing creativity. *Journal of Creative Behavior*, 25, 194–204.

Costa, P. T., & McCrae, R. R. (1992). Normal personality assessment in clinical practice:

The NEO personality inventory. *Psychological Assessment, 4*, 5–13.

Cramond, B. (1993). The Torrance Tests of Creative Thinking: From design through establishment of predictive validity. In R. F. Subotnik & K. D. Arnold (Eds.), *Beyond Terman: Contemporary longitudinal studies of giftedness and talent* (pp. 229–254). Norwood, NJ: Ablex.

Csikszentmihalyi, M. (1988). Society, culture, and person: A systems view of creativity. In R. J. Sternberg (Ed.), *The nature of creativity: Contemporary psychological perspectives* (pp. 325–339). New York: Cambridge University Press.

Davidovitch, N., & Milgram, R. M. (2006). Creative thinking as a predictor of teacher effectiveness in higher education. *Creativity Research Journal, 18*, 385–390.

Davis, G. A. (1973). *Psychology of problem solving: Theory and practice.* New York: Basic Books.

Davis, G. A. (1989). Testing for creative potential. *Contemporary Educational Psychology, 14*, 257–274.

Davis, G. A. (1992). *Creativity is forever* (3rd ed.). Dubuque, IA: Kendall/Hunt.

de Bono, E. (1971). *Lateral thinking for management.* New York: McGraw-Hill.

de Bono, E. (1985). *Six thinking hats.* Boston: Little Brown.

Dollinger, S. J., Burke, P. A., & Gump, N. W. (2007). Creativity and values. *Creativity Research Journal, 19*, 91–103.

Dollinger, S. J., & Shafran, M. (2005). Note on Consensual Assessment Technique in creativity research. *Perceptual and Motor Skills, 100*, 592–598.

Dollinger, S. J., Urban, K. K., & James, T. A. (2004). Creativity and openness: Further validation of two creative product measures. *Creativity Research Journal, 16*, 35–47.

Dombroski, T. W. (1979). *Creative problem-solving: The door to progress and change.* Hicksville, NY: Exposition Press.

Domino, G. (1970). Identification of potentially creative persons from the Adjective Check List. *Journal of Consulting and Clinical Psychology, 35*, 48–51.

Domino, G. (1994). Assessment of creativity with the ACL: An empirical comparison of four scales. *Creativity Research Journal, 7*, 21–33.

Duncker, K. (1945). On problem solving. *Psychological Monographs, 58*(5), ix–113.

Eisen, M. L. (1989). Assessing differences in children with learning disabilities and normally achieving students with a new measure of creativity. *Journal of Learning Disabilities, 22*, 462–464, 451.

Feist, G. J. (1998). A meta-analysis of personality in scientific and artistic creativity. *Personality and Social Psychology Review, 2*, 290–309.

Feldhusen, J. F., & Clinkenbeard, P. R. (1986). Creativity instructional materials: A review of research. *Journal of Creative Behavior, 20*, 153–182.

Fodor, E. M., & Carver, R. A. (2000). Achievement and power motives, performance feedback, and creativity. *Journal of Research in Personality, 34*, 380–396.

Forbes, J. B., & Domm, D. R. (2004). Creativity and productivity: Resolving the conflict. *S.A.M. Advanced Management Journal, 69*, 4–27.

Fox, L. H. (1985). Review of Thinking Creatively with Sounds and Words. In J. V. Mitchell, Jr. (Ed.), *Ninth mental measurements yearbook* (pp. 1622–1623). Lincoln, NE: University of Nebraska.

Gagné, F. (1994). Are teachers really poor talent detectors? Comments on Pegnato and Birch's (1959) study of the effectiveness and efficiency of various identification techniques. *Gifted Child Quarterly, 38*, 124–126.

Gardner, H. (1988). Creativity: An interdisciplinary perspective. *Creativity Research Journal, 1*, 8–26.

Gardner, H. (1993). *Creating minds.* New York: Basic Books.

Getzels, J. W., & Jackson, P. W. (1962). *Creativity and intelligence: Explorations with gifted students.* New York: Wiley.

Gick, M. L., & Holyoak, K. J. (1980). Analogical problem solving. *Cognitive Psychology, 12*, 306–355.

Gist, M. E., & Mitchell, T. R. (1992). Self-efficacy: A theoretical analysis of its determinants and malleability. *Academy of Management Review, 17*, 183–211.

Gough, H. G. (1979). A creative personality scale for the Adjective Check List. *Journal of Personality and Social Psychology, 37*, 1398–1405.

Guilford, J. P. (1967a). Creativity: Yesterday, today, and tomorrow. *Journal of Creative Behavior, 1*, 3–14.

Guilford, J. P. (1967b). *The nature of human intelligence.* New York: McGraw-Hill

Guilford, J. P. (1968). *Intelligence, creativity and their educational implications.* New York: Robert R. Knapp.

Guilford, J. P., & Hoepfner, R. (1966). Creative potential is related to measure of IQ and verbal comprehension. *Indian Journal of Psychology*, 41, 7–16.

Hall, W., & MacKinnon, D. W. (1969). Personality inventory correlates of creativity among architects. *Journal of Applied Psychology*, 53, 322–326.

Harrington, D. M. (1975). Effects of explicit instructions to "be creative" on the psychological meaning of divergent thinking test scores. *Journal of Personality*, 43, 434–454.

Hattie, J. (1980). Should creativity tests be administered under testlike conditions? An empirical study of three alternative conditions. *Journal of Educational Psychology*, 72, 87–98.

Heausler, N. L., & Thompson, B. (1988). Structure of the Torrance Tests of Creative Thinking. *Educational and Psychological Measurement*, 48, 463–468.

Hébert, T. P., Cramond, B., Spiers-Neumeister, K. L., Millar, G., & Silvian, A. F. (2002). *E. Paul Torrance: His life, accomplishments, and legacy*. Storrs, CT: The University of Connecticut, National Research Center on the Gifted and Talented.

Helson, R. (1971). Women mathematicians and creative personality. *Journal of Consulting and Clinical Psychology*, 36, 210–220.

Hennessey, B. A. (1994). The Consensual Assessment Technique: An examination of the relationship between ratings of product and process creativity. *Creativity Research Journal*, 7, 193–208.

Hickey, M. (2001). An application of Amabile's consensual assessment technique for rating the creativity of children's musical compositions. *Journal of Research in Music Education*, 49, 234–244.

Hocevar, D. (1979a). A comparison of statistical infrequency and subjective judgment as criteria in the measurement of originality. *Journal of Personality Assessment*, 43, 297–299.

Hocevar, D. (1979b, April). *The development of the Creative Behavior Inventory*. Paper presented at the annual meeting of the Rocky Mountain Psychological Association. (ERIC Document Reproduction Service No. ED 170 350)

Hocevar, D. (1979c). Ideational fluency as a confounding factor in the measurement of originality. *Journal of Educational Psychology*, 71, 191–196.

Hocevar, D. (1979d). The unidimensional nature of creative thinking in fifth grade children. *Child Study Journal*, 9, 273–277.

Hocevar, D. (1981). Measurement of creativity: Review and critique. *Journal of Personality Assessment*, 45, 450–464.

Hocevar, D., & Bachelor, P. (1989). A taxonomy and critique of measurements used in the study of creativity. In J. A. Glover, R. R. Ronning, & C. R. Reynolds (Eds.), *Handbook of creativity* (pp. 53–75). New York: Plenum Press.

Hocevar, D., & Michael, W. B. (1979). The effects of scoring formulas on the discriminant validity of tests of divergent thinking. *Educational and Psychological Measurement*, 39, 917–921.

Hoepfner, R., & Hemenway, J. (1973). *Test of creative potential*. Hollywood, CA: Monitor.

Holland, J. L. (1959). Some limitations of teacher ratings as predictors of creativity. *Journal of Educational Psychology*, 50, 219–223.

Holland, J. L., & Nichols, R. C. (1964). Prediction of academic and extracurricular achievement in college. *Journal of Educational Psychology*, 55, 55–65.

Holland, J. L., & Richards, J. M., Jr. (1965). Academic and nonacademic accomplishment: Correlated or uncorrelated? *Journal of Educational Psychology*, 56, 165–174.

Holly, K. A., Michael, W. B. (1972). The relationship of Structure-of-Intellect factor abilities to performance in high school modern algebra. *Educational and Psychological Measurement*, 32, 447–450.

Horn, J. L. (1967). On subjectivity in factor analysis. *Educational and Psychological Measurement*, 27, 811–820.

Horn, J. L., & Knapp, J. R. (1973). On the subjective character of the empirical base of Guilford's structure of intellect model. *Psychological Bulletin*, 80, 33–43.

Horn, D., & Salvendy, G. (2006a). Consumer-based assessment of product creativity: A review and reappraisal. *Human Factors and Ergonomics in Manufacturing*, 16, 155–175.

Horn, D., & Salvendy, G. (2006b). Product creativity: Conceptual model, measurement and characteristics. *Theoretical Issues in Ergonomics Science*, 7, 395–412.

Howieson, N. (1981). A longitudinal study of creativity – 1965–1975. *Journal of Creative Behavior*, 15, 117–134.

Hunter, S. T., Bedell, K. E., & Mumford, M. D. (2007). Climate for creativity: A quantitative review. *Creativity Research Journal*, 19, 69–90.

Hunsaker, S. L., & Callahan, C. M. (1995). Creativity and giftedness: Published instrument uses and abuses. *Gifted Child Quarterly*, 39, 110–114.

Ignatz, M. (1982). Sex differences in predictive ability of tests of Structure-of-Intellect factors relative to a criterion examination of high school physics achievement. *Educational and Psychological Measurement*, 42, 353–360.

Isaksen, S. G., & Treffinger, D. J. (1985). *Creative problem-solving: The basic course*. Buffalo, NY: Bearly Limited.

James, L. R., Ellison, R. L., Fox, D. G., & Taylor, C. W. (1974). Prediction of artistic performance from biographical data. *Journal of Applied Psychology*, 59, 84–86.

Jaussi, K. S., Randel, A. E., & Dionne, S. D. (2007). I am, I think I can, and I do: The role of personal identity, self-efficacy and cross-application of experiences in creativity at work. *Creativity Research Journal*, 19, 247–258.

Kaufman, J. C., & Baer, J. (2005). The amusement park theory of creativity. In J. C. Kaufman, & J. Baer (Eds.), *Creativity across domains: Faces of the muse*. (pp. 321–328). Mahwah, NJ: Erlbaum.

Kaufman, J. C., Baer, J., Cole, J. C., & Sexton, J. D. (2008). A comparison of expert and nonexpert raters using the consensual assessment technique. *Creativity Research Journal*, 20, 171-178.

Kaufman, J. C., Baer, J., & Cole, J. C. (2009). Expertise, domains, and the Consensual Assessment Technique. *Journal of Creative Behavior*, 43, 223–233.

Kaufman, J. C., Gentile, C. A., & Baer, J. (2005). Do gifted student writers and creative writing experts rate creativity the same way? *Gifted Child Quarterly*, 49, 260–265.

Kaufman, J. C., Plucker, J. A., & Baer, J. (2008). *Essentials of creativity assessment*. New York: Wiley.

Kaufman, J. C., & Sternberg, R. J. (Eds.). (2006). *The international handbook of creativity*. New York: Cambridge University Press.

Kelly, K. E. (2004). A brief measure of creativity among college students. *College Student Journal*, 38, 594–596.

King, L. A., McKee Walker, L., & Broyles, S. J. (1996). Creativity and the five-factor model. *Journal of Research in Personality*, 30, 189–203.

Kirton, M. J. (2006). *Adaptation-innovation in the context of diversity and change*. New York: Routledge.

Kogan, N., & Pankove, E. (1974). Long-term predictive validity of divergent-thinking tests: Some negative evidence. *Journal of Educational Psychology*, 66, 802–810.

Lee, J., Day, J. D., Meara, N. M., & Maxwell, S. (2002). Discrimination of social knowledge and its flexible application from creativity: A multitrait-multimethod approach. *Personality and Individual Differences*, 32, 913–928.

Lim, W., & Plucker, J. (2001). Creativity through a lens of social responsibility: Implicit theories of creativity with Korean samples. *Journal of Creative Behavior*, 35, 115–130.

MacKinnon, D. W. (1965). Personality correlates of creativity. In M. J. Aschner, & C. E. Bish (Eds.), *Productive thinking in education* (pp. 159–171). Washington, DC: National Education Association.

MacKinnon, D. W. (1975). IPAR's contribution to the conceptualization and study of creativity. In I. A. Taylor, & J. W. Getzels (Eds.), *Perspectives in creativity* (pp. 60–89). Chicago: Aldine.

MacKinnon, D. W. (1978). *In search of human effectiveness: Identifying and developing creativity*. Buffalo, NY: The Creative Education Foundation.

Maier, N. R. F. (1945). Reasoning in humans. III. The mechanisms of equivalent stimuli and of reasoning. *Journal of Experimental Psychology*, 35, 349–360.

Makel, M. C., & Plucker, J. (2007). An exciting – but not necessarily comprehensive – tour of the globe: A review of The International Handbook of Creativity. *Psychology of Aesthetics, Creativity, and the Arts*, 1, 49–51.

Mednick, S. A. (1962). The associative basis for the creative process. *Psychological Review*, 69, 220–232.

Mehta, R., & Zhu, R. (2009). Blue or red? exploring the effect of color on cognitive task performances. *Science*, 323(5918), 1226–1229.

Meeker, M. (1969). *The Structure-of-Intellect: Its interpretation and uses*. Columbus, OH: Charles & Merrill.

Meeker, M., & Meeker, R. (1982). *Structure-of-Intellect Learning Abilities Test: Evaluation, leadership, and creative thinking*. El Segundo, CA: SOI Institute.

Michael, W. B., & Bachelor, P. (1992). First-order and higher-order creative ability factors in Structure-of-Intellect measures administered to sixth-grade children. *Educational and Psychological Measurement*, 52, 261–273.

Milgram, R. M., & Hong, E. (1994). Creative thinking and creative performance in adolescents as predictors of creative attainments in adults: A follow-up study after 18 years. In R. F. Subotnik & K. D. Arnold (Eds.), *Beyond Terman: Contemporary longitudinal studies of giftedness and talent* (pp. 212–228). Norwood, NJ: Ablex.

Milgram, R. M., & Milgram, N. A. (1976). Creative thinking and creative performance in Israeli students. *Journal of Educational Psychology*, 68, 255–259.

Milgram, R. M., & Rabkin, L. (1980). Developmental test of Mednick's associative hierarchies of original thinking. *Developmental Psychology*, 16, 157–158.

Myford, C. M. (1989). *The nature of expertise in aesthetic judgment: Beyond inter-judge agreement*. Unpublished doctoral dissertation, University of Georgia Press.

Nemiro, J. E. (2001). Assessing the climate for creativity in virtual teams. In M. M. Beyerlein, D. A. Johnson, & S. T. Beyerlein (Eds.), *Eighth annual University of North Texas symposium on individual, team, and organizational effectiveness* (pp. 59–84). Oxford: Elsevier Science/JAI Press.

Nie, Y. G., & Zheng, X. (2005). A study on the developmental characteristics of children's and adolescent's creative personality. *Psychological Science*, 2, 356–361.

Niu, W., & Sternberg, R. J. (2001). Cultural influence of artistic creativity and its evaluation. *International Journal of Psychology*, 36, 225–241.

Okuda, S. M., Runco, M. A., & Berger, D. E. (1991). Creativity and the finding and solving of real-world problems. *Journal of Psychoeducational Assessment*, 9, 45–53.

Osborn, A. A. (1963). *Applied imagination* (3rd ed.). New York: Scribner.

Parnes, S. J., Noller, R. B., & Biondi, A. M. (1977). *Guide to creative action*. New York: Scribner's.

Pearlman, C. (1983). Teachers as an informational resource in identifying and rating student creativity. *Education*, 103, 215–222.

Pegnato, C. W., & Birch, J. W. (1959). Locating gifted children in junior high schools: A comparison of methods. *Exceptional Children*, 25, 300–304.

Plucker, J. (1998). Beware of simple conclusions: The case for content generality of creativity. *Creativity Research Journal*, 11, 179–182.

Plucker, J. A. (1999a). Is the proof in the pudding? Reanalyses of Torrance's (1958 to present) longitudinal study data. *Creativity Research Journal*, 12, 103–114.

Plucker, J. A. (1999b). Reanalyses of student responses to creativity checklists: Evidence of content generality. *Journal of Creative Behavior*, 33, 126–137.

Plucker, J. A.. (2004). Generalization of creativity across domains: Examination of the method effect hypothesis. *Journal of Creative Behavior*, 38, 1–12.

Plucker, J. A., Beghetto, R. A., & Dow, G. (2004). Why isn't creativity more important to educational psychologists? Potential, pitfalls, and future directions in creativity research. *Educational Psychologist*, 39, 83–96.

Plucker, J. A., & Dow, G. T. (in press). Attitude change as the precursor to creativity enhancement. In R. Beghetto & J. Kaufman (Eds.), *Creativity in the classroom*. New York: Cambridge University Press.

Plucker, J. A., Kaufman, J. C., Temple, J. S., & Qian, M. (2009). Do experts and novices evaluate movies the same way? *Psychology and Marketing*, 26, 470–478.

Plucker, J. A., & Renzulli, J. S. (1999). Psychometric approaches to the study of human creativity. In R. J. Sternberg (Ed.), *Handbook of creativity* (pp. 35–60). New York: Cambridge University Press.

Plucker, J. A., & Runco, M. A. (1998). The death of creativity measurement has been greatly exaggerated: Current issues, recent advances, and future directions in creativity assessment. *Roeper Review*, 21, 36–39.

Plucker, J. A., Runco, M. A., & Lim, W. (2006). Predicting ideational behavior from divergent thinking and discretionary time on task. *Creativity Research Journal*, 18, 55–63.

Priest, T. (2006). Self-evaluation, creativity, and musical achievement. *Psychology of Music*, 34, 47–61.

Pyryt, M. (2004). Pegnato revisited: Using discriminant analysis to identify gifted children. *Psychology Science*, 46, 342–347.

Qian, M., Plucker, J. A., & Shen, J. (in press). A model of Chinese adolescents' creative personality. *Creativity Research Journal*.

Randel, A. E., & Jaussi, K. S. (2003). Functional background identity, diversity, and individual performance in cross-functional teams. *Academy of Management Journal*, 46, 763–774.

Reis, S. M., & Renzulli, J. S. (1991). The assessment of creative products in programs for gifted and talented students. *Gifted Child Quarterly*, 35, 128–134.

Reis, S. M., & Renzulli, J. S. (1999). Research relating to the development of creative productivity using the enrichment triad model. In A. S. Fishkin, B. Cramond, & P. Olszewski-Kubilius (Eds.), *Investigating creativity in youth: Research and methods* (pp. 367–387). Cresskill, NJ: Hampton Press.

Renzulli, J. S. (1976). *New directions in creativity.* New York: Harper & Row.

Renzulli, J. S. (1978). What makes giftedness? Reexamining a definition. *Phi Delta Kappan*, 60, 180–184, 261.

Renzulli, J. S. (1985). Review of Thinking Creatively in Action and Movement. In J. V. Mitchell, Jr. (Ed.), *Ninth mental measurements yearbook* (pp. 1619–1621). Lincoln, NE: University of Nebraska Press.

Renzulli, J. S. (1994). *Schools for talent development: A practical plan for total school improvement.* Mansfield Center, CT: Creative Learning Press.

Renzulli, J. S., Owen, S. V., & Callahan, C. M. (1974). Fluency, flexibility, and originality as a function of group size. *Journal of Creative Behavior*, 8, 107–113.

Renzulli, J. S., Hartman, R. K., & Callahan, C. M. (1981). Teacher identification of superior students. In W. B. Barbe & J. S. Renzulli (Eds.), *Psychology and education of the gifted* (3rd ed.) (pp. 151–156). New York: Irvington Publishers.

Renzulli, J. S., & Reis, S. M. (1985). *The schoolwide enrichment model: A comprehensive plan for educational excellence.* Mansfield Center, CT: Creative Learning Press.

Renzulli, J. S., Smith, L. H., White, A. J., Callahan, C. M., Hartman, R. K., & Westberg, K. L. (2002). *Scales for Rating the Behavioral Characteristics of Superior Students. Technical and administration manual* (Rev. ed.). Mansfield, CT: Creative Learning Press.

Rhodes, M. (1961). An analysis of creativity. *Phi Delta Kappan*, 42, 305–311.

Rickards, T. J. (1994). Creativity from a business school perspective: Past, present, and future. In S. G. Isaksen, M. C. Murdock, R. L. Firestien, & D. J. Treffinger (Eds.), *Understanding and recognizing creativity: The emergence of a discipline* (pp. 331–368). Norwood, NJ: Ablex.

Rimm, S. B. (1983). *Preschool and Kindergarten Interest Descriptor.* Watertown, WI: Educational Assessment Service.

Rosen, C. L. (1985). Review of Creativity Assessment Packet. In J. V. Mitchell, Jr. (Ed.), *Ninth mental measurements yearbook* (p. 1621). Lincoln, NE: University of Nebraska Press.

Rotter, D. M., Langland, L., & Berger, D. (1971). The validity of tests of creative thinking in seven-year-old children. *Gifted Child Quarterly*, 4, 273–278.

Runco, M. A. (1984). Teachers' judgments of creativity and social validation of divergent thinking tests. *Perceptual and Motor Skills*, 59, 711–717.

Runco, M. A. (1986a). Divergent thinking and creative performance in gifted and nongifted children. *Educational and Psychological Measurement*, 46, 375–384.

Runco, M. A. (1986b). Maximal performance on divergent thinking tests by gifted, talented, and nongifted children. *Psychology in the Schools*, 23, 308–315.

Runco, M. A. (1987a). The generality of creative performance in gifted and nongifted children. *Gifted Child Quarterly*, 31, 121–125.

Runco, M. A. (1987b). Interrater agreement on a socially valid measure of students' creativity. *Psychological Reports*, 61, 1009–1010.

Runco, M. A. (1989a). The creativity of children's art. *Child Study Journal*, 19, 177–189.

Runco, M. A. (1989). Parents' and teachers' ratings of the creativity of children. *Journal of Social Behavior & Personality*, 4, 73–83.

Runco, M. A. (1991). The evaluative, valuative, and divergent thinking of children. *Journal of Creative Behavior*, 25, 311–309.

Runco, M. A. (1999) Divergent thinking. In M. A. Runco & S. Pritzker (Eds.), *Encyclopedia of creativity: Vol. 1. Ae-h* (pp. 577–582). San Diego: Academic Press.

Runco, M. A. (2007a). Correcting the research on creativity. *Creativity Research Journal*, 19, 321–327.

Runco, M. A. (2007b). *Creativity: Theories and themes: Research, development, and practice.* San Diego, CA: Elsevier Academic Press.

Runco, M. A. (2008). Divergent thinking is not synonymous with creativity [Commentary]. *Psychology of Aesthetics, Creativity, and the Arts*, 2, 93–96.

Runco, M. A., & Albert, R. S. (1985). The reliability and validity of ideational originality in the divergent thinking of academically gifted and nongifted children. *Educational and Psychological Measurement*, 45, 483–501.

Runco, M. A., & Basadur, M. (1993). Assessing ideational and evaluative skills and creative styles and attitudes. *Creativity & Innovation Management*, 2, 166–173.

Runco, M. A., & Chand, I. (1994). Problem finding, evaluative thinking, and creativity. In

M. A. Runco (Ed.), *Problem finding, problem solving, and creativity* (pp. 40–76). Norwood, NJ: Ablex.

Runco, M. A., & Johnson, D. J. (2002). Parents' and teachers' implicit theories of children's creativity: A cross-cultural perspective. *Creativity Research Journal*, 14, 427–438.

Runco, M. A., McCarthy, K. A., & Svenson, E. (1994). Judgments of the creativity of artwork from students and professional artists. *The Journal of Psychology*, 128, 23–31.

Runco, M. A., & Mraz, W. (1992). Scoring divergent thinking tests using total ideational output and a creativity index. *Educational and Psychological Measurement*, 52, 213–221.

Runco, M. A., Noble, E. P., & Luptak, Y. (1990). Agreement between mothers and sons on ratings of creative activity. *Educational and Psychological Measurement*, 50, 673–680.

Runco, M. A., & Okuda, S. M. (1988). Problem finding, divergent thinking, and the creative process. *Journal of Youth and Adolescence*, 17, 211–220.

Runco, M. A., & Okuda, S. M. (1991). The instructional enhancement of the flexibility and originality scores of divergent thinking tests. *Applied Cognitive Psychology*, 5, 435–441.

Runco, M. A., Okuda, S. M., & Thurston, B. J. (1987). The psychometric properties of four systems for scoring divergent thinking tests. *Journal of Psychoeducational Assessment*, 2, 149–156.

Runco, M. A., Plucker, J. A., & Lim, W. (2000–2001). Development and psychometric integrity of a measure of ideational behavior. *Creativity Research Journal*, 13, 393–400.

Runco, M. A., & Smith, W. R. (1992). Interpersonal and intrapersonal evaluations of creative ideas. *Personality and Individual Differences*, 13, 295–302.

Runco, M. A., & Vega, L. (1990). Evaluating the creativity of children's ideas. *Journal of Social Behavior and Personality*, 5, 439–452.

Ruscio, J., Whitney, D. M., & Amabile, T. M. (1998). Looking inside the fishbowl of creativity: Verbal and behavioral predictors of creative performance. *Creativity Research Journal*, 11, 243–263.

Schaefer, C. E., & Anastasi, A. (1968). A biographical inventory for identifying creativity in adolescent boys. *Journal of Applied Psychology*, 52, 42–48.

Seddon, G. M. (1983). The measurement and properties of divergent thinking ability as a single compound entity. *Journal of Educational Measurement*, 20, 393–402.

Simonton, D. K. (1988b). *Scientific genius: A psychology of science*. Cambridge, MA: Harvard University Press.

Smith, J. M., & Schaefer, C. E. (1969). Development of a creativity scale for the Adjective Check List. *Psychological Reports*, 34, 755–758.

Snyder, A., Mitchell, J., Bossomaier, T., & Pallier, G. (2004). The creativity quotient: An objective scoring of ideational fluency. *Creativity Research Journal*, 16, 415–420.

Soldz, S., & Vaillant, G. E. (1999). The big five personality traits and the life course: A 45-year longitudinal study. *Journal of Research in Personality*, 33, 208–232.

Speedie, S. M., Treffinger, D. J., & Houtz, J. C. (1976). Classification and evaluation of problem solving tasks. *Contemporary Educational Psychology*, 1, 52–75.

Sternberg, R. J. (2003). *Wisdom, intelligence, and creativity synthesized*. New York: Cambridge University Press.

Sternberg, R. J. (2005). Creativity or creativities? *International Journal of Human-Computer Studies*, 63, 370–382.

Sternberg, R. J., & Davidson, J. E. (1992). Problem solving. In M. C. Aikin (Ed.), *Encyclopedia of educational research*. (Vol. 3, pp. 1037–1045). New York: Macmillan.

Sternberg, R. J., & Grigorenko, E. L. (2000–2001). Guilford's Structure of Intellect model and model of creativity: Contributions and limitations. *Creativity Research Journal*, 13, 309–316.

Sternberg, R. J., Kaufman, J. C., & Pretz, J. E. (2001). The propulsion model of creative contributions applied to the arts and letters. *Journal of Creative Behavior*, 35, 75–101.

Sternberg, R. J., Kaufman, J. C., & Pretz, J. E. (2002). *The creativity conundrum*. New York: Psychology Press.

Sternberg, R. J., Kaufman, J. C., & Pretz, J. E. (2003). A propulsion model of creative leadership. *Leadership Quarterly*, 14, 455–473.

Sternberg, R. J., & Lubart, T. I. (1995). *Defying the crowd: Cultivating creativity in a culture of conformity*. New York: Free Press.

Sternberg, R. J., & O'Hara, L. A. (1999). Creativity and intelligence. In R. J. Sternberg (Ed.), Handbook of creativity (pp. 251–272). New York: Cambridge University Press.

Taylor, C. W. (1964). *Widening horizons in creativity*. New York: Wiley.

Taylor, C. W. (1988). Various approaches to and definitions of creativity. In R. J. Sternberg (Ed.), *The nature of creativity* (pp. 99–121). New York: Cambridge University Press.

Taylor, C. W., & Barron, F. (1963a). Preface. In C. W. Taylor & F. Barron (Eds.), *Scientific creativity: Its recognition and development* (pp. xiii–xix). New York: Wiley.

Taylor, C. W., & Barron, F. (Eds.). (1963b). *Scientific creativity: Its recognition and development.* New York: Wiley.

Taylor, C. W., & Ellison, R. L. (1966). *Alpha Biological Inventory.* Salt Lake City: Institute for Behavioral Research.

Taylor, C. W., & Ellison, R. L. (1967). Predictors of scientific performance. *Science,* 155, 1075–1079.

Taylor, C. W., & Williams, F. E. (Eds.). (1966). *Instructional media and creativity.* New York: Wiley.

Thompson, B., & Anderson, B. V. (1983). Construct validity of the divergent production subtests from the Structure-of-Intellect Learning Abilities Test. *Educational and Psychological Measurement,* 43, 651–655.

Thorndike, R. L. (1972). Review of Torrance Tests of Creativity Thinking. In O. K. Buros (Ed.), *The seventh mental measurements yearbook* (pp. 838–839). Highland Park, NJ: Gryphon Press.

Tierney, P., & Farmer, S. M. (2002). Creative self-efficacy: Its potential antecedents and relationship to creative performance. *Academy of Management Journal,* 45, 1137–1148.

Tighe, E., Picariello, M. L., & Amabile, T. M. (2003). Environmental influences on motivation and creativity in the classroom. In J. Houtz (Ed.), *The educational psychology of creativity* (pp. 199–222). Cresskill, NJ: Hampton Press.

Torrance, E. P. (1962). *Guiding creative talent.* Englewood Cliffs, NJ: Prentice-Hall.

Torrance, E. P. (1969). Prediction of adult creative achievement among high school seniors. *Gifted Child Quarterly,* 13, 223–229.

Torrance, E. P. (1970). *Encouraging creativity in the classroom.* Dubuque, IA: William C. Brown.

Torrance, E. P. (1971). Stimulation, enjoyment, and originality in dyadic creativity. *Journal of Educational Psychology,* 62, 45–48.

Torrance, E. P. (1972a). Can we teach children to think creatively? *Journal of Creative Behavior,* 6, 114–143.

Torrance, E. P. (1972b). Career patterns and peak creative achievements of creative high school students 12 years later. *Gifted Child Quarterly,* 16, 75–88

Torrance, E. P. (1972c). Predictive validity of "bonus" scoring for combinations on repeated figures tests of creative thinking. *The Journal of Psychology,* 81, 167–171.

Torrance, E. P. (1974). *Torrance Tests of Creative Thinking: Norms-technical manual.* Bensenville, IL: Scholastic Testing Service.

Torrance, E. P. (1976). Creativity testing in education. *The Creative Child and Adult Quarterly,* 1, 136–148.

Torrance, E. P. (1979). Unique needs of the creative child and adult. In A. H. Passow (Ed.), *The gifted and talented: Their education and development. 78th NSSE Yearbook* (pp. 352–371). Chicago: The National Society for the Study of Education.

Torrance, E. P. (1981a). Empirical validation of criterion-referenced indicators of creative ability through a longitudinal study. *Creative Child and Adult Quarterly,* 6, 136–140.

Torrance, E. P. (1981b). Predicting the creativity of elementary school children (1958–1980) – and the teacher who "made a difference." *Gifted Child Quarterly,* 25, 55–62.

Torrance, E. P. (1981c). *Thinking creatively in action and movement.* Bensenville, IL: Scholastic Testing Service.

Torrance, E. P. (1982). Misperceptions about creativity in gifted education: Removing the limits on learning. In S. N. Kaplan, A. H. Passow, P. H. Phenix, S. M. Reis, J. S. Renzulli, I. S. Soto, L. H. Smith et al. (Eds.), *Curriculum for the gifted: Selected proceedings of the first national conference on curricula for the gifted/talented* (pp. 59–74). Ventura, CA: Office of the Ventura County Superintendent of Schools.

Torrance, E. P. (1988). The nature of creativity as manifest in its testing. In R. J. Sternberg (Ed.), *The nature of creativity: Contemporary psychological perspectives* (pp. 43–75). New York: Cambridge University Press.

Torrance, E. P., & Ball, O. E. (1984). *Torrance Tests of Creative Thinking: Streamlined administration and scoring manual* (rev. ed.). Bensenville, IL: Scholastic Testing Service.

Torrance, E. P., & Khatena, J. (1970). What kind of person are you? *Gifted Child Quarterly,* 14, 71–75.

Torrance, E. P., Khatena, J., & Cunnington, B. F. (1973). *Thinking creatively with sounds and words*. Bensenville, IL: Scholastic Testing Service.

Torrance, E. P., & Safter, H. T. (1989). The long range predictive validity of the Just Suppose Test. *Journal of Creative Behavior, 23*, 219–223.

Torrance, E. P., Tan, C. A., & Allman, T. (1970). Verbal originality and teacher behavior: A predictive validity study. *The Journal of Teacher Education, 21*, 335–341.

Torrance, E. P., & Wu, T. H. (1981). A comparative longitudinal study of the adult creative achievement of elementary school children identified as highly intelligent and as highly creative. *Creative Child and Adult Quarterly, 6*, 71–76.

Treffinger, D., Young, G., Selby, E., & Shepardson C. (2002). *Assessing creativity: A guide for educators*. Storrs, CT: The National Research Center on the Gifted and Talented.

Wallach, M. A. (1976, January-February). Tests tell us little about talent. *American Scientist*, 57–63.

Wallach, M. A., & Kogan, N. (1965). *Modes of thinking in young children: A study of the creativity-intelligence distinction*. New York: Holt, Rinehart & Winston.

Wallach, M. A., & Wing, C. W., Jr. (1969). *The talented student: A validation of the creativity-intelligence distinction*. New York: Holt, Rinehart & Winston.

Wang, X. (2003). *A study about students' creative tendency and their perception of teachers' classroom behavior*. Unpublished master's thesis. Beijing Normal University, Beijing, China.

Wasik, J. L. (1974). Teacher perceptions of behaviors associated with creative problem solving performance. *Educational and Psychological Measurement, 34*, 327–341.

Weisberg, R. W. (1993). *Creativity: Beyond the myth of genius*. New York: W. H. Freeman.

Wheatley, T., & Wegner, D. M. (2001). Psychology of automaticity of action. In N. J. Smelser & P. B. Baltes (Eds.), *International encyclopedia of the social and behavioral sciences*, (pp. 991–993). Oxford, UK: Elsevier Science.

Williams, F. E. (1979). Assessing creativity across Williams' "cube" model. *Gifted Child Quarterly, 23*, 748–756.

Williams, F. E. (1980). *Creativity assessment packet*. Buffalo, NY: DOK Publishers.

Williams, R. L. (1999). Operational definitions and assessment of higher-order cognitive constructs. *Educational Psychology Review, 11*, 411–427.

Yamada, H., & Tam, A. Y.-W. (1996). Prediction study of adult creative achievement: Torrance's longitudinal study of creativity revisited. *Journal of Creative Behavior, 30*, 144–149.

CHAPTER 4

The Roles of Creativity in Society

Seana Moran

According to an emerging consensus among psychologists, creativity is defined as a novel yet appropriate solution to a problem or response to a situation (e.g., Amabile, 1996; Campbell, 1960; Feldman, Csikszentmihalyi, & Gardner, 1994; Runco, 2004). Creativity also includes the proactive devising, formulating, or framing of problems themselves (Getzels & Csikszentmihalyi, 1976; Kaufmann, 2003; Runco & Chand, 1994). Examples of creativity are ubiquitous. We see creativity in

- everyday cleverness, especially among children;
- the arts and sciences, with an abundant stream of paintings, dramas, theories, and concepts;
- business, with innovative products such as Federal Express's overnight delivery, 3M's Post-It Note, and Google;

Howard Gardner has helped me to develop these ideas, particularly as regards the potential of creativity to be put to constructive or destructive use. I thank him for his help – he barely escaped being a coauthor.

- social interaction, most recently with Web sites like MySpace and Twitter;
- education as charter schools and non-school venues, such as children's museums, arise around the world; and
- public policy as countries try to govern and promote their cultural assets and intellectual capital in more systematic ways, such as England's cultural industries initiatives.

As technology takes care of most routine tasks, we increasingly hear a clarion call for creativity in current and future generations of workers and citizens (e.g., Chen, Moran & Gardner, 2009; Florida, 2002; Friedman, 2005; Tepper, 2002).

Psychological research on creativity can be categorized according to cognitive, personality, developmental, and social sources (e.g., Gardner, 1988; Sawyer, 2006; Simonton, 2000); along Wallas's (1926) "four P's" of creative person, process, product, and press (e.g., Moran, 2009a); by methodologies such as psychometric, psychodynamic, and experimental paradigms (Feldhusen & Goh, 1995; Mumford, 2003; Plucker & Runco,

1998); and by the potential for creativity versus the performance of creativity (e.g., Runco & Charles, 1993). Several handbooks attest to the breadth and diversity of scholarly approaches (e.g., Rickards, Runco, & Moger, 2009; Runco, 1997; Sternberg, 1999).

Despite all of this creativity-related discourse and activity among practitioners, policymakers, and scholars, surprisingly little attention has been paid to the question of *why*. Why value creativity? What is the role of creativity in society? This line of questioning views creativity as a *cause* in social and intellectual endeavors, not just as an effect of individual differences, social support, or cognitive processes.

The Definition of Role

Role is a "part played." It describes a relationship that sets up "shoulds," or expectations for behavior (Biddle, 1986). The more common uses of the term might describe interpersonal responsibilities between two people, as in marriage or friendship, or the term might indicate how a person should perform on the job in the relationship between a person and organization. Yet a role could set up expectations between any two entities. In this chapter, I use this term to describe the relationship that obtains between an activity (creativity) and its environment writ large (society). This relationship defines what the activity is for.

A role can be thought of as having three interrelated dimensions. First, a role involves a *position* within a social network that links it to other positions. It provides connection. For example, there are the interconnected positions of dancer, choreographer, and lighting technician in a troupe stage production. The dancer position is more visible than the other two, and it often enjoys more fame. However, the choreographer is often considered the creative force of the troupe and is accorded considerable power and influence. The lighting technician usually is considered secondary in terms of influence and necessity.

Second, a role involves a *function* that has an effect on the wider community. It serves or contributes in some way to a greater system. A choreographer conceives and maps the bodily movement and spatial arrangement of a dance composition for the dancer to perform and the audience to enjoy. Without a dancer, the choreographer's work cannot be demonstrated. Without lighting, the choreographer's and dancer's work cannot be seen.

Third, a role involves a *purpose* that incorporates values, orients goals, and drives behavior. It provides meaning and direction. A choreographer's purpose may be to display the ways a body can make art through three-dimensional space; or it may be to highlight the athleticism and energy of movement. A dancer may dance for fun, for exercise, or for conveyance of emotion. A lighting technician aims to make visible to the audience a dancer's movements and mood.

Many creativity scholars, as well as the public, implicitly have relied primarily on the positional dimension. For example, many researchers focus on the roles of artist or scientist as "special" or "genius" parts played in society. Creativity is set aside in these roles, which are often considered marginal positions away from the mainstream of daily life (Bourdieu, 1993). "Gifted" individuals with "potential" are found to take on these special positions, and they are studied for their unusual qualities. (See Barron & Harrington, 1981; Feldhusen & Treffinger, 1980; Park, Lubinski, & Benbow, 2007; Milgram, 1999; Runco, 1999, 2003; Simonton, 1994; Torrance, 1972, for examples.)

In fact, individuals can be creative or noncreative in any domain. There are creative lighting experts, and plenty of artists (even prima donnas) who are not creative. Indeed, creativity can be seen as a possibility in any domain that allows novelty and has mechanisms for evaluating that novelty relative to the domain's current state and, ideally, the wider society in which the domain operates (Csikszentmihalyi, 1988; Gardner, Csikszentmihalyi & Damon, 2001). Creativity is perhaps more likely to arise when the activity has a purpose of difference, change, or cultural evolution. Then it is intentional and proactive (Kaufmann, 2003). Gruber (1989), in particular, focused on purpose as a key aspect of creativity.

In this chapter, I focus on the functional and, especially, purposeful dimensions of the role of creativity. What does creativity *do* for society? Why should society *care* about creativity? What does creativity *gain* us? I argue that creativity can assume two apparently different roles in society. One, which I call the improvement role, emphasizes the large-scale societal consequences of a creation. The other, which I term the expression role, focuses on the significance of the activity for the individual creator. In the end, I suggest a framework in which these two roles interact, emphasizing how individual and societal creative purposes are more complementary than competitive.

The Value of Creativity

Purpose is based in values. Values signify the relative importance of goals or ideals. A focus on purpose is both timely and revealing since people tend to exhibit ambivalence about creativity. On the one hand, creative persons, institutions, and inventions are touted by politicians, leaders, educators, and the media as "saviors" for the ills of society. In addition, people often say they would like the opportunity to be more creative on the job or in leisure. Yet studies of creativity and values over the past 40 years show that American adults, including teachers, do not value creativity very highly (Hitt, 1975; Kasof, Chen, Himsel, & Greenberger, 2007; Moran, 2010a; Sternberg & Lubart, 1995; Torrance, 2003). Creativity is often associated with deviance, rebelliousness, daring, and independence (see also Cropley, 1996; Keniston, 1960; Moran, 2010a; Sternberg & Lubart, 1995): Creators "go their own way" and may not be dependable or reliable. They hold different values (Dollinger, Burke, & Gump, 2007).

Creativity involves moving beyond what exists now, using resources brought from the past to devise potentially better options for the future (e.g., Craft, 2003). Creativity is perceived to create a disjunct between present and future – it makes tomorrow less predictable. Our relationship with the future can be a key indicator of our attitudes toward creativity. Torrance's (1991, 1993, 2004) 30-year longitudinal study of "beyonders" found that a person's image of the future, and the role of oneself in that future, is more predictive of later creative achievements than are past achievements or traits such as intelligence.

By examining the "why" of creativity, I bring to the fore the relationship of creativity to the future. This relationship is often described in terms of the hopes and the risks of creativity. Hope signifies a desired future state. It involves optimism, thriving, and anticipated positive change. Hope instills balance, providing a more psychologically stable path toward the future. Creativity breeds both hope and benefits from hope because it provides a way to realize that hope. With creativity, a person can become more agentic in bringing the desired state into being. He or she is more self-directed.

Risk signifies the possibility of loss or hazard. It involves uncertainty, consequences, and trust. Risk upsets balance, bringing to mind unknowns that are like potholes in the path toward the future. Creativity involves uncertainty because it is difficult to know the consequences of something truly new. Dr. Faust, for example, discovered to his horror that creations cannot always be controlled. The belief is that novelty makes a situation more uncertain for the rest of us, which gives rise to anxiety (Jaques, 1990; Stacey, 1996). Anxiety is fear without an explicit object. It's being afraid of something but not knowing quite what we fear. To some extent, we must trust that creations are benevolent for them to be allowed to come into existence.

Gardner (1993) has argued that creativity is amoral: Novel, useful ideas or products could bring benefits or wreak havoc. Devastating examples are Nazi scientific experiments, superior technology in warfare that "improves" the ability to kill, agitprop propaganda masquerading as art, and in the 2000s the no-documentation ninja mortgages, credit default swaps, and other "creative products" in financial markets. At the time a novel product is introduced, we don't know its rippling effects. This is why, in recent work, Gardner and colleagues (2007; Gardner et al., 2001) have sought to yoke the realm of creativity with the imperative of responsibility (see also Moran, 2010b). As Winston Churchill said, "The price of greatness is responsibility."

The root of the word "responsibility" means to respond or to answer. To whom does the creator or creative product answer to? Whom or what does his or her work impact? There seems to be a critical time when a potential creator's passions and concerns hook in with society's goals and momentum to make a difference not only to the self but to society (Moran & Gardner, 2006). Responsibility shows that what we do matters, that we are all interconnected and affect each other. Creativity is a particularly visible way of impacting others in our communities because it changes the status quo for individuals and sometimes for the entire group.

Thus, creativity creates a bumpier ride: The result is more unpredictable than if the situation is stable and we can count on tomorrow to be much like today was. Our optimism holds that new will be better, but the law of unintended consequences says we might want to hedge our bets. Still, creativity is often considered good because it invents and perhaps controls the future. With creativity, the future becomes an opportunity, not a threat – at least for the creators. Opportunities are favorable circumstances for success. Whether we can recognize a situation as an opportunity may depend in part on what our purpose is. Through our activities, we position ourselves in our future. Purpose can enable or constrain our ability to re-cognize – that is,

think again and perhaps differently – about a situation. And that re-cognition is often where opportunity lays – in the ability to transform a crisis into a learning experience, an obstacle into a challenge, a support into an asset (Moran, 2008).

The Roles of Society in Creativity

Before delving into the roles of creativity in society, it may be helpful to describe the reciprocal perspective: What roles does society play in creativity? Creativity's impact depends in part on power: Who gets to say what its role in society is? And who gets to decide who can be creative? Power entails the differential relationships among positional roles within society: Who can control the flow of resources, including information, social influence, and funding? Under the sway of scholarly paradigms that assumed creativity was the sole result of individuals (e.g., psychometric, psychodynamic, and early cognitive models), the societal influence on creativity was ignored. In the past 30 years, the interactive, contextualized nature of how creativity arises has become of more interest (e.g., Becker, 1982; Bourdieu, 1993; Csikszentmihalyi, 1988; Gardner, 1993; Hunter, Bedell, & Mumford, 2007; Zuckerman, 1977).

Csikszentmihalyi (1996), Gardner (1993), and Simonton (2003) discuss particular societies and historical time periods where creativity flourished and floundered. Ancient Greece, Renaissance Italy, and late twentieth-century America are examples of thriving creative societies, whereas Stalinist Russia and Maoist China are considered creativity-thwarting environments (except perhaps in domains that advanced a political or military agenda). Creativity needs a society that values novelty and appropriateness concurrently. If creativity is not allowed to exist or be recognized, then its role in society is moot. Thus, the role of creativity in society depends in part on the society in which a potential for creativity exists.

In general, society's impact can be parsed among three roles: benefactor, regulator, and consumer. These roles come into play at different times in the process of a novel idea's or product's creation. They are like ripples that the novel idea or product must pass through to become successful.

Creativity benefactors, such as funders, venture capitalists, incubators, and suppliers, influence the beginning of creativity. They provide resources enabling creativity to occur. Gardner (1993) and Becker (1982), for example, both show how the artist – far from being a "lone genius" – requires a network of emotional, financial, and material supports to create. Similarly, Zuckerman (1977) shows how science arises from beneficial relationships. Benefactors help stimulate the "novel" aspect of creativity. They create a space for creativity to have the possibility to arise.

Creativity regulators are the bottleneck of creativity. These powerful individuals are responsible for selecting, from among the myriad potential new ideas and products in their fields, which ideas and products are worthy of support, development, and dissemination. Csikszentmihalyi (1988), Amabile (1982), Bourdieu (1993), and Sosa and Gero (2004) have put forth theories and methods to assess how these "gatekeeping" decisions are made. These theories suggest that individuals are socialized into the field to produce works similar to what is already in use. Because practitioners are initially taught to think in similar ways, evaluations of products, even if they are subjective, are often reliable indicators of creativity (Amabile, 1982; Kaufman, Lee, Baer, & Lee, 2007). That is, experts tend to agree on what is creative. However, gatekeeping is imprecise (e.g., Delmestri, Montanari, & Usai, 2005; Licuanan, Dailey, & Mumford, 2007; Marsh, Jayasinghe, & Bond, 2008). The more novel the product, the harder it is for gatekeepers to evaluate and the more the creator must devise a way for the product to be seen as acceptable to others (Bourdieu, 1993; Gardner & Nemirovsky, 1991). Thus, creative work and creative fields include considerable political skill – either by the creator or by a benefactor – to persuade others to overcome their anxieties and value something unfamiliar (Kasof, 1995; Runco, 1995).

Regulators also help manage the risk of creativity. They provide a safety check by weeding out products or producers that may potentially harm the field or the consumers the field serves. This function is more visible in products and services to the public, such as inspections in transportation or food, and clinical trials in pharmaceuticals. But it also operates in professional fields where the consumers are other professionals, such as peer review in academia and the bar exam in law (e.g., Johnson, 2008). Regulators take care of the "appropriate" aspect of creativity. To be appropriate means the environment, both other people and the symbolic body of knowledge practitioners work with, is taken into consideration (Runco & Chand, 1994; Runco & Charles, 1993). The issue is whether and how field members and the public can trust gatekeepers (Gardner, Benjamin, & Pettingill, 2006).

Creativity consumers are the end game of creativity. In esoteric or difficult-to-master fields, the consumers may be a tiny group. For example, Einstein's theory of relativity had to be accepted only by the dozen leading physicists of the day. More commonly, however, judgments of creativity are made over time by a much larger cohort. When a creative idea or product captures the hearts, minds, and/or wallets of a critical mass of people, it "wins" the game of acceptance and adoption, which can bring fame and even fortune to the creator or promoter (Sternberg & Lubart, 1995). Consumers can range from early adopters who pick up the "latest, greatest" items to laggards who won't buy an item until it's already out of fashion (Rogers, 1995). The balance of a product's novelty and appropriateness helps determine how many people will want it: too much novelty and only the early adopters partake; too much appropriateness and consumers may not even notice it since there probably are already many other similar products available.

Eventually, the benefits to early adopters with "cultural capital," who are not afraid of a little risk in trying something new, reach the majority of consumers. The product is no longer a luxury, but becomes a necessity: indoor lights, telephones, refrigerators, cars, televisions, computers, cell phones, and credit cards, to name a few. The idea or product becomes part of the mainstream, part of the social fabric. It has become accepted, standardized, or appropriate. Enough time has passed since its introduction that people who are risk averse can read reviews or talk to others who have used the product so they can know in advance what they are buying. Thus, creativity signifies a state or period in a temporal process when an idea or product, which holds promise of being beneficial, is introduced. However, an idea or product does not remain creative indefinitely because it eventually becomes the standard for later ideas or products.

A Dichotomy of Purposes Based on Differing Perspectives

Given ambivalent values about creativity and the societal roles of benefactor, regulator, and consumer in creativity, I propose two overarching roles that creativity, in turn, plays in society. I focus on modern, primarily European and American society. One role – improvement – is usually championed by creativity regulators, as trustees for a group, or more democratically by creativity consumers. The other role – expression – is usually championed by creativity benefactors and often creators themselves. Thus, roles are related to perspectives. Whose view should we privilege – the group's or the individual's?

The societal perspective of the group emphasizes an "objective" account of the functions and purposes of creativity. This account is based implicitly on intersubjective agreement and common understanding (Rogoff, 1990), usually as promoted by those in powerful positions. It emphasizes novelty at the group level with appropriateness yoked to group goals. This perspective is interested in finding the select individuals who can "make history" through great contributions – "big-C" creativity. The psychometric (e.g., Wilson, Guilford, & Christensen, 1953), personality (e.g., Barron & Harrington, 1981), historiometric (Simonton, 1994), cognitive (e.g., Gardner, 1993; Perkins, 1981), and management (e.g., Agars & Kaufman, 2005; Amabile, 1996; Stonehouse & Minocha, 2008) approaches depict creativity as an individual ability or trait to be assessed and harnessed by society (or the group) to make great leaps forward in productivity, technology, and innovation.

The individual perspective emphasizes a "subjective" account of the functions and purposes of creativity. This account is based on the idiosyncratic meanings a person derives from particular experiences (Feldman, 1994; Vygotsky, 1978), with little credence given to external evaluations. It emphasizes novelty and appropriateness for the individual but not necessarily for the group. This perspective is interested in "making a mark" in the world through personal contributions – "little-c" creativity. Humanistic (e.g., Maslow, 1970), educational (e.g., Craft, 2003; Feldman, 1994; Runco, 2003), and health (e.g., Davis, 1987; Mirowsky & Ross, 2007; Richards, 2007; Runco & Richards, 1998) researchers show a growing appreciation for creativity as expression in general problem solving and self-development that is less norm-comparative and more inclusive. The psychoanalytic (e.g., Rothenberg, 1990) and sociological (e.g., Becker, 1963; Stebbins, 1971) approaches seem mostly interested in the individual perspective, but in relation to the societal perspective. However, their emphasis is on how the two perspectives differ. They focus on self-expression, but often in terms of pathology or deviance from a norm.

I explore these two perspectives as dichotomous influences on creativity's role in society. From the societal perspective, creativity's role is improvement; from the individual perspective, creativity's role is expression.

Creativity's Role Is Improvement

"We need new ideas to solve our country's pressing problems."

"We need workers who can 'think outside the box' – especially in science and technology – to be competitive in today's global economy."

"What drives the world today is change."

From the societal perspective, often voiced by political and business leaders, the function of creativity is to improve society. The purpose or intention is competitive advantage: The business, state, or nation will compare favorably to others if new ideas are implemented (e.g., Prajogo, 2006; Stonehouse & Minocha, 2008). The belief is that a novel, appropriate solution will create a positive spiral of productivity and achievement. For example, several government leaders have argued that modern societies live or die depending on their nurturing and valuing of creativity. Thus, they have established plans to stimulate creativity in education and economics (e.g., the New England Council in Boston [2001], the National Advisory Committee on Creative and Cultural Education [1999] in the United Kingdom, and the National Program of Educational Reform and Development in China [see Shen, 1996]). The Matthew effect (Merton, 1968), where those with the most get more and those with the least get even less, will commence, and the society will be on the more privileged path. The underlying value assumption is that if workers and citizens come up with new ideas, life will be better.

In general, Western cultures are considered more product oriented and tend to take this perspective (Lubart, 1999). However, most cultures aim to improve. Within a particular culture, "improve" might translate into different manifestations. Some link improvement to carrying on tradition, whereas others link it to change. Chinese students, for example, improve their artistic skill by better imitating the classics, whereas American students improve their artistic skill by darting forth in unexpected directions (Gardner, 1989).

The societal perspective reinforces beliefs that power is hierarchical and a society should strive to be on top. Central control of societal resources by experts and authorities can be more thoughtfully and strategically allocated and coordinated toward desired ends. Opportunities should be carefully evaluated, and the optimum ones implemented. Outcomes of successful opportunities should be preserved for current and future generations to further build on. This approach calls for educational programs that select for and nurture individuals with the highest potential to be innovative in various domains (see also Chen, Moran, & Gardner, 2009; Moran, 2009b).

Over the course of time, societies parse into fields of expertise – professions, industries, and the like – who oversee a particular domain of culture. Practitioners jostle for power and influence over policy, standards, and the valuation of work products. For efficiency, practitioners develop procedures and norms to reinforce conformity. Thus, creativity eventually gives way to standardization. Creativity pulls society forward to a new stable state. Regulators and consumers come to depend on the resulting consistency. For example, a new painting style spawns imitators, and a "school of art" arises (e.g., Martindale, 1990). A new category of technology – for example, cell phones – eventually settles on standardized cables and protocols and makes usage easier and cheaper. A scientific method – for example, genetic blueprinting – is developed, equipment is built, and one or a few labs ascend to be the standard-setters.

Creativity's role as improver brings to the fore the evaluation aspect of creativity. In recent years scholars have devoted considerable attention to evaluation (e.g., Elsbach & Kramer, 2003; Paletz & Peng, 2008; Runco & Charles, 1993). Evaluation is the mechanism that gatekeepers use to determine appropriateness. Evaluation is external to the product and creator, imposed by others in the field (i.e., experts, colleagues) or outside the field (i.e., government, consumers). Creators and creative products should expect to be subjected to feedback from others.

Evaluation is necessary because creativity requires the use of often scarce resources. Therefore, leaders need to allocate resources to those most likely to do well with them. In the past (and continuing in the present), criteria for resource allocation have included intelligence, giftedness, and talent as assessed through various measures (e.g., Park et al., 2007; Terman et al., 1925; Torrance, 2003; Wilson et al., 1953). These instruments sort people. People have potential that can be realized (e.g., Runco, 2003). Exemplars are those select individuals whose potential is more fully realized; they have gone further to turn their potential into achievements (Csikszentmihalyi, 1996; Gardner, 1993; John-Steiner, 1985). Evaluation sorts creativity by amount; for example, children are often assessed based on how much creative potential or creative achievement they have as depicted in a score (Runco, 2003). But eventually, if a person reaches a threshold, evaluation sorts creativity by kind; eminent creators who transform a domain – such as Shakespeare in theater, or Newton in physics, or the Wright brothers in aviation – are considered a different *kind* of person than people who devise personal or small-scale innovations or inventions.

With creativity's role as improver, the important thing is the goal and what counts as progress toward it. Because most fields do not have clear criteria for evaluating truly novel products, what counts as "good" can vary across individuals. What field practitioners or experts consider good may differ significantly from what consumers or novices think is good (Caroff & Besancon, 2008; Kaufman, Baer, Cole, & Sexton, 2009). This discrepancy is often seen in the divergent opinions of awards committees and viewers in the film, television, and advertising industries (e.g., Delmestri et al., 2005). What some field members consider good may vary from other field members. This discrepancy is often seen in peer review of academic publications (Marsh et al., 2008).

These various constituents have different values that underlie their evaluations and their conceptions of improvement.

People who believe that improvement is the role of creativity may have difficulty with the moral and responsibility aspects of creativity; creativity cannot be coincident with improvement, on the one hand, and yet concurrently moral-free. Agreeing with Gardner's earlier work, I argue that creativity cannot and is not automatically associated with benevolence. Creators issue new acts and products for all kinds of reasons. Many do not care about their social consequences, and even those that do often have little or no control over how their creations are used. Did Einstein anticipate the use of his equation to create nuclear weapons? Did Watson and Crick anticipate genetic engineering?

However, the essential amorality of creativity does not relieve individuals or societies of the obligation to attempt to direct or regulate the uses of innovations. The innovation is one step; its publication and application is a separate step. Einstein did not have to write President Roosevelt about the potential uses of nuclear fission; nor did he have to join various organizations devoted to peace and disarmament. These are morally guided choices that he made – either in his role as a scientist or in his role as a citizen. James Watson did not have to join the human genome project; nor did he have to propose that 3–5% of the budget be devoted to ethical issues.

I argue that if people want to affect the course of history, if they take the societal perspective of creativity-as-improvement, then they assume the attendant responsibility. Those who steal the fire from the gods have a moral obligation to attend to its uses and, where possible, direct those uses to noble ends (Gardner et al., 2001; Gardner, 2007).

Creativity's Role Is Expression

"I stretch myself in my work, see what happens."

"My art reveals a side of me I didn't know I had."

"I throw out my ideas, my experiences, and hope others can understand who I am."

From the individual perspective, often voiced by creative practitioners and laypeople (e.g., Sternberg, 1985), the function of creativity is to manifest latent aspects of the self. Because individuals are assumed to be unique, this function leads to variation, a complex buzz of concurrent possibilities (Campbell, 1960). The purpose or intention is to make meaning. The individual understands something in a personally significant way and shares that meaning through some type of product. The belief is that a novel idea or product validates a person's existence in that he or she has "made a mark" on the world. The person has contributed to his or her immediate environment. The underlying value assumption is that difference is important: If individuals express what is "inside" them – their potential – then they will feel better. Creativity is positive surprise.

Within a particular culture, "express" might translate into different manifestations. Some cultures are more tolerant of individuality and self-expression, especially if the self is expressing something beyond the cultural norm. The value of freedom of speech in the United States tends to protect a wide variety of expressions, whereas many traditional cultures severely limit the content and timing of expressions. Even within America there are differences: San Francisco tends to allow wider latitude of self-expression than Peoria. Although conventional wisdom states that Western cultures are generally more oriented to the individual, Eastern cultures tend also to take this perspective and see creativity's role as that of self-expression (Lubart, 1999).

The underlying belief of this perspective is that creativity should not be limited to unequivocally domain-transforming geniuses, such as Einstein, Picasso, or T.S. Eliot (as in, e.g., Gardner, 1993). Rather, almost anyone can come up with new ways to address a common life problem or think in terms of possibilities rather than only perceiving and reacting to "what is." Self-expression relates to externalization, or how one shows the world his or her interpretations of cultural meanings (Engestrom, 1999; see also Moran & John-Steiner, 2003). In this vein, Maslow (1970) included creativity as part of self-actualization in his theory of motivation, Runco (1996) promotes the notion of "personal creativity," Richards (2007) emphasizes "everyday creativity," and Craft (2003) advocates for "little-c" creativity. Although this emphasis on self-expression aims to make creativity less elitist than the improvement role, it also makes creativity more solipsistic than contributory. It disconnects individuals from responsibility to a greater good.

The individual perspective reinforces more egalitarian beliefs: We're all different, but we can coexist. It's better if we're connected in a positive way, so long as we don't constrain each other's expression. We need not seek a common goal. What is important is experience – who we are, what we're doing now, what it feels like, where it takes us existentially. Power is not hierarchical, but networked. We don't have to be better than each other; our differences can be complementary. Collaborations are viewed in terms of their internal benefits and not their external accomplishments. People self-expressing together can catalyze and enhance the expressions, motivation, and identities of their partners (John-Steiner, 2000; Moran & John-Steiner, 2004).

With creativity's role as expression, what is important is the self – what are the qualities being expressed? Society is viewed as a nurturer of individuality. Societies offer education and training, support, and "safe spaces" for people to explore their interests, preferences, and experiences. This role of creativity-as-expression has been a particular emphasis in educational circles. In many countries, the purpose of education has become more about releasing children's creative capacities than in training them in the dominant culture (e.g., Chen et al., 2009; Craft, 2003; Moran, 2009b). Evaluation, if it is done, should be based on subjective criteria that take into account the process of becoming, not just the end product of achievement. Thus, sometimes this role of creativity-as-expression mixes the concepts of learning and creativity (see Moran, 2010a).

Of particular note is how this creativity role is more often called on when focusing on "special populations" – that is, individuals from groups that are assumed not to be able to contribute to the "common good" through normal channels. These individuals include children (who are too young and may lack the expertise and judgment to contribute; Moran, 2007) and the sick or disabled (who are too feeble to contribute). It also used to include women (Kirschenbaum & Reis, 1997). Can children be active cultural agents or is their "creativity" an error or misunderstanding (Craft, 2003)? Can cancer patients create meaning for their experiences (Visser & Op't Hoog, 2008)? Can employees with lower autonomy stay healthier through creativity (Mirowsky & Ross, 2007)?

Creativity-as-expression is a way of coping with life's challenges (Cropley, 1996). Traditionally, it provided a means for those without power to have some say in society. Scott's (1990) study of mechanisms of resistance takes a sociological stance on the productive role that the creation of rumors, rituals, and so forth plays in helping people who cannot directly state their views. This purpose may still hold. Technology is changing how people can express themselves, especially for people formerly excluded from societal interaction, such as youth who have not reached majority age (see Moran, 2007).

Creativity here is seen as a separate side effect or outlet for people who are not allowed or don't want to contribute directly to societal norms or goals. Consider the beatnik writers of mid twentieth-century America (see Moran, 2009c), the jester in medieval courts, the joker in Shakespeare's plays, or the coyote in Southwest Native American stories. Creativity here means "play" or "of no real consequence." Of course, play has been linked to creativity both theoretically and empirically (e.g., Goldmintz & Schaefer, 2007; Moran & John-Steiner, 2003; Russ, Robins, & Christiano, 1999).

This role, taken to its extreme, is perhaps best seen in the phenomenon of the internet. What would it look like if everyone were creative? YouTube. MySpace. Facebook. Blogs. Wikis. There are no gatekeepers other than the sense of propriety, fairness, or other values that Internet users negotiate or force on each other. In such an environment, different mechanisms of trust must evolve. For example, eBay, yelp, Amazon, and similar retail and review sites have developed "reputations" for users to assess the validity of other people's expressions. Thus, someone can put almost anything up on the Web, but it may or may not have much meaning to others depending on the creator's reputation with other users. Responsibility pertains less to a norm or the future and more to policing each other in the present. The assumption is that, overall, the different expressions and opinions will coagulate into some type of coherence; but the process of development remains preeminent. For example, wiki pages are rarely considered "done" because people are expressing new ideas and perspectives daily. With creativity-as-expression, the point is motion and momentum, not a product that can be put on a pedestal as an exemplar.

Creativity, Society, Wisdom, and Further Possibilities

Two perspectives take the extremes of creativity's role in society. The first perspective articulates a relatively linear society "center" marching toward greatness. The individual is a tool for historical development. The underlying metaphor is of transporting society across the "border" into a better future with the norm shifted to a "higher" or "stronger" position. The political, business, and scientific headlines focus on improvement, progress, and making an aspect *of* society better. Leaders believe creativity drives that improvement. They want innovation and flexibility for competitive advantage. Products and services become more convenient, cheaper, faster, and better.

The second perspective articulates a subjective individual experiencing novelty and distinction from others. The culture is a tool for personal development. Statements of artists, educators, and workers focus on expression, variation, and potentially making a difference *in* society. The metaphor is that of blossoming. These individuals believe that creativity manifests the latent aspects of the self through work and play. They want authenticity, stimulation, and opportunities to be true to themselves.

From a dynamic-systems approach (see, e.g., Guastello, 2007), the two perspectives of creativity as improvement or expression are not extremes of one dimension. Rather, they are seen as different levels of analysis – individual and society interact over time to bring new ideas and products into the realm of culture (e.g., Campbell, 1960; Moran & John-Steiner, 2003). In a dynamic system, creative ideas, products, and solutions are creative only temporarily – when they are introduced and judged. But over time, they become seen as standard and conventional because they have been internalized by a majority of minds of cultural members. These ideas, products, or solutions are no longer new, even if they retain the label of having once been innovative. The challenge is for people who seek creativity – both improvement and expression – to have the foresight to consider the wider ramifications of these purposes on themselves, others, institutions, communities, and the environment.

Vygotsky argued that creativity is the construction and synthesis of experience-based meanings and cognitive symbols (the individual perspective) embodied in cultural artifacts (i.e., creative products) that endure over time to be appropriated by future generations (the societal perspective) (see Moran & John-Steiner, 2003). Thus, from a time-sensitive, dynamic perspective, creativity is a temporary misalignment of society and individual as they learn from and develop each other (Gardner et al., 2001; Moran & John-Steiner, 2003; see also Moran, 2010b). That misalignment readjusts into a new alignment with the world more knowledgeable in some way than it was before.

The roles of creativity raise the issue of the relationship between creativity and wisdom. At first glance, these two perspectives seem to pull in somewhat different directions (Craft, Gardner, & Claxton, 2008; Sternberg, 2001). In creativity, novelty and acceptance are key – "defying" then "charming" the crowd to follow. Wisdom, on the other hand, seems to entail three features: 1) a broad, systemic view, usually based on considerable experience; 2) a recognition of both human possibilities and limitations, or a sense of awe and humility; and 3) an application or use that goes beyond individual or group advantage and seeks instead to do what is right in the situation, often for a "greater good" (Baltes & Smith, 2008; Craft et al., 2008; Connell & Moran, 2008; Sternberg, 2001).

Some scholars suggest that wisdom takes creativity a step further by recognizing the need for both change and stability in a social and symbolic system (e.g., Sternberg, 2001). This claim emphasizes the novelty aspect of creativity and relegates the acceptance aspect more to wisdom.

Yet both creativity and wisdom address problem solving, both can include a "twist" in thinking, and both tend to have a transformative effect, to some degree, on those involved. For example, the classic wisdom scenario in the Bible of King Solomon shows both creativity and wisdom. Two women both claimed to be the mother of a baby. Solomon looked at the issue in an unusual way and suggested cutting the baby in half to solve the dispute. The real mother, willing to give up custody rather than see the baby harmed, was revealed.

Another relevant story is when Jesus intervened in the imminent stoning of an adulteress. Jesus basically conducted a "mirror test" (Gardner et al., 2001) on the men by pointing out that all of them, like the woman, were sinners. If she must die for her transgression, so too must they. Gandhi's campaign to erode British power in India through nonviolence rather than through fighting is a nonreligious example of the same interplay of creativity and wisdom. Solomon, Jesus, and Gandhi challenged people's assumptions and beliefs about the situation, and this challenge drove new actions. The creative product or service, or the wise decision or action, has psychological leverage – people's understandings are different afterward (Simonton, 2008; Sternberg, 2001). The meaning of what creators do (in the present and the future), as well as the benevolence of those actions and their effects, is what can turn creativity into wisdom (Helson & Srivastava, 2002).

Recently, purpose has been conceived as a link between the individual and society. Purpose is an intention and a reason for activity that is both meaningful to the individual and that contributes positively to society (Damon, 2008). In this light, the improvement and expression roles of creativity are different purposes interacting to evolve possibilities into opportunities, opportunities into activity, and activity into cultural artifacts. Realized possibilities that positively affect the greater good are wise. Artifacts, in turn, can stimulate even further possibilities in a cycle of cultural progress. As Newton said, "I have stood on the shoulders of giants." He recognized the function and purposes of prior generations' creations on his work. They made his work possible; he took their foundation and added to the laws of physics in a transformative way. His equations later made possible Einstein's equations, which allowed for relativity and not just absoluteness, as Newton's equations implied.

Feldman's (1994) "transformational imperative" suggests that people have a need and desire to make something of themselves and to have an effect on the world. They seek resources, niches, and opportunities to do so. The variation that this imperative creates eventually shifts the average, the norm. Csikszentmihalyi's (1988) "where is creativity?" systems model, Bourdieu's (1993) cultural production theory, and Feldman's (1994) universal-to-unique continuum describe how those imperatives filter through larger "ripples" of social organization. Feldman's continuum can be thought of in terms of the number of people who hold an idea, which can run from unique, when only one person knows, to universal, when everyone knows or should know the idea. Moving from the unique and idiosyncratic end toward the cultural and universal end represents a widening influence of a creation (i.e., a person's variation) on others. His or her self-expression increasingly becomes an improvement among increasingly larger ripples of society.

Creativity results from a community. For it to arise, there must be a confluence of both individual and societal forces (Seitz, 2003). Cultural progress is not "full steam ahead." Self expression is not "do whatever." We need to recognize the checks and balances in social systems. There is a call for both openness and regulation. Too much openness can lead to chaos. Too much regulation can lead to stagnation. Neither scenario is conducive to creativity that is significant, meaningful, and responsible. Neither total freedom nor total security works.

We do not seek to control or mandate how the imagination works and what products it may fashion – whether ideas, objects, strategies, or experiences. Yet we must acknowledge that each of us lives within a particular society, as well as an increasingly interconnected global society. As citizens of these societies, we cannot close our eyes to the uses and interpretations that follow on creations, be they of individual or historical dimensions.

An act of self-expression, no less than a Nobel Prize-winning discovery, may have wide consequences. I suggest that, far from diminishing the province of creativity, this state of affairs actually enhances it. For yoked to the act of creativity is an additional challenge, namely, how to increase the likelihood that the creation is put to positive ends. The function and purpose of creativity become more important than traits or positions. Rather than creativity diminished, we instead have creativity multiplied.

References

Agars, M. D., & Kaufman, J. C. (2005). Creativity in the workplace: Introduction to the special issue. *Korean Journal of Thinking & Problem Solving*, 15(2), 5–6.

Amabile, T. (1982). Social psychology of creativity: A consensual assessment technique. *Journal of Personality and Social Psychology*, 43, 997–1013.

Amabile, T. (1996). *Creativity in context*. Boulder, CO: Westview Press.

Baltes, P. B., & Smith, J. (2008). The fascination of wisdom: Its nature, ontogeny, and function. *Perspectives on Psychological Science*, 3(1), 56–64.

Barron, F., & Harrington, D. (1981). Creativity, intelligence, and personality. *Annual Review of Psychology*, 32, 439–476.

Becker, H. S. (1963). *Outsiders*. Glencoe, IL: The Free Press.

Becker, H. S. (1982). *Art worlds*. Berkeley: University of California Press.

Biddle, B. J. (1986). Recent developments in role theory. *Annual Review of Sociology*, 12, 67–92.

Bourdieu, P. (1993). *The field of cultural production*. New York: Columbia University Press.

Campbell, D. T. (1960). Blind variation and selective retention in creative thought as in other knowledge processes. *Psychological Review*, 67, 380–400.

Caroff, X., & Besancon, M. (2008). Variability in creativity judgments. *Learning and Individual Differences*, 18, 367–371.

Chen, J.-Q., Moran, S., & Gardner, H. (2009). *Multiple intelligences around the world*. San Francisco: Jossey-Bass.

Connell, M., & Moran, S. (2008, August). *"All the wiser": Wisdom from a systems perspective*. Invited talk at the University of Chicago, Arete Initiative, Chicago, IL.

Craft, A. (2003). The limits to creativity in education: Dilemmas for the educator. *British Journal of Educational Studies*, 51(2), 113–127.

Craft, A., Gardner, H., & Claxton, G. (Eds.). (2008). *Creativity, wisdom, and trusteeship: Exploring the role of education*. Thousand Oaks, CA: Corwin Press.

Cropley, A. J. (1996). Recognizing creative potential: An evaluation of the usefulness of creativity tests. *High Ability Studies*, 7(2), 203–219.

Csikszentmihalyi, M. (1988). Society, culture, and person: A systems view of creativity. In R. J. Sternberg (Ed.), *The nature of creativity* (pp. 325–339). New York: Cambridge University Press.

Csikszentmihalyi, M. (1996). *Creativity*. New York: HarperCollins.

Damon, W. (2008). *The path to purpose*. New York: Free Press.

Davis, B. W. (1987). Some roots and relatives of creative drama as an enrichment activity for older adults. *Educational Gerontology*, 13(4), 297–306.

Delmestri, G., Montanari, F., & Usai, A. (2005). Reputation and strength of ties in predicting commercial success and artistic merit of independents in the Italian feature film industry. *Journal of Management Studies*, 42(5), 975–1002.

Dollinger, S. J., Burke, P. A., & Gump, N. W. (2007). Creativity and values. *Creativity Research Journal*, 19(2–3), 91–103.

Elsbach, K. D., & Kramer, R. M. (2003). Assessing creativity in Hollywood pitch meetings: Evidence for a dual-process model of creativity judgments. *Academy of Management Journal*, 46(1), 283–301.

Engestrom, Y. (1999). Activity theory and individual and social transformation. In Y. Engestrom, R. Miettinen, & R.-L. Punamaki (Eds.), *Perspectives on activity theory* (pp. 19–38). Cambridge: Cambridge University Press.

Feldhusen, J. F., & Goh, B. E. (1995). Assessing and accessing creativity: An integrative review of theory, research and development. *Creativity Research Journal*, 8, 231–247.

Feldhusen, J. F., & Treffinger, D. J. (1980). *Creative thinking and problem solving in gifted education*. Dubuque, IA: Kendall/Hunt.

Feldman, D. H. (1994). *Beyond the universals of cognitive development* (2nd Ed.). Norwood, NJ: Ablex.

Feldman, D. H., Csikszentmihalyi, M., & Gardner, H. (1994). *Changing the world: A framework for the study of creativity*. Westport, CT: Praeger.

Florida, R. (2002). *The rise of the creative class*. New York: Basic Books.

Friedman, T. L. (2005). *The world is flat*. New York: Farrar, Straus, & Giroux.

Gardner, H. (1988). Creativity: An interdisciplinary perspective. *Creativity Research Journal*, 1, 8–26.

Gardner, H. (1989). *To open minds: Chinese clues to the dilemma of contemporary education.* New York: Basic Books.

Gardner, H. (1993). *Creating minds.* New York: Basic Books.

Gardner, H. (Ed.). (2007). *Responsibility at work.* San Francisco: Jossey-Bass.

Gardner, H., Csikszentmihalyi, M., & Damon, W. (2001). *Good work: When excellence and ethics meet.* New York: Basic Books.

Gardner, H., Benjamin, J., & Pettingill, L. (2006). An examination of trust in contemporary American society. In B. Kellerman (Ed.), *Center for Public Leadership Working Papers*, Harvard University. Spring 2006.

Gardner, H., & Nemirovsky, R. (1991). From private intuitions to public symbol systems: An examination of the creative process in Georg Cantor and Sigmund Freud. *Creativity Research Journal*, 4(1), 1–21.

Getzels, J. W., & Csikszentmihalyi, M. (1976). *The creative vision: A longitudinal study of problem finding in art.* New York: John Wiley & Sons.

Goldmintz, Y., & Schaefer, C. E. (2007). Why play matters to adults. *Psychology and Education: An Interdisciplinary Journal*, 44(1), 12–25.

Gruber, H. E. (1974). *Darwin on man: A psychological study of scientific creativity.* New York: Dutton.

Gruber, H. E. (1989). The evolving systems approach to creative work. In D. B. Wallace & H. E. Gruber (Eds.), *Creative people at work* (pp. 3–24). New York: Oxford University Press.

Guastello, S. J. (2007). Non-linear dynamics and leadership emergence. *The Leadership Quarterly*, 18, 357–369.

Helson, R., & Srivastava, S. (2002). Creative and wise people: Similarities, differences, and how they develop. *Personality and Social Psychology Bulletin*, 28, 1430–1440.

Hitt, M. A. (1975). The creative organization: Tomorrow's survivor. *Journal of Creative Behavior*, 9(4), 283–290.

Hunter, S. T., Bedell, K. F., & Mumford, M. D. (2007). Climate for creativity: A quantitative review. *Creativity Research Journal*, 19(1), 69–90.

Jaques, E. (1990). *Creativity and work.* Madison, WI: International Universities Press.

John-Steiner, V. (1985). *Notebooks of the mind: Explorations of thinking.* Albuquerque, NM: University of New Mexico Press.

John-Steiner, V. (2000). *Creative collaboration.* New York: Oxford University Press.

Johnson, V. E. (2008). Statistical analysis of the National Institutes of Health peer review system. *PNAS Proceedings of the National Academy of Sciences of the United States of America*, 105(32), 11076–11080.

Kasof, J. (1995). Explaining creativity: The attributional perspective. *Creativity Research Journal*, 8(4), 311–366.

Kasof, J., Chen, C., Himsel, A., & Greenberger, E. (2007). Values and creativity. *Creativity Research Journal*, 19(2–3), 105–122.

Kaufman, J. C., Baer, J., Cole, J. C., & Sexton, J. D. (2009). A comparison of expert and nonexpert raters using the Consensual Assessment Technique. *Creativity Research Journal*, 20(2), 171–178.

Kaufman, J. C., Lee, J., Baer, J., & Lee, S. (2007). Captions, consistency, creativity, and the Consensual Assessment Technique: New evidence of reliability. *Thinking Skills and Creativity*, 2(2), 96–106.

Kaufmann, G. (2003). What to measure? A new look at the concept of creativity. *Scandinavian Journal of Educational Research*, 47(3), 235–252.

Keniston, K. (1960). *The uncommitted.* New York: Dell.

Kirschenbaum, R. J., & Reis, S. M. (1997). Conflicts in creativity: Talented female artists. *Creativity Research Journal*, 10(2–3), 251–263.

Licuanan, B. F., Dailey, L. R., & Mumford, M. D. (2007). Idea evaluation: Error in evaluating highly original ideas. *Journal of Creative Behavior*, 41(1), 1–27.

Lubart, T. I. (1999). Creativity across cultures. In R. J. Sternberg (Ed.), *Handbook of creativity* (pp. 339–350). New York: Cambridge University Press.

Marsh, H. W., Jayasinghe, U. W., & Bond, N. W. (2008). Improving the peer-review process for grant applications: Reliability, validity, bias, and generalizability. *American Psychologist*, 63(3), 160–168.

Martindale, C. (1990). *The clockwork muse: The predictability of artistic styles.* New York: Basic Books.

Maslow, A. (1970). *Motivation and personality.* New York: Harper & Row.

Merton, R. K. (1968). The Matthew effect in science. *Science*, 159, 56–63.

Milgram, R. M. (1999). Creative out-of-school activities in intellectually gifted adolescents as predictors of their life accomplishments in young adults: A longitudinal study. *Creativity Research Journal*, 12, 77–88.

Mirowsky, J., & Ross, C. E. (2007). Creative work and health. *Journal of Health and Social Behavior*, 48(4), 385–403.

Moran, S. (2007, November). *Commitment and democracy: Are researchers capturing what young people commit to civically and politically?* Paper presented at the conference of the Association for Moral Education, New York, NY.

Moran, S. (2008, November). Opportunity recognition. Invited talk at Babson College, Wellesley, MA.

Moran, S. (2009a). Creativity: A systems perspective. In T. Richards, M. Runco, & S. Moger (Eds.), *The Routledge companion to creativity* (pp. 292–301). London: Routledge.

Moran, S. (2009b). Why multiple intelligences? In J.-Q. Chen, S. Moran, & H. Gardner (Eds), *Multiple intelligences around the world* (pp. 365–373). San Francisco: Jossey-Bass.

Moran, S. (2009c). What role does commitment play among writers with different levels of creativity influence? *Creativity Research Journal*, 21(2–3), 243–257.

Moran, S. (2010a). Creativity in school. In K. S. Littleton, C. Wood, & J. K. Staarman (Eds.), *International handbook of educational psychology: New perspective on learning and teaching*. Bingley, England: Emerald.

Moran, S. (2010b). Returning to the GoodWork Project's roots: Can creative work be humane? In H. Gardner (Ed.), *GoodWork: Retrospectives and opportunities*. GoodWork Project working paper.

Moran, S., & Gardner, H. (2006). Extraordinary cognitive achievements: A developmental and systems analysis. In W. Damon (Series Ed.) & D. Kuhn & R. S. Siegler (Vol. Eds.), *Handbook of child psychology: Vol. 2. Cognition, perception, and language* (6th ed., pp. 905–949). New York: Wiley.

Moran, S., & John-Steiner, V. (2003). Creativity in the making: Vygotsky's contemporary contribution to the dialectic of development and creativity. In R. K. Sawyer, V. John-Steiner, S. Moran, R. J. Sternberg, D. H. Feldman, J. Nakamura et al. (Eds.), *Creativity and development* (pp. 61–90). New York: Oxford University Press.

Moran, S., & John-Steiner, V. (2004). How collaboration in creative work impacts identity and motivation. In D. Miell & K. Littleton (Eds.), *Collaborative creativity: Contemporary perspectives* (pp. 11–25). London: Free Association Books.

Mumford, M. D. (2003). Where have we been, where are we going? Taking stock in creativity research. *Creativity Research Journal*, 15, 107–120.

National Advisory Committee on Creative and Cultural Education. (1999). *All our futures: Creativity, culture and education*. London: Department for Children, Schools, and Families.

New England Council. (2001). *The creative economy initiative: A blueprint for investment in New England's creative economy*. Boston: Report of the New England Council.

Paletz, S. B. F., & Peng, K. (2008). Implicit theories of creativity across cultures: Novelty and appropriateness in two product domains. *Journal of Cross-Cultural Psychology*, 39, 286–302.

Park, G., Lubinski, D., & Benbow, C. P. (2007). Contrasting intellectual patterns predict creativity in the arts and sciences: Tracking intellectually precocious youth over 25 years. *Psychological Science*, 18(11), 948–952.

Perkins, D. N. (1981). *The mind's best work*. Cambridge, MA: Harvard University Press.

Plucker, J. A., & Runco, M. A. (1998). The death of creativity measurement has been greatly exaggerated: Current issues, recent advances, and future directions in creativity assessment. *Roeper Review*, 21, 36–39.

Prajogo, D. I. (2006). The relationship between innovation and business performance: A comparative study between manufacturing and service firms. *Knowledge & Process Management*, 13(3), 218–225.

Richards, R. (2007). *Everyday creativity and new views of human nature: Psychological, social, and spiritual perspectives*. Washington, DC: American Psychological Association.

Rickards, T., Runco, M. A., & Moger, S. (Eds.). (2009). *The Routledge companion to creativity*. London: Routledge.

Rogers, E. M. (1995). *Diffusion of innovations* (4th ed.). New York: Free Press.

Rogoff, B. (1990). *Apprenticeship in thinking: Cognitive development in social context*. New York: Oxford University Press.

Rothenberg, A. (1990). *Creativity and madness: New findings and old stereotypes*. Baltimore, MD: Johns Hopkins University Press.

Runco, M. A. (1995). Insight for creativity, expression for impact. *Creativity Research Journal*, 8(4), 377–390.

Runco, M. A. (1996). Personal creativity: Definition and developmental issues. *New Directions for Child Development*, 72, 3–30.

Runco, M. A. (Ed.). (1997). *The creativity research handbook* (Vol. 1). Cresskill, NJ: Hampton.

Runco, M. A. (1999). A longitudinal study of exceptional giftedness and creativity. *Creativity Research Journal*, 12(2), 161–164.

Runco, M. A. (2003). Education for creative potential. *Scandinavian Journal of Educational Research*, 47(3), 317–324.

Runco, M. A. (2004). Creativity. *Annual Review of Psychology*, 55, 657–687.

Runco, M. A., & Chand, I. (1994). Problem finding, evaluative thinking, and creativity. In M. A. Runco (Ed.), *Problem finding, problem solving, and creativity* (pp. 40–68). Norwood, NJ: Ablex.

Runco, M. A., & Charles, R. (1993). Judgments of originality and appropriateness as predictors of creativity. *Personality and Individual Differences*, 15, 537–546.

Runco, M. A., & Nemiro, J. (1993). Problem finding and problem solving. *Roeper Review*, 16(4), 235–241.

Runco, M. A., & Richards, R. (Eds.). (1998). *Eminent creativity, everyday creativity, and health*. Norwood, NJ: Ablex.

Russ, S. W., Robins, D., & Christiano, B. (1999). Pretend play: Longitudinal prediction of creativity and affect and fantasy in children. *Creativity Research Journal*, 12, 129–139.

Sawyer, R. K. (2006). *Explaining creativity: The science of human innovation*. New York: Oxford University Press.

Scott, J. C. (1990). *Domination and the arts of resistance: Hidden transcripts*. New Haven, CT: Yale University Press.

Seitz, J. A. (2003). A communitarian approach to creativity. *Mind, Culture, and Activity*, 10(3), 245–249.

Shen, Z. L. (1996). Historical review of aesthetic education, *Researches in Higher Education of Light Industry*, 24, 3–7.

Simonton, D. K. (1994). *Greatness: Who makes history and why*. New York: Guilford.

Simonton, D. K. (2000). Creativity: Cognitive, personal, developmental, and social aspects. *American Psychologist*, 55(1), 151–158.

Simonton, D. K. (2003). Creative cultures, nations, and civilizations: Strategies and results. In P. B. Paulus & B. A. Nijstad (Eds.), *Group creativity: Innovation through collaboration* (pp. 304–325). New York: Oxford University Press.

Simonton, D. K. (2008). Creative wisdom: Similarities, contrasts, integration, and application. In A. Craft, H. Gardner, & G. Claxton (Eds.), *Creativity, wisdom, and trusteeship: Exploring the role of education* (pp. 68–76). Thousand Oaks, CA: Corwin Press.

Sosa, R., & Gero, J. S. (2004). Diffusion of creative design: Gatekeeping effects. *International Journal of Architectural Computing*, 2(4), 517–531.

Stacey, R. D. (1996). *Complexity and creativity in organizations*. San Francisco: Berrett-Koehler.

Stebbins, R. A. (1971). *Commitment to deviance*. Westport, CT: Greenwood.

Sternberg, R. J. (1985). Implicit theories of intelligence, creativity, and wisdom. *Journal of Personality & Social Psychology*, 49(3), 607–627.

Sternberg, R. J. (Ed.). (1999). *The handbook of creativity*. New York: Cambridge University Press.

Sternberg, R. J. (2001). What is the common thread of creativity? Its dialectical relation to intelligence and wisdom. *American Psychologist*, 56(4), 360–362.

Sternberg, R. J., & Lubart T. (1995). *Defying the crowd: Cultivating creativity in a culture of conformity*. New York: Free Press.

Stonehouse, G., & Minocha, S. (2008). Strategic processes @ Nike – Making and doing knowledge management. *Knowledge and Process Management*, 15(1), 24–31.

Terman, L. M. et al. (1925). *Mental and physical traits of a thousand gifted children* (Vol. 1 of *Genetic studies of genius*, L. M. Terman, Ed.). Stanford, CA: Stanford University Press.

Tepper, S. J. (2002). Creative assets and the changing economy. *The Journal of Arts Management, Law, and Society*, 32(2), 159–168.

Torrance, E. P. (1972). Career patterns and peak creative achievements: High school students twelve years later. *Gifted Child Quarterly*, 16, 15–88.

Torrance, E. P. (1991). The beyonders and their characteristics. *Creative Child and Adult Quarterly*, 16, 69–79.

Torrance, E. P. (1993). The beyonders in a thirty year longitudinal study of creative achievement. *Roeper Review*, 15, 131–134.

Torrance, E. P. (2003). Reflection on emerging insights on the educational psychology of creativity. In J. C. Houtz (Ed.), *The educational psychology of creativity* (pp. 273–286). Cresskill, NJ: Hampton Press.

Torrance, E. P. (2004). Great expectations: Creative achievements of the sociometric stars in a 30-year study. *The Journal of Secondary Gifted Education*, 26(1), 5–13.

Visser, A., & Op't Hoog, M. (2008). Education of creative art therapy to cancer patients: Evaluation and effects. *Journal of Cancer Education*, 23(2), 80–84.

Vygotsky, L. S. (1978). *Mind in society: The development of higher psychological processes* (M. Cole, V. John-Steiner, S. Scribner, & E. Souberman, Eds.). Cambridge, MA: Harvard University Press.

Wallas, G. (1926). *The art of thought*. New York: Harcourt.

Wilson, R. C., Guilford, J. P., & Christensen, P. R. (1953). The measurement of individual differences in originality. *Psychological Bulletin*, 50, 362–370.

Zuckerman, H. (1977). *Scientific elite*. New York: Free Press.

Section II

DIVERSE PERSPECTIVES ON CREATIVITY

CHAPTER 5

Cognition and Creativity

Thomas B. Ward and Yuliya Kolomyts

Creativity is a multifaceted phenomenon requiring a multitude of approaches to understand it. As the chapters in this volume attest, there are individual, situational, social, and cultural factors that work together to determine the likelihood and the magnitude of a creative outcome. This chapter focuses on a particular ingredient in the creative mix, namely, the thought processes that individuals bring to bear on the problems they confront. More particularly, it focuses on the creative cognition approach, which views creativity through the lens of cognitive science (see, e.g., Finke, Ward, & Smith, 1992; Ward, Smith, & Finke, 1999). Creative cognition is concerned with explicating how fundamental cognitive processes, available to virtually all humans, operate on stored knowledge to yield ideas that are novel and appropriate to a task at hand.

Cognitive processes and knowledge are, one way or another, addressed in most approaches to understanding creativity, including a variety of confluence models (e.g., Amabile, 1983a, 1983b; Csikszentmihalyi, 1999; Lubart & Sternberg, 1995). Amabile's approach includes both domain general and domain specific knowledge and skills in addition to a balance between intrinsic and extrinsic motivation (Amabile, 1983a, 1983b; Collins & Amabile, 1999). Csikszentmihalyi's systems model includes the individual, domain, and field, and notes that individuals use acquired domain knowledge along with cognitive abilities to make advances to domains, with the worth of those contributions judged by the gatekeepers of the domain or field (Csikszentmihalyi, 1999). The investment model notes that intellectual abilities, knowledge, and thinking styles combine with other components to produce creative outcomes (Lubart & Sternberg, 1995).

The creative cognition approach is deeply rooted in its parent disciplines of cognitive psychology and cognitive science. Rather than focusing broadly on the range of contributing factors, as in confluence models, it concentrates instead on the cognitive ingredient in depth. The approach is consonant with the broadly agreed-on notion that existing knowledge plays a role in creativity at all levels, and that the quality of creative outcomes will be influenced by the extent of a person's knowledge and the manner in which elements of that knowledge are accessed and combined (Cropley, 1999; Feldhusen, 1995, 2002; Munford & Gustafson, 1988; Sternberg & Lubart, 1995).

The Geneplore Framework

A general, descriptive framework for creative cognition is the Geneplore model (Finke et al., 1992), which characterizes the development of novel and useful ideas as resulting from an interplay of *generative* processes that produce candidate ideas of varying degrees of creative potential and *exploratory* processes that expand on that potential. Rather than focusing on *the* creative process as a singular entity, the model identifies a cluster of basic cognitive processes, which combine in a variety of ways to influence the probability of a creative outcome.

The generative processes that have been identified include retrieval of various types of information, such as specific category exemplars, general knowledge, images, source analogs, and so on (e.g., Gentner, 1989; Holyoak & Thagard, 1995; Perkins, 1981; Smith, 1995; Ward, 1994) as well as association (Mednick, 1962) and combining of concepts and images (Baughman & Mumford, 1995; Finke, 1990; Hampton, 1987; Murphy, 1988). These processes are assumed to result in candidate ideas, sometimes referred to as *preinventive forms*, that are not necessarily complete creative solutions to the problem at hand, but rather represent possible starting points that can either facilitate or inhibit creative outcomes. The model assumes that people can use properties, such as apparent novelty and aesthetic appeal, to determine which preinventive forms should be retained for further processing. The creative potential of selected ideas is then developed by way of other specific exploratory processes that modify, elaborate, consider the implications, assess the limitations, or otherwise transform the candidate ideas.

An important feature of the creative-cognition approach is the specificity with which it characterizes both the nature of basic cognitive processes and how they operate on knowledge structures to produce ideas. For example, rather than relying solely on more global cognitive descriptors, such as "divergent thinking," the creative-cognition approach seeks to specify the basic component processes that lead to divergent productions. When a person achieves a certain fluency score on a divergent-thinking task by listing items in response to a prompt (e.g., alternate uses for a shoe), for example, the listed items may have been derived from the application of a wide range of processes, including episodic retrieval (e.g., recalling having used a shoe to kill a bug), mental imagery (e.g., scanning a mental image of a shoe, noting that it has laces, and realizing that they could serve a specific purpose), analysis of features (e.g., noting that shoes have the property of being heavy and therefore could be used as doorstops), abstraction (e.g., interpreting a shoe as a container, with the consequence that it could be used to store things), or analogy (e.g., noting that shoes cover feet like gloves cover hands so a shoe might be used to keep hands warm too), among many other possibilities. At a still more specific level, creative cognition attempts to identify the detailed operation of those component processes. For example, although an individual might produce a divergent idea by way of analogy to some other knowledge domain, analogy is itself just a global descriptor for more fundamental processes such as alignment, retrieval, mapping, and projection of information from a source to a target domain (e.g., Gentner, 1989). The point is not that any one participant uses all of these specific processes, but rather that it is the underlying processes that are doing the work and therefore are of most interest; the divergent-thinking score is simply the end result.

There is nothing wrong with using divergent thinking as a general label for the type of ability individuals must possess to be creative (e.g., Csikszentmihalyi, 1999). Nor is it necessarily inappropriate to use divergent-thinking scores as indicators of creative capacity. Indeed, there is at least some evidence that divergent-thinking scores predict real-world creativity (e.g., Kim, 2008; Plucker, 1999). However, a more precise characterization of creativity will require a detailed consideration of the processes used in generating the items leading to that score. By extension, it is essential to understand the basic underlying processes that lead to all forms of creativity.

Creative thinking can thus be characterized in terms of how various specific processes are employed or combined. For example, a writer might generate the beginnings of a new plot line by mentally combining familiar and exotic concepts, and then explore the ramifications of the combination in fleshing out the details of the story (see, e.g., Donaldson, 1992; Ward, Finke, & Smith, 1995). Similarly, a scientist might generate candidate analogies designed to understand one domain in terms of another, and then rigorously scrutinize those analogies to test their descriptive or explanatory utility (e.g., Gentner et al., 1997).

A Convergence Approach

As a general guide to developing studies of creative processes, the creative cognition approach makes use of a convergence strategy (Ward, 2001; Ward et al., 1995). Using that strategy, anecdotes or historical accounts of creative achievements or creative failures are examined to provide hints about potentially relevant processes and conceptual structures. Those processes and structures are then defined operationally in terms of experimental procedures and outcomes in a way that allows controlled experiments to be conducted to investigate them.

Combining the types of information available from anecdotes and laboratory studies can provide a much more complete picture of creativity and the factors that can inhibit or facilitate it than can be obtained by relying exclusively on one approach or the other. Anecdotes about real world instances of creative success or failure are essential in that they provide hints about processes that may have some ecological validity. On the other hand, such accounts are often based on retrospective reports of the creative individuals involved (Dunbar, 1997). It is difficult to verify the extent to which particular processes were actually used and the extent to which they were causally associated with the real world accomplishments or failures. Even when there is corroborating evidence to support retrospective accounts, there remains the "compared to what" problem (Ward, 2001; Ward et al., 1995). That is, even if a creative accomplishment operated in exactly the way it appears in an anecdotal account, it does not necessarily follow that the identified processes played a causal role in the relative extent to which the outcome was a success or failure. There is no way to know whether some other process might have resulted in a better or worse idea, and without that knowledge there is no way to make factually grounded recommendations about the best ways to facilitate future creative endeavors.

A strength of laboratory studies is that they allow a manipulation of independent variables thought to be of interest, precise control over any extraneous variables (at least those the experimenter is cognizant of), and careful measurement of outcome or dependent variables. The vagaries of real world settings are removed, and it becomes possible to establish a direct causal link between a process and an outcome. In addition, because such studies are typically grounded in previous theory and research, the rich knowledge in the field about a given process or structure aids in the devising of the study and the interpretation of its results. However, there is also the risk that in the very act of gaining control over the variables, an artificial situation is created that makes any results obtained of questionable value for understanding real world phenomena. Just because we can manipulate something about which the field of cognitive psychology has come to learn a great deal does not mean that that variable bears any relation to factors that matter in real world design situations. But, by devising laboratory investigations with an eye toward insights obtained from anecdotal accounts, laboratory studies have a better chance of assessing relevant processes in reasonably valid ways.

Thus, using a convergence approach it is possible to balance the strengths and weaknesses of anecdotal and laboratory procedures against one another. The result can be a more compelling account of the cognitive processes and structures, as well as any situational and interpersonal factors associated with more or less creative outcomes. However, it should also be noted that "convergence" is the name of the approach and not necessarily its outcome. That is, it is quite possible that laboratory findings would contradict a given creator's report that a particular thought process was beneficial or causal in leading to a specific creative accomplishment. At that point, either the process would be brought into question or differences between the real world and laboratory settings would need to be considered in interpreting the "divergent" results.

Types and Levels of Creativity

It is important to recognize that there are enormous individual differences in the extent to which people generate creative products. There is no doubt that some individuals produce more and higher quality creative outcomes than others, and a limited few achieve extreme levels of accomplishment (see, e.g., Eysenck, 1995; Simonton, 1994). In addition, creativity is diverse in the sense that there are clearly directions, degrees, and domains of creative contributions (Csikszentmihalyi, 1996, 1998; Kaufman & Baer, 2005; Sternberg, 1999; Sternberg, Kaufman, & Pretz, 2002). For example, Sternberg et al.'s (2002) propulsion model distinguishes among types of creative contribution, such as replication (reproducing existing works), forward incrementation (moving a domain ahead by a small extent), and reinitiation (moving a domain to a completely new starting point). A related distinction is between little-c or everyday creativity and Big-C or eminent creativity, as well as the recent Four C Model (Kaufman & Beghetto, 2009) that adds mini-c and Pro-c creativity as beginning and intermediate manifestations of creativity. Inspired by Runco's (1996) notion of personal creativity, mini-c captures the idea that even very young individuals and those without a large amount of domain knowledge construct personal understandings of the world, and that the proclivities that lead to those constructions can be, with appropriate experiences and feedback over time, precursors of little-c or even Big-C creative productivity. Pro-c is a level between little-c and Big-C creativity. Those engaged in Pro-c creativity have developed the knowledge, skills, and motivation to make creative advances in a chosen profession, although their creative products do not generally reach the revolutionary level of Big-C eminent contributions. Finally, it is clear that there are special types of processes that are particularly relevant for single domains of creativity, such as music, acting, art, mathematics, engineering, and other domains represented in Kaufman and Baer's (2005) edited volume on domain specific aspects of creativity.

With distinctions about directions, degrees, and domains in mind, it is important to note that the creative-cognition approach has been concerned largely with fundamental processes, such as abstraction, conceptual combination, and analogy, which can operate to yield creative outcomes from the most mundane to the most extraordinary across a wide range of domains. A central tenet of creative cognition is that individual differences and variations in the extent of creative contributions are largely understandable in terms of variations in the use of specifiable processes or combinations of processes, the intensity of application of such processes, the richness or flexibility of stored cognitive structures to which the processes are applied, the capacity of memory systems, such as working memory, and other known and observable fundamental cognitive principles (see Ward, Smith, & Vaid, 1997, and see Simonton, 1997, for a counterpoint). Creative cognition explicitly rejects the notion that extraordinary forms of creativity are the products of minds that operate according to principles that are fundamentally different than those associated with normative cognition, and that are largely mysterious and unobservable. Moreover, it has to date been concerned with domain-general processes and knowledge rather than processes more restricted to specific domains. Several processes, including retrieval of information at different levels of abstraction, conceptual combination, analogy, and problem finding will be used to illustrate the creative-cognition approach.

Retrieval of Specific versus General Information

An organizing framework for considering the retrieval of information at different levels of abstraction or generality is the *path-of-least-resistance model* (Ward, 1994, 1995; Ward, Dodds, Saunders, & Sifonis, 2000; Ward, Patterson, Sifonis, Dodds, & Saunders, 2002). The model states that, when people develop new ideas for a particular domain, the predominant tendency is to access fairly specific, basic-level exemplars from that domain as starting points, and to project many of the stored properties of the instances onto the novel ideas being developed. For example, in devising a new sport, the predicted predominant tendency would be for people to retrieve specific known instances of sports, such as baseball and football, and to pattern the new sport after those instances. Following the path is expected to result in reduced originality of the new ideas, in contrast to other more abstract approaches to accessing knowledge. On the other hand, there may be benefits to relying on specific instances in terms of the practicality or feasibility of the new ideas.

The path of least resistance is similar to, and largely consistent with, the associationist view of creativity (e.g., Mednick, 1962) in that it suggests that some items are likely to come to mind in a given situation more readily than others, but it also differs in emphasis. First, it focuses specifically on the internal structure of categories, that is, the hierarchical, taxonomic relations between a category and its various members (e.g., between fruit and apple) rather than the more thematic (e.g., needle and thread), opposite (hot and cold), or lexical-phrase (blue cheese) types of associations that have typically been discussed as part of the association approach. Second, the path of least resistance is more concerned with normative patterns across individuals than with individual differences in the steepness of association hierarchies. Finally, the emphasis in the path of least resistance is on using representativeness to predict the likelihood of a person relying on a given exemplar in a creative generation task rather than on the idea that more remote responses are, per se, more original. Basing an imaginary fruit on a less representative instance, such as a kumquat, could well yield a product that would be rated as more novel than one based on a more representative instance, such as an apple, but that is not a *necessary* prediction from the path of least resistance.

There are interesting anecdotal/historical accounts that reveal the possible constraints imposed by relying on specific known instances as well as the possible advantages. For example, in the 1830s, when passenger rail travel was just getting started in the United States, designers seem to have patterned the first railway passenger cars directly on horse-drawn stagecoaches of the day, including the fact that conductors had to sit on the outside of the car (White, 1978). This approach was efficient in the sense that railway passenger cars became available quickly, but because the conductors were seated on the outside, several of them fell off and were killed. Thus, a property of an existing domain instance that was unnecessary and potentially harmful was nevertheless carried over into the new idea being developed. As another example, anyone who has had to scroll down and then back up in reading a pdf version of a journal article in a format that mimics the two-column arrangement of its hard-copy counterpart knows that the copying of that exact format into electronic form is less than optimal from the point of view of the reader. The two-column format works well when one need only move one's eyes from the bottom of one column to the top of the next on a page. But, in an electronic format, unless one has a giant screen, the top of the second column disappears as one scrolls to the bottom of the first column, requiring a scroll back up to continue. Thus, a property of the old format (hard copy) was carried over to the new format (electronic) when it might have been more helpfully left behind.

In the cases mentioned in the previous paragraph, accessing and relying on specific exemplars of earlier knowledge got in the way of innovation. However, there is ample evidence from historical accounts that many nonproblematic advances in a wide range of domains also were based on a slow incremental process of patterning new ideas after very specific earlier ones (see, e.g., Basalla, 1988; Ward et al. 1995). An example noted by Basalla is the close connection between Eli Whitney's Cotton Gin, designed to separate the seeds from the cotton fiber, and a previously existing device, the charka, which performed a similar function. Another example is that Edison's light bulb was a close variant on preexisting designs of which Edison was cognizant (Friedel, Israel, & Finn, 1986). The approach of relying heavily on specific existing products in developing new ones may favor practicality over extreme, but potentially impractical, originality.

To approximate real-world creative endeavors of the type described in the previous section, researchers have devised several laboratory techniques in which participants are required to develop more complete creative products than in typical divergent-thinking tasks. Such open-ended products have included collages (Amabile, 1982), stories, and drawings based on specific prompts (Lubart & Sternberg, 1995), designs for novel toys (Smith, Ward, & Schumacher, 1993), sketches and descriptions of possible extraterrestrials or other imagined entities (Ward, 1994), inventions for various domains (Finke, 1990), and logos for new products (Jaarsveldt & van Leeuwen, 2005), among many others. The productions are generally rated for their creativity, originality, and practicality as well as for the pres-

ence of other specific types of properties. However, the ratings themselves are not the main issue. Rather, they are used primarily as markers to provide evidence about the combinations of external and internal factors that influence creative performance, as well as the cognitive processes and structures that are most commonly used and that are associated with more or less creative outcomes.

Laboratory research findings using these types of creative generation paradigms mirror the real-world phenomena. First, there is the general finding that, when given the task of devising a new domain instance, people develop products that bear a striking similarity to known domain instances. For example, when asked to envision animals on other planets, the vast majority of college students produce descriptions and drawings that resemble typical Earth-animals, including such pervasive properties as eyes, legs, and bilateral symmetry (Ward, 1994), and they do so even when given instructions that encourage more originality (Ward & Sifonis, 1997). In addition, just as the innovators noted previously seem to have been influenced by examples they were exposed to (e.g., stagecoaches, light-bulb designs, the charka), so too are individuals in laboratory studies found to copy features of examples they are exposed to (Marsh, Landau, & Hicks, 1996; Marsh, Ward, & Landau, 1999; Sifonis, Ward, Gentner, & Houska, 1997; Smith, Ward, & Schumacher, 1993), and they do so even when features of the examples are identified as being problematic (Jansson & Smith, 1991). It appears that innovation can be constrained by chronically accessible domain instances as well as those made more accessible through recent exposure.

This tendency to base novel entities on specific, basic-level exemplars has also been shown for the domains of fruit and tools (Ward et al., 2002). In addition, although investigators have not always assessed their participants' approaches to creative idea generation, the tendency of novel ideas to be structured in predictable ways by existing conceptual frameworks is a robust one that has also been observed in young children (Cacciari, Levorato, & Cicogna, 1997; Karmiloff-Smith, 1990), gifted adolescents (Ward, Saunders, & Dodds, 1999), science-fiction authors (Ward, 1994), design engineers (Condoor, Brock, & Burger, 1993), and other creative individuals (Ward, 1995; Ward et al., 1995). The phenomenon has also been shown to extend to a variety of conceptual domains, such as imaginary coins (Rubin & Kontis, 1983) and faces (Bredart, Ward, & Marczewski, 1998). Thus, it is reasonable to assume that the tendency to retrieve and rely on basic level domain instances is a general one underlying this broad range of structured imagination phenomena (Ward, 1994, 1995).

Subsequent studies have also revealed the impact of several different aspects of conceptual structures. For example, Ward (1994) explored the influence of correlated attributes as a structuring principle in creative imagination. Traditional studies on categorization have shown that certain groups of features tend to occur together in natural, real-world categories (e.g., Rosch, Mervis, Gray, Johnson, & Boyes–Braem, 1976). For instance, in animal categories, the feature "wings" tends to occur more often with "feathers" than with "fur." To determine whether similar types of feature correlations would occur in creative exemplar generation, Ward had subjects imagine and draw animals from a planet described as being completely different from Earth, and different groups were told either that the creature had feathers, scales, or fur, or they were given no information about its attributes.

The participants in the "feather" condition were significantly more likely to include wings and beaks as additional features, whereas those in the "scales" condition were significantly more likely to include fins and gills, relative to those in the "fur" or control conditions. Self-reports collected after subjects created their animals indicated that they tended to base them on particular instances of known birds, fish, or mammals, in the feather, scales, and fur conditions, respectively. Thus, the different instructions led to the retrieval of different instances of earth animals, whose properties were then mapped onto the novel entities.

Laboratory findings also reveal some of the properties of existing conceptual structure that are most influential in guiding the form of new ideas. For the three distinct conceptual domains of animals, fruit, and tools, Ward et al. (2002) had separate groups of college students perform a noncreative task of listing all of the domain instances they could think of, and a creative task of imagining, drawing, and describing novel instances of those categories that might exist on another planet. Data from the listing task were used to derive a measure of representativeness, namely, Output Dominance, or the number of participants who listed any given exemplar. Exemplars listed by more people can be taken as more representative of the domain. In the creative-imagination task, after producing their novel products, participants described the kinds of things they used as the basis for their ideas, and references to specific domain exemplars (e.g., dogs, hammers, oranges) were tabulated to derive a measure of Imagination Frequency for each exemplar. The more people who reported relying on a particular exemplar in the creative task, the higher the Imagination Frequency, and the more that exemplar can be seen as influencing creative generation.

Additional research supporting the value of avoiding readily accessible instances and accessing more abstract levels of representation reveals that people can be induced to adopt more abstract approaches in conceptual expansion tasks and that they develop more original creations as a result (Ward, Patterson, & Sifonis, 2004). For example, participants who were asked to imagine life on other planets developed more original designs when they were asked to consider abstract attributes of living things (e.g., need for nutrition to support biological processes) than when they were asked to keep in mind specific Earth animals or were given no special instructions (Ward et al., 2004). Similarly, procedures that preclude reliance on the most readily accessible specific solutions by imposing constraints have been shown to increase originality (Moreau & Dahl, 2005).

Although accessing abstract information, in contrast to relying on specific domain instances, is linked to greater originality, it is essential to consider another important ingredient of innovative ideas, namely, their usefulness or practicality in meeting the need at hand. A recent study suggests that reliance on specific instances may be more beneficial in terms of practicality. In particular, when participants were given the task of devising new sports, those who reported relying on specific known sports developed ideas that were rated as more playable than those developed by individuals who reported other, more abstract approaches (Ward, 2008). More generally, originality and playability were significantly negatively correlated. To create a scenario to illustrate why that might be true, consider, for example, that "ball" might be part of the representation of the specific sport of "basketball," whereas "object contended for" might be the comparable abstract feature in the higher-level concept "sport." A new sport patterned on the former might include the very practical object of a ball, whereas one patterned on the latter might include an original but less sensible object that teams contend for, with the result that it would be judged less playable. In either case, an attribute from the accessed concept is projected onto the new situation, but one fosters practicality whereas the other fosters originality.

Thus, even though individuals who naturally adopt more abstract approaches to creative generation tasks, or who are encouraged via experimental manipulations to do so (e.g., Ward et al., 2004) produce more original outcomes, that originality may come at a cost of practicality (Ward, 2008). It should be noted that originality and practicality (in the sense of appeal to consumers) are not always negatively correlated (e.g., Dahl & Moreau, 2002). Nevertheless, both properties need to be considered in assessing the relative merits of reliance on specific instances versus more abstract levels of knowledge.

In the Ward (2008) study, participants also rated their own knowledge about sports and took a brief test of sport knowledge.

Sport knowledge was found to be significantly positively correlated with the rated playability of the sports they developed. That is, the more knowledgeable individuals appear to have been better able to exploit their knowledge in service of devising ideas for sports that others might actually like to play.

Far from rejecting existing knowledge, idea generation in service of innovation requires its judicious use. Whether more specific or more abstract knowledge will be most helpful may depend on the relative value assigned to originality or practicality in the project being undertaken, but it is likely that in most cases accessing multiple levels of abstraction will be helpful. In the next section, I sketch some properties of a tool that might aid in that access.

Although one might have assumed that the accessibility of exemplars was reasonably stable, evidence actually points to the fact that it is dynamic and changeable, at least within limits. For one thing, when people list category exemplars in two separate sessions one week apart, correlations between responses are positive and large enough that the listing procedure would be thought of as a reliable measure of a consistent internal structure, but they are far from perfect, indicating that the relative accessibility of any given item is not identical across experimental settings (e.g., Bellezza, 1984). In addition, exposure to exemplars early in an experimental session has been shown to increase their likelihood of being listed in a subsequent exemplar-listing task (e.g., Graf, Shimamura, & Squire, 1985). Furthermore, primed increases in accessibility have functional consequences, such as increases in false recall (e.g., Smith, Ward, Tindell, Sifonis, & Wilkenfeld, 2000).

The fact that the accessibility of exemplars can be manipulated has been used to establish a more direct causal link between that property and performance in creative tasks. Ward and Wickes (2009) used a pleasantness rating task to prime particular exemplars of fruit and tools, and examined the extent to which those primed items were used in a creative generation task. After exposure to some items from each category in that rating task, participants generated imaginary instances from those domains and reported retrospectively on the factors that influenced their creations. The basic finding was that for both conceptual domains, people were more likely to base their imagined creations on exemplars that had been presented in the rating task than exemplars that had not been presented in that task. The finding extends previous research showing that the information used in creative generation can be *predicted* on the basis of accessibility data. The information used can also be *controlled*, at least to some extent, by manipulating the accessibility of category items in a prior task

To summarize, research using the creative-cognition convergence approach does reveal that the findings from laboratory studies converge with anecdotal accounts. There is a general tendency to rely on specific domain instances in developing new products, and that tendency is associated with more originality, but less practicality.

Conceptual Combination

A particular domain general process interest in explicating creativity is conceptual combination, a process whereby previously separate ideas, concepts, or other forms are mentally merged. The elements to be combined can be words, concepts, visual forms, and other simple elements, or at a more abstract level, they can be hypothetical scientific constructs, musical styles, artistic genres, and so on. Whether in science, technology, art, music, literature, or other creative realms, combinations are seen as stimulants to creativity, and they have been mentioned frequently in historical accounts of creative accomplishments (e.g., Rothenberg, 1979; Thagard, 1984; Ward, 2001; Ward et al., 1995). Rothenberg in particular has argued that simultaneously entertaining or integrating two opposing ideas, a process termed Janusian thinking, underlies creative acts as diverse as the paintings of da Vinci, the symphonies of Mozart, and the scien-

tific reasoning of Einstein. In addition, combining concepts is a crucial component in several process models of creative functioning (e.g., Davidson & Sternberg, 1985; Mumford, Mobley, Uhlman, Reiter-Palmon, & Doares, 1991; Sternberg, 1988), and because the capacity to interpret and produce combinations is a fundamental one that underlies our use of language, it has been the focus of intense scrutiny by cognitive psychologists (see e.g., Costello & Keane, 2000; Gagne, 2000; Hampton, 1987, 1997; Murphy, 1988; Wisniewski, 1997a, 1997b).

Combination is directly relevant as a process underlying creativity because combinations are not mere summations of the elements being merged. Instead, they can yield *emergent features*. That is, combinations can produce or make salient properties that are either absent from or very low in salience for the representations of either of their components elements. Even a simple combination, such as "pet bird," might include an emergent property, namely, "talks," which would not typically be thought of as an attribute of "pets" or "birds" in general.

A more intriguing example of the power of combining simple concepts taken from the realm of literature is the case of Stephen Donaldson, a noted fantasy writer, who attributed the inspiration for his series on *Thomas Covenant, The Unbeliever* to the combined concepts of *unbelief* and *leprosy*. Unbelief is an unwillingness to accept the possibility of alternatives to our observed physical reality. Donaldson had wanted to write a story about unbelief but was stymied until he combined that concept with the disease of leprosy, at which point his "brain took fire" (Donaldson, 1992). The reason it was so powerful a combination for Donaldson is that his knowledge of leprosy told him that a person with leprosy would be extremely vigilant to detect unsensed but potentially life-threatening injuries and would be loath to accept the reality of a fantasy world, even one in which he had a hero's status and apparent relief from the disease. The dynamic tension between Covenant's need for continued self-vigilance and the attraction of the fantasy world sets the stage for a powerful series of books.

Donaldson went on to note that combinations of exotic and familiar concepts were particularly potent for him, echoing the view from other historical and anecdotal observations that discrepant and even opposing combinations hold the most potential for creativity (see e.g., Rothenberg, 1979). A question for creative cognition is whether or not the power of combinations, particularly those composed of dissimilar or opposing pairs, to produce emergent ideas can be demonstrated in a laboratory study with nonexpert participants.

As a source of converging evidence of the emergent power of combinations, a wide range of laboratory studies have asked participants to define, interpret, list properties of, or otherwise process novel or familiar combinations or conjunctions of concepts. Although many of the studies have been concerned primarily with language processing, a persistent phenomenon relevant to understanding creativity is that emergent properties appear in the combinations that were either nonevident or completely absent from either of the constituents of the combination. So, for example, Harvard-educated carpenters are sometimes deemed to be nonmaterialistic, whereas neither Harvard-educated people nor carpenters alone are so characterized (Kunda, Miller, & Claire, 1990). Likewise, culturally anomalous combinations, such as Republican social worker (see e.g., Hastie, Schroeder, & Weber, 1990), and truly exotic conjunctions, such as furniture that is also fruit (Hampton, 1997), lead to emergent properties not characteristic of the separate elements of the combination. One interpretation of the findings is that participants have to generate explanations or otherwise reconcile the discrepancies of the component concepts, which leads them to postulate novel properties. Although these studies did not require participants to develop stories, much like Donaldson's "unbelieving leper," the more discrepant combinations seem to suggest more creative possibilities than more stereotypic combinations (e.g., Harvard-educated lawyer).

Estes and Ward (2002) provided evidence directly consistent with Rothenberg's suggestion about Janusian thinking. They had a sample of college students interpret various types of adjective-noun combinations. Of most interest, when the adjectives and nouns were opposing in meaning (e.g., healthy illness), the participants' interpretations contained more emergent properties than when the terms represented more typical pairings (e.g., harmful illness). A healthy illness, for example, might be one that temporarily incapacitates its victim, thereby preventing the person from engaging in some activity that could have resulted in more harm (e.g., taking a fateful trip). A harmful illness, by contrast, is just one that causes some harm to the body – not a particularly novel construct.

Additional laboratory research also reveals that concepts need not be specifically opposite or contradictory in meaning to provoke emergence. Instead, more generally, the dissimilarity of the components of a combination determines the extent to which they will yield emergent properties (Wilkenfeld & Ward, 2001). In the Wilkenfeld and Ward study, participants interpreted combinations that varied in similarity, and the number of emergent features was assessed. The college-student participants were given 16 pairs of words and asked to write two separate definitions of each. Eight of the pairs were composed of similar concepts (e.g., guitar harp) and eight were composed of dissimilar concepts (e.g., airplane puddle). Because definitions alone would not be expected to reveal a large number of attributes that people deemed to be true of the combined concepts, participants were also asked to list features that something would need in order to be considered a good instance of the defined concept. The set of features could then be used to determine whether there are novel properties that emerge from combining the concepts and whether they are more pervasive in dissimilar combinations.

To provide the needed features for assessing emergence, a separate group of participants listed the characteristic features of each of the separate concepts that comprised the 16 similar and dissimilar combinations. The participants were asked to list at least six features that describe each word. Features mentioned by even one person were noted in order to produce a list of features of the component concepts that was as comprehensive as possible. The resulting database contained more than 11,000 features. Features were considered to be emergent if they were in the list for a combination but not for either of its constituent concepts alone.

Consistent with the expectations regarding the role of constituent similarity, Wilkenfeld and Ward found that dissimilar combinations resulted in more emergent properties than similar combinations. They also found that second interpretations resulted in more emergent properties, especially for similar pairs, indicating that people may use up their easiest interpretation first and then engage in more creative exploration to produce a second interpretation. Thus, the laboratory results confirm and extend the anecdotal accounts.

Combination processes also include more than just interpreting noun-noun or adjective-noun combinations, and laboratory studies have been devised to examine various combinatorial processes. For example, sometimes combination involves figuring out how to integrate sets of objects that ordinarily are not grouped together into a single coherent concept. Mobley, Doares, and Mumford (1992) used a paradigm to approximate that type of combination process, in which participants were given four exemplars from each of three categories (e.g., furniture: chair, couch, table, stool) and had to develop concepts to explain the grouping of all of them together. They were to label, define, and list new exemplars of the combined category. In some problems, the three starting categories were closely related, and in others they were not. When the component objects were more dissimilar, people generated more original outcomes, but the outcomes were also judged to be of lower quality. Apparently, then, as with the results of studies already described,

the need to integrate more discrepant pieces of information provided a boost to originality, though not necessarily to overall quality. As with studies in the creative-generation section of this paper, the findings point to the need for ratings of products along multiple dimensions, including the key creativity ingredients of originality and practicality.

Creative combination in real-world settings also includes combining of larger knowledge structures. Importantly, Scott, Lonergan, and Mumford (2005) have also shown that this type of paradigm can be extended to examine combinations of more complex structures. In that study, college students were asked to combine information from descriptions of education programs to develop their own ideas for curricula.

Mumford's work is also important in that it reveals that the outcome of conceptual combination depends on what people are instructed to consider. Considering shared attributes across the exemplars appears to be more effective for closely related concepts, whereas considering more metaphoric kinds of interpretations is effective with discrepant ones (Mumford, Baughman, Maher, Costanza, & Supinski, 1997). This makes sense because related concepts share many attributes, whereas discrepant ones do not, and integrating them may require people to go beyond ordinary meanings toward more metaphoric ones.

Research also shows that a combination does not have to involve verbal units at all to be a stimulus for creativity. Merging visually presented abstract forms, for example, can also lead to emergent new ideas. Rothenberg and Sobel (1980) showed that participants who viewed two images superimposed on one another created metaphors that were rated as more creative than those produced by participants who saw the same images next to one another. Finke (1990) also showed that people who mentally combined randomly selected visual forms were able to develop ideas for inventions and discoveries for a variety of domains under a wide range of procedures. Although superimposed or merged images do not always lead to more creative outcomes (e.g., Sobel & Rothenberg,

1980), the results are suggestive that combined images can, at least under some circumstances, be a stimulus to originality.

Finke's (1990) research also reveals important information about the conditions that can facilitate or impede creativity when people combine visual forms. Participants were given sets of three geometric forms and were asked to mentally integrate them into more complex ones that could be interpreted as inventions or new products for domains, such as furniture, vehicles, or tools (see also Roskos-Ewoldsen, Intons-Peterson, & Anderson, 1993). When they chose the category or were assigned a category in advance of generating the form, they produced fewer creative inventions (rated as original and practical by judges) than when the relevant category was specified only after they developed the forms. There seem to be creative benefits of combining visual materials without a specific goal in mind and then later interpreting them in an exploratory phase of processing.

Analogy

The intense focus on retrieval at abstract and specific levels and on conceptual combination should not be taken as an indicator that it is those processes that are the only sources of novel ideas. Another process with a special link to creativity that has also undergone careful experimental examination is analogical reasoning or transfer, the application or projection of structured knowledge from a familiar domain to a novel or less familiar one (see, e.g., Gentner, Holyoak, & Kokinov, 2001; Holyoak & Thagard, 1995).

Commonly cited examples of analogy in creative endeavors abound, such as Rutherford's use of a solar system as a model for how the hydrogen atom was structured, and Robbins, Laurents, Bernstein, and Sondheim's adaptation of Shakespeare's *Romeo and Juliet* to the context of a 1950's New York City gang conflict in *West Side Story*. Meticulous case studies have also detailed the role of analogy in major creative accomplishments, such as Kepler's reasoning about planetary motion (Gentner et al., 1997), Edison's development of an electric light distribution system (Basala, 1988; Friedel et al., 1986), and the Wright brothers' efforts to craft a workable flying machine (Crouch, 1992). Not surprisingly, then, analogy has been a key ingredient in proposals for enhancing creativity (e.g., Gordon, 1961) and has been listed as a component process in cognitive-process models of creativity (e.g., Finke et al., 1992).

The transformational power of analogies derives, at least in part, from the fact that good analogies connect the familiar and novel domains at very deep levels, not merely at the surface (e.g., Gentner, 1983, 1989; Gentner & Toupin, 1986). Consider the solar system/atom analogy. It means that, just as planets orbit around a more massive central body, the sun, electrons may orbit around a more massive central body, the nucleus. But the nucleus and electrons do not resemble the sun and planets in any superficial way. The nucleus of an atom does not appear yellow like the sun, nor does it have a high surface temperature. The electrons are not as big as planets. What matters is that there are corresponding objects that bear particular relations to one another. Likewise, New York City of the 1950s did not have to resemble Verona of centuries earlier, and Maria did not have to look or dress like Juliet. What mattered is that two young people were in love, but were also connected to larger groups that were in conflict with one another.

As with conceptual combination, there are various manifestations of analogy and multiple purposes to which analogies might be put. The most obvious purpose is applying the knowledge from one domain as a kind of model to help in understanding or developing ideas in another domain, but another purpose is to communicate a new idea to others in a concise, understandable way. Dunbar's (1997) on-line observations of the reasoning of intact molecular-biology lab groups, for example, led him to conclude that analogies between distant domains (e.g., solar system/atom) are quite rare, and that many creative advances are instead the result of analogies between close conceptual domains (e.g., between two different viruses). Specifically, Dunbar found that, out of 99 analogies observed, only 2 could be characterized as mapping knowledge between distant domains, that is, between the organism of interest to the lab and some nonbiological domain. The others were all analogies using comparisons within the same organism under consideration or between two different organisms. Furthermore, the two nonbiological analogies were not used to develop an understanding of something, but instead served a more communicative goal of explaining something.

An important implication of the Dunbar findings is that anecdotal accounts of the use of distant analogies to facilitate discovery may be overblown. They may instead be used more in service of communicating an idea than in formulating it. In effect, a "convergence" approach yielded a "divergent" result. In any case, the findings show that advances in understanding creative activities are more likely to come from using evidence from multiple methods than from the application of one type of method to the exclusion of others.

Dunbar went on to argue that distant analogies may be developed subsequent to a major discovery and serve as a means of communicating the new concept to others. So, for example, Rutherford may not have gotten the idea for how an atom might be structured by considering the structure of the solar system. Rather, he may have chosen that analogy as way of describing his idea, which had its origins in some other source. The right analogy can be very persuasive, as, for example, when proponents of intervention in the Gulf War compared the situation to the early days of World War II, and warned about the dangers of appeasement.

Research using such online methods also makes it clear that the picture is not as simple as one might think. In particular, Christensen and Schunn (2007) examined the functioning of design engineers working on a design project within a firm noted for its creative accomplishments. The par-

ticular group whose meetings were examined had the task of developing completely new features for the product that was being designed. In contrast to Dunbar's results, Christensen and Schunn found distant analogies to occur as commonly as near analogies. In addition, although distant analogies were used for explanation, as in the Dunbar work, they were also used for problem solving, a function much more linked to the creative process itself and not just an after-the-fact account of the process. Thus, the use of the in vivo method has helped draw attention to the idea that the use of various processes and their value in those endeavors depends on the type of creative task involved.

Problem Formulation

There is, of course, more to being creative than combining concepts, using analogies, and applying other transformational processes. At least since the groundbreaking work of Csikszentmihalyi and Getzels (1971) showing a link between the exploratory activities of artists and the quality of their subsequent creations, creativity researchers have been sensitive to the idea that the way people formulate problems or tasks is an important component of the creative process. Several models of creativity include steps such as problem construction, problem definition, and problem discovery (see, e.g., Basadur, 1994, 1997; Mumford et al., 1991; Runco & Chand, 1994, 1995; Sternberg, 1988; Treffinger, Isaksen, & Dorval, 1994). Implicit or explicit in these models is the belief that the way people conceptualize a problem strongly influences their likelihood of achieving an original or creative solution.

By distinguishing between processes associated with initial problem formulation and subsequent procedures, such models draw attention to the fact that creativity may be more than just problem solving. Particularly in real-world settings, in which people are confronted with ill-defined tasks, creative behavior requires several steps. Generally, innovators are not simply handed clearly delineated problems, which they then begin to solve. Instead, doing something creative often requires people to construct, formulate, or otherwise define the problem or task to be accomplished, to retrieve from memory or seek out relevant information, and to generate and evaluate potential courses of action.

Mumford, Reiter-Palmon, and Redmond (1994) provided experimental evidence that engaging in problem formulation increases the quality and originality of problem solutions. They had college students perform a creative-generation task in which they were to develop a marketing survey and advertisements for a fictitious product. Students in a problem-construction condition were instructed to a) list important factors to consider, and b) restate the problem prior to engaging in the task, whereas those in the no-problem construction condition were not. Importantly, those in the former condition produced ideas that were higher in quality and originality than those in the latter condition. Mumford et al. suggested that problem-construction activities allowed students to consider a range of options rather than jump at the first idea that came to mind.

Culture, Language, and Concepts

The discussion of cognitive processes has, to this point, been culture-centric in the sense that it has assumed that the conceptual processes and structures involved are universal ones. However, because culture and language are linked to conceptual functioning, the creative-cognition approaches must begin to include not just normative looks at how concepts are utilized in a given task, as shown in the work considered in previous sections, but also how individuals with diverse backgrounds process the same information differently. Here we illustrate the point with a consideration of taxonomic versus thematic ways of conceptualizing (e.g., Markman & Hutchinson, 1984).

A taxonomic mode of organizing the world is based on "decontextualized" reasoning where the relationship between objects is not important but their category membership or the similarity of their attributes is. A thematic mode, on the other hand, is based on "contextualized" reasoning where causal, spatial, or temporal relationships between the objects are more important than the individual objects or the hierarchical categories of which they are members. Consider a cup, a plate, and some milk. Which two of the three entities go together best conceptually or are most closely related? A taxonomic way of organizing information might link the cup and plate because they are both in the category of "tableware," whereas a thematic mode of thought might link the cup and milk based on the relational notion that the milk goes in the cup.

The specific types of ideas that occur to individuals in developing novel products can reasonably be expected to differ depending on which of these modes of thought they use. The work considered in this chapter so far, showing that people tend to retrieve and rely on highly accessible category instances when they develop new ideas, implicitly assumes that people are largely oriented toward and concerned with taxonomic, categorical types of information. If they were all adults from Western cultures and, in particular, from the United States, then that might be a safe assumption. However, there is compelling evidence that individuals with different cultural backgrounds do not always organize information that way, and may well prefer to think in terms of thematic relations among objects rather than their categorical membership (Nisbett, Peng, Choi, & Norenzayan, 2001). In other words, what have been taken as universal characteristics of the operation of basic category processes in creativity may be more narrowly limited to individuals from specific cultures. Consequently, studies of creative cognition need to focus on cultural and other differences in the way individuals conceptualize the entities under consideration, how those differences affect the ideas that they generate, and how variations across individuals affect ultimate outcomes.

Nisbett et al. (2001) reviewed research demonstrating that participants from American samples usually attend to objects' properties (e.g., perceptual properties) and use a taxonomic approach to categorization, whereas participants from East Asian samples attend to the relationship between the objects and use a thematic approach. There is also evidence for other variations between American and Asian samples in basic cognitive processing, including the use of formal logic versus experiential knowledge, a preference for rules versus family resemblance for structuring categories, and a reliance on category membership in guiding inductive inference. How those variations relate to the outcomes of creative endeavors has not received empirical attention but must be considered for a complete picture to emerge.

Pragmatically, it is also important to know whether the types of variations in processing that have been observed are more linked to culture or to language. Ji, Zhang, and Nisbett (2004) conducted a study designed to reveal the degree to which language and culture respectively affect the choice of the reasoning strategy in categorization. In their study, the researchers used American monolinguals and two types of East Asian bilinguals: *compound*, who tend to acquire their second language early and in the same context as their first; versus *coordinate*, who tend to acquire their second language later and in a different context.

To examine the roles that language and culture play in categorization, Ji et al. (2004) used a verbal categorization task that consisted of triads of words with participants being asked to select the two out of three that were most closely related. This task was chosen because it allowed the researchers to see whether participants' would be inclined to make taxonomic choice, such as *monkey* and *panda*, or thematic choices, such as *monkey* and *bananas*. In an attempt to separate the language effect from the culture effect, the researchers administered this task to bilingual participants in both their native language (L1) and English (L2). The authors reasoned that if bilingual participants consistently use a thematic approach regardless of the testing language, it would constitute evidence of the cultural influence on

their reasoning, whereas if their preference for the thematic approach was less obvious when they were tested in English, it would be evidence of the language influence. It was anticipated that the language effect would be observed for coordinate bilinguals but not for compound bilinguals because the former may have two separate cognitive representations for their two languages, whereas compound bilinguals may have a single common one. All of the original hypotheses were supported by the results of the study, and the performance of the East Asians showed a robust cultural effect regardless of the language in which they were tested. East Asian participants consistently categorized objects based on relationships between them, whereas American participants grouped objects based on the similarity of attributes that the objects possessed. The fact that a cultural effect was found when bilinguals were tested in both L1 and L2 means that differences between East Asians and Americans are not caused merely by differences in the languages in which they are tested. However, when coordinate bilinguals were tested in their native language, they based their groupings primarily on relationships, whereas when they were tested in English, this tendency was weaker. This means that besides a strong cultural effect, there was also a language effect that was observed for coordinate bilinguals. No language effect was found for compound bilinguals. The fact that coordinate bilinguals used a thematic approach more often when tested in their native language led the authors to suggest that the language of testing had a priming effect on the participants. In other words, having to read and write in Chinese activated the thematic character of the objects bilinguals were presented with and doing the same in English activated the taxonomic properties of objects.

There have been differences observed between Chinese and American individuals in performance on some of the types of tasks considered in this chapter as well as on a range of other creativity-relevant beliefs and behaviors (e.g., Lau, Hui, & Ng, 2004; Niu & Sternberg, 2001, 2002). For example, Niu and Sternberg (2001) found that Chinese college students generated imagined aliens that were rated as less original than those generated by American college students. The reasons for the discrepancy are not certain, and it is clear that the advantage does not always go to individuals from western cultures, but regardless of the pattern of similarities and differences, attention to similarities and differences in basic conceptual processes may yield important insights into the phenomenon.

Other Processes and a Path to Progress

A host of other processes that have been investigated by cognitive psychologists also have the potential to serve creative purposes. These include the reorganization of existing category knowledge to form ad hoc or goal-derived categories to meet a particular need (e.g., Barsalou, 1983, 1991; Mumford et al., 1994), metaphoric interpretation, which can yield emergent properties (e.g., Tourangeau & Rips, 1991), reasoning from unexpected observations (Dunbar, 1997), and the constructive forgetting of interfering information during incubation (e.g., Smith, 1995). In spite of the progress made in understanding these processes and the ones considered in more detail in the present chapter, much remains to be done to understand the cognition of creativity. Applying a convergence approach and bringing together the ecological validity of real-world examples with the experimental rigor of cognitive-science research can provide the path to continued progress on this important goal.

References

Amabile, T. M. (1982). Social psychology of creativity: A consensual assessment technique. *Journal of Personality and Social Psychology*, 43, 997–1013

Amabile, T. M. (1983a). *The social psychology of creativity*. New York: Springer-Verlag.

Amabile, T. M. (1983b). Social psychology of creativity: A componential conceptualization. *Journal of Personality and Social Psychology*, 45, 357–377.

Barker, J. (1993). *Paradigms: The business of discovering the future*, New York: HarperBusiness.

Barsalou, L. W. (1983). Ad hoc categories. *Memory & Cognition*, 11, 211–227.

Barsalou, L. W. (1985). Ideals, central tendency, and frequency of instantiation. *Journal of Experimental Psychology: Learning, Memory, and Cognition*, 11, 629–654.

Barsalou, L. W. (1991). Deriving categories to achieve goals. In G. H. Bower (Ed.), *The psychology of learning and motivation: Advances in research and theory* (Vol. 27, pp. 1–64). New York: Academic Press.

Basadur, M. (1994). Managing the creative process in organizations. In M. A. Runco (Ed.), *Problem finding, problem solving, and creativity* (pp. 237–268). Norwood, NJ: Ablex.

Basalla, G. (1988). *The evolution of technology*. London: Cambridge University Press.

Baughman, W. A., & Mumford, M. D. (1995). Process-analytic models of creative capacities: Operations influencing the combination and reorganization processes. *Creativity Research Journal*, 8, 37–62.

Beghetto, R. A., & Kaufman, J. C. (2007). Toward a broader conception of creativity: The case for "mini-c" creativity. *Psychology of Aesthetics, Creativity, and the Arts*, 2, 73–79.

Bredart, S., Ward, T. B., & Marczewski, P. (1998). Structured imagination of novel creatures' faces. *American Journal of Psychology*, 111, 607–725.

Bellezza, F. S. (1984). Reliability of retrieval from semantic memory: Common categories. *Bulletin of the Psychonomic Society*, 22, 3324–326.

Cacciari, C., Levorato, M. C., & Cicogna, P. (1997). Imagination at work: Conceptual and linguistic creativity in children. In T. B. Ward, S. M. Smith, & J. Vaid (Eds.), *Creative thought: An investigation of conceptual structures and processes* (pp. 145–177). Washington, DC: American Psychological Association.

Christensen, B. T., & Schunn, C. D. (2007). The relationship of analogical distance to analogical function and pre-inventive structure: The case of engineering design. *Memory & Cognition*, 35, 29–38.

Collins, M. A., & Amabile, T. M. (1999). Motivation and creativity. In R. J. Sternberg (Ed.), *Handbook of creativity* (pp. 297–312). Cambridge: Cambridge University Press.

Condoor, S. S., Brock, H. R., & Burger, C. P. (1993, June). *Innovation through early recognition of critical design parameters.* Paper presented at the meeting of the American Society for Engineering Education, Urbana, IL.

Costello, F. J., & Keane, M. T. (2000). Efficient creativity: Constraint guided conceptual combination. *Cognitive Science,* 24, 299–349

Cropley, A. J. (1999). Creativity and cognition: producing effective novelty. *Roeper Review,* 21(4), 253–265.

Crouch, T. D. (1992). Why Wilbur and Orville? Some thoughts on the Wright brothers and the process of invention. In R. J. Weber & D. N. Perkins (Eds.), *Inventive minds* (pp. 80–92), London: Oxford University Press.

Csikszentmihalyi, M. (1996). *Creativity: Flow and the psychology of discovery and invention.* New York: Haper Collins.

Csikszentmihalyi, M. (1998). Reflections on the field. *Roeper Review,* 21, 80–81.

Csikszentmihalyi, M. (1999). Implications of a systems perspective for the study of creativity. In R. J. Sternberg (Ed.), *Handbook of creativity* (pp. 313–335). Cambridge: Cambridge University Press.

Csikzentmihalyi, M., & Getzels, J. W. (1971). Discovery-oriented behavior and the originality of creative products: A study with artists. *Journal of Personality and Social Psychology,* 19, 47–52.

Dahl, D., & Moreau, P. (2002). The influence and value of analogical thinking during new product ideation. *Journal of Marketing Research,* 39, 47–60

Davidson, J. E., & Sternberg, R. J. (1985). Competence and performance in intellectual development. In E. Neimark, R. de Lisi, & J. H. Newman (Eds.), *Moderators of competence* (pp. 43–76). Hillsdale, NJ: Erlbaum.

Donaldson, S. R. (1992). *The real story* (Afterword). New York: Bantam Books.

Dunbar, K. (1997). How scientists think: On-line creativity and conceptual change in science. In T. B. Ward, S. M. Smith, & J. Vaid (Eds.), *Creative thought: An investigation of conceptual structures and processes* (pp. 461–494). Washington, DC: American Psychological Association.

Estes, Z., & Ward, T. B. (2002). The emergence of novel attributes in concept modification. *Creativity Research Journal,* 14, 149–156.

Eysenck, H. J. (1995). *Genius: The natural history of creativity.* Cambridge, England: Cambridge University Press.

Feldhusen, J. F. (1995). Creativity: a knowledge base, metacognitive skills, and personality factors. *Journal of Creative Behavior,* 29(4), 255–268.

Feldhusen, J. F. (2002). Creativity: the knowledge base and children. *High Ability Studies,* 13(2), 179–183.

Finke, R. A. (1990). *Creative imagery: Discoveries and inventions in visualization.* Hillsdale, NJ: Erlbaum.

Finke, R. A., Ward, T. B., & Smith, S. M. (1992). *Creative cognition: Theory, research, and applications.* Cambridge, MA: MIT Press.

Friedel, R. D., Israel, P., & Finn, B. S. (1986). *Edison's electric light: Biography of an invention.* New Brunswick, NJ: Rutgers University Press.

Gagne, C. L. (2000). Relation-based combinations versus property-based combinations: A test of the CARIN theory and the dual-process theory of conceptual combination. *Journal of Memory and Language,* 42, 365–389.

Gentner, D. (1983). Structure mapping: A theoretical framework for analogy. *Cognitive Science,* 7, 155–170.

Gentner, D. (1989). The mechanisms of analogical learning. In S. Vosniadou & A. Ortony (Eds.), *Similarity and analogical reasoning.* Cambridge: Cambridge University Press.

Gentner, D., Brem, S., Ferguson, R., Wolff, P., Markman, A. B., & Forbus, K. (1997). In T. B. Ward, S. M. Smith, & J. Vaid (Eds.), *Creative thought: An investigation of conceptual structures and processes* (pp. 403–460). Washington, DC: American Psychological Association.

Gentner, D., Holyoak, K., & Kokinov, B. (2001). *The analogical mind: Perspectives from cognitive science.* Cambridge, MA: MIT Press.

Gentner, D., & Toupin, C. (1986). Systematicity and surface similarity in the development of analogy. *Cognitive Science,* 10, 277–300

Getzels, J. W., & Csikszentmihalyi, M. (1976). *The creative vision: A longitudinal study of problem finding in art.* New York: Wiley.

Gordon, W. (1961). *Synectics: The development of creative capacity.* New York: Harper & Row.

Graf, P., Shimamura, A. P., & Squire, L. R. (1985). Priming across modalities and priming across category levels: Extending the domain of preserved function in amnesia. *Journal of Experimental Psychology: Learning, Memory, and Cognition,* 11, 386–396.

Hampton, J. A. (1987). Inheritance of attributes in natural concept conjunctions. *Memory and Cognition,* 15, 55–71.

Hampton, J. A. (1997). Emergent attributes in combined concepts. In T. B. Ward, S. M. Smith, & J. Vaid (Eds.), *Creative thought: An investigation of conceptual structures and processes* (pp. 83–110). Washington, DC: American Psychological Association.

Hastie, R., Schroeder, C., & Weber, R. (1990). Creating complex social conjunction categories from simple categories. *Bulletin of the Psychonomic Society*, 28, 242–247.

Holyoak, K., & Thagard, P. (1995). *Mental leaps: Analogy in creative thought.* Cambridge, MA: MIT Press

Ishibashi, K., & Takeshi, O. (2007). Exploring the effect of copying incomprehensible exemplars on creative drawings. In *Proceedings of the Cognitive Science Society.* Cognitive Science Society.

Jaarsveld, S., & van Leeuwen, C. (2005). Sketches from a design process: Creative cognition inferred from intermediate products. *Cognitive Science*, 29, 79–101.

Jansson, D. G., and Smith, S. M. (1991). Design fixation. *Design Studies*, 12, 3–11.

Ji, L. J., Zhang, Z., & Nisbett, R. E. (2004). Is it culture or is it language? Examination of language effects in cross-cultural research on categorization. *Journal of Personality and Social Psychology*, 87, 57–65.

Karmiloff-Smith, A. (1990). Constraints on representational change: Evidence from children's drawing. *Cognition*, 34, 57–83.

Kaufman, J. C., & Baer, J. (2005). *Creativity across domains: Faces of the muse.* Mahwah, NJ: Erlbaum.

Kaufman, J. C., & Beghetto, R. A. (2009). Beyond big and little: The Four C model of creativity. *Review of General Psychology*, 13, 1–12.

Kim, K. H. (2008). Meta-analyses of the relationship of creative achievement to both IQ and divergent thinking test scores. *Journal of Creative Behavior*, 42, 106–130.

Kunda, Z., Miller, D. T., & Claire, T. (1990). Combining social concepts: The role of causal reasoning. *Cognitive Science*, 14, 551–577.

Lau, S., Hui, A. N. N., & Ng, G. Y. C. (Eds.). (2004). *Creativity: When East meets West.* Singapore: World Scientific Publishing.

Lubart, T. I., & Sternberg, R. J. (1995). An investment approach to creativity. In S. M. Smith, T. B. Ward, & R. A. Finke (Eds.), *The creative cognition approach* (pp. 269–302). Cambridge, MA: MIT Press.

Markman, E., & Hutchinson, J. (1984). Children's sensitivity to constraints on word meaning: Taxonomic versus thematic relations. *Cognitive Psychology*, 16, 1–27.

Marsh, R. L., Landau, J. D., & Hicks, J. L. (1996). How examples may (and may not) constrain creativity. *Memory & Cognition*, 24, 669–680.

Marsh, R. L., Ward, T. B., & Landau, J. D. (1999). The inadvertent use of prior knowledge in a generative cognitive task. *Memory & Cognition*, 27, 94–105.

Mednick, S. A. (1962). The associative basis of the creative process. *Psychological Review*, 69, 220–232.

Mobley, M. I., Doares, L. M., & Mumford, M. D. (1992). Process analytic models of creative capacities: Evidence for the combination and reorganization process. *Creativity Research Journal*, 5, 125–155.

Moreau, C. P., & Dahl, D. W. (2005), Designing the solution: The impact of constraints on consumers' creativity, *Journal of Consumer Research*, 32 (1), 13–22.

Mumford, M. D., Baughman, W. A., Maher, M. A., Costanza, D. P., & Supinski, E. P. (1997). Process-based measures of creative problem-solving skills: IV. Category combination. *Creativity Research Journal*, 10, 59–71.

Mumford, M. D., Blair, C. S., & Marcy, R. T. (2006). Alternative knowledge structures in creative though. In J. C. Kaufman & J. Baer (Eds.), *Creativity and reason in cognitive development* (pp. 117–136). Cambridge: Cambridge University Press.

Mumford, M. D., & Gustafson, S. B. (1988). Creativity Syndrome: Integration, application, and innovation. *Psychological Bulletin*, 103, 27–43.

Mumford, M. D., Mobley, M. I., Uhlman, C. E., Reiter-Palmon, R., & Doares, L. M. (1991). Process analytic models of creative thought. *Creativity Research Journal*, 4, 91–122.

Mumford, M. D., Reiter-Palmon, R., & Redmond, M. R. (1994). Problem construction and cognition: Applying problem representations in ill-defined problems. In M. A. Runco (Ed.), *Problem finding, problem solving, and creativity* (pp. 3–39). Norwood, NJ: Ablex Publishing Company.

Murphy, G. L. (1988). Comprehending complex concepts. *Cognitive Science*, 12, 529–562.

Nisbett, R. E., Peng, K., Choi, I., & Norenzayan, A. (2001). Culture and systems of thought: Holistic versus analytic cognition. *Psychological Review*, 108, 291–310.

Niu, W., & Sternberg, R. J. (2001). Cultural influences on artistic creativity and its evaluation.

International Journal of Psychology, 36, 225–241.

Niu, W., & Sternberg, R. (2002). Contemporary studies on the concept of creativity: the East and the West. *Journal of Creative Behavior*, 36, 269–288.

Perkins, D. N. (1981). *The mind's best work.* Cambridge, MA: Harvard University Press.

Plucker, J. A. (1999). Is the proof in the pudding? Reanalysis of Torrance's (1958 to present) longitudinal data. *Creativity Research Journal*, 12, 103–114.

Rosch, E., Mervis, C. B., Gray, W. D., Johnson, D. M., & Boyes-Braem, P. (1976). Basic objects in natural categories. *Cognitive Psychology*, 8, 382–439.

Roskos-Ewoldsen, B., Intons-Peterson, M. J., & Anderson, R. A. (Eds.). (1993). *Imagery, creativity, and discovery: A cognitive perspective.* Amsterdam: Elsevier Science (North-Holland).

Rothenberg, A. (1979). *The emerging goddess.* Chicago, IL: University of Chicago Press.

Rothenberg, A, & Sobel, R. S. (1980). Creation of literary metaphors as stimulated by superimposed versus separated visual images. *Journal of Mental Imagery*, 4, 79–91.

Rubin, D. C., & Kontis, T. C. (1983). A schema for common cents. *Memory & Cognition*, 11, 335–341.

Runco, M. A. (1993). Divergent thinking, creativity, and giftedness. *Gifted Child Quarterly*, 37, 16–22.

Runco, M. A. (1996). Personal creativity: Definition and developmental issues. *New Directions for Child Development*, 72, 3–30.

Runco, M. A., & Chand, I. (1994). Conclusions concerning problem finding, problem solving, and creativity. In M. A. Runco (Ed.), *Problem finding, problem solving, and creativity* (pp. 217–290). Norwood, NJ: Ablex Publishing Company.

Runco, M. A., & Chand, I. (1995). Cognition and creativity. *Educational Psychology Review*, 7, 243–267

Schooler, J. W., & Melcher, J. (1995). The ineffibility of insight. In S. M. Smith, T. B. Ward, & R. A. Finke (Eds.), *The creative cognition approach* (pp. 97–133). Cambridge, MA: MIT Press.

Scott, G. M., Lonergan, D. C., & Mumford, M. D. (2005). Conceptual combination: Alternative knowledge structures, alternative heuristics. *Creativity Research Journal*, 17, 79–98.

Sifonis, C. M., Ward, T. B., Gentner, D., & Houska, M. (1997). Relation versus object mapping in creative generation. In M. G. Shafto & P. Langley (Eds.), *Proceedings of the nineteenth annual conference of the Cognitive Science Society.* Hillsdale, NJ: Erlbaum.

Simonton, D. K. (1994). *Greatness: Who makes history and why.* New York: Guilford.

Simonton, D. K. (1997). Creativity in personality, developmental, and social psychology: Any links with cognitive psychology. In T. B. Ward, S. M. Smith, & J. Vaid (Eds.), *Creative thought: An investigation of conceptual structures and processes* (pp. 309–324). Washington, DC: American Psychological Association.

Smith, S. M. (1995). Fixation, incubation, and insight in memory and creative thinking. In S. M. Smith, T. B. Ward, & R. A. Finke (Eds.), *The creative cognition approach* (135–156). Cambridge, MA: MIT Press.

Smith, S. M., & Vela, E. (1991). Incubated reminiscence effects. *Memory & Cognition*, 19, 168–176.

Smith, S. M., Ward, T. B., Tindell, D. R., Sifonis, C. M., & Wilkenfeld, M. J. (2000). Category structure and created memories. *Memory & Cognition*, 28, 386–395.

Smith, S. M., Ward, T. B., & Schumacher, J. S. (1993). Constraining effects of examples in a creative generation task. *Memory & Cognition*, 21, 837–845.

Sobel, R. S., & Rothenberg, A. (1980). Artistic creation as stimulated by superimposed versus separated visual images. *Journal of Personality and Social Psychology*, 39, 953–961.

Sternberg, R. J. (1988). A three-facet model of creativity. In R. J. Sternberg (Ed.), *The nature of creativity: Contemporary psychological perspectives* (pp. 125–147). Cambridge, UK: Cambridge University Press

Sternberg, R. J. (1999). A propulsion model of creative contributions. *Review of General Psychology*, 3, 83–100.

Sternberg, R. J., Kaufman, J. C., & Pretz, J. E. (2002). *The creativity conundrum.* Philadelphia: Psychology Press.

Sternberg, R. J., & Lubart, T. (1995). *Defying the crowd.* New York: Free Press.

Sternberg, R. J., & Lubart, T. I. (1996). An investment theory of creativity and its development. *Human Development*, 34, 1–31.

Thagard, P. (1984). Conceptual combination and scientific discovery. In P. Asquith & P. Kitcher (Eds.), *PSA: Proceedings of the Biennial Meeting of the Philosophy of Science Association*

(Vol. 1). East Lansing, MI: Philosophy of Science Association.

Tourangeau, R., & Rips, L. (1991). Interpreting and evaluating metaphors. *Journal of Memory and Language*, 30, 452–472.

Treffinger, D. J., Isaksen, S. G., & Dorval, K. B. (1994). Creative problem solving: An overview. In M. A. Runco (Ed.), *Problem finding, problem solving, and creativity* (pp. 223–236). Norwood, NJ: Ablex.

Ward, T. B. (1994). Structured imagination: The role of conceptual structure in exemplar generation. *Cognitive Psychology*, 27, 1–40.

Ward, T. B. (1995). What's old about new ideas? In S. M. Smith, T. B. Ward, & R. A. Finke (Eds.), *The creative cognition approach* (pp. 157–178). Cambridge, MA: MIT Press.

Ward, T. B. (1998). Analogical distance and purpose in creative thought: Mental leaps versus mental hops. In K. Holyoak, D. Gentner, & B. Kokinov (Eds.), *Advances in analogy research: Integration of theory and data from the cognitive, computational, and neural sciences* (pp. 221–230). Sofia: New Bulgarian University.

Ward, T. B. (2001). Creative cognition, conceptual combination and the creative writing of Stephen R. Donaldson. *American Psychologist*, 56, 350–354.

Ward, T. B. (2008). The role of domain knowledge in creative generation. *Learning and Individual Differences*. 18, 363–366.

Ward, T. B., Dodds, R. A., Saunders, K. N., & Sifonis, C. M. (2000). Attribute centrality and imaginative thought. *Memory & Cognition*, 28, 1387–1397

Ward, T. B., Finke, R. A., & Smith, S. M. (1995). *Creativity and the mind: Discovering the genius within*. New York: Plenum Publishing.

Ward, T. B., Patterson, M. J., & Sifonis, C. (2004). The role of specificity and abstraction in creative idea generation. *Creativity Research Journal*, 16, 1–9.

Ward, T. B., Patterson, M. J., Sifonis, C. M., Dodds, R. A., & Saunders, K. N. (2002). The role of graded category structure in imaginative thought. *Memory & Cognition*, 30, 199–216.

Ward, T. B., Saunders, K. N., & Dodds, R. A. (1999). Creative cognition in gifted adolescents. *Roeper Review*, 21, 260–265.

Ward, T. B., & Sifonis, S. M. (1997). Task demands and generative thinking: What changes and what remains the same? *Journal of Creative Behavior*, 31, 245–259.

Ward, T. B., Smith, S. M., & Finke, R. A. (1999). Creative cognition. In R. J. Sternberg (Ed.), *Handbook of creativity*. Cambridge: Cambridge University Press.

Ward, T. B., Smith, S. M., & Vaid, J. (Eds.). (1997). *Creative thought: An investigation of conceptual structures and processes*. Washington, DC: American Psychological Association.

Ward, T. B., & Wickes, K. N. S. (2009). Stable and dynamic properties of graded category structure in Imaginative thought. *Creativity Research Journal*, 21, 15–23.

White, J. H. (1978). *The American Railroad Passenger Car*. Baltimore: Johns Hopkins University Press.

Wilkenfeld, M. J., & Ward, T. B. (2001). Similarity and emergence in conceptual combination. *Journal of Memory and Language*, 45, 21–38.

Wisniewski, E. J. (1997a). Conceptual combination: Possibilities and esthetics. In T. B. Ward, S. M. Smith, & J. Vaid (Eds.), *Creative thought: An investigation of conceptual structures and processes* (pp. 51–81). Washington, DC: American Psychological Association.

Wisniewski, E. J. (1997b). When concepts combine. *Psychonomic Bulletin & Review*, 4, 167–183.

CHAPTER 6

The Function of Personality in Creativity

The Nature and Nurture of the Creative Personality

Gregory J. Feist

- The cave paintings of Lascaux.
- The great Pyramids of Egypt.
- Plato's philosophical works.
- Copernicus's heliocentric astronomy.
- Shakespeare's plays.
- Newton's calculus and theories of gravity and mechanics.
- Beethoven's and Mozart's symphonies.
- Darwin's (and Wallace's) theory of natural selection.
- Einstein's theory of relativity.
- Watson and Crick's discovery of the DNA molecule.

These are just a few of the truly creative accomplishments of our species. When truly creative ideas, pieces of art, or behavior occur, we all want to know: How did that happen? Who created that? Why didn't I think of that?! Assuming one's curiosity is peaked, then the next set of questions that comes up is, What qualities of thought or personality does that person have that the rest of us do not have? What makes him or her so special?

Creativity of that magnitude is special and exceedingly rare. Yet creativity comes in many different forms, shades, and hues.

First, the creativity of great artists and scientists is what attracts most attention, and for good reason. These enterprises are cornerstones of culture and provide mileposts of our cultural development and progress. And yet, not everyone who is an artist or scientist is equally creative, nor are all creative people either artists or scientists. Some are creative in business, in their understanding of other people, or simply in living. In short, the qualities of creativity that are both fascinating and yet frustrating are its complexity and variability. This chapter reviews the current (last 10 years of) research on personality and creativity that mostly supports but occasionally calls for modifications in the model I proposed in both qualitative and quantitative reviews of the late 1990s (Feist, 1998, 1999).

Personality and Creativity Defined

As a long-time creativity researcher, I often hear, especially from artists, that creativity is inherently unknowable, mysterious, and immeasurable. Hence, the argument continues, researchers can't agree even on what

creativity means. It may be true that creativity is difficult to measure and to quantify,
but it's not impossible and it is false to say no
consensual definition has emerged on how
to define it. In fact, creativity researchers
have for the last 60 years been nearly unani-
mous in their definition of the concept (e.g.,
Amabile, 1996; Feist, 2006; Guilford, 1950;
Kaufman & Baer, 2004; MacKinnon, 1970;
Runco, 2004; Simonton, 2008; Sternberg,
1988): Creative thought or behavior must be
both novel/original and useful/adaptive. It
is easy to see why originality per se is not
sufficient – there would be no way to distinguish eccentric or schizophrenic thought
from creative. To be classified as creative,
thought or behavior must also be useful or
adaptive. Usefulness, however, is not meant
in merely a pragmatic sense, for behavior or
thought can be judged as useful on purely
intellectual or aesthetic criteria.

What about personality? How do we
define that? When psychologists use the
term *personality*, they are referring to the
unique and relatively enduring set of behaviors, feelings, thoughts, and motives that
characterize an individual (Feist & Feist,
2009; Roberts & Mroczek, 2008). There are
two key components to this definition. First,
personality is what distinguishes us from one
another and makes us unique. Second, personality is relatively enduring, or consistent.
In sum, personality is the relatively enduring unique ways that individuals think, act,
and feel. As it turns out, recent research has
begun to demonstrate that unique and consistent differing styles of behaving (i.e., personalities) are found within many different
species of animal, from octopus and mice to
birds and horses (Dingemanse, Both, Drent,
Van Oers, & Van Noordwijk, 2002; Gosling
& John, 1999; Morris, Gale, & Duffy, 2002).
Personality is not just a trait of humans, but
of most mammals and some birds, reptiles,
and fish.

Functional Model of Personality and Creativity

As I proposed in the late 1990s, personality
influences creativity by lowering behavioral

thresholds (Feist, 1998, 1999). In my model,
genetic differences influence both brain
structures and temperamental differences,
leading to personality variability (social, cognitive, and motivational-affective, and now
clinical traits), which in turn effects creative
thought and behavior. The idea was and
still is that a particular constellation of personality traits function to lower the thresholds of creative behavior, making it more
rather than less likely (cf., Allport, 1937;
Brody & Ehrlichman, 1998; Ekman, 1984;
Feist, 1998; Rosenberg, 1998). As I wrote in
1998: "One purpose of this meta-analysis was
to provide the raw material – the empirical consensus – so that future researchers
can make educated guesses as to where to
begin their search for the potential underlying physiological and psychological mechanisms of highly creative behavior" (Feist,
1998, p. 305). The part of the model that has
been most intensively investigated over the
last decade since the model was first proposed is the biological-foundations component, especially genetic and neuroscientific
foundations. However, one component of
the model is completely new, reflecting even
greater growth in research, namely, the clinical personality traits of psychoticism, schizotypal personality, latent inhibition, and negative priming. Hence, this review will give
more weight to these components than the
others.

My functional model builds ties between
biology and personality variability and
argues for the causal primacy of biological
factors in personality in general and the creative personality in particular, much as other
personality theorists have done (Eysenck,
1990; Krueger & Johnson, 2008; McCrae &
Costa, 2008). To be clear, my updated model
of the creative personality includes six main
latent variables, in order of causal priority:

- Genetic and epigenetic influences on per-
  sonality
- Brain Qualities
- Cognitive Personality Traits
- Social Personality Traits
- Motivational-Affective Personality Traits
- Clinical Personality Traits

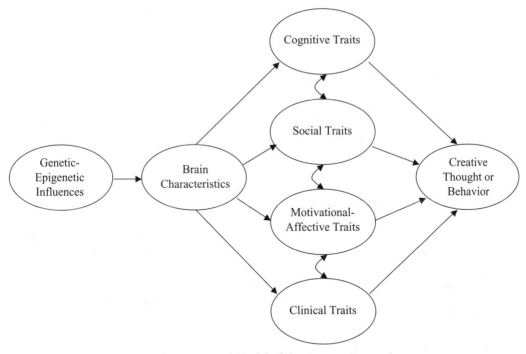

Figure 6.1. Functional Model of the Creative Personality

By combining the biological and the function-of-traits arguments, I present in Figure 6.1 an updated model for the paths from specific biological processes and mechanisms to psychological dispositions to creative thought and behavior. The basic idea is that causal influence flows from left to right, with genetic and epigenetic influences having a causal effect on brain influences. Brain-based influences in turn causally influence the four categories of personality influence: cognitive, social, motivational, and clinical. These traits individually and collectively lower thresholds for creative thought and behavior, making each more likely in those individuals who possess that cluster of traits.

A modest amount of research from the 1970s to 1990s focused on the genetic and biologically based personality influences on creative personality, but biologically based explanations were still a minority perspective. A decade ago, therefore, I shied away from going into a detailed review of the biological aspects of the model, and even argued that "the paths of influence from genetic disposition and temperament to per-

sonality dispositions to creative behavior are long, precarious, and in need of much more prospective, longitudinal, and wherever possible experimental research" (Feist, 1998, p. 302).

In the late 1990s, however, with the growth in neuroscience and evolutionary perspectives, a clear shift occurred not only in personality research, but in psychological research as a whole. Most models of personality now include some form of neuroscientific or biological component, and combined nature and nurture models are more the norm than exception. Ten years later, therefore, the growth of research allows me the luxury of diving into rather than shying away from reviewing the biological research on creative personality, thought, and behavior.

Genetic and Epigenetic Influences on Personality

For a long time, genetic explanations of personality were thought to be deterministic. Genes were immutable; therefore, if there were a genetic component to thought, behavior, or personality, it was deterministic and immutable. Both laypeople and many scientists eschew the inferred lack of freedom that genetic explanations appeared to have.

We now know this view is outdated and misleading (Pinker, 2002). First of all, there is no simple path from genetics to behavior, and this is even more true for the path from genetics to personality. Genetic influence on personality is polygenic, meaning dozens if not hundreds of genes are often involved in shaping each trait (Rutter, 2006). There is no such thing as an "extraversion" gene, but there are many genes that are involved in the production of hormones and neurotransmitters that affect extraversion.

The evidence for genetic effects on creativity is somewhat indirect. Few researchers have directly investigated genetic influences on creative achievement. Researchers have, however, investigated its influence on both personality and intelligence, and because personality and intelligence are related to creativity, this body of research ultimately illuminates a genetic influence on creative achievement.

The most impressive and comprehensive work on this topic is a recent paper by Dean Simonton (2008). In it he develops a quantitative model of talent and specifies the genetic underpinning of talent as it goes through intelligence and personality. Simonton argues that scientific talent is produced by both genetic and training/experience and calculates its genetic influence in science. He does so by obtaining effect sizes from meta-analytic studies and heritabilities from behavioral genetic studies. By multiplying and summing effect sizes (between personality and intelligence with a creativity outcome) and the heritability of the personality or intelligence dimension, one can obtain an estimate of the genetic influence of talent on creative achievement in science. By Simonton's calculations, the genetic aspect of personality contributes between 3 and 9% of the variability in scientific training and performance, and the genetic aspect of

intelligence contributes between 10 and 20%. Moreover, these are independent effects; taken together, genetically based personality and intelligence factors account for between 13 to 29% of the variation in scientific talent.

As Simonton (2008) points out, there are ways that natural endowment can affect talent and creativity both genetically and nongenetically (Benbow, 1988). Prenatal hormonal influence is one such nongenetic influence. But a more general and newly uncovered nongenetic process is epigenesis, meaning "beyond genetics." Epigenesis occurs when events change how our genes get expressed – that is, get turned on or off – without altering the sequence of DNA (Rutter, 2006). More specifically, chemical markers (methyl groups) attach to the A, C, G, T sequences on the double helix and enhance, silence, or change "the volume" of particular genes. These markers are activated by environmental events, such as diet, stress, and drugs. In fact, prenatal hormones almost certainly operate epigenetically. The mother is exposed to high levels of stress, virus, drugs, or other toxins, and this results in immune and hormonal responses in her body that lead to markers attaching to her DNA and that of her developing fetus (Watters, 2006). These markers in turn affect the timing and degree of genetic expression, more often than not turning off genes that result in phenotypic and behavioral changes.

The evidence most relevant for creativity comes from epigenetic influences on intelligence. Toxins ingested by the mother, either intentionally or unintentionally, may influence the child's intelligence. Alcohol, drugs, and viral infections in a pregnant woman can seriously lower her child's overall intelligence (Jacobson & Jacobson, 2000; Ruff, 1999; Steinhausen & Spohr, 1998). For example, heavy alcohol consumption during pregnancy can lead to mental retardation in the child (Streissguth, Barr, Sampson, Darby, & Martin, 1989). Prenatal exposure to high levels of lead, mercury, or manganese may lead to serious impairments in a child's intelligence (Dietrich, Succop, Berger, & Hammond, 1991; Jacobson & Jacobson, 2000). As much research has reported, moderately high levels of intelligence are a necessary but not sufficient condition for creative thought and behavior (see Batey & Furnham, 2006, for a recent review of the literature).

Brain Influences on the Creative Personality

Just as epigenetics has revolutionized our view of the interplay between nature and nurture at a genetic level, brain plasticity has done the same at a neuroscientific level. Our brains are very much a product of our environment, in particular during fetal development and the first few years of postnatal development (Baltes, Reuter-Lorenz, & Rösler, 2006; Perry, 2002).

Genes build proteins that create every structure in the body, including the brain, neurotransmitters, and hormones, the three biological structures most strongly affecting behavior and personality. Neuroscientists over the last decade have begun to uncover the particular brain regions most active during problem solving and creativity, and two main findings have emerged: The frontal lobes and the right hemisphere are most centrally engaged during creative thought and problem solving. Another conclusion from neuroscience supports the idea that creative thought comes about not simply by greater activity *within* particular regions of the brain, but rather by the more complex and dense neural connectivity *between* major regions of the brain.

Frontal Lobes

The lobes above and behind the eyes – the prefrontal cortex – are what make our species unique. They form the seat of the higher reaches of human nature, namely, consciousness, creativity, personality, and morality (Dunbar, 1993; Fuster, 2002; Kras-

negor, Lyon, & Goldman-Rakic, 1997; Miller & Cummings, 1999; Mithen, 1996; Stone, Baron-Cohen, & Knight, 1998; Stuss, Picton, & Alexander, 2001).

The evidence for the unique role of the frontal lobes in creative thought and personality has been mounting for the last 20 years. As is often the case, the first evidence came from brain injured individuals. Chow and Cummings reviewed neuropsychological evidence that demonstrates loss of creative thought, impaired set shifting, and an increase in stimulus bound behavior as a result of dorsolateral and anterior cingulate lesions in the frontal lobes (Chow & Cummings, 1999). Bruce Miller and his colleagues reported a case of a female painter who developed frontal-temporal dementia. As an apparent result of this condition, her paintings went from amateurish to quite sophisticated and more creative (Mell, Howard, & Miller, 2003). One explanation offered by the authors was that some forms of visual creativity may be somewhat inhibited by the language regions in the left frontal-temporal area and that these inhibitions were removed with the dementia.

More recently brain-imaging studies on noninjured people have borne out the connection between creativity and the frontal lobes. Another such study was conducted by Carlsson, Wendt, and Risberg (2000), who compared frontal functioning in high- and low-creativity groups. A creativity measure (the Creative Functioning Test, CFT) was administered to 60 right-handed male undergraduates, and the 12 highest- and 12 lowest-scoring participants formed the two groups. Measuring regional cerebral blood flow (rCBF) in the brain, Carlsson and colleagues found that during an unusual-uses task (brick), highly creative participants showed bilateral activation of the prefrontal cortex, whereas the less creative participants showed unilateral (left side) activation of the same area. Finally, Goel and Vartanian (2005; Vartanian & Goel, 2007) present recent brain-imaging evidence that generating hypotheses, set shifting, and creative cognition (i.e., insight) first and foremost involve activity in the prefrontal cortex (PFC) in the right hemisphere (Brodmann's Area 47).

Right-Hemisphere Activity

As is already implied by much of the neuroscientific research on brain function and creative problem solving, the two hemispheres of the brain are not equal partners in this enterprise. There is more activity during creative insight in the right hemisphere than in the left. Technically speaking, such asymmetrical activity in known as "laterality" (Bradshaw, 1989).

Regarding cognitive differences between the hemispheres, we now know that the right hemisphere (RH) is more active when processing novel, diffuse, heuristic, and global (early-stage) information than the left hemisphere (LH). The LH, on the other hand, is more active when processing routinized, analytic, and focused (late-stage) information (Beeman, Bowden, & Gernsbacher, 2000; Bowden & Beeman, 1998; Bradshaw, 1989; Fiore & Schooler, 1998; Galin, 1974; Martindale, Hines, Mitchell, & Covello, 1984). This general finding does suggest more right-hemisphere activation in expansive and creative associations to novel problems (Katz, 1986; Martindale et al., 1984). Moreover, the right hippocampus appears to play an important role during insights into difficult problems (Luo & Nikki, 2003; Schneider et al., 1996).

In general, these conclusions support the notion that the two hemispheres are functionally different, with the LH being more involved in "analytic" problems and the RH more involved in "holistic" problems and thought (Vartanian & Goel, 2007).

Other research has examined the relation between creative thinking and right-hemispheric dominance by means of a lexical decision task and a dichotic listening task. In the lexical decision task, words or nonsense words are projected slightly to the right or to the left of a fixed point on a screen. The participants tap either the right arrow, left arrow, or space key depending on whether they see a word on the right, on the left, or no word at all. Similarly, in the dichotic listening task, participants are exposed for 300 ms to six consonant-vowel syllables (e.g., "ba," "ta," and "ka," etc.) to either their right or left ears. Immediately prior to the auditory consonant–vowel syllable, the participants are exposed to a visual stimulus of the same syllables. If the visual stimulus matches the sound they hear in the right ear, the participants respond "right." If the visual stimulus matches the sound they hear in the left ear, the participants respond "left." If it matched neither one, the participant responded "none." These two tasks measure "laterality," that is, a dominance of one hemisphere over the other. One prediction tested with such research is that more-creative people are more right-hemisphere dominant than less-creative people. The few studies that have tested this hypothesis using these techniques have found support for the right-hemisphere dominance of creative people (Weinstein & Graves, 2001, 2002).

Finally, researchers experimentally manipulated which hemisphere processed a problem and then compared solution rates (Beeman & Bowden, 2000; Bowden & Jung-Beeman, 2003). They found that when the problem was projected to the left visual field and hence processed by the RH, insight solutions occurred much more frequently than when projected to the right visual field and processed by the LH. In short, right-hemisphere activity causes more creative insights. Together, these findings provide relatively strong evidence that these brain regions play a causal role in creative insight. They are not effects of creative thinking.

There are, however, a couple of important qualifications to this generalization. First of all, one has to be careful not to conclude that the "right-brain" is the seat of creativity. That is a gross and distorting simplification. Second, as Martindale noted, "it would seem that creative people rely more on the right hemisphere than on the left only during the creative process and not in general" (1999, p. 148).

Neural Complexity

A final conclusion from the neuroscience of creativity is a more general one: The highly creative brain may be most marked by neural circuits that are more complex and more highly interconnected than the less creative brain (Andreasen, 2005; Heilman, Nadeau, & Beversdorf, 2003). That is, rather than having simply a more active right-frontal or temporal area, they may have greater connectivity between all major associative regions of the brain. Such a finding would be consistent with one of their most consistent and robust abilities, namely, creative people generate many more ideas, and the ideas they generate are looser and more remote in their associations. They are more cognitively fluent. This may be so because of a brain that simply has more connections, making rich associations more likely. Idea generation is as much about making connections as anything. Indeed, the frontal lobes themselves may well be especially important in this overall greater neural connectivity given that the frontal lobes do more to connect various regions of the brain than any other lobe (Kaufer & Lewis, 1999).

The history of art and science is replete with creative geniuses who were able to generate numerous creative ideas, but one of my favorite is the great inventor Nikola Tesla. Among Tesla's most long-lasting inventions are alternating current (AC), the radio, microwaves, generators, and the Tesla coil (Pickover, 1998). He had a tremendously strong visual sense and would often simply visualize every minute detail of machines and apparatuses that he would later invent (or not, sometimes being satisfied or too overworked to bring the idea into physical form). He generated so many ideas that he only seldom actually carried out and made the invention. He was also probably a synesthete, that is, someone whose sensory modalities cross, resulting in seeing smells or tasting colors. For Tesla, dropping small strips of paper into a liquid resulted in a horrible taste in his mouth (Pickover, 1998). Synesthesia is more common in highly creative people than the population as a whole (Ramanchandran & Hubbard, 2003).

One explanation for synesthesia is that it results from a cross-wiring or cross-activation of sensory neurons in various parts of the brain (Ramachandran & Hubbard, 2003). Cross-activation occurs when two areas of the brain, normally kept separate, get activated at the same time by the same stimulus. So brain regions involved in color perception get cross-activated with sensations of numbers. As it turns out, one region of the temporal lobe is active in processing both color sensations and numbers, and is therefore the most likely area of cross-activation in this form of synesthesia (Hubbard & Ramachandran, 2005; Ramachandran & Hubbard, 2003). Similarly, the OFC in the frontal lobes has many bimodal neurons (Rolls, 2000), which are neurons that respond to more than one sense – such as taste, smell, touch, and vision – and may become cross-activated in synesthesia (Radeau & Colin, 2004). Creativity and synesthesia share neural complexity in common.

Is Brain Activation a Cause or Effect of Creative Thinking?

Of course, these findings really just beg the question: Are the changes causes or effects of creative insight? Are people who are most consistently creative different in these regions from those who are not? If so, how did these brain differences arise? Genetics? Brain plasticity? The only way to examine these questions is to conduct brain studies on those who are "highly creative" and compare them to baselines of those low in creativity. If we assume that these groupings could be made validly, then seeing consistent brain activation differences in the creative compared to the less creative group would support the idea that these regions are causes rather than effects of creative insight.

It is important to point out, however, that even if the anatomical (regional) brain differences do act causally on creative thinking, this does not mean that these differences come about purely from biological forces, such as genetics. Knowing what we now know about how genes get turned on or off by environmental factors (epigenetics) and how much experience shapes the brain and its connections, we would be foolish to argue that brain differences are hardwired. Genes and the brain interact with experiences and are as much effects as they are causes of behavior (Moffitt, Caspi, & Rutter, 2005). What happens while we are in the womb, after the genome has been determined, plays a very important role in brain development (Ptito, & Desgent, 2006).

Personality Influences on Creativity

In fact, the causal nature of brain influences is precisely what the early model of personality and creativity assumed (Feist, 1998, 1999). These brain differences function to make creative traits more or less likely, which in turn make creative thought and behavior more or less likely. So personality traits mediate the relationship between brain and creative thought and behavior. By having genetic dispositions that create CNS differences that facilitate creative thinking, highly creative people also develop a set of personality traits consistent with their biological dispositions. In addition, although personality and intelligence are key predictors of creative achievement (Batey & Furnham, 2006), some recent evidence suggests that personality may trump intelligence as a predictor of lifetime creative achievement (Feist & Barron, 2003).

Building on the qualitative and quantitative reviews of personality and creativity from 10 years ago, the personality traits most consistently connected to creativity are clustered into cognitive, social, motivational-affective, and clinical groups. Clinical traits are new to the model and therefore will get more attention than the other three classic trait dimensions.

Cognitive Personality Traits

I classify particular traits as "cognitive" because they deal with how people habitually process information, solve problems, and respond to new situations. Chief among the cognitive personality traits is "openness to experience."

As John and colleagues (2008) recently described it, openness is "the breadth, depth, originality, and complexity of an individual's mental and experiential life" (p. 120). Open people tend to be imaginative and curious, and so it is not surprising that open people are more creative. This is not just a theoretical connection but also an empirical one. In addition to the large empirical literature supporting this claim up until the mid 1990s, much recent research continues to build the case for the association between openness and creativity (Burch, Hemsley, Pavelis, & Corr, 2006; Charyton & Snelbecker, 2007; Dollinger, Urban, & James, 2004; Furnham, 1999; Gelade, 1997; George & Zhou, 2001; Perrine & Brodersen, 2005; Prabhu, Sutton, & Sauser, 2008; Reuter et al., 2005; Soldz & Valliant, 1999; Wolfradt & Pretz, 2001; Wutrich & Bates, 2001).

A recent representative study of personality and creativity was conducted with college students (Dollinger et al., 2004). It examined the Big Five personality dimensions and their relation to creativity as measured by a Test for Creative Thinking-Drawing Production (TCT-DP) task. The TCT-DP presents the participant five geometric figures (e.g., a semi-circle, a right angle, a dashed line) in a box drawn on a sheet of paper. The participants are told that an artist started the drawing and they are asked to "continue with this drawing. You are allowed to draw anything you wish" (Dollinger et al., 2004, p. 38). These drawings, in turn, were evaluated by three artist judges and three psychologist judges on 10 different creativity dimensions, such as "new elements," "connections," and "unconventionality." In addition to also completing John and Donahue's Big Five Inventory (BFI), the participants also completed Hocevar's Creative Behavior Inventory (CBI), Gough's Creative Personality Scale (Cps) and Domino's Creativity Scale (Cr). The last two are personality scales of creativity scored from Gough's Adjective Check List.

Results showed that none of the personality dimensions, with the exception of Openness, consistently correlated with the creative personality scales, creative behavior, and the creative drawing task. The only other personality dimension that had some reliable association with creative production, behavior, and personality was Extraversion. But it correlated only with some of the CBI subscales and both of the creative personality scales (Cps and Cr). It did not correlate with the creative drawings.

However, there have been some interesting and important qualifications to the straight and positive relationship between openness and creativity. For example, Prabhu and colleagues (2008) provide an interesting qualification to the relationship between openness and creativity: It is mediated by intrinsic motivation. As with other research reviewed here, Prabhu and colleagues report significant positive correlations between both openness and intrinsic motivation with creativity. However, the zero-order relationship between openness and creativity decreases somewhat (β from .33 to .25; $z = 2.28$; $p. = .02$) when it goes through intrinsic motivation, suggesting a mediating effect of intrinsic motivation.

Another interesting and recent qualification of the relationship between openness and creativity was reported by George and Zhou (2001). They reported that creative behavior was highest if very open participants were given tasks that were open and somewhat undefined. In other words, highly open people are not creative in all work environments. They are most creative when the situation and task is ambiguous and not well defined. People high in openness not only work more creatively in unstructured

environments, they also tend to have more creative hobbies than people low in openness (Wutrich & Bates, 2001). Finally, some recent evidence suggests there may be a biological basis for openness, or at least one main subcomponent of openness – sensation seeking – and the hormone testosterone (Reuter et al., 2005). Those high in sensation seeking tend to have higher baseline levels of testosterone.

Social Personality Traits

Social traits of personality involve first and foremost behaviors and attitudes that concern one's relationships to other people, such as questioning or accepting what authority figures say, being comfortable or uncomfortable around strangers and large groups of people, being warm or hostile toward others, and believing one is better or worse than others. The trait terms that summarize these tendencies are norm-doubting, nonconformity, independence, extraversion-introversion, aloofness, hostility, coldness, and dominance/self-confidence/arrogance.

As I made clear with the meta-analysis on personality and creativity, the general factor of extraversion does not quite reflect its accurate relationship with creativity. When one splits extraversion, however, into two of its main components – sociability-gregariousness and confidence-assertiveness – a clearer association emerges. Highly creative people are generally not sociable and outgoing, but they are independent, confident, and assertive (Chávez-Eakle, Lara, & Cruz-Fuentes, 2006; Feist, 1999). The recent angle on confidence and assertiveness has morphed into research on self-efficacy and creativity. As proposed by Bandura (1986), self-efficacy is the personal belief that one is capable of doing something or carrying out some source of action. Highly creative people, as Bandura argued, possess a definite and strong sense of self-efficacy, if not in general than at least in the domain of their expertise. Research has supported this idea (Hill, Tan, & Kikuchi, 2008; Jaussi,

Randel, & Dionne, 2007; Prabhu et al., 2008; Tierney & Farmer, 2002).

Conservatism and conformity continue to conflict with creativity (Feist & Brady, 2004; Nettle, 2006; Peterson & Pang, 2006; Rubinstein, 2003). Conservatism is the opposite pole of norm-doubting and reflects a tendency to value tradition and authority. Rubinstein (2003), for instance, examined authoritarianism and creativity in Israeli college students (design, behavioral science, and law). Creativity was measured by the Tel-Aviv Creativity Test (TACT; Milgram, Milgram, & Landau, 1974), a variation of Wallach and Kogan's classic test of creativity. The TACT asks for as many ideas as a person can come up with in a limited amount of time concerning unusual uses of four everyday objects; it also asks for all of the different things an abstract painting could represent. As predicted, Rubinstein found strong negative relationships between creativity and authoritarianism as well as a linear relationship between career choice (major) and authoritarianism. Law students were more authoritarian than behavioral science students, who were more authoritarian than design students. Similarly, Dollinger (2007) reported that in a sample of more than 400 students, the more politically conservative students were less likely to have reported creative hobbies or accomplishments, and their photo essays and drawings were judged as less creative than the liberal students. Highly creative people doubt, question, and often reject norms, traditions, and conservative ideology. Indeed, one could argue these findings validate both constructs, for creativity concerns producing novel and unusual ideas and conservatism/authoritarianism values tradition.

Motivational-Affective Personality Traits

Motivational traits are defined by a person's desire to persist in activities and to be successful in his or her activities. Trait terms characteristic of motivation are persistent, driven, ambitious, and impulsive. That some

people are driven to be creative is both undeniable and perplexing. Why do people want to create? Some people are willing to forego social relationships and economic well-being to create lasting works. Going back to psychoanalysts and continuing with modern terror-management theorists, some have argued that behind the need to create is the unconscious fear of death and the desire to overcome our necessarily limited time on this earth (Arndt, Greenberg, Solomon, Pyszczynski, & Schimel, 1999; Rank, 1932/1989). There is little doubt that awareness of mortality is behind some of the need to leave a legacy, and that one way to leave a legacy is by creating poems, songs, paintings, novels, theories, and scientific discoveries that continue to have an impact after we are dead.

If those who have a desire to produce works that leave a mark on the world are to succeed, they also need to be driven, focused, and ambitious. They are not the kind of person who gives up easily in the face of hindrances and roadblocks. And that is generally what the research on drive and creativity continues to show: Creative artists, businesspeople, and scientists are driven, ambitious, and persistent (Adelson, 2003; Batey & Furnham, 2006; Chávez-Eakle et al., 2006; Harris, 2004; Shalley & Gilson, 2004).

But what kinds of things motivate them? Need to know? Self-Expression? Success? Recognition? Money? Joy from the process? It could be each of these depending on the nature of the creative task. Scientists are probably driven more by the need to know and artists more by the need for self-expression. And both are often driven by the pleasure the process of discovery or expression brings, otherwise known as intrinsic motivation. Indeed, intrinsic motivation is often associated with highly creative thought or behavior, and quite a body of research supports this idea (Amabile, 1996; Hennessey, 2000, 2003; Moneta & Siu, 2002; Prabhu et al., 2008). That is, when pleasure and excitement are the drive and energy behind a task, then the end product often is more creative than if the drive is lacking or extrinsic. Amabile's classic work on motivation and creativity has reported that extrinsic motivation (reward, surveillance, or recognition) can often have a detrimental effect on creative achievement. Experimentally, this effect has been demonstrated by offering people rewards for a creative task and comparing the creativity of the outcome to those not offered rewards for doing the task. The typical finding is that the nonrewarded group members produce products judged to be more creative than the rewarded group (Amabile, 1996). Similarly, positive affect (feeling good) seems to facilitate creative thinking (Amabile, Barsade, Mueller, & Staw, 2005; Fredrickson, 2001; Isen, 2000). Indeed, so much evidence has accumulated on this general association between intrinsic motivation, positive affect, and creativity that Amabile and her colleagues refer to it as the "intrinsic motivation principle of creativity" (Amabile, 1996; Hennessey, 2000).

Yet it is clear even to those who established the intrinsic-motivation principle of creativity that positive affect and intrinsic motivation do not always facilitate creative thought, just as extrinsic motivation does not always hinder it. Other researchers, for example, have argued that reward, which leads to positive affect, is unconnected to creativity. Eisenberger and his colleagues have conducted much of this research, and when they inform participants in a reward condition that they will not just be rewarded but rather be rewarded for producing a *creative* product, then reward does increase rather than decrease the creative performance (Eisenberger & Rhoades, 2001; Eisenberger & Shanock, 2003). If people are told explicitly that they are being rewarded for producing something creative, reward can apparently facilitate creative thinking. Given the complex nature of the findings on intrinsic and extrinsic motivation and creativity, it is probably safest to conclude that it is drive and ambition that matter most, and whether the reward is internal (pleasure) or external (reward, money, or recognition) is not as important as the drive and ambition to create something new and worthwhile.

Clinical Personality Traits

One of the biggest changes in the field of personality and creativity over the last 10 years – besides the steady rise in neuroscientific studies – is the tremendous growth in research on personality disorders, mental health, and creative thought and behavior. The influences of mental health on creative thought and behavior are so robust now that I must add a new dimension to the three major trait groupings from my previous model. So now in addition to cognitive, social, and motivational-affective, I include a clinical-traits group that includes the normal personality dimension of psychoticism and its related concept of schizotypy. I should make a qualification, however. The evidence for the connection between clinical-personality traits and creativity is stronger in the arts than in the sciences (Jamison, 1993; Ludwig, 1995; Rawlings & Larconini, 2008).

Eysenck's well-known model of personality proposed psychoticism to be the third of the three superfactors of personality. People high in psychoticism are cold, aloof, eccentric, hostile, impulsive, and egocentric (Eysenck, 1982, 1990). Moreover, Eysenck argued that psychoticism is the personality dimension most closely aligned with creative thought and behavior (Eysenck, 1993, 1995). Empirical investigations continue to provide support for Eysenck's general theoretical model linking psychoticism to creative thought and behavior (Aguilar-Alonso, 1996; Merten & Fischer, 1999; Schuldberg, 2005; Stavridou & Furnham, 1996). Interestingly, Martindale (2007) reported a significant positive correlation between psychoticism and creativity for men but not for women.

Consistent with Eysenck's theory, Martindale (2007) and Weinstein and Graves (2002) theorized that the thread tying schizotypal personality disorder and creativity together is the loose semantic processing of information in the RH. Therefore, ideas are associated in a global and holistic manner rather than in a narrow and analytic way. In their words, "increased availability of distant or less common semantic associations can result in both higher creativity scores on certain tests (e.g., of remote associates and verbal fluency) and also in higher scores on positive schizotypy tests (e.g., of magical ideation and unusual perceptual experiences)" (Weinstein & Graves, 2002, p. 138). The idea, consistent with a lot of the research on heightened right-hemispheric activity in highly creative people, is that there is a relative weakening of the LH and strengthening of right-hemisphere processing. Moreover, latent inhibition and primordial thinking are commonly found elements both in creative thought and schizotypal personality (Carson, Peterson, & Higgins, 2003; Eysenck, 1995; Martindale, 2007). Latent inhibition is the ability to selectively attend to only the most relevant sensory experience and tune out the irrelevant. Highly creative people are often less able to tune out the irrelevant information. In this sense, failure to screen out irrelevant sensory experiences and ideas might enrich one's source for ideas, which would explain the greater ideational fluency of creative people.

Eysenck's three-dimensional model of personality concerned normal rather than abnormal personality structure. However, as he pointed out, the odds of personality disorders or mental health problems increased asymptotically as one moved higher and higher toward the high end of the psychoticism dimension. Recently, some researchers have begun to question the validity of Eysenck's psychoticism dimension, especially as it relates to pathology, and instead have turned their attention to a more specific (and narrower) clinical personality dimension – schizotypy or schizotypal personality disorder (Chapman, Chapman, & Kwipal, 1994; Martindale & Dailey, 1996; Nettle, 2006). A person with schizotypal personality disorder is isolated and asocial, but in addition has very odd or magical thoughts and beliefs (APA, 2000). For instance, people with schizotypal personality disorder may believe that stories on television or in the newspaper were written directly about them or that people they don't know are saying things about them behind their backs.

During the last decade or so, many researchers have examined the connection between schizotypal personality disorder and creativity (Batey & Furnham, 2008; Burch, Pavelis Hemsley, & Corr, 2006; Fisher et al., 2004; Martindale & Dailey, 1996; Nettle, 2006; Rawlings & Locarnini, 2008; Weinstein & Graves, 2002; Wutrich & Bates, 2001). The most common and validated measure of schizotypy is the O-LIFE (Oxford-Liverpool Inventory of Feelings and Experiences; Mason, Claridge, & Jackson, 1995). It consists of four subscales: Unusual Experiences, Cognitive Disorganization, Introvertive Anhedonia, and Impulsive Nonconformity. Unusual experiences involve unusual perceptions, hallucinations, and delusions. Cognitive disorganization involves attention, whereas introvertive anhedonia describes a lack of enjoyment and affect. Finally, impulsive nonconformity assesses the extent to which the person is likely to exhibit violent, reckless, and self-abusive behaviors. Creative artists, more than scientists, tend to have elevated schizotypy scores. For example, poets and visual artists score higher than nonartists on most of the O-LIFE scales, especially unusual experiences, cognitive disorganization, and impulsive nonconformity (Nettle, 2006). Moreover, there is a curvilinear relationship with degree of involvement in poetry and visuals arts. Serious amateurs show the highest levels, with professionals being next, followed by hobbyists. In another study, visual artists and musicians had higher scores on unusual experiences than biological and physical scientists (Rawlings & Locarnini, 2008).

Conclusions

The research and theory on the connection between personality and creativity remains a vital topic of investigation for psychological scientists. The basic conclusions from 10 years still hold and yet two areas of research – brain influences and clinical traits – have grown so drastically that they deserve being added to the functional model in Figure 6.1. The model proposes that genetic and epigenetic factors create conditions in the central nervous system that make particular personality traits more likely. These personality traits cluster into cognitive, social, motivational-affective, and clinical groups. Being high or low in certain personality dispositions makes creative thought and behavior more or less likely.

The literature on the genetic and brain influences has expanded as well as the literature on clinical traits of psychoticism and schizotypy. Simonton recently analyzed the genetic contributions to scientific talent and creativity and concluded that personality independent of intelligence contributes between 3 and 9% of the variability in scientific training and performance. Moreover, these are independent effects; therefore, genetically based personality and intelligence factors may together account for between 13 and 29% of the variation in scientific talent. One of the more exciting new areas of investigation concerns epigenetics, or how markers tag the base-pair sequences of DNA and turn on or off particular genes. These markers respond to environmental experiences such as diet, drink, or prenatal influences. Epigenetic influences moderate levels of intelligence. The main conclusions from neuroscience research demonstrate the importance of frontal lobe functioning, greater neural complexity, and increased right-hemisphere activity in highly creative people or during creative problem solving.

These biological markers in turn make the emergence of higher levels of certain personality traits more likely. The cognitive traits (openness and cognitive flexibility), social traits (norm-doubting, nonconformity, independence, extraversion-introversion, aloofness, hostility, coldness, and dominance, self-confidence/arrogance), motivational-affective traits (drive, persistence, intrinsic motivation, and positive affect), and clinical traits (psychoticism, latent inhibition, and schizotypy) all function to make creative thought, behavior, and achievement more probable.

In the 1970s and 1980s, some psychologists argued that personality was a dying or even dead field, falsely concluding that Mischel's classic book *Personality and Assessment* (1968) had shown that personality dispositions do not exist (Ross & Nisbett, 1991). Personality does exist and traits are not mere hypothetical concepts with no effect on behavior. Traits function to lower behavioral thresholds. Creative behavior is no exception, and future researchers will no doubt continue to investigate the complex connection between personality and creativity.

References

Adelson, B. (2003). Issues in scientific creativity: Insight, perseverance and personal technique profiles of the 2002 Franklin institute laureates. *Journal of the Franklin Institute*, 340(3), 163–189.

Aguilar-Alonso, A. (1996). Personality and creativity. *Personality and Individual Differences*, 21, 959–969.

Allport, G. W. (1937). *Personality: A psychological interpretation*. New York: Holt, Rinehart, & Winston.

Amabile, T. (1996). *Creativity in context*. Boulder, CO: Westview.

Amabile, T., Barsade, S., Mueller, J., & Staw, B. (2005). Affect and creativity at work. *Administrative Science Quarterly*, 50(3), 367–403.

American Psychiatric Association (APA) (2000). *DSM-IV-TR*. Washington, DC: Author.

Andreasen, N.C. (2005). *The creative brain: The science of genius*. London: Plume Books.

Arndt, J., Greenberg, J., Solomon, S., Pyszczynski, T., & Schimel, J. (1999). Creativity and terror management: Evidence that creative activity increases guilt and social projection following mortality salience. *Journal of Personality and Social Psychology*, 77(1), 19–32.

Baltes, P.B., Reuter-Lorenz, P.A., & Rösler, F. (Eds.). (2006). *Lifespan development and the brain: The perspective of biocultural co-constructivism*. New York: Cambridge University Press.

Bandura, A. (1986). *Social foundations of thought and action: A social cognitive theory*. Englewood Cliffs, NJ: Prentice-Hall.

Batey, M., & Furnham, A. (2006). Creativity, intelligence, and personality: A critical review of the scattered literature. *Genetic, Social and General Psychology Monographs*, 132, 355–429.

Batey, M., & Furnham, A. (2008). The relationship between measures of creativity and schizotypy. *Personality and Individual Differences*, 45, 816–821.

Beeman, M.J., & Bowden, E. (2000). The right hemisphere maintains solution-related activation for yet-to-be solved insight problems. *Memory and Cognition*, 28, 1231–1241.

Beeman, M.J., Bowden, E.M., & Gernsbacher, M.A. (2000). Right and left hemisphere cooperation for drawing predictive and coherence inferences during normal story comprehension. *Brain and Language*, 71, 310–336.

Benbow, C. (1988). Sex differences in mathematical reasoning ability in intellectually talented preadolescents: Their nature, effects, and possible causes. *Behavioral and Brain Sciences*, 11(2), 169–232.

Bowden, E.M., & Beeman, M.J. (1998). Getting the right idea: Semantic activation in the right hemisphere may help solve insight problems. *Psychological Science*, 6, 435–440.

Bowden, E.M., & Jung-Beeman, M. (2003). Aha! Insight experience correlates with solution activation in the right hemisphere. *Psychonomic Bulletin and Review*, 10, 730–737.

Bradshaw, J.L. (1989). *Hemispheric specialization and psychological function*. Chichester, Australia: Wiley.

Brody, N., & Ehrlichman, H. (1998). *Personality psychology: The science of individuality*. Upper Saddle River, NJ: Prentice-Hall.

Burch, G. St. J., Hemsley, D.R., Pavelis, C., & Corr, P.J. (2006). Personality, creativity, and latent inhibition. *European Journal of Personality*, 20, 107–120.

Burch, G. St.J., Pavelis, C. Hemsley, D.R, & Corr, P.J. (2006). Schizotypy and creativity in visual artists. *British Journal of Psychology*, 97, 177–190.

Carlsson, I., Wendt, P.E., & Risberg, J. (2000). On the neurobiology of creativity: Differences in frontal activity between high and low creative subjects. *Neuropsychologia*, 38, 873–885.

Carson, S.H., Peterson, J.B., & Higgins, D.M. (2003). Decreased latent inhibition is associated with increased creative achievement in high-functioning individuals. *Journal of Personality and Social Psychology*, 85, 399–406.

Chapman, J.P., Chapman, L.J., & Kwapil, T.R. (1994). Does the Eysenck Psychoticism dimension predict psychosis? A ten year longitudinal study. *Personality and Individual Differences*, 17, 369–375.

Charyton, C., & Snelbecker, G.E. (2007). Engineers' and musicians' choices of self-descriptive adjectives as potential indicators of creativity by gender and domain. *Psychology of Aesthetics, Creativity, and the Arts*, 1, 91–99.

Chávez-Eakle, R.A., Lara, M.C., & Cruz-Fuentes, C. (2006). Personality: A possible bridge between creativity and psychopathology. *Creativity Research Journal*, 18, 27–38.

Choi, J.N. (2004). Individual and contextual predictors of creative performance: The mediating role of psychological processes. *Creativity Research Journal*, 16, 187–199.

Chow, T.W., and Cummings, J.L. (1999). Frontal-subcortical circuits. In B.L. Miller & J.L. Cummings (Eds.). *The human frontal lobes: Functions and disorders* (pp. 3–26). New York: Guilford Press.

Dietrich, K., Succop, P., Berger, O., & Hammond, P. (1991). Lead exposure and the cognitive development of urban preschool children: The Cincinnati Lead Study cohort at age 4 years. *Neurotoxicology and Teratology*, 13(2), 203–211.

Dingemanse, N.J., Both, C., Drent, P.J., Van Oers, K., & Van Noordwijk, A.J. (2002). Repeatability and heritability of exploratory behaviour in great tits from the wild. *Animal Behaviour*, 64, 929–938.

Dollinger, S.J. (2007). Creativity and conservatism. *Personality and Individual Differences*, 43, 1025–1035.

Dollinger, S.J., Urban, K.K., & James, T.A. (2004). Creativity and openness: Further validation of two creative product measures. *Creativity Research Journal*, 16, 35–47.

Dunbar, R.I.M. (1993). Coevolution of neocortical size, group size and language in humans. *Behavioral and Brain Sciences*, 16, 681–735.

Eisenberger, R., & Rhoades, L. (2001). Incremental effects of reward on creativity. *Journal of Personality and Social Psychology*, 81, 728–741.

Eisenberger, R., & Shanock, L. (2003). Rewards, intrinsic motivation, and creativity: A case study of conceptual and methodological isolation. *Creativity Research Journal*, 15, 121–130.

Ekman, P. (1984). Expression and the nature of emotion. In K.R. Scherer & P. Ekman (Eds.). *Approaches to emotion* (pp. 319–344). Hillsdale, NJ: Erlbaum.

Eysenck, H.J. (1982). *Personality, genetics and behavior: Selected papers*. New York: Praeger.

Eysenck, H.J. (1990). Biological dimensions of personality. In L.A. Pervin (Ed.), *Handbook of personality: Theory and research* (pp. 244–276). New York: Guilford.

Eysenck, H.J. (1993). Creativity and personality: Suggestions for a theory. *Psychological Inquiry*, 4, 147–178.

Eysenck, H.J. (1995). *Genius: The natural history of creativity*. New York: Cambridge University Press.

Feist, G.J. (1998). A meta-analysis of the impact of personality on scientific and artistic creativity. *Personality and Social Psychological Review*, 2, 290–309.

Feist, G.J. (1999). Personality in scientific and artistic creativity. In R.J. Sternberg (Ed.), *Handbook of human creativity* (pp. 273–296). Cambridge, England: Cambridge University Press.

Feist, G.J. (2006). How development and personality influence scientific thought, interest, and achievement. *Review of General Psychology*, 10, 163–182.

Feist, G.J., & Barron, F. (2003). Predicting creativity from early to late adulthood: Intellect, potential, and personality. *Journal of Research in Personality*, 37, 62–88.

Feist, G.J., & Brady, T. (2004). Openness, nonconformity and the preference for abstract art. *Empirical Studies of Arts*, 22, 77–89.

Feist, J., & Feist, G.J. (2009). *Theories of personality*. New York: McGraw-Hill.

Fisher, J.E., Mohanty, A., Herrington, J.D., Koven, N.S., Miller, G.A., & Heller, W. (2004). Neuropsychological evidence for dimensional schizotypy: Implications for creativity and psychopathology. *Journal of Research in Personality*, 38, 24–31.

Fiore, S.M., & Schooler, J.W. (1998). Right hemisphere contributions to creative problem solving: Converging evidence for divergent thinking. In M. Beeman & C. Chiarello (Eds.), *Right hemisphere language comprehension: Perspectives from cognitive neuroscience*. Mahwah, NJ: Erlbaum.

Fredrickson, B. (2001). The role of positive emotions in positive psychology: The broaden-and-build theory of positive emotions. *American Psychologist*, 56(3), 218–226.

Furnham, A. (1999). Personality and creativity. *Perceptual and Motor Skills*, 88, 407–408.

Fuster, J.M. (2002). Frontal lobe and cognitive development. *Journal of Neurocytology*, 31, 373–385.

Galin, D. (1974). Implications for psychiatry of left and right cerebral specialization: A neurophysiological context for unconscious processes. *Archives of General Psychiatry*, 31, 572–583.

Gelade, G. (1997). Creativity in conflict: The personality of the commercial creative. *Journal of Genetic Psychology*, 165, 67–78.

George, J.M., & Zhou, J. (2001). When openness to experience and conscientiousness are related to creative behavior: An interactional approach. *Journal of Applied Psychology*, 86, 513–524.

Goel, V., & Vartanian, O. (2005). Dissociating the roles of right ventral lateral and dorsal lateral prefrontal cortex in generation and maintenance of hypotheses in set-shift problems. *Cerebral Cortex*, 15, 1170–1177.

Gosling, S.D., & John, O.P. (1999). Personality dimensions in non-human animals: A cross-species review. *Current Directions in Psychological Science*, 8, 69–75.

Gräff, J., & Mansuy, I. (2008). Epigenetic codes in cognition and behaviour. *Behavioural Brain Research*, 192(1), 70–87.

Guilford, J.P. (1950). Creativity. *American Psychologist*, 5, 444–454.

Harris, J.A. (2004). Measured intelligence, achievement, openness to experience, and creativity. *Personality and Individual Differences*, 36, 913–929.

Heilman, K.M., Nadeau, S.E., & Beversdorf, D.O. (2003). Creative innovation: Possible brain mechanisms. *Neurocase*, 9, 369–379.

Hennessey, B. (2000). Self-determination theory and the social psychology of creativity. *Psychological Inquiry*, 11(4), 293–298.

Hennessey, B. (2003). The social psychology of creativity. *Scandinavian Journal of Educational Research*, 47(3), 253–271.

Hill, A., Tan, A., & Kikuchi, A. (2008). International high school students' perceived creativity self-efficacy. *Korean Journal of Thinking & Problem Solving*, 18(1), 105–115.

Hubbard, E.M., & Ramachandran, V.S. (2005). Neurocognitive mechanisms of synesthesia, *Neuron*, 48, 509–520.

Isen, A.M. (2000). Positive affect and decision making. In M. Lewis & J.M. Haviland-Jones (Eds.), *Handbook of emotions* (2nd ed., pp. 417–435). New York: Guilford.

Jacobson, S., & Jacobson, J. (2000). *Teratogenic insult and neurobehavioral function in infancy and childhood*. Mahwah, NJ: Erlbaum.

Jamison, K.R. (1993). *Touched with fire: Manic-depressive illness and the artistic temperament*. New York: Free Press.

Jaussi, K., Randel, A., & Dionne, S. (2007). I am, I think I can, and I do: The role of personal identity, self-efficacy and cross-application of experiences in creativity at work. *Creativity Research Journal*, 19(2), 247–258.

John, O.P., Naumann, L.P., & Soto, C.J. (2008). Paradigm shift to the integrative Big Five trait taxonomy. In O.P. John, R.W. Robins, & L.A. Pervin (Eds.), *Personality handbook: Theory and research* (pp. 114–158). New York: Guilford.

Katz, A.N. (1986). The relationship between creativity and cerebral hemisphericity for creative architects, scientists, and mathematicians. *Empirical Studies of the Arts*, 4, 97–108.

Kaufer, D.I., & Lewis, D.A. (1999). Frontal lobe anatomy and cortical connectivity. In B.L. Miller & J.L. Cummings (Eds.), *The human frontal lobes: Functions and disorders* (pp. 27–44). New York: Guilford.

Kaufman, J.C., & Baer, J. (2004). Hawking's haiku, Madonna's math: Why it is hard to be creative in every room of the house. In R.J. Sternberg, E.L. Grigorenko, & J.L. Singer (Eds.), *Creativity: From potential to realization.* Washington, DC: APA Books.

Krasnegor, N.A., Lyon, G.R., & Goldman-Rakic, S. (Eds.). (1997). *Development of the prefrontal cortex: Evolution, neurobiology, and behavior.* Baltimore, MD: Paul H. Brookes.

Krueger, R.F., & Johnson, W. (2008). Behavioral genetics and personality: A new look at the integration of nature and nurture. In O.P. John, R.W. Robins, & L.A. Pervin (Eds.), *Personality handbook: Theory and research* (pp. 287–310). New York: Guilford.

Ludwig, A.M. (1995). *The price of greatness.* New York: Guilford.

Luo, J., & Niki, K. (2003). Function of hippocampus in 'insight' of problem solving. *Hippocampus*, 13(3), 316–323.

MacKinnon, D.W. (1970). Creativity: A multi-faceted phenomenon. In J. Roslanksy (Ed.), *Creativity* (pp. 19–32). Amsterdam: North-Holland.

Martindale, C. (1999). Biological bases of creativity. In R.J. Sternberg (Ed.), *Handbook of creativity* (pp. 137–152). Cambridge, UK: Cambridge University Press.

Martindale, C. (2007). Creativity, primordial cognition, and personality. *Personality and Individual Differences*, 43, 1777–1785.

Martindale, C., & Dailey, A. (1996). Creativity: Primary process cognition and personality. *Personality and Individual Differences*, 20, 409–414.

Martindale, C., Hines, D., Mitchell, L., & Covello, E. (1984). EEG alpha asymmetry and creativity. *Personality and Individual Differences* 5, 77–86.

Mason, O., Claridge, G., & Jackson, M. (1995). New scales for the assessment of schizotypy. *Personality and Individual Differences*, 1, 7–13.

McCrae, R.R., & Costa, P.T., Jr. (2008). The five-factor theory of personality. In O.P. John, R.W. Robins, & L.A. Pervin (Eds.), *Personality handbook: Theory and research* (pp. 159–181). New York: Guilford.

Mell, J.C., Howard, S.M., & Miller, B.L. (2003). Art and the brain: The influence of frontotemporal dementia on an accomplished artist. *Neurology*, 60, 1707–1710.

Merten, T., & Fischer, I. (1999). Creativity, personality, and word association responses: Associative behavior in forty supposedly creative persons. *Personality and Individual Differences*, 27, 933–942.

Milgram, R., Milgram, N.N., & Landau, E. (1974). *Identifying gifted children in Israel: A theoretical and empirical research.* Tel-Aviv: Tel-Aviv University.

Miller, B.L., & Cummings, J.L. (Eds.). (1999). *The human frontal lobes: Functions and disorders.* New York: Guilford.

Mischel, W. (1968). *Personality and assessment.* New York: Wiley.

Mithen, S. (1996). *The prehistory of the mind: The cognitive origins of art and science.* London: Thames & Hudson.

Moffitt, T., Caspi. A., & Rutter, M. (2005). Strategy for investigating interactions between measured genes and measured environments. *Archives of General Psychiatry*, 62, 473–481.

Moneta, G., & Siu, C. (2002, September). Trait intrinsic and extrinsic motivations, academic performance, and creativity in Hong Kong college students. *Journal of College Student Development*, 43(5), 664–683.

Morris, P.H., Gale, A., & Duffy, K. (2002). Can judges agree on the personality of horses? *Personality and Individual Differences*, 33, 67–81.

Nettle, D. (2006). Schizotypy and mental health amongst poets, visual artists, and mathematicians, *Journal of Research in Personality*, 40, 876–890.

Pascual-Leone, A. (2001). The brain that plays music and is changed by it. *Annals of the New York Academy of Sciences*, 930, 315–329.

Perrine, N., & Brodersen, R.M. (2005). Artistic and scientific creative behavior: Openness and the mediating role of interests. *Journal of Creative Behavior*, 39, 217–236.

Perry, B.D. (2002). Childhood experience and the expression of genetic potential: What childhood neglect tells us about nature and nurture. *Brain and Mind*, 3, 79–100.

Peterson, B.E., & Pang, J.S. (2006). Beyond politics: Authoritarianism and the pursuit of leisure. *Journal of Social Psychology*, 146, 443–461.

Pickover, C.A. (1998). *Strange brains and genius: The lives of eccentric scientists and madmen*. New York: Plenum Trade.

Pinker, S. (2002). *The blank slate: The modern denial of human nature*. New York: Viking.

Ptito, M., & Desgent, S. (2006). Sensory input-based adaptation and brain architecture. In P.B. Baltes, P.A. Reuter-Lorenz, & F. Rösler (Eds.), *Lifespan development and the brain: The perspective of biocultural co-constructivism* (pp. 111–133). New York: Cambridge University Press.

Prabhu, V., Sutton, C., & Sauser, W. (2008). Creativity and certain personality traits: Understanding the mediating effect of intrinsic motivation. *Creativity Research Journal*, 20(1), 53–66.

Radeau, M., & Colin, C. (2004). On ventriloquism, audiovisual neurons, neonates, and the senses. *Behavioral and Brain Sciences*, 27, 889–890.

Ramachandran, V.S., & Hubbard, E.M. (2003, May). Hearing colors, tasting shapes. *Scientific American*, 288, 52–59.

Rank, O. (1989). *Art and artist: Creative urge and personality development*. New York: Knopf. (Original work published 1932)

Rauch, A., & Frese, M. (2007). Let's put the person back into entrepreneurship research: A meta-analysis on the relationship between business owners' personality traits, business creation, and success. *European Journal of Work and Organizational Psychology*, 16(4), 353–385.

Rawlings, D., & Locarnini, A. (2008). Dimensional schizotypy, autism, and unusual word associations in artists and scientists. *Journal of Research in Personality*, 42, 465–471.

Reuter, M., Panksepp, J., Schnabel, N., Kellerhoff, N., Kempel, P., & Hennig, J. (2005). Personality and biological markers of creativity. *European Journal of Personality*, 19, 83–95.

Roberts, B.W., & Mroczek, D. (2008). Personality trait change in adulthood. *Current Directions in Psychological Science*, 17, 31–35.

Rolls, E.T. (2000). The orbitofrontal cortex and reward. *Cerebral Cortex*, 10, 284–294.

Rosenberg, E.L. (1998). Levels of analysis and the organization of affect. *Review of General Psychology*, 2, 247–270.

Ross, L., & Nisbett, R.E. (1991). *The person and the situation: Perspectives of social psychology*. New York: McGraw-Hill.

Rubinstein, G. (2003). Authoritarianism and its relation to creativity: A comparative study among students of design, behavioral sciences and law. *Personality and Individual Differences*, 34, 695–705.

Ruff, H. (1999). Population-based data and the development of individual children: The case of low to moderate lead levels and intelligence. *Journal of Developmental & Behavioral Pediatrics*, 20(1), 42–49.

Runco, M. (2004). Everyone has creative potential. In R.J. Sternberg, E.L. Grigorenko, & J.L. Singer (Eds.), *Creativity: From potential to realization* (pp. 21–30). Washington, DC: APA Books.

Rutter, M. (2006). *Genes and behavior: Nature-nurture interplay explained*. Malden, MA: Blackwell.

Schneider, F., Gur, R.E, Alavi, A., Seligman, M., Mozley, L., Smith, R., et al., (1996). Cerebral blood flow changes in limbic regions induced by unsolvable anagram tasks. *American Journal of Psychiatry*, 153(2), 206–212.

Schuldberg, D. (2005). Eysenck Personality Questionnaire scales and paper-and-pencil tests related to creativity. *Psychological Reports*, 97, 180–182.

Shalley, C.E., & Gilson, L.L. (2004). What leaders need to know: A review of social and contextual factors that can foster or hinder creativity? *The Leadership Quarterly*, 15, 33–53.

Simonton, D. (2008). Scientific talent, training, and performance: Intellect, personality, and genetic endowment. *Review of General Psychology*, 12(1), 28–46.

Soldz, S., & Vaillant, G. E. (1999). The big five personality traits and the life course: A 45 year longitudinal study. *Journal of Research in Personality*, 33, 208–232

Steinhausen, H., & Spohr, H. (1998). Long-term outcome of children with fetal alcohol syndrome: Psychopathology, behavior, and intelligence. *Alcoholism: Clinical and Experimental Research*, 22(2), 334–338.

Sternberg, R.J. (1988). A three-facet model of creativity. In R.J. Sternberg (Ed.), *The nature of creativity* (pp. 125–147). Cambridge, England: Cambridge University Press.

Stone, V.E., Baron-Cohen, S., & Knight, R.T. (1998). Frontal lobe contributions to theory of mind. *Journal of Cognitive Neuroscience*, 10, 640–656.

Stavridou, A., & Furnham, A. (1996). The relationship between psychoticism, trait-creativity, and the attentional mechanism of cognitive inhibition. *Personality and Individual Differences*, 21, 143–153.

Streissguth, A., Barr, H., Sampson, P., Darby, B., & Martin, D. (1989). IQ at age 4 in relation to maternal alcohol use and smoking during pregnancy. *Developmental Psychology*, 25(1), 3–11.

Stuss, D.T., Picton, T.W., & Alexander, M.P. (2001). Consciousness and self-awareness, and the frontal lobes. In S.P. Salloway, P.F. Malloy, & J.D. Duffy (Eds.), *The frontal lobes and neuropsychiatric illness* (pp. 101–109). Washington, DC: American Psychiatric Publishing.

Tierney, P., & Farmer, S.M. (2002). Creative self-efficacy: Its potential antecedents and relationship to creative performance. *Academy of Management Journal*, 45, 1137–1148.

Vartanian, O., & Goel, V. (2007). Neural correlates of creative cognition. In C. Martindale, P. Locher, & V.M. Petrov (Eds.), *Evolutionary and neurocognitive approaches to aesthetics, creativity and the arts* (pp. 195–207). Amityville, NY: Baywood.

Watters, E. (2006, November 22). DNA is not destiny. *Discover*, Retrieved online on January 27, 2010 from http://discovermagazine.com/2006/nov/cover.

Weinstein, S., & Graves, R.E. (2001). Creativity, schizotypy, and laterality. *Cognitive Neuropsychiatry*, 6, 131–146.

Weinstein, S., & Graves, R.E. (2002). Are creativity and schizotypy products of a right hemisphere bias? *Brain and Cognition*, 49, 138–151.

Wolfradt, U., & Pretz, J. (2001). Individual differences in creativity: Personality, story writing, and hobbies. *European Journal of Personality*, 15, 297–310.

Wutrich, V., & Bates, T.C. (2001). Schizotypy and latent inhibition: Nonlinear linkage between psychometric and cognitive markers. *Personality and Individual Differences*, 30, 783–798.

CHAPTER 7

How Does a Visual Artist Create an Artwork?

Paul J. Locher

Introduction

Extensive study has taught us much about the factors that contribute to artistic creativity, such as an artist's perceptual abilities, drawing skills, and his/her personal history and personality (see Kozbelt & Seeley, 2007, for a review of this literature). But investigations of the actual working processes engaged in by visual artists as they make art are very few by comparison. Most of what is known about the contribution of the various factors mentioned to the process of artistic creation comes from two types of case study research, namely, *archival case studies* and *real-life case studies*. Archival case studies involve the analyses of completed art works and use as stimuli different versions of a single painting, such as the recorded development of Picasso's painting *Guernica* (Weisberg, 2004), which I describe later in "Archival Case Studies of Art Making." These studies are obviously limited because they do not capture directly the actual art-making process. This is achieved by real-life case studies that use a variety of tech-niques to record an artist's creative production from start to completion. For example, Miall and Tchalenko (2001) simultaneously measured a painter's eye and hand movements and coupled these observations with a filmed record of an emerging portrait to illuminate the artist's on-going art-making processes.

This chapter presents an overview of empirical findings of recent archival and real-life case studies undertaken to provide insights into the way a visual artist creates an artwork. It describes the different research methodologies (viz., eye-movement recordings, sketch analysis, X-ray analysis, and brain-scan research) used to investigate the art-making process. The findings illuminate how an artist develops conceptual themes, how pictorial elements are selected and arranged in a painting during its genesis, and the role of "good composition" (i.e., pictorial balance) in such an endeavor. The influences of an artist's perceptual skills, drawing techniques, and his/her personal history and personality on the artistic process are also described.

A Descriptive Model of the Art-Making Process

Mace and Ward (2002) generated a descriptive model of the art-making process based on interviews conducted with professional visual artists as they completed a self-initiated artwork. The researchers conducted two real-life studies: the first one provided an initial data source, which was used to generate the model, and the second study was conducted to determine its validity. Artists in both studies were interviewed on three occasions spaced over the course of the developing artwork – when it was first initiated, at the midpoint in the process, and when the work was being finished. Transcriptions of the interviews were analyzed and their contents categorized in terms of patterns of behavior from which a four-phase model of the unfolding developmental process of making an artwork emerged. The four phases identified by the researchers from the interviews are Phase 1 – Artwork Conception, Phase 2 – Idea Development, Phase 3 – Making the Artwork, and Phase 4 – Finishing the Artwork and Resolution. According to the model, an artist initially engages in various activities of idea conception to identify an idea or feeling that could be a potential artwork. At some point, reflection results in a decision to select one of the potential ideas that have arisen for execution. Once a particular artwork idea has been chosen, it is then developed both conceptually and physically in a complex set of interactive processes involving the structuring, extending, restructuring, and evaluating of the composition's form and content. An essential aspect of this concept-development phase for most artists is the making of preliminary drawings or sketches of the emerging artwork, which give the work an initial tentative pictorial structure. When the envisioned final version of the work has been decided on, initiation of the actual artwork begins and the same set of processes used during the idea-development phase are employed in its creation. As a result of evaluative processes, the artist decides at some point that the work

is considered either "complete" or as nonviable, which leads to its postponement or abandonment. Mace and Ward emphasize that the art-making process is dynamically interactive, with feedback loops between developmental phases; that is, the artist can, and frequently does, return to an earlier phase of construction as new artwork ideas arise either conceptually or from the emergence of the tentative pictorial structure. The processes involved in each phase and among phases of art making briefly described here are illustrated in greater detail by the research findings presented throughout the rest of this chapter.

Archival Case Studies of Art Making

The Process of Creating an Artwork

When different phases of the development of an artwork have been recorded, either as a series of sketches or photographs of the emerging composition, there are several ways these images can be used to generate empirical insights into artists' thought and working processes as they create a work of art. One approach is Weisberg's (2004) archival case study of Picasso's development of his painting *Guernica*. Picasso dated and numbered 45 preliminary sketches for the painting. Once he began work on the actual painting, the canvas was photographed eight times from start to completion of the creative task. Weisberg tallied the number of times the images depicted the overall structural organization of the composition and the number of times they focused on one of the key characters or components of the composition's subject matter (i.e., horse, bull, mother and child, woman, man, statue hand, statue head). The summaries of these elements in the preliminary sketches and in the photographed versions of the painting constituted the quantitative data for Weisberg's analyses of the chronological development of the work.

With respect to the sketches, which Picasso completed over three time periods, Weisberg (2004) observed that during the idea-development phase of the painting's creation the first 11 sketches were split between studies of the overall structural arrangement of the composition and studies of the central figure of a horse, which is stabbed by a lance and raises its head in a scream of agony. During the second and third time periods Picasso shifted his focus from the structure of the composition to a concentration on the development of the individual characters depicted. Specifically, studies of the bull and of the mother and child take precedence in the second period, and most of the artist's efforts are devoted to the solitary woman and the falling person in the last of the preliminary sketches. Weisberg notes that of the eight early sketches that focus on the overall composition, seven are clearly organized structurally in the same way as is the finished painting. In addition, all main characters are present in the first and last state of the painting itself, and changes made to the painting across the eight photographs are relatively small-scale and can be ascribed to demands of the developing structural arrangement of the composition.

According to Weisberg (2004), the full set of observations suggests that Picasso had the "skeleton" of *Guernica* in mind when he began the work and that the process of creation of the composition can best be characterized as an elaboration of a kernel idea, rather than the generation of numerous different ideas (i.e., "false starts and wild experiments," see Simonton, 1999) from which the final creative product emerged. As additional support for this assertion, Weisberg presents evidence that the kernel idea and the thought processes underlying the evolution of *Guernica* were likely derived from contents of Picasso's earlier paintings, especially his painting titled *Minotauromachy*. He points out the similarity between the characters and the spatial organization of the two works and suggests that *Guernica* can be seen as a variation of *Minotauromachy*. Weisberg also shows correspondences between the characters in *Guernica* and three paintings by Goya, using these observations to support his assertion that Picasso's thought processes in creating *Guernica* were struc-

tured by art he was familiar with. This view is consistent with Mace and Ward's (2002) assertion, based on their interviews with artists, that an "artwork does not arise from a conceptual void, nor is it largely determined in advance. Rather, the genesis of an artwork arises from a complex context of art making, thinking, and ongoing experience" (p. 182). This is a theme that appears in the findings of most of the studies reported in this chapter.

Another approach to archival research on art making was employed by Kozbelt (2006). In his study, undergraduate art students and nonartists examined 22 in-progress states (photographs) of Henri Matisse's painting *Large Reclining Nude* and rated each of these states on 26 items. The items measured the constructs of originality, technique, arousal potential, primordial thought, and the overall quality of the work at each stage of creation. Kozbelt observed a different pattern of aesthetic judgment criteria between the art students and nonartists as the painting progressed, with the greatest difference between the two groups being in terms of the quality of the painting in its final stages of development. Nonartists' judgments emphasized realism and technique, and they evaluated the painting less favorably as Matisse transformed the composition from a realistic nude into an increasingly more abstract work. In contrast, the art students placed greater emphasis on the aesthetic-judgment criteria of originality and abstraction, and they rated the final version of the painting as both the very best and most original of all, whereas the nonartists rated it the poorest in quality.

Kozbelt (2006) reports that art students' judgments, and those of the nonartists to a lesser degree, showed a jagged trajectory in the composition's quality, which he suggests reflects Matisse's use of a complex decision-making process to elaborate the work and gradually transform it by structuring and restructuring processes into a satisfying finished painting in the artist's view. However, despite fluctuations in the perceived quality of the painting by the art students as it emerged, Kozbelt notes that there is remarkable consistency in the appearance of the painting as a whole from its start to finish, as seen across the 22 recorded versions. He states that this is consistent with Weisberg's (2004) contention that the creative process for artists appears to be largely one of elaborating a kernel idea, rather than the generation of many different ideas during the creative process. According to Kozbelt, Matisse seems neither to have planned the painting entirely in advance, thus working directly toward a final envisioned composition, nor to have had sudden insights about the content and overall structural organization of the work as its creation progressed. The incremental changes in the appearance of the painting are, according to Kozbelt, likely responsible for the "temporary" increases and decreases in the work's perceived quality by the art students in his study.

Influence of an Artist's Personal History on Art Making

There is a long history of interest, which continues to this day, in the psychological connection between an artist's personal history and his or her resulting motives for creating an artwork, as well as its content and style. Thousands of biographies and articles describing the "life and work" of an artist attempt to explain the connections between the two in a manner that uniquely fits the artist in question. One recent example is the archival case study by Gunderman and Hawkins (2008) titled *The Self-Portraits of Frida Kahlo*. They describe how this well-known Mexican artist's life and paintings were profoundly influenced by her many illnesses and the radiological images of her body that she encountered as a patient. As the result of a serious accident at age 18, the amputation of her right leg for gangrene later in life, and the many other major medical problems she endured, Kahlo underwent 32 separate operations during her life. Additionally, she spent a great deal of time in plaster casts and orthopedic braces, or confined to bed. She died at age 47. Gunderman and Hawkins describe how Kahlo's

life experiences contributed to the medical themes of pain and suffering that frequently appear in her art, especially in her self-portraits. Using the pictorial content of three of Kahlo's paintings, they show how seeing radiographs of her own spine, pelvis, and leg exerted a powerful influence on the visual representation of herself, which frequently conveyed deeply personal feelings and perspectives about her illnesses.

Gunderman and Hawkins (2008) caution that their artistic and biographic interpretations of Kahlo's art are just that – interpretations – and they may or may not accurately reflect the artist's motives and resulting creation process. The study of artistic biography, which makes for very interesting reading, lacks scientific rigor. According to Machotka (2003), what is needed in this area of research are real-life case studies of art making and its relationship to personality; these case studies should be conducted in controlled settings and should contrast many individuals on a number of explanatory variables grounded in a theoretical foundation. This is exactly what Machotka has done in a research project that I describe below in "Art Making and Analysis."

Seeing Through a Painting – X-Ray Analysis

Important techniques for museum conservators, conservation scientists, and art historians for studying the way a painting is developed, or its authenticity, are X-ray radiography and infrared reflectography. These techniques are valuable because they reveal *pentimenti* – the image(s) that preceded the visible one – and do this in a way that does not alter or damage the painting. With these techniques, one can see through the surface image of a painting to its underdrawings and detect changes in composition made by the artist during the idea-development phase of the creative task. The first laboratory devoted to the study of paintings by X-ray was established in 1925 at the Fogg Museum at Harvard University. Shortly thereafter most of the major museums in Europe joined with the Fogg Museum to obtain and exchange technical information about the use of X-rays (Burroughs, 1938, 1965). When Burroughs published his book *Art Criticism from a Laboratory* in 1938, the Fogg Museum library file of radiographic images (referred to then as shadowgraphs) contained the names of 650 European artists and approximately 3,200 shadowgraphs. Since then, countless case studies of individual paintings have appeared in the literature, and it is likely that the works of all major and minor artists from the Medieval and Renaissance periods up to works created by contemporary artists have been subjected to some form of spectroscopic examination. One recent example reports the findings of an infrared reflectography study of one panel of an enormous fifteenth-century altarpiece (Biersdorfer, 2008). The preparatory underdrawings of the panel's chief artist, Fernando Gallego, show his use of strong, confident lines and attention to details of the composition of the panel, known as *The Raising of Lazarus*, from start to finish. Additionally, Gallego left notes for his workshop assistants in his sketched underdrawing showing what colors he wanted and where he wanted them, such as the word *blanco* written on the shroud of Lazarus, indicating the master's desire for white paint to be used for this pictorial detail.

With respect to the topic of this chapter, art historians have been able to identify the working methods of an artist at the early phases in the painting process by studying comparatively the artist's changes in style and content within a single underdrawing, differences in the underdrawings of variants of a painting, and different works by the artist. Interpretation of the early sketches and the final version is made in the light of historical knowledge about an artist's workshop practices and about conventions of pictorial execution common at the time – all contributing factors to the art-making process. Space does not permit the details of one such case study to be presented here. The reader is referred to Kirsh and Levenson's (2000) book *Seeing through Paintings* for examples of X-ray studies of the working process of artists such as Chardin, El Greco, Constable, and Mondrian. The book also provides an excellent annotated bibliography of many studies performed in this field as well as a list of videotapes that illustrate technical examination procedures and artists' techniques.

Real-life Case Study Research

Perceptual/Cognitive and Drawing Processes during Art Making

Miall and Tchalenko (2001) conducted a study to identify the picture-production processes of British portrait artist Humphrey Ocean, who was known for his skill in producing detailed and realistic portraits of models from life. When an artist draws from life, his or her gaze shifts back and forth many hundreds of times between the sitter and the emerging drawing. To capture the nature of this process the researchers employed an eyetracker to record the artist's visual exploration strategies, a sensor recording the movements of the artist's pencil, and a close-up video filming of the emerging portrait. The study consisted of five parts, which correspond to the sequence of phases included in Mace and Ward's (2002) model of the art-making process. First, the artist, wearing the eyetracker, looked at each of the four prospective male sitters, one at a time, to select a model. It was observed that Ocean initially fixated on the left eye of each candidate, after which he made a number of fixations that rested mostly on a candidate's eyes. Fixation durations were of approximately 400 ms during this selection process. Following this, the artist drew each candidate in a small sketchpad for between 1 and 2 minutes to help him in making a selection of the model. Average fixation duration during this task was 1,000 ms, a rather long duration compared to when he was just looking at the candidates (400 ms). This suggests that the artist carefully selected the features of each candidate to include in his sketch. During the art-making phase of the study, Ocean drew the portrait on a vertical drawing pad positioned on an easel. His eye fixations were recorded for 15 minutes each hour, after which he worked normally without the eyetracker for 30 to 40 minutes, followed by a 10- to 15-minute rest period for the artist and model. Five sets of recordings were made, which spanned the entire time taken to draw the portrait. During the third and fifth eye-fixation recording periods, a motion-tracking monitor was attached to the back of the artist's hand to record the spatial locations of the pencil relative to the drawing pad and the timing of all hand movements.

The drawing process that emerged from the combined observations of the artist's eye and hand movements across the entire course of artistic creation is the following. For the first 35 seconds, Ocean scanned the blank paper with occasional glances at the model, suggesting he initially visualized the composition. He then began to draw the model's right eye, which he worked on for about 1 hour. During this period the artist utilized a pattern of regular fixations on the model's face, each of which lasted for between 600 ms and 1,000 ms. Throughout the remaining hours of the sitting, some subtle variations of this basic fixation pattern appeared as the artist drew the hair, lips, and other facial features, which suggested to the researchers that there may be a relationship between the complexity of the visual object being viewed (the model's eye vs. his hair) and the viewing pattern. Additionally, the artist's eye frequently returned to the same feature on the model at a rate that would indicate visual memory of that feature was refreshed approximately every 5 seconds.

Analyses of the artist's hand movements revealed that drawing was frequently accompanied by repeated practice strokes for periods lasting from between 5 and 20 seconds, during which the artist drew in the air just above the paper's surface. During these periods, shorter, more rapid fixations were used to examine the detail on the model's drawn face or on another part of the drawing before returning to follow the movement of the pencil tip just above the paper. Occasionally, these movements produced faint pencil marks on the paper. These practice strokes likely aided the artist

in deciding on the exact location and form of the line to be drawn. In the artist's words, "If the line lands a millimeter to the right or a millimeter to the left, it changes the weight, in some way, or the shape that it is describing. So when the line lands, you just want it to land in the right position, whatever that is" (Miall & Tchalenko, 2001, p. 39). It should be noted that despite this careful attention to the details of a feature in the model's face, few lines in the portrait represented actual lines on the model's face, suggesting that the artist considered the artistic and aesthetic qualities of the work as the composition was created.

During the next phase of the experiment, Ocean drew three portraits each within a relatively short period of about 10 minutes so that the eye and hand movements could be monitored throughout the entire period of creation. The artist's drawing processes during this task were similar to those recorded for the creation of the main portrait.

In the last part of the study, Ocean and three individuals untrained in the visual arts made a series of brief 1-minute sketches from a black-and-white photograph of a face. Both eye movements and pencil movements were recorded. The artist's fixation durations remained between 600 ms and 1,000 ms, whereas those of the untrained participants were approximately half as long. Additionally, untrained individuals did not show precise fixation on individual details of the face, frequently examining two or more areas of the face when looking at it, whereas the artist's fixations were precisely targeted on selected details of the face.

What do the data observed in this case study suggest concerning the way the artist selected, organized, and arranged pictorial elements during the creation of the portraits? Miall and Tchalenko (2001) offer the following answer to this question. All of Ocean's actions suggest that visual information about the model is selected and integrated into the composition detail by detail, rather than in a more holistic manner, and that the eye and eye–hand actions are essentially driven by the drawing's progress. Each element and detail is of intrinsic importance.

Ocean remarked, "I'm sure of what I am see-ing, I'm not quite sure what I am going to do about it. So I make a decision. The final result is made up of a great many decisions" (p. 39).

In another real-life case study, Yokochi and Okada (2005) investigated the ongoing creative processes of art making by a tradi-tional Chinese ink painter (Mr. K) who had approximately 20 years of experience in this style of painting. In the first of two stud-ies, conducted in a temple, the artist drew a picture of a mountain and valley across four large sliding doors with brush and Chi-nese ink. Video cameras were set up on both sides of the doors to capture his drawing pro-cess. Sensors in the mats on which the artist walked while drawing produced a record of where and in what order he moved about in front of the doors while completing the artwork. In a second study, conducted in the artist's studio, Mr. K drew eight pictures on blank paper and eight pictures on sheets of paper that contained 15 random lines. The artist's task in the latter scenario was to incorporate the 15 lines into each composi-tion, a procedure that produced constraints on the composition's structural organiza-tion. The theme of the set of artworks was the four seasons. The artist spent between 20 and 30 minutes completing each drawing. Once again, the emerging artwork and the drawing process were recorded.

Analyses of the ongoing processes used by Mr. K to create the picture on the slid-ing doors revealed his art-making strategy. Initially, he drew the central part of the left doors for about 22 minutes (43% of the total 51 minutes spent creating the work), after which he stepped back to view the entire picture that had thus far been created. The global image during the first phase of the work's development was gradually formed as the artist drew local images one by one. He then began to draw on the right panels, often stepping back to see the whole com-position. As he completed the picture, Mr. K moved back and forth very frequently to view the entire work, adding a few lines here and there. These behaviors, together with an interview with the artist, indicated that he formed his plans for the structural organiza-tion of the painting as the work progressed. He did not begin the task with a completed artwork in mind; rather, the art-making pro-cess consisted of a series of interactive pro-cesses involving structuring, evaluating, and restructuring the content and form of the artwork.

Analysis of the duration and timing of Mr. K's drawing movements during the second task revealed that the artistic process con-sisted of cycles of drawing followed by short or long pauses (operationally defined based on the data set as less or more than 9 sec-onds in duration, respectively). Short pauses were associated with movement of the brush from one place to another or to the ink plate, and the less frequently occurring long pauses likely reflect the artist taking time to think about the design and plan and monitor his drawing process. Yokochi and Okada (2005) observed significant differences in these pro-cesses as a function of the lines on the paper. First, the mean time for drawing on the blank paper was longer than the mean time for drawing on the lined paper ($Ms = 18$ min. vs. 10 min., respectively). Additionally, more pauses occurred in the lined-paper condition than in the blank-paper condition, but there was about the same number of both types of pauses during the first and second half of each artwork's development. This latter finding is seen by the researchers as indicat-ing that the artist planned and monitored his drawing throughout construction of the artworks. Furthermore, it was observed that Mr. K frequently moved his brush in the air before he actually drew any lines on paper. The percentage of pauses with hand move-ment was 59% in the blank-paper condi-tion, whereas it was 86% in the lined-paper condition. The researchers suggest that by moving the brush in the air so frequently in the lined-paper condition, the artist gen-erated mental images to facilitate incorpo-rating the lines into the composition. The artist described this process in the follow-ing way, "Although I do not draw any actual objects on the paper, through drawing the form in the air, I can judge if the balance of the objects is OK" (p. 251). Finally, the compositions created on blank paper were rated by college students as better composed, more focused, and better balanced than were those drawn on the lined paper. Pictures in the lined-paper condition were characterized by liveliness and dynamism, characteristics different from those of traditional Chinese ink paintings. Thus, the lines seem to have produced constraints for the artist and forced him to create a new style for these compositions.

We turn now to an experimental investigation by Cohen (2005) of the relationship between the visual analysis component of the drawing process and an artist's ability to render realistic drawings. In each of four studies, university art majors and non–art majors were asked to realistically render the images in two photographs of the heads of males seen from the shoulders up. Each participant's eye movements were video recorded as he or she looked back-and-forth between the photograph and the drawing; the location of the gaze (photograph, drawing, neither) and the time spent fixating that region were used for analyses. In Experiment 1, participants were given 10 minutes to draw each stimulus using whatever strategy they desired (i.e., unregulated gaze-frequency condition). In the remaining three experiments, gaze frequency was manipulated by an apparatus in which participants could alternately see the to-be-drawn photograph or their drawings as they were being created. The speed of alternation between the two views was experimentally manipulated at intervals of 1, 3, 5, 8, or 15 seconds across experiments to vary gaze frequency.

In general, results revealed that the art-trained students made more alternations between the drawing and the stimulus than did untrained students. For both groups, high gaze frequencies were positively associated with more accurate drawings as rated by a group of nonartists. Cohen (2005) suggests that higher gaze frequencies (relatively fast alternations) for artists contribute to their drawing process and its accuracy by (1) providing the perceptual system with only a small amount of pictorial information in working memory to be transferred

to the drawing; (2) reducing memory distortions of perceptual information contained in working memory, which is known to begin to distort very shortly after the removal of the stimulus; and (3) facilitating the reduction of stimulus interpretation and context effects through focused attention (brought about by inattentional blindness and void viewing), which results in only a very small portion of a stimulus being "visible."

Sketching and the Design Process: Creative Discovery

Most artists begin work on a composition with one or more study sketches of what will become the completed work. These might be a series of drawings like the 45 preliminary sketches Picasso created prior to starting work on *Guernica* or preparatory underdrawings of paintings produced directly on the canvas. Progressive changes in preliminary sketches are made during the developmental phase of art making until the structural organization of what the artist believes will become the final composition is realized. Sketching is also considered an essential part of the creative process in all areas of design (e.g., fashion, product design, industrial design, architecture, and engineering). In fact, more is known about the processes of sketching and drawing used by designers than by artists because of the relevance of such research to the education and skill development of students and practitioners in these applied fields. This literature has led to many theoretical frameworks and models that explain the interactive contributions of the aesthetic and technical factors to the design process in all applied fields of design (see, e.g., Eckert & Stacey, 2003; Locher, Overbeeke, & Wensveen, in press).

The first phase of the design process – the concept-development phase – is characterized by the generation of concept sketches that provide an initial pictorial representation of a design. Sketches serve as external memories of design ideas for later inspection, and they provide visual cues "on the fly" for the association of structural and functional issues associated with the artifact being developed. Sketching, if effective, is a cyclical, dialectic process that results in the continuous emergence of new knowledge and reinterpretations of a potential design. It is often envisaged as "visual thinking." As one example of a real-life case study in this field, Tovey and Porter (2003) investigated the drawing techniques and sketching process of six professional automotive designers at the Ford Motor Company design studio. The designers were instructed to reflect aloud on the physical and mental processes they were going through as they created a concept sketch for an automobile; their sketching behavior and verbal commentaries were video recorded. It was observed that the concept-design process began with the use of structured lines and forms. As the sketch evolved desired lines were emphasized with a heavier stroke and form shading. In terms of their visuomotor process, the actions used by the designers consisted of strong sweeping movements that were frequently made through the air above the pad before touching pen to the paper. The designers' comments made it clear that they engaged with their sketches in an interactive way that allowed the designs to emerge on paper. The creative process was not an externalization of a design conceived at the start of a project in the designers' head and seen in their mind's eye; rather, the creative process generated design features in their minds throughout the development of the artifact. These are the same ongoing art-making processes reported by artist participants in the studies already described.

With respect to the focus of this volume – creativity – it is interesting to note that despite the availability and continual improvements of very sophisticated commercial computer-aided design (CAD) systems, freehand sketching continues to be considered the primary tool at the initial concept-design stage for students and professionals across design domains (e.g., Bilda & Demirkan, 2003). The major criticism of CAD-system use at the conceptual stage of design is that such systems do not foster creativity and may, in fact, inhibit it. They are typically technical drawing tools

geared to production needs, such as automation, accuracy, and efficiency of routine drawing tasks, all of which may reduce the designer's creative options. If such systems are to contribute to creative sketching activity, future systems will have to foster "constructive perception" that promotes changes in conceptualization and external representation of the design being developed. To date, however, computer and information sciences are only just now starting to investigate creativity support software tools that can extend designers' capabilities to create innovative designs at their conceptual stage. Shneiderman (2007, p. 24) points out that the Association for Computing Machinery's *Computing reviews classification system* still does not include the terms creativity, exploration, discovery, or innovation among its 1,500 entries, and many design professionals and artists still question whether computer-based creativity support is an achievable goal for the initial phase of the design process.

Art-Making and Personality

Are different approaches to image making (i.e., artistic styles) associated with an artist's personality? Machotka (2003, 2006) employed a very comprehensive real-life case-study approach to answer this question. University students who were variously accomplished in the visual arts were recruited from art and psychology classes as "artists" in the study. Participants individually selected one of six photographs of landscapes, which they then transformed into "a work of art" on a computer using retouching software (Adobe Photoshop program) to manipulate and transform the image. While participants worked on the picture, their image making was followed in detail by an experimenter who noted the Photoshop tool in use, the operation performed, and all comments made by the participant about "what was going on." In addition, progressive transformations of each artwork were saved in such a way that its development could be reconstructed. When individuals decided they had completed their artwork, they answered questions about the process, their motives and intentions, and the picture's meaning. Following this, participants' personalities were studied clinically by means of an extensive psychodynamic interview.

Machotka's (2003) research team reviewed the personality data together with the set of recorded images and formulated a tentative connection between the personality profiles of participants and their approaches to picture making. To verify this relationship statistically, the researchers rated each image and the process by which it was made on 21 distinguishable and recurrent image characteristics, which were reduced by factor analysis to five dimensions called image-based narrative, timidity, flowing process, formality, and expansiveness. They then looked to see how the image clusters fit the clinical interpretations, that is, if the clinical interpretations were consistent within clusters and different between them. Cluster analysis found that personal data fit the clusters closely; it identified seven different approaches to picture making by the participants.

As one example, in the cluster entitled *Narrative informality and compensatory longings* the images produced by participants were narrative and without form; they showed little emphasis on texture, organization, or composition. They conveyed a certain up-beat mood, but exhibited very little idiosyncrasy or originality. Such images were consistently produced by people with strong compensatory longings. Their childhoods "were marked by inconsistency and loss or illness, and they grew up to dedicate themselves to improving the lives of others – and the images they made for us were fantasies, attempts to create a better past than the one they had had. We saw their main impulses as wish-fulfilling and reparative, and so strong that they overwhelmed any desire – if there had been one – to think of their images in more detailed, formal terms" (Machotka, 2006, p. 75). Another cluster of participants who exercised relentless control over major issues in their lives produced dense, collaged images, and yet another group whose prominent concerns

reflected a strong need to integrate their lives produced well-composed and well-formed compositions. Machotka concluded that the style of the artworks, such as their abstractness, formality, or fluid boldness, reliably reflected what he called the map of each participant's interpersonal world. However, no single mode of creating an art work was expected or found.

Of particular relevance to the topic of this chapter was the finding that there were some artists in each cluster. Four artists formed a small cluster of their own labeled *Consistent style and the need to integrate*, which was defined by attention to form and style of the pictures in a way that integrated their personal concerns and history. Thus, Machotka's (2006) study demonstrates empirically that a painting is at least a partial expression of an artist's personality and that the personality clusters observed in his study function in different ways to influence picture characteristics, as was the case for the nonartists in the sample.

Art Making and the Brain

Making art draws on many brain areas, including those that carry out functions that contribute to visual creativity, to planning the structural organization of an artifact, and to the motor planning and drawing skills used to carry out the artistic production. In addition to these visuomotor processes, regions of the brain involved in the formation of symbolic and linguistic concepts, drives, and emotions are also involved in the artistic process. Neuroscientists working within the emerging discipline known as neuroaesthetics (see Skov & Vartanian, 2008) have begun to investigate the brain mechanisms that underlie artists' abilities to produce artworks. An expanding research literature is providing insights into the regional brain contributions to artistic production. This literature consists of the growing body of case studies showing the emergence and evolution of visual creativity in talented artists and nonartists with progressive degenerative dementias (e.g., Mell, Howard, & Miller, 2003; and see Miller &

Hou, 2004, for a review of this literature). It is now well documented that each of the degenerative dementias, such as Alzheimer's disease and different subtypes of frontotemporal dementia, leads to predictable changes in some patients' patterns of artistic skills. For example, often patients with frontotemporal dementia who have no background in painting develop a spontaneous interest in art making, resulting in their creation of progressively more complex and visually precise paintings. Many often exhibit a compulsive need to paint, which drives their visual creativity; this in turn helps these patients perfect their artistic skills. Their paintings are usually realistic or surrealistic without significant symbolic or abstract components. Also, despite progressive social and cognitive impairment, such patients exhibited increased interest in the fine detail of faces, objects, and shapes. Many frequently employ the colors purple, yellow, or blue.

According to Miller and Hou (2004), case studies of patients with dementia have and will continue to provide a window into the neurology underlying the artistic process. However, as with archival case studies in other areas of investigation, such observations do not provide direct evidence of the ongoing art-making process, and research that examines the brain regions involved during real-life artistic production is almost nonexistent. One notable exception is the study conducted by Solso (2001) to determine how the brain activity of a skilled portrait artist differed from a nonartist as they drew a series of faces. Solso took functional magnetic resonance imaging (fMRI) scans of the leading British portrait artist Humphrey Ocean (the same participant in Miall & Tchalenko's, 2001, study already discussed) and a nonartist volunteer as they sketched drawings of faces and complex geometric figures. Data collected for the geometric figures were subtracted from the scans for faces to control for the perceptual-motor activity required to sketch the faces. Clear and important differences in activity occurred in two regions of the brain as each participant drew the faces, namely, in the right-posterior parietal and in the right-

middle frontal areas. The right-posterior parietal area was activated in both participants, but the degree of activation was greater (i.e., increase in blood flow activity) in the nonartist than in the artist. This confirms that an area of the brain associated with facial processing activity was indeed activated when both participants looked at faces but not activated during visual processing of the geometric figures. Important for the present discussion is the finding that a lower level of activation was seen in the artist, suggesting that he was more efficient than the nonartist when processing facial features. This may be explained by the fact that, because of the portrait artist's professional experience viewing faces, he may require little involvement by the area of the brain associated with facial perception when looking at the faces. Given that a nonartist lacks this type of experience with faces, he may require greater involvement of this area of the brain, as was found in the study.

The second and related finding was that the artist showed greater activation in the right-middle frontal area of the brain than the nonartist, which is an area associated with more complex associations, manipulation of visual forms, and planning of the fine motor responses of the hands. According to Solso (2001), this suggests that a skilled portrait artist, one who frequently sees and draws faces, engages in a "higher order" interpretation of a model's face, that is, he sees beyond the features of a face. Taking the two major findings together, Solso concludes that "the artist 'thinks' portraits more than he 'sees' them" (p. 34), whereas the nonartist seems to be merely copying the face.

Compositional Balance

Thus far, the focus of this chapter has been on the contribution of an artist's characteristics to the creative processes involved in art making. We turn now to the influence on the artist of standards of good composition (i.e., the "visually right"; see Locher, 2003), which are always a consideration, even if the artist chooses to violate them. In the view of many art theoreticians and artists (e.g., Arnheim, 1988; Bouleau, 1980; Kandinsky, 1926/1979), balance is the most important design principal in the visual arts because it unifies the structural elements of a pictorial display into a cohesive organization or framework that helps determine the role of each element within a composition. A composition is said to be balanced when its elements and their qualities (e.g., size, shape, color, directionality) are poised about a balancing center so that their visual forces or tensions compensate one another and appear anchored and stable. Given the hypothesized importance of balance to the creation of an artwork, are artists compelled to balance their composition, or are they free not to do so? Arnheim's reply to this question is that "balance is necessary to make the artist's statement definitive. If a composition is unbalanced, it will appear to be an interrupted movement, an action paralyzed in its striving toward a state of rest. Similar to what musicians call a half-cadence, such an intermediate state will make the viewer sense that the needed solution is in the offing but not actually supplied. Thus if the artist wishes his work to convey its meaning itself rather than simply stimulate the viewer to embark on some shaping of his own, the composition will have to be in equilibrium" (p. 66).

Empirical evidence supports the importance of balance in an artist's compositional efforts. For example, Firstov, Firstov, Voloshinov, and Locher (2007) investigated whether artists' spatial control of color within a composition results in the location of the colorimetric barycenter corresponding to the geometric center of a painting. The colorimetric barycenter is the "center of gravity" for all compositional colors and the areas they occupy within the color mass of the entire pictorial field of a painting. Firstov et al. computed the location of the colorimetric barycenter for each of 1,332 paintings by Russian artists. The set of compositions studied included 1,174 works by modern painters of the late twentieth century, 30 landscapes and 70 portraits created in the late nineteenth and early twentieth centuries, and 58 nonrepresentational

paintings by avant-garde painters of the early twentieth century. The researchers observed that the artists' manipulation of color within a composition resulted in the location of its center of colorimetric mass corresponding closely to its geometric center for both representational and abstract paintings. This finding demonstrates the power of the center of a pictorial field to function as an "anchor" or balancing point about which artists exert spatial control over color. It provides empirical evidence that they are strongly influenced in their use of color by the timeless standard of good composition – balance. However, Firstov et al.'s observations do not demonstrate *how* balance is achieved during the art-making process. This was the purpose of a real-life study by Locher, Cornelis, Wagemans, and Stappers (2001), the findings of which provide a quantitative account of the influence of balance on artists' compositional strategies as they created visual designs.

Participants in Locher et al.'s (2001) study were students enrolled in an Academy of Fine Arts who had completed an average of 3 years of study in either painting, sculpture, ceramics, or graphics. The artists were asked to create four "interesting" designs using planar black plastic triangles or quadrilaterals, which varied in degree of orientation potential on a white display field whose format was either circular or rectangular. Videotape recordings of the development from start to finish of each design completed by each artist were made and used to assess the distribution of physical weight about the principal axes of each design and the location of its balance center. A digitized version of each design created by each artist was produced from its videotape record at 20% intervals of the total time taken for completion (i.e., 20%, 40%, 60%, 80%, and 100% – the completed design).

Locher et al. (2001) found that almost all of the designs were begun with a few shapes placed in the pictorial field and developed by the addition of one or two elements at a time that typically resulted in adjustment to the overall structural organization. Approximately the first 50% of total construction time was spent "building" the design. Once all elements were placed in the field, the artist used both hands to continuously slide elements from one location to another. To determine whether the artists' designs were balanced, and at what point during the development of a design, the researchers computed a quantitative balance index about the four principal axes of each design. The index is the percentage of a design's area (pixels) covered by the black shapes on one side of a central axis. A perfectly balanced composition has 50% of the black area created by the shapes on both sides of an axis; any distribution other than this, say a 60% – 40% distribution, would indicate a less than perfectly balanced design.

It was found that regardless of element type, format, or phase of construction, the balance center of a design was closely aligned with the geometric center of the pictorial field. Furthermore, the structural or physical weight of the compositional elements measured quantitatively was evenly distributed (balanced) about the four principal axes of the designs throughout their construction. These findings demonstrate empirically once again that the center of a pictorial field functions as the balancing point about which a design's structural skeleton is organized by artists. And, most importantly for the present discussion, Locher et al.'s (2001) findings demonstrate that some universal principles of good composition are likely, such as balance, and that these principles are taken into consideration by visual artists during art making, especially when they are working within certain artistic styles.

Conclusions

Empirical investigations of the actual working processes engaged in by visual artists as they make art are very limited in number. As is true with all case studies, it is not possible to know how well results of such studies might generalize. Despite these limitations, the findings of both archival and real-life case studies reported in this chapter pro-

vide converging empirical evidence of the nature of the art-making process outlined in Mace and Ward's (2002) model, as explained throughout the chapter. In sum, there is agreement in the studies reviewed that the artist participants did not have the completed image of the artwork in their minds before starting to sketch or paint it but gradually developed a plan for the composition during the idea-development and art-making phases of the entire creative process. Pictorial elements were selected and integrated into a composition detail by detail, guided simultaneously during the ongoing development of the work by its intended meaning, the artist's procedural knowledge, the information provided by the current stage of the work's pictorial content and structural organization, and by motor planning. All of these factors contribute to the finished work in a dynamically interactive way.

Additionally, the findings support Kozbelt and Seeley's (2007) Visuomotor Skill Model, which postulates two main sources of an artist's skills for making art. The first of these is the specialized knowledge needed for artistic production, which is initially acquired in the form of declarative knowledge and becomes procedural knowledge through practice. The second skill is motor planning, also acquired with extensive practice. As demonstrated by the review, these skills play complementary roles in influencing the perceptual and thought processes that underlie artistic production at all phases of art making.

Finally, as is the case for any type of behavior, research evidence reported herein demonstrates that the processes and products of art making are mediated by a number of factors in addition to the motor, perceptual, and cognitive mechanisms employed during artistic production. These included an artist's personality and personal history, and the universal convention of pictorial execution for good design – balance. In addition to the factors described in this review, there are many other autobiographical, motivational, cultural, and historical factors that are thought to contribute to the content and style of an artwork and the creative processes employed during its production. A comprehensive understanding of art making by visual artists awaits a great many additional real-life case-study and experimental investigations of these highly interactive and interdependent factors.

References

Arnheim, R. (1988). *The power of the center: A study of composition in the visual arts*. Berkeley: University of California Press.

Biersdorfer, J. D. (2008, June 8). What lies beneath can tell another tale. *The New York Times*, Arts & Leisure Section, p. 26.

Bilda, Z., & Demirkan, H. (2003). An insight on designers' sketching activities in traditional versus digital media. *Design Studies*, 24, 27–49.

Bouleau, C. (1980). *The painter's secret geometry*. New York: Hacker Books.

Burroughs, A. (1938, 1965). *Art criticism from a laboratory*. Westport, CT: Greenwood Press.

Cohen, D. (2005). Look little, look often: The influence of gaze frequency on drawing accuracy. *Perception & Psychophysics*, 67, 997–1009.

Eckert, C., & Stacey, M. (2003). Adaptation of sources of inspiration in knitwear design. *Creativity Research Journal*, 15, 355–384.

Firstov, V., Firstov, V., Voloshinov, A., & Locher, P. (2007). The colorimetric barycenter of paintings. *Empirical Studies of the Arts*, 25, 209–217.

Gunderman, R. B., & Hawkins, C. M. (2008). The self-portraits of Frida Kahlo. *Radiology*, 247, 303–306.

Kandinsky, V. (1979). *Point and line to plane* (H. Dearstyne & H. Rebay, Trans.). New York: Dover. (Original work published 1926)

Kirsh, A., & Levenson, R. (2000). *Seeing through paintings: Physical examination in art historical studies*. New Haven, CT: Yale University Press.

Kozbelt, A. (2006). Dynamic evaluation of Matisse's 1935 *Large Reclining Nude*. *Empirical Studies of the Arts*, 24, 119–137.

Kozbelt, A., & Seeley, W. (2007). Integrating art historical, psychological, and neuroscientific explanations of artists' advantages in drawing and perception. *Psychology of Aesthetics, Creativity, and the Arts*, 1, 80–90.

Locher, P. J. (2003). An empirical investigation of the visual rightness theory of picture perception. *Acta Psychologica*, 114, 147–164.

Locher, P., Cornelis, E., Wagemans, J., & Stappers, P. (2001). Artists' use of compositional balance for creating visual displays. *Empirical Studies of the Arts*, 19, 213–227.

Locher, P., Overbeeke, C., & Wensveen, S. (in press). A framework for aesthetic interaction. *Design Issues*.

Mace, M., & Ward, T. (2002). Modeling the creative process: A ground theory analysis of creativity in the domain of art making. *Creativity Research Journal*, 14, 179–192.

Machotka, P. (2003). *Painting and our inner world: The psychology of image making*. New York: Kluwer Academic/Plenum.

Machotka, P. (2006). Artistic styles and personalities: A close view and a more distant view. *Empirical Studies of the Arts*, 24, 71–80.

Mell, J. C., Howard, S., & Miller, B. (2003). Art and the brain: The influence of frontotemporal dementia on an accomplished artist. *Neurology*, 60, 1707–1710.

Miall, R., & Tchalenko, J. (2001). A painter's eye movements: A study of eye and hand movement during portrait drawing. *Leonardo*, 34, 35–40.

Miller, B., & Hou, C. (2004). Portraits of artists: Emergence of visual creativity in dementia. *Archives of Neurology*, 61, 842–844.

Schneiderman, B. (2007). Creativity support tools: Accelerating discovery and innovation. *Communications of the ACM*, 50, 20–32.

Simmonton, D. K. (1999). *Origins of genius*. New York: Oxford.

Skov, M., & Vartanian, O. (2008). *Neuroaesthetics*. Amityville, NY: Baywood.

Solso, R. (2001). Brain activities in a skilled versus a novice artist: An fMRI study. *Leonardo*, 34, 31–34.

Tovey, M., & Porter, S. (2003). Sketching, concept development and automotive design. *Design Studies*, 24, 135–153.

Weisberg, R. (2004). On structure in the creative process: A quantitative case-study of the creation of Picasso's Guernica. *Empirical Studies of the Arts*, 22, 23–54.

Yokochi, S., & Okada, T. (2005). Creative cognitive process of art making: A field study of a traditional Chinese ink painter. *Creativity Research Journal*, 17, 241–255.

CHAPTER 8

Organizational Creativity

A Systems Approach

Gerard J. Puccio and John F. Cabra

Introduction

Organizational creativity has been defined as "the creation of a valuable, useful new product, service, idea, procedure, or process by individuals working together in a complex social system" (Woodman, Sawyer, & Griffin, 1993, p. 293). The creative act is sufficiently complex when carried out by an individual alone, such as the artist, photographer, writer, and so on; imagine the heightened amount of dynamism reached when individuals attempt to create within organizational systems. This chapter explores some of the fundamental factors that influence the manifestation of creativity in the workplace. We take a systems approach in that we endeavor to understand the complex whole as it is formed and influenced by individual components. We begin by discussing the reasons why there has been a burgeoning interest in organizational creativity. The remainder of the chapter uses a systems model as a framework to review literature relevant to organizational creativity.

Why Organizational Creativity Is Hot

In his 1975 article "The creative organization," Hitt observed that "although voluminous research exists in the field of creativity as it relates to the individual, little has been done relative to organizational creativity and its necessity" (p. 283). How things have changed! There are now numerous journal articles on the topic of organizational creativity. Indeed, there is a refereed journal dedicated to this very topic. Established in the early 1990s, the aim of the *Creativity and Innovation Management* journal is to bridge "the gap between the theory and practice of organizing imagination and innovation." Commensurate with the growth in journal publications, there also has been an increase in books on organizational creativity authored by those in university centers (i.e., Bilton, 2007; Davis & Scase, 2001; DeGraff & Lawrence, 2002; Hargadon, 2003; Thompson & Choi, 2005; Zhou & Shalley, 2008).

Why has there been an increased interest in organizational creativity? There are at least two main trends that appear to have fostered growth in this area of creativity research. One trend responds to the need for organizations to adapt quickly to change; the other trend reflects a concern for innovation. Although interconnected, we briefly discuss each trend in turn.

There is no escaping the fact that we live in an ever-changing world and that large-scale change occurs at an ever-faster pace. This is exemplified by the fact that more than half of the major, life-altering, technological and social innovations introduced to the world came into being in the past 200 years (Albery & Yule, 1989; Henry, 2001; Makridakis, 1989). Before the 1800s it would have been possible, indeed probable, that many generations could live without experiencing the impact of a single significant technological or social invention. In contrast, a person born in the early 1960s would have already experienced the impact of civil rights, space exploration, organ transplants, personal computers, mobile phones, the Internet, cloning, genetic engineering, e-mail, and much more.

Organizations and their members have not escaped the impact of transformative change. According to Hitt (1975), organizations exist to provide solutions to society's needs and problems. As society evolves at a breakneck pace, organizations are forced to respond quickly; those incapable of change will quickly find themselves replaced by organizations that are more responsive. As Hitt (1975) observed, "In order to avoid extinction, organizations must change and *adapt* to changes in order to remain viable. To do so requires utilization of all available resources, especially the most creative – the human resource" (p. 284). Organizations do not adapt to change; rather it is the people within organizations who are required to change. Therefore, it is not surprising that a number of studies and reports have identified creative thinking and creative problem solving as fundamental workplace skills. One of the earliest studies to do so took place in the 1980s (Carnevale, Gainer, & Meltzer, 1990). This three-year-long national study sought to identify the skills necessary for success in the workplace. Analysis of the data yielded by a cross-industry sample of organizations led to the identification of seven distinct skill sets. One of the skill sets, labeled "adaptability," included two specific skills related to creativity – creative thinking and problem solving. Similarly, a U.S. Labor Department report focusing on the skills essential for workers to be productive in the new millennium included the following thinking skills: thinking creatively, making decisions, solving problems, knowing how to learn, and reasoning (SCANS Commission, 1991).

The call for creative thinking in the workplace has continued. A group of leaders from public and private organizations, such as American Society for Curriculum Development, Dell, Educational Testing Service, Microsoft, and Verizon, published a report in 2008 entitled *21st Century Skills, Education & Competitiveness* (Partnership for 21st Century Skills, 2008). As with previous studies and reports, this more recent list of work skills once again highlighted the central role creativity plays in today's organizations. The specific creativity-related skills articulated in this report were solving complex, multidisciplinary, open-ended problems; creativity and entrepreneurial thinking; and making innovative use of knowledge, information, and opportunities. Why are creativity skills so highly touted in today's organizations? As noted earlier, in order to survive, organizations must provide solutions to society's changing needs, and the increased pace of change places a premium on employees' creativity skills. No longer do employees spend their entire careers dedicated to the refinement and elaboration of a single product or service. There has been a dramatic decrease in product life cycles. For instance, Hunter and Schmidt (1996) reported that manufactured products are subject to fundamental redesign every 5 to 10 years. In high-tech industries, this time line shrinks to every 6 to 12 months. This observation led Williams and Yang (1999) to conclude that "today, workers must adapt quickly as they switch from performing one specialized task to performing another equally specialized task"

(p. 375). It would seem generally accepted that for organizations to adapt, they must have employees who are flexible, adaptive, imaginative, and able to tolerate ambiguity – in short, they must be creative.

Another major trend that has fostered a burgeoning interest in organizational creativity, especially among those in the private sector, has been a desire to become more innovative. It is now widely argued that to remain competitive, organizations must not only adapt to change but also drive change through innovative business practices, processes, products, and services. Apple, Google, Toyota, General Electric, Microsoft, Pfizer, Disney, SONY, and other leading companies understand that their bottom-line success relies on an ability to innovate. Janzen (2000) suggested that "after the age of efficiency in the 1950s and 1960s, quality in the 1970s and 1980s, and flexibility in the 1980s and 1990s, we now live in the age of innovation" (p. 3). As clear evidence for this focus on innovation, a global survey of 2,468 senior executives carried out by the Boston Consulting Group revealed that 66% of the respondents ranked innovation among the top three strategic priorities for their companies (Andrew, Sirkin, Haanæs, & Michael, 2007). Similarly, Vardis and Selden (2008) reported 55% of the 513 executive level officers they surveyed identified innovation as one of their top three current strategic priorities.

Schumpeter (1934) provided one of the first systematic definitions of innovation. In his view, innovation was the successful commercialization of new combinations, such as new materials and components, the introduction of new processes, the development of new markets, and the creation of new organizational forms. A contemporary description of innovation was extracted from IBM's in-depth interviews of 765 chief executive officers (IBM Global CEO Study, 2006). These executives outlined three discrete forms of innovation: business model innovation (i.e., new structures or financial models); operational innovation (i.e., new ideas that improve the effectiveness and efficiency of processes

and functions); and product/service/market innovation (i.e., new products, services or "go-to-market" activities). Many now make the case that innovation, in whatever form, does not occur without creativity. For example, Amabile, Burnside, and Gryskiewicz (1999) suggested that "creativity is the crucial 'front-end' of the innovation process; before innovation can happen, the creative ideas must be generated by individuals and teams so that they can be successfully implemented" (p. 1). Taking a broader approach, Rickards (1996) suggested that creativity is required throughout the entire innovation process. He specifically noted that

> the linear model mind-set always results in the assumption that creativity "exists" at the front end of a two-stage idea generation and implementation innovation process. This article makes the case for a long-needed break with this assumption. In the new paradigm, ideas and actions occur and interact as long as innovation is being pursued. Creativity continues as long as action continues. This is not just desired, it is necessary for as long as the innovation processes continue in a competitive environment in the absence of perfect knowledge about outcomes of actions. (p. 24)

The Connection between Creativity and Innovation: Some Empirical Evidence

It is one thing to suggest that creativity is theoretically linked to innovation, and quite another to demonstrate empirically that creativity indeed spawns innovation. A small number of studies have endeavored to demonstrate the practical link between organizational creativity and innovation. Perhaps the earliest study to undertake this question was carried out by Blau and McKinley (1979). In this study, the researchers examined, among other variables, whether the work motif, that is, the main design ideas, pursued by an architectural firm predicted the extent to which the firm's work was objectively perceived as being innovative (e.g., industry awards for innovation). Results indicated that work motif was a significant predictor of innovation awards; in

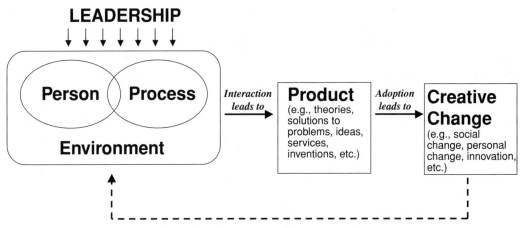

Figure 8.1. Creativity: A Systems Model

particular, firms whose design ideas challenged the constraints outlined by their clients generated more innovative architectural designs. Moreover, Blau and McKinley discovered that the most innovative firms "rarely standardize design concepts from project to project, and attempt continually to evolve new and creative solutions to particular problems" (pp. 216–217).

Bharadwaj and Menon (2000) carried out a study in which they examined the specific kinds of creativity found in organizations and their impact on innovation. These researchers broke creativity down into two specific areas, *individual creativity mechanisms*, defined as activities individual employees pursued on their own to develop personal creativity, and *organizational creativity mechanisms*, or the practices and formal procedures adopted by organizations to promote creative behavior. These researchers then compared the amount of innovation reported across organizations. Bharadwaj and Menon's findings showed that the highest levels of innovation, as reported by employees, were found among those organizations that were identified as having high amounts of both individual and organizational creativity mechanisms. Although Bharadwaj and Menon concluded that both types of creativity contribute to innovation, they suggested that "organizational creativity mechanisms seem to have a stronger association with innovation performance" (p. 430).

Where Bharadwaj and Menon (2000) relied on employees' perception of innovative performance, Soo, Devinney, Midgley, and Deering (2002) ranked some 317 firms on innovation and then compared the variables that contributed to innovation, as well as the financial benefits associated with innovation. An analysis across these organizations showed that the most innovative firms were those that were most active in using creativity to generate new knowledge. Specifically, Soo et al. concluded that "creativity in problem solving is the main driver of new knowledge creation and innovation" (p. 145). These researchers also examined the benefits of innovation and found that the most innovative firms enjoyed significantly greater market share and return on assets. These findings support the important role creativity plays in fostering innovation and the tangible benefits organizations derive from innovation.

Models of Organizational Creativity

At the very beginning of this chapter we offered a passing comment about the complex nature of organizational creativity. Figure 8.1 presents a model useful in understanding the nature of organizational creativity. Originally offered by Puccio, Murdock, and Mance (2007), we believe the *creative change model*, which utilizes a systems approach, provides a useful framework for reviewing the sets of variables related to organizational creativity. Relating this model to organizations, innovation comes about as the result of the interaction among people, the processes they engage in, and the environment in which they work. The *person* facet in this model refers to individual skills, background, experience, personality, knowledge, motivation, and so forth. *Process* relates to the stages of thought people engage in when working alone or with others to creatively address predicaments and opportunities at work. The *environment* relates both to the psychological and physical setting in which a person works. Puccio et al. (2007) suggested that it is the interplay among these variables that leads to the formation of an intangible or tangible product (i.e., solution to a problem, expression of a new idea, development of a new service, an original product concept, an invention, etc.). Not until the product of creative thinking has been adopted is creative effort fully realized – change has been adopted, at least temporarily. When adopted internally, these creative changes can lead to cost reduction, improved policies or procedures, new business models, and so forth. Products with an external focus result in a change in the marketplace, such as the successful introduction of an innovative product or service. This is an iterative model, as the adoption of an internal or external change has a subsequent impact on the organization and thus potentially influences people, processes, and the environment in that organization.

The literature review found in the remainder of this chapter is organized around this model. We selected this model because it subsumes the oft-referred to four fundamental aspects of creativity, namely, person, process, product, and environment (see Brown, 1989; MacKinnon, 1978; Rhodes, 1961; Stein, 1968), which also appear in many organizational creativity models (see Schoenfeldt & Jansen, 1997). To these core elements of creativity we add leadership. Recent literature has especially emphasized the impact leaders have on group and organizational creativity (e.g., Amabile, Schatzel, Moneta, & Kramer, 2004; Gumus-luoglu & Ilsev, 2009; Redmond, Mumford, & Teach, 1993; Sosik, 1997; Sternberg, 2003), and in their review of various organizational creativity theories, Schoenfeldt and Jansen (1997) comment on the need to include leadership in interactionist models of organizational creativity. The remainder of this chapter explores the research literature related to the main elements in this model that interact to yield a creative product or outcome within the workplace, specifically person, process, environment, and leadership.

Person

Perhaps the area that has received the greatest attention within the field of creativity studies has been the examination of the qualities, skills, traits, and other attributes that distinguish highly creative individuals from their less creative counterparts. Many of the pioneering creativity researchers, such as MacKinnon (1962), Torrance (1974), Barron (1969), and Guilford (1970), dedicated their research to the distillation of those factors that set creative people apart. It is not our intention to summarize the extensive literature available on the creative person; instead, we focus on the specific factors that predispose someone to be successfully creative within the organizational context. Here Amabile's (1983a, 1983b, 1988) research stands out.

Amabile has carried out a series of investigations that have examined the role individual creativity plays with respect to organizational creativity. Amabile (1988) could not have been clearer about the crucial nature of employees' creativity and its relationship to innovation when she summarized some of her early research:

> The entire process of individual creativity must be considered as a crucial element in the process of organizational innovation. . . . It is individual creativity that provides the raw material for organizational innovation and, therefore, individual creativity must be central to the organizational model. (p. 150)

This statement reinforces the position that organizational innovation does not happen without the emergence of creativity at an individual level. To that end, Amabile interviewed employees from a variety of work settings to unearth the individual factors that contributed to creative accomplishment in the workplace (Amabile, 1988; Amabile & Gryskiewicz, 1988). The following list summarizes the qualities associated with individual creativity: various personality traits (e.g., persistence, curiosity, and energy); self-motivation; special cognitive abilities; risk-orientation; expertise in the area; qualities of the group; diverse experience; social skill; brilliance; and naiveté. Positive affect can now be added to this list of individual factors that promote creativity. A recent study by Amabile, Barsade, Mueller, and Staw (2005) found a simple-linear relationship between positive mood and peer-rated creativity.

This investigation, in conjunction with other studies carried out by Amabile (1987), led to the formulation of a componential model of individual creativity. The model comprises three core features: domain-relevant skills, creativity-relevant skills, and intrinsic task motivation. To create, an individual must understand his or her discipline, job, or field. Domain-relevant skills refer to knowledge, technical skills, and special talents associated with one's area of work. Domain-relevant skills are necessary but not sufficient for creativity to occur. To produce work that is original, individuals must also possess creativity-relevant skills, such as suspending judgment, self-discipline, perseverance, and nonconformity. Finally, to achieve creative outcomes the employee must be highly motivated. As Amabile (1988) noted, "No amount of skill in the domain or in the methods of creative thinking can compensate for a lack of appropriate motivation to perform an activity" (p. 133). Motivation toward a task can be sorted into three categories: no motivation, an intrinsic orientation (i.e., pursuing a task for its own sake), and an extrinsic orientation (i.e., focusing on reasons external to the task, such as rewards, expected evaluation, and competition). In

general, individuals who are engaged in a task for intrinsic reasons are more likely to generate creative outcomes, whereas an extrinsic focus tends to undermine creativity. Dewett's (2007) recent study helped provide insight into the motivation-creativity relationship in the workplace. Dewett's research demonstrated that increased levels of intrinsic motivation among research and development (R&D) personnel enhanced risk taking and experimentation, which in turn positively impacted individual creativity. It should be noted that over time Amabile has revised her thoughts about the deleterious effects of extrinsic motivation. Under certain conditions extrinsic rewards can serve to accentuate intrinsic motivation (see Amabile, 1993; Hennessey & Amabile, 1998).

Chuang (2007) tested the applicability of Amabile's model with some of the most innovative companies in Taiwan. Twelve high-level managers involved directly in innovation efforts participated in in-depth interviews. These companies included Toyota, Fubon Bank, and Tong-yi Starbucks. According to Chuang, the analysis revealed, as predicted in Amabile's model, that individual factors, such as employee creativity and mindset, were directly related to organizational innovation. Additionally, Chuang found that the inclusion of organizational (i.e., organizational resources, culture and structure) and environmental factors (i.e., customers, technology, competitors, etc.) strengthened Amabile's model. As Chuang suggested, "Individual, organizational, and environmental factors mutually complement and interact with one another; they affect the organizational innovation process" (p. 886). These findings support the contention, as outlined in this chapter, that models of organizational creativity must take a systems approach and should consider the interaction among the fundamental facets of individuals, the surrounding environment, and the stages of the creative process. Ford (1995) put forward a similar argument, stating that he believes "this love affair with creators has led researcher [sic] to focus too narrowly on characteristics of individuals that lead them to commit creative acts" (p. 21). Based on this assertion, Ford proposed that the creative act could be likened to a crime. That is, creativity involves motive, means, and opportunity. To underscore the importance of the latter variable, Ford noted that a positive work environment can even serve to draw out creativity among those who would not ordinarily pursue creative acts. Amabile's own research acknowledges the crucial influence the work environment has on employee creativity (Amabile et al., 1999; Amabile & Gryskiewicz, 1988). The next section reviews some of the literature that has delineated the aspects of environment that are conductive to creativity in the workplace.

The Creative Work Environment

Over the years, research in the field of creativity has transitioned from a fairly narrow focus on creativity as an individual quality to a concern for the impact of the environment on creative behavior. MacKinnon (1978) referred to this area of inquiry as the "creative situation" and described the purpose of this line of research as the identification of "those characteristics of the life circumstances and of the social, cultural, and work milieux that facilitate or inhibit the appearance of creative thought and action" (p. 52). Since early efforts to explore creativity in organizational contexts, researchers have sought to understand how factors associated with the work environment affect employee creativity (Abbey & Dickson, 1983; Amabile & Gryskiewicz, 1988; Ekvall, 1983; Rickards & Bessant, 1980; Siegel & Kaemmerer, 1978). These efforts have culminated in lists of attributes of the work environment that are believed to have a profound influence on employee creativity. Table 8.1 summarizes some of the dimensions determined to be apposite to a creative work environment. In some cases, these lists correspond directly to variables included in well-established and widely used measures of the work environment, most notably Amabile's KEYS

(Amabile et al., 1999), Ekvall's Creative Climate Questionnaire (Ekvall, 1996), and Anderson and West's Team Climate Inventory (1998).

Work environment is a broad, all-encompassing term. As scholars have closely examined conditions found in the work environment, more specific constructs have emerged that are subsumed under this general, catchall category. We review some of the constructs that have been related specifically to the work environment; we progress from broad to more concrete constructs. We begin our review with national culture.

National Culture

National culture is defined as the traditions, values, symbols, heroes, and rituals that shape behavior and cultivate desired perceptions of the world (Adler, 2002). Hofstede (2001) stated that "culture can be defined as the interactive aggregate of common characteristics that influence a human group's response to its environment" (p. 10). Rudowicz (2003) argued that sociocultural systems cannot be separated from creative output. Ng (2001) provided a detailed description of how Western and Eastern cultures have differential effects on individuals' psychological make-up and, as a consequence, determine how easy or difficult it is for individuals to be creative within their native culture. According to Ng, Eastern cultures emphasize control by the environment (i.e., conformity, harmony, etc.), whereas Western cultures focus more on autonomy and individuality. As a result, Ng suggested that Asians are more likely to develop a psychological make-up that includes such qualities as cautiousness, self-criticism, and conservative values, which makes it more challenging to engage in creative behavior.

With increased globalization, more and more organizations are crossing cultural boundaries. Consider German automaker Daimler's purchase of Chrysler, or more recently, the Belgian company InBev's acquisition of Anheuser-Busch. These expansions bring together different cultures, which may give rise to conflict, especially if attempts

Table 8.1: Comparison of Dimensions Deemed To Be Important to the Creative Environment

Ekvall & Tangeberg-Andersson (1986)	Rickards & Bessant (1980)	Siegel & Kaemmerer (1978)	Amabile, Burnside, & Gryskiewicz (1999)	VanGundy (1987)	Basadur (1987)	Cabra & Joniak (2006)	Anderson & West (1998)	Soriano de Alencar & Bruno-Faria (1997)
Challenge Support for Ideas Dynamism Playfulness Debate Conflict Trust Freedom Pressure of Work Achievement Risk-taking	Management Style Communication Reward System	Support for Creativity Tolerance of Differences Personal Commitment	**STIMULANTS:** Organizational Encouragement Supervisory Encouragement Work Group Supports Sufficient Resources Challenging Work Freedom **OBSTACLES:** Organizational Impediments Workload Pressure **CRITERION SCALES:** Creativity Productivity	Autonomy Performance Reward Dependency Risk-taking Support for Creativity Personal Commitment Top Management Support High Responsibility for Initiating Ideas Job Security Moderate Degree of Ambiguity	**BARRIERS:** Limited Time Limited or Invisible Funds Inadequate Upward Communication Inadequate Downward Communication Physical Environment Inadequate Contact with Technical Activities Organizational Structure Lack of Technical Critique Low Risk-taking Lack of Creative Processes and Training	Resources Trust Responsiveness Leadership Style Freedom Synergy Dynamism Idea Time Self Confidence Building Support Organized Creativity Influence Management Norms Belonging Sense of Equity Response to Social Political Cultural Conditions Envy/Jealousy	Vision Participative Safety Task Orientation Support for Innovation	**STIMULANTS:** Challenges Colleagues' Support Freedom & Autonomy Organizational Structure Organization Support Physical Environment Salaries & Benefits Support from the Boss Technological & Material Resources Training **OBSTACLES:** Boss Characteristics Lack of Equipments & Other Material Resources Lack of Training Organization Culture Organization Structure Personal Relationships Physical Environment Political & Administrative Influences Salaries & Benefits Task Characteristics Volume of Tasks

are not made to grasp and address the integration of different norms and traditions (Lubart, 1999; Rapaille, 2001; Westwood & Low, 2003). Such differences are likely to relate to dissimilar approaches, perceptions, and values as related to creativity. For example, Mostafa and El-Masry's (2008) study of 125 future marketing managers illustrated how Egyptian and British managers differed in their attitudes about organizational barriers to creativity. A 17-item Barriers to Creativity measure was used to examine differences in perceived obstacles to organizational creativity between the two populations. The barriers measured by these items included such factors as risk aversion, fear of failure, time pressure, and management rejection of suggestions. The overall results revealed significant differences on 16 of the 17 items. Mostafa and El-Masry provided descriptions of how some of the underlying cultural differences, especially the individualistic nature of Western cultures versus the collectivistic orientation found in Egyptian society, might explain their findings. Given these differences, these authors suggested that management practices with respect to creativity must vary according to the culture. Where freedom, self-directed decision making, and an overall focus on the outcome are beneficial in Western cultures, the high power distance of Arab cultures might require managers to provide more direction, particularly in regard to how a team approaches a task and the strategies used to achieve the desired outcome.

A majority of the research into the conditions of work environments conducive to creativity has been carried out in organizations in North America and Europe. Cabra, Talbot, and Joniak (2005) undertook a study to explore the creative work environment in Colombian organizations. These researchers did not presume that previously identified dimensions would be relevant to the Colombian employees' experience and therefore took a qualitative approach, thus allowing the most pertinent factors to emerge. Their results revealed environmental factors in keeping with past research, such as Idea Time, Freedom, and Trust.

However, they discovered a number of dimensions that had not been identified in previous research, such as Envy/Jealousy, Financial Support (a subscale under the general heading Support), and Influence Management Norms. With respect to Financial Support, Cabra, Talbot, and Joniak discovered that material incentives in Colombian organizations brought about innovation, suggesting that extrinsic motivation can propel employee creativity when unmet basic needs weigh heavily on an organizational member's mind.

It is generally accepted that work environments that feature autocratic leadership styles will stifle ideas and creativity (Miller, 1988). In contrast, in their qualitative study Cabra, Talbot, and Joniak (2005) found that some interviewees perceived directive leadership behaviors as being helpful to workplace creativity so long as the leader was respectful and benevolent. Hofstede (2001) reported that those in collectivistic societies, such as Colombia, are expected to sacrifice their personal goals for the sake of group goals, and thus a more directive style of leadership is embraced.

In their study of 1,228 individuals in 30 countries, Shane, Venkataraman, and MacMillan (1995) determined that those who preferred avoiding uncertainty were more likely to desire idea champions to aid them in navigating ideas through the organization; idea champions are typically savvy at maneuvering ideas through a firm's political process. Shane et al. found similar results when they examined additional cultural values, namely, high power distance and collectivism. Organizations in countries that valued a greater distance between those who wield power and those who do not favored the use of idea champions, as was the case for those employees in collectivistic societies.

The few studies mentioned here have important implications concerning cross-cultural deployment of creativity research, models, and concepts. Westwood and Low (2003) identified three problems associated with the application of creativity concepts across cultures. One problem concerns the

tendency to force universalistic interpretations of creative processes, structures, and
functions. Second is the tendency to laud
one approach to creativity and innovation in
a particular culture, while devaluing a perspective on creativity that already exists in
another. The third problem relates to falla-
ciously bolstering differences through sim-
plified explanatory models. In their review
and critique of cross-cultural issues pertinent to creativity, Westwood and Low concluded that "culture can and does impact
on creative and innovation processes, but
the relationship should not be considered
universalistically, simplistically or unreflex-
ively" (p. 235).

External Environment

Isaksen, Lauer, Ekvall, and Britz (2000–2001)
defined the external environment as "any
condition or situation that is outside the
organization itself (e.g., the market, global
financial conditions, government, the larger
political and social system, technological
and scientific developments) but can exert
an influence on the organization's performance" (p. 173). Conversely, organizations
generally exert little influence in regard to
conditions found in the external environment. Unlike cultural values and traditions,
which are developed over long periods of
time and are not easily changed, the external
environment is more temporal. Political and
social conditions can emerge and go away,
such as in the case of changes in governmental leadership or an economic downturn.

In an extensive study of cities throughout the United States, Florida (2002) examined factors that contributed to a munic-
ipality's ability to attract creative talent;
suggestive in his findings were social and
political dynamics that fall outside the control of organizations yet do much to ensure
a ready pool of highly creative workers.
According to Florida (2002), creative people
"prefer places that are diverse, tolerant
and open to new ideas" (p. 223). Additionally, Florida's research into the "creative class" showed, among other variables,
that such workers desire places that afford

a socially rich lifestyle, offer structured
opportunities for social interaction, provide authentic experiences, and are tolerant
of diverse ethnic groups, ages, and sexual
orientations.

On a wider scope, other studies have suggested that a country's governmental policies, processes, and decisions can have deleterious effects on organizational creativity.
De Soto (2000), for example, reported on
the extensive challenges to establishing a
legal business in Latin America. He examined the process steps required to register a
garment shop in Lima, Peru, which, after
following all prerequisites, took 289 days,
with an average of 6 hours of effort per
day. In Hungary, for example, Inzelt (2003)
maintained that policymakers created practices that hampered Hungary's transition
process to a postsocialist economy. Hun-
garian banks, for instance, placed too many
conditions on loans taken out for industrial
R&D and created funding mechanisms that
undermined innovation.

As for the United States, Kao (2007)
has argued that there is a need for a
national innovation policy to improve our
innovation process, a process that currently
is trumped by bureaucracy and resources
that are siphoned elsewhere to more reactionary types of initiatives. Estrin (2009), former chief technology officer at Cisco Systems, provided a cogent argument for the
important role government plays in igniting
and sustaining creativity and innovation in
organizations:

> Our nation's leaders decisively influence
> the health of the country's Innovation
> Ecosystem. Politicians influence day-to-day
> business processes through laws and reg-
> ulations. They control funding and policy
> that directly affect our educational system
> and the research community.... Federal
> and state policies have a significant impact
> on the Ecosystem. Legislation, SEC regu-
> lations, litigation rules, healthcare require-
> ments, and tax incentives all affect the abil-
> ity of businesses to innovative effectively.
> (pp. 49–50)

South Korea provides a good example of
a country that has enacted a series of

policy measures to integrate relationships among academia, industry, and the public research sector. Its government has further refined legal and institutional conditions to supplement R&D efforts, and South Korea is now one of the largest investors in R&D worldwide (Chung, 2003). For further information on ways in which countries can encourage innovation, see Forbes and Wield (2002), Edquist and Hommen (2008), and Kao (2007).

Organizational Culture

As in national culture, organizations over time create and preserve values, traditions, and beliefs. What delineates organizational from national culture is its reach. That is, organizational cultures within a national culture vary. Google, for instance, may espouse an open and informal organizational culture, whereas General Motors may value a more closed and formal culture. Thus, organizational culture is confined, whereas national culture is far-reaching and may affect many organizations. Lundy and Cowling (1996) provided a straightforward definition of organizational culture when they stated that "it is the way that things are done around here" (p. 168). Organizational traditions and beliefs can be reinforced by organizational structures (e.g., centralized, decentralized, virtual) and by physical space (e.g., mobile furniture, corporate playgrounds, workspace visibility).

In regard to organizational culture and creativity, Martins and Terblanche (2003) identified five major factors related to organizational culture that promote creativity: 1) an innovation strategy that explicitly focuses on the development and implementation of new products and services, which is derived through an organization's vision and mission; 2) the organizational structure, which includes such variables as flexibility, freedom, and cooperative teams; 3) organizational support mechanisms, such as reward and recognition programs, as well as availability of resources (e.g., time, information technology, creative people); 4) behavior that encourages innovation, consisting of response to failure, idea generation, spirit of continuous learning, risk-taking, competitiveness, support for change, and conflict management; and 5) open communication.

Amazon.com provides a good example of an organizational culture that is conducive to creativity. Amazon.com subscribes to a customer-centric strategy (Burrows, 2008). A centrally held belief at Amazon.com is that they should not imitate their competitors, as this approach would produce reactionary creativity. Therefore, employees are encouraged to experiment and find new ways to provide added value to customers. Google is another excellent example of an organizational culture that supports workplace creativity. Its organizational structure is informal; lava lamps and large rubber balls can be found in the workplace. Fun and play are encouraged. Its offices were designed around clusters to promote the flow of information. Additionally, Google provides each of its engineers 20% of their work time to experiment with their ideas (Elgin, 2005).

The importance of organizational culture in regard to organizational creativity was reinforced by the Boston Consulting Group's survey of senior managers (Andrew et al., 2007). When asked about the obstacles to innovation, 38% of the 2,468 senior managers identified a risk-averse corporate culture as the number one barrier to innovation in their organizations.

Organizational Structures

Organizational structures relate to the hierarchy found within an organization; as such, they outline relationships among organizational components and communicate lines of responsibility and authority. Lafley and Charan (2008) documented several different structures within one company, Procter and Gamble (P&G), designed to promote innovation. Future Works make up a multidisciplinary unit run by a general manager. Its mission is to seek discontinuous ideas that can lead to a new business that is adjacent to an existing category or one that runs across several category businesses. A sponsor is assigned to the innovation, which assures the innovation has a home and a champion. Another structure is the New Business Development (NBD) organization. Whereas Future Works can cross business categories, the NBD targets a specific unit. Innovation project teams are charged with developing and pipelining innovations that improve existing products and are funded by the respective business units. The External Business Unit (EBU) explores ideas outside of the organization. Ideas can come from vendors, other organizations, entrepreneurs, and other outside sources. EBUs serve as brokerage houses. Innovation Hot Zones are simulated homes and supermarkets or any other setting where P&G products are likely to be housed. They are located around the world at P&G locations or in locations owned by partners and other retailers. An ethnographic approach is employed to gain insight from watching consumers. These observations are used to generate new product concepts. Another structure is called Connect and Develop. This is an internet network-based organizational structure that taps into all of P&G's relationships, such as retirees, other companies, retail customers, suppliers, nonretail customers, and its competitors.

Holt (1987) provided further thoughts about how to structure organizations and teams in a way that increases the likelihood of innovation. In his paper, Holt discusses such structures as matrix organizations, the independent project team, and the venture team. And for empirical studies on the relationships among organizational structure, creativity, and innovation, see, for example, Prakash and Gupta (2008), Freeman and Engel (2007), and Sumanski, Kolenc, and Markic (2007).

Climate

An examination of Table 8.1 shows that the dimensions of the work environment represent a cross-section of various environmental concepts reviewed here. For example, com-

munication and reward systems, which can be considered part of the organizational culture (Martins & Terblanche, 2003), are highlighted by a number of scholars (Basadur, 1987; Rickards & Bessant, 1980; VanGundy, 1987). Basadur's (1987) dimensions include specific references to organizational structure and physical setting. In their study of Brazilian organizations, Soriano de Alencar and Bruno-Faria (1997) cited organizational structure, salaries and benefits, physical environment, and training among those work environment dimensions most closely related to creativity. A large number of the dimensions found in Table 8.1 seem to align most closely with what has been referred to as "climate." "Culture" and "climate" are often used interchangeably, as have been the dimensions associated with these environmental constructs, yet some have argued that these are conceptually distinct aspects of environment (Glick, 1985; Isaksen, 2007). Isaksen and Ekvall (2007) offered a simple point of differentiation when they noted that climate is what organizational members experience, whereas culture is defined as what organizational members value. Climate consists of the behaviors, feelings, and attitudes that distinguish life in an organization (Ekvall, 1983). Ekvall (1983) posited that "each organization member perceives the climate, and can describe it in light of his or her own perception" (p. 2). Some have been critical of the use of the term "climate." Guion (1973) suggested that climate is a broad concept that has been loosely defined, and Glick (1985) maintained that climate is a generic term that targets many dimensions and consequently makes the concept almost useless. As a remedy, Glick (1985) proposed that the most effective use of the term is to frame it within a targeted area of analysis or concern (e.g., climate for job satisfaction, security, production, safety, or creativity).

One of the leading scholars with respect to the climate for creativity has been Ekvall (1983, 1996, 1997). Ekvall (1983) suggested that climate affects how organizational members communicate, solve problems, make decisions, handle conflicts, learn, and motivate, and thus can be reflected in the efficiency and productivity of the organization. Ekvall identified 10 dimensions related to a creative climate, namely, Dynamism, Challenge, Freedom, Trust and Openness, Idea Support, Conflict, Debate, Idea Time, Playfulness/Humor, and Risk-Taking. Using his measure of the creative climate, the Creative Climate Questionnaire, Ekvall has demonstrated significant differences between organizations and units within organizations with respect to their creative output. In one of his most elaborate studies, Ekvall (1991) had independent researchers from a business school apply their model for assessing innovation to 27 different organizations. The application of the innovation criteria enabled the researchers to place each organization into one of three categories: innovative, average, or stagnant. Employees in these organizations also completed Ekvall's climate measure. The results were clear. The most positive climates for creativity were found among those employees in organizations identified as being innovative. Not surprisingly, the perceptions of the most oppressive work climates were found for those employees in organizations that had been identified as being stagnant. For other studies that have examined the efficacy of Ekvall's dimensions, see Ekvall and Ryhammar (1999), Isaksen et al., (2000–2001), and Sellgren, Ekvall, and Tomson (2008).

Anderson and West (1998) developed the Team Climate Inventory (TCI) to measure work-group climate for innovation. The TCI targets team development initiatives that are meant to foster creativity. This measure assesses four climate factors: Vision (the extent to which clarity exists between team goals and visions); Participative Safety (the extent to which shared decision making exists in teams and the environment is perceived as nonthreatening); Task Orientation (the extent to which team members share similar concerns regarding excellence in quality of task performance); and Support for Innovation (the extent to which practical support is provided to

new ways of doing things). The TCI was created using items extracted from other measures, such as the Siegel Scale of Support for Innovation (Siegel & Kaemmemer; 1978), and its psychometric properties have been evaluated by other researchers (see Mathisen & Einarsen, 2004). Additionally, the TCI has been translated and tested in other languages, such as Norwegian and Swedish (Mathisen, Einarsen, Jørstad, & Brønnick, 2004).

Physical Space

As innovation has climbed the strategic priorities list in organizations, there has been greater attention given to the physical features within an organization and how workspaces might be designed to inspire creative thinking. It would seem that some organizations recognize that the physical structures created under the mechanistic models of organizations are not appropriate in the innovation age. IDEO, a California-based design firm, has garnered great attention by showcasing its nontraditional physical spaces. At IDEO, employees are encouraged to create their own workspaces; here, employees' work areas are adorned with prototypes from past projects, artifacts from their favorite hobbies, and knickknacks. As Kelley (2001), general manager of IDEO, observed, "This may sound a bit extreme, but companies that depend on the creativity of their staff give them free reign when it comes to space" (p. 125). At Oticon, a midsize Danish manufacture of hearing aids, workers are able to concentrate on any project and are free to join any team (Ewing, 2007). Desks and filing cabinets are not fixed. They are pushed to new locations, reconfigured into new spaces for workers to organize themselves. Workers band together around natural leaders as a way to be drawn to the most exciting projects. The United Kingdom's Royal Mail has established an award-winning innovation lab that features white curved walls suitable for capturing ideas, musical instruments, online brainstorming technology, material for prototype construction, movable furniture, digital recording devices, and a team of expert facilitators.

The creation of creative workspaces appears to be outpacing scholars' ability to document and describe the nature and impact of such spaces. That said, a few authors have offered their reflections on the physical setting for creativity (Haner, 2005; Kristensen, 2004; Lewis & Moultrie, 2005; Moultrie et al., 2007). Lewis and Moultrie (2005) maintained that physical structures provide a competitive advantage to organizations that leverage these spaces to improve their performance and innovation efforts. The marketplace has become highly dynamic, and thus organizational spaces that are designed well are apt to be more responsive and flexible than those that are not. Kristensen (2004) emphasized that physical spaces influence an employee's emotional well-being. A positive association with the surrounding physical space, therefore, will enhance creative work. Haner (2005) posited that physical space can serve as a source of inspiration and motivation. An attractive space can spark innovation strategies and signal to employees that creativity is expected.

Lewis and Moultrie (2005), using a case-study approach, examined three U.K.-based innovation laboratories. Preliminary findings indicated that physical structures were conducive to innovation when malleable – space that can be broken down, changed, or reconfigured at a moment's notice in response to an organizational need or marketplace demand. Similarly, Haner (2005) argued that a hybrid space, one that can accommodate both private and group work, as well as divergent and convergent processes, is optimal for innovation. Finally, Moultrie et al. (2007) provide a framework that helps practitioners and researchers better understand the roles, goals, and various design features of physical spaces that promote organizational creativity. Each component in their framework contains a list of variables organizational leaders should consider in designing space that promotes creativity.

Process

Organizations can hire creative talent and develop a creative work environment, but these actions do not guarantee creative outcomes. To increase the probability of successful creative thinking, many organizations have adopted management practices, outlined creative methods and strategies that are applied in groups, and introduced training programs all designed to help employees more effectively and skillfully engage in the creative process. The aim here is to undertake deliberate approaches that do not leave creativity to chance. At its core, creativity is an applied area of study – many scholars and practitioners seek to understand better how creativity comes to fruition so that ultimately it can be facilitated, directed, and nurtured in a manner that increases the likelihood that individuals and groups in organizations can quickly generate creative breakthroughs to problems.

Can the creative process be directed at will? In surveying engineers, Ekvall (2000) discovered that, indeed, organizations can adopt particular practices that promote creative thinking. Among the engineers in his study, 88% reported that the use of project groups and continuous improvement methods enhanced creativity, and 85% indicated that the application of creative problem-solving methods in meetings had positive effects as well. Where Ekvall conducted a survey across many organizations, Mahmoud-Jouini and Charue-Duboc (2008) conducted a case-study analysis of a new unit created to pursue discontinuous innovation (i.e., radically new ideas that depart from existing products and services) within one automotive company. These researchers were particularly interested in the design and organizational creativity processes that enabled this unit to achieve its mission. These authors carefully documented the creative process followed by this team, from its inception through to the identification and subsequent funding of five exploratory projects deemed likely to succeed. Based on this research, a detailed description emerged in regard to the activities subsumed in each stage of this team's creative process (i.e., scope definition, knowledge sharing, conceptual design, and embodiment design). Furthermore, Mahmoud-Jouini and Charue-Duboc outlined four broader organizational practices that supported the eventual success of this team: 1) the creation of a broad scope for the innovation unit; 2) the dual role of the members of the unit, dedicating a percentage of their time to the project while carrying out ongoing work responsibilities, which encouraged boundary spanning; 3) the back and forth flow between knowledge and concept development during the creativity process; and 4) the role and cross-divisional nature of the exploratory projects that emerged from the innovation unit.

Further evidence for the value of adopting deliberate creative-process strategies can be found in a study briefly cited earlier in this chapter (Bharadwaj & Menon, 2000). Recall that Bharadwaj and Menon compared individual versus organizational creativity mechanisms and found that the latter had a stronger relationship to innovation performance. The organizational creativity mechanisms included such practices as a widely shared process for creative problem solving, formal creativity and idea-generation programs, a designated innovation center, and facilitators assigned to lead idea-generation efforts. Based on their findings, these researchers called on managers "to formalize creativity approaches and techniques in organizations to improve innovation output" (p. 431). Moreover, they suggested that organizations look at "creativity expenditures as an investment, rather than treat it as an expenditure" (p. 431).

Through the years, numerous creative processes have been developed and subsequently adopted in organizations. These creative processes offer models and techniques that can be followed by individuals and groups to improve creative output. These creativity methodologies are designed to provide employees with structured approaches that endeavor to make the creative process less mysterious and more easily facilitated in a predictable and repeatable manner. We briefly review some of the more widely known creative process models and approaches.

Creative Problem Solving

Originally developed by Osborn (1953), creator of Brainstorming, Creative Problem Solving is one of the earliest, most widely adopted and thoroughly researched creative-process models (Isaksen & Treffinger, 2004; Puccio, Murdock, & Mance, 2005). In the creativity literature, readers will come across lower-case references to the term "creative problem solving." In such situations, the author is usually making a general reference to efforts undertaken by individuals and teams to resolve open-ended problems through creative thinking, such as the studies carried out by Ekvall (2000) and Bharadwaj and Menon (2000) cited above. In contrast, when capitalized as a proper noun, "Creative Problem Solving" (CPS) refers to the name given to the creative-process model introduced by Osborn (1953) and enhanced by others mainly associated with the International Center for Studies in Creativity at the State University of New York – Buffalo State (Isaksen & Treffinger, 1985; Noller, Parnes, & Biondi, 1976; Puccio et al., 2007). As a creative process model with a more than 50-year history, CPS has been subjected to ongoing development and continuous refinement. For a detailed description of the various versions of CPS, see Puccio et al. (2005), Isaksen and Treffinger (2004), and Puccio and Cabra (2009). The current version of CPS, used at the International Center for Studies in Creativity, is called the Thinking Skills Model (Puccio et al., 2007) and features the following steps: Exploring the Vision, Formulating Challenges, Exploring Ideas, Formulating Solutions, Exploring Acceptance, and Formulating a Plan. Additionally, one metacognitive step, called Assessing the Situation, is used to help individuals and groups determine where to begin in CPS and then how to proceed through this process. This version is referred to as the Thinking Skills Model, as it articulates the kinds of thinking and affective skills developed through and employed by CPS. Although the names of the steps in the CPS process have changed over the years, several features have remained constant. First, each step of the process begins with a divergent phase, the search for many, novel, and diverse options, which is followed by a convergent phase, the identification and development of the most promising alternatives. Second, the model includes efforts to clarify the problem, generate ideas, develop solutions, and plan for action, which closely parallels descriptions of the stages included in individuals' natural creative-process efforts. In this way, CPS is intended to provide individuals and groups with an explicit creativity model that complements and enhances their innate creative-thinking skills.

Two meta-analytic studies have confirmed the positive value of CPS (Rose & Lin, 1984; Scott, Leritz, & Mumford, 2004). In fact, Scott et al. (2004) found that creativity training based on cognitive models, such as CPS, were the most effective at enhancing attitude, problem solving, creative performance, and divergent thinking. Basadur has carried out a robust research program in which he has tested the efficacy of CPS training within organizational settings. Using his version of CPS, Basadur found that CPS training significantly improved fluency in generating new product concepts (Basadur, Graen, & Green, 1982), attitudes toward divergent thinking (Basadur, Graen, & Scandura, 1986), and union-management negotiations (Basadur, Pringle, Speranzini, & Bacot, 2000). Furthermore, Basadur has reported similar positive effects of CPS training in other cultures, specifically Japan (Basadur, Wakabayashi, & Takai, 1992) and South America (Basadur, Pringle, & Kirkland, 2002).

Beyond Basadur's work, a number of other creativity researchers have explored the value of CPS training in organizational settings. For a review of the empirical research focused on CPS training in the workplace, see Puccio, Firestien, Coyle, and Masucci (2006).

de Bono Techniques

One of the most ardent proponents for the trainability of creativity is de Bono (1992). For more than four decades, de Bono has authored books designed to teach readers how to be more creative. Two of his most well-known concepts are lateral thinking (de Bono, 1977) and the six thinking hats (de Bono, 1999). Lateral thinking refers to a shift in thinking or perception; it is a complete break from previous thoughts or paradigms. The sudden breakthrough associated with lateral thinking cannot be produced through logical thinking; therefore, de Bono has devised strategies designed to assist individuals and groups to generate radically new ideas that depart from entrenched ways of viewing a situation.

Where there are specific lateral-thinking tools that are applied to particular challenges, the six thinking hats operate more akin to a creative process. Each hat represents a different kind of thinking a person is to adopt. For instance, the white hat relates to information and facts. When wearing the red hat, metaphorically speaking, the person is to focus his or her thinking on the emotional aspects of a situation. The green hat is associated with creative thinking and idea generation. And so on. The hats are designed to foster "parallel thinking" during group problem-solving efforts. The same hat, or way of thinking, is adopted by all group members, thus creating a shared focus. De Bono (1999) considered the hats as "direction labels for thinking" (p. 4). The group applies the thinking associated with the hats as necessary to deliberately manage their process.

A recent study by Birdi (2004) examined the impact of a creativity-training program on employees in a civil-service organization in the United Kingdom. The training program consisted of three 2-day workshops. One workshop, called Business Beyond the Box, focused on helping participants set radical goals and develop strategies for achieving these goals. Two workshops were dedicated to de Bono's methods, one workshop focused on lateral thinking and the other on the six thinking hats. Analysis of a post-program survey revealed that whereas the Business Beyond the Box workshop had the greatest impact on attitude toward innovation, those workshops based on de Bono's methods did more to improve participants' knowledge of creativity techniques. The de Bono workshops also showed greater impact on work-related idea generation. Birdi's (2004) study withstanding, it would appear that empirical research into the efficacy of de Bono's methods lags behind their wide diffusion and popularity. In her recent review of de Bono's methods, Dingli (2009) indicated that de Bono places much greater emphasis on the "practical and effective application of his methods" (p. 345).

Appreciative Inquiry

Cooperrider and Srivastva (1987) were the first to describe an organizational-development process that begins by looking at what is working well, as opposed to what needs to be fixed. This process is called Appreciative Inquiry (AI) and is an affirmative approach used to explore opportunities for organizational development and to sustain high levels of performance. AI assumes that it is simpler to expand the "positive" than it is to get rid of the "negative." The AI process is comprised of the following stages: Discovery (i.e., identifying organizational processes and practices that are currently working well); Dream (i.e., identifying ways to expand or further deploy the processes and practices that are working well); Design (i.e., co-constructing the ideal future processes and practices); and Destiny (i.e., identifying ways to execute the proposed ideal processes and practices). Given the fact that the AI process begins by focusing on positive organizational attributes, it has been shown to be particularly useful in groups and organizations that are experiencing an adversarial work climate (Cooperrider & Srivastva, 1987).

In a meta-case study of AI interventions, Bushe and Kassam (2005) found that the AI process led to transformational change in 7 of 20 cases. Based on the review of these case applications, Bushe and Kassam (2005) concluded that "the forms of engagement that have evolved in AI practice may not, in the end, turn out to be the best way to engage collective ideation, but these cases demonstrate that doing so appears to be central to transformational change" (p. 176). To address this shortcoming, Cabra-Vidales (2004) described the integration of CPS and AI in a manner that would be useful in organizational development efforts. Elsewhere, Peelle (2006) conducted a quasi-experiment with six work teams to compare the effects of CPS and AI on group identification and group potency. Working on real business tasks, three cross-functional teams, comprising six members, followed the AI process, while three teams of similar composition employed CPS. Results showed that both CPS and AI improved posttask group potency and group identification. However, direct comparisons between the two methodologies indicated that the AI process demonstrated greater effects on the affective disposition of these teams. For instance, Peelle (2006) observed that members of the AI teams had a "shared sense of liberation and empowerment not fully shared by teams employing CPS" (p. 460).

AI has been used with many organizations and on a wide range of organizational challenges. Cooperrider, Whitney, and Stavros (2005) provide examples of the use of AI with such companies as British Airways, McDonalds, and GTE. In the case of GTE, these authors report on the creation of more than 10,000 innovations through the application of AI. See Cooperrider et al. (2005) and Cooperrider and Sekerka (2003) for additional information on AI.

Design Thinking

Design thinking capitalizes mostly on a user-centric approach to problem solving. Innovation is achieved mainly through careful observations of unmet consumer needs.

Consumers' experiences with products and services often provides clues to implicit gaps, unarticulated sources of frustration, and opportunities for new approaches. Design can be inspired also by what Fulton-Suri (2005) described as the "thoughtless" acts of everyday life (e.g., throwing a jacket over a chair, positioning a laptop for more comfortable use while lying in bed, resting a coffee cup on the floor while seated in a classroom desk). Design thinking begins with the step Understand, which comprises learning as much as possible about the use of a particular product or service (Ko & Kasaks, 2007). During this step a complete list of the product or service's features is created. The next step is called Observe. Here the individual or team is encouraged to engage in "ethnographic" observation of users. This step also involves finding and interviewing people willing to share their experiences with the product or service under question. This is followed by the step called Point of View. In this step, meaning is drawn from the observations made in the prior step. Next comes the step Visualize, which involves brainstorming sketches of solutions to the challenges and insights associated with the product or service. After the best solutions are identified, then physical solutions are created in the Prototype step. In the final step, Test and Reiterate, individuals and teams solicit feedback on the prototype and make changes accordingly.

Design thinking has generated much interest. Take, for instance, an ABC News *Dateline* story, "Deep Dive," which reported on the design firm IDEO. So popular was the news report – as measured by the record number of transcript requests – that it compelled ABC to rebroadcast this show 5 months later (Koppel, 1999). Additionally, the increased interest in design thinking has led to the recent creation of many design schools at universities around the world. *BusinessWeek* now ranks annually the top design schools globally; it has been argued that companies are now turning to these schools to recruit creative and talented managers (Woyke & Atal, 2007). For a description of the integration of design thinking into business school programs and courses, see Bisoux (2007).

Synectics

Gordon (1960) introduced a creative process model, called Synectics, based primarily on the use of analogies. This process encourages participants to dialogue through metaphor by using tools such as the direct analogy (i.e., the individual thinks of ways similar to how problems in technology or biology, e.g., have been solved); personal analogy (i.e., the individual imagines him/herself as the problem); symbolic analogy (i.e., the problem solver uses images that symbolically represent the essence of the problem under consideration); and fantasy analogy (i.e., the individual identifies the perfect and most outrageous solution and then works backward to reach the ideal goal). Gordon (1960) argued that creative people engage in a thinking process based on nonrational, free-association models that occur in the preconscious levels of thought. Synectics, therefore, was developed to make this process explicit and to overcome mental blocks to creative thinking through the use of analogical thinking.

Since its introduction in the 1960s, publications on Synectics have been sparse. A recent study by Gassmann and Zeschky (2008) carefully analyzed situations in which analogical thinking successfully led to new product innovation. Their findings highlighted the specific organizational conditions that are necessary to promote effective use of analogies; for instance, the firm must begin by having a deep understanding of the problem at hand and top management must be open to external solutions. For recent descriptions of this creative process methodology and its use, see Prince (2002), Nolan (2003), and Rickards (2003).

TRIZ

Where Synectics taps into the subjective free-associative processes of the mind, TRIZ, also known as the Theory of Inventive Problem Solving, is based on objective and repeatable engineering principles and practices. TRIZ was designed to take an algorithmic approach to invention, innovation, and creativity. The origin of TRIZ dates back to the 1940s, when an official of the Soviet Navy patent department, Genrich Altshuller (2001), reviewed thousands of patents and identified patterns among these inventions. This analysis led to the formation of 40 principles of invention that are at the core of the TRIZ process (Mann, 2001; Moehrle, 2005). These principles are intended to enable individuals to resolve engineering contradictions that are at the essence of the problem. The problem solver reviews the list of 40 principles and then selects a principle that best fits the problem or uses a matrix to help in selecting the most appropriate invention principle (Moehrle, 2005). An example of a TRIZ principle is Dynamicity. Here, the problem solver identifies a product's attributes, then selects one that is deemed immoveable, and thinks of ways to make it moveable.

TRIZ has evolved as it has integrated other creative practices to tackle a wide range of nontechnical problems, including those in the area of customer service (Zhang, Chair, & Tan, 2005) and the field of biology (Vincent, Bogatyreva, Pahl, Bogatyrev, & Bowyer, 2005). TRIZ has been widely adopted in organizations, and as such there are numerous papers that describe the use of this method. For examples of TRIZ applications to various business challenges in 2008 alone, see Akay, Demiray, and Kurt (2008); Chang, Tseng, and Wu (2008); and Su and Lin (2008). Additionally, León-Rovira, Heredia-Escorza, and Lozano-Del Río (2008) conducted an empirical study that tested the impact of TRIZ training on engineering students.

Deliberate Creativity: Some Future Directions

Since the early introduction of structured methods for promoting creative thinking in the 1950s and 1960s, it would seem that at no time has there been a greater demand for and application of these methods. The literature abounds with case examples of applications of such methods as TRIZ, design thinking, CPS, and AI. The preponderance of documented cases of the successful application of these methods in organizations provides a compelling story for their usefulness. However, as application has greatly outpaced scholarship, there is a clear need to close the gap between practice and research. Why would this be a concern? First, these methods are not all identical. It is likely that they have different strengths and, as a result, some may work better under certain conditions and on particular kinds of challenges. Empirical studies would be instrumental in illuminating the respective value of these creative methodologies. Second, there seem to be great disparities in the number of empirical investigations of the training effects of these methodologies. Whereas CPS has been examined in approximately 20 empirical studies in organizational contexts, there appears to be a paucity of research into de Bono's methods, design thinking, AI, and TRIZ. Research is needed to expand the investigations into CPS and to take up the issue of training effects in regard to the other methodologies. Finally, research needs to be carried out that examines the degree to which such creativity methodologies can move beyond their limited use as tools – that is, as strategies employed only when a difficult task presents itself – and can be woven into the very fabric of an organization. That is to make the cognitive and affective principles that operate underneath these methods part of the organizational culture. It is likely that when such attitudes and thought processes become part of the culture, an organization will become a truly creative system, thus encouraging creativity to arise in all units and at any time.

Leadership

A major trend within the area of organizational creativity has been the increased attention given to the role leadership plays in fostering creativity in the workplace. Many writers now argue that one of the most prominent variables within the organizational context that either promotes or undermines creativity is leadership behavior. Recent surveys of top-level managers carried out by McKinsey (Barsh, Capozzi, & Davidson, 2008) and the Boston Consulting Group (Andrew et al., 2007) pointed to the crucial role top management plays in bringing about innovation in organizations. For instance, in the conclusion of their Boston Consulting Group report, Andrew et al. summed up their findings by stating that

most critically, it will mean demonstrating to the rest of the organization – through the leader's words and actions – that innovation is a personal priority. This is truly a case of walking the walk and talking the talk, because employees are unlikely to believe a leader who says one thing and does another. (p. 27)

Numerous other writers have pointed out the impact of leadership at the broad organizational level (Blau & McKinley, 1979; Hitt, 1975; VanGundy, 1987), and more specifically on group creativity (Mumford, 2000; Oldham & Cummings, 1996; Rickards & Moger, 2000). Indeed, the link between leadership behavior and organizational and group creativity has led to a burgeoning body of research (see, e.g., Amabile et al., 2004; Basadur, 2004; Boehlke, 2008; Chen, 2007; Gumusluoglu & Ilsev, in press; Jaussi & Dionne, 2003; Jung, 2000–2001; Mumford, Scott, Gaddis, & Strange, 2002; Shalley & Gilson, 2004; Shin & Zhou, 2007; Sternberg, 2003; Sternberg, Kaufman, & Pretz, 2003; Wu, McMullen, Neubert, & Yi, 2008). Additionally, many of the dimensions featured in Table 8.1 highlight the important role leadership plays in establishing a work environment conducive to creativity (e.g., Amabile et al., 1999; Rickards & Bessant, 1980; VanGundy, 1987).

The intensified focus on the influence of leaders has led to the articulation of leadership behaviors, abilities, and qualities thought to be conducive to creativity and, ultimately, innovation. Based on the work carried out at the Boston Consulting Group, Andrew and Sirkin (2006) argued that lead-

ers who wish to turn creative ideas into innovation tend to possess a particular set of qualities that would be less prevalent in other leadership activities and responsibilities. They identified these qualities and skills as follows: tolerance for ambiguity; ability to assess and be comfortable with risk; ability to quickly and effectively assess an individual; ability to balance passion and objectivity; and ability to change.

A qualitative study of employees' daily diaries by Amabile et al. (2004) yielded a detailed description of leader behaviors that supported or undermined employees' creativity. Some of the positive leader behaviors included showing support for a team member's actions, addressing subordinates' negative feelings, providing constructive positive feedback on work done, maintaining regular contact with and providing general guidance to subordinates, and asking for team members' ideas and opinions. Examples of the leader behaviors identified by Amabile et al. that inhibited employee creativity included checking on the status of assigned work too often, not providing enough clarity about an assignment, changing assignments or objectives too frequently, and displaying lack of interest in subordinates' work or ideas.

With the increased concern for managing creativity, leadership theories and models have been empirically tested for their relevance to this group and organizational outcome. The model of charismatic leadership, originally introduced by House (1977) and extended by Conger and others (see Conger, 1999; Conger & Kanungo, 1988; Hunt & Conger, 1999), offers a set of personal qualities that seem germane to creativity and innovation management. Murphy and Ensher (2008) examined the degree to which the characteristics ascribed to charismatic leaders were prevalent among successful television directors and their efforts to promote creative productions. The qualitative analysis of interviews conducted with 21 directors of well-known national television shows revealed that many of the qualities ascribed to charismatic leadership were prevalent in the creative work led by these individuals. Visioning, for example, assisted in setting a work climate conducive to creative thinking. The directors demonstrated a sensitivity to group member's needs and used a higher than average amount of praise in discussions with others. The leaders in this study also described the use of unconventional behaviors as a means to inspire group loyalty.

Perhaps the leadership theory that has received the greatest attention with respect to organization creativity is the transformational-leadership model (Burns, 1978). Transformational leaders assist followers in developing their fullest potential. Transformational leaders motivate others to do more than what is expected or to transcend their own self-interests. In summarizing the qualities of a transformational leader, Northouse (2004) provided some clear connections between this leadership approach and creativity:

> It includes leadership that stimulates followers to be creative and innovative, and to challenge their own beliefs and values as well as those of the leader and the organization. This type of leadership supports followers as they try new approaches and develop innovative ways of dealing with organizational issues. (p. 177)

Numerous research studies have examined the positive effects of transformational leadership on group creativity. Jung (2000–2001) found that small groups led by transformational leaders were significantly more fluent and flexible in generating ideas to a problem than groups subjected to a transactional leader (i.e., a leader-follower exchange based on a quid pro quo relationship). Sosik (1997) tested and found that groups working under the high transformational leadership condition generated more original solutions to an open-ended task than did groups working under a low-transformational leadership condition. Similarly, Sosik, Kahai, and Avolio (1998) showed that the high transformational leadership approach led to higher levels of idea elaborations and original solutions in small groups.

The studies cited above involved undergraduate students working on open-ended problems for which they had little ownership, but does transformational leadership make a difference in real organizations? A growing body of literature has examined this precise issue. Shin and Zhou (2003) found that Korean employees exhibited higher levels of creativity under transformational leaders. In a more recent study of R&D teams, the same authors (Shin & Zhou, 2007) demonstrated that employees' observations of the amount of transformational leadership behavior exhibited by their immediate supervisor predicted team creativity (i.e., newness of ideas, significance of ideas, and usefulness of ideas). Specifically, these authors found that transformational leadership had a particular interaction effect with educational specialization heterogeneity such that team creativity went up when there were high levels of transformational leadership and high levels of educational diversity. Jung, Chow, and Wu (2003) reported that transformational leadership had a significant positive effect on organizational innovation as measured by R&D expenditures and patents obtained over a 3-year period. Gumusluoglu and Ilsev (2009) studied 43 different Turkish firms and found that transformational leadership behaviors, controlling for job tenure and education, had a significant positive relationship with employee creativity. The same researchers also found that higher levels of transformational leadership predicted organizational innovation. Gumusluoglu and Ilsev demonstrated that the ratio of sales generated by product innovation to total sales, and the ratio of sales generated by product innovation to expenditures for innovative efforts, were linked to transformational leadership behavior.

Puccio et al. (2007) have argued that the fields of leadership and creativity have become inextricably linked, and that the shared bond between these two concepts is change. Creativity, the introduction of original and useful ideas, is a process that leads to change. And leadership often acts as the catalyst for change (Puccio et al.,

2007). Those who lead teams and organizations in the ever-changing social, technical, business, and global environments must generate original responses themselves and facilitate the creative thinking of others, both greatly enhanced through creative thinking and problem solving. This has led some researchers, such as Mumford, Zaccaro, Harding, Jacobs, and Fleishman (2000), to conclude that the main task for today's leaders is to resolve complex social problems. To do so, leaders must be creative problem solvers. Mumford and colleagues (e.g., Mumford, Baughman, Maher, Costanza, & Supinski, 1997; Mumford, Baughman, Supinski, & Maher, 1996; Mumford, Baughman, Threlfall, Supinski, & Costanza, 1996; Mumford, Supinski, Threlfall, & Baughman, 1996; Reiter-Palmon & Illies, 2004) have carried out research that has unpacked the cognitive abilities associated with creative problem solving, and Puccio et al. have outlined the thinking skills and strategies leaders can use to become more effective at resolving open-ended problems and, ultimately, to bring about change. Given the important relationship between leadership and creativity, especially with respect to organizational creativity, it is highly likely that leadership will continue to receive great attention by those interested in how creativity manifests itself in teams and organizations. Simply put, leadership behavior has emerged as the one of the most potent variables in predicting creativity in teams and organizations.

Conclusion

In 1975, Hitt lamented the paucity of research in the area of organizational creativity. And now, a little more than three decades later, it is impossible to summarize the voluminous breadth of literature in a single chapter. This research has enabled a great deal of knowledge to be amassed about the individual qualities of employees that contributes to creativity in the workplace. There is a better understanding of the types of creativity methodologies that can be used

to facilitate creative thinking and problem solving in teams and organizations. There is much greater recognition of the impact of the work environment on organizational creativity and the specific dimensions that either facilitate or undermine creativity in organizational settings. Finally, recent work has illuminated the central role leadership behavior plays in promoting workplace creativity.

These research efforts have spawned a vast body of knowledge, knowledge that when applied can do much to uplift a very important organizational resource – employee creativity. Organizations are designed to solve society's problems. Those organizations that are richer in ideas and more imaginative are likely to be more effective at meeting society's demands and more adept at adapting to changing circumstances. The field of creativity, in large measure, is an applied science. As such, the insights gained through more than 30 years of research into organizational creativity can do much to bolster organizations' efforts to promote creativity. Leaders who employ strategies and knowledge associated with individual creativity, creativity processes, and creative environments stand a greater chance in bringing about organizational creativity that will ultimately lead to higher levels of both internal and external innovation.

References

Abbey, A., & Dickson, J. W. (1983). R&D work climate and innovation in semiconductors. *Academy of Management Journal*, 26, 362–368.

Adler, N. J. (2002). *International dimensions of organizational behavior* (4th ed.). Cincinnati, OH: Southwestern.

Akay, D., Demiray, A., & Kurt, M. (2008). Collaborative tool for solving human factors problems in the manufacturing environment: The theory of inventive problem solving technique (TRIZ) method. *International Journal of Production Research*, 46, 2913–2925.

Albery, N., & Yule, V. (1989). *Encyclopaedia of social inventions*. London: The Institute for Social Inventions.

Altshuller, G. (2001). *And suddenly the inventor appeared: TRIZ, the theory of inventive problem solving* (L. Shulyak, Trans.). Worcester, MA: Technical Innovation Center.

Amabile, T. M. (1983a). *The social psychology of creativity*. New York: Springer-Verlag.

Amabile, T. M. (1983b). Social psychology of creativity: A componential conceptualization. *Journal of Personality and Social Psychology, 45,* 357–377.

Amabile, T. M. (1987). The motivation to be creative. In S. G. Isaksen (Ed.), *Fontiers of creativity research: Beyond the basics* (pp. 223–254). Buffalo, NY: Bearly Ltd.

Amabile, T. M. (1988). A model of creativity and innovation in organizations. *Research in Organizational Behavior, 10,* 123–167.

Amabile, T. M. (1993). Motivational synergy: Toward a new conceptualization of intrinsic and extrinsic motivation in the workplace. *Human Resource Management Review, 3,* 185–201.

Amabile, T. M., Barsade, S. G., Mueller, J. S., & Staw, B. M. (2005). Affect and creativity at work. *Administrative Science Quarterly, 50,* 367–403.

Amabile, T. M., Burnside, R. M., & Gryskiewicz, S. S. (1999). *User's manual for assessing the climate for creativity: A survey from the center for creative leadership*. Greensboro, NC: Center for Creative Leadership.

Amabile, T. M., & Gryskiewicz, S. S. (1988). Creative human resources in the R&D laboratory: How environment and personality affect innovation. In R. L. Kuhn (Ed.), *Handbook of creative and innovative managers* (pp. 501–524). New York: McGraw-Hill.

Amabile, T. M., Schatzel, E. A., Moneta, G. B., & Kramer, S. J. (2004). Leader behaviors and the work environment for creativity: Perceived leader support. *The Leadership Quarterly, 15,* 5–32.

Anderson, N. R., & West, M. A. (1998). Measuring climate for work group innovation: Development and validation of the team climate inventory. *Journal of Organizational Behavior, 19,* 235–258.

Andrew, J. P., & Sirkin, H. L. (2006). *Payback: Reaping the rewards of innovation*. Boston, MA: Harvard Business School Press.

Andrew, J. P., Sirkin, H. L., Haanæs, K., & Michael, D. C. (2007, August). *Innovation 2007: A BCG senior management survey (BCG Report)*. Boston: Boston Consulting Group.

Barron, F. (1969). *Creative person and creative process*. New York: Holt, Rinehart & Winston.

Barsh, J., Capozzi, M., & Davidson, J. (2008, January). Leadership and innovation. The McKinsey Quarterly. Retrieved January 27, 2010, from http://www.mckinseyquarterly.com/Leadership_and_innovation_2089.

Basadur, M. (1987). Needed research in creativity for business and industrial applications. In S. G. Isaksen (Ed.), *Frontiers of creativity research: Beyond the basics* (pp. 390–416). Buffalo, NY: Bearly Ltd.

Basadur, M. (2004). Leading others to think innovatively together: Creative leadership. *The Leadership Quarterly, 15,* 103–121.

Basadur, M., Graen, G. B., & Green, G. (1982). Training in creative problem solving: Effects on ideation and problem finding and solving in an industrial research organization. *Organizational Behavior and Human Performance, 30,* 41–70.

Basadur, M., Graen, G. B., & Scandura, T. A. (1986). Training affects on attitudes toward divergent thinking amongst manufacturing engineers. *Journal of Applied Psychology, 71,* 612–617.

Basadur, M., Pringle, P., & Kirkland, D. (2002). Crossing cultures: Training effects on the divergent thinking attitudes of Spanish-speaking South American managers. *Creativity Research Journal, 14*(3&4), 395–408.

Basadur, M., Pringle, P., Speranzini, G., & Bacot, M. (2002). Collaborative problem solving through creativity in problem definition: Expanding the pie. *Creativity and Innovation Management, 9*(1), 54–76.

Basadur, M., Wakabayashi, M., & Takia, J. (1992). Training effects on the divergent thinking attitudes of Japanese managers. *International Journal of Intercultural Relations, 16*(3), 329–345.

Bharadwaj, S., & Menon, A. (2000). Making innovation happen in organizations: Individual mechanisms, organizational creativity mechanisms or both? *Journal of Product Innovation Management, 17,* 424–434.

Bilton, C. (2007). *Management and creativity: From creative industries to creative management*. Malden, MA: Blackwell.

Birdi, K. S. (2004). No idea? Evaluating the effectiveness of creativity training. *Journal of European Industrial Training, 29,* 102–111.

Bisoux, T. (2007). Design thinking @ innovation U. *BizEd, 6,* 24–31.

Blau, J. R, & McKinley, W. (1979). Ideas, complexity, and innovation. *Administrative Science Quarterly*, 24, 200–219.

Boehlke, S. (2008). The Politics of Creativity: Four Domains for Inquiry and Action by Leaders in R&D. *Creativity and Innovation Management*, 17(1), 77–87.

Brown, R. T. (1989). Creativity: What are we to measure? In J. A. Glover, R. R. Ronning, & C. R. Reynolds (Eds.), *Handbook of creativity* (pp. 3–32). New York: Plenum.

Burns, J. M. (1978). *Leadership*. New York: Harper & Row.

Burrows, P. (2008, April 17). Bezos on innovation. *Business Week*. Retrieved January 27, 2010, from http://www.businessweek.com/magazine/content/08_17/b4081064880218.htm.

Bushe, G. R., & Kassam, A. F. (2005). When is appreciative inquiry transformational?: A meta-case analysis. *Journal of Applied Behavioral Science*, 41, 161–181.

Cabra-Vidales, J. F. (2004). Complementary application of appreciative inquiry and organizational creative problem solving. *Revista Escuela de Administración de Negocios* [Journal of Business School of Administration], Bogotá, Colombia, 53, 96–100.

Cabra, J. F., Talbot, R. J., Joniak, A. J. (2005, January–June). Exploratory study of creative climate: A case from selected Colombian companies and its implications on organizational development. *Cuadernos de Administración*, Bogotá, Colombia, 18(29), 53–86.

Carnevale, A. P., Garner, L. J., & Meltzer, A. S. (1990). *Workplace basics: The essential skills employers want*. San Francisco: Jossey-Bass.

Chang, W. T., Tseng, C. H., & Wu, L. L. (2008). Conceptual innovation of a prosthetic hand using TRIZ. *Journal of the Chinese Society of Mechanical Engineers*, 29, 111–120.

Chen, M. H. (2007). Entrepreneurial leadership and new ventures: Creativity in entrepreneurial teams. *Creativity and Innovation Management*, 16, 239–249.

Chuang, L. (2007). The social psychology of creativity and innovation: Process theory (PT) perspective. *Social Behavior and Personality*, 35, 875–888.

Chung, S. (2003). Innovation in Korea. In L. V. Shavinina (Ed.), *The international handbook on innovation* (pp. 890–90). Oxford: Pergamon.

Conger, J. A. (1999). Charismatic and transformational leadership in organizations: An insider's perspective on these developing streams of research. *The Leadership Quarterly*, 10, 145–179.

Conger, J. A., & Kanungo, R. N. (1988). Behavioral dimensions of charismatic leadership. In J. A. Conger & R. N. Kanungo (Eds.), *Charismatic leadership* (pp. 78–97). San Francisco: Jossey-Bass.

Cooperrider, D. L., & Sekerka, L. E. (2003). Toward a theory of positive organizational change. In K. S. Cameron, J. E. Dutton, & R. E. Quinn (Eds.), *Positive organizational scholarship: Foundations of a new discipline* (pp. 225–240). San Francisco: Berrett-Koehler.

Cooperrider, D. L., & Srivastva, S. (1987). Appreciative inquiry in organizational life. *Research in Organizational Change and Development*, 1, 129–169.

Cooperrider, D. L., & Whitney, D., & Stavros, J. (2005). *Appreciative Inquiry Handbook: The first in a series of workshops for leaders of change*. Euclid, OH: Crown Custom Publishing.

Davis, H., & Scase, R. (2001). *Managing creativity: The dynamics of work and organization*. Buckingham, UK: Open University Press.

de Bono, E. (1977). *Lateral thinking*. Harmondsworth, England: Penguin Books.

de Bono, E. (1992). *Serious creativity: Using the power of lateral thinking to create new ideas*. New York: HarperCollins.

de Bono, E. (1999). *Six thinking hats* (revised). Boston: Little, Brown.

DeGraff, J., & Lawrence, K. A. (2002). *Creativity at work: Developing the right practices to make innovation happen*. San Francisco, CA: Jossey-Bass (University of Michigan Business School Management Series).

De Soto, F. (2000). *The mystery of capital: Why capitalism triumphs in the West and fails everywhere else*. New York: Basic Books.

Dewett, T. (2007). Linking intrinsic motivation, risk taking, and employee creativity in an R&D environment. *R&D Management*, 37, 197–208.

Dingli, S. (2009). Thinking outside the box: Edward de Bono's lateral thinking. In T. Rickards, M. A. Runco, & S. Moger (Eds.), *The Routledge companion to creativity* (pp. 338–350). London: Routledge.

Edquist, C., & Hommen, L. (Eds.). (2008). *Small country innovation systems: Globalization, change and policy in Asia and Europe*. Cheltenham, UK: Edward Edgar.

Ekvall, G. (1983). *Climate, structure and innovativeness of organizations: A theoretical framework and experiment*. Stockholm, Sweden:

The Swedish Council for Management and Work Life Issues.

Ekvall, G. (1983). *Climate, structure and innovativeness in organizations: A theoretical framework and an experiment* [Rep. 1]. Stockholm: Faradet.

Ekvall, G. (1991). The organizational culture of idea-management: A creative climate for the management of ideas. In J. Henry & D. Walker (Eds.), *Managing innovation* (pp. 73–79). London: Sage.

Ekvall, G. (1996). Organizational climate for creativity and innovation. *European Journal of Work and Organizational Psychology*, 5, 105–123.

Ekvall, G. (1997). Organizational conditions and levels of creativity. *Creativity and Innovation Management*, 6, 195–205.

Ekvall, G. (2000). Management and organizational philosophies and practices as stimulants or blocks to creative behavior: A study of engineers. *Creativity and Innovation Management*, 9, 94–99.

Ekvall, G., & Ryhammar, L. (1999). The creative climate: Its determinants and effects at a Swedish university. *Creativity Research Journal*, 12, 303–310.

Ekvall, G., & Tångeberg-Andersson, Y. (1986). Working climate and creativity: A study of an innovative newspaper office. *Journal of Creative Behavior*, 20(3), 215–225.

Elgin, B. (2005, October 3). Managing Google's idea factory. *BusinessWeek*, pp. 88–90.

Estrin, J. (2009). *Closing the innovation gap: Reigniting the spark of creativity in the global economy*. New York: McGraw-Hill.

Ewing, J. (2007, August 20). No cubicle culture. *BusinessWeek*. Retrieved January 27, 2010, from http://www.businessweek.com/magazine/content/07_34/b4047412.htm.

Florida, R. (2002). *The rise of the creative class: And how it is transforming work, leisure, community, and everyday life*. New York: Basic.

Forbes, N., & Wield, D. (2002). *From followers to leaders: Managing technology and innovation in newly industrializing countries*. London: Routledge.

Ford, C. M. (1995). Creativity is a mystery: Clues from the investigators' notebooks. In C. M. Ford & D. A. Gioia (Eds.), *Creative action in organizations: Ivory tower visions & real world voices* (pp. 12–49). Thousand Oaks, CA: Sage.

Freeman, J., & Engel, J. S. (2007). Models of innovation: Startups and mature corporations. *California Management Review*, 50, 94–119.

Fulton-Suri, J. (2005). *Thoughtless acts? Observations on intuitive design*. San Francisco, CA: Chronicle Books.

Gassmann, O., & Zeschky, M. (2008). Opening up the solution space: The role of analogical thinking for breakthrough product innovation. *Creativity and Innovation Management*, 17(2), 97–106.

Glick, W. H. (1985). Conceptualizing and measuring organizational and psychological climate: Pitfalls in multi-level research. *Academy of Management Review*, 10(3), 601–616.

Gordon, W. J. J. (1960). *Synectics*. New York: Harper & Row.

Guilford, J. P. (1970). Traits of creativity. In P. E. Vernon (Ed.), *Creativity* (pp. 167–188). Middlesex, England: Penguin.

Guion, R. M. (1973). A note on organizational climate. *Organizational Behavior and Human Performance*, 9, 120–125.

Gumusluoglu, L., & Ilsev, A. (2009). Transformational leadership, creativity, and organizational innovation. *Journal of Business Research*, 62, 461–473.

Haner, U.-E. (2005). Spaces for creativity and innovation in two established organizations. *Creativity and Innovation Management*, 14(3), 288–298.

Hargadon, A. (2003). *How breakthroughs happen: The surprising truth about how companies innovate*. Boston: Harvard University Press.

Hennessey, B. A., & Amabile, T. A. (1998). Reality, intrinsic motivation, and creativity. *American Psychologist*, 53, 674–675.

Henry, J. (2001). *Creativity and perception in management*. London: Sage.

Hitt, M. A. (1975). The creative organization: Tomorrow's survivor. *The Journal of Creative Behavior*, 9, 283–290.

Hofstede, G. (2001). *Cultures consequences: comparing values, behaviors, institutions, and organizations across nations* (2nd ed.). Thousand Oaks, CA: Sage.

Holt, K. (1987). *Innovation: A challenge to the engineer*. Oxford: Elsevier.

House, R. J. (1977). A 1976 theory of charismatic leadership. In J. G. Hunt & L. L. Larson (Eds.), *Leadership: The cutting edge* (pp. 189–207). Carbondale: Southern Illinois University Press.

Hunt, J. G., & Conger, J. A. (1999). From where we sit: An assessment of transformational and charismatic leadership research. *The Leadership Quarterly*, 10, 335–343.

Hunter, J. E., & Schmidt, F. L. (1996). Intelligence and job performance: Economic and social implications. *Psychology, Public Policy, and Law, 2*, 447–472.

IBM Gobal CEO Study (2006). *Expanding the innovation horizon*. Somers, NY: IBM.

Inzelt, A. (2003). Innovation process in Hungary. In L. V. Shavinina (Ed.), *The international handbook on innovation* (pp. 859–880). Oxford: Pergamon.

Isaksen, S. G. (2007). The climate for transformation: Lessons for leaders. *Creativity and Innovation Management, 16*(1), 3–15.

Isaksen, S. G., & Ekvall, G. (2007). *Assessing your context for change: A technical manual for the SOQ – Enhancing performance of organizations, leaders and teams for over 50 years* (2nd ed.). Orchard Park, NY: The Creative Problem Solving Group.

Isaksen, S. G., Lauer, K. J., Ekvall, G., & Britz, A. (2000–2001). Perceptions of the best and worst climates for creativity: Preliminary validation evidence for the Situational Outlook Questionnaire. *Creativity Research Journal, 13*, 171–184.

Isaksen, S. G., & Treffinger, D. J. (1985). *Creative problem solving: The basic course*. Buffalo, NY: Bearly Ltd.

Isaksen, S. G., & Treffinger, D. J. (2004). Celebrating 50 years of reflective practice: Versions of creative problem solving. *The Journal of Creative Behavior, 38*, 75–101.

Janzen, F. (2000). *The age of innovation*. London: Prentice-Hall.

Jaussi, K. S., & Dionne, S. D. (2003). Leading for creativity: The role of unconventional leader behavior. *The Leadership Quarterly, 14*, 475–498.

Jung, D. I. (2000–2001). Transformational and transactional leadership and their effects on creativity in groups. *Creativity Research Journal, 13*, 185–196.

Jung, D. I., Chow, C., & Wu, A. (2003). The role of transformational leadership in enhancing organizational innovation: Hypotheses and some preliminary findings. *The Leadership Quarterly, 14*, 525–544.

Kao, J. (2007). *Innovation nation: How America is losing its innovation edge, why it matters, and what we can do to get it back*. New York: Simon & Schuster.

Kelley, T. (2001). *The art of innovation*. New York: Doubleday.

Ko, A., & Kazaks, A. (2007). Use your noodle: An instant guide to design. *Ambidextrous, 7*, 26–27.

Koppel, T. (Producer). (July 13, 1999). Deep dive. *Nightline*. [Television series episode]. New York: ABC News.

Kristensen, T. (2004). The physical context of creativity. *Creativity and Innovation Management, 13*(2), 89–96.

Lafley, A. G., & Charan, R. (2008). *Gamechanger: How you can drive revenue and profit growth with innovation*. New York: Crown.

León-Rovira, N., Heredia-Escorza, Y., & Lozano-Del Río, L. (2008). Systematic creativity, challenge-based instruction and active learning: A study of its impact on freshman engineering students. *International Journal of Engineering Education, 24*, 1051–1061.

Lewis, M., & Moultrie, J. (2005). The organizational innovation laboratory. *Creativity and Innovation Management, 14*(1), 73–83.

Lubart, T. I. (1999). Creativity across cultures. In R. J. Sternberg (Ed.), *Handbook of creativity*, (pp. 339–350). Cambridge: Cambridge University Press.

Lundy, O., & Cowling, A. (1996). *Strategic human resource management*. London: Routledge.

MacKinnon, D. W. (1962). The nature and nurture of creative talent. *The American Psychologist, 17*, 484–495.

MacKinnon, D. W. (1978). *In search of human effectiveness*. Buffalo, NY: Creative Education Foundation.

Mahmoud-Jouini, S. B., & Charue-Duboc, F. (2008). Enhancing discontinuous innovation through knowledge combination: The case of an exploratory unit within an established automotive firm. *Creativity and Innovation Management, 17*, 127–135.

Makridakis, S. (1989). Management in the 21st century. *Long Range Planning, 21*(2), 37–53.

Mann, D. (2001). An introduction to TRIZ: The theory of inventive problem solving. *Creativity and Innovation Management, 10*(2), 123–125.

Martins, E. C., & Terblanche, F. (2003). Building organizational culture that stimulates creativity and innovation. *European Journal of Innovation Management, 6*(10), 64–74.

Mathisen, G. E., & Einarsen, S. (2004). A review of instruments assessing creative and innovative environments within organizations. *Creativity Research Journal, 16*, 119–140.

Mathisen, G. E., Einarsen, S., Jørstad, K., & Brønnick, K. (2004). Climate for work group creativity and innovation: Norwegian validation of the team climate inventory (TCI). *Scandinavian Journal of Psychology, 45*, 383–392.

Miller, W. C. (1988). The strategic innovation management assessment profile. In Y. Ijiri & R. L. Kuhn (Eds.), *New directions in creative and innovative management: Bridging theory and practice* (pp. 287–302). Cambridge, MA: Ballinger.

Moehrle, M. G. (2005). What is TRIZ? *Creativity and Innovation Management*, 14(1), 3–13.

Mostafa, M. M., & El-Masry, A. (2008). Perceived barriers to organizational creativity: A cross-cultural study of British and Egyptian future marketing managers. *Cross Cultural Management*, 15(1), 81–93.

Moultrie, J., Nilsson, M., Dissel, M., Haner, U.-E., Janssen, S., & Van Der Lugt, L. (2007). Innovation spaces: Towards a framework for understanding the role of the physical environment in innovation. *Creativity and Innovation Management*, 16, 53–65.

Mumford, M. D. (2000). Managing creative people: Strategies and tactics for innovation. *Human Resources Management Review*, 10, 313–351.

Mumford, M. D., Baughman, W. A., Maher, M. A., Costanza, D. P., & Supinski, E. P. (1997). Process-based measures of creative problem-solving skills: IV. Category combination. *Creativity Research Journal*, 10, 59–71.

Mumford, M. D., Baughman, W. A., Supinski, E. P., & Maher, M. A. (1996). Process-based measures of creative problem-solving skills: II. Information encoding. *Creativity Research Journal*, 9, 77–88.

Mumford, M. D., Baughman, W. A., Threlfall, K. V., Supinski, E. P., & Costanza, D. P. (1996). Process-based measures of creative problem-solving skills: I. Problem construction. *Creativity Research Journal*, 9, 63–76.

Mumford, M. D., Scott, G. M., Gaddis, B., & Strange, J. M. (2002). Leading creative people: Orchestrating expertise and relationships. *The Leadership Quarterly*, 13, 705–750.

Mumford, M. D., Supinski, E. P., Threlfall, K. V., & Baughman, W. A. (1996). Process-based measures of creative problem-solving skills: III. Category selection. *Creativity Research Journal*, 9, 395–406.

Mumford, M. D., Zaccaro, S. J., Harding, F. D., Jacobs, T. O., & Fleishman, E. A. (2000). Leadership skills for a changing world: Solving complex problems. *The Leadership Quarterly*, 11, 11–35.

Murphy, S. E., & Ensher, E. A. (2008). A qualitative analysis of charismatic leadership in creative teams: The case of television directors. *The Leadership Quarterly*, 19, 335–352.

Nolan, V. (2003). Whatever happened to Synectics? *Creativity and Innovation Management*, 12, 24–27.

Noller, R. B., Parnes, S. J., & Biondi, A. M. (1976). *Creative actionbook: Revised edition of the creative behavior workbook*. New York: Scribner.

Northouse, P. G. (2004). *Leadership: Theory and practice* (3rd ed.). Thousand Oaks, CA: Sage.

Ng, A. K. (2001). *Why Asians are less creative than Westerners*. Singapore: Prentice-Hall.

Oldham, G. R., & Cummings, A. (1996). Employee creativity: Personal and contextual factors at work. *Academy of Management Journal*, 39, 607–634.

Osborn, A. F. (1953). *Applied imagination: Principles and procedures of creative problem-solving*. New York: Scribner.

Partnership for 21st Century Skills (2008). *21st century skills, education & competitiveness: A resource and policy guide*. Tuscon, AZ: Partnership for 21st Century Skills.

Peelle, H. E. (2006). Appreciative inquiry and creative problem solving in cross-functional teams. *The Journal of Applied Behavioral Science*, 42, 447–467.

Prakash, Y., & Gupta, M. (2008). Exploring the relationship between organization structure and perceived innovation in the manufacturing sector in India. *Singapore Management Review*, 30, 55–76.

Prince, G. M. (2002). *Your life is a series of meetings . . . Get good at life*. Weston, MA: 1st Books Library.

Puccio, G. J., & Cabra, J. F. (2009). Creative problem solving: Past, present, and future. In T. Rickards, M. A. Runco, & S. Moger (Eds.), *The Routledge companion to creativity* (pp. 327–337). London: Routledge.

Puccio, G. J., Firestien, R. L., Coyle, C., & Masucci, C. (2006). A review of the effectiveness of CPS training: A focus on workplace issues. *Creativity and Innovation Management*, 15, 19–33.

Puccio, G. J., Murdock, M. C., & Mance, M. (2005). Current developments in Creative Problem Solving for organizations. *The Korean Journal of Thinking & Problem Solving*, 15, 43–76.

Puccio, G. J., Murdock, M. C., & Mance, M. (2007). *Creative leadership: Skills that drive change*. Thousand Oaks, CA: Sage.

Rapaille, G. (2001). *7 secrets of marketing in a multi-cultural world*. Provo, UT: Executive Excellence Publishing.

Redmond, M. R., Mumford, M. D., & Teach, R. (1993). Putting creativity to work: Effects of leader behavior on subordinate creativity. *Organizational Behavior and Human Decision Processes*, 55, 120–151.

Reiter-Palmon, R., & Illies, J. J. (2004). Leadership and creativity: Understanding leadership from a creative problem-solving perspective. *The Leadership Quarterly*, 15, 55–77.

Rhodes, M. (1961, April). An analysis of creativity. *Phi Delta Kappan*, pp. 305–310.

Rickards, T. (1996). The management of innovation: Recasting the role of creativity. *European Journal of Work and Organizational Psychology*, 5, 13–27.

Rickards, T. (2003). Synectics: Reflections of a little-s practitioner. *Creativity and Innovation Management*, 12, 28–31.

Rickards, T., & Bessant, J. (1980). The creativity audit: Introduction of a new research measure during programmes for facilitating organizational change. *R&D Management*, 10, 67–75.

Rickards, T., & Moger, S. (2000). Creative leadership processes in project team development: An alternative to Tuckman's stage model. *British Journal of Management*, 11, 273–283.

Rose, L. H., & Lin, H.-T. (1984). A meta-analysis of long-term creativity training programs. *The Journal of Creative Behavior*, 18(1), 11–22.

Rudowicz, E. (2003). Creativity and culture: A two way interaction. *Scandinavian Journal of Educational Research* 47(3), 273–290.

SCANS Commission (1991). *What work requires of schools: A SCANS report for America 2000*. The Secretary's Commission on Achieving Necessary Skills. Washington, DC: U.S. Department of Labor.

Schoenfeldt, L. F., & Jansen, K. J. (1997). Methodological requirements for studying creativity in organizations. *The Journal of Creative Behavior*, 31, 73–90.

Schumpeter, J. A. (1934). *The Theory of Economic Development*. Cambridge, MA: Harvard University Press.

Scott, G., Leritz, L. E., & Mumford, M. (2004). The effectiveness of creativity training: A quantitative review. *Creativity Research Journal*, 16(4), 361–388.

Shalley, C. E., & Gilson, L. L. (2004). What leaders need to know: A review of social and contextual factors that can foster or hinder creativity. *The Leadership Quarterly*, 15, 33–53.

Sellgren, S. F., Ekvall, G., & Tomson, G. (2008). Leadership behaviour of nurse managers in relation to job satisfaction and work climate. *Journal of Nursing Management*, 16, 578–587.

Shane, S., Venkataraman, S., & MacMillan, I. (1995). Cultural differences in Innovation championing strategies. *Journal of Management*, 21(5), 931–952.

Shin, S. J., & Zhou, J. (2003). Transformational leadership, conservation, and creativity: Evidence from Korea. *Academy of Management Journal*, 46, 703–714.

Shin, S. J., & Zhou, J. (2007). When is educational specialization heterogeneity related to creativity in research and development teams? Transformational leadership as a moderator. *Journal of Applied Psychology*, 92, 1709–1721.

Siegel, S. M., & Kaemmerer, W. F. (1978). Measuring the perceived support for innovation in organizations. *Journal of Applied Psychology*, 63, 553–562.

Soo, C., Devinney, T., Midgley, D., & Deering, A. (2002). Knowledge management: Philosophy, processes, and pitfalls. *California Management Review*, 44, 129–150.

Soriano de Alencar, E. M. L., & Bruno-Faria, M. D. F. (1997). Characteristics of an organizational environment which stimulates and inhibits creativity. *Journal of Creative Behavior*, 31, 271–281.

Sosik, J. J. (1997). Effects of transformational leadership and anonymity on idea generation in computer-mediated groups. *Group & Organizational Management*, 22, 460–487.

Sosik, J. J., Kahai, S. S., & Avolio, B. J. (1998). Transformational leadership and dimensions of creativity: Motivating idea generation in computer-mediated groups. *Creativity Research Journal*, 11, 111–121.

Stein, M. I. (1968). Creativity. In E. F. Boragatta & W. W. Lambert (Eds.), *Handbook of personality theory and research* (pp. 900–942). Chicago: Rand McNally.

Sternberg, R. J. (2003). WICS: A model of leadership in organizations. *Academy of Management Learning and Education*, 2, 386–401.

Sternberg, R. J., Kaufman, J. C., & Pretz, J. E. (2003). A propulsion model of creative leadership. *The Leadership Quarterly*, 14, 455–473.

Su, C. T., & Lin, C. S. (2008). A case study on the application of fuzzy QFD in TRIZ for service quality improvement. *Quality & Quantity*, 42, 563–578.

Sumanski, M. M., Kolenc, I., & Markic, M. (2007). Teamwork and defining group structures. *Team Performance Management*, 13, 102–116.

Thompson, L., & Choi, H. S. (Eds.). (2005). *Creativity and innovation in organizational teams.* Mahwah, NJ: Erlbaum.

Torrance, E. P. (1974). *Torrance tests of creative thinking: Norms and technical manual.* Bensenville, IL: Scholastic Testing Services.

VanGundy, A. (1987). Organizational creativity and innovation. In S. G. Isaksen (Ed.), *Frontiers of creativity research: Beyond the basics* (pp. 358–379). Buffalo, NY: Bearly Ltd.

Vardis, H., & Seldon, G. L. (2008). A report card on innovation: How companies and business schools are dealing with it. In G. J. Puccio, C. Burnett, J. F. Cabra, J. M. Fox, S. Keller-Mathers, M. C. Murdock, & J. A. Yudess (Eds.), *Creativity and innovation management: An international conference* (pp. 239–258). Buffalo, NY: International Center for Studies in Creativity.

Vincent, J. F. V., Bogatyreva, O., Pahl, A.-K, Bogatyrev, N., & Bowyer, A. (2005). Putting biology into TRIZ: A database of biological effects. *Creativity and Innovation Management,* 14(1), 66–72.

Westwood, R., & Low, D. R. (2003). The multicultural muse: Culture, creativity, and innovation. *International Journal of Cross Cultural Management,* 3(2), 235–259.

Williams, W. M., & Yang, L. T. (1999). Organizational creativity. In R. J. Sternberg (Ed.), *Handbook of creativity* (pp. 226–250). Cambridge, UK: Cambridge University Press.

Woodman, R. W., Sawyer, J. E., & Griffin, R. W. (1993). Toward a theory of organizational creativity. *Academy of Management Review,* 18(2), 293–321.

Woyke, E., & Atal, M. (2007, October 4). The talent hunt: Design programs are shaping a new generation of creative managers. *BusinessWeek.* Retrieved January 27, 2010, from http://www.businessweek.com/innovate/content/oct2007/id2007104_575219.htm.

Wu, C., McMullen, J. S., Neubert, M. J., & Yi, X. (2008). The influence of leader regulatory focus on employee creativity. *Journal of Business Venturing,* 23, 587–602.

Zhang, J., Chair, K.-H., & Tan, K.-C. (2005). Applying TRIZ to service conceptual design: An exploratory study. *Creativity and Innovation Management,* 14(1), 34–42.

Zhou, J., & Shalley, C. E., (2008). *Handbook of organizational creativity.* New York: Lawrence Erlbaum Associates.

CHAPTER 9

Creativity in Highly Eminent Individuals

Dean Keith Simonton

Creativity can assume many guises. There's the creativity that appears in everyday problem solving – how to revise a favorite recipe when one required spice is absent from the kitchen cabinet; how to plan a surprise party for a special someone when it requires that every one assemble simultaneously at an exotic locale; or how to reorganize office operations to reduce expenditures by 20% while still maintaining productivity and morale. The solutions to these problems may yield a memorable cake, event, or organization chart, but any influence is most often transient and delimited. The ad hoc recipe may not yield a prizewinning cake, the event may not set a new trend in celebrations, and the new office structure may work only for the specific personnel at a particular point in time.

In contrast, creativity can sometimes be of such importance that its effects endure for decades, centuries, even millennia. This is the magnitude of creativity seen in the epic poem *Iliad*, the ceiling frescoes of the Vatican's Sistine Chapel, the philosophical treatise *Discourse on the Method*, the scientific monograph *Principia Mathematica*, the Symphony No. 5 in C Minor, Op. 67, the novel *War and Peace*, or the film *The Seventh Seal*. So monumental are these creative products that they have earned their creators immortal fame. Not just the products but the names of their authors have left a lasting mark on history – names like Homer, Michelangelo, Descartes, Newton, Beethoven, Tolstoy, and Bergman.

This latter degree of creativity is sometimes styled Big-C Creativity, to be distinguished from little-c creativity mentioned in the previous paragraph (Simonton, 2000b). However, the expression Big-C Creativity can be also applied to cases that are not nearly so outstanding. Anyone creative enough to publish a poem in a major literary magazine, have an application approved by the U.S. Patent Office, publish a highly cited scientific article in a top-tier journal, or write the score to a mainstream feature film might be said to exhibit lower levels of Big-C Creativity. In other words, the latter label might be attached to all creators who generated an identifiable product without necessarily rendering the person highly eminent. So when we talk about the creativity at the highest level we are really talking about **Boldface-C** Creativity – the creativity of highly eminent individuals.

It's easy to provide a crude operational definition of this grade of creativity. It's called the "Google test." Pick a given *creative* individual and then use google.com to search the creator's *name*. If you get thousands of internet sites – perhaps including a link to a corresponding Wikipedia article – the person has passed the preliminary exam. If the links include at least one site dedicated specifically to that individual, then Google certification attains the highest level of confidence. To illustrate, consider Hildegard von Bingen, the twelfth-century abbess, philosopher, scientist, physician, artist, poet, and composer: Can she be considered a **Boldface-C** Creator? The answer, as any reader can verify, is yes. Hundreds of thousands of hits plus her very own Wikipedia entry and dedicated Web site (http://www.hildegard.org)!

Most often these highly eminent creators are recognized as creative geniuses. As a consequence, I devote most of this chapter to discussing these special people. Yet at the chapter's close I briefly examine the creativity found in highly eminent persons who cannot properly be referred to as exemplars of creative genius.

Creative Genius

Creative geniuses become highly eminent because they have contributed at least one product that is widely viewed as a masterwork in an established domain of creative achievement. Because these domains are quite varied, we must begin by discussing the diverse *varieties* of creative genius. The next topic concerns the psychological *correlates* – both dispositional and developmental – of creative achievement in these diverse domains. The last subject turns to *grades* of creative genius. Even among **Boldface-C** creators there exists variation

in the extent of creative accomplishment. Although there's no doubt Hildegard von Bingen belongs in this exclusive club, she's certainly not the club's president.

Varieties

If a creative genius is someone who becomes eminent by making a contribution to a major domain of creative achievement, what are these domains? The ancient Greeks were perhaps the first to address this question. The answer took the form of the Muses who were thought to inspire each creative genius. Traditionally, there was a Muse responsible for heroic or epic poetry (Calliope), lyric and love poetry (Erato), sacred poetry (Polyhymnia or Polymnia), tragedy (Melpomene), comedy (Thalia), music (Euterpe), dance (Terpsichore), history (Clio), and astronomy (Urania). Presumably, other forms of creativity, such as philosophy or the visual arts, required no Muse!

Modern researchers have tried to identify the main domains of achievement according to those forms that have attracted the highest levels of creativity in a given civilization or civilizations. Francis Galton's (1869) *Hereditary genius* included chapters on scientists, creative writers, poets (as a separate group!), painters, and composers. Catharine Cox's (1926) *Early Mental Traits of Three Hundred Geniuses* classified her creators as scientists, philosophers, informative creative writers (essayists, critics, and historians), imaginative creative writers (poets, dramatists, and novelists), artists (painters and sculptors), and composers. Alfred Kroeber's (1944) *Configuration of Culture Growth* grouped geniuses from the major world civilizations into the fields of philosophy, science, philology, literature, drama (as a separate group, too), sculpture, painting, and music. More recently, Charles Murray's (2003) *Human Accomplishment* classified a worldwide sample of eminent creators into the domains of science, mathematics, medicine, technology, philosophy, literature, art, and music.

Although there seems to be some agreement on certain core domains – especially the broad categories of science, philosophy, literature, music, and the visual arts – it is important to recognize that specific non-Western civilizations will often include forms of creativity that are not particularly appreciated in Western civilization. For instance, Chinese civilization includes the highly regarded categories of calligraphers and artisans (Simonton, 1988a), and Japanese civilization includes the highly honored categories of ceramicists and sword makers (Simonton, 1997b). This point should be remembered when researchers try to compare the relative creativity of civilizations or cultures (e.g., Galton, 1869; Murray, 2003). Lots of creativity is channeled into areas that are overlooked because of ethnocentric blinders (a problem with assessing the achievements of women creators as well).

Sometimes, too, alternative modes of creativity are dismissed because their products are too ephemeral. Examples might include choreography, fashion design, wine-making, and haute cuisine. Even if creators in these areas can become highly eminent in their own lifetime, that eminence dissipates quickly with the passage of time. Who besides an expert in the history of ballet even remembers the choreographer for the debut performance of Tchaikovsky's *The Nutcracker*? In comparison, how many of my readers have heard of either Tchaikovsky or *The Nutcracker*?

Although many creators attain eminence in one and only one inclusive domain of creative achievement, it is clear that some can attain distinction in more than one. In addition to Hildegard von Bingen, such universal or omnibus creators include Omar Khayyám, Leonardo da Vinci, Blaise Pascal, Johann Wolfgang von Goethe, and Benjamin Franklin. But how common is such creative versatility? It turns out that it is fairly frequent (Simonton, 1976; White, 1931). This fact was most recently established in Cassandro's (1998) study of 2,102 creative geniuses. The creators were assessed on their versatility, defined by having achieved eminence in more than one domain or subdo-

main. Although 61% were not versatile by this definition, 15% were eminent in more than one subdomain within a domain (e.g., poetry and drama within literature), and fully 24% were eminent in more than one domain (e.g., literature and science). Hence, more than one third exhibited creative versatility of some kind. Shakespeare was a creator in the first category of versatility (poet and dramatist), whereas Goethe was a creator in the second category (poet, dramatist, novelist, and natural scientist).

Creative geniuses who contribute to more than one domain or subdomain can be said to have "balanced portfolios." Their eminence does not depend on their contributions to any single domain. This is very fortunate. Although Goethe was proudest of his scientific work (most notably his *Theory of Colors*), it is manifest that his current reputation rests far more on his literary greatness.

Correlates

Why does someone choose to attain fame (and perhaps fortune) in one domain rather than another? Is it a matter of mere chance, or are there certain variables that are associated with the choice? Could Picasso just as well have grown up to become an Einstein and vice versa? Or was the creative growth of these two eminent individuals deflected toward divergent domains?

As it happens, the latter is the case. Specific factors tend to direct creativity toward particular domains of achievement. These factors fall into two categories: dispositional and developmental (Simonton, 2009c).

DISPOSITIONAL CORRELATES
Human beings vary on a large number of intellectual and personality variables, some of which correlate with the domain of creative achievement. Perhaps the single most intriguing example is psychopathology. Since the time of Aristotle people have speculated about the "mad genius." There seems to be some grain of truth to the association. For example, creative achievement appears to be positively correlated with

elevated scores on the clinical scales of the Minnesota Multiphasic Personality Inventory (Barron, 1963) as well as the psychoticism scale of the Eysenck Personality Questionnaire (Eysenck, 1995). Even so, it is also the case that any inclinations toward mental illness are contingent on the domain of creative achievement. According to Ludwig (1998), the frequency and magnitude of psychopathology typical of a domain corresponds to the nature of the creativity in the domain: Creators in domains that "require more logical, objective, and formal forms of expression tend be more emotionally stable than those in . . . [domains] that require more intuitive, subjective, and emotive forms" (p. 93). Ludwig then showed that this principle applied at multiple levels of "magnification," that is, the occurrence of mental illness exhibited the fractal pattern of "self-similarity." Consider the following four levels:

Level 1: Scientists have lower lifetime rates of mental illness than do artists (see also Post, 1994; Raskin, 1936);

Level 2: (a) in the sciences, natural scientists have lower rates than do social scientists (see also Ludwig, 1995); and (b) in the arts, creators in the formal arts (e.g., architecture) have lower rates than those in the performing arts (e.g., music and dance), who in their turn have lower rates than those in the expressive arts (e.g., literature and the visual arts);

Level 3: Within a specific expressive art like literature, nonfiction writers display lower rates than do fiction writers, who in their turn have lower rates than do poets (cf. Jamison, 1989; Simonton & Song, 2009); and

Level 4: Within any specific artistic domain (e.g., painting, sculpture, and photography), those who create in a formal style will exhibit lower rates than those creating in a symbolic style, and the latter exhibit yet lower rates than those creating in an emotive style. So of all varieties of creativity, poets writing in a highly emotionally

expressive style should have the highest propensity for pathology (cf. Kaufman, 2000–2001, 2001; Martindale, 1972; Simonton & Song, 2009).

An analogous variety of Level 4 magnification can be found in the relation between psychopathology and scientific creativity in paradigmatic disciplines. In particular, scientists who display some degree of psychopathology are more likely to attain eminence as revolutionaries who reject the current paradigm, whereas scientists who exhibit no pathology are more prone to become famous for making contributions that preserve the current paradigm (Ko & Kim, 2008).

I must stress that these differentiations can be applied to other dispositional characteristics besides psychopathology. Unfortunately, these contrasts tend to involve a subset of disciplines rather than the rather comprehensive distinctions that Ludwig (1998) offered. In fact, most relevant investigations concentrate on contrasts among scientific disciplines. Even so, it is useful to contemplate the following two interdomain differences. First, Chambers (1964) found that creative psychologists were more likely to score higher than creative chemists on Factor M of the 16 Personality Factors (see also Cattell & Drevdahl, 1955). This means that chemists are less bohemian, introverted, unconventional, imaginative, and creative in thought and behavior relative to psychologists. Second, in Roe's (1953) study of 64 eminent scientists (using the Thematic Apperception Test), the social scientists (psychologists and anthropologists) were shown to be less factual, more emotional, and more rebellious than the physical scientists (physicists and chemists).

Interestingly, dispositional traits divide even subdisciplines of the same overall discipline (i.e., "Level 4" magnification). An example is Suedfeld's (1985) content analysis of addresses delivered by presidents of the American Psychological Association (APA). The speeches were scored on integrative complexity, a measure of how many divergent perspectives a person can take into consideration and whether the person can integrate these perspectives into a coherent viewpoint. Those APA presidents who were natural-science oriented (e.g., behaviorists) demonstrated lower levels of integrative complexity than those who were human-science oriented (e.g., humanistic psychologists).

DEVELOPMENTAL CORRELATES

At least in part, dispositional traits must have some foundation in the early environmental experiences that shape creative development. Disposition is as much a function of nurture as nature, if not more. It should come as no surprise, therefore, that highly eminent individuals who contribute to distinct domains of creative achievement also tend to differ in their developmental backgrounds (Simonton, 2009c). In a sense, the creators in each domain exhibit distinctive biographical profiles.

This fact is immediately apparent in research on the family backgrounds of Nobel laureates (Berry, 1981). If we exclude the prizes for peace (because it does not represent a recognized form of creativity) and for physiology/medicine (because it is a very heterogeneous category), we find that 28% of the laureates in physics are most likely to have come from homes where the father was an academic professional. The corresponding figures for the chemistry and literature laureates are 17% and 6%, respectively. Even more striking are the differences in partial orphanhood – losing their fathers while still young. The figures are physics 2%, chemistry 11%, and literature 17%. The contrast in the family backgrounds of the physicists and creative writers is especially striking: 30% of the literature laureates "lost at least one parent through death or desertion or experienced the father's bankruptcy or impoverishment," whereas "the physicists... seem to have remarkably uneventful lives" (p. 387; see also Simonton, 1986; cf. Raskin, 1936).

Another study of over 300 twentieth-century eminent personalities found that fiction and nonfiction authors tended to come from unhappy home environments, whereas better home conditions produced scientists

and philosophers (Simonton, 1986). In addition, the eminent scientists had the most formal education and artists and performers the least. A comparable investigation of an earlier sample of eminent scientists and creative writers showed that the former tended to have appreciably more formal education than the latter (see also Raskin, 1936). There is also some tentative evidence that creative artists, relative to creative scientists, are prone to have been exposed to a greater diversity of mentors (Simonton, 1984, 1992). Last but not least, eminent artists may be somewhat more likely to be nurtured by unstable and heterogeneous sociocultural systems than is the case for scientific creators (Simonton, 1975, 1997b). Sociocultural stability and homogeneity more favor the creative development of eminent scientists.

If we focus on contrasts among scientific domains, we encounter such findings as (a) eminent psychologists, relative to chemists, were much more likely to have been rebellious toward their parents (Chambers, 1964; see also Roe, 1953) and (b) physical scientists showed early interests in mechanical and electrical gadgets, whereas social scientists were more inclined toward literature and the classics, and often exhibited an early desire to become creative writers (Roe, 1953). These divergences continue into adulthood. Whereas 41% of eminent social scientists experienced divorce, only 15% of eminent biologists did so, and the corresponding figure for eminent physical scientists was 5% (Roe, 1953).

Perhaps the most fascinating developmental correlate is a creator's ordinal position in the family. Galton (1874) was the first to document how firstborns are disproportionately represented among eminent scientists, and subsequent researchers have replicated this result (Eiduson, 1962; Roe, 1953; Terry, 1989). Indeed, the firstborn predominance appears particularly strong among eminent women psychologists (Simonton, 2008b). At the same time, there is reason to believe that revolutionary scientists have a higher likelihood of having been laterborns (Sulloway, 1996). That's because laterborns are supposedly more rebellious, more open to new ideas, and less conforming to conventions. This difference is reflected in aesthetic forms of creative eminence as well. Whereas classical composers are more disposed to be firstborns (Schubert, Wagner, & Schubert, 1977), creative writers are more inclined to be laterborns (Bliss, 1970). Presumably creativity in the former domain is more formal and conventional than creativity in the latter domain.

This pattern of differences closely mirrors what we previously saw with respect to dispositional traits. It is possible to array various scientific and artistic disciplines along a single bipolar dimension (Simonton, 2009c). At one pole are domains where creativity tends to be more logical, objective, formal, and conventional; at the other pole are domains where creativity tends to be more intuitive, subjective, emotive, and unconventional. This bipolar dimension then allows us to arrange all domains of creative achievement according to their respective dispositional and developmental traits. To illustrate, eminent creativity in domains near the former pole, like physics and chemistry, should be associated with a greater frequency of firstborns, lower psychopathology and parental loss, and higher levels of formal education, whereas eminent creativity in domains near the opposite pole, like fiction and poetry, should be associated with a greater frequency of laterborns, higher psychopathology and parental loss, and lower levels of formal education. Of course, these are mere tendencies that operate only on the average. These are statistical regularities rather than hard and fast rules. Nevertheless, the disposition and development of someone who attains eminence near one pole will often differ from the disposition and development of someone who attains eminence near the opposite pole.

Grades

Too often the term "genius" is applied as a dichotomous term. Either you have genius or you don't. This all-or-none usage is especially commonplace in psychometric definitions of genius. Thus, Terman (1925–1959) defined genius as someone who earned a score of 140 or higher on the Stanford-Binet Intelligence Scale. This psychometric threshold even appears in the *American Heritage Dictionary* (1992) where a genius is "A person who has an exceptionally high intelligence quotient, typically above 140." Naturally, people might quibble about the precise cutoff. Some may put it as low as 130, whereas others might put it as high as 160. The decision is clearly arbitrary. Or, rather, the only guiding principle seems to be that the qualifying score has to be low enough to admit its advocate into the ranks of genius!

Yet when we turn to *creative* genius, it becomes more obvious that we must deal with a quantitative rather than qualitative attribute. This reality is apparent in the most favored definition of creativity, namely, that it must produce an idea that is both (a) original, novel, or surprising and (b) adaptive or functional (Simonton, 2000b). So Einstein's general theory of relativity is highly creative because it was highly original (i.e., constituting a substantial break with Newtonian physics) as well as highly functional (e.g., it solved a problem in Mercury's orbit that hitherto lacked any workable solution). It should be clear that these two components are continuous rather than discrete variables. Creative products, in particular, can vary in both originality and adaptiveness. Moreover, the variation in these two dimensions does not have to go together. Some ideas may be highly original but nonadaptive, or highly adaptive but completely unoriginal. The first of these outcomes is perhaps the most interesting. An illustration is Einstein's unified field theory: It was extremely original, but it simply failed to work, yielding predictions that were manifestly false.

Given that creative genius is a quantitative rather than qualitative trait (i.e., even geniuses can vary in the amount of creativity they display), we should expect it to be associated with other quantitative variables. And it does. Below I provide examples that fall into three categories: achieved eminence, creative productivity, and grade predictors.

ACHIEVED EMINENCE

Cattell (1903) was the first person to demonstrate empirically how much geniuses can differ in the attainment of fame. Using several standard reference works, he compiled a list of the 1,000 most eminent creators and leaders in Western civilization, where the 1,000 were ranked ordered according to the amount of space they received. The top-ranked creative genius on the list (#2) was William Shakespeare, a big name that needs no introduction (first place went to a leader). And the bottom ranked? The nineteenth-century French historian, philologist, and critic named Claude Charles Fauriel, who came in 998th (the 999th and 1,000th were both leaders). I must confess that I had no idea who this person was until I wrote this paragraph. But Fauriel does pass the Google test! So Shakespeare and Fauriel define the end points in eminence for creative geniuses in this distinguished sample.

One might object that such space measures do not represent the best way to assess the achievement of such geniuses. Certainly one reason why Shakespeare is ranked so high is that it is easy to devote many lines to synopses of his plays and sonnets. Yet the extreme variation in achievement eminence appears if we use alternative operational definitions. An interesting illustration is to be found in Hart's (2000) book *The 100: A Ranking of the Most Influential Persons in History*. Here the author attempted to identify the top 100 in terms of worldwide influence and then rank them. In his (subjective) opinion, the highest ranked creative genius was Isaac Newton, who came in second place (after a leader), whereas Shakespeare was pushed down to 31st. The lowest ranked creative genius was Homer, who came in at 98th (99th and 100th were leaders). Because this was a top-100 rather than top-1,000 list, Homer has far better name recognition than Fauriel. The least influential scientist on Hart's list, at 82nd, is Gregory Pincus, the person credited with the first practical birth control pill!

Both Cattell (1903) and Hart (2000) differentiated creative geniuses along an ordinal scale. This practice actually underestimates

the magnitude of the variation in achieved eminence. In the case of Cattell (1903), for example, a genius ranked #1 is as far from one ranked #2 as a genius ranked #999 is from one ranked #1,000. But if he had published the raw space measures – the number of lines or pages devoted to each individual, he would have obtained far different results. The gap between #1 and #2 would be far, far greater than that between #999 and #1,000. That's because the cross-sectional distribution of eminence is extremely skewed (Martindale, 1995; Zusne, 1985). The overwhelming majority of creative geniuses are rather obscure, and just a handful stick out, with only one or two situated at the apex of acclaim.

Martindale (1995) provided an excellent illustration with respect to the number of books devoted to 602 British poets. A total of 34,516 books were written, or an average 57 books apiece. However, 9,118 of these books, or fully 26%, are about William Shakespeare. The two leading runners-up are Milton at 1,280, or 4%, and Chaucer at 1,096, or 3%. At the bottom end, 134 poets, or 22%, were the subject of not a single book. Accordingly, if we ranked these poets Shakespeare, Milton, and Chaucer would come in 1st, 2nd, and 3rd, whereas 134 poets would all be tied for last place. Although Shakespeare can be said to be over six times as famous as Milton by the book counts, his rank is only one score higher. At the other end, the 134 nonentities are all equally unknown. The only way to distinguish among them would be to adopt a more refined space measure. Instead of counting the number of monographs, we could count the number of lines each receives in encyclopedias or biographical dictionaries dedicated to English literature. A poet who ranked 602nd by this measure would probably represent a Big-C but regular-font creator. He or she might demarcate absolute zero on the **Boldface-C** temperature scale.

CREATIVE PRODUCTIVITY

From a psychological perspective, there's something a bit odd about the above distribution. Ever since Galton (1869), researchers have been accustomed to believe that most psychological variables are normally distributed. Instead, eminence is often so skewed that the modal score rests at the very bottom of the distribution and the highest scores dwell at the end of an enormously long upper tail. Frequently there is no lower tail whatsoever! How can this be?

The answer gets back to what I said was a minimal requirement for Big-C Creativity: the contribution of at least one creative product to a recognized domain. Although occasionally there exist one-hit wonders who make one and only one contribution (Kozbelt, 2008), it is rare for these creators to rise to the highest ranks. The reputation of Homer rests on more than his *Iliad*, Michelangelo on more than his Sistine Chapel frescoes, Descartes on more than the *Discourse on the Method*, Newton on more than the *Principia Mathematica*, Beethoven on more than the Fifth Symphony, Tolstoy on more than *War and Peace*, and Bergman on more than *The Seventh Seal*. Indeed, each has contributed additional creative products that alone would have ensured their place in the pantheon of **Boldface-C** Creators. Try the *Odyssey*, the *Pietà*, the *Les passions de l'âme*, the *Opticks*, the 9th Symphony, *Anna Karenina*, and *Cries and Whispers*, respectively. These geniuses are far from one-hit wonders.

This brings me to one of the hallmarks of creative genius: productivity (Albert, 1975). Creators of the highest order tend to be extremely prolific, producing work after work after work. Besides maintaining an exceptional rate of output, they tend to initiate output at an unusually young age and not end their output until quite advanced in years (Simonton, 1997a). So phenomenal is their output that a relatively small number of creators tend to dominate their chosen domain. Typically, the top 10% in total lifetime output are responsible for about half of all contributions, whereas the bottom 50% in total lifetime output can be credited with only 15% or less of all contributions (Simonton, 2009b). To show how extraordinary this dominance can be, Thomas Edison held patents to more than 1,000 inventions, and to this very day he holds the most approved applications of anyone else in the history of the U.S. Patent Office.

Admittedly, the foregoing findings apply to total lifetime output regardless of the quality of that output. Might it not be possible that some individuals are nothing more than mass producers who generate one worthless work after another? And might it also be possible that other individuals are perfectionists who offer the world just a handful of masterpieces – all wheat and no chaff? Yes, both are possible, but both are also exceedingly rare (Simonton, 2004). The norm is for the creators who produce the most works to also produce the most masterworks. That means, in effect, that even the greatest creative geniuses will generate lesser, even mediocre products. In other words, output tends to be uneven, high quality products rubbing shoulders with low quality products (Simonton, 2000a). Einstein is generally viewed as one of the all-time superlative geniuses. Even so, his career by no means consisted of an uninterrupted series of successes. I already mentioned his biggest failure – the unified field theory. He also penned a large number of unsuccessful attacks on quantum theory. In fact, one of those critiques woefully failed because he neglected to take into consideration his own theory of relativity!

In any case, the cross-sectional distribution of high-impact contributions corresponds very closely to that of low-impact contributions (Simonton, 1997a). Because both distributions are highly skewed, with a small elite credited with most of the work, we obtain a partial explanation for the similarly skewed distribution of eminence. Highly prolific creators generate most of the work, good or bad, but obviously it is their best work that ensures their posthumous reputation (e.g., Simonton, 1977, 1991a, 1991b). I say that the explanation is only "partial" because the distribution of eminence is even more skewed than the distribution of productivity (Martindale, 1995). Other factors operate to stretch the upper tails of eminence well beyond what can be explicated by creative output alone.

No doubt Einstein was the preeminent theoretical physicist of his day. But it is likely that his fame today relative to that of, say, Enrico Fermi or Niels Bohr, is out of proportion to their respective contributions. How many times have you seen a T-shirt or wall poster with the face of Fermi or Bohr?

GRADE PREDICTORS

We have just learned that the primary basis for variation in eminence is variation in lifetime output. Those who make more total contributions to their chosen domain are more likely to make more notable contributions, and it is on the latter that their eminence is largely founded. Hence, the next question is whether creative geniuses differ on other variables that predict how they vary in productivity and eminence. This question is particularly critical from a psychological perspective. One could argue that the individual differences in fame and output reflect the operation of sociological rather than psychological processes. For instance, sociologists have shown how the process of accumulative advantage – where the rich get richer and the poor get poorer – can produce skewed productivity distributions in the absence of any individual differences in talent or ability (e.g., Allison, Long, & Krauze, 1982; Allison & Stewart, 1974). But if we can identify predictors of genius grade that dwell inside individuals, then psychological explanations become more justified.

Fortunately, psychologists have in fact identified several variables that predict the level of creative achievement. Some of these variables – such as inclination toward some degree of psychopathology and ordinal position in the family – also differentially predict attainment according to domain (Simonton, 2009c). Yet other predictors appear to be universal. Most conspicuously, creative genius does appear to be positively associated with general intelligence, as assessed by historiometric IQ. The correlation tends to be somewhere between .20 and .30 (Cox, 1926; Simonton, 1976, 1991c, 2008a; Simonton & Song, 2009; Walberg, Rasher, & Hase, 1978). It is almost unheard of for a creative

genius to have an IQ below 120, and the overwhelming majority has IQs above 140.

But high general intelligence alone does not guarantee genius-grade creativity. The person must also possess tremendous energy, drive, persistence, and determination (Cox, 1926; Galton, 1869; Helmreich, Spence, & Pred, 1988; Simonton, 1991c). One reason why this is so crucial is because exceptional creative achievement requires an awesome amount of work. First, it takes about a decade of intensive study and practice to acquire the necessary domain-specific expertise (Ericsson, 1996). History-making creative achievements are not produced by amateurs or novices. Second, churning out product after product can be grueling business, especially when successes are punctuated by failures (e.g., Simonton, 2000a). One cannot hope to produce pathbreaking work if one is unwilling to take big risks, and sometimes such risks do not pay off.

Undoubtedly, to some extent the personal attributes of creative geniuses can be attributed to heredity. That attribution is justified because almost all traits have substantial heritability coefficients (Simonton, 1999, 2008c). In this sense, genius is inborn. Yet is also the case that creative genius is made. The inventory of environmental experiences that contribute to creative development is quite large (Simonton, 2009b). It includes family background factors, educational and training experiences, and early career opportunities, the specifics partly dependent on the domain of achievement. The significant point is that the most illustrious creative geniuses differ on a diversity of variables. This fact, in combination with the dispositional differences, implies that the magnitude of creativity displayed has a psychological foundation.

To be sure, given that so many psychological variables tend to be normally distributed, one might wonder how these variables can account for the skewed distributions of eminence and productivity. Although a number of explanations have been offered (Simonton, 1997a, 1999), one is of special interest here. If an outcome variable is the additive function of a large number of normally distributed variables, then that outcome variable will also have a normal distribution. But what if that outcome variable is a *multiplicative* function of those same normally distributed variables? In that case the outcome variable will display a highly skewed lognormal distribution (Simonton, 2003). This distribution can then explain the cross-sectional distribution in lifetime output. The creative geniuses found in the extreme upper tail are those who happen to register the highest on all of the predictor variables. The multiplicative manner in which those predictors are integrated serves to exaggerate their extremity. The upshot is an Albert Einstein, Jean-Paul Sartre, James Joyce, Pablo Picasso, or Igor Stravinsky.

Other Geniuses?

I have concentrated on creative geniuses because creativity is most obviously the basis of their extraordinary eminence. If you take away the creative products of Einstein, Sartre, Joyce, Picasso, and Stravinsky, their status as historic figures evaporates. At best they would constitute a collection of obscure eccentrics. But are there are other kinds of geniuses besides those who exhibit exceptional creativity? Here I discuss three possibilities: athletes, performers, and leaders.

Athletes

Athletes are an interesting group insofar as Galton (1869) included them in his *Hereditary Genius* – to wit, famous wrestlers and oarsmen. But did they also have to be creative to be eminent? Although I know of no research addressing this issue, it should be evident to anyone who follows sports that it probably depends on the domain. Some sports require that athletes demonstrate appreciable problem-solving ability, whereas others emphasize a finely honed skill. In the former category might be a point guard in basketball or a quarterback in American football, whereas in the latter

category might be a sprinter or shot putter in track and field competitions. I very much doubt that Galton's wrestlers and oarsmen had to exhibit anything more than abundant strength, endurance, and special training.

In team sports in which coaches play a critical role, some creative genius may be operative at a higher level. For instance, some elite coaches in the U.S. National Football League have attained some status of this kind. Coach Bill Walsh, who led the San Francisco 49ers to three Super Bowl championships, has been credited with creating the "West Coast Offense." Can he be considered to have been a creative genius in sports? Or perhaps to have demonstrated creative leadership?

Perhaps the safest conclusion at this point is that it is rare for creativity to carry the primary weight in attaining eminence as an athlete or coach in sports.

Performers

Performers form a group of eminent individuals probably even more heterogeneous than the athletes. In this category can be placed musicians and virtuosi (in classical, jazz, rock, country, R&B, hip/hop, pop, etc.), male and female actors in theater and film, comedians, and entertainers of diverse varieties (acrobats, jugglers, mimes, clowns, etc.). As in the instance of athletes, the contribution of creativity to eminence likely hinges on the domain. Thus, jazz musicians have much more latitude for the exercise of creativity than do classical musicians. Indeed, for top-notch jazz players is it even possible to draw a distinction between music performance and compositional creativity? Yet even within a single domain there may be appreciable variation. Some comedians write most of their own material, and others largely don't, for example.

It is worth pointing out that when college students are asked to name people who exemplify creativity, they come up mostly with creative geniuses, such as Leonardo da Vinci, Picasso, Michelangelo, Mozart, Steven Spielberg, Shakespeare, Beethoven, Walt Disney, Salvador Dali, Sigmund Freud, and Alexander Graham Bell (Paulhus, Wehr, Harms, & Strasser, 2002). Yet the resulting list of creativity exemplars also included the performers Michael Jackson, Robin Williams, and Madonna. The first of these was even ranked between Shakespeare and Beethoven! Nonetheless, relatively little empirical research has been carried out on these more marginal manifestations of eminent creativity. So the best conclusion that can be drawn right now is that creativity has a subordinate role to play in their attaining eminence.

Leaders

Galton's (1869) *Hereditary Genius* devotes almost as much space to great leaders as it does to great creators. Similarly, more than one-third of Cox's (1926) 301 geniuses were politicians, commanders, revolutionaries, and religious leaders – and that was after deleting all hereditary monarchs from her sample! The question then arises as to whether the eminence of such leaders also depends on creativity. Can politics, war, revolution, and religion be placed alongside science, philosophy, literature, music, and the visual arts as major domains of creative achievement?

To some extent, the answer is affirmative. That's because many of the correlates and predictors identified for creative genius reappear for geniuses in domains of leadership (Simonton, 2009a). May the following four examples suffice to make the point:

1. General intelligence appears to be about as important in predicting achieved eminence in leaders as it does in creators (Simonton, 1983, 2006). The only qualification is that it requires somewhat less intelligence to attain distinction in leadership positions than in creative domains. Military commanders, in particular, require less outstanding intellect than the rest (Cox, 1926; Simonton & Song, 2009). Leaders can even be too bright to lead (Simonton, 1985).

2. Earlier I noted how APA presidents could be differentiated into natural-science and human-science psychologists according to the integrative complexity displayed by their presidential addresses (Suedfeld, 1985). Integrative complexity is also positively associated with both exceptional creativity (Feist, 1994) and outstanding leadership (Suedfeld, Guttieri, & Tetlock, 2003). No matter whether you are a creator or a leader, it is imperative to view your domain in a fully integrated yet finely differentiated manner.

3. Motivation, drive, persistence, and determination are no less critical for leader eminence as for creative eminence (Cox, 1926; Simonton, 1991c). The principal stipulation here is that the specific nature or emphasis of the motive may change. Because creators tend to be more introverted and leaders more extroverted, extraordinary leadership is more strongly linked to the need for power (Winter, 2003). Where creators want to organize ideas and images, leaders desire to control other individuals.

4. Family background factors for creative geniuses have echoes among genius-grade leaders (Simonton, 2009a). For example, traumatic experiences in childhood and adolescence, such as parental loss, also appear to play some role in the development of historic leaders (Berrington, 1974; Eisenstadt, 1978). Perhaps even more intriguing is the impact of birth order: Whereas status quo political leaders are more likely to be firstborns (Zweigenhaft, 1975), revolutionary leaders are more likely to be laterborns (Stewart, 1977; Sulloway, 1996). This differentiation closely parallels what was found for creative geniuses (e.g., scientists vs. artists; revolutionary vs. normal scientists; classical composers vs. creative writers).

The above four parallels apply to all kinds of creators and leaders. Additional correspondences have been found in empirical research regarding one particular type of political leadership: presidents of the United States. First of all, expert ratings of presidential performance are correlated with independent evaluations of the chief executive's creativity, where the latter is gauged by his willingness to introduce new programs and legislation (Simonton, 1988b). Moreover, presidential performance is positively associated with openness to experience (Simonton, 2006), the dimension of the Big Five Personality model that is most strongly correlated with everyday creativity (Harris, 2004; McCrae, 1987). Creativity is also positively related to ratings of presidential charisma (Simonton, 1988b).

The latter subjective evaluations, furthermore, correspond to objective computer content analyses of presidential addresses. More specifically, the speeches delivered by highly charismatic U.S. presidents tend to score high in primary-process or "primordial" imagery (Emrich, Brower, Feldman, & Garland, 2001). In fact, the investigators used the same Regressive Imagery Dictionary that Martindale (1990) devised to assess the psychological dynamics of changes in literary styles. Regression into this form of cognitive thought is conducive to enhanced originality. Better yet, poetry that scores higher on this same variable tends to be deemed more creative than that scoring lower (Simonton, 1989). Great, creative, and charismatic presidents deliver speeches that are more akin to art than science.

All told, unlike illustrious athletes and performers, highly eminent leaders seem not too distant from highly eminent creators. Both creators and leaders may require a high degree of creativity to achieve a high degree of distinction. Perhaps the biggest contrast is that the leaders, unlike the creators, seldom leave behind a discrete product that can be highly valued for its creativity divorced from the historical context in which it was written. Perhaps the only exception to this generalization is when a leader leaves a great speech to posterity. Lincoln's Gettysburg Address comes to mind. Yet even here this product cannot be fully appreciated without comprehending the context in which it was written. In contrast, Shakespeare's plays and sonnets can be treasured without knowing the exact circumstances in which they were created. Indeed, **Boldface-C** creativity can be viewed as that which transcends a given place and time. If so, then creative geniuses alone define the exemplars of creativity among highly eminent individuals.

References

Albert, R. S. (1975). Toward a behavioral definition of genius. *American Psychologist, 30,* 140–151.

Allison, P. D., Long, J. S., & Krauze, T. K. (1982). Cumulative advantage and inequality in science. *American Sociological Review, 47,* 615–625.

Allison, P. D., & Stewart, J. A. (1974). Productivity differences among scientists: Evidence for accumulative advantage. *American Sociological Review, 39,* 596–606.

American heritage electronic dictionary (3rd ed.). (1992). Boston: Houghton Mifflin.

Barron, F. X. (1963). *Creativity and psychological health: Origins of personal vitality and creative freedom.* Princeton, NJ: Van Nostrand.

Berrington, H. (1974). Review article: The Fiery Chariot: Prime ministers and the search for love. *British Journal of Political Science, 4,* 345–369.

Berry, C. (1981). The Nobel scientists and the origins of scientific achievement. *British Journal of Sociology, 32,* 381–391.

Bliss, W. D. (1970). Birth order of creative writers. *Journal of Individual Psychology, 26,* 200–202.

Cassandro, V. J. (1998). Explaining premature mortality across fields of creative endeavor. *Journal of Personality, 66,* 805–833.

Cattell, J. M. (1903). A statistical study of eminent men. *Popular Science Monthly, 62,* 359–377.

Cattell, R. B., & Drevdahl, J. E. (1955). A comparison of the personality profile (16 P. F.) of eminent researchers with that of eminent teachers and administrators, and of the general population. *British Journal of Psychology, 46,* 248–261.

Chambers, J. A. (1964). Relating personality and biographical factors to scientific creativity. *Psychological Monographs: General and Applied, 78* (7, Whole No. 584).

Cox, C. (1926). *The early mental traits of three hundred geniuses.* Stanford, CA: Stanford University Press.

Eiduson, B. T. (1962). *Scientists: Their psychological world.* New York: Basic Books.

Eisenstadt, J. M. (1978). Parental loss and genius. *American Psychologist, 33,* 211–223.

Emrich, C. G., Brower, H. H., Feldman, J. M., & Garland, H. (2001). Images in words: Presidential rhetoric, charisma, and greatness. *Administrative Science Quarterly*, 46, 527–557.

Ericsson, K. A. (1996). The acquisition of expert performance: An introduction to some of the issues. In K. A. Ericsson (Ed.), *The road to expert performance: Empirical evidence from the arts and sciences, sports, and games* (pp. 1–50). Mahwah, NJ: Erlbaum.

Eysenck, H. J. (1995). *Genius: The natural history of creativity*. Cambridge, England: Cambridge University Press.

Feist, G. J. (1994). Personality and working style predictors of integrative complexity: A study of scientists' thinking about research and teaching. *Journal of Personality and Social Psychology*, 67, 474–484.

Galton, F. (1869). *Hereditary genius: An inquiry into its laws and consequences*. London: Macmillan.

Galton, F. (1874). *English men of science: Their nature and nurture*. London: Macmillan.

Harris, J. A. (2004). Measured intelligence, achievement, openness to experience, and creativity. *Personality and Individual Differences*, 36, 913–929.

Hart, M. H. (2000). *The 100: A ranking of the most influential persons in history* (Rev. & Updated ed.). Secaucus, NJ: Citadel Press.

Helmreich, R. L., Spence, J. T., & Pred, R. S. (1988). Making it without losing it: Type A, achievement motivation, and scientific attainment revisited. *Personality and Social Psychology Bulletin*, 14, 495–504.

Jamison, K. R. (1989). Mood disorders and patterns of creativity in British writers and artists. *Psychiatry*, 52, 125–134.

Kaufman, J. C. (2000–2001). Genius, lunatics and poets: Mental illness in prize-winning authors. *Imagination, Cognition & Personality*, 20, 305–314.

Kaufman, J. C. (2001). The Sylvia Plath effect: Mental illness in eminent creative writers. *Journal of Creative Behavior*, 35, 37–50.

Ko, Y., & Kim, J. (2008). Scientific geniuses' psychopathology as a moderator in the relation between creative contribution types and eminence. *Creativity Research Journal*, 20, 251–261.

Kozbelt, A. (2008). One-hit wonders in classical music: Evidence and (partial) explanations for an early career peak. *Creativity Research Journal*, 20, 179–195.

Kroeber, A. L. (1944). *Configurations of culture growth*. Berkeley: University of California Press.

Ludwig, A. M. (1995). *The price of greatness: Resolving the creativity and madness controversy*. New York: Guilford.

Ludwig, A. M. (1998). Method and madness in the arts and sciences. *Creativity Research Journal*, 11, 93–101.

Martindale, C. (1972). Father absence, psychopathology, and poetic eminence. *Psychological Reports*, 31, 843–847.

Martindale, C. (1990). *The clockwork muse: The predictability of artistic styles*. New York: Basic Books.

Martindale, C. (1995). Fame more fickle than fortune: On the distribution of literary eminence. *Poetics*, 23, 219–234.

McCrae, R. R. (1987). Creativity, divergent thinking, and openness to experience. *Journal of Personality and Social Psychology*, 52, 1258–1265.

Murray, C. (2003). *Human accomplishment: The pursuit of excellence in the arts and sciences, 800 B.C. to 1950*. New York: HarperCollins.

Paulhus, D. L., Wehr, P., Harms, P. D., & Strasser, D. I. (2002). Use of exemplar surveys to reveal implicit types of intelligence. *Personality and Social Psychology Bulletin*, 28, 1051–1062.

Post, F. (1994). Creativity and psychopathology: A study of 291 world-famous men. *British Journal of Psychiatry*, 165, 22–34.

Raskin, E. A. (1936). Comparison of scientific and literary ability: A biographical study of eminent scientists and men of letters of the nineteenth century. *Journal of Abnormal and Social Psychology*, 31, 20–35.

Roe, A. (1953). *The making of a scientist*. New York: Dodd, Mead.

Schubert, D. S. P., Wagner, M. E., & Schubert, H. J. P. (1977). Family constellation and creativity: Firstborn predominance among classical music composers. *Journal of Psychology*, 95, 147–149.

Simonton, D. K. (1975). Sociocultural context of individual creativity: A transhistorical time-series analysis. *Journal of Personality and Social Psychology*, 32, 1119–1133.

Simonton, D. K. (1976). Biographical determinants of achieved eminence: A multivariate approach to the Cox data. *Journal of Personality and Social Psychology*, 33, 218–226.

Simonton, D. K. (1977). Eminence, creativity, and geographic marginality: A recursive structural equation model. *Journal of Personality and Social Psychology*, 35, 805–816.

Simonton, D. K. (1983). Intergenerational transfer of individual differences in hereditary monarchs: Genes, role-modeling, cohort, or sociocultural effects? *Journal of Personality and Social Psychology*, 44, 354–364.

Simonton, D. K. (1984). Artistic creativity and interpersonal relationships across and within generations. *Journal of Personality and Social Psychology*, 46, 1273–1286.

Simonton, D. K. (1985). Intelligence and personal influence in groups: Four nonlinear models. *Psychological Review*, 92, 532–547.

Simonton, D. K. (1986). Biographical typicality, eminence, and achievement style. *Journal of Creative Behavior*, 20, 14–22.

Simonton, D. K. (1988a). Galtonian genius, Kroeberian configurations, and emulation: A generational time-series analysis of Chinese civilization. *Journal of Personality and Social Psychology*, 55, 230–238.

Simonton, D. K. (1988b). Presidential style: Personality, biography, and performance. *Journal of Personality and Social Psychology*, 55, 928–936.

Simonton, D. K. (1989). Shakespeare's sonnets: A case of and for single-case historiometry. *Journal of Personality*, 57, 695–721.

Simonton, D. K. (1991a). Career landmarks in science: Individual differences and interdisciplinary contrasts. *Developmental Psychology*, 27, 119–130.

Simonton, D. K. (1991b). Emergence and realization of genius: The lives and works of 120 classical composers. *Journal of Personality and Social Psychology*, 61, 829–840.

Simonton, D. K. (1991c). Personality correlates of exceptional personal influence: A note on Thorndike's (1950) creators and leaders. *Creativity Research Journal*, 4, 67–78.

Simonton, D. K. (1992). The social context of career success and course for 2,026 scientists and inventors. *Personality and Social Psychology Bulletin*, 18, 452–463.

Simonton, D. K. (1997a). Creative productivity: A predictive and explanatory model of career trajectories and landmarks. *Psychological Review*, 104, 66–89.

Simonton, D. K. (1997b). Foreign influence and national achievement: The impact of open milieus on Japanese civilization. *Journal of Personality and Social Psychology*, 72, 86–94.

Simonton, D. K. (1999). Talent and its development: An emergenic and epigenetic model. *Psychological Review*, 106, 435–457.

Simonton, D. K. (2000a). Creative development as acquired expertise: Theoretical issues and an empirical test. *Developmental Review*, 20, 283–318.

Simonton, D. K. (2000b). Creativity: Cognitive, developmental, personal, and social aspects. *American Psychologist*, 55, 151–158.

Simonton, D. K. (2003). Scientific creativity as constrained stochastic behavior: The integration of product, process, and person perspectives. *Psychological Bulletin*, 129, 475–494.

Simonton, D. K. (2004). *Creativity in science: Chance, logic, genius, and zeitgeist*. Cambridge, England: Cambridge University Press.

Simonton, D. K. (2006). Presidential IQ, openness, intellectual brilliance, and leadership: Estimates and correlations for 42 US chief executives. *Political Psychology*, 27, 511–639.

Simonton, D. K. (2008a). Childhood giftedness and adulthood genius: A historiometric analysis of 291 eminent African Americans. *Gifted Child Quarterly*, 52, 243–255.

Simonton, D. K. (2008b). Gender differences in birth order and family size among 186 eminent psychologists. *Journal of Psychology of Science and Technology*, 1, 15–22.

Simonton, D. K. (2008c). Scientific talent, training, and performance: Intellect, personality, and genetic endowment. *Review of General Psychology*, 12, 28–46.

Simonton, D. K. (2009a). Genius, creativity, and leadership. In T. Rickards, M. Runco, & S. Moger (Eds.), *Routledge companion to creativity* (pp. 247–255). London: Taylor & Francis.

Simonton, D. K. (2009b). *Genius 101*. New York: Springer.

Simonton, D. K. (2009c). Varieties of (scientific) creativity: A hierarchical model of disposition, development, and achievement. *Perspectives on Psychological Science*, 4, 441–452.

Simonton, D. K., & Song, A. V. (2009). Eminence, IQ, physical and mental health, and achievement domain: Cox's 282 geniuses revisited. *Psychological Science*, 20, 429–434.

Stewart, L. H. (1977). Birth order and political leadership. In M. G. Hermann (Ed.), *The psychological examination of political leaders* (pp. 205–236). New York: Free Press.

Suedfeld, P. (1985). APA presidential addresses: The relation of integrative complexity to historical, professional, and personal factors.

Journal of Personality and Social Psychology, 47,
848–852.

Suedfeld, P., Guttieri, K., & Tetlock, P. E. (2003).
Assessing integrative complexity at a distance:
Archival analyses of thinking and decision
making. In J. M. Post (Ed.), *The psychological assessment of political leaders: With profiles of Saddam Hussein and Bill Clinton* (pp.
246–270). Ann Arbor: University of Michigan
Press.

Sulloway, F. J. (1996). *Born to rebel: Birth order,
family dynamics, and creative lives.* New York:
Pantheon.

Terman, L. M. (1925–1959). *Genetic studies of
genius* (Vols. 1–5). Stanford, CA: Stanford
University Press.

Terry, W. S. (1989). Birth order and prominence in the history of psychology. *Psychological Record, 39,* 333–337.

Walberg, H. J., Rasher, S. P., & Hase, K. (1978).
IQ correlates with high eminence. *Gifted
Child Quarterly, 22,* 196–200.

White, R. K. (1931). The versatility of genius. *Journal of Social Psychology, 2,* 460–489.

Winter, D. G. (2003). Measuring the motives
of political actors at a distance. In J.
M. Post (Ed.), *The psychological assessment
of political leaders: With profiles of Saddam Hussein and Bill Clinton* (pp. 153–
177). Ann Arbor: University of Michigan
Press.

Zusne, L. (1985). Contributions to the history of
psychology: XXXVIII. The hyperbolic structure of eminence. *Psychological Reports, 57,*
1213–1214.

Zweigenhaft, R. L. (1975). Birth order, approval-
seeking, and membership in Congress. *Journal
of Individual Psychology, 31,* 205–210.

CHAPTER 10

Everyday Creativity

Process and Way of Life – Four Key Issues

Ruth Richards

One may ask: Would we humans value *everyday creativity* more – the "originality of everyday life" – if we knew how much it could do for us, for example, improve our physical and psychological health, boost our immune function, and give us greater life satisfaction and meaning? In fact, there is evidence for this and more (e.g., Richards, 2007a, in press-a; Runco & Pritzker, 1999).

Everyday creativity can be operationally defined using only two *product* criteria (after Barron, 1969): first, *originality* (or relative rarity of a creation within a given reference group) and, second, *meaningfulness* (being comprehensible to others, not random or idiosyncratic, and thus being socially meaningful). Everyday creativity thus defined appears to offer value for human beings over time and culture (Abraham, 2007; Arons,

2007; Eisler, 2007; Sundararajan & Averill, 2007). It is not possible to cover everything about everyday creativity (see edited volumes by Runco & Richards, 1998, and Richards, 2007a, for further perspectives). Rather, this chapter is structured around four key issues:

1. **The construct of everyday creativity.** Its features and adaptive basis are described, along with one assessment approach, including a focus on both creative *product* and creative *process*, at work and at leisure.

2. **Healthy benefits of everyday creativity.** Varied healthy benefits are considered, followed by seemingly paradoxical findings on creativity and illness.

3. **Alternative ways of knowing and creativity.** Diverse perspectives on intuition and creative insight provide added perspective on everyday creative *process*, and even on certain of the earlier health benefits.

4. **"Creative normalcy" versus conformity in everyday life.** Societal norms are

The author wishes to acknowledge key individuals who have helped advance this work and indeed have made it possible, including, especially, Dennis Kinney and Sandow Sacks Ruby, along with Maria Benet, Heidi Daniels, Ruth Arnon Hanham, Seymour Kety, Inge Lunde, Karen Linkins, Ann Merzel, and Steven Matthysse.

considered toward healthier applications of everyday creativity, avoidance
of its "dark side," and work toward
greater human benefit.

Defining Everyday Creativity

The construct of everyday creativity is
defined in terms of human originality at
work and leisure across the diverse activities of everyday life. It is seen as central to
human survival, and, to some extent, it is
(and must be) found in everyone. Because
everyday creativity is not just about *what*
one does, but also *how*, creative process as
well as product are observed.

Universal Quality That Helps Us Survive

Many people say, "I can't draw – I'm not
creative!" Or they cannot sing, act, or write
poetry, and therefore they believe they have
"no creativity." Creativity for them is largely
about the arts, or perhaps the sciences.
Their standards, furthermore, are unrealistic. The portrait they paint should stand
with Rembrandt's, their novel should equal
Jane Austen's. Creativity, they assume, concerns only a small group of celebrated
or eminent people; it does not concern
them.

Everyday creativity, by contrast, is for all
of us. It is not only universal, but necessary
to our very survival as individuals and as a
species (e.g., Richards, 1998; Richards, Kinney, Benet, & Merzel, 1988). We humans are
not creatures of instinct who all build our
nests the same way. Throughout our day,
whether at home or at work, we humans
adapt and innovate, improvise flexibly, at
times acting from our "gut feelings," at times
from options we imagine and systematically
try out, one after the other. Our creativity
may involve anything from making break-
fast to solving a major conflict with one's
boss.

The biologist Edward Sinott (1959) described a primrose that puts out red flowers when the weather is cold and white
flowers when it gets warmer. We humans
have vastly more options than the primrose to adapt within our own environments
and adapt those environments to us. With
everyday creativity, we manifest what evolutionary biologist Theodosius Dobzhansky
(1962) called our "phenotypic plasticity," our
many potentialities within the constraints
of our genetic endowment (Richards, 1998;
Richards, Kinney, Benet et al., 1988). Our
everyday creativity can help us survive
physically – to find food when starving,
heat when freezing, or to escape from the
woods when lost. It also may enhance our
reproductive fitness (Gabora & Kaufman,
Chapter 15, this volume; Runco & Richards,
1998).

The larger systems picture is important
too. Through everyday creativity we and
others can fill "ecological niches" in our
culture (Tooby & DeVore, 1987), where
we each identify a place in the world to
contribute our talents and skills and hopefully find satisfaction. The norm-referenced
construct of everyday creativity acknowledges this social role (Montuori, Combs,
& Richards, 2004; Montuori & Purser, 1999;
Richards, 1998). (See Gabora & Kaufman,
Chapter 15, this volume, for more detailed
treatment of evolutionary issues.)

An Operationalization: The Lifetime Creativity Scales

The two criteria, *originality* and *meaningfulness*, became the basis for the *Lifetime
Creativity Scales (LCS)*, developed and validated with Dennis Kinney and others
at McLean Hospital and Harvard Medical
School. The LCS has shown a very high
degree of interrater reliability and multiple indicators of construct validity (Kinney,
Richards, & Southam, in press; Richards,
Kinney, Benet et al., 1988; Shansis et al.,
2003). The LCS is presented here as an
example of one rigorous operationalization
of *everyday creativity* at both work and
leisure, although other measures do exist
(e.g. Torrance, 1972). Some key creativity
findings with the LCS will be discussed
later in the discussion of mental health and
creativity.

Criteria of *originality* and *meaningfulness* can be applied to most real-life outcomes at work and leisure (these involve products, performances, and ideas, and all must be "major enterprises"). Norm-referenced assessment is based on extensive interview data – where self-report has proven a strong measure of real-life creativity (Hocevar & Bachelor, 1989; Kinney et al., in press).

CREATIVE PRODUCT AND PROCESS ARE BOTH CONSIDERED

Creative *process* is considered in assessing creative *product*. Participants assessed with the LCS were asked not only about *what* they do but *how* they do it – a critical point. The same task can be done in many different ways. There can be, for example, a world of difference between how one person fixes a car versus how another fixes it, the difference manifesting in a high or low bill, or a car that runs for years, or dies down the block. One of our validation participants was not only a successful auto mechanic but even invented some of his own tools.

Assessments may be done for any outcome from home repairs to counseling a friend, helping one's child with a report, reorganizing an office, teaching a class, or landscaping a home. Indeed, and at the everyday level, painting that portrait or writing a poem also qualify. The arts are again included. They are just a smaller slice – too small a slice many might say – of our everyday life (Richards, 2007d).

To reemphasize the point, everyday creativity is not only about *product* but is also about *process*, about *how* one does a task. Many things that we do each day appear common, prosaic, and seemingly uneventful. Yet not only is this unnecessary, but we can live better if we use conscious creative approaches, meeting each situation afresh in our lives, from the meals we create to how we organize things at the office (Richards, 2007a). Our validation participants (Richards, Kinney, Benet et al., 1988) included people doing a range of ordinary and extraordinary things – including the above-mentioned auto mechanic, a homemaker who made innovative clothes on a tight budget, and a World War II resistance fighter who smuggled to safety people fleeing from the Nazis. One can see, in this last case most poignantly, how everyday creativity can save lives.

OVERALL "PEAK CREATIVITY" (ORIGINALITY) IS THE CENTRAL MEASURE

The LCS has scores for vocational and avocational creativity and overall creativity. Quality ("peak creativity") and quantity ("extent of involvement") are assessed for each of these. Yet the focus remains on *originality*, with Overall "Peak Creativity" the most useful measure.

The centrality of originality was borne out in validation studies with three large samples, where we found quality (Peak Creativity) strongly correlated with quantity (Richards, Kinney, Benet et al., 1988). With divergent production measures, *fluency*, too, has emerged a strong predictor for *originality* (e.g., Richards, 1976; Wallach & Kogan, 1965) – the more ideas one has, the greater chance they will be original. This makes intuitive sense.

Yet it is interesting that, for the LCS, vocational and avocational creativity emerged more independently of each other. (Richards, Kinney, Benet et al., 1988). One may, for instance, be creative at the office, and come home to relax. We found that persons at risk for bipolar (e.g., Richards, Kinney, Benet et al., 1988; Richards, Kinney, Daniels, & Linkins, 1992) and schizophrenia spectrum disorders (Kinney et al., 2000–2001) were more apt to manifest their highest creativity at work and at leisure, respectively. The first group tends to be more active in the world, the second more withdrawn.

For some measures of creative products, "meeting a need" is a required feature. Yet here, everyday creative outcomes needn't be immediately useful – although they typically are. The focus is to discern the maximum real-life realization of underlying creative potential for a person through their creative accomplishment, whether it meets an immediate need or not. Some innovations fade, whereas others show value slowly

over time. Consider the unwelcome innovations of some headstrong teens when they
"should" be doing their homework or chores.
(Might that secret project in the garage actually be the next big IT innovation?) Our
immediate concern was tapping underlying
innovative capacity as manifested in real-life
creative accomplishment – whether or not
the outcomes were immediately useful or
wanted.

One Creativity or Many?

Is there some central creative quality, intellectual or nonintellective, rather like "g" in
general intelligence? The debate continues
about what aspects of creativity may be
domain specific and multiple (e.g., literary
or musical ability) or may, by contrast, cross
domains and show generality (e.g., Gardner,
1983; Plucker & Beghetto, 2004; Sternberg,
Grigorenko, & Singer, 2004). Amabile (1996)
usefully distinguishes between creativity-
relevant and domain-relevant skills. More
general factors, often involving nonintellective traits or cognitive styles, do appear
across multiple domains and have even
been called "core characteristics" of creativity (e.g., Barron & Harrington, 1981; Helson,
1999). *Openness to experience* is one such general capacity relevant to creativity (Kinney &
Richards, 2007; Sundararjan & Averill, 2007),
which is one factor in the Five Factor Theory
of Personality (Costa & Widiger, 1994).

Family patterns can also be telling,
whether a similarity is genetic or environmental in basis. Unlike the Bach family
where there were dozens of musicians, high
everyday-creativity families can be found
with diverse accomplishments – perhaps in
teaching, in music, in business, again suggesting more general factors are involved
(e.g., Andreasen, 1987; Richards et al., 1988b;
see Richards, 2007a). Beyond this, diverse
creative capacities within a single eminently
creative individual, crossing domains, have
also been addressed, such as artists who also
write (Zausner, 2007a, 2007b). Barron (1969,
1995) went further to suggest that originality
seems habitual with highly creative people.

Relation to General Intelligence

Intelligence is not the same thing as creativity, as Terman's studies of high IQ individuals showed (Terman & Oden, 1959).
How unfortunate that many programs for
"gifted and talented" youth still lean on IQ
or standardized achievement tests as the sole
means to identify their creatively talented
students (Richards, in press-b; see Kim, Cramond, & VanTassel-Baska, Chapter 21, this
volume).

Nonetheless, IQ-related characteristics,
such as memory or logical operations, are
still useful in creativity. Yet what gives
creativity its special flavor? With psychometric tests of divergent thinking, only
low positive correlations (in the 0.3 range)
with IQ estimates are found (Barron, 1969;
Barron & Harrington, 1981; Richards, 1976,
1981).

Important, too are indications of *neces-
sary-but-not-sufficient* relationships of IQ on
measures on creativity, whether involving heteroscedastic (triangular) scatterplots
(e.g., Guilford, 1968; Richards, 1976) or an
IQ threshold, as in the IQ score of about 120
found by Barron (1969) and associates with
distinguished creators across fields. Here
was a necessary intelligence level, but one
beyond which further IQ increments didn't
seem to matter that much.

In our own validation work on the LCS
(Richards, Kinney, Benet et al., 1988), everyday creativity and a cluster of education-
intelligence-SES estimates loaded on different factors. Furthermore, certain results
regarding bipolar disorders held true, even
after IQ, SES, and education estimates
were covaried out (Richards, Kinney, Lunde
et al., 1988). The relationship of intelligence
to creativity remains controversial with at
least five different categories of potential association, as suggested by Sternberg
(Kaufman, Plucker, & Baer, 2008; Sternberg
& O'Hara, 1999). Yet whatever the resolution, and the adjunctive importance of
general intelligence, it does not appear to
provide the unique and distinctive key to
creativity.

TWO OTHER BROAD-BASED APPROACHES TO CREATIVE PROCESS AND PRODUCT

Of the many constructs for and approaches to creativity (see Plucker, this volume), two provide useful contrasts here: (a) *personal or mini-c creativity*, and (b) *self-actualizing creativity*. Each concerns both creative product and process.

PERSONAL CREATIVITY/MINI-C CREATIVITY

The first is termed *personal creativity* (Runco, 1996, 2007) or *mini-c creativity* (Beghetto & Kaufman, 2007), where the *mini-c* name acknowledges that everyday creativity is sometimes called *little-c* and eminent creativity *Big-C*. A fourth proposed possibility, called *Pro-C*, involves the subpopulations from which Big-C creativity may emerge (Kaufman & Beghetto, 2009). *Mini-c/Personal creativity* is a self-referenced construct attracting new interest (e.g., Sundararajan, 2009), and one that will hopefully be operationalized. A teacher, for example, may want to assess learning based on where the students started, looking at creative *product* and the *process* steps along the way. Too often the focus is on bringing every student to the same standard rather than looking at individual gains and personal bests. This self-referenced construct could nicely complement the norm-referenced construct of *everyday creativity*

SELF-ACTUALIZING CREATIVITY

In the next, well-known example, Abraham Maslow's (1968, 1971) *self-actualizing creativity* is theoretically available to everyone but falls further along a developmental path where everyday creativity may help point the way. Many believe that creativity can help us grow and develop further as human beings (Combs & Krippner, 2007; Loye, 2007; Ray & Anderson, 2000; Rogers, 1961; Richards, 2007a, 2007c). From a humanistic perspective (e.g., Maslow, 1968, 1971; Richards, Kinney, Benet et al., 1988; Wink, 1999), Maslow, who wrote of *self-actualizing* persons, placed *self-actualization* at the pinnacle of his hierarchy of needs. Interestingly,

he saw self-actualizing *creativity* essentially as a byproduct of the self-actualizing process, stating that (Maslow, 1968, p. 145).

SA [self-actualizing] creativity stresses first the personality rather than its achievements, considering these achievements to be epiphenomena.... It stresses characterological qualities like boldness, courage, freedom, spontaneity, perspicuity, integrity, self-acceptance... [and] the expressive or Being quality... rather than its problem-solving or problem making quality. (p. 145)

More research is needed on diverse populations to explore, for example, when the creative process becomes central to one's way of life, and under what circumstances it might also provide a potential path of personal and even spiritual development. When, for example, might *deficiency* creativity transform into *being* creativity, as problems are solved and individuals find higher purpose in their efforts (Rhodes, 1990; Richards, 1998, 2007, in press-a; Sundararajan & Averill, 2007)? A further path may be seen, for example, with the Zen arts (Loori, 2004; Pritzker, 1999). When creative process brings us more fully into the moment, beyond preconceptions, fears, and distorting ideas of self and world, toward richer contact with the phenomenal world, what new awarenesses might arise?

Value of Everyday Creativity as a Broad-Based Dependent Variable

Everyday creativity, as a construct, is not, as some think, confined to the trivia of life. This is an important misunderstanding. It concerns almost *anything* to which one brings originality, any time creation occurs in an everyday context, including major projects. Nor are eminent and exceptional creators excluded. Everyday creativity can be seen as the ground from which (a later and) more publicly celebrated accomplishment can grow (Richards, 1998, 2007a). In fact, many an important invention, equation, or painting that has changed culture started with a fleeting image or wild idea on an everyday walk or hike.

The construct of everyday creativity, operationalized here with the LCS, is not unique but resonates with other broad-based real-life measures of creativity and behavioral checklists (Andreasen, 1987; Helson, Roberts, & Agronick, 1995; Torrance, 1972), albeit the LCS takes the approach further. The LCS became the first broad-based measure of real-life creativity, broadly applicable at work or leisure, that could be used with unselected populations, and could tap their creativity – and again this is very important – *wherever* it might emerge. If one is looking, for instance, at a population of persons living on the street, and asking about creativity, one must be ready to find it in whatever form it takes – be this in selling papers or other items for cash, or helping at a homeless shelter.

Interestingly *everyday creativity* and the LCS were even featured in the Tuesday Science Times section of *The New York Times* (Goleman, 1988b). This was in part because of new kinds of mental health problems that could be addressed with creativity as *dependent variable*. Many previous studies *chose* people for specialized creativity (e.g., in art, writing, leadership – often eminent people), and used it as the *independent variable*. They thereby limited the population to which results could be generalized – only those active in a particular domain or who could perform a specialized activity (e.g., writing, or scientific discovery). The approach assumes *this* behavior, furthermore, would be the best sample of a person's underlying creative potential (e.g., is writing a story the best assessment for a musician?).

STUDYING NEW POPULATIONS
One can now sample from populations that are diverse except for the selection variable. Consider, as we did, persons diagnosed with a "bipolar mood disorder" or "schizophrenia spectrum" diagnosis, along with certain of their relatives – results to be discussed in the section "Creativity as 'Compensatory Advantage' to Bipolar Spectrum Disorders"

(Kinney et al., 2000–2001; Richards & Kinney, 1990; Richards et al., 1992; Richards, Kinney, Lunde et al., 1988).

The target population can become persons carrying a certain diagnosis of, for example, ADHD or dyslexia, or all members of a certain family, or individuals who were home schooled versus conventionally schooled. The populations can be sampled and compared using the same scale. Instead of a smaller group of people (however interesting or exceptional they may be), results can be generalized to literally millions of people in the population at large.

Summary

The construct of everyday creativity was presented as universal and central to human survival, and to the development of self and culture, with focus both on creative *product* and *process*. Everyday creativity, operationalized using the LCS, involves a norm-referenced perspective on meaningful originality across all areas of human endeavor, both at work and leisure. In the next section, we look at some of its beneficial aspects.

Everyday Creativity and Health

All else being equal, does creativity tend to work in the service of health – and what then of the apparent exceptions? To be considered are the expressive arts, guided imagery, creative appreciation, issues of bipolar disorders and creativity, and patterns of resilient coping with problems.

Creativity, Arts, and Health

Can expressive creative writing actually improve physical health, as well as psychological well-being? Might it even boost immune function? Remarkably, the answer is "yes." Here is our mind–body connection shown in bold relief. Pennebaker's expressive writing studies and those of his associates (e.g., Pennebaker, Glaser, & Kiecolt-Glaser, 1988) have now been multiply replicated and extended (e.g., Pennebaker, 1995; Lepore & Smyth, 2002). The benefits are definitely there. In addition, other work with visual arts, with imagery, and even with the appreciation of creativity show benefit.

Expressive-Writing Paradigm

Imagine if you were asked to write about something so traumatic you had not told anyone about it. The control group wrote about something neutral. In the original Pennebaker study, experimental and control group both wrote for only 20 minutes a day, four times total. Perhaps some in the expressive group had not even fully disclosed their dreaded experience and feelings to themselves, to their own conscious minds. Yet now it came out. What did they write about? Examples involved stress coming to college, loss and loneliness, conflicts with the opposite sex, parents, death, divorce, and trauma (Pennebaker et al., 1988).

Shortly after writing, expressive writers typically felt troubled, anxious, and depressed. But for many, at least, it didn't last; six weeks later, on the average they scored significantly higher than controls on a measure of psychological well-being. Plus, they had made fewer visits than controls to the college health center. And compared to the control group – a finding remarkable to some people unfamiliar with mind–body medicine (e.g., Freeman & Lawlis, 2001) – participants were significantly higher than controls on two measures of T-cell function, indices of immune competence. Even their bodies – their immune systems, their white blood cells – know the difference! Through their writing, amazingly enough, these participants, compared to controls, emerged more resistant to disease.

Findings could logically generalize to everything from private journaling to blogs to Facebook and other social networking sites that allow emotional catharsis, processing, and shared understanding. At best, this is about *resilience* – where the capacity to face, address, integrate, and transform one's worst fears and darkest moments can, going forward, lead to new strength and empowerment. One can even learn to gain pleasure from such mastery (Richards, 1998; Russ, 1999). Think of important pieces of world literature – such as J.M. Barrie's *Peter Pan* – that harken back to early childhood issues; some authors cope with such trauma by transforming it through writing (Morrison & Morrison, 2006).

Elaborations on the design of the Pennebaker research paradigm have shown that expressive writing can integrate fragmented mental structures and increase working memory (e.g., Klein, 2002). It appears it takes more than emotional catharsis to heal most deeply (Sundararajan & Richards, 2005); conscious, controlled, and deliberate processing, as in narrative construction, leads to a deeper understanding and lower reactivity. In art therapy as well as writing, verbally processing one's visual creations leads to greater gains (McNiff, 1992).

OPENING PANDORA'S BOX

One's creative expression, whether in writing or another modality, can open, and may in fact be designed to open, a Pandora's box of material from our unconscious (Progoff, 1975; Richards, 2007b; Zausner, 2007b). It can take great courage to confront this. Working it through appears to be a key ingredient. Poets, whose work gives less chance for narrative construction and further processing, may show fewer of the health benefits found among other writers (Kaufman & Sexton, 2006). When our deep-seated issues are not addressed, through habitual suppression, denial, avoidance, or other defenses, there can be serious and ongoing health risks (e.g., Singer, 1990; Wickramasekera, 1998).

Turning to arts and arts medicine, one finds a growing literature, albeit one characterized at one time by a predominance of case studies and anecdotal reports rather than controlled research (e.g., McNiff, 1992; Richards, 2004, 2007a, 2007d; Sonke-Henderson, Brandman, Serlin, & Graham-Pole, 2008), but this is changing. The multimodal facing and working through of one's situation, be it from grief, shock, fear of illness, conflict or crisis, depression or anxiety, or ongoing stress with cancer, loss,

AIDS and other illnesses, using visual arts, writing, combined arts approaches, interpersonal sharing, and creatively helping others to deal with these issues in turn, can be invaluable (N. Rogers, 1993; Shapiro, 2009; Zausner, 2007a, 2007b).

The healing effects of arts were underscored by presentations and demonstrations from persons with mental health challenges in a moving event at The Carter Presidential Center in Atlanta, called "Arts and Self-Expression in Mental Health," where I gave a related talk (Richards, 2004). Goals included reduction of the stigma of mental illness. The presentation of few findings on creativity and on the healthy effects of self-expression underscored this. for the benefit of people who still believe that creativity in the context of psychopathology must somehow itself be problematic. One reason for this assumption may derive from problems some people have in acknowledging their own unconscious and irrational mental contents (which may indeed come forth in creativity) may project this material onto others instead (Richards, 1996, 1998, 2004). The more we learn about arts and healing, about our own unconscious and conscious creative process, and about the bravery that can be involved in creatively facing our depths, the more we can realize our common humanity as well as celebrate the health that can shine through in our resilient creative coping.

GUIDED IMAGERY AND MEANING MAKING

One needn't do arts to plumb one's inner depths or to heal. Guided imagery is an increasingly common modality in health and healing (e.g., Achterberg, 2002). According to Freeman and Lawlis (2001), such imagery is "the very foundation of all mind-body interactions and effects. . . . (and) plays a critical role in all health care." Guided imagery has been used with many problems, including eczema, diabetes, breast cancer, and more. "Targeted imagery," in fact, has been shown to lead to specific physiological change (Freeman & Lawlis, 2001).

This work can employ one's fullest creative mind; the most effective images are personally relevant and *self-created* (Freeman & Lawlis, 2001; Richards, 2007a; Singer, 2006). Interestingly, author Ezra Pound (in Freeman & Lawlis, 2001) said of such imagery that "the image is more than an idea. It is a vortex or cluster of fused ideas and is endowed with energy" (p. 261).

Dreamwork, psychotherapy, and work with "personal mythology," which can make conscious and transform certain images and beliefs, can be life changing. One can construct narratives and new integrations, find self-defining memories, discover key images and alter them, and even revision one's life-directing stories. This can lead to new freedom, health, and greater life meaning (Feinstein & Krippner, 1997; Krippner & Waldman, 1999; McAdams, 1993; Singer, 2006).

CREATIVE ACTIVITY, APPRECIATION, AND LONGEVITY

Creative activity of many types seems relevant to successful aging, greater acceptance of one's situation, finding purpose and alternatives, feeling empowered, and discovering satisfaction and meaning (Adams-Price, 1998; Adler, 1995; Langer, 1989). Indeed, complex environments in animal studies have led to brain growth, higher blood flow, and healthy neurochemicals (Levy & Langer, 1999).

A major study involving everyday populations examined what the authors called *vicarious creativity*, which we have elsewhere called *appreciation of creativity* – and is correlated with everyday creativity. The study looked at 12,000 people in Sweden comparing those who attended more creative events, such as plays and concerts, and visited sites exhibiting the creativity of others, including museums and galleries, with those who were less culturally active. There were controls for several confounding factors. Whatever the full explanation, those more active, involved, and artistically aware elder on the average, *lived longer* (Levy & Langer, 1999). Earlier we noted the creativity possible in *appreciation* of creativity (Pritzker, 2007; Richards, 2007a; Zausner, 2007b) and how active it, in itself, can be. Now one sees how healthy it can be as well.

Creativity as "Compensatory Advantage" to Bipolar Spectrum Disorders

Then what of the exceptions? Is there truth to the popular belief that bipolar disorder (such as manic-depressive illness) and creativity go together? Yes and no. Furthermore, the story for *everyday creativity* is not necessarily the same as for eminent-level creativity. It connects, as well, to some findings from brain studies in the next section.

MODEL: SICKLE-CELL ANEMIA

First, consider sickle-cell anemia, a simple genetic model of *compensatory advantage*. The present situation is probably more complicated than this simple model. But the model is useful. With sickle-cell, if a child inherits an allele from both parents, it is a bad situation – there is severe anemia, painful crises, and early death. If the child inherits only one allele, and is a carrier, the child may have a mild anemia at worst. But there still is the *compensatory advantage* of resistance to malaria. There are more carriers than those with the full syndrome.

This model had been discussed for schizophrenia (Kinney & Matthysse, 1978). We wondered if it might hold for bipolar disorders, where twin and adoption studies had shown an important genetic contribution (e.g., Wender et al., 1986). Was there a compensatory advantage – this time for *creativity*? Might relatives of people with full bipolar disorder, relatives who were not as ill, yet perhaps had just a few loose associations, or deeper emotions, or excess energy and confidence, as well as the executive functions to pull it all together show such an advantage?? We postulated for both groups an *inverted-U relationship* such that people with milder symptomatology would carry the creative advantage. In many ways, our findings supported this.

NEW PERSPECTIVES ON RELATIONS BETWEEN CREATIVITY AND BIPOLAR DISORDERS

Our various studies, using the LCS, included both individuals diagnosed with bipolar I disorder (with major mood elevations and depressions) cyclothymic personality disorder (smaller and more ongoing mood swings), and unipolar depression (with and without bipolar risk), as well as psychiatrically normal relatives and controls. (For further details on this and related topics, see Kinney & Richards, 2007; Richards, 1998, 1999; Runco & Richards, 1998) and chapters by Silvio and Kaufman, and Simonton, in this volume. For information on the bipolar spectrum of disorders, see Akiskal & Akiskal, 2007; Akiskal et al., 2006; and Akiskal & Mallya, 1987.) Three key points can be noted here (Richards & Kinney 1990; Richards, Kinney, Lunde, Benet, & Merzel, 1988, Richards et al., 1992; see also Richards, 1998; Kinney et al., 2000–2001; the special 2000–2001 issue of *Creativity Research Journal*, "Creativity and the Schizophrenia Spectrum"; and other studies that are supportive – e.g., Andreasen, 1987; Eckblad & Chapman, 1986; Fodor, 1999; Jamison, 1989, 1993; Jamison, Gerner, Hammen, & Padesky, 1980; Schuldberg, 1990, 2000–2001).

First: The evidence supports a compensatory advantage *involving creativity, linked to risk for bipolar disorders. An evident relation exists between risk for bipolar disorder and higher everyday creativity, in fact fitting the "inverted-U" pattern and* compensatory advantage. *It was not the sicker people who were more creative. Better functioning individuals – or people during better functioning mood states – showed the highest creativity. (A peak diagnosis for creativity was cyclothymia, not manic-depressive illness; a peak mood state was mild mood elevation, not mania.) With creativity and the schizophrenia spectrum, we again found – here, more preliminary and in somewhat different form, for example, involving magical thinking – support for a* compensatory advantage *for everyday creativity.*

Second: Both personal and family psychiatric history need to be considered. Here we found two surprises. A creative advantage isn't necessarily always about illness. A compensatory advantage was also suggested for psychiatrically normal first-degree relatives of bipolar probands. In addition, the bipolar history may manifest only in a family member and not the person. Further, individuals who have a history of unipolar depression with a family history of bipolar disorder showed higher everyday creativity than individuals lacking this family history. (Subclinical mood elevations might help explain these results.)

Third: Everyday creativity appears to work in the service of health. All else being equal, creativity may be positive, even protective, rather than making people sick. The data can only suggest this through the finding that better-functioning people show higher creativity, and further research is needed. Everyday creativity might also be studied as a mind–body intervention for mood disordered persons and kids at risk.

If everyday creativity in fact represents a *compensatory advantage* to risk for bipolar disorders, creativity is an adaptive characteristic – an advantage, not a disadvantage. Results generalize not just to a handful of famous people but to literally millions of individuals in this country alone, where up to 5% may have a bipolar spectrum disorder. Indeed, as many as two thirds of individuals diagnosed as "unipolar" depressed may actually have a subtle bipolar spectrum disorder (Akiskal et al., 2006; Akiskal & Mallya, 1987). Evolutionary advantages have been suggested for bipolar disorders (Akiskal & Akiskal, 2007; Gartner, 2005; Goodwin & Jamison, 1990; Richards, Kinney, Lunde, Benet, & Merzel, 1988) and perhaps for schizophrenia as well (Nettle & Clegg, 2006).

The Schizophrenia Spectrum and Creativity. Although replication is needed, Kinney et al. (2000–2001) have shown higher everyday creativity among better-functioning individuals with low-level symptoms from the "schizophrenia spectrum," findings

that again fit the *inverted-U* or *compensatory advantage* profile. Of related interest is work by Fleck and colleagues (2008) with a nonclinical population, showing that individuals high in *transliminality* – allowing unconscious processes to enter consciousness – showed both (a) features such as magical ideation, and belief in the paranormal, similar to the clinical sample, and (b) EEG patterns including certain temporal-lobe changes consistent with patterns in schizotypy and schizophrenia spectrum disorders.

A creative "compensatory advantage" linked to either bipolar or schizophrenia spectrum disorders is a vital area for further research – one that could help ease the pain of many, decrease stigma, and give hope.

Resilient Creative Coping

Within the broader population, one may turn to personal problems and *resilience*. Table 10.1 has five logical possibilities, which can also be multiple or overlapping, for ways creativity can relate to personal problems (or pathology). These include both direct and indirect relationships (Richards, 1981, 1999).

The last option of a *third factor that can affect both* creativity and problems can include the situation of *compensatory advantage* just discussed. The third factor, here mediating creativity and pathology (e.g., genetic factors), is not necessarily positive or negative and can manifest in different ways.

Two other composite patterns (involving #1 and #2, *direct and indirect relationships, where problems generate creativity*, and then #3 and #4, *direct and indirect relationships where creativity generates problems*) concern whether creativity is helpful or not for an individual. Early conflict and difficulty is frequent in exceptional creativity and yet is somehow overcome (e.g., Goertzel & Goertzel, 1962). Success may be due to many factors including resilient personal response, or resources and supports (e.g., Flach, 1990; Werner & Smith, 2001). When issues are conscious and processed, not suppressed, avoided, or denied, and when there is support and executive functioning to hold

Table 10.1: Typology of Relations of Creativity to Problems/Pathology

---

1) Direct Relationship: Problems Lead to Creativity   (P → C)

Here, problems can directly influence the *content* or *process* of creativity. Kay Jamison, in *An Unquiet Mind*, wrote about her own bipolar disorder. The content came directly from her experience. The process might at times have been affected by mild mood symptoms affecting cognition, affect, or motivation (e.g., looser associations, deeper feelings, enhanced energy or motivation). As another example, consider a young woman who just escaped an abusive situation and immediately and creatively helps a sibling escape.

2) Indirect Relationship: Problems Lead to a Situation
(Third Factor) That Leads to Creativity   (P → T → C)

Here problems lead to an event or realization (Third Factor) that generates new creative goals or accomplishments. Consider someone who got painfully divorced and is writing regularly in a journal, for catharsis and understanding. S/heThis individual discovers hidden potential, pleasure from writing, and the wish to share with others around more universal themes – and comes to write a blog that helps many people. Nobelist John Cheever is another example, who wrote as a youth about family and school difficulties, and later in life shared some of this more broadly in his books. With growth beyond personal issues and greater concern for the human condition, these examples also concern *deficiency* creativity turning into a more altruistic *being* creativity (Rhodes, 1990).

3) Direct Relationship: Creativity Leads to Problems   (C → P)

This one can go either way. Problems are almost guaranteed for some types of creativity, such as visual art or writing therapies that open up hidden recesses and reveal unconscious material. Often we seek this in arts, in psychotherapy, in dreamwork, or in talking with a friend. But what happens next? Why is one person resilient (Flach, 1990), coping with personal disruption and reintegration, while another is not? Humanistic psychologist Rollo May (1975) wrote about anxiety that can accompany creative revelations and the need for *courage* to move ahead with creativity. Difficult results of one's creativity may ultimately be healthy, if worked through (as in the preceding section). If not this can lead to escapes and various problems, as one sees in the section that follows.

4) Indirect Relationship: Creativity Leads to a Situation
(Third Factor) That Ends Up Generating Problems   (C → T → P)

Here a problem becomes too much, even if resilient attempts were made to cope (or defend). Unlike the Pennebaker (1995) studies where expressive-writing participants worked things through toward increased well-being, here major discomfort remains untreated. This could lead to depression, alcohol or drug abuse, avoidance, etc. Another sad case involves ostracism of creative youth in schools, by peers, and sometime by teachers who misunderstand their presentations (Cramond, 2005). They may cope by withdrawal, clowning, and other defenses, as may some employees in similar situations.

5) Third Factor, Which Can Affect Both Creativity and Problems   (C ← T → P)

Familial liability or a diathesis for bipolar-spectrum mood disorders affects perhaps more than 5% of the population (Akiskal & Akiskal, 2007; Akiskal & Mallya, 1987). (Consider too other major pathologies that run in families and might show a *compensatory advantage*.) Enhanced creative potential isn't necessarily related to degree of illness, or even to illness at all – just to underlying familial risk. There may be effects on cognition, affect, or motivation. It may even follow (e.g., Richards & Kinney, 1990) that early creative exposures for children at risk could lower the emergence or expression of pathology. Other examples include many early childhood conflicts. These can at times leadto resilient coping (e.g., Goertzels & Goertzels, 1962; Werner & Smith, 2001), at other times to decompensation. It is vital to clarify what makes the difference, and how one can intervene to help people.

Note: **P** signifies personal problems, illnesses, pathologies, conflicts; **C** stands for creative process and manifestation; **T** represents a third/intervening factor, single or multiple, mediating a relationship. Table is adapted from Richards (1999), p. 40.

things together, creativity may be able act in the service of health (Richards, 2007a). Alas, it doesn't always happen. We may consider two general possibilities.

> *First pattern: When creativity helps (#1 and #2)*. Here, problems lead to a desire to cope (third factor), which fuels a creative working through. The first pattern (#1) may fit with this, too, when the individual capitalizes directly on their difficult experience for creative use and transformation, for example, from a breakup, a death, or other major conflict.

> *Second pattern: When creativity hurts (#3 and #4)*. This time, #3, a decompensation from creative activity, may come first, and the resilient coping typical of #2 doesn't happen. Hence a further problem emerges, as per #4, for example, anxiety leading to substance use and then abuse, or conflicts with superiors leading to truancy or job difficulty.

The big question here concerns what makes the difference. Why do some people cope creatively and others fall by the wayside? How can we boost resilient and creative coping (Flach, 1990; Richards, 1998)? Studies of *compensatory advantage* (Kinney & Richards, 2007) and related traits may provide certain leads, as do key case studies (Zausner, 2007b). Longitudinal work (e.g., Werner & Smith, 2001) is invaluable, yet with a few notable exceptions (e.g., Helson et al., 1995) it has not focused enough on creativity.

Summary

Although everyday creativity may require much of us in terms of personal risk-taking, there are many indications that it can be healthy in expressive arts activities and beyond. Although one hears about "creativity and psychopathology," creativity may serve as a healthy *compensatory advantage* to the risk for bipolar disorder and perhaps for schizophrenia. We also have chances for resilient creative coping with our problems. The next section looks more deeply at what may be happening personally during insightful creative moments.

Alternative Ways of Knowing and Creativity

This section primarily concerns intuition and the subsequent moment of insight that may follow, considered by many to be the "core" of creative functioning. This focus may also help explain certain "health" findings above. There are many perspectives (e.g., Myers, 2002; Sternberg & Davidson, 1999) including special-process and multiple-process views. Pink's (2005) *A whole new mind: Why right-brainers will rule the future* addresses one aspect, while suggesting the topic is vitally important for us all (see also Richards, 2007d).

Intuition and Insight

How does one *intuit*, or "arrive at the solution of a problem *without* reasoning toward it" (Damasio, 1994, p. 188). Humans seem to use intuition often – to size up someone new, assess a product in a store, or decide if someone is telling the truth. Intuition is quick and global. We may "get it," and in a flash. We may often be right, but it may take logic a long time to explain why (e.g., Myers, 2002). It is a worthy problem, however, and one key to our universal everyday creativity.

Intuition appears to draw on hemispheric specialization and a number of other factors: unconscious knowledge, procedural as well as declarative memory, experiential knowledge, holistic impressions, and affective as well as cognitive material (Damasio, 1994; Myers, 2002; Sternberg & Davidson, 1999). Some even believe there are transpersonal and subtle quantum-mechanical dimensions in the process (Laszlo, in press; Miller & Cook-Greuter, 2000; Osho, 2001).

Policastro (1999) distinguished intuition from creative insight: "Intuition entails vague and tacit knowledge, whereas insight involves sudden and usually clear awareness" (p. 90). We may find sudden insight invaluable in an emergency. We may also discover a slower and sometimes vague and early intuitive sense about our work. It can persist in a subterranean stratum, allowing intuition to guide our work along the way.

Taking Wallas's (in Dacey & Lennon, 1998) four stages of *preparation, incubation, illumination,* and *verification* as our model, we are looking at the middle two stages, at *incubation,* when we are not consciously aware of the processing, and *illumination,* or that sudden Aha! moment. Jonas Salk said of creativity as a whole that it is based on a "merging of intuition and reason" (in Damasio, 1994, p. 189). Here, however, we are in pursuit of the Aha! of illumination.

After the following example, the discussion touches on some stylistic issues, newer brain findings, a model from chaos theory, and issues of states of consciousness.

EXAMPLE

Lehrer (2008) relates a poignant life-or-death true story: In 1949, on the hottest day ever recorded in Montana, 15 firefighters parachuted into a remote gulch to battle a fire supposed to be small. With a shift of wind, the fire suddenly went out of control, jumped the watery gulch, and, now fanned by fierce winds, raced in an updraft toward the firefighters. The leader yelled for everyone to flee up to the ridge, but soon saw a wall of flame 50 yards behind, and closing fast. He had only seconds. In an incredible instant he stopped, lit a match, and ignited the ground right before him; with a wet handkerchief to mouth, he lay down in the just burned ground waiting for the fire to pass over. Remarkably, he (and one other person) survived. In this case, the near-instantaneous processing and insight were lifesaving.

Intentional and Stylistic Approaches to Creativity

How did the leader find this solution? Could anyone have done it?

Some features may predict for this capacity, such as being open to one's "gut feelings," or having facility in intrapersonal intelligence (Policastro, 1999) to tune in to such inner processes. S. B. Kaufman (2009) found that "faith," or confidence, in using one's

intuition is also valuable. Among participants in a high-functioning group, individuals showing decreased *latent* inhibition – a drop in a preconscious gating mechanism that screens from one's attention those stimuli previously found irrelevant – had greater "faith" in intuition. Participants were more open to new material, had ways to control it, and the confidence to use it.

Low latent inhibition is found in certain persons diagnosed schizophrenic. Yet in the service of creativity, it has also been linked to "openness to experience" (Peterson & Carson, 2000). Adaptive use of "latent inhibition" may not be unlike "regression in the service of the ego" (Kris, 1976). It may also be consistent with stylist features such as "preference for complexity" or "tolerance of ambiguity" (Barron, 1969), which involve staying open to new material while maintaining adaptive control. Relevant too are the findings of a creative "compensatory advantage" in healthier parts of the schizophrenia spectrum, as mentioned in the previous section (Kinney et al., 2000–2001).

This section underscores the importance of work on (a) cognitive style and creativity, and on (b) a compensatory advantage for creativity linked to certain milder clinical syndromes but in itself possibly useful and adaptive.

Tracking Intuition and Insight – Patterns of Mentation

It is significant that certain covert creative processes are beginning to yield to scientific analysis. For instance, a series of studies using EEG and often fMRI contrast (a) a more rapid holistic and relatively unconscious creative process of solving a problem with (b) a more conscious deliberate and logical strategy – the *insight* versus *analytic* strategies. Tasks used problems (anagrams, or remote associate tests after Mednick) that could be solved with either strategy. In one study (Subramaniam, Kounios, Parrish, & Jung-Beeman, 2008) involving an anagram task, participants worked in their own chosen way and later reported on strategy.

Participants chose one strategy or the other (or both in alteration) when presented with the task. Related brain changes were found just *before* the moment of insight. This fits more complex models of insight (see Sternberg & Davidson, 1999) where the Aha! moment is just the end of a sequence.

Another study (Kounios et al., 2008) looked at "initial resting brain state" and showed differences in resting EEG. Again there were different brain states early on, in this case *prior* to the activity! People with a more intuitive style were perhaps already "getting ready" neurologically. Notably, findings support patterns of attentional diffusion and right-lateralized hemisphericity found earlier in a study by Martindale (1999). In this more receptive creative phase, Martindale also found (a) low cortical activation; (b) more dominant right hemispheric activation; and (c) low frontal activity, including slow theta waves. The subjective counterpart involves defocused attention, associative thought, and many simultaneous representations – quite resonant with the findings of Kounois et al. (2008).

Of further interest, insight strategies (but not analytic performance) have been shown to correlate with embedded figures performance and identifying out-of-focus pictures (see Bowden, Jung-Beeman, Fleck, & Kounios, 2005). These are more holistic right-brain tasks.

Finally, keeping in mind, first, that (a) *mild mood elevation* (vs. extreme elevation, neutrality, or depression) was the preferred creative state for participants with bipolar disorders (Richards & Kinney, 1990) and eminent creators in the arts (Jamison, 1989; Ludwig, 1995), and, second, that (b) for all of us, a *positive* mood also spurs creative thinking (e.g., Isen, Daubman, & Nowicki, 1987), one may note two other compelling findings (Subramaniam et al., 2008): Participants who were in a *positive mood* while doing Mednick-type remote associate problems (a) solved *more* problems in general compared to controls and (b) solved more problems using an *insight* strategy rather than an analytic strategy. Such findings on mental state and style, and cognition and

affect, appear relevant to the everyday creativity of all of us.

Models from Chaos Theory: The Aha! Moment

Models utilizing nonlinear-dynamical-systems (chaos) theory provide yet a different lens on the sudden dynamics of the Aha! moment, at minimum metaphorically. The context is one of bifurcation and self-organizing neural events and potentials; change can happen in a flash, since chaotic systems are far from being at equilibrium and are poised for transformation (e.g., Abraham, 1996, 2007; Briggs & Peat, 1989; Richards, 1996 1998, 2000–2001; Schuldberg, 1999, 2007; Zausner, 1996).

THE "BUTTERFLY EFFECT"

Consider the so-called "butterfly effect," a term that has entered popular culture. As the story goes, an innocent butterfly flaps its wings over Moscow, and a storm system erupts over New York City. We see global weather patterns, interconnected around the earth and resting on the edge of change. A small puff of air produces a big reaction. Of course this happens only at special times – for example, when the last snowflake lands and precipitates an avalanche. But there are many phenomena in the natural world, from storms to stock-market crashes, that have been attributed to the butterfly effect (Robertson & Combs, 1995). One sees a complex dynamic system with highly interdependent and recursive relationships between the parts, which suddenly bifurcates to a new solution.

In this context, one may consider the Aha! phenomenon. There is evidence for so-called chaotic ground states in neural electrical activity, where new *attractors* (that is, the state to which a system in phase space may settle down) can develop in an instant. This has been shown, for example, with new sensory input for new odors (sweet, bitter orange, vinegar) in studies of the olfactory bulb (Skarda & Freeman, 1987). New solution may be quickly generated. Abraham (1996) noted three types of *bifurcations* (to new solutions) that could potentially be operative in creativity. He also discussed how the tension between divergent and convergent thinking (typical of creativity) could generate a context for such events (see also Krippner, Richards, & Abraham, 2009). One should note that it is the extended brain that collaborates here when innovation occurs, in response to new information, and not some tiny brain locus.

Such insights may evidently occur along with a burst of brain activity (Lehrer, 2008), as cells across the cortex reform into a new network, which is able to enter consciousness. Policastro (1999) speculates that, in intuition, an implicit code of associative strengths among neural units becomes an "explicit code of symbolic rules" (p. 91). All the more true this would be, then, in sudden insight.

HOW MIGHT A CREATIVE PERSON EXPERIENCE SUCH A MOMENT?

A useful analogy for creative insight may be found in the popping of popcorn, where each exploded kernel represents a creative insight. When we load corn into a popper, we don't know which kernel will explode or when. But we do expect more popping if we turn the heat up. We raise the odds for cooking (or for frequency of creative insights).

With the brain, we may have strategies that, statistically, make insight more likely. If we are open to experience, bravely welcoming whatever may occur, we may effectively be turning the heat up. We come closer to an "edge of chaos" where new solutions can suddenly be present. One would expect creative personality traits such as tolerance for ambiguity or preference for complexity to expand the possibilities. Yet we also have ego strength (Barron, 1969) or executive functioning to keep the lid on the popper and make sure nothing gets burned.

Creative States of Consciousness

One can take another, more experiential, look at mental states that can enhance creativity and that may potentially relate to earlier brain findings. Intuition can come,

for instance, when we are not working, not expecting it, taking a walk, or taking a shower. We relax to allow it, and may need, as writer Anne Lamott (1994) said, to stop the chatter of the rational mind. Some creators purposefully take a walk along with one's muse (see Richards, 1998), play music, and so on. Yet at other times the creator must work hard to maintain creative concentration in the mental state that is most generative. Rainer Maria Rilke addressed this difficulty in a remarkable letter (Rilke, in Barron, Montuori, & Barron, 1997, p. 53):

> I am experiencing yet again the awful, inconceivable polarity between life and all-encompassing work. How far from me is the work, how far the angels!.... Please do not expect me to speak to you of my inner labor... of all the reversals I will have to undergo in my struggle for concentration.

What are the relevant mental states we ourselves experience? Varied "states of consciousness" occur in normal life, for example, in sleep, dreaming, or meditation (Krippner, 1999). It is interesting that widely varied states of consciousness have entered psychology textbooks (e.g., Zimbardo, Johnson, & Weber, 2006) yet are infrequently mentioned in connection with creative intuition or insight. Important exceptions include Csikszentmihalyi's (1990, 1996) groundbreaking work on *flow*, and Martindale's (1999) electrical brain research.

According to Baruss (2003), major alterations of consciousness involve "changes in the ordinary waking state along any number of dimensions... (for example) the stream of thoughts, feelings, and sensations" (p. 8). Alterations of some sort may occur in our everyday life and in our everyday creativity. Is facility at state modulation even part of our creative capacity (Richards, 2007c)? For example, practices related to the Zen arts (e.g., Loori, 2004; Pritzker, 1999; Sekida, 1977) have been said to involve "active" meditative approaches.

In fact, meditative approaches – beyond their use in spiritual practice and mind–body medicine (e.g., Kabat-Zinn, 1994) – may offer useful models for some stages of creativity. The receptive creative phase is perhaps more consistent with mindful (vs. concentrative) approaches (e.g., Goleman, 1988a; see Richards, 2007c).

Frederick Franck, author of books including *Zen Seeing, Zen Drawing: Meditation in Action* (1993) links creative discipline with "active" meditative discipline. Walsh and Shapiro (2006) stressed that "meditation has major implications for an understanding of such central psychological issues as cognition and attention, mental training and development" (p. 227). A recent study (Horan, 2009) attempted to further characterize creativity in terms of the two major categories of mindfulness and concentrative meditation and suggested functions of different EEG frequencies. Surely, useful work lies ahead.

BEYOND STEREOTYPES, BEYOND CONCEPTUAL MIND

As meditators are aware, as one becomes more free of conceptual mind, there are further openings toward more direct knowing, which go beyond the concepts, labeled images, biases, prejudices, gender and ethnic stereotypes, fears and expectations, memories, structures of consciousness, and entire realms of a conceptual superstructure – which signify not only living in a past of labeled experience, but in *our* conditioned past and limited world; we unwittingly create such experience (in conjunction with culture), replacing and dividing the vast fullness of manifest reality (e.g. Combs & Krippner, 2007; Kapleau, 1980; Richards, 2007c; Tarthang Tulku, 1978; Thich Nhat Hanh, 1998; Wilber, 2006).

Is this about creativity? In Zen arts (Loori, 2004; Pritzker, 1999), *everyday creative process* is very much the point, being freshly and fully present, whether one is in the garden or the tearoom. In tune with Eastern views of creativity (Sundararajan & Averill, 2007), one is creating conditions such that something greater and profoundly authentic comes through, trailing hints of greater possibility – brushwork in calligraphy, lofty peaks in Chinese landscape, immediacy of a Haiku, a sip of tea.

The calligrapher learns great skill for the practiced craft. Yet this is precisely so the craftsperson may step aside. The book *The Zen of Archery* (Herrigel, 1953) gives beautiful examples of this. This may seem different than our Western view of individual creativity (e.g., Sundararajan & Averill, 2007). Yet is this mystery and awe fully remote from Western acts, and products, of creativity? Or does it sometimes occur, and we just imbue it with a different story?

Summary

It was asked: Do we use varied ways of knowing and can these help us understand and enhance creativity? One finds new areas of work offering fresh understanding, including stylistic features, brain studies, chaos theory and self-organizing processes, and applications of varied states of consciousness. Areas of overlap with studies on psychopathology also occur. The next section asks if creative people have social disadvantages, as well as advantages, in pursuing such directions.

Creative Normalcy Versus Conformity

In our usual social settings, how tolerant and, indeed, how welcoming are we of divergence and the colorful ways in which creative people may present themselves? How healthy are our societal norms? The answer is relevant to many issues, including the issue of nurturing versus discouraging creativity in educational settings, where the nonconformist innovator is not always welcomed by teachers or even peers (see Beghetto, Chapter 23, this volume). Where and how often do we push away the creative person in our lives because of inconvenience or threat? And how often do we distance ourselves because of "difference," sometimes even pathologizing the "abnormal" when it is not "pathological" at all, but "usefully exceptional"?

Broadening the Acceptable Limits of Normality

This concern is not just about a *central tendency* for socially desirable behaviors, but also about *variation*. How much do we honor the diversity of the nonconformist creator? What is the normative presentation we accept and how much divergence around this norm do we, in our culture, allow – or even celebrate? It has been suggested that we need both to *further value human uniqueness and to broaden our acceptable limits of normality* (Richards, 1998).

It can be natural to resist change at times, but how aware are we of conscious and unconscious, and group as well as individual, pressures against an innovator to desist (e.g., Richards, 2007b)? Sometimes, at the group level, these forces are even powerfully self-organizing. Our creator is, in some sense, a revolutionary, wanting not just to construct but to deconstruct, and thus to threaten something in our environment. We all typically know the bosses, teachers, and parents – probably including ourselves at times – who may energetically resist this disruption. But do we, in our culture, teach about these forces and counterforces, and the roles and values of change? Recognize it is worth noting how healthy for us a certain amount of change can be. Rather than marginalize the innovator, perhaps we can be a bit more flexible. More attention to these issues is needed (Montuori & Purser, 1999; Richards, in press-a).

In a more clinical context, how often do we project false stereotypes of "creativity and madness" onto what may be a healthy divergence? There are, after all, many roads to creativity (Richards, 1981). Yet tragically, some well-functioning creative people may romanticize and imitate such clinical images to their detriment, believing the creator must suffer, be depressed, and be eccentric to succeed. Some who need it even refuse what could be lifesaving treatment (Jamison, 1993; Richards, 1996, 1998, in press-a). Others who are functioning well fear that being creative will, despite themselves, make them bizarre or unhealthy, and as a result they don't fully develop their creativity.

What stereotypes abound: Think of an absentminded professor running into walls, or a distracted person with hair out at all angles, as if she or he cannot be creative and also manage real world needs. Or consider the mad scientist or the bizarre artist. By implication they are strange, perhaps unhealthy, out of contact with reality. Yet the opposite may often be true. As Frank Barron (1969) said:

> It appears that creative individuals have a remarkable affinity for what in most of us is unconscious and preconscious ... to find hints of emerging form in the developmentally more primitive and less reasonable structured aspects of his own mental functioning. (p. 88)

What then are the consequences? Let us repeat one of Barron's (1963) most famous quotes:

> The creative person is both more primitive and more cultivated, more destructive and more constructive, occasionally crazier and yet adamantly saner, than the average person. (p. 234)

Social Support of Creativity

As society's focus turns more from eminent to everyday creativity (or mini-c or personal creativity), from product to process, and from arts and sciences more exclusively to creativity in many aspects of life, the images of creative people may become more varied and healthier. In this information age, in businesses and organizations, creativity is increasingly coveted in growing economies around the globe (Florida, 2005) and involves not just a few exceptional people in a narrow range of occupational levels. Of interest regarding creative divergence, some top cities for creative opportunity also may be more accepting of divergent lifestyles (Florida, 2002, 2005). Commitment to creativity can also extend to the highest governmental levels. In up-and-coming

New Zealand (Clark, 2002), creativity was not only made one of its top social priorities a few years ago, at all levels of participation, but even became a centerpiece of the prime minister's address.

In our interdependent society, the study of social creativity is on the rise, and participatory and collaborative structures and conditions have become an important focus (see Amabile, 1996; Goerner, 2007; Montuori & Purser, 1999; Richards, 2007a, 2007c; Sawyer, 2007). The healthy collaborative aspect should also improve the creator's image. Interpersonal and interactional creativity becomes all the more intriguing, since the criteria for everyday creativity of (a) *originality* and (b) *meaningfulness* apply quite nicely to authentic interchanges in the moment – to what one might call creative encounter (May, 1975; Richards, 2007e). Here indeed is a healthy and beneficial perspective. Furthermore, the introduction of *caring* relationships into the creativity conversation, in contexts ranging from a psychotherapeutic duo to a whole society (e.g., Goerner, 2007; Richards, 2007c, 2007e), shows the universal importance of everyday creativity in human encounter. Significantly, caring relationships linked with early education for creativity catalyze not only novel products, but richer neural connections and ongoing creative potential in the creative and developing young person – with benefits for all of society (Eisler, 2007; Goleman, 2006; Siegel, 2007). Such phenomena can mitigate indeed against negative stereotypes of creativity.

Notably, creativity is discouraged in rigid hierarchical structures in business or society, where only a few at the top innovate and others follow their lead (Abraham, 1996; Eisler, 2007; Goerner, 2007). By contrast, a participatory setting that evolves and grows creatively should show everyday creativity at all levels, indeed as a norm of the culture. The phenomenon should start at the grass-roots level. Creative *appreciation* is one aspect, so that new advances are adopted, adapted to individual needs, and can take root (Richards, 2007a), In our country, the so-called *cultural creatives* (Ray & Anderson,

2000), estimated at about one fourth of the population, may help play this important role.

There can be active creative variants of passive appreciation, where one is very engaged in processing an innovation, even if outwardly silent to the observer (Pritzker, 2007; Zausner, 2007a). Everyday creativity at the grass-roots level is thus all the more relevant. Creativity is truly a conversation, and it changes and grows with time. A systems view helps encompass this "metabolism of the new" – and the different roles involved (Csikszentmihalyi, 1988; Montuori & Purser, 1999; Richards, 1996, 1998). If the extent of our cultural creativity were more widely discussed, this creativity might be seen as healthy – indeed necessary – for a democratic society.

Yet, simultaneously, some say we live in a reality characterized by "survival of the fittest," and we at times live even by norms of "might makes right." How, one might ask, do healthy and collaborative creative systems fit in here? Perhaps this is the wrong question. Charles Darwin himself (Gruber & Barrett, 1981; Loye, 2007), as it emerges, was moving toward other dominant values specific to the more collaborative and, hopefully, principled, human species. These included caring and collaboration. For example, in *The descent of man*, Darwin writes of love 95 times, moral sensitivity 92 times, and mutuality or mutual aid (cooperation) 24 times, and "survival of the fittest" only 3 times (Loye, 2007). This does not seem odd when one recalls that Darwin the scientist also prepared for the ministry (Richards, 2007a, 2007c). Today, it is all the more true that, in a shrinking globe with massive problems, we need collaborative values and group creativity (Loye, 2007; Richards, 2007c). Such work could change not only our views of the creative individual but of humanity's entire future.

Price of Conformity

Yet blind conformity can work against much of this process. Indeed, creativity has no guarantees of wise or benevolent use (McLaren, 1999; Richards, 1993; and see Cropley & Cropley, Chapter 16, this volume). Meanwhile, we humans are social creatures who can operate according to unconscious conformist tendencies. We need to be more conscious and self-conscious, to resist malevolent influences, to take a stand when needed, and even work as individuals and groups toward our *conscious evolution* as a species (Barron, 1995; Ornstein & Ehrlich, 1989; Richards, 1998). But first we must know what we now do.

The price and the peril of human conformity was shown in bold relief in the Stanford Prison Experiment (Zimbardo, 2008), and indeed by the real life abuses at Abu Ghraib and Guantanamo Bay, or in a number of historical events where a great many people "just went along." In the Stanford Prison Experiment, researchers assigned some students to be prisoners and others to be guards in an experimental role-play designed to last 2 weeks. What actually happened was frightening; the participants and the researchers overidentified with their roles, leading to shocking brutality, on the one hand, and fear and terror, on the other. The experiment was terminated early.

Along such lines, great tragedies of history have harnessed, and are still harnessing, our "normative" human tendencies to conform to group pressure in a situation, aided by our potential for mindlessness, automaticity, and ability to do "what is expected" in a context. Who then is less apt to do this? And how do we find more of them? Who is the nonconformist, the one who is more field independent and challenging of authority, the one who generates new ideas and alternative plans? Who is willing to "stand apart" and radically deconstruct what we have become accustomed to in our daily life, while presenting new (and not necessarily welcome) alternatives (Dacey & Lennon, 1998; Richards, 2007a; Richards & Kinney, 1989)? Surely these are our highly creative people. Those persons we call "normal" (as in the statistical median or mean) may at times be mindless and outright dangerous. By contrast, those sometimes colorful and eccentric creative people may be just the

ones to see truly what is happening, and to help us all. The call, again, is for a different, and a "creative" normalcy, and a conscious move in that direction by a society that nurtures everyday creativity toward its own higher development.

Toward Higher Purpose

Can creativity take us even further as human beings? Abraham Maslow (1968, 1971) went beyond everyday creativity to study *self-actualizing creativity* – with many aspects of everyday creativity appearing along the way. Maslow found, not only innovation, but many positive signs of personal growth and development. Not only were his self-actualizing people happier, more at peace, more spontaneous, and more fulfilled, but as Maslow (1971) said, they were "motivated in other higher ways" (p. 289). This included what Maslow called "being values," such as *truth, goodness, beauty, justice,* and one called *aliveness,* which can be seen in terms of dynamic process and is very much related to the rich immediate presence and awareness already discussed. (One can also, if so inclined, reframe this presence and awareness as part of a meditative or spiritual path [Richards, 2007c, 2007d].) Surely such creators could more strongly resist being misled by malevolent influences. Maslow's self-actualizing creators further showed a deep commitment to their work, which was not necessarily distinguished from play and seemed to serve a broader purpose, be it advancement of knowledge or the betterment of the human condition.

More work is needed in the important area of ongoing adult development, with broader populations, longitudinal studies, and more diverse methods. Some studies of self-actualization and creativity exist (Runco, 1999). Humanistic psychology and positive psychology (e.g., Peterson, 2006; Schneider, Bugental, & Pierson, 2001) have made great strides toward finding more positive possibilities in human nature and join with world and religious leaders in asking how we can live better lives, be more at peace, and care more for each other, thereby creating a better world (Carter, 2001; Dalai Lama, 1999; Tarthang Tulku, 1991; Thich Nhat Hanh, 1997, 2002). Everyday creativity is not just about a good idea, but about a process and a way of life. Let us put more energy into exploring how it can change us and our troubled times for the better.

Summary

How tolerant and, indeed, welcoming are we of divergence and colorful interest in each other? How nurturing of this is our culture? At the same time, how conscious and careful are we about a malevolent side of creativity, as well as our own mindless and conformist tendencies? If the study and practice of creativity can send us in a more positive direction, as individuals and as cultures, let us continue research to understand the positive qualities involved, more collaborative ways of creating and living, and how we can better value and honor each other and the healthy diversity in our world.

Conclusion

This chapter has considered four issues involving everyday creativity:

(1) **Identifying everyday creativity.** The construct involves our potential for *originality* and *meaningfulness* at work or at leisure, our "phenotypic plasticity" as human beings, being both necessary and universal, born in the need for survival, its fruition in our higher human development. Viewed as a *process*, its benefits are particularly evident.

(2) **Everyday creativity and health.** Creativity is often healthy, available to everyone, and can manifests in the present moment beyond our preconceptions, fears, and self-concerned views of self, where it can open us to new awareness, both from the world and our own depths. Expressive arts, imagery, even creative appreciation may facilitate this. For certain people carrying family risk for psychopathology, who themselves

are better functioning, everyday creativity may represent a *compensatory advantage* (as with sickle-cell anemia, which yields resistance to malaria). Meanwhile we all have problems but have potential for resilient creative response.

(3) **Alternative ways of knowing.** Through stylistic patterns, new brain discoveries, phenomena of chaos theory, and states of consciousness, our everyday creativity, particularly in its intuitive and insight phases, may make broad use of our mental capacities and mind–body connections, along with related states of mind, thereby offering new routes to understanding and enhancing creativity.

(4) **Creative normalcy versus conformity.** What are the normative and accepted ways of behaving in our culture? *Everyday creativity* offers norms that are more open, healthy, and participatory – and more immune to some of the mindless conformist behaviors our species has been, at its worst, prey to. If certain employers, teachers and others now pathologize creative behaviors, perhaps eventually, with greater perspective, we will find that it is how we *lived in the past* that was more truly *pathological*.

Happier, fuller, and healthier times may lie ahead if we learn to value everyday creativity, both in ourselves and in our culture. only will it help us adapt to an unpredictable future but to shape that future to our lasting benefit.

References

Abraham, F. (1996). The dynamics of creativity and the courage to be. In W. Sulis & A. Combs (Eds.), *Nonlinear dynamics in human behavior. Studies of nonlinear phenomena in life sciences* (Vol. 5; pp. 364–400). Singapore: World Scientific.

Abraham, F. (2007). Cyborgs, cyberspace, cybersexuality: The evolution of everyday creativity. In R. Richards (Ed.), *Everyday creativity and new views of human nature* (pp. 241–259). Washington, DC: American Psychological Association.

Achterberg, J. (2002). *Imagery in healing: Shamanism and modern medicine*. Boston: Shambhala.

Adams-Price, C. E. (Ed.). (1998). *Creativity and successful aging*. New York: Springer.

Adler, L. P. (1995). *Centennarians: The bonus years*. Santa Fe, NM: Health Press.

Akiskal, H. S., & Akiskal, K. K. (2007). In search of Aristotle: Temperament, human nature, melancholia, creativity and eminence. *Journal of Affective Disorders, 100*, 1–6.

Akiskal, H. S., Akiskal, K. K., et al. (2006). Validating the bipolar spectrum in the French National EPIDEP Study: Overview of the phenomenology and relative prevalence of its clinical prototypes. *Journal of Affective Disorders, 96*(3), 197–205.

Akiskal, H. S., & Mallya, G. (1987). Criteria for the "soft" bipolar spectrum: Treatment implications. *Psychopharmacology Bulletin, 23*, 67–73.

Amabile, T. (1996). *Creativity in context*. New York: Westview/Perseus.

Andreasen, N. (1987). Creativity and mental illness: Prevalence in writers and their first-degree relatives. *American Journal of Psychiatry, 144*, 1288–1292.

Arons, M. (2007). Standing up for humanity: Upright body, creative instability, and spiritual balance. In R. Richards (Ed.), *Everyday creativity and new views of human nature* (pp. 175–193). Washington, DC: American Psychological Association.

Barron, F. (1963). *Creativity and psychological health*. Princeton, NJ: Van Nostrand.

Barron, F. (1969). *Creative person and creative process*. New York: Holt, Rinehart, & Winston.

Barron, F. (1995). *No rootless flower: An ecology of creativity*. Creskill, NJ: Hampton Press.

Barron, F., & Harrington, D. (1981). Creativity, intelligence, and personality. *Annual Review of Psychology, 32*, 439–476.

Barron, F., Montuori, A., & Barron, A. (1997). *Creators on creating: Awakening the cultivating the imaginative mind*. New York: Tarcher/Putnam.

Baruss, I. (2003). *Alterations of consciousness: An empirical analysis for social scientists*. Washington, DC: American Psychological Association.

Beghetto, R., & Kaufman, J. (2007). Toward a broader conception of creativity: A case for "mini-c" creativity. *Psychology of Aesthetics, Creativity, and the Arts, 1*(2), 73–79.

Bowden, E. M., Jung-Beeman, M., Fleck, J., & Kounios, J. (2005). New approaches to demystifying insight. *Trends in Cognitive Sciences, 9*(7), 322–328.

Briggs, J., & Peat, F. D. (1989). *Turbulent mirror: An illustrated guide to chaos theory and the science of wholeness*. New York: Perennial/Harper & Row.

Carter, J. (2001). *Living faith*. New York: Three Rivers Press.

Clark, H. (2002). Prime minister's statement to Parliament. Retrieved February 1, 2010, from http://www.executive.govt.nz/minister/clark/innovate/speech.htm.

Combs, A., & Krippner, S. (2007). Structures of consciousness and creativity: Opening the doors of perception. In R. Richards (Ed.), *Everyday creativity and new views of human nature* (pp. 131–149). Washington, DC: American Psychological Association.

Costa, P. T., & Widiger, T. A. (1994). *Personality disorders and the five-factor model of personality*. Washington, DC: American Psychological Association.

Cramond, B. (2005). *Fostering creativity in gifted students*. Waco, TX: Prufrock Press.

Csikszentmihalyi, M. (1988). Society, culture, and person: A systems view of creativity. In R. Sternberg (Ed.), *The nature of creativity* (pp. 325–339). New York: Cambridge University Press.

Csikszentmihalyi, M. (1990). *Flow: The psychology of optimal experience*. New York: HarperPerennial.

Csikszentmihalyi, M. (1996). *Creativity: Flow and the psychology of discovery and invention*. New York: HarperCollins.

Dacey, J., & Lennon, K. H. (1998). *Understanding creativity*. San Francisco: Jossey-Bass.

Dalai Lama, His Holiness. (1999). *Ethics for a new millennium*. New York: Riverhead Books.

Damasio, A. R. (1994). *Descartes' error: Emotion, reason, and the human brain*. New York: Grosset/Putnam.

Dobzhansky, T. (1962). *Mankind evolving*. New Haven, CT: Yale University Press.

Eckblad, M., & Chapman, L. J. (1986). Development and validation of a scale for hypomanic personality. *Journal of Abnormal Psychology, 3*, 214–222.

Eisler, R. (2007). Our great creative challenge: Rethinking human nature, and recreating society. In R. Richards (Ed.), *Everyday creativity and new views of human nature* (pp. 261–285). Washington, DC: American Psychological Association.

Feinstein, D., & Krippner, S. (1997). *The mythic path*. New York: Tarcher.

Flach, F. (1990). Disorders of the pathways involved in the creative process. *Creativity Research Journal*, 3, 158–165.

Fleck, J. I., Green, D. L., Stevenson, J. L., Payne, L., Bowden, E., Jung-Beeman, M., et al. (2008). The transliminal brain at rest: Baseline EEG, unusual experiences, and access to unconscious mental activity. *Cortex*, 44, 1353–1363.

Florida, R. (2002). *Rise of the creative class*. New York: Basic Books.

Florida, R. (2005). *Flight of the creative class*. New York: HarperBusiness

Fodor, E. (1999). Subclinical inclination toward manic-depression and creative performance on the Remote Associates Test. *Personality and Individual Differences*, 27, 1273–1283.

Franck, F. (1993). *Zen seeing, Zen drawing: Meditation in action*. New York: Bantam.

Freeman, L., & Lawlis, G. F. (2001). *Mosby's complementary and alternative medicine: A research-based approach*. St. Louis, MO: Mosby.

Gardner, H. (1983). *Frames of mind*. New York: Basic Books.

Gartner, J. D. (2005). *The hypomanic edge: The link between (a little) craziness and (a lot of) success in America*. New York: Simon & Schuster.

Goerner, S. (2007). A "knowledge ecology" view of creativity: How integral science recasts collective creativity as a basis of large-scale learning. In R. Richards (Ed.), *Everyday creativity and new views of human nature* (pp. 221–239). Washington, DC: American Psychological Association.

Goertzel, V., & Goertzel, M. (1962). *Cradles of eminence*. Boston: Little, Brown.

Goleman, D. (1988a). *The meditative mind*. New York: Tarcher/Putnam.

Goleman, D. (1988b, September 13). A new index illuminates the creative life. *The New York Times*, pp. C1, C9.

Goleman, D. (2006). *Social intelligence*. New York: Bantam.

Goodwin, F., & Jamison, K. R. (1990). *Manic-depressive illness*. New York: Oxford University Press.

Gruber, H., & Barrett, P. (1981). *Darwin on man: A psychological study of scientific creativity* (2nd ed.). Chicago: University of Chicago Press.

Guilford, J. P. (1968). *Intelligence, creativity, and their educational implications*. San Diego: Knapp.

Helson, R. (1999). Personality. In M. A. Runco & S. R. Pritzker (Eds.), *Encyclopedia of creativity* (Vol. 2, pp. 361–373). San Diego: Academic Press.

Helson, R., Roberts, B. W., & Agronick, G. S. (1995). Enduringness and change in the creative personality and the prediction of occupational creativity. *Journal of Personality and Social Psychology*, 69, 1173–1181.

Herrigel, E. (1953). *Zen in the art of archery*. New York: Vintage.

Hocevar, D., & Bachelor, P. (1989). A taxonomy and critique of measurements used in the study of creativity. In J. A. Glover, R. R. Ronning, & C. R. Reynolds (Eds.), *Handbook of creativity* (pp. 53–74). New York: Plenum.

Horan, R. (2009). The neuropsychological connection between creativity and meditation. *Creativity Research Journal*, 21(2–3), 199–222.

Isen, A., Daubman, K. A., & Nowicki, G. P. (1987). Positive affect facilitates creative problem-solving. *Journal of Personality and Social Psychology*, 52, 1122–1131.

Jamison, K. R. (1989). Mood disorders and patterns of creativity in British artists and writers. *Psychiatry*, 52, 125–134.

Jamison, K. R. (1993). *Touched with fire*. New York: Free Press.

Jamison, K. R., Gerner, R., Hammen, C., & Padesky, C. (1980). Clouds and silver linings: Positive experiences associated with primary affective disorders. *American Journal of Psychiatry*, 137, 198–202.

Kabat-Zinn, J. (1994). *Wherever you go, there you are: Mindfulness meditation in daily life*. New York: Hyperion.

Kapleau, P. (1980). *The three pillars of Zen*. New York: Anchor Books.

Kaufman, J. C. (2001). Genius, lunatics, and poets: Mental illness in prizewinning authors. *Imagination, Cognition, and Personality*, 20, 305–314.

Kaufman, J., & Beghetto, R. (2009). Beyond big and little: The Four-C Model of Creativity. *Review of General Psychology*, 13, 1–12.

Kaufman, J., Plucker, J., & Baer, J. (2008). *Essentials of creativity assessment*. Hoboken, NJ: Wiley

Kaufman, J., & Sexton, J. D. (2006). Why doesn't the writing cure help poets? *Review of General Psychology*, 10(3), 268–282.

Kaufman, S. B. (2009). Faith in intuition is associated with decreased latent inhibition in a sample of high-achieving adolescents. *Psychology of Aesthetics, Creativity, and the Arts*, 3(1), 28–34.

Kinney, D. K., & Matthysse, S. M. (1978). Genetic transmission of schizophrenia. *Annual Review of Medicine*, 29, 459–473.

Kinney, D. K., & Richards, R. (2007). Artistic creativity and affective disorders: Are they connected? In C. Martindale, P. Locher, & V. M. Petrov (Eds.), *Evolutionary and neurocognitive approaches to aesthetics, creativity, and the arts* (pp. 225–237). Amityville, NY: Baywood Publ. Co.

Kinney, D. K., Richards, R., Lowing, P., LeBlanc, D., Zimbalist, M., & Harian, P. (2000–2001). Creativity in offspring of schizophrenics and controls. *Creativity Research Journal*, 11, 17–25.

Kinney, D. K., Richards, R., & Southam, M. (in press). Everyday creativity, its assessment, and The Lifetime Creativity Scales. In M. Runco (Ed.), *The handbook of creativity*. Cresskill, NJ: Hampton Press.

Klein, K. (2002). Stress, expressive writing, and working memory. In S. J. Lepore & J. M. Smyth (Eds.), *The writing cure* (pp. 135–155). Washington, DC: American Psychological Association.

Kounios, J., Fleck, J., Green, D. L., Payne, L., Stevenson, J., Bowden, E., & Jung-Beeman, M. (2008). The origins of insight in resting brain activity. *Neuropsychologia*, 46(1), 281–291.

Krippner, S. (1999). Altered and transitional states. In M. A. Runco & S. R. Pritzker (Eds.), *Encyclopedia of creativity* (Vol. 1, pp. 45–52). San Diego: Academic Press.

Krippner, S., Richards, R., & Abraham, F. D. (2009, August). *Creativity and chaos in waking and dreaming states*. Paper presented at the annual meeting of The Society for Chaos Theory in Psychology and the Life Sciences, Milwaukee, WI.

Kris, E. (1976). On preconscious mental processes. In A. Rothenberg & C. Hausman (Eds.), *The creativity question* (pp. 135–143). Durham, NC: Duke University Press.

Lamott, A. (1994), *Bird by bird: Some instructions on writing and life*. New York:Pantheon.

Langer, E. (1989). *Mindfulness*. Reading, MA: Addison-Wesley.

Laszlo, E. (in press). In defense of intuition: Exploring the physical foundations of spontaneous apprehension. *Journal of Scientific Exploration*.

Lehrer, J. (2008, July 28). The Eureka hunt: Why do good ideas come to us when they do? *The New Yorker*, 84, 40–45.

Lepore, S. J., & Smyth, J. M. (Eds.). (2002). *The writing cure: How expressive writing promotes health and emotional well-being*. Washington, DC: American Psychological Association.

Levy, B., & Langer, E. (1999). Aging. In M. Runco & S. Pritzker (Eds.), *Encyclopedia of creativity* (Vol. 1, pp. 45–52). San Diego: Academic Press.

Loori, J. D. (2004). *The Zen of creativity: Cultivating your artistic life*. New York: Ballantine.

Loye, D. (2007). Telling the new story: Darwin, evolution, and creativity versus conformity in science. In R. Richards (Ed.), *Everyday creativity and new views of human nature* (pp. 153–173). Washington, DC: American Psychological Association.

Ludwig, A. (1995). *The price of greatness*. New York: Guilford.

McAdams, D. P. (1993). *The stories we live by: Personal myths and the making of the self*. New York: Guilford.

McLaren, R. B. (1999). Dark side of creativity. In M. Runco & S. Pritzker (Eds.), *Encyclopedia of creativity* (Vol. 1, pp. 483–491). San Diego: Academic Press.

McNiff, S. (1992). *Art as medicine: Creating a therapy of the imagination*. Boston: Shambhala.

Marks-Tarlow, T. (1999). The self as dynamical system. *Nonlinear Dynamics, Psychology, and the Life Sciences*, 3, 311–345.

Martindale, C. (1999). Biological bases of creativity. In R. Sternberg (Ed.), *Handbook of creativity* (pp. 137–152). New York: Cambridge University Press.

Maslow, A. (1968). *Toward a psychology of being*. New York: Van Nostrand Reinhold.

Maslow, A. (1971). *The farther reaches of human nature*. New York: Penguin.

May, R. (1975). *The courage to create*. New York: Bantam Books.

Miller, M., & Cook-Greuter, S. (2000). *Creativity, spirituality, and transcendence: Paths to integrity and wisdom in the mature self*. Stamford, CT: Ablex.

Montuori, A., Combs, A., & Richards, R. (2004). Creativity, consciousness, and the direction for human development. In D. Loye (Ed.), *The great adventure: Toward a fully human theory of evolution* (pp. 197–236). Albany, NY: SUNY Press.

Montuori, A., & Purser, R. (1999). *Social creativity* (Vol. 1). Cresskill, NJ: Hampton Press.

Morrison, D., & Morrison, S. L. (2006). *Memories of loss and dreams of perfection: Unsuccessful childhood grieving and adult creativity.* Amityville, NY: Baywood.

Myers, D. G. (2002). *Intuition.* New Haven, CT: Yale Nota Bene/Yale University Press.

Nettle, D., & Clegg, H. (2006). Schizotypy, creativity and mating success in humans. *Proceedings of the Royal Society Britain,* 273, 611–615.

Ornstein, R., & Ehrlich, P. (1989). *New world, new mind: Moving toward conscious evolution.* New York: Touchstone.

Osho (2001). *Intuition: Knowing beyond logic.* New York: St. Martin's Griffin.

Pennebaker, J. (Ed.). (1995). Emotion, *disclosure, and health.* Washington, DC: American Psychological Association.

Pennebaker, J., Kiecolt-Glaser, J., & Glaser, R. (1988). Disclosure of trauma and immune function: Health implications for psychotherapy. *Journal of Consulting and Clinical Psychology,* 56, 239–245.

Peterson, C. (2006). *A primer in positive psychology.* New York: Oxford University Press.

Peterson, C., & Carson, S. (2000). Latent inhibition and openness to experience in a high-achieving student population. *Personality and Individual Differences,* 28, 323–332.

Pink, D. (2005). *A whole new mind: Why right-brainers will rule the future.* New York: Riverhead.

Plucker, J. A., & Beghetto, R. A. (2004). Why creativity is domain general, why it looks domain specific, and why the distinction does not matter. In R. Sternberg, E. Grigorenko, & J. Singer (Eds.), *Creativity: From potential to realization* (pp. 153–167). Washington, DC: American Psychological Association.

Policastro, E. (1999). *Intuition.* In M. Runco & S. Pritzker (Eds.), *Encyclopedia of creativity* (Vol. 2, pp. 89–93). San Diego: Academic Press.

Pritzker, S. R. (2007). Audience flow: Creativity in television watching with applications to teletherapy. In R. Richards (Ed.), *Everyday creativity and new views of human nature* (pp. 109–129). Washington, DC: American Psychological Association.

Pritzker, S. R. (1999). Zen. In M. Runco & S. Pritzker (Eds.), *Encyclopedia of creativity* (Vol. 2, pp. 745–750). San Diego: Academic Press.

Progoff, I. (1975). At a journal workshop: *Basic text and guide for using the Intensive Journal process.* New York: Dialogue House Library.

Ray, P., & Anderson, S. R. (2000). *The cultural creatives.* New York: Three Rivers Press.

Rhodes, C. (1990). Growth from deficiency creativity to being creativity. *Creativity Research Journal,* 3(4), 287–299.

Richards, R. (1976). Comparison of selected Guilford and Wallach-Kogan tests of creative thinking in conjunction with measures of intelligence. *Journal of Creative Behavior,* 10, 151–164.

Richards, R. (1981). Relationships between creativity and psychopathology: An evaluation and interpretation of the evidence. *Genetic Psychology Monographs,* 103, 251–324.

Richards, R. (1993). Seeing beyond: Issues of creative awareness and social responsibility. *Creativity Research Journal,* 6, 165–183.

Richards, R. (1996). Does the lone genius ride again? Chaos, creativity, and community. *Journal of Humanistic Psychology,* 36(2), 44–60.

Richards, R. (1998). When illness yields creativity. In M. Runco & R. Richards (Eds.), *Eminent creativity, everyday creativity, and health* (pp. 485–540). Greenwich, CT: Ablex.

Richards, R. (1999). Affective disorders. In M. Runco & S. Pritzker (Eds.), *Encyclopedia of Creativity* (Vol. 1, pp. 31–43). San Diego: Academic Press.

Richards, R. (2004). The arts and self-expression in mental health. *Invited presentation, Carter Presidential Center,* Atlanta, GA. Reprinted in *Elites Magazine* (Italian).

Richards, R. (2000–2001). Millennium as opportunity: Chaos, creativity, and J. P. Guilford's Structure-of-Intellect model. *Creativity Research Journal,* 13 (3 & 4), 249–265.

Richards, R. (2001). A new aesthetic for environmental awareness: Chaos theory, the natural world, and our broader humanistic identity. *Journal of Humanistic Psychology,* 41, 59–95.

Richards, R. (Ed.). (2007a). *Everyday creativity and new views of human nature: Psychological, social, and spiritual perspectives.* Washington, DC: American Psychological Association.

Richards, R. (2007b). Everyday creativity: Our hidden potential. In R. Richards (Ed.), *Everyday creativity and new views of human nature* (pp. 25–53). Washington, DC: American Psychological Association.

Richards, R. (2007c). Twelve potential benefits of living more creatively. In R. Richards (Ed.), *Everyday creativity and new views of human nature* (pp. 289–319). Washington, DC: American Psychological Association.

Richards, R. (2007d). Everyday creativity and the arts. *World Futures*, 63, 500–525.

Richards, R. (2007e). Relational creativity and healing potential: The power of Eastern thought in Western clinical settings. In J. Pappas, B. Smythe, & A. Baydala (Eds.), *Cultural healing and belief systems*. Calgary, Alberta: Detselig Enterprises.

Richards, R. (in press-a). Everyday creativity in the classroom: A trip through time with seven suggestions. In R. A. Beghetto & J. C. Kaufman (Eds.), *Nurturing creativity in the classroom*. New York: Cambridge University Press.

Richards, R. (in press-b). Who is gifted and talented, and what should we do about it? *National Association of Gifted Children Newsletter, Creativity Division*.

Richards, R., & Kinney, D. K. (1989). Creativity and manic-depressive illness (letter). *Comprehensive Psychiatry*, 30, 272–273.

Richards, R., & Kinney, D. K. (1990). Mood swings and creativity. *Creativity Research Journal*, 3, 203–218.

Richards, R., Kinney, D. K., Benet, M., & Merzel, A. (1988). Assessing everyday creativity: Characteristics of the Lifetime Creativity Scales and validation with three large samples. *Journal of Personality and Social Psychology*, 54, 476–485.

Richards, R., Kinney, D. K., Daniels, H., & Linkins, K. (1992). Everyday creativity and bipolar and unipolar affective disorder. *European Psychiatry*, 7, 49–52.

Richards, R., Kinney, D. K. Lunde, I., Benet, M., & Merzel, A. (1988). Creativity in manic-depressives, cyclothymes, their normal relatives, and control subjects. *Journal of Abnormal Psychology*, 97, 281–288.

Robertson, R., & Combs, A. (1995). *Chaos theory in psychology and the life sciences*. Mahwah, NJ: Erlbaum.

Rogers, C. (1961). *On becoming a person*. Boston: Houghton Mifflin.

Rogers, N. (1993). *The creative connection: Expressive arts as healing*. Palo Alto, CA: Science & Behavior Books.

Runco, M. (1996). Personal creativity: Definition and developmental issues. *New Directions for Child Development*, 72, 3–30.

Runco, M. (1999). Self-actualization and creativity. In M. Runco & S. Pritzker (Eds.), *Encyclopedia of Creativity* (Vol. 2, pp. 533–536). San Diego: Academic Press.

Runco, M. (2007). To understand is to create: An epistemological perspective on human nature and personal creativity. In R. Richards (Ed.), *Everyday creativity and new views of human nature* (pp. 91–107). Washington, DC: American Psychological Association.

Runco, M., & Pritzker, S. R. (Eds.). (1999). *Encyclopedia of creativity* (Vols. 1–2). San Diego: Academic Press.

Runco, M., & Richards, R. (Eds.). (1998). *Eminent creativity, everyday creativity, and health*. Greenwich, CT: Ablex.

Russ, S. (Ed.) (1999). *Affect, creative experience, and psychological adjustment*. Philadelphia, PA: Brunner/Mazel.

Sawyer, K. (2007). *The creative power of collaboration*. New York: Basic Books.

Schneider, K., Bugental, J., & Pierson, J. F. (2001). *Handbook of humanistic psychology: Leading edges in theory, research, and practice*. Thousand Oaks, CA: Sage.

Schuldberg, D. (1990). Schizotypal and hypomanic traits, creativity, and psychological health. *Creativity Research Journal*, 3(3), 218–230.

Schuldberg, D. (1999). Chaos theory and creativity. In M. A. Runco & S. R. Pritzker (Eds.), *Encyclopedia of Creativity* (Vol. 1, pp. 259–272). San Diego: Academic Press.

Schuldberg, D. (2000–2001). Six subclinical "spectrum traits" in "normal" creativity. *Creativity Research Journal*, 13(1), 5–16.

Schuldberg, D. (2007). Living well creatively: What's chaos got to do with it? In R. Richards (Ed.), *Everyday creativity and new views of human nature* (pp. 55–73). Washington, DC: American Psychological Association.

Sekida, K. (Ed. and Trans.). (1977). *Two Zen classics: Mumonkan and Hekiganroku*. New York: Weatherhill.

Serlin, I. A. (Ed.). (2008). *Whole person healthcare* (Vols. 1–3). Westport, CT: Praeger.

Shansis, F., Fleck, M., Richards, R., Kinney, D., Izquierdo, I., Mattevi, B., et al. (2003). Desenvolvimento da versao para o Portugues das Escalas de Criatividade ao Longo da Vida (ECLV). [Development of the Portuguese language version of the Lifetime Creativity Scales.] *Revista de Psiquiatria do Rio Grande do Sul*, 25(2), 284–296.

Shapiro, A. B. (2009). *Healing into possibility: The transformational lessons of a stroke.* Novato, CA: New World Library.

Siegel, D. J. (2007). *The mindful brain: Reflection and attunement in the cultivation of well-being.* New York: W.W. Norton.

Singer, J. (1990). *Repression and dissociation.* Chicago: University of Chicago Press.

Singer, J. (2006). *Imagery in psychotherapy.* Washington, DC: American Psychological Assoc.

Sinott, E. W. (1959). The creativeness of life. In H. H. Anderson (Ed.), *Creativity and its cultivation* (pp. 12–29). New York: Harper & Row.

Skarda, C., & Freeman, W. J. (1987). How brains make chaos in order to make sense of the world. *Behavioral and Brain Sciences,* 10, 161–173.

Sogyal Rinpoche (1994). *The Tibetan book of living and dying.* New York: HarperSanFrancisco.

Sonke-Henderson, J., Brandman, R., Serlin, I. A., & Graham-Pole, J. (Eds.). (2008). *Whole person healthcare* (Vol. 3). Westport, CT: Praeger.

Sternberg, R., & Davidson, J. E. (1999). Insight. In M. Runco & S. Pritzker (Eds.), *Encyclopedia of creativity* (Vol. 2, pp. 57–69). San Diego: Academic Press.

Sternberg, R., Grigorenko, E., & Singer, J. (Eds.). (2004). *Creativity: From potential to realization.* Washington, DC: American Psychological Association.

Sternberg, R. J., & O'Hara, L. A. (1999). Creativity and intelligence. In R. J. Sternberg (Ed.), *Handbook of creativity* (pp. 251–272). Cambridge, MA: Cambridge University Press.

Subramaniam, K., Kounios, J., Parrish, T. B., & Jung-Beeman, M. (2008). A brain mechanism for facilitation of insight by positive affect. *Journal of Cognitive Neuroscience,* 21(3), 415–432.

Sundararajan, L. (2009, August). *The Chinese notion of savoring as a process model.* Paper presented at the 117th annual convention of the American Psychological Association, Toronto, Ontario, Canada.

Sundararajan, L. L., & Averill, J. (2007). Creativity in the everyday: Culture, self, and emotions. In R. Richards (Ed.), *Everyday creativity and new views of human nature* (pp. 195–220). Washington, DC: American Psychological Association.

Sundararajan, L. L., & Richards, J. A. (2005, August). *Expressive writing and health.* Paper presented at the 113th annual meeting of the American Psychological Association, Washington, DC.

Tart, C. T. (1994). *Living the mindful life.* Boston: Shambhala.

Tarthang Tulku. (1978). *Openness mind.* Berkeley, CA: Dharma.

Tarthang Tulku. (1991). *Skillful means: Patterns for success* (2nd ed.). Berkeley: Dharma.

Teasdale, J., Siegel, Z., Williams, J. M., Ridgeway, V. A., Soulsby, J. M., & Lau, M. A. (2000). Prevention of relapse/recurrence in major depression by mindfulness-based cognitive therapy. *Journal of Consulting and Clinical Psychology,* 68(4), 615–623.

Terman, L. M., & Oden, M. H. (1959). *Genetic studies of genius: Vol. 5. The gifted group at midlife.* Stanford, CA: Stanford University Press.

Thich Nhat Hanh. (1997). *Teachings on love.* Berkeley, CA: Parallax Press.

Thich Nhat Hanh. (2002). *Touching peace.* Berkeley: Parallax Press.

Tooby, J., & DeVore, I. (1987). The reconstruction of hominid behavioral evolution through strategic modeling. In W. G. Kinsey (Ed.), *The evolution of human behavior: Primate models* (pp. 183–237). Albany: SUNY Press.

Torrance, E. P. (1972). Creative young women in today's world. *Exceptional Children,* 38, 597–603.

Wallace, B. A. (2006). *The attention revolution: Unlocking the power of the focused mind.* Boston: Wisdom.

Wallach, M. A., & Kogan, N. (1965). *Modes of thinking in young children.* New York: Holt, Rinehart, & Winston.

Walsh, R., & Shapiro, S. L. (2006). The meeting of meditative disciplines and Western psychology. *American Psychologist,* 61, 227–239.

Wender, P., Kety, S. S., Schulsinger, F., Rosenthal, D., Ortman, F., & Lunde, I. (1986). Psychiatric disorders in the biological and adoptive families of adopted individuals with affective disorders. *Archives of General Psychiatry,* 43, 923–929.

Werner, E. E., & Smith, R. S. (2001). *Journeys from childhood to midlife: Risk, resilience, and recovery.* Ithaca, NY: Cornell University Press.

Wickramasekera, I. (1998). Secrets kept from the mind, but not the body and behavior. *Independent Practitioner,* 18, 38–42.

Wilber, K. (2006). *Integral spirituality.* Boston: Shambhala.

Wink, P. (1999). Self processes and creativity. In M. Runco & S. Pritzker (Eds.), *Encyclopedia of creativity* (Vol. 2, pp. 537–541). San Diego: Academic Press.

Zausner, T. (1996). The creative chaos: Speculations on the connection between nonlinear dynamics and the creative process. In W. Sulis & A. Combs (Eds.), *Nonlinear dynamics in human behavior* (pp. 343–349). Singapore: World Scientific.

Zausner, T. (2007a). *When walls become doorways: Creativity and the transforming illness.* New York: Harmony/Random House.

Zausner, T. (2007b). Artist and audience: Everyday creativity and visual art. In R. Richards (Ed.), *Everyday creativity and new views of human nature*: (pp. 75–89). Washington, DC: American Psychological Association.

Zimbardo, P. (2008). *The Lucifer Effect: Understanding how good people turn evil.* New York: Random House Trade Paperbacks.

Zimbardo, P. G., Johnson, R. L., & Weber, A. L. (2006). *Psychology: Core concepts.* Boston: Allyn & Bacon.

CHAPTER 11

The Neurobiological Foundation of Creative Cognition

Allison B. Kaufman, Sergey A. Kornilov, Adam S. Bristol, Mei Tan, and Elena L. Grigorenko

Introduction

Psychology's fundamental assumption that cognition is biologically grounded is now widely accepted and, with the exception of a few esoteric interpretations of cognition, is treated as an axiom that can be found in virtually any psychology textbook. Therefore, it can be assumed that, for any facet of cognition, it should be theoretically possible to elucidate its neural mechanisms and establish how the brain implements them. This is what the relatively new fields of cognitive neuroscience and cognitive neurogenetics strive to do. The primary goals in the field of cognitive neuroscience are to identify the brain networks involved in the various types and aspects of cognition, and to describe how those brain networks operate, both independently and interactively, in order for that facet of cognition to emerge. The primary goal in the field of cognitive neurogenetics is to reveal the genetic mechanisms that underlie the formation and function of cognition-related brain networks. Recent technical advances,

such as human neuroimaging and human genomics and genetics, together with the more traditional approaches of human neuropsychology as well as developmental and cognitive psychology, offer a promising start to understanding the neurobiological foundations of cognition.

Arguably, few aspects of human cognition are as fascinating or as perplexing as creativity. From one point of view, creativity, it could be argued, is the highest level of human cognitive ability, the engine that drives artistic, cultural, scientific, and technical advances. From another point of view, creativity is simply inherent in each aspect of cognition whenever our "thinking apparatus" engages with novelty, either within the task itself or in the way this apparatus approaches this task. But how does the brain engage in such activity? In this chapter, we summarize recent work on the neurobiological bases of creativity, bringing into the discussion two main sources of data, namely, the fields of neuroscience and neurogenetics. We begin with a discussion of how creativity is defined and measured, with an emphasis on the measures used in neurobiological approaches to creativity. Next, we attempt to synthesize two distinct views on the neural basis of creativity: the hypothesis that (a) the faculties for creative cognition reside predominately in the right hemisphere; and (b) creative cognition is derived from a reduction in network inhibition, which originates in the frontal lobe. As we shall see, despite the supporting evidence for both theories, each remains somewhat oversimplified and imprecise as to its actual neurophysiological underpinnings. Finally, we look to more recent advances from animal and human studies in neuroscience and neurogenetics for clues both to the evolution of creative cognition and to its neurobiological foundation.

Defining and Measuring Creativity

One complication in determining the neurobiological foundation of creativity is that exactly what counts as "creative" is not so easily defined. Indeed, there are several competing explanations as to what being creative entails (i.e., what is defined as the *process* of creativity) and what creative output should look like (i.e., what the *product* of creativity might or should be).

While considering the *process* of creativity, we assume here that creativity is a sequence of cognitive operations that gives rise to novel insights or ideas (Sternberg, Kaufman, & Pretz, 2002). When the *product* of creativity is considered, the creative norms for achievement in a field or discipline must be taken into account (Csikszentmihalyi, 1996). Note that, with both process and product approaches, there is a significant element of dependency on the historical and cultural contexts in which creativity is considered. This is because what is judged to be a novel insight or idea or a creative product today may not be considered so at a different time or in a different culture. The classic example is Gregor Mendel's studies of inheritance in pea pods; his work was regarded with indifference during his lifetime yet lauded as revolutionary

nearly a half a century later. Of course, as the field of genetics matured, it became clear that although Mendel's discoveries gave us a springboard to subsequent discoveries, his ideas are really relevant to only a limited number of phenotypic traits, and complex human behaviors fall outside of this number.

Thus, in examining the creative process or product, we are not restricted *a priori* to any specific, predefined sets of cognitive operations. Rather, we often "work backward" from the process that led to the novel idea or product that is judged creative, and try to understand whether the process or product (or both!) met the definition of being creative then (at that time and in that cultural context). There is no *a priori* expectation of a match between the "then" and "now" in either of these approaches. In fact, what might have been a creative product or process "then" might not be so "now," and the other way around. For example, nearly all inventions that are produced and adopted in our everyday life have this fate. There is evidence that ink was first used about 5,000 years ago in ancient China for the purposes of highlighting the raised surfaces of pictures and texts carved in stone. Whoever thought of using berries, plants, minerals, or some of their derivatives for this purpose at that time was clearly engaged in a creative process and generated a creative product. Today, however, the usage of ink per se, or the usage of something else as an ink, might not be (and probably is not) considered creative. Yet throughout the development of human civilization, many other types of ink have been developed (and are being developed); these incremental changes toward the development of ink of better quality, longevity, non-toxicity, and so forth could also be considered creative now, but they probably would not have been considered creative then, or they may not have been possible at all because the particular level of technological development necessary for its production was not available in ancient China.

Moreover, there are creative processes and products that appear to be transient across epochs and cultures. Most of such examples of creativity are related to the arts (e.g., music), but even there, tastes change. For example, not all judges consider the first written records of musical expression, called Samaveda music (Parpola, 1973), to be creative. Likewise, it is easy to imagine a large disparity between adults and youth who are asked to rate the creativity of rap music.

Focusing on either the process or the product (or both) can be and has been useful in studies of creativity. Each approach imposes different requirements on the definition of creativity and, correspondingly, calls for different methods in studying creative cognition. Similarly, because creativity can be studied in different disciplines, each discipline might determine a preference for either of these two aspects of creativity. For example, creative products might be of more interest to studies of creativity in the context of the history of the arts, but creative processes might be of more interest to studies of creativity in psychology.

Similarly, cognitive neuroscience, given its orientation toward understanding the biological "machinery" supporting cognition in general and creative cognition in particular, is more apt to view creativity through an examination of its processes and to assume that the general biological mechanisms of creativity are at work to some degree in all individuals and across all domains.

Thus, studies carried out in the context of cognitive neuroscience or cognitive neurogenetics tend to divide participants into "more-creative" and "less-creative" groups (conceptualizing creativity as a continuous variable), and then try to study the cognitive mechanisms that might underlie this group differentiation and possibly explain these quantitative individual differences in creativity. From this point of view, the process of creativity is assumed to generalize across individuals, although the level of creativity, or the level of creative performance, may very well differ depending on factors such as, among others, innate intellectual ability, cognitive styles, knowledge, personality, and motivation (e.g., Sternberg & Lubart, 1996).

Assuming, then, that researchers working in the fields of neuroscience and neurogenetics restrict themselves to studying the creative process rather than the creative product, the following questions arise: What occurs cognitively during the creative process? And what biological mechanisms or structures might be supporting this process?

First, it has been argued (Martindale, 1999) that creative inspiration occurs in a mental state where attention is defocused, when thought is associative, and when a large number of mental representations are simultaneously activated. Defocused attention refers to the ability to consider numerous elements simultaneously, rather than limiting attention to only a few elements. Associative thoughts or thought hierarchies are the probabilistic relationships that exist between the elements of cognition (e.g., words, images, numbers, concepts, natural laws). Shallow associative hierarchies indicate that the associative strength linking various elements are relatively weak, thus allowing for more variable recall, pairwise, or other combinations of cognition elements. In a similar vein, Mednick (1962) suggested that creative thinking is characterized by facilitated access to multiple word meanings and relationships, and that tasks that tap into this capacity can be used to quantify creativity. Empirically, this can be shown by comparing the performance of participants ranked at a variety of levels of creativity on a test requiring the resolution of verbal ambiguity (Atchley, Keeney, & Burgess, 1999).

In this section, we have briefly outlined a few of the cognitive constituents or cognitive "building blocks" that are believed to be part of the overall creative process: defocused attention, associative thinking, and the simultaneous generation of multiple mental representations. Outlining these fundamental processes is important because many neurobiological approaches to creativity examine these elemental faculties. This is particularly true for the hemispheric asymmetry hypothesis of creativity, to which we will turn next. In this case, the notion that the neurobiological basis of creativity is seated in the right hemisphere comes indirectly from accumulated evidence that the right hemisphere predominates in tasks that are somehow related to creativity (e.g., visual pattern recognition).

But nevertheless, one issue that is important to note in all these studies is the difficulty of deciding what is creative or who is creative and who is not – a problem that has plagued the field of creativity research since its inception (Sternberg et al., 2002). Because there is no standard to determine what is creative (and what is not), comparisons of results across studies using "creative" and "noncreative" participants, processes, and products become problematic and imprecise.

Creativity and Hemispheric Asymmetry

Original theories of hemispheric asymmetry as they relate to creative cognition asserted that higher cognitive constructs such as creativity come from distinct workings of each hemisphere, which are subsequently integrated via the corpus callosum (Bogen & Bogen, 1969). Specifically, the hemispheric-asymmetry hypothesis posits that creativity is a result of neural functioning within the right hemisphere. This notion is embedded in the long-standing belief that the two sides of the cerebral hemispheres are functionally dissociable, with each responsible for different cognitive processes, either wholly or predominantly (Carlsson, 1990).

Notions of hemispheric asymmetries go back at least as far as the turn of the twentieth century (for a review, see Gazzangiga, 2008). At that time, psychiatry dealt with the possibilities of multiple or suppressed personalities, and educators advocated the instruction of the nondominant side of the brain and promoted ambidextrous training (Crichton-Browne, 1897, as cited in Jay & Neve, 1999). In neurology, doctors conferred about the accumulating evidence provided by patients with unilateral brain damage. Popular culture embraced ideas of a dual nature of being, the most famous example

being Robert Louis Stevenson's tale of Dr. Jekyll and Mr. Hyde, written in 1886. The cognitive differences between the left and right hemispheres have been characterized as "propositional vs. appositional," "analytic vs. holistic," and defined in several other ways (Bogen, 1977; Bogen & Bogen, 1969).

These ideas sparked interest in educational spheres as well, with the generally accepted idea that conventional schooling is aimed at the development of the logical (left) hemisphere, but is rather neglectful of the capabilities of the right hemisphere (Kaufman & Baer, 2006). The notion that people were "left-brained," meaning analytical, math/science-oriented, perhaps socially rigid, or "right-brained," being free-spirited, artistic individuals who eschew details and think holistically, has permeated American popular culture to some extent (e.g., see http://www.drawright.com).

Is there experimental evidence supporting the hemispheric-asymmetry hypothesis with regard to studies of creativity? The hemispheric-asymmetry hypothesis gained renewed popularity during the 1970s following Roger Sperry and his colleagues' examination of epileptic patients who had undergone a surgical procedure that severed their corpus collosum, the main neural tract connecting the two halves of the brain (Sperry, 1974). These "split-brain patients," as they were called, afforded the opportunity to investigate the consequences of disrupted interhemispheric communication for various behavioral and cognitive capacities never before studied in such a special pool of individuals. In addition, using lateralized stimuli, the investigators could interrogate the functioning of one hemisphere independently. This analysis was possible because of the lateralization of some aspects of sensory processing; for example, visual input from the left visual field is processed exclusively by the left hemisphere, and visual input from the right visual field is processed by the right hemisphere. The work of Sperry and his colleagues inspired a reevaluation of older neurological data as well as new investigations of hemispheric specialization in animals.

There are now extensive data indicating that the right hemisphere specializes in global, parallel, holistic processes, whereas the left hemisphere specializes in sequential and analytical processes. Based on this body of work, some researchers (Brittain, 1985; Katz, 1978, 1983, 1985; Razumnikova, 2007; Vol'f, Razumnikova, & Golubev, 1997) asserted that the processes in the right hemisphere are responsible for the generation of novel ideas, which are then communicated by the left hemisphere. Experimental studies have shown that participants who excel in divergent thinking (Razumnikova & Larina, 2005) and creativity-related tasks (Jausovec & Jausovec, 2000) show, as per their EEG, higher right-hemisphere facilitation (Faust & Lavidor, 2003), right-hemisphere dominance in band synchronization (Bhattacharya & Petsche, 2005), more coherence between occipital and frontopolar areas (Petsche, 1996), and phase coupling (Grabner, Fink, & Neubauer, 2007; Jausovec, 2000).

Similarly, right-hemisphere engagement was also registered in studies of creativity measuring event-related potentials (ERPs). To illustrate, Aghababyan and colleagues (2007) registered changes in the amplitude of the N200 negative component of the ERP during a subject's performance of a verbal creative task. They found that the N200, a response component that is thought to reflect various discrimination, classification, and executive functions, was significantly increased in the frontal and anterior frontal areas of the left hemisphere and in the temporo-parieto-occipital area of the right hemisphere. Collectively, findings from these electrophysiological studies corroborate the importance of right-hemispheric cortical networks in creative cognition.

Recent neuroimaging studies using fMRI have also provided evidence for a special role of the right hemisphere in creativity. For example, capitalizing on the Graded Salience Hypothesis (GSH), which predicts a selective right-hemisphere involvement in the processing of novel, nonsalient meanings, Mashal and colleagues (Mashal, Faust, Hendler, & Jung-Beeman, 2007) developed sets of related word pairs forming literal, novel, and conventional metaphorical expressions, and sets of unrelated word pairs. Typical adult participants were then asked to read the four types of linguistic expressions and decide which relationship existed between the two words (metaphoric, literal, or unrelated). The idea behind this design was that novel metaphorical expressions represented nonsalient interpretations, whereas conventional metaphors and literal expressions represented salient interpretations. A direct comparison of the novel metaphors versus the conventional metaphors revealed significantly stronger activity in the right posterior superior temporal sulcus, the right inferior frontal gyrus, and the left middle frontal gyrus. Similarly, Howard-Jones and colleagues, using fMRI methods (Howard-Jones, Blakemore, Samuel, Summers, & Claxton, 2005), implicated specific areas of the right prefrontal cortex in an activity that called for approaching a story-generation task creatively (i.e., demonstrating divergent semantic processing).

Considering the neuropsychology, electrophysiological, and neuroimaging results we have just discussed, one is compelled to ask: How might this neural lateralization of brain function have evolved? Is it found in other species and, if so, are the cognitive specializations found in the human brain present in related or rudimentary form in other animals? A brief discussion of the evolution of neural lateralization will provide a foundation for our later discussion of creativity-like behavior in animals.

Some hypothesize that lateralization evolved because the ability to process two "tasks" at once was extremely advantageous. For example, normal chicks are able to use their right eye (left hemisphere) in a foraging task, while simultaneously using their left eye (right hemisphere) to monitor their surroundings for predators (Hunsaker, Rogers, & Kesner, 2007). If the right hemisphere is specialized to attend to novelty, using this hemisphere would be advantageous for predator detection, leaving the left available for the classification and character-ization required in the foraging task. Chicks whose lateralization was disrupted during development by incubation in the dark are unable to carry out these tasks simultane-ously (Hunsaker et al., 2007).

It appears that lateralization has selec-tive and evolutionary consequences for prey species as well. If a species tends to favor one eye/side for environmental monitoring or escape behavior, the animal that preys on it may become aware of this. It therefore becomes advantageous for a single individ-ual within a population to do the opposite of the group (run the other way or increase vig-ilance in other direction) (Rogers, 2000, 2002, 2006; Rogers, Zucca, & Vallortigara, 2004). Much like creativity, this "going against the grain" may lead to individual- versus population-level asymmetries, in which one person in a group favors a different hemi-sphere or behavior consistently despite the overall preference of the population as a whole (Rogers et al., 2004), thus engaging in a behavior that is both novel (relative to the rest of the population) and appropriate (to the task of not being eaten). Having the right ratio of creative and noncreative thinkers at the population level can be extremely important to a group, as demon-strated in a study that employed the com-puter modeling of ant colonies (Rogers et al., 2004). Returning to the original point, the evolutionary benefit of hemispheric lateral-ization at an individual level, this asymme-try may allow for simultaneous processing of multiple types of information (Rogers, 2000). The ability to be creative while at the same time watching to make sure you don't fall down the stairs (although some of us may not be very well lateralized for this!), and the ability of one hemisphere to be dominant over the other and thereby prevent incompatible behaviors (Hunsaker, Rogers, & Kesner, 2007), (which may in turn relate to the theories of Martindale to be dis-cussed in the next section on "Disinhibition Hypotheses"), might be examples of such simultaneous processing.

And yet, clearly, the idea that creativity is uniquely a property of the right hemi-sphere is an oversimplification. The neuro-logist Joseph Bogen, who participated in Sperry's original studies involving the split-brain patients, and who most actively pro-moted the hemispheric asymmetry per-spective, posited that the neural basis of creativity was the result of both the func-tional specialization of the two hemispheres *and* the subsequent combinatorial interac-tion of the hemispheres, which requires the corpus collosum (Bogen & Bogen, 1988). Thus, one needs both right and left sides of the brain for fruitful creativity. In Bogen's framework, an absence of creativity could be a result of any of three possible condi-tions: (a) an impoverished left hemisphere (or propositional mind), leading to a defi-ciency in the technical competence needed to adequately carry out a creative task; (b) an impoverished right hemisphere (or apposi-tional mind), leading to a deficiency in inno-vative or imagination abilities despite tech-nical skills; or (c) a transient or permanent disruption in interhemispheric communica-tion (Bogen & Bogen, 1988).

Recent research in creativity seems to support Bogen's idea that processes assumed to be grounded in both hemispheres are necessary for creativity. Specifically, it has long been argued that experience is nec-essary for creativity (Hayes, 1989). More specifically, it has been observed that a minimum of 10 years of experience and knowledge in a field is required to make a creative contribution (Simonton, 1997). Without the acquired tacit professional knowledge to build on, it seems impossible to create the novel combinations of existing ideas that begin the creative process. Such an acquisition requires a heavy engagement of the left hemisphere, which is typically associated with gathering and storing log-ical, factual information (Vauclair, Fagot, & Depy, 1999). Indeed, from this point of view, creativity may be viewed as a process in which straightforward, traditionally "left-brain" processes of information acquisition and storage interact with processes associ-ated with the "right brain," such as abstract and novel integration. In other words, cre-ativity in this interpretation requires both the sequential and interactive engagement of both hemispheres, an interdisciplinary project between two "experts." Therefore, it might not be surprising that, although as yet limited, there is emerging evidence for the involvement of the left hemisphere in various creative tasks (Aghababyan et al., 2007; Bechtereva et al., 2004).

Disinhibition Hypotheses and the Role of the Frontal Lobes

A second prominent theory of creative cognition, pioneered by Hans Eysenck (1967) and investigated most thoroughly by Colin Martindale (1999), emphasizes cognitive disinhibition, or the ability to shed the schematic constraints and biases that impede creative thought (Martindale, 1971, 1989). This idea has deep historical roots, going back to the nineteenth-century concept of degeneration and psychoticism advocated by Morel (1857), which emphasized that the atrophy of the higher inhibitory centers of the brain result in a constellation of symptoms such as criminality and overemotionality. Indeed as Martindale (1971) pointed out, the traits used by early theorists to characterize degeneration overlap considerably with those used to describe eccentric, highly creative individuals. Eysenck's (1993) original theory held that the greater cognitive flexibility seen in creative people was a static personality trait, whereas Martindale (1999) believed that it could change in accordance with the situation.

To update this concept into neurobiological terms, this view posits that creative cognition is the result of a brain state characterized by low levels of cortical activation, because cortical activation, as measured in EEG studies, is generally believed to inhibit other systems in the brain (Martindale, 1977; Martindale & Greenough, 1973; Martindale & Hines, 1975). Therefore, the disinhibition hypothesis states that cortical activation gates the cognitive processes occurring in other brain regions such that (a) increased cortical activation suppresses the processes needed to access remote associates (i.e., new possibilities and novel recombinations), whereas (b) reduced cortical activation would effectively disinhibit or release these cognitive mechanisms and allow creative cognition to occur.

The majority of direct empirical evidence for the cognitive disinhibition hypothesis comes from the work of Colin Martindale and his collaborators. In a review summarizing six published studies, Martindale noted a consistent finding that creative people show lower levels of cortical arousal (i.e., less inhibition of "abnormal" behavior) in the form of alpha waves that remain the same or increase during creative tasks. By contrast, in noncreative situations, these participants exhibited the same alpha-wave blocking as noncreative participants, suggesting that creative people are able to enter into a cognitive state that is conducive to creativity when the task demands it (Martindale, 1977).

Additional indirect evidence for the disinhibition hypothesis comes from studies that show that increases in stress and arousal, which presumably increase levels of cortical activation, result in decreases in originality and creativity. For example, several investigations using word-association tasks and other creativity tests have shown that stress produces decreases in performance (Coren & Schulman, 1971; Krop, Alegre, & Williams, 1969). Moreover, group "brainstorming" sessions, originally conceived to increase creative output, often have the opposite effect owing, in the disinhibition framework, to the heightened cortical arousal that accompanies the group-session work environment (Lindgren & Lindgren, 1965).

The disinhibition hypothesis is also consistent with studies showing that highly creative people are overly reactive to a variety of stimuli (Martindale, Anderson, Moore, & West, 1996). For example, Martindale (1977) found that a series of mild electric shocks was rated as more intense by creative participants. Additionally, he and his colleagues showed that emotional arousal in creative participants, as measured by galvanic skin responses,[1] was greater than for less-creative participants in response to a series of moderately intense auditory tones. Moreover, the creative participants took twice as long to habituate to the tones (Martindale et al., 1996). Recent work on speed of information processing also supports this finding, showing that creative participants, when presented with a task and a distracter, had longer reaction times than did controls. Creative participants in these studies had increased difficulty mitigating the impact of distractions, and this was manifested in increased reaction times (Dorfman, Martindale, Gassimova, & Vartanian, 2008; Vartanian, Martindale, & Kwiatkowski, 2007).

There is also some EEG evidence that highly creative individuals have higher basal levels of cortical arousal than do less-creative individuals, but the relationship is not strong (Martindale, 1977). Martindale (1990) reviewed the literature on creativity and EEG measures and found that, although a significant difference in cortical arousal was found in two studies, a trend for highly creative participants to have higher basal cortical arousal was apparent in all studies.

In general, increases in arousal lead to decreases in creativity, originality, and variability of behavior. However, the basal level of cortical arousal may not be the important difference between more- and less-creative participants, but rather the *variability* in cortical arousal. In general, creative people show *lower* levels of cortical arousal, as indicated by EEG alpha-wave activity (an inverse of cortical arousal) during periods of creative cognition. For example, researchers recorded EEG measures while high- and low-creative participants engaged in the Alternate Uses Test (a divergent thinking test), the Remote Associates Test (a verbally based creativity and intelligence test) and a basic intelligence test. They found that highly creative participants had the highest alpha-wave activity (lowest cortical arousal) during the Alternate Uses Test, rel-

ative to the baseline conditions and during the periods when engaged in the other tasks requiring less creativity. By contrast, the medium- and low-creative groups showed low alpha-wave activity (high cortical arousal) during all three tests (Martindale & Hines, 1975). Thus, it is very possible that creative and less-creative people differ not only in basal level of cortical arousal, but also in the cortical arousal response during specific circumstances: the inspirational stages of the creative process.

The physiological evidence that creative people are overly reactive or overly sensitive to stimuli, which was previously addressed, may help explain why creative people often isolate themselves, sometimes to the point of stimulus deprivation and lowered cortical arousal. Somewhat paradoxically, however, highly creative people are usually novelty seekers (Martindale, 1999). Martindale believes that the reason presumably oversensitive creative people seek stimulation and novelty is because withdrawal, which results in a lowering level of arousal, eventually leads to a craving for novelty and stimulation (Martindale, 1999).

The question arising from these ideas is whether creative individuals are capable of "controlling" their level of cortical arousal (consciously or not) via their environment. In fact, it has been argued (Kris, 1952) that it is easier for people who are creative to shift between primary-process and secondary-process thinking (a state of primary-process thinking being necessary for creativity). However, in early studies of EEG and biofeedback, it was found that highly creative individuals were typically worse than less-creative controls at learning to control EEG patterns (Martindale & Armstrong, 1974; Martindale & Hines, 1975). Consistent with these biofeedback results, most accounts of highly creative people stress disinhibition and lack of self-control (Martindale, 1972, 1989). Martindale even traces the acknowledgment of these traits in creative people back to the early psychiatric notions of degeneration, a construct similar to psychosis (Martindale, 1999). Indeed,

---

1   Method of measuring the electrical resistance of the skin.

from this perspective, creative achievements seem not to be based on self-control, but rather on unintentional inspiration. This process appears to be similar to that involved in insight. Yet researchers (e.g., Vartanian & Goel, 2007) have investigated this relationship and differentiate insight from creativity. Creative solutions tend to be the result of multiple rounds of idea generation and evaluation; insights are not totally open ended (there is an answer), whereas creativity does not require or generate answers; and it appears that insights are more emotion provoking than is creativity per se. This general idea that diffused attention and disinhibition are characteristic features of creative cognition is also indirectly supported by various findings from functional brain studies exploring the prefrontal and frontal responses to novel stimuli (Daffner et al., 2006; Dias & Honey, 2002; Yamaguchi, Hale, D'Esposito, & Knight, 2004). However, the nature and specifics of the involvement of the prefrontal and frontal areas of the brain with processing novel stimuli are unclear.

Thus, the literature at this point can be interpreted in more than one way. For example, it was mentioned previously that it seems that creative people appear, at least at times, to be hermetic, attempting to avoid stimulation overload and, correspondingly, an excess cortical arousal (Martindale, 1999). Yet, there are also systematic findings linking creative activities with novelty seeking (Feist, 1999). Compounding this is the idea that it is possible that both associations are true, but might be sequential and time dependent – recall that it has been argued that creative people seek stimulation and novelty after extended periods of withdrawal (Martindale, 1999). Yet, there is the alternative or additional possibility that self-stimulation and novelty seeking occur during the interim period between different stages of creative cognition, but not because of a general need to compensate for stimulus deprivation but because new experiences and new ideas are needed as nourishment for subsequent stages of the creative process and realization of creative products.

The disinhibition hypothesis has attracted and still attracts the attention of many researchers of creativity. Yet, regardless of how nearly true or accurate it is, it seems to focus only on the first step of creative cognition, setting up the necessary prerequisites for the "real" creative cognition that occurs in other brain regions. It might be regulating the creativity-related networks in such a way that the prefrontal and frontal areas, having processed novel information, get disengaged so that the subsequent processing that is likely to occur – for instance, in sensory integration centers of the association cortices and the memory centers in the medial temporal lobe – can unfold to generate new associations, insights, and, ultimately, creative products.

Thus, theoretically, the hemispheric-asymmetry and disinhibition hypotheses can be integrated under the assumption that these hypotheses address different stages of creative cognition, and that a reduction in cortical activation, specifically in the frontal lobe, results in a selective disinhibition of particular areas of the right hemisphere that have been or will be implicated as associated with various facets of creativity.

Creativity and Mental Illness

It is impossible to discuss the neurobiology of creativity without reference to the possible link between creativity and mental health. These links are related to two lines of research. First, there is a long-standing tradition in the developed world of correlating high levels of creativity with mental illnesses (Richards, 1981). The stereotype of the "mad genius" is entrenched in Western culture (despite a body of literature disputing the idea, see Plucker, Beghetto, & Dow, 2004) and has been the subject of an entire literature of creativity theories (Andreasen, 1987).

Empirically, there is speculation that creativity, certain aspects of cognition (e.g., disinhibition and latent inhibition[2]), and particular personality traits (e.g., psychoticism) are related (Martindale & Dailey, 1996). In turn, similar characteristics of cognition and personality appear to be characteristic of madness. Many studies focus on low latent inhibition as a common factor in creative individuals, and then, in turn, correlate low latent inhibition with mental illness (Baruch, Hemsley, & Gray, 1988; Lubow, Ingberg-Sachs, Zalstein-Orda, & Gerwitz, 1992). For example, studies show that a reduced pattern of activation in the frontal lobes is characteristic of latent inhibition and, in turn, both are associated with bipolar disorder (Lloyd-Evans, Batey, Furnham, & Columbus, 2006); furthermore, patients with very high or very low schitzotypy show low levels of latent inhibition (Wuthrich & Bates, 2001). It has also been proposed that the link between latent inhibition and creativity and mental illnesses is mediated by intelligence. There may be a trade-off in people with reduced latent inhibition such that higher intelligence may lead to a creative personality, and lower intelligence to psychoticism (Carson, Peterson, & Higgins, 2003; Peterson, Smith, & Carson, 2002).

Martindale et al. (1996) have argued that much of the correlation between creativity and mental illness is a result of the fact that highly creative individuals are oversensitive and slower to habituate to novelty. As a result, these creative people are drawn to novelty as an alternative to repetition. This is counterintuitive to the idea that they are drawn to novelty by the boredom caused by high rates of habituation (Martindale, 1999).

Genetic and Evolutionary Bases of Creativity

There is substantial interest in understanding the genetic bases of creativity (Chavez-

Eakle, 2007). As yet, however, the published literature on the genetic basis of creativity is limited, although the development of genome-wide association studies will likely change (see, e.g., Simon-Sanchez & Singleton, 2008). Three lines of evidence are typically cited in the context of understanding the links between genes and creativity.

The first line is related to the relationship between brain asymmetry and the association between mental illnesses and creativity. It is, perhaps, pertinent that genetic investigations of a variety of developmental disorders such as autism, attention deficit hyperactivity disorder (ADHD), schizophrenia, bipolar illness, specific language impairment (SLI), and dyslexia suggest possible genetic overlap. In addition, many of these conditions are characterized by lack of common hemisphere asymmetry and anomalous brain lateralization (Klimkeit & Bradshaw, 2006), as well as dysfunction of the frontal lobes and their prefrontal areas (Bradshaw & Sheppard, 2000). Correspondingly, it has been hypothesized that there could be some shared genetic mechanisms that contribute to these shared manifestations of creativity, mental illnesses, and peculiarities of the brain structures (Folley, Doop, & Park, 2003).

Specifically, it has been proposed (Smalley, Loo, Yang, & Cantor, 2005) that atypical cerebral asymmetry (ACA) and the absence of left-hemisphere dominance for language may be a shared phenotype resulting from genes located in regions of overlap. In fact, a whole-genome investigation of the ACA phenotype has resulted in the identification of two regions of interest in the human genome, at 9q33–34 and 16p13. Indeed, these regions in turn have been featured in a number of neuropsychiatric conditions. Interestingly, interpreting their findings, the authors suggest that, because ACA is associated with certain aspects of creativity, such risk genes may also be enhancer genes for creativity (Smalley et al., 2005).

Similarly, although limited, there is evidence from quantitative genetic studies of

2 Latent inhibition is a cognitive process of "learned irrelevance" or the ability to disregard or inhibit responses to a particular stimulus or stimuli to prevent information overload or engage in associate learning or memory formation.

various types of relatives that supports the presumed molecular-genetic link between creativity and mental disorders. In particular, Kinney, Richards, Lowing, LeBlanc, and Zimbalist (2001) compared 36 index adult adoptees of biological parents with schizophrenia and 36 demographically matched control adoptees with no biological family history of psychiatric hospitalization. The researchers rated the participants' real-life creativity. It was reported that individuals with indicators of genetic liability for schizophrenia – such as schizotypy, schizoid personality disorder, and multiple schizotypal signs, but not schizophrenia itself – had significantly higher creativity than other participants.

Yet in a different study, Simeonova et al. (2005) compared creativity, as measured by the Barron-Welsh Art Scale (BWAS), in bipolar parents ($n = 40$) and their offspring ($n = 20$) with bipolar disorder (BD), and bipolar offspring with ADHD ($n = 20$) with healthy control adults ($n = 18$) and their children. Higher creativity scores were reported in both the adults (120% higher) and offspring with BD (107% higher), and in offspring with ADHD (91% higher) as compared to healthy control children. The researchers concluded that their results supported an association between BD and creativity.

These and other similar empirical findings, as well as various theoretical explorations, have triggered a series of studies in which creativity and mental illness are linked together and treated as "elements" of evolutionary biology and human nature. For example, it has been proposed (Akiskal & Akiskal, 2007) that affective disorders (e.g., mania, associated psychotic states, schizophrenia) serve as a genetic reservoir from which "genes for genius" are drawn.

The second line of research into the genetic bases of creativity stems from traditional behavior-genetic studies. This research employs two main methods, the twin method and the family method, with the assumptions being that the utilization of the first method permits researchers to estimate heritability, whereas the utilization of the second method permits estimating familiality (familial resemblance).

To illustrate some of the relevant studies, consider the following examples. Using 10 various creativity tests, including five from J. P. Guilford, researchers Reznikoff et al. (1973) worked with 37 identical (monozygotic, MZ) and 70 fraternal (dizygotic, DZ) twin pairs. Although, in general, the intraclass correlations for MZ twins were higher than for those for DZ twins, indicating the presence of genetic influences, the overall pattern of results did not provide convincing evidence of a genetic component in creativity. Similar results were found in a separate study using a different set of creativity tests. In an overview of 10 early twin studies of creativity (Canter, 1973), average correlations of 0.61 for MZ and 0.50 for DZ twins were presented. Yet it was argued that, if present, genetic influences on creativity can be primarily accounted for by the correlation between creativity and IQ (Nichols, 1978).

In a later study that utilized the Torrance indicators of creativity, the findings were similar (Grigorenko, LaBuda, & Carter, 1992). Although the MZ twins' resemblance was higher (.86) than that of the DZ twins (.64), the overall estimates of heritability, although statistically significant and different from zero in this study, were moderate (.43 ± .13). Similar observations were made in other twin studies of creativity (e.g., Egorova, 2000).

Likewise, findings from family studies are not consistent. There is evidence both for (Dacey, 1989; Scheinfeld, 1973; Vernon, 1989) and against the familial transmission of creativity (Bramwell, 1948).

Again, although limited in numbers, these studies suggest that, if heritable, creativity may be an emergent property; that is, it emerges from the synergistic interaction among a cluster of more fundamental characteristics, rather than being a single trait in itself (Estes & Ward, 2002). They further suggest that, to a large extent, creativity can be enhanced by the environment (Dockal, 1996).

The only molecular-genetic study of creativity (Reuter, Roth, Holve, & Hennig, 2006) investigated genetic associations between a measure of "inventiveness" from the "Berlin Intelligence Structure Test" (BIS; Jäger, 1982) and three genetic polymorphisms, all located in different genes (the VAL158MET polymorphism in the COMT gene,[3] the TAQ IA polymorphism in the DRD2[4] gene, and the TPH-A779C polymorphism in the TPH1[5] gene). The study was done in a small sample ($n = 92$) of adults. The results indicated the presence of a genetic association between genetic variation in the DRD2 and TPH1 genes and verbal and numerical creativity, respectively. However, given the number of nonreplicable findings in the field of genetics of complex behavior, these results, although of interest, require confirmation in a larger independent sample. Moreover, in the theory underlying the BIS, creativity is explicitly viewed as a subcomponent of intelligence. Thus, this study presents a precedent for rather than a definitive implication of the genes contributing to genetic variability in creativity.

The third and final line of research that will be discussed here is once again built on various ideas that have already been discussed in previous sections. This line of research has unfolded primarily within the framework of evolutionary biology. In this context, creativity is often viewed as dealing with novelty and concerning mental and behavioral flexibility (Reader & Laland, 2003). The basis of this research is the association between brain size and the development and introduction of innovations, and it has been studied in a variety of animal models (Lefebvre, Reader, & Sol, 2004; Reader & Laland, 2002). With respect to identifying candidate genes or gene clusters that might be involved in forming the biological foundation for creativity, this work implies that such an identification should start with those genes that influence the temporal regulation of neuronal and myelin growth and those genes that control the growth of the brain (Seldon, 2007).

Brain size has been directly correlated to innovative abilities in a variety of species including birds, primates, and predatory bats (Lefebvre et al., 2004). Note that in "wild" situations, innovation has been judged on the practical applications of the observed behavior, which is similar to the appropriateness criteria in the definition of creativity used by many human creativity researchers. For example, in both nonhuman primates and songbirds, the innovation rate is positively correlated with structures that are comparable to the mammalian neocortex, namely, the neocortex and striatum in nonhuman primates, and their avian analogs, the hyperstriatum ventrale and neostriatum (Rehkamper et al., 1991) in songbirds (Lefebvre et al., 2004). Lefebvre and colleagues (1997) have developed a measure of innovation rate that correlates forebrain size specifically to foraging innovation. Using this measure, several research teams have noted a positive relationship between innovative abilities as manifested in bower (nest) complexity and cerebellum size in Bowerbirds (*Ptilonorhynchidae* spp.) (Day, Westcott, & Olster, 2005; Madden, 2001).

Sol and colleagues have put forth the "brain size-environmental change" hypothesis (Sol et al., 2005) that there is a positive correlation between the size of an animal's brain and its ability to adapt to new environments, and studies in both birds and mammals have provided support for it (Sol, Bacher, Reader, & Lefebvre, 2008; Sol, Timmermans, & Lefebvre, 2002). This idea has important implications for the study of the evolution of neural mechanisms and cognitive capacities relating to creativity and innovation; being an invasive species requires novel and appropriate solutions to new challenges (e.g., new ways to get food in an unfamiliar environment). Additionally, increased innovative ability allows animals to stay in one place year round and not waste energy migrating, which may explain why residential species tend to be more innovative and why more reports of innovation occur during winter months (Lefebvre et al.,

3   Catechol-O-methyltransferase.
4   Dopamine D_2 receptor.
5   Tryptophan hydroxylase 1.

2004). Drawing a connection with creativity in humans, one researcher suggests that extensive experience in a particular field (or environment/location for an animal) is required for significant creativity or innovation in that field or area (Hayes, 1989).

To summarize, both behavior studies as well as molecular-genetic and evolutionary studies of creativity-related cognitive processes present the field with a pattern of interesting but also contradictory (at least at this point in time) results. Clearly, more research is needed to crystallize these findings.

Concluding Remarks

The products and processes of creative thinking remain difficult to define and are subject to the judgments of history and culture, but the greatest advances continue to inspire awe and sometimes appear born from mystical or divine sources. In our view, continued examination of the genetic and neurophysiological bases of creativity has not diminished this sense of wonderment; it has only enhanced it.

Our survey of the predominant theories describing how the brain works to produce creative activity – the hemispheric-asymmetry and disinhibition hypotheses – poses the possibility that the two are not mutually exclusive and may, in fact, work in tandem. Additionally, overlapping behaviors or phenotypes between creative individuals and those diagnosed with genetically based mental disorders has allowed us to consider the genetic bases of creative cognition – a link that allows us to investigate the possibility of genetic inheritance of creative abilities and the evolutionary forces that may shape this process.

Hence, the attempt to understand the etiology of creativity, its neuroscience and neurogenetics, unfolds in parallel with the continuing evolution of definitions and theories of creativity. Even while observing and defining creative activities, examining the outcomes of creative cognition, and developing various tools to measure them,

the field has plunged into explorations of the etiological cases of creativity in order to better understand the intricacies of its existence and development. So although much remains enigmatic about creativity, the field's understanding of it has been enhanced by our view of it through the neurobiological lens.

Author Note

This work was supported in part by general funds from Karen Jensen Neff and Charlie Neff.

References

Aghababyan, A. R., Grigoryan, V. G., Stepanyan, A. Y., Arutyunyan, N. D., & Stepanyan, L. S. (2007). EEG reactions during creative activity. *Human Physiology*, 33, 252–253.

Akiskal, H. S., & Akiskal, K. K. (2007). In search of Aristotle: Temperament, human nature, melancholia, creativity and eminence. *Journal of Affective Disorders*, 100, 1–6.

Andreasen, N. C. (1987). Creativity and mental illness: Prevalence rates in writers and their first-degree relatives. *American Journal of Psychiatry*, 144, 1288–1292.

Atchley, R. A., Keeney, M., & Burgess, C. (1999). Cerebral hemispheric mechanisms linking ambiguous word meaning retrieval and creativity. *Brain and Cognition*, 40, 479–499.

Baruch, I., Hemsley, D. R., & Gray, J. A. (1988). Latent inhibition and 'psychotic proneness' in normal subjects. *Personality and Individual Differences*, 9, 777–783.

Bechtereva, N. P., Korotkov, A. D., Pakhomov, S. V., Roudas, M. S., Starchenko, M. G., & Medvedev, S. V. (2004). PET study of brain maintenance of verbal creative activity. *International Journal of Psychophysiology*, 53, 11–20.

Bhattacharya, J., & Petsche, H. (2005). Drawing on mind's canvas: Differences in cortical integration patterns between artists and non-artists. *Human Brain Mapping*, 26(1), 1–14.

Bogen, J. E. (1977). Some educational implications of hemispheric specialization. In M. C. Wittrock (Ed.), *The human brain* (pp. 133–152). Englewood Cliffs, NJ: Prentice-Hall.

Bogen, J. E., & Bogen, G. M. (1969). The other side of the brain III: The corpus callosum and creativity. *Bulletin of the Los Angeles Neurological Society*, 34, 191–220.

Bogen, J. E., & Bogen, G. M. (1988). Creativity and the corpus callosum. *Psychiatric Clinics of North America*, 11(3), 293–301.

Bradshaw, J. L., & Sheppard, D. M. (2000). The neurodevelopmental frontostriatal disorders: evolutionary adaptiveness and anomalous lateralization. *Brain & Language*, 73, 297–320.

Bramwell, B. S. (1948). Galton's "Hereditary Genius"; and the three following generations since 1869. *Eugenics Review*, 39, 146–153.

Brittain, A. W. (1985). Creativity and hemispheric functioning: A second look at Katz's data. *Empirical Studies of the Arts*, 3, 105–107.

Canter, S. (1973). Personality traits in twins. In G. Claridge, S. Canter, & W. I. Hume (Eds.), *Personality Differences and Biological Variations* (pp. 21–51). New York: Pergamon.

Carlsson, I. (1990). Lateralization of defense mechanisms related to creative functioning. *Scandinavian Journal of Psychology*, 31, 241–247.

Carson, S. H., Peterson, J. B., & Higgins, D. M. (2003). Decreased latent inhibition is associated with increased creative achievement in high-functioning individuals. *Journal of Personality and Social Psychology*, 85, 499–506.

Chavez-Eakle, R. A. (2007). Creativity, DNA, and cerebral blood flow. In C. Martindale, P. Locher, & V. M. Petrov (Eds.), *Evolutionary and neurocognitive approaches to aesthetics, creativity and the arts* (pp. 209–224.). Amityville, NY: Baywood.

Coren, S., & Schulman, M. (1971). Effects of an external stress on commonality of verbal associates. *Psychological Reports*, 28, 328–330.

Csikszentmihalyi, M. (1996). *Creativity: Flow and the psychology of discovery and invention*. New York: HarperCollins.

Dacey, J. S. (1989). Discriminating characteristics of the families of highly creative adolescents. *Journal of Creative Behavior*, 23, 263–271.

Daffner, K. R., Ryan, K. K., Williams, D. M., Budson, A. E., Rentz, D. M., Wolk, D. A., et al. (2006). Increased responsiveness to novelty is associated with successful cognitive aging. *Journal of Cognitive Neuroscience*, 18, 1759–1773.

Day, L. B., Westcott, D. A., & Olster, D. H. (2005). Evolution of bower complexity and cerebellum size in bowerbirds. *Brain, Behavior, and Evolution*, 66, 62–72.

Dias, R., & Honey, R. C. (2002). Involvement of the rat medial prefrontal cortex in novelty detection. *Behavioral Neuroscience*, 116, 498–503.

Dockal, V. (1996). Is creativity independent of heredity? *Studia Psychologica*, 38, 107–119.

Dorfman, L., Martindale, C., Gassimova, V., & Vartanian, O. (2008). Creativity and speed of information processing: A double dissociation involving elementary versus inhibitory cognitive tasks. *Personality and Individual Differences*, 44, 1382.

Egorova, M. S. (2000). Сопоставление дивергентных и конвергентных особенностей когнитивной сферы детей (возрастной и генетический анализ). [A comparison of divergent and convergent characteristics of cognition in children: An analysis of their development and genesis.] *Voprosy Psychologii*, 1, 36–46.

Estes, Z., & Ward, T. B. (2002). The emergence of novel attributes in concept modification. *Creativity Research Journal*, 14(2), 149–156.

Eysenck, H. J. (1967). *The biological basis of personality*. Springfield, IL: Charles C. Thomas.

Faust, M., & Lavidor, M. (2003). Semantically convergent and semantically divergent priming in the cerebral hemispheres: Lexical decision and semantic judgment. *Cognitive Brain Research*, 17, 585–597.

Feist, G. J. (1999). The influence of personality on artistic and scientific creativity. In R. J. Sternberg (Ed.), *Handbook of creativity* (pp. 273–296). Cambridge: Cambridge University Press.

Folley, B. S., Doop, M. L., & Park, S. (2003). Psychoses and creativity: Is the missing link a biological mechanism related to phospholipids turnover? *Prostaglandins Leukotrienes & Essential Fatty Acids*, 69, 467–476.

Gazzangiga, M. F. (2008). *Human: The science behind what makes us unique*. New York: HarperCollins.

Grabner, R. H., Fink, A., & Neubauer, A. C. (2007). Brain correlates of self-rated originality of ideas: evidence from event-related power and phase-locking changes in the EEG. *Behavioral Neuroscience*, 121, 224–230.

Grigorenko, E. L., LaBuda, M. C., & Carter, A. S. (1992). Similarity in general cognitive ability, creativity, and cognitive style in a sample of adolescent Russian twins. *Acta Geneticae Medicae et Gemellologiae*, 41(1), 65–72.

Hayes, J. R. (1989). *The complete problem solver* (2nd ed.). Hillsdale, NJ: Erlbaum.

Howard-Jones, P. A., Blakemore, S. J., Samuel, E. A., Summers, I. R., & Claxton, G. (2005).

Semantic divergence and creative story generation: An fMRI investigation. *Cognitive Brain Research*, 25, 240–250.

Hunsaker, M. R., Rogers, J. L., & Kesner, R. P. (2007). Behavioral characterization of a transection of dorsal CA3 subcortical efferents: Comparison with scopolamine and physostigmine infusions into dorsal CA3. *Neurobiology of Learning and Memory*, 88(1), 127–136.

Jäger, A. O. (1982). *Berliner Intelligenzstruktur-Test (BIS-Test)*. Göttingen, Germany: Hogrefe.

Jausovec, N. (2000). Differences in cognitive processes between gifted, intelligent, creative, and average individuals while solving complex problems: An EEG study. *Intelligence*, 28, 213–237.

Jausovec, N., & Jausovec, K. (2000). Differences in resting EEG related to ability. *Brain Topography*, 12, 229–240.

Jay, M., & Neve, M. (Eds.). (1999). *1900: A fin-de-siecle reader*. London: Penguin.

Katz, A. N. (1978). Creativity and the right cerebral hemisphere: Towards a physiologically based theory of creativity. *Journal of Creative Behavior*, 12, 253–264.

Katz, A. N. (1983). Creativity and individual differences in asymmetric cerebral hemispheric functioning. *Empirical Studies of the Arts*, 1, 3–16.

Katz, A. N. (1985). Setting the record right: Comments on creativity and hemispheric functioning. *Empirical Studies of the Arts*, 3, 109–113.

Kaufman, J. C., & Baer, J. (Eds.). (2006). *Creativity and reason in cognitive development*. Cambridge: Cambridge University Press.

Kinney, D., Richards, R., Lowing, P., Leblanc, D., & Zimbalist, M. E. (2001). Creativity in offspring of schizophrenic and control parents: An adoption study. *Creativity Research Journal*, 13, 17–25.

Klimkeit, E. I., & Bradshaw, J. L. (2006). Anomalous lateralisation in neurodevelopmental diorders. *Cortex*, 42, 113–116.

Kris, E. (1952). *Psychoanalytic explorations in art*. New York: International Universities Press.

Krop, H. D., Alegre, C. E., & Williams, C. D. (1969). Effects of induced stress on convergent and divergent thinking. *Psychological Reports*, 24, 895–898.

Lefebvre, L., Reader, S. M., & Sol, D. (2004). Brains, innovations, and evolution in birds and primates. *Brain, Behavior, and Evolution*, 63, 233–246.

Lefebvre, L., Whittle, P., Lascaris, E., & Finklestein, A. (1997). Feeding innovations and forebrain size in birds. *Animal Behavior*, 53, 549–560.

Lindgren, H. C., & Lindgren, F. (1965). Brainstorming and orneriness as facilitators of creativity. *Psychological Reports*, 16, 577–583.

Lloyd-Evans, R., Batey, M., Furnham, A., & Columbus, A. (2006). *Bipolar disorder and creativity: Investigating a possible link*. Hauppauge, NY: Nova Science Publishers.

Lubow, R. E., Ingberg-Sachs, Y., Zalstein-Orda, N., & Gerwitz, J. C. (1992). Latent inhibition in low and high "psychotic-prone" normal subjects. *Personality and Individual Differences*, 15, 563–572.

Madden, J. (2001). Sex, bowers, and brains. *Proceedings of the Royal Society of London Series B Biological Sciences*, 268, 833–838.

Martindale, C. (1971). Degeneration, disinhibition, and genius. *Journal of the History of the Behavioral Sciences*, 7(2), 177–182.

Martindale, C. (1972). Femininity, alienation, and arousal in the creative personality. *Psychology*, 9, 3–15.

Martindale, C. (1977). Creativity, consciousness, and cortical arousal. *Journal of Altered States of Consciousness*, 3(1), 69–87.

Martindale, C. (1989). Personality, situation and creativity. In J. Glover, R. Ronning, & C. Reynolds (Eds.), *Handbook of creativity* (pp. 211–232). New York: Plenum.

Martindale, C. (1990). Creative imagination and neural activity. In R. Kunzendorf & A. Sheikh (Eds.), *Psychophysiology of mental imagery: Theory, research, and application* (pp. 89–108). Amityville, NY: Baywood.

Martindale, C. (1999). Biological basis of creativity. In R. J. Sternberg (Ed.), *Handbook of creativity* (pp. 137–152). Cambridge, UK: Cambridge University Press.

Martindale, C., Anderson, K., Moore, K., & West, A. N. (1996). Creativity, oversensitivity, and rate of habituation. *Personality and Individual Differences*, 20, 423–427.

Martindale, C., & Armstrong, J. (1974). Relationship of creativity to cortical activation and its operant control. *Journal of Genetic Psychology*, 124(2), 311–320.

Martindale, C., & Dailey, A. (1996). Creativity, primary process cognition and personality. *Personality and Individual Differences*, 20, 409–414.

Martindale, C., & Greenough, J. (1973). The differential effect of increased arousal on creative and intellectual performance. *Journal of Genetic Psychology*, 123(2), 329–335.

Martindale, C., & Hines, D. (1975). Creativity and cortical activation during creative, intellectual and EEG feedback tasks. *Biological Psychology*, 3(2), 91–100.

Mashal, N., Faust, M., Hendler, T., & Jung-Beeman, M. (2007). An fMRI investigation of the neural correlates underlying the processing of novel metaphoric expressions. *Brain & Language*, 100, 115–126.

Mednick, S. A. (1962). The associative basis of the creative process. *Psychological Review*, 69, 220–232.

Morel, B. A. (1857). *Traite des degenerescences physiques, intellectuelles et morales de l'espece humaine*. Paris: Bailliere.

Nichols, R. C. (1978). Twin studies of ability, personality and interests. *Homo*, 29, 158–173.

Parpola, A. (1973). The literature and study of the Jaiminiya Samaveda in retrospect and prospect. *Studia Orientalia*, 43, 6.

Peterson, J. B., Smith, K. W., & Carson, S. (2002). Openness and extraversion are associated with reduced latent inhibition: Replication and commentary. *Personality and Individual Differences*, 33, 1137–1147.

Petsche, H. (1996). Approaches to verbal, visual and musical creativity by EEG coherence analysis. *International Journal of Psychophysiology*, 24, 145–159.

Plucker, J. A., Beghetto, R. A., & Dow, G. T. (2004). Why isn't creativity more important to educational psychologists? Potential, pitfalls, and future directions in creativity research. *Educational Psychologist*, 39, 83–97.

Razumnikova, O. M. (2007). Creativity related cortex activity in the remote associates task. *Brain Research Bulletin*, 73, 96–102.

Razumnikova, O. M., & Larina, E. N. (2005). Полушарные взаимодействия при поиске оригинальных вербальных ассоциаций: особенности когерентности биопотенциалов коры у креативных мужчин и женщин. [Hemispheric interactions during the search for novel verbal analogies: particularities of brain potentials' coherence in creative men and women.] *Zhurnal Vysshei Nervnoi Deiatelnosti Imeni I. P. Pavlova*, 55(6), 785–795.

Reader, S. M., & Laland, K. N. (2002). Social intelligence, innovation, and enhanced brain size in primates. *Proceedings of the National Academy of Sciences*, 99, 4436–4441.

Reader, S. M., & Laland, K. N. (Eds.). (2003). *Animal innovation*. Oxford: Oxford University Press.

Rehkämpera, G., Frahma, H. D., & Zillesa, K. (1991). Quantitative development of brain and brain structures in birds (galliformes and passeriformes) compared to that in mammals (insectivores and primates). *Brain, Behavior and Evolution*, 37, 125–143.

Reuter, M., Roth, S., Holve, K., & Hennig, J. (2006). Identification of first candidate genes for creativity: A pilot study. *Brain Research*, 1069(1), 190–197.

Reznikoff, M., Domino, G., Bridges, C., & Honeyman, M. (1973). Creative abilities in identical and fraternal twins. *Behavior Genetics*, 3, 365–377.

Richards, R. L. (1981). Relationships between creativity and psychopathology: an evaluation and interpretation of the evidence. *Genetic Psychology Monographs*, 103, 261–324.

Rogers, L. J. (2000). Evolution of hemispheric specialization: Advantages and disadvantages. *Brain and Language*, 73, 236–253.

Rogers, L. J. (2002). Lateralization in vertebrates: Its early evolution, general pattern, and development. *Advances in the Study of Behavior*, 31, 107–161.

Rogers, L. J. (2006). Factors influencing development of lateralization. *Cortex*, 42, 107–109.

Rogers, L. J., Zucca, P., & Vallortigara, G. (2004). Advantages of having a lateralized brain. *Proceedings of the Royal Society of London Series B-Biological Sciences*, 271, S420–S422.

Scheinfeld, A. (1973). *Twins and supertwins*. Oxford, England: Penguin.

Seldon, H. L. (2007). Extended neocortical maturation time encompasses speciation, fatty acid and lateralization theories of the evolution of schizophrenia and creativity. *Medical Hypotheses*, 69, 1085–1089.

Simeonova, D. I., Chang, K. D., Strong, C., & Ketter, T. A. (2005). Creativity in familial bipolar disorder. *Journal of Psychiatric Research*, 39, 623–631.

Simón-Sánchez, J., & Singleton, A. (2008). Genome-wide association studies in neurological disorders. *The Lancet Neurology*, 7, 1067–1072.

Simonton, D. K. (1997). Creative productivity: A predictive and explanatory model of career trajectories and landmarks. *Psychological Review*, 104, 66–89.

Smalley, S. L., Loo, S. K., Yang, M. H., & Cantor, R. M. (2005). Toward localizing genes underlying cerebral asymmetry and mental health. *American Journal of Medical Genetics. Part B, Neuropsychiatric Genetics*, 135, 79–84.

Sol, D., Bacher, S., Reader, S. M., & Lefebvre, L. (2008). Brain size predicts the success of mammal species introduced into novel environments. *American Naturalist*, 172, S63–71.

Sol, D., Duncan, R. P., Blackburn, T. M., Cassey, P., & Lefebvre, L. (2005). Big brains, enhanced cognition, and response of birds to novel environments. *Proceedings of the National Academy of Sciences*, 102, 5460–5465.

Sol, D., Timmermans, S., & Lefebvre, L. (2002). Behavioral flexibility and invasion success in birds. *Animal Behavior*, 60, 495–502.

Sperry, R. W. (1974). Lateral specialization in the surgically separated hemispheres. In F. Schmitt & F. Worden (Eds.), *Third neurosciences study program* (Vol. 3, pp. 5–19). Cambridge: MIT Press.

Sternberg, R. J., Kaufman, J. C., & Pretz, J. E. (2002). *The creativity conundrum: A propulsion model of kinds of creative contributions*. Philadelphia, PA: Psychology Press.

Sternberg, R. J., & Lubart, T. I. (1996). Investing in creativity. *American Psychologist*, 51(7), 677–688.

Vartanian, O., & Goel, V. (2007). Neural correlates of creative cognition. In C. Martindale, P. Locher, & V. M. Petrov (Eds.), *Evolutionary and neurocognitive approaches to aesthetics, creativity and the arts* (pp. 195–207). Amityville, NY: Baywood.

Vartanian, O., Martindale, C., & Kwiatkowski, J. (2007). Creative potential, attention, and speed of information processing. *Personality and Individual Differences*, 43, 1470.

Vauclair, J., Fagot, J., & Depy, D. (1999). Nonhuman primates as models of hemispheric specialization. In M. Haug & R. E. Whalen (Eds.), *Animal models of human emotion and cognition* (pp. 247–256). Washington, DC: American Psychological Association.

Vernon, P. E. (1989). The nature-nurture problem in creativity. In J. A. Glover, R. R. Ronning, & C. R. Reynolds (Eds.), *Handbook of creativity* (pp. 93–110). New York: Plenum.

Vol'f, N. V., Razumnikova, O. M., & Golubev, A. M. (1997). Специфика изменений ритмов ЭЭГ и эффективность вербальной мнестической деятельности у мужчин и женщин. [The dynamic of EEG changes and effectiveness of verbal mnemonic activity in males and females.] *Bulletin of the Siberian Section of the Russian Academy of Sciences*, 2, 83–86.

Wuthrich, V., & Bates, T. C. (2001). Schizotypy and latent inhibition: Non-linear linkage between psychometric and cognitive markers. *Personality and Individual Differences*, 30, 783–798.

Yamaguchi, S., Hale, L. A., D'Esposito, M., & Knight, R. T. (2004). Rapid prefrontal-hippocampal habituation to novel events. *Journal of Neuroscience*, 24, 5356–5363.

CHAPTER 12

Developmental Approaches to Creativity

Sandra W. Russ and Julie A. Fiorelli

Can children be creative? Can we see the creative process at work in children? If so, what are the processes that are developing in children that contribute to their creativity? What are the major developmental approaches to creativity? What facilitates creativity and what interferes with it? These are the main questions this chapter will address.

Contemporary approaches to creativity view the creative product to be a result of a complex interaction of the person and the environment. There are a number of processes within the individual that help a person be creative. Different theorists focus on and study different variables. Some of these cognitive and affective processes are divergent thinking, problem solving, flexibility of thought, access to emotion, and access to affect in fantasy. Personality variables of self-confidence, risk-taking, and openness to experience are also involved in creativity. Many of these processes can be observed and measured in children.

Just as there is no one overarching theory of creativity, there is no one comprehensive theory of the development of creativity. Approaches tend to focus on a specific area or process, like divergent thinking or problem solving. But we must remember that it is the whole child who is developing and integrating many processes and outside influences. How these processes crystallize and enable creative products to be formed is a challenging question for the field.

Developmental Approaches to Creativity in Children

One of the first questions to be addressed in thinking about creativity in children is whether or not children can actually be creative. Creativity is defined as the ability to produce work that is novel, of high quality, and useful or appropriate according to the particular task or discipline (Sternberg, Kaufman, & Pretz, 2002). The concept of "Big-C" and "little-c" creativity is also a common way of thinking about creative acts. (Richards, 2001) "Big-C" creativity makes a major contribution in a domain and usually results after a total immersion in the area so a new discovery can occur. "Little-c" creativity is a new or novel approach to a problem that is interesting and useful, but does not make a major impact on a field. In the area of everyday creativity (Richards, 1999), "little-c" creativity occurs all the time. When we consider creativity in children, there are many examples of "little-c" and everyday creativity. For example, a child might figure out a new way to train a puppy or a faster route home from school. There are not many examples of "Big-C" creativity in children. Children have not had time to master the knowledge base of a domain and make major contributions to a field. And they are typically not mature enough to make complex transformations or sublimations. There are, of course, rare exceptions. For example, Mozart was a child prodigy who made some contributions to music as a young person. But most creative children do not make major contributions to a field. Rather, they produce useful or good products that are novel and good "for their age group" (Runco, 1996; Russ, 1993). Even Mozart's works as a child were not among his greater ones.

Runco (1999a, 2007) has differentiated between theories of the development of creativity that involve discontinuous stages and those that are continuous.

Stage Theories

Stage theorists hold the view that children must pass through various stages, usually in a fixed order, and make discontinuous leaps to the next stage (Siegler, Deloache, & Eisenberg, 2006). One of the most influential stage theorists was Piaget, especially in the area of cognitive development. Piaget proposed that there is a qualitative change in children's thinking as they go through different stages (Piaget, 1932). Important to the area of creativity is the preoperational stage, from 2 to 7 years old, where children begin to use mental imagery and symbolic representation. For example, the block can be used as a telephone because one object can stand for another. Runco (2007) pointed out that Piaget's theory of adaptation is relevant to the development of creativity. The

theory of adaptation involves both the process of assimilation and accommodation as important developmental functions. Singer and Revenson (1996) described adaptation as "the continuous process of using the environment to learn and learning to adjust to changes in the environment "(p. 15). Assimilation is the taking in of information and the fitting of that information into existing notions and frameworks about the world. Accommodation is revising one's world view to fit the new information. Runco stressed that in order for adaptation to begin to occur; there must be a sense of disequilibrium leading the child to go into action. Runco (1999b) has written extensively on the importance of disequilibrium to the creative process for both children and adults. There must be some tension or perceived problem to begin the creative process. For children, there must be a challenge or problem for the child to manage in order to trigger the adaptation process.

Another major stage theory of child development is Freud's psychosexual stage theory. This theory was a model for conceptualizing child development as progressing from one stage to another sequentially. Freud's stage theory focused on the emotional development of the child and the development of defenses. The development of the defense of repression is especially important to the area of creativity. Developmentally, children are learning to integrate primitive, disorganized primary-process thinking and secondary-process thought. Freud (1915/1958) first conceptualized primary-process thought as an early, primitive system of thought that was drive laden and not subject to rules of logic or oriented to reality. One example of primary-process thinking is the kind of thought that occurs in dreams. Access to primary-process thought has been hypothesized to be important in creativity because associations are fluid and primitive images can be accessed and used in creative work (Holt, 1977; Kris, 1952; Martindale, 1981). This psychoanalytic theory is based on Freud's (1926/1959) formulation that repression of "dangerous" drive-laden material leads to a more general intellectual restriction. A large body of research with children and adults has found a relationship between access to primary-process thought and creativity (see Russ, 2002, for a review). This empirical support for the link between primary-process thinking and creativity implies that children must find a balance between using repression effectively so they can function with daily stresses and using repression flexibly so they can also think about a wide range of images and emotions that can be helpful in creative expressions and problem solving.

Runco (1999a, 2007) identified the most useful discontinuity theory that applies to creativity as that of Kohlberg's model of changes in conventionality. Runco discussed Kohlberg's (1987) stage theory of development, which proposes a preconventional stage, conventional stage, and postconventional stage. For children in middle childhood, when social norms and expectations carry great weight, unconventional ideas and behaviors are normally inhibited. Torrance (1968) described what appears to be a fourth-grade slump in original thinking that occurs around the age of 9. The fourth-grade slump is a reduction in original thinking in fourth-grade children when compared with younger and older children. The fourth-grade slump has been found in both longitudinal and cross-sectional studies (Guignard & Lubart, 2006). This frequently observed phenomenon is consistent with Kolberg's stage theory at the point when children in middle childhood are in the conventional-thinking stage. Runco (2007) postulated that the association process, which is so important for divergent thinking (generating ideas) and creativity, might be cut short at this stage because of the pressure of conventionality. He also wondered if brain development could be a factor as well. Lubart and Lautrey (1996) proposed that the development of reasoning ability and logical thought processes might account for the fourth-grade slump. They found that divergent thinking decreased in 9-year-olds as reasoning increased. They speculated that there may be development in reasoning processes during the ninth year that affects creative performance. Nevertheless, there are many individual differences in the degree to which conventional thinking dominates the child and how pervasive this inhibition is across situations. For example, pretend play or forms of artistic expression or activities (movies, comic books, videogames) may serve as safe venues for original, unconventional thinking. Other dimensions in child development also come into play. Children who are less repressed and more open to experience may be able to tolerate and express unconventional thoughts and feelings better than children with a more repressive style (Russ, 1993, 2004). Piaget made an interesting statement that is relevant to this issue as well. He said (1962) that "the creative imagination, which is the assimilation activity in a state of spontaneity, does not diminish with age, but, as a result of the correlative progress of accommodation, is gradually reintegrated in intelligence, which is thereby correspondingly broadened" (p. 289). Perhaps if we used more comprehensive measures of creativity, rather than, divergent thinking for example, we could see the development of the creative imagination. There may not be a fourth-grade slump in the creativity of story narratives? Further research on this interesting question is important.

Theories Emphasizing Continuity of Development

Vygotsky (1967) was a major sociocultural theorist who saw child development as continuous, involving quantitative changes in the child that developed within an interpersonal context (Siegler, Deloache et al., 2006). Vygotsky (1978) and Piaget (1932) believed that interaction through peers fosters problem solving and play development. Vygotsky (1978) identified a zone of proximal development, which includes tasks that are too difficult for the child individually, but are possible with guidance by adults or more skilled peers when the child is playing. Hirsh-Pasek and Golinkoff (2003) cited a study by McCune, Dipane, Fireoved, and Fleck (1994) demonstrating that the level of a child's play increased with adult involvement, but not control. With guidance and demonstration from the researcher, children engaged in more complex and creative make-believe play and abstract thinking. Through these interactions, children are encouraged to participate to solve more advanced problems and increase the complexity of play. Children are then able to adapt these newly learned skills and incorporate them into future interactions (Tudge & Rogoff, 1989).

In many areas of child development, processes are viewed as being on a continuum of development, becoming more complex or elaborate over time. Many processes involved in creativity seem continuous in nature. Keegan (1996) used a case-study method to support the continuity of development of processes involved in creativity. He stated that "the accumulation of knowledge, the sense of purpose, and the love of work exhibited by adults who produce something of extraordinary novelty and value are approximated by children and adolescents in their pursuits and underpin their creative productions" (p. 65).

Plucker and Beghetto (2004) conceptualized creativity as consisting of a combination of abilities and processes. Some of these processes are domain general and others are domain specific. For example, the ability to generate a variety of original ideas might be domain general, whereas musical talent is domain specific.

Russ (1993, 2004) identified many processes that are developing in children involved in the creative act. A number of cognitive, affective, and personality processes have been identified in the literature as being important in creativity (Russ, 1993). All of these creative abilities and processes are incubating in the developing child. Runco (2007) spoke of the uneven development of some of these processes and the continuous development of others. Stage models might apply to some cognitive processes, whereas other processes undergo a continuity of development. Because creativity involves many different processes and

configurations, no one model applies to all. There are many profiles of creative individuals and many different routes to creativity (Russ, 1993).

Developmental Processes Important in Creativity

There is a general consensus in the field of creativity about what specific processes and abilities are important to creative production.

Cognitive Processes

Two cognitive processes important in creativity are divergent thinking and transformation abilities. Both of these processes were identified by Guilford (1968) as being important in and unique to creative problem solving. Divergent thinking is thinking that goes off in different directions and that generates a variety of ideas. For example, a typical item on a divergent-thinking test would be "how many uses for a button can you think of?" Transformation abilities involve reorganizing information, breaking out of old ways of thinking, breaking a set, and revising what one knows into new patterns. These abilities can be measured in children and are relatively independent of intelligence (Runco, 1991). Tests such as Wallach and Kogan's adaptation of Alternate Uses Test (1965) or Torrance Tests of Creativity (Torrance, Ball, & Safter, 1992) are valid and reliable measures of divergent-thinking processes.

Divergent thinking is thought to be important across domains. Milgram and Livne (2006) consider divergent thinking to be a critical component of creative talent in every domain. They also did an extensive review and concluded that divergent thinking does relate to real-life problem solving. Divergent thinking is relatively stable over time in children. In a study by Russ, Robins, and Christiano (1999) there was a significant association between divergent thinking in first- and second-grade children and their divergent-thinking scores 4 years later (r = .46 for spontaneous flexibility). Interestingly, there were no significant differences between the means of the divergent-thinking test when comparing first- and second-grade scores with fifth- and sixth-grade scores. Other studies have found higher divergent-thinking scores in older children. Runco and Pezdek (1984) found a significant difference between the third-grade and sixth-grade divergent-thinking scores in two different samples of children. Runco and Albert (1986) also concluded that the ability to generate new ideas develops over time.

Other cognitive processes that are important in, but not unique to, creativity are sensitivity to problems and problem finding (Getzels & Csikszentmihalyi, 1976), task persistence and trying alternative problem solving approaches (Weisberg, 1988), breadth of knowledge and wide range of interests (Barron & Harrington, 1981), insight and synthesizing abilities (Sternberg,1988), and evaluative ability (Guilford, 1950).

Problem finding is the ability to identify the problem to be solved, which others may have missed, before tackling the problem. Runco and Okuda (1988) explored the link between problem finding and creativity. Adolescents provided solutions to given problems as well as to problems they were asked to create. Results indicated that the adolescents provided significantly more-creative responses to the self-generated problems. They emphasized the importance of both problem-finding and problem-solving ability to real-world creativity. Runco and Okuda found a greater difference between the discovered and presented problem scores compared to Wakefield's (1985) results with fifth-grade children. These findings suggest that problem finding and problem solving may become more distinct skills in adolescence. Creativity might not only increase with age but also change qualitatively.

Pretend play ability has been related to a number of cognitive processes important in creativity in a variety of studies (see Dansky,

1999; Russ, 2004; Singer & Singer, 1990, for reviews). Pretend play involves pretending, the use of fantasy and make-believe, and the use of symbolism. Fein (1987) stated that pretend play is symbolic behavior in which "one thing is playfully treated as if it were something else" (p. 282). Fein viewed play as a natural form of creativity in children. The associations between play and creativity make theoretical sense from a variety of perspectives. Many of these creative cognitive processes occur in play and are fostered through play.

Affective Processes

Affect expression and affective fantasy themes are also important processes in creativity–especially in the arts. Openness to one's own emotions is involved in many of the performing arts (theater, music, dance). Access to emotional memories helps the creative process of the writer and poet (Russ, 2009). Research on mood states and creativity finds that positive affect, and at times negative affect, enhances the creative process (Isen, Daubman, & Nowicki, 1987). Although the mechanisms are not clear, the consensus is that the involvement of emotions broadens the process of associations and improves creativity on a variety of creativity measures.

There are many ways that the developing child can come to feel comfortable with emotions, emotional memories, and fantasies. Pretend play also helps with affect expression. As Fein (1987), Vygotsky (1967), and Singer and Singer (1990) have stressed, play is a safe arena where feelings and fantasy can be expressed and worked with at the child's own pace. Piaget also thought of symbolic play as a place where children expressed emotions that were out of awareness. The child could then dissociate the act or thought from the context and assimilate it into behavior (Singer & Revenson, 1996). This type of play then became compensatory play.

A number of personality variables are also important in creativity. Openness to experience (McCrae & Costa, 1987), intrinsic motivation (Amabile, 1983), self-confidence (Sternberg, 1988), and risk-taking (Sternberg) are a few that emerge in the literature and can be assessed in children.

Much of what has been written about the development of creativity in children has focused on the development of play. This is because play and creativity are intertwined (Fein, 1987; Sawyer, 1997; Vygotsky, 1930/1967). Because so many of the cognitive and affective processes important in creativity also occur in pretend play, we now turn to play and the development of play.

Play Processes and Creativity

Sawyer (1997) conceptualized pretend play in young children as being improvisational. Improvisation is important in adult creativity. Sawyer pointed out that pretend play is unscripted yet has loose outlines to be followed. Singer and Singer (1990) conceptualized play as practice with divergent thinking. Vygotsky (1930/1967) theorized that imagination developed out of children's play (Smolucha, 1992). He stated that "the child's play activity is not simply a recollection of past experience but a creative reworking that combines impressions and constructs from them new realities addressing the needs of the child" (1930/1967, p. 7). Through play, children develop combinatory imagination – the ability to combine elements of experience into new situations and behaviors. Combinatory imagination is important in both artistic and scientific creativity. Research findings support the relationship between pretend play ability and creativity in children. There are many studies from many different researchers that found significant, positive relationships between play and different components of creativity such as divergent thinking (Lieberman, 1977; Russ & Grossman-Mckee, 1990), insight (Vandenberg, 1980), and flexibility (Pellegrini, 1992). For example, in a longitudinal study, imagination in play was related to divergent thinking over a 4-year period, independent of verbal intelligence. Play in the first and second grade was related to divergent

thinking in the fifth and sixth grade (Russ, Robins, & Christiano, 1999). This longitudinal study supported the stability of the association between pretend play and divergent thinking.

Fein (1987) and Russ (1993, 2004) have stressed the importance of affect in play in the link to creativity. Fein proposed an affect symbol system that gets activated in pretend play and is important in creativity. An affective symbol stores information about emotional events and is manipulated and worked with in pretend play. Russ (1993), from a psychodynamic framework, stressed the importance of pretend play in helping children access emotional memories and fantasies. In my research, affect expression in play has related to divergent thinking (Russ & Grossman-McKee, 1990), to teachers' ratings of fantasy ability (Kaugars & Russ, 2009), and to emotion in memory narratives (Russ & Schafer, 2006).

DEVELOPMENTAL TRENDS IN
CHILDREN'S PLAY

Hirsh-Pasek and Golinkoff (2003) concluded that around the age of 2, children begin to discover pretend play. They are able to pretend to hear a voice from the telephone, for instance. In the third and fourth years, pretend play is especially evident. Children are able to think symbolically, not be confined to a single use of an object, and consider worlds outside their own. They are now able to recognize that although a plate is typically used to hold food, it can also be used as a steering wheel for an imaginary car. Play follows developmental stages in which a child moves from reacting to characteristics of objects to exploring objects to symbolically using objects (Belsky & Most, 1981).

As children develop, their play becomes more complex. Dansky (1999) pointed out that in high-level play, children display all seven dimensions of original thinking described by Milgram (2006): associative fluency; imagery; curiosity; fantasy; problem finding; metaphoric production; and selective attention deployment. He concluded that individual differences in play have implications for individual differences in creativity. Dansky also theorized that adopting the "as if" frame in play may open the door to a mode of problem solving where one can play with ideas and possibilities, which is so important in creativity.

Just as it is important in creativity to play with ideas and images, it is also important to play with affective processes. Affect expression in play occurs from a very young age. Interestingly, when we compare affect expression in the play narrative in children from 6 to 10 years of age, we do not find developmental differences in the amount of affect expression over these years. In terms of stability of affect expression, Russ, Robins, et al. (1999) found significant relations between affect expression in children in play when they were first and second graders, and affect expression in play narratives when they were sixth and seventh graders. This finding suggests some stability in the tendency to express emotion and emotional themes in narratives across time.

Piaget (1951) emphasized the importance of peers in the development of problem-solving skills but suggested the peers need not be more advanced. Through interactions with others at a similar developmental stage, children learn different perspectives, discuss possible resolutions, and decide on the best solution. Children develop problem-solving skills, as well as advance their play skills, through this resolution process.

Harris (1989) proposed that imaginative understanding may help children understand others' mental states and affective experiences. This is consistent with the developing theory of mind in children whereby they build an understanding of how the mind works and understand the minds of others (Siegler et al., 2006; Wellman, 1990). Harris (2000) and other researchers have found that engaging in make-believe enables children to learn to take the perspective of the other.

These developmental theorists suggest and research supports that it is within play that children are able to create and solve problems for themselves, learn how to interact with others, discover a sense of power,

learn how to cope with life events, and develop language (Hirsh-Pasek & Golinkoff, 2003). Research demonstrates that play and play interventions lead to an improvement in problem-solving ability (Drewes, 2006; Fisher, 1992). In one study, Sylva, Bruner, and Genova (1976) demonstrated through the use of chalk and sticks that self-guided play serves to teach problem solving. In another study, 4-year-olds were either given an opportunity to play or a training experience, followed by a task requiring problem solving. On the first task, participants given the play opportunity performed as well as those participants trained in the specific task. The second task was related, but more complex than the first. On this task, children who had the play opportunity were faster and required fewer hints than those who were trained on a similar yet less difficult task (Smith & Dutton, 1979).

Research demonstrates that divergent thinking, associated with creativity and more advanced problem solving, improves through divergent play (Pepler & Ross, 1981). Children who first engaged in divergent play were much more successful at the subsequent divergent task of building a city from a pile of blocks. Through such play, children are able to create and solve new problems, an essential process to the development of problem-solving skills. The children who engaged in convergent activities prior were discouraged by the problem-solving task. They were less likely to think outside of the box, often getting stuck on one incorrect solution, and were much more likely to give up before the task's completion. This suggests that without proper play, the creative processes may be hindered. If a child is never given opportunities to creatively find solutions to problems or engage in activities that have more than one answer, they are likely preventing full development of such processes.

Wyver and Spence (1999) examined the relationship between play and problem solving further and identified an element of reciprocity. They found that the development of divergent problem solving facilitates the development of play skills and vice versa.

Elkind (2007) suggested that the problem-solving process occurs only if children are developmentally ready. The most effective way to develop this skill is through child-initiated and child-guided play, not at the instruction or control of the more advanced adult. As Hirsh-Pasek and Golinkoff (2003) suggested, a child begins to consider symbolic play only after fully exploring the objects in his or her world, not at the instruction of the parent. Similarly, it seems problem solving can begin to occur only once the child has developed an understanding of his or her surroundings. In other words, an elementary understanding is necessary to develop such skills. As children increasingly engage in pretend play during the preschool years, they are also developing skills to problem solve. Furthermore, children are developing the skills to interact, play, and problem solving cooperatively with their peers (Ashley & Tomasello, 1998; Brownell & Carriger, 1990, 1991).

Other Developmental Influences

There is evidence that creative thinking is inherited to some degree. Runco (2007) reviewed the literature. Twin studies have concluded that about 22% of the variance in creativity is due to the influence of genes (Waller, Bouchard, Lykkens, Tellegen, & Blacker, 1993) Genes that influence neural transmission may be key, such as dopamine receptors (Reuter et al., 2005).

Dietrich (2004) concluded that creative thinking involves the prefrontal cortex. As the technology of cognitive neuroscience advances, we will learn more about the neurological mechanisms underlying creativity and the role that early experiences play in influencing the developing brain.

Enhancing Creativity in Children

In general, creativity training programs have focused on divergent thinking (Lubart & Guignard, 2004). There has been some success, but there are questions as to whether increases in divergent thinking will gener-alize from one task or domain to another (Baer, 1998).

Also, it is not clear whether short-term interventions can effect lasting change in creativity. Some research suggests that changes in creativity occur over long periods of time and do not fluctuate in response to short-term interventions (Runco & Pezdek, 1984). On the other hand, there have been successful short-term interventions. In Italy, a carefully conceptualized creativity-enhancement program was developed by Antonietti and Cerioli (1996). This program was carried out by teachers with elementary-school children and was based on story-telling activities. They concluded that children can learn to be creative but only if teachers "employ instructional methods that are consistent with the complex nature of creativity stressed by recent research" and that are not simply based on repetitive activities (Antonietti & Cornoldi, 2006, p. 157). They also stressed the importance of considering emotions in developing creativity-enhancement programs.

One Way to Foster Creativity in Children is Through Facilitation of Pretend Play Skills

There have been successful efforts to improve children's play skills. Many of these play-training studies have been in an academic context rather than a therapeutic context. Smilansky's (1968) was one of the first to demonstrate that teachers could teach play skills. She worked with kindergarten children from low SES backgrounds in Israel for 90 minutes a day, 5 days a week, for 9 weeks. The children who engaged in socio-dramatic play, with help from their teachers, showed significant cognitive improvement when compared with other groups. The teachers helped the children develop their play by commenting, making suggestions, and giving demonstrations. Play training has been found to be effective with mentally retarded populations (Hellendoorn, 1994; Kim, Lombardino, Rothman, & Vinson, 1989). Additionally, Hartmann and Rolett (1994) reported positive results with elementary-school children in Austria, where teachers instructed low-SES children in play 4 hours per week. When compared with a comparable control class, the play intervention group had better divergent thinking and were happier in school.

One of the methodological problems with many studies in the play-facilitation area is the lack of adequate control groups. Smith (1988, 1994) has consistently raised this issue in reviewing the play-intervention literature. Smith stressed that adequate research design requires the inclusion of a control group that involves experimenter–child interaction of a form other than pretend play. He concluded that when this kind of control group is included, usually both the play group and the control group improve with no significant differences between them. Dansky (1999) reached a different conclusion after reviewing the play-training literature. He concluded that many studies that found significant results did have adequate control groups (Dansky, 1980; Shmukler, 1984–1985; Udwin, 1983). Dansky concluded that there were consistently positive results in studies with adequate control groups, demonstrating that play tutoring, over a period of time, did result in increased imaginativeness in play and increased demonstrated creativity

Russ, Moore, and Pearson (2007) investigated the effects of play-intervention techniques on children's play skills and associations with divergent thinking. Participants were 50 first- and second-grade children in an inner city school (99% African-American). Children were randomly assigned to either an imagination play group, an affect play group, or a puzzles/coloring control group. Each participant met five times with a play trainer in individual sessions. A standardized play intervention was used for each play group. A major hypothesis was that children in the play conditions would have significantly better play ability than children in the control group. Specified *a priori* contrasts were used to analyze the play variables. The affect play group showed greater cognitive and affective play skills than the control group. The imagination play group showed greater affective play skills than the control group. There was a significant effect of group on divergent thinking. Although the sample size was small, the results are promising that a brief standardized play intervention can improve children's play skills, which may improve divergent thinking.

When Moore and Russ (2008) did a follow-up study of these children 4 to 8 months later, the imagination group had improved play skills over time. The increase in divergent thinking did not hold over this period. We are continuing to investigate whether or not divergent thinking can be facilitated through play and whether there will be generalized, long-lasting effects.

A classic longitudinal study by Harrington, Block, and Block (1987) tested the principles put forth by Rogers (1954), who stated that creativity in children was most likely to occur when three conditions were present: openness to experience, internal locus of evaluation, and the ability to toy with elements and concepts. He thought that these three internal conditions were fostered by two external conditions: psychological safety and psychological freedom. In the Harrington et al. study, 106 children and their families were followed in a longitudinal study. Researchers categorized child-rearing practices based on data collected when the children were preschoolers. The child-rearing practices data were based on parent questionnaires and observations of parent–child interactions. Child-rearing practices that were consistent with Roger's approach encouraged expression of feelings, gave time to daydream and loaf, encouraged curiosity and exploration, let the child make their own decisions, and permitted questions and discussion. Relationships were investigated between child-rearing practices and a creative potential index of the child as a preschooler and as a young adolescent. The creative-potential index was based on teacher's ratings and on personality Q-sorts. There was a correlation of .33 between the preschool creative-potential score and the adolescent potential score, indicating some stability of the construct. The main finding of the study was that parents who used child-rearing practices consistent with Rogers's theory had children who were more creative than children of parents whose practices and attitudes were not consistent with Rogers's theory. After using path-analysis techniques, the authors concluded that Rogers's childrearing practices approach contributed significantly to adolescent creative potential scores after gender, IQ, and preschool creativity scores were controlled for. They concluded that environments that foster the child's autonomy and self-confidence should also foster creativity. These findings are consistent with those of Csikszentmihalyi and Rathunde (Adler, 1991), who found that a home environment that combined support and optimal challenge was essential for creative development. Families of teenagers that promoted creative functioning showed five characteristics: clarity of expectations; interest in what the child was currently doing; offering choices; commitment; and providing complex opportunities for action (challenge). Studies by Lubart and colleagues found that families with flexible rules have children with greater creativity than families with rigid rules, regardless of socioeconomic level (Lubart & Lautry, 1998; Lubart, Mouchiroud, Tordjman, & Zenasni, 2003).

Singer and Singer (1990) followed preschoolers and did home visits for an in-depth study of parents and home environment. They reported that imaginative children had parents who were more resourceful, adventuresome, and creative based on self-descriptions. They also used child-rearing that used reasoning instead of physical discipline, had clear rules and orderly routines, and had more sitting-down time and reading time with their children.

Humor has also emerged as enhancing creativity. Milgram and Livne (2006) reviewed research by Ziv (1976), who found that a humorous atmosphere enhanced creativity in adolescents.

Obstacles to Creativity

Albert tackled the difficult question of why so many gifted and talented children do not evolve into adults who make major creative contributions. For example, these children might become adults who display much everyday creativity or "little-c" creativity, but not various degrees of "Big-C" creativity. Albert (1996) concluded that the use of defenses in childhood that distort reality interferes with creative development. He discussed the importance of being able to tolerate the gaps and tensions of problem identification necessary to creative work. He proposed that early ability to "create" transitional objects that helped with separation from others and to tolerate frustrations and challenges was important in developing the ability to work alone and autonomously so common in creative adults. Albert proposed that the use of defenses that result in distortion and repression interfered with creative potential and behavior. The use of these defenses does not help the child develop tolerance for negative affect and difficult memories, and it interferes with learning to use creative behaviors to help resolve problems.

Morrison and Morrison (2006) described how trauma such as loss of a parent or sibling can interfere with imagination and limit it to "compensatory themes that are repetitive attempts to understand and master the past" (p. 14). If this important difficult affect-laden content is repressed, then imagination can be restricted and, eventually, memory can be limited.

These ideas are similar to those of psychoanalytic theory, reviewed earlier, which state that the use of repression will interfere with creative ability. Freud's formulation was that repression of "dangerous" drive-laden material leads to more general intellectual restriction (1926/1959). Kris's (1952) concept of "regression in the service of the ego" postulated that creative individuals could regress or have access to a fluid, primitive, and affective mode of thinking (primary process) in a controlled fashion. A lack of repression should lead to greater flexibility in thinking. For a more contemporary cognitive-affective perspective, access to emotion-laden images and emotion broadens the associative process, important in creativity (Isen, Daubman, & Nowicki, 1987). There is strong research evidence supporting this hypothesis in children and adults (see Russ 1993; Russ & Schafer, 2006). In children the expression of primary process (affective images) on the Rorschach was related to divergent thinking (Russ & Grossman-McKee, 1990) and to ability to shift sets in problem solving (Russ, 1982). Affect expression in pretend-play narratives showed a relation to divergent thinking in preschoolers (Kaugars & Russ, in press) and elementary-school children (Russ & Grossman-McKee) and over a 4-year period (Russ, Robins, & Christiano, 1999). The ability to express affective themes appears to be cross-situational in that affect in play related to affect on the Rorschach (Russ & Grossman-McKee) and to affect in memory descriptions (Russ & Schafer). These theories and research are supportive of Albert's conceptualization that other processes "kick in" in adolescence or adulthood that determine whether or not creative potential is realized in an individual. How affect is dealt with is one variable. Perhaps what we might label the "affective style" of an individual is especially important. In a recent meta-analysis of mood-creativity research with children and adults, Baas, De Dreu, and Nijstad (2008) concluded that positive moods, especially those that are activating with approach motivation (happiness), are related to or facilitate creative thinking. Negative affect usually does not facilitate creativity, but the picture is complex. And, affect-laden memories or fantasies, where a mood state may not be aroused, could function in different ways than mood states (Russ, 2002).

Another important characteristic is passion for the work. Passion and the tendency to become absorbed in the task has been identified as crucial by many creativity researchers (Amabile, 1983; Csikszentmihalyi, 1990; Roe, 1952). To let this kind of pas-

sion in an area and a joy of learning develop in children is becoming increasingly difficult in our culture because of overscheduling and intense focus on academic content. Yet love of the task is necessary to help the individual tolerate all of the negative and frustrating components of the creative process necessary to make a major contribution. In order to deal with the frustrations of mastering the knowledge base, dealing with small and large failures, tolerating the tensions in the problem-solving process, one needs to have a love of the work. Children also must have time and opportunity to follow developing interests so they can fully develop their talents and abilities (Feinstein, 2006).

The lack of time to engage in pretend play is also an obstacle to developing creativity. Society continually minimizes the importance of free play. Over the past few decades, the amount of free play for a child has decreased (Hirsh-Pasek & Golinkoff, 2003; Hirsh-Pasek, Golonkoff, Berk, & Singer, 2009). The American Academy of Pediatrics (2006), in a clinical report, has expressed concern about the loss of child-driven play time owing to a hurried lifestyle and an increased focus on academics and enrichment activities. Parents are more apt to overschedule structured activities and enroll their children in academic-focused preschools to strengthen what the parents believe to be intellectual development (Hirsh-Pasek & Golinkoff). The decrease in unstructured play time has occurred throughout the world. Singer, Singer, D'Agnostillo, and Mallikarjumm (2007) conducted interviews with parents in a number of different countries. They found that children do not have enough opportunities to be involved in unstructured activities. Play deprivation is associated with depression and increased hostility in children (Hirsh-Pasek & Golinkoff). Also, if children are not given sufficient opportunities to play, they may not fully develop the resource of play that has been related to so many areas of adaptive functioning, including creativity (Russ, 2004). Tegano, Lookabaugh, May, and Burdette (1991) found an increase in constructive play when the structure was child-imposed, but when the teacher imposed structure, there was a significant decrease in constructive play. Less constructive, creative play indicates fewer opportunities to problem solve and generate their own ideas. Although the long-term effects of less play remain unknown, previous findings suggest they may be harmful (Hirsh-Pasek & Golinkoff).

However, even considering the shift in focus and opportunities to play, Elkind (2007) suggests that children maintain the same desire to play. Although there are fewer spaces and less designated areas of play, children continue to play games and create learning experiences where and when they can. They reinvent outdoor areas for make-believe games and change routine activities into games of finishing first or lasting the longest. Although it is difficult to generalize, it seems many children continue to foster their creativity and problem solving through play.

Recent findings by Russ and Dillon (2009) are consistent with Elkind's view that children desire to play and are resourceful in finding outlets. Russ and Dillon reviewed 13 studies from 1986 to 2008 with different school-based populations that used the same standardized play task, instructions, and scoring system (Affect in Play Scale, Russ 1993, 2004). The pretend play comprised a 5-minute task that was videotaped. Using cross-temporal meta-analysis, they found that the organization of the play narrative and amount of affect expression has remained stable over this 20-year period. Imagination in the play narrative significantly increased in recent years. These findings suggest that children are finding ways to develop abilities to express imagination and affective expression, even though there is less unstructured time available to them. Perhaps the complexities of contemporary culture are motivating the adaptation process that Piaget identified, to the benefit of creativity in children. Nevertheless, other processes important to creativity need to be supported as well. Children need time to immerse themselves in creative activities

and explore with no goal in sight. Unstructured time is necessary for the child to experience the pleasure of coming up with something creative.

Concluding Thoughts

Research suggests that children are able to be creative, in the sense that they are able to come up with novel ideas in the context of their age and abilities. Although there is general agreement about which processes and abilities are important for the development of creativity, fully understanding the development of each process and its role in creativity is a more complex task. The research is not conclusive as to precisely how creativity develops and what exactly is essential in fostering this development.

Evidence of creativity in children also occurs in the realm of play. From early on, children demonstrate their ability to pretend, use their imagination, express and manipulate affect, and problem solve through play. Improved play skills are associated with divergent thinking and creativity. Studies demonstrate that interventions are able to successfully improve play, which suggests that similar techniques may be helpful in the development of creativity.

Ultimately, many factors contribute to a child's creativity and the development of that creativity. Innate biological processes, personality factors, home life, and society are important in the successful development of creativity. Although the current trend seems to be that parents typically focus less on free play and that society places greater emphasis on involvement in structured activities, many children continue to demonstrate creative processes and find ways to utilize and advance these skills. Because of this more recent trend, there seems to be a greater need to understand and emphasize the importance of creativity, as well as the factors that foster or hinder its development. One important research question for the future is whether the field of the development of creativity should focus on developing techniques to directly facilitate creative processes or, rather, on identifying and developing the parenting and environmental conditions in which creativity can flourish. Perhaps creativity research needs to focus on both of these issues in the immediate future.

In the meantime, based on the research and scholarly literature, our prescription for developing creativity in children is the following:

1. Give children time to engage in pretend play.
2. Encourage exploration of different domains of activities so the child can find what they deeply enjoy and develop their talents and abilities.
3. Foster an environment in which a child feels safe and comfortable to express ideas that are unconventional.
4. Reinforce and enjoy acts of everyday creativity.
5. Encourage independence in problem solving, keeping in mind the principles of optimal challenge and frustration.
6. Encourage expression of feelings in verbal exchange, in pretend play, and in other media, so the child learns to feel comfortable with feelings and to integrate them into easily accessible memories.

Helping children develop a variety of processes involved in creativity during childhood will increase the probability that they will make genuine creative contributions as adults.

References

Adler, T. (1991, September). Support and challenge: Both key for smart kids. *APA Monitor*, 10–11.

Albert, R. (1996). Some reasons why childhood creativity often fails to make it past puberty into the real world. In M. Runco (Ed.), *Creativity from childhood through adulthood: The developmental issues* (pp. 43–56). San Francisco: Josey-Bass.

Amabile, T. (1983). *The social psychology of creativity*. New York: Springer-Veclay.

Antonietti, A., & Cerioli, L. (Eds.). (1996). *Creativi a scuola* [To be creative at school]. Milan: Franco Angeli.

Antonietti, A., & Cornoldi, C. (2006). Creativity in Italy. In J. Kaufman & R. Sternberg (Eds.), *The international handbook of creativity* (pp. 124–166). New York: Cambridge University Press.

Ashley, J., & Tomasello, M. (1998). Cooperative problem-solving and teaching in preschoolers. *Social Development, 7,* 143–163.

Baer, J. (1998). The case for domain specificity of creativity. *Creativity Research Journal, 11,* 173–177.

Barron, F., & Harrington, D. (1981). Creativity, intelligence, and personality. In M. Rosenzweig & L. Porter (Eds.), *Annual Review of Psychology* (Vol. 32, pp. 439–476). Palo Alto, CA: Annual Reviews.

Baas, M., De Dreu, C., & Nijstad, B. (2008) A meta-analysis of 25 years of mood-induction research: Hedonic tone, activation, or regulatory focus? *Psychological Bulletin, 34,* 779–806.

Belsky, J., & Most, J. (1981). From exploration to play: A cross-sectional study of infant free play behavior. *Developmental Psychology, 17,* 630–639.

Brownell, C. A., & Carriger, M. S. (1990). Changes in cooperation and self-other differentiation during the second year. *Child Development, 61,* 1164–1174.

Brownell, C. A., & Carriger, M. S. (1991). Collaborations among toddler peers: Individual contributions to social contexts. In L. B. Resnick, J. M. Levine, & S. D. Teasley (Eds.), *Perspectives on socially shared cognition* (pp. 365–383). Washington, DC: American Psychological Association.

Csikszentmihalyi, M. (1990). *Flow: The psychology of optimal experience*. Grand Rapids, MI: Harper & Row.

Dansky, J. (1980). Make-believe: A mediator of the relationship between play and associative fluency. *Child Development, 51,* 576–579.

Dansky, J. (1999). *Play*. In M. Runco & S. Pritzker (Eds.), *Encyclopedia of creativity* (pp. 393–408). San Diego: Academic Press.

Dietrich, A. (2004, December 11). The cognitive neuroscience of creativity. *Psychonomic Bulletin and Review*, pp. 1011–1026.

Drewes, A. (2006). Play-based interventions. *Journal of Early Childhood and Infant Psychology, 2,* 139–156.

Elkind, D. (2007). *The power of play: Learning what comes naturally*. New York: Da Capo Press.

Fein, G. (1987). Pretend Play: Creativity and consciousness. In P. Gorlitz & J. Wohlwill (Eds.), *Curiosity, imagination, and play* (pp. 281–304). Hillsdale, NJ: Erlbaum.

Feinstein, J. (2006). *The nature of creative development*. Stanford: Stanford University Press.

Fisher, E. (1992). The impact of play on development: A meta-analysis. *Play and Culture*, 5, 159–181.

Freud, S. (1958). The unconscious. In J. Strachey (Ed. & Trans.), *The standard edition of the complete psychological works of Sigmund Freud* (Vol. 14, pp. 159–215). London: Hogarth Press. (Original work published 1915)

Freud, S. (1959). Inhibition symptoms, and anxiety. In J. Strachey (Ed. & Trans.), *The standard edition of the complete psychological works of Sigmund Freud* (Vol. 20, pp. 87–172). London: Hogarth Press. (Original work published 1926)

Getzels, S., & Csikszentmihalyi, M. (1976). *The creative vision: A longitudinal study of problem finding in art*. New York: Wiley-Interscience.

Ginsburg, K. (2006). The importance of play in promoting healthy child development and maintaining strong parent–child bonds. Clinical Report. *American Academy of Pediatrics*.

Guignard, J., & Lubart, T. (2006). Is it reasonable to be creative? In J. Kaufman & J. Bare (Eds.), *Creativity and reason in cognitive development* (pp. 269–281). New York: Cambridge University Press.

Guilford, J. P. (1950). Creativity. *American Psychologist*, 5, 444–454.

Guilford, J. P. (1968). *Intelligence, creativity and their educational implications*. San Diego: Knapp.

Harrington, D. M., Block, J. W., & Block, J. (1987). Testing aspects of Carl Rogers' theory of creative environments: Childrearing antecedents of creative environments in young adolescents. *Journal of Personality and Social Psychology*, 52, 851–856.

Harris, P. (1989). *Children and emotion: The development of psychological understanding*. Cambridge: Blackwell.

Harris, P. (2000). *The work of the imagination*. Oxford, UK: Blackwell.

Hartmann, W., & Rollett, B. (1994). Play: Positive intervention in the elementary school curriculum. In J. Hellendoorn, R. van der Kooij, & B. Sutton-Smith (Eds.), *Play and intervention* (pp. 195–202). Albany: State University of New York Press.

Hellendoorn, V. (1994). Imaginative play training for severely retarded children. In J. Hellendoorn, R. van der Kooij, & B. Sutton-Smith (Eds.), *Play and intervention* (pp. 113–122). Albany: State University of New York Press.

Hirsh-Pasek, K., & Golinkoff, R. M. (2003). *Einstein never used flashcards: How our children really learn – and why they need to play more and memorize less* (Rev. ed.). Pennsylvania: Rodale.

Hirsh-Pasek, K., Golinkoff, R., Berk, L., & Singer, D. (2009). *A mandate for playful learning*. Oxford: Oxford University press.

Holt, R. (1977) A method for assessing primary process manifestations and their control in Rorschach responses. In M. Rickers-Ovsiankina (Ed.), *Rorschach psychology* (pp. 375–420). New York: Kreiger.

Isen, A., Daubman, K., & Nowicki, G. (1987). Positive affect facilitates creative problem solving. *Journal of Personality and Social Psychology*, 52, 1122–1131.

Kaugers, A., & Russ, S. (2009). Assessing preschool children's pretend play: Preliminary validation of the Affect on Play Scale-preschool version. *Early Education and Development*, 20, 733–755.

Keegan, R. (1996). Creativity from childhood to adulthood: A difference in degree not of kind. In M. Runco (Ed.), *Creativity from childhood to adulthood: The developmental issues* (pp. 57–66). San Francisco: Josey-Bass.

Kim, Y. T., Lombardino, L. J., Rothman, H., & Vinson, B. (1989). Effects of symbolic play intervention with children who have mental retardation. *Mental Retardation*, 27, 159–165.

Kohlberg, L. (1987). The development of moral judgment and moral action. In L. Kohlberg (Ed.), *Child psychology and childhood education. A cognitive developmental view*. New York: Longman.

Kris, E. (1952). *Psychoanalytic explorations in art*. New York: International Universities Press.

Lieberman, J. N. (1977). *Playfulness: Its relationship to imagination and creativity*. New York: Academic Press.

Lubart, T., & Guignard, J. (2004). The generality-specificity of creativity: A multivariate approach. In R. Sternberg, E. Grigorenko, & J. Singer (Eds.), *Creativity: From potential to realization* (pp. 43–56). Washington, DC: APA Books.

Lubart, T., & Lautrey, J. (1996). *Development of creativity in 9- to 10-year old children*. Paper presented at the Growing Mind Congress, Geneva, Switzerland .

Lubart, T., & Lautrey, J. (1998, July). *Family environment and creativity*. Paper presented at the 15th biennial meetings of the International Society for the Study of Behavioral Development, Berne, Switzerland.

Lubart, T., Mouchiroud, C., Tordjman, S., & Zenasni, F. (2003). *Psychologie de la creativite* [Psychology of creativity]. Paris: Colin.

Martindale, C. (1981) *Cognition and consciousness*. Homewood, Il.: Dorsey Press.

McCrae, R. R., & Costa, P. T. (1987). Validation of the five model across instruments and observers. *Journal of Personality and Social Psychology*, 52, 81–90.

McCune, L., Dipane, D., Fireoved, R., & Fleck, M. (1994). Play: A context for mutual regulation within mother-child interaction. In A. Slade & D. Palmer (Eds.), *Children at play: Clinical and developmental approaches to meaning and representation* (pp. 148–166). New York: Oxford University Press.

Milgram, R., & Livne, N. (2006). Research on creativity in Israel: A chronicle of theoretical and empirical development. In J. Kaufman & R. Sternberg (Eds.), *The international handbook of creativity* (pp. 307–336). New York: Cambridge University Press.

Moore, M., & Russ, S. (2008). Follow-up of pretend play intervention: Effects on play, creativity, and emotional processes in children. *Creativity Research Journal*, 20, 427–436.

Morrison, D., & Morrison, S. (2006) *Memories of loss and dreams of perfection*. Amityville: Baywood Publishing.

Pellegrini, A. (1992). Rough and tumble play and social problem solving flexibility. *Creativity Research Journal*, 5, 13–26.

Pepler, D., & Ross, H.S (1981). The effects of play on convergent and divergent problem solving. *Child Development*, 52, 1202–1210.

Piaget, J. (1932). *The moral judgement of the child*. London: Routledge & Keegan Paul.

Piaget, J. (1951). *Principal factors determining intellectual evolution from childhood to adult life*. New York: Columbia University Press.

Piaget, J. (1962). *Play, dreams, and imagination in childhood*. New York: W.W. Norton.

Plucker, J., & Beghetto, R. (2004). Why creativity is domain general, why it looks domain specific, and why the distinction does not matter.

In R. Sternberg, E. Grigorenko, & J. Singer (Eds.), *Creativity: From potential to realization* (pp.153–167). Washington, DC: APA Books.

Rathunde, K., & Csikszentmihalyi, M. (1991). Adolescent happiness and family interaction. In K. Pillemer & K. McCartney (Eds.), *Parent-child relations throughout life* (pp. 143–162). Hillsdale, NJ: Erlbaum.

Reuter, M., Panksepp, J., Schnabel, N., Kellerhoff, P., Kempel, P., & Henning, J. (2005). Personality and biological markers of creativity *European Journal of Personality*, 19, 83–95.

Richards, R. (1999) Everyday creativity. In M. Runco & S. Pritzker (Eds.), *Encyclopedia of creativity* (Vol. 1, pp. 683–687). San Diego: Academic Press.

Richards, R. (2001). Creativity and the schizophrenia spectrum: More and more interesting. *Creativity Research Journal*, 13, 111–132.

Roe, A. (1952). A psychologist examines 64 eminent scientists. *Scientific American*, 187, 21–25.

Rogers, C. (1954). Towards a theory of creativity. *E.T.C. A Review of General Semantics*, 16, 249–263.

Runco, M. A. (1991). *Divergent thinking*. Norwood, NJ: Ablex.

Runco, M. (1996). Personal creativity: Definition and developmental issues. In M. Runco (Ed.), *Creativity from childhood through adulthood: The developmental issues* (pp. 3–30). San Francisco: Jossey-Bass.

Runco, M. (1999a). Developmental trends in creative abilities and potentials. In M. Runco & S. Pritzker (Eds.), *Encyclopedia of creativity* (pp. 537–540). San Diego: Academic Press.

Runco, M. (1999b). Tension, adaptability, and creativity. In S. Russ (Ed.), *Affect, creative experience, and psychological adjustment* (pp. 165–194). Philadelphia: Brunner/Mazel.

Runco, M. (2007). *Creativity*. San Diego: Elsevier.

Runco, M., & Albert, R. (1986). The threshold theory regarding creativity and intelligence. An empirical test with gifted and nongifted children. *Creative Child and Adult Quarterly*, 11, 212–218. The adapted version is in M. Runco (Ed.), *Divergent thinking* (pp. 165–172). Norwood, NJ: Ablex Publishing Corporation.

Runco, M., & Okuda, S. (1988). Problem discovery, divergent thinking, and the creative process. *Journal of Youth and Adolescence*, 17, 211–220. The adapted version is in M. Runco (Ed.), *Divergent thinking* (pp. 69–77). Norwood, NJ: Ablex.

Runco, M., & Pezdek, K. (1984). The effects of television and radio on children's creativity. *Human Communication Research*, 11, 109–120. The adapted version is in M. Runco (Ed.), *Divergent thinking* (pp. 31–40). Norwood, NJ: Ablex.

Russ, S. (1982). Sex differences in primary process thinking and flexibility in problem solving in children. *Journal of Personality Assessment*, 46, 569–577.

Russ, S. (1993). *Affect and creativity: The role of affect and play in the creative process*. Hillsdale, NJ: Erlbaum.

Russ, S. (2002). Gender differences in primary process thinking and creativity. In R. Bornstein & J. Masling (Eds.), *The psychodynamics of gender role* (pp. 53–80). Washington DC: APA Books.

Russ, S. (2004). *Play in child development and psychotherapy: Toward empirically supported practice*. Mahwah, NJ: Erlbaum.

Russ, S. (2009). Pretend play, emotional processes, and developing narratives. In J. Kaufman & S. Kaufman (Eds.), *The psychology of creative writing* (pp. 247–263). New York: Cambridge University Press.

Russ, S., & Dillon, J. (2009, March). *Changes in children's play processes over 20 years*. Paper presented at the Society for Personality Assessment. Chicago.

Russ, S., & Grossman-McKee, A. (1990). Affective expression in children's fantasy play, primary process thinking on the Rorschach, and divergent thinking. *Journal of Personality Assessment*, 54, 756–771.

Russ, S., Moore, M. E., & Pearson, B. L. (2007). *Effects of play intervention on play Skill and adaptive functioning: A pilot study*. Manuscript submitted for publication.

Russ, S., Robins, D., & Christiano, B. (1999). Pretend play: Longitudinal prediction of creativity and affect in fantasy in children. *Creativity Research Journal*, 12, 129–139.

Russ, S., & Schafer, E. (2006). Affect in fantasy play, emotion in memories, and divergent thinking. *Creativity Research Journal*, 18, 347–354.

Sawyer, P. K. (1997). *Pretend play as improvisation*. Mahwah, NJ: Erlbaum.

Siegler, R., Deloace, J., & Eisenberg, N. (2006) *How children develop*. New York: Worth.

Shmukler, D. (1984–1985). Structured vs. unstructured play training with economically disadvantaged preschoolers. *Imagination, Cognition, & Personality*, 4, 293–304.

Singer, D., & Revenson, T. (1996). *A Piaget primer*. New York: Plume Books.

Singer, D. G., & Singer, J. L. (1990). *The house of make-believe: Children's play and the developing imagination*. Cambridge, MA: Harvard University Press.

Singer, J., Singer, D., D'Agostino, N., & Mallikarjun, R. (2007). *Giving our children the right to be children: A mother's perspective: A global report*. New York: Strategy One.

Smilansky, S. (1968). *The effects of sociodramatic play on disadvantaged preschool children*. New York: Wiley.

Smith, P. (1988). Children's play and its role in early development; a re-evaluation of the "play ethos." In A. Pellegrini (Ed.), *Psychological bases for early education* (pp. 207–226). Chichester, UK: Wiley.

Smith, P. (1994). Play training: An overview. In J. Hellendoorn, R. van der Kooij, & B. Sutton-Smith (Eds.), *Play and intervention* (pp. 185–192). Albany: State University New York Press.

Smith, P. K., & Dutton, S. (1979). Play and training in direct and innovative problem solving. *Child Development*, 50, 830–836.

Smolucha, F. (1992). A reconstruction of Vygotsky's theory of creativity. *Creativity Research Journal*, 5, 49–67.

Sternberg, R. (1988). A three-facet model of creativity. In R. Sternberg (Ed.) *The nature of creativity* (pp. 125–147). Cambridge: Cambridge University press.

Sternberg, R. J., Kaufman, J. C., & Pretz, J. E. (2002). *The creativity conundrum*. New York: Psychology Press.

Sylva, K., Bruner, J., & Genova, P. (1976). The role of play in the problem solving of children 3–5 years old. In J. Bruner, A. Jolly, & K. Sylva (Eds.), *Play – Its role in evolution and development*. New York: Penguin Books.

Tegano, D., Lookabaugh, S., May, G., & Burdette, M. (1991). Constructive play and problem-solving: The role of structure and time in the classroom. *Early Child Development and Care*, 68, 27–35.

Torrance, E. P. (1968). A longitudinal examination of the fourth-grade slump in creativity. *Gifted Child Quarterly*, 5, 195–199.

Torrance, E. P., Ball, E. O., & Safter, H. T. (1992). *Torrance Tests of Creative Thinking: Streamlined score guide Figural A and B*. Bensenville, IL: Scholastic Testing Service.

Tudge, J., & Rogoff, B. (1989). Peer influences on cognitive development: Piagetian and Vygotskian perspectives. In M. Bornstein &

J. Bruner (Eds.), *Interaction in human development* (pp. 17–40). Hillsdale, NJ: Erlbaum.

Udwin, O. (1983). Imaginative play training as an intervention method with institutionalized preschool children. *British Journal of Educational Psychology*, 53, 32–39.

Vandenberg, B. (1980). Play, problem-solving, and creativity. *New Directions for Child Development*, 9, 49–68.

Vygotsky, L. S. (1967). *Imagination and creativity in childhood*. Moscow: Prosvescheniye. (Original work published in 1930)

Vygotsky, L. S. (1967). Play and its role in the mental development of the child. *Soviet Psychology*, 5, 6–18.

Vygotsky, L. (1978). Interaction between learning and development. In M. Cole (Ed.), *Mind in society* (pp. 79–91). Cambridge, MA: Harvard University Press.

Wakefield, J. (1985). Towards creativity: Problem finding in a divergent-thinking exercise. *Child Study Journal*, 15, 265–270.

Wallach, M., & Kogan, M. (1965). *Modes of thinking in young children: A study of the creativity-intelligence distinction*. New York: Holt, Rinehart, & Winston.

Waller, N. G., Bouchard, T. J., Lykkens, D. T., Tellegen, A., & Blacker, D. M. (1993). Creativity, heritability, familiality: Which word does not belong? *Psychological Inquiry*, 4, 235–237.

Weisberg, R. (1988). Problem solving and creativity. In R. Sternberg (Ed.), *The nature of creativity* (pp. 148–176). Cambridge: Cambridge University Press.

Wellman, H. M. (1990). *Children's theories of mind*. Cambridge, MA: MIT Press.

Wyver, S. R., & Spence, S. H. (1999). Play and divergent problem solving: Evidence supporting a reciprocal relationship. *Early Education and Development*, 10, 419–444.

Ziv, A. (1976). Facilitating effects of humor on creativity. *Journal of Educational Psychology*, 68, 318–322.

CHAPTER 13

Educational Creativity

Jeffrey K. Smith and Lisa F. Smith

A veteran teacher recently told us of a student with learning challenges who was working on a multiplication problem. The problem was 5 × 13. The student kept looking at the clock, and then turned and said, "The answer is 65." The teacher congratulated the student on a correct answer and then inquired as to why he seemed to turn to the clock for help. He replied, "Well, I've been learning how to tell time and I know that the 12 means 60 minutes, 5 for each number. So 13 would be one more 5 and that would be 65."

In a workshop discussion on how to encourage participation and engagement of students in classroom activities, a biology teacher offered this tip: "I use 'biology bucks.' Here's how it works. First, I make a bunch of copies of dollar bills, but with my picture instead of Washington's. I keep them in my drawer. When I get a particularly good contribution in class, I say, 'That's worth a biology buck!' I take a dollar out of the drawer, sign it, and give it to the student. Then, if a student gets an 88 on a test, which is a B+ for me, she can turn in two biology bucks, and her grade

goes up to 90, which is an A-. Students learn quickly how to make good contributions, and I don't have to do any record-keeping."

We were once engaged in a scaffolding discussion with the most "scientific" of our children on a science fair project. He was trying to invent a device that would rapidly warm the interior of an automobile in February before the car heater finally warmed the car up. The best idea he could generate was to turn the inside of the car into a large microwave oven and then mist it with water, and turn on the microwave capability. This seemed somewhat impractical and potentially lethal. Then our "literary" child came along and said, "Why don't you just change the plug on a hair dryer so that it will fit into that cigarette lighter thing? Wouldn't that work?"

What these vignettes have in common is that they might be examples of educational creativity. Then again, they might not be. But they do represent the three basic aspects of creativity that researchers see as generally comprising the overlap between creativity and education. Respectively, they are

- The use of creativity (or insight) to solve problems in other subject areas;
- Creative ideas for teaching; and,
- Teaching for or attempting to enhance the creativity of children.

This chapter looks at creativity from the perspective of those involved with education and at education from the perspective of those involved in creativity research. Our goal is to examine several critical issues in creativity research and in the realities of schooling to see where the relationship between the two can be made stronger. That is, how can creativity become a more central aspect of the educational enterprise? The relationship between education and creativity would seem to be a natural one, almost obvious in its degree of "fit." But, to a great extent, this appears not to be the case (Makel, 2009; Plucker, Beghetto, & Dow, 2004). There is something of an on-again, off-again relationship between creativity and education. Creativity is, and historically has been, important in areas such as early childhood education and gifted and talented education. It has been important at certain times in education generally, most notably the 1960s and 1970s, and there is evidence that creativity is more influential in education in countries other than the United States, but fundamentally, the influence of creativity on education has been intermittent and irregular (Feldman & Benjamin, 2006). As will be seen, there are a number of current efforts to rectify the situation, but creativity simply is not at the forefront of the educational debate today.

From the perspective of educators, creativity is often viewed not as an end, but as a means toward ends such as improving problem-solving ability, engendering motivation, and developing self-regulatory abilities. Although the idea of creativity is attractive to educators, there is pitfall as well as promise. From an educational perspective, creativity is a mixed blessing. At the same time that it can promote the development of curiosity, ingenuity, and problem-solving skills, it holds the potential to disrupt classroom processes, such as the orderly progression of the class through the curriculum or the orderly working of the class through the school day. Educators are attracted to creativity, but they sometimes feel that they should not get too close, so as not to end up as a moth to a flame.

Turning to look at the issue from the perspective of creativity researchers, a corollary can be found. Scholars interested in the contributions of exceptional individuals ("Big-C" in creativity terminology) (e.g., Simonton, 1994; Weisberg, 1993) might well be hard-pressed to see the relevance of their work for a group of 10-year-olds learning to identify leaves in their neighborhood, or how to multiply fractions. Even those who look at creativity in everyday life ("little-c") (e.g., Richards, 2007) do not readily offer educational applications. This is not to say that this kind of work never happens, and it certainly is not meant to imply that creativity researchers consider themselves "above" such scholarly endeavors. It is rather to say that there are inherent difficulties here. These difficulties are theoretical as well as practical. Take, for instance, the example above of the teacher who uses biology bucks. Is that an example of creativity in education (in particular, creativity in teaching)? Well, it might seem to be the first time that teacher did it, but what about the tenth year he used it? Is it still creative? What about another teacher who uses the same idea, or adapts it to her own classroom? Or the student who used the clock to solve a math problem; was that being creative or simply having an insight? In addition to conceptual/theoretical issues, as any educational psychologist can attest to, conducting research in schools brings with it a host of challenges (random assignment – of children!?); doing research in an area such as creativity brings with it additional challenges such as "whose creativity?" and "creativity to what end?"

Thus, creativity and education sit and look at one another from a distance, much like the boys and girls at the seventh-grade dance, each one knowing that a foray across the gym floor might bring great rewards but is fraught with peril. Occasionally, a brave soul chooses to venture forth, all too often not the individual the rest of the group would have chosen as an emissary. In recent years, the addition to the educational enterprise of the ubiquitous No Child Left Behind has sucked all of the air out of the ruminations of educators who might embrace creativity in the United States. We live for the annual mandated state assessments. Education and creativity have enough trouble getting together in the best of times, and these are not the best of times. This seems to us to be a particularly distressing state of affairs, as the creativity research community has never been more vibrant and productive. In this chapter, we want to look at the issues involved and present some ideas that may lead to a realization of the incredible potential that creativity holds for education.

This chapter contains five sections. The first section takes a brief look at the relationship of creativity research and educational concerns over time. The second section examines the relationship between creativity and education today. In this section, we discuss the findings of an informal set of interviews with a sample of teachers and administrators concerning their views on creativity in schooling. The third section reviews a number of models of creativity in the literature that seem to us to have particular utility for educational practice. The fourth section brings those models to educational practice to see what some of the consequences might be. In this section, we highlight what we feel are the key issues that need to be appreciated by both creativity researchers and educators in order for the dialogue between them to be productive. The fifth section presents aspects of a research agenda for creativity research that we believe will help promote creativity to a more prominent role in educational practice. We present some ideas on how the current scholarship in creativity might be productively brought to the field of education in an effort to see teachers teaching creatively, teaching creativity, and teaching for creativity in learning.

A Very Brief History of the Relationship between Creativity and Education

Although the issue of creativity and considerations of it in various guises (ingenuity, inventiveness, etc.) can be seen throughout history, most creativity theorists use the 1950 Presidential Address of J. P. Guilford to the American Psychological Association as the beginning of modern creativity research (e.g., Fasko, 2001–2002; Sternberg, 2006). In this address, Guilford called on psychologists to investigate the issues of creativity, one of which, he argued, was the relationship between creativity and learning. Guilford is probably best known today for his Structure of Intellect model (Guilford, 1985), but he also contributed much to our understanding of creativity, in particular with regard to giftedness and the measurement of creativity (Guilford, 1975). Also interested in the assessment of creativity, but taking a somewhat different approach to the questions of creativity, Paul Torrance looked at creative teaching and creative thinking in children (Torrance, 1972, 1981). Torrance (1966) also developed the Torrance Tests of Creative Thinking, which still dominate approaches to creativity testing in the United States. Together, Guilford and Torrance can rightly be considered the pioneers of modern creativity theory and research.

Feldman and Benjamin (2006) provided an excellent discussion of the history of the relationship between creativity and education in the United States. They argued that at various points in time and in various areas within education, creativity has played a more or less prominent role. As Feldman and Benjamin point out, the importance of creativity in early childhood education has been a paramount consideration among educators since the influential work of Pestalozzi in Switzerland, Froebel in Germany, and Peabody in the United States, albeit some of those approaches seem only marginally creative by modern standards. And in the 1960s and 1970s, the open education movement and like-minded endeavours (Duckworth, 1972; Silberman, 1973) were influential, even if creativity might not have been the primary goal of this work. But, Feldman and Benjamin argued, " . . . creativity researchers (with rare exceptions) have neglected educational aims and means" (p. 320). We feel that may be something of an overstatement, and we think the blame for a lack of impact on education of creativity research should be shared between creativity researchers and educators. The 1980s brought a back-to-basics mentality to education, and in America, at least, No Child Left Behind pushed most educational activities that did not lead directly to gains in literacy and numeracy out of the curriculum. Creativity may be undergoing a renaissance of importance in education globally, and in particular in the United Kingdom (Craft, 2005), but it is difficult at this point to separate out hard evidence of such a renaissance from calls that it really needs to be, or ought to be, happening (e.g., Florida, 2002, 2005).

Although we agree that the impact of creativity research on education has not been as strong as it might be, it is clear that there has been substantial work since Guilford's call. In addition to the work of Guilford and Torrance, a number of scholars have diligently promoted the potential of a stronger presence of creativity in education, most notably Getzels and Jackson (1962), Duckworth (1972), Davis (1982), Amabile (1986), Runco (1992), Renzulli (1992), and Sternberg (2003). (Note that only a single, exemplary citation is listed for each of these scholars; all have published many more on the intersection of creativity and issues that bear on education.) Furthermore, even in the face of impediments to progress such as No Child Left Behind, we see today a number of very promising efforts to bring creativity to classrooms. Some of these can be seen in the chapter by Beghetto in this volume. But

there is more work to be done and there are obstacles to overcome. We turn now to looking at the issues of creativity from the perspective of educators.

Creativity at the Chalkface

Our New Zealand "Kiwi" colleagues who are practicing teachers define themselves as working at the "chalkface" (a U.K. term that is an allusion to the hardscrabble life of miners working at the "coalface"). How do workers at the chalkface view creativity? Although the relationship between creativity and educational practice is a tenuous one, that does not mean that creativity is not highly valued by teachers. Indeed, it is a concept that receives wide attention in educational circles. It simply seems to be the case that it does not make it into the classroom with any great frequency or consistency. Thus, it is not the case that educators look on creativity in the way that the townsfolk looked at the Tsar in the prayer of the Jewish community in *Fiddler on the Roof*: "God bless and keep the Tsar far from our village." Educators *do* like creativity. They particularly like aspects of creativity found in certain settings, such as insight in problem solving, the generation of a wide variety of ideas when thinking of a topic for a writing assignment, or a novel connection between what is being learned now and what was learned previously. But, there are aspects to creativity that don't fit well with how classrooms and schools typically operate. And they operate in that fashion not because teachers are naturally repressive or don't have the best interests of children at heart. It has much more to do with organizing and managing the activities of 25 children for 6 hours, keeping them physically and emotionally intact, and making sure that they learn how to read and do mathematics all at the same time. If you asked if and when teachers might really appreciate a truly creative idea, they might ruefully say, "That would be wonderful, but could you hold it off until Thursday after lunch?"

If we are to look at creativity in education today, it might be useful to start with a shared understanding of what we mean by creativity. We think that one of the critical points of miscommunication between researchers and the educational community has to do with what creativity means to each group. Kaufman and Sternberg (2007) defined creative ideas as consisting of three components: "First, those ideas must represent something different, new, or innovative. Second, they need to be of high quality. Third, creative ideas must also be appropriate to the task at hand. Thus, a creative response to a problem is new, good, and relevant" (p. 55). Versions of this definition are probably the most widely used in creativity research today, but they are not the only ones that have been offered over the years. Various definitions have involved ideational fluency and divergent thinking. Atchley, Keeney, and Burgess (1999) discussed the ability to develop remote ideational associations, and Edwards (2001) included the willingness to explore the unknown. Plucker, Beghetto, and Dow (2004) developed an entire table of varying definitions that include how people approach problems.

How do practicing educators define creativity? In preparing to work on this chapter, we interviewed (in small groups) 48 teachers and principals in a training seminar as to what kinds of school and classroom activities they engage in that are creative. We apologize for the informality and lack of rigor in sampling of our approach; still, the results are revealing. We basically found four types of responses.

First, a number of teachers mentioned specific programs that they employ. The two most common responses in this category are the Multiple Intelligences approach of Howard Gardner (1983, 1993), and the Thinking Hats approach of Edward de Bono (1992). Other responses that might be categorized here include, perhaps somewhat strangely, Bloom's taxonomy of educational objectives (Bloom, 1956) and modern variants of it, and Csikszentmihalyi's (1996)

concept of flow. The reader familiar with the scholarship on creativity may be a bit perplexed by what "gets counted" as creativity here. Certainly de Bono's approach involving lateral thinking and approaching an issue or problem from different perspectives (the different hats) would be categorized as creativity in education. But what about Gardener's Multiple Intelligence theory? Is it really fundamentally about creativity? Or Bloom's taxonomy? Does that not seem to stretch the definition of creativity to the breaking point?

The second response from teachers with regard to creativity has to do with specific techniques that they use to encourage students to be creative. Brainstorming, mind maps, thinking outside the box, and collaborative activities are the most frequently mentioned here. Also in this category would be specific activities that are designed to promote creativity such as science fairs, art activities, poetry, and story writing. This response is a kind of, "Yes, we often do creative things in class." It is creativity qua creativity – a kind of "Tuesday, 11:00 – 11:50: Creativity" approach to creativity.

The third response concerns being open to students' comments and ideas as a part of regular teaching. Teachers see being open to and using unexpected student responses to questions as being responsive to student creativity. Thus, this view of creativity in the classroom is fundamentally a reactive approach to creativity as opposed to a proactive approach.

The fourth response has to do with creative teaching. The responses here are particularly interesting. Teachers by nature are scavengers and hoarders of ideas – particularly ideas that might be useful in their teaching. To them, creative ideas for teaching are ones *they don't currently know about that they think might be useful for them*. They fundamentally do not care where they came from. When they teach in a fashion that is new and different for them, they are being creative in their teaching. As one teacher succinctly put it: "Everything was creative once."

What do these responses mean? Can we put them together to get a working definition of how practicing educators define, or at least perceive, creativity? First, it is clear that teachers have a rather expansive notion of what creativity is (and thus a very simple definition of the term). To understand that expansiveness, it must be remembered that they practice their craft in a highly routinized set of circumstances. Their work schedule rarely varies. The curriculum is often highly prescribed, and they interact with the same cast of characters each day. It also has to be recognized that they have enormous responsibilities, and that among these responsibilities, enhancing, promoting, or valuing creativity are not typically high on the list, at least, not higher in priority than ensuring that the curriculum is taught and learned. In fact the phrase, "He is a very creative teacher" might well be a left-handed compliment. And describing a student as "highly creative" may be code for "hard to handle." At the elementary level, teachers are responsible for teaching children how to read, do long division, spell (and not creatively), write, get along with others, learn about science, and so on. Most of what they work on with children would fall within the three lowest levels of Bloom's taxonomy (knowledge, comprehension, application). Their approaches to classroom activities are typically drawn from a repertoire of the tried and true. This is not because they don't value innovation, but because they feel a great sense of responsibility for their charges and will not blithely venture into instructional terra incognita that might not be as effective as what is familiar. At the high school level, there is the additional press of specifications for what courses should be covering. Standards-based instruction, which is universally popular in American education, is usually quite specific in terms of what should be taught (at all levels of schooling).

Thus, when the issue of creativity is broached, teachers think of those things that exist outside of the realm of the ordinary. Creative is *different*. It is seductive. Creative is high heels as opposed to sensible shoes – they look great, but do they really have a place in the classroom? The idea of *different* often substitutes for the idea of *novelty* in teacher definitions of creativity. It is very much context dependent. If a student comes up with an idea that is new to the student, then it is creative. Like a recently purchased used car, "new to me" often will suffice for creative in an educational context. This would apply to how teachers view teaching as well. Trying a new teaching idea, even if it is one that was just presented at a professional development workshop, is being creative to many, perhaps most, teachers. Thus, "different" substitutes for "novel" and "new to me" substitutes for "new" in the educational definition of creativity. For Kaufman and Sternberg (2007), the second criterion was that ideas be of high quality, or simply, "good." That isn't really necessary for educators. To be certain, a good creative idea is better than a bad creative idea, but for most teachers, both are creative. "Outside of the box" is fine even if it comes from "out of left field." Teachers find value in most student ideas, and they often find great value in things that don't work. The places where students' ideas go astray are often the most informative to teachers about how the students are thinking about the problem or content under consideration. They are windows to the thinking processes of the students. Thus a "good" bad idea is rich with interpretive and ultimately instructional potential. Furthermore, a bad idea is one step further along the creative path than no idea at all. Teachers are in the business of starting wherever a child is and working from there. If a teacher can help a child see why an idea isn't a good one, then the child has the potential to see that the next idea might be good. Thus, the bad idea is father to the good one.

Kaufman and Sternberg's (2007) third component is relevance. The idea has to be relevant to the situation under consideration. Most educators would agree. An idea doesn't have to actually work to be creative, and it only has to be new to the person involved; but, it does have to be pertinent to the task at hand. None of this is meant as a critique of the Kaufman and Sternberg definition; it is perfectly reasonable and widely accepted. The point here is to argue that when teachers envision creativity, they are looking at a slightly different beast.

To sum up – and probably to a degree unfairly – an educational perspective on creativity is that it is a double-edged sword. It may well be good in some situations, but not in others. This might be attributable to the idea that teachers don't usually consider "good" to be a criterion for "creative." To be creative, something has to be appropriate to the situation (relevant) and new or different to that person. In our discussions with teachers, we basically came up with four different notions of creativity in education. For some teachers, creative is actually the *consolation prize*. Creative is the label on the bin of ideas that sounded great but didn't pan out. "It was a creative idea, but it didn't work out." For other teachers, creativity is primarily a *means to an end*. Creative thinking can be a vehicle for improving reading, math, or science skills. Although creativity may be worthwhile, it neither takes precedence nor is valued over learning how to read. So if it is part of the process of achieving literacy or numeracy, then it is worthwhile.

Teaching for creativity because creativity is valued exists in pockets within education, most notably in early childhood education, gifted and talented education, and in the arts curricula. *Creative teaching*, in the minds of teachers, has to do with trying something new and different to them. Creative teaching ideas are often approached with some trepidation, as they typically mean giving up or altering, at least for a while, the approach that the teacher currently has the most faith in with regard to efficacy (think of your dentist saying, "I'd like to try a really creative way of pulling that molar.")

If there are natural impediments to creativity in teaching and learning, there are equally great areas of promise. To investigate these, we look at several theoretical approaches to creativity research popular today that hold potential for translation to educational practice.

Current Thinking in Creativity

The early work of Guilford (1950, 1975) and Torrance (1966, 1972) led, in part, to what is often referred to as the psychometric approach to creativity. That is, because both Guilford and Torrance developed approaches to measuring creativity or creative potential, those measures in essence became operational definitions of the theories that they represented. Thus, the concepts of ideational *fluency* (how many ideas could be generated from a prompt), *flexibility* (how many distinct categories of thinking these ideas represented), and *originality* (how original or novel these ideas were) became a kind of working definition for researchers in the field. Note that what Guilford and Torrance have are measures of characteristics or traits of individuals or persons. People have more of the characteristics of creativity, or less of them. Other approaches (e.g., Amabile, 1979, 1996) took different perspectives on the issue of creativity measurement but operated within the same general framework of looking at creativity from the perspective of how much of it persons have.

Contrast this with the approach of Kaufman and Sternberg (2007), who define the characteristics not of persons, but of the creative ideas, or products, that they generate (new, good, relevant). In a similar vein, Richards (2007), following Barron (1969), defined creative products as needing only two characteristics, *originality* and *meaningfulness to others*. Originality might be considered synonymous with new, and meaningful might incorporate both good and relevant, but meaningfulness *to others* connotes a social context that is not necessarily present in the Kaufman and Sternberg definition. Thus, the two characteristics proffered by Richards might be more involved than the three from Kaufman and Sternberg.

The issue is actually more complicated than simply wondering if we are talking about ideas, processes, or persons. Creativity researchers usually talk about "the four P's" of creativity: person, process, product, and press (Rhodes, 1961/1987, as cited in Runco, 2004). These four P's resonate well with the rhythms of classroom life. Persons are teachers and children in education; processes are classroom instructional processes, as well as the processes that children employ in going about addressing the tasks of school life and broadening their repertoire of knowledge and skills; products are the tangible evidences of student efforts: the tests, essays, posters, book reports, presentations, and homework that students produce; and press is the classroom (and home) environments in which student learning and growth takes place. The four P's are easily translatable to life in classrooms, teaching, and even the study of educational psychology. Using this conceptualization as a basis, we can examine some of the current thinking in creativity that might be particularly applicable to educational settings and concerns. It should be noted that there are many theories about creativity; they are examined in depth in other chapters in this volume. The purpose here is to select a few that appear to have particularly strong potential for applicability to educational issues.

Because several theories bear aspects in common, they are presented here in three clusters: person-oriented models, process-oriented models, and product-oriented models. In considering the classifications that we made for the models, it occurred to us that the originators/proponents of each model would probably object to its classification. That is because all of the models involve more than one of the processes, and to a degree, all of them. Our classification is based on where we see the model's evolution – what was the basis for the development of the model. For example, Guilford's (1985) Structure of Intellect model, which has a strong creativity component, is fundamentally talking about

the nature of individuals, or what they are like. The same is true with Sternberg's Successful Intelligence approach (Sternberg & Grigorenko, 2007). Even though Sternberg has used his model to develop approaches to teaching successful intelligence, it is basically about what people are like and what they might be like with certain kinds of instructional interventions. On the other hand, Richards' (2007) approach "everyday creativity" is classified under product. Although Richards talks extensively about process and press, the model starts with a contrast of everyday acts of creativity as compared to Nobel Laureate type acts of creativity. These fundamentally are looking at the product of the creative process, big or small. So, with an apology to all of our colleagues for the classifications of their work, we take a brief look at some of the models we find most interesting to and appropriate for education. All of these models are discussed in more depth elsewhere (e.g., Runco, 2004), as well as in this volume, often by their originators (in particular, a review of them can be found in Kozbelt, Beghetto, and Runco, this volume), so we just mention them here and highlight aspects pertinent to our discussion. We encourage the reader to examine any interesting model in depth and hoped to have enticed the reader to do so.

Person-oriented Models

The first model we consider is Sternberg's (Sternberg & Grigorenko, 2007) Successful Intelligence model, which is rooted in the work of Guilford and Thurstone. Guilford's (1985) Structure of Intellect model is an extension of Thurstone's (1938) Primary Mental Abilities work, which had seven primary abilities, and in which creativity was not a player. Guilford's model, on the other hand, included ideational fluency and adaptive flexibility as key components, each of which is directly linked to the notion of creativity. Although it would be too far a stretch to argue that Sternberg's Successful Intelligence model was based on the Structure of Intellect model, Sternberg acknowledges the influence of Guilford on his thinking (Sternberg & Grigorenko, 2000–2001). The Successful Intelligence model focuses on three processing skills that are essential contributors to successful intelligence: analytical, creative, and practical (Sternberg, 1999). These processing skills allow for individuals to capitalize on their strengths, as well as to ameliorate and correct weaknesses. Individuals vary on their levels of these three processing skills, which is why we have classified this as a person-oriented approach. Sternberg argues that successful intelligence is intelligence that allows people to succeed in life on their own terms and in their own environment. With creativity as an essential component of the model, and with the nature of how that component relates to success explained theoretically and explored empirically (Sternberg, 2002; Sternberg & Grigorenko, 2004), creativity is not an add-on to other educational pursuits and goals; it is positioned as an essential element to the attainment of those goals.

This model is particularly attractive for education because it appeals to the "creativity as a means to an end" segment of the educational community. It shows how creativity is essential to succeed in life. At the same time, if creativity *is* essential to succeed in life, then it is important on its own terms. The logic here is quite appealing: creativity is an important component of problem solving and other important skills; therefore it is important in its own right.

Process-oriented Models

Process-oriented models focus on how creativity happens – what are the steps involved? Cropley and Cropley (2008) proposed a "phase" model based on very early work by Wallas (1926), which involves a series of seven phases of the creative process: preparation, activation, cogitation, illumination, verification, communication, and validation. These phases can be seen in other guises throughout the creativity literature. The authors relate each of these phases to the four P's of creativity (person, process,

product, press) to look at how the phases are realized in creativity. De Bono (1992), on the other hand, presented creativity in terms of what he calls lateral thinking and the use of "six thinking hats." His work is not widely cited in academic circles, but he is one of the most frequently mentioned names among teachers when you ask about engaging in creativity in the classroom. His writing focuses on a step-by-step approach to enhancing creative thinking and is rich with metaphors and examples. His clear explanations and strong advocacy of his techniques in his writings appeal to teachers. He provides encouragement and confidence to try something new in the classroom. It is difficult to find strong evidence of the efficacy of his approaches other than their popularity (which is certainly a form of evidence). Teachers are fundamentally engaged in process; that is what they do. Ultimately, for a model to be successful with teachers, it has to seriously address the process dimension of creativity.

Product-oriented Models

A number of models approach the notion of creativity by defining the nature of creative products. Simonton (1994) has studied the contributions of those whom we would consider to have made outstanding contributions to society. This type of creativity is often referred to as "Big-c" creativity. In contrast to this, some scholars talk about "little-c" creativity, meaning those contributions that are clearly useful and perhaps important, but not earth shaking. And then, more recently, Kaufman and Beghetto (2007, 2009) have put forward the notion of "mini-c" creativity, or creativity that exists at a personal level. They define mini-c creativity as the "novel and personally meaningful interpretation of experiences, actions, and events" (p. 3).

Mini-c shares a perspective with everyday creativity (Richards, 2007) and what Runco calls personal creativity (Runco, 1996, 2003). Runco (2003) argued that the processes that underlie creativity should be kept conceptually distinct from the expression of those processes and from their recognition of being creative from a social perspective. This also seems to us to be a particularly useful distinction in looking at creativity from an educational perspective. We find the Beghetto and Kaufman (2007) mini-c approach to creativity to be completely consistent with the perspective on creativity that we found in the teachers that we interviewed. Mini-c ideas basically form the seeds of creativity that teachers can nurture and grow into more readily recognizable forms of creativity.

Bringing Current Thinking to Education

The various approaches to creativity taken by the leading creativity researchers have different implications for educational creativity. Bringing powerful ideas from creativity research to educational practice requires, perhaps, a bit of an iterative process, working back and forth between creativity issues and issues from education. In our review of the creativity literature and examination of models of creativity, we found a number of ideas, large and small (some even "mini"), that seem to us to have great potential for having an impact on education. We review four of those ideas here.

We could begin with the student with learning challenges presented at the beginning of this chapter as a good example of the utility of the concept of personal creativity for education. The teacher who related that story to us was able to work with that spark of creativity in a number of ways. She was able to confirm and extend the ideas of the relationships between telling time and the multiplication tables. She was also able to take that wonderful leap from one setting to another, and work with the student on how to use that kind of thinking in other settings. And she was able to celebrate the student's success that was engendered by taking the problem into his own hands and thinking creatively about it. Finally, she was able to store away in her teacher's mental file on this student that such creativity might be a strength to build on in the future, and maybe even with other students.

But was this idea really creative according to the definitions of creativity? In this case, the idea was novel for the student, and practical and useful as well. But it was only so on a personal level. That is why we think that the idea of mini-c creativity (Beghetto & Kaufman, 2007) is so promising. It is what classroom teachers think creativity is in students, and furthermore, it is an idea they can work with. Teachers understand the generation of an idea that *might* be useful in a given context. To us, evaluating its utility, convincing others of its utility, or having it be useful in a social context puts too many requirements on what can be called creativity to be useful when talking about 7-year-olds. We think that these are useful components of a process that brings a creative idea into reality and realizes its potential, but we are happy to call an initial idea, new and different to the student, and relevant to the issue at hand, *creative*. Thus, mini-c, and its precursors in the product-oriented models described, provide a good starting point for bringing education and creativity together.

If creativity for education might be defined as mini-c, what about the other aspects of creativity that are discussed in the creativity literature? Well, we like those, but we see them as a part of a development and learning process. For example, the ability to judge the usefulness of a new idea is an extremely important skill. It is one that can be developed independently of the generation of new ideas (and usually is). It is quite different from concepts such as ideational fluency and flexibility. And it is different again from modifying and revising ideas to make them more useful. If creativity is defined, and consequently emphasized in schools, as the more limited generation of ideas in the context of a task, then it can be viewed as an integral component in developing problem-solving ability in children. Creativity can then be teamed with critical thinking and evaluative skills, social skills, and so on to produce the fuller and better-developed products of creativity. Mini-c facilitates the conversation between researchers and educators without either having to give up cherished notions of creativity or children.

A second area where the research on creativity seems to us to hold great potential for education is Sternberg's (2002) Successful Intelligence model. In this model, bringing creativity to bear on problems and issues is a central component of being successful in life. The argument that creativity is not a frill or an add-on but is essential to thinking and problem solving is an argument that educators are willing to listen to. Runco (2003) goes so far as to say, "The basic idea is that any thinking or problem solving that involves the construction of new meaning is creative. This may sound contrary to theories of creativity which emphasise originality and usefulness, but there is no incompatibility if you keep in mind that a personal construction will likely be original and useful to that one individual" (p. 318). Within this paradigm, consider the notion of "choosing creativity" (Sternberg, 2000). Choosing creativity is an incredibly powerful problem-solving technique. It is a choice we often make as adults when other approaches to solving a problem do not seem to be effective. This might occur individually or when working with a group of people. It occurs when we say, individually or collectively, "this isn't working, maybe I need to get creative here for a while." People we think of as being creative are, in part, people who turn to this option more readily and in more situations than others do. Students can be taught how to approach choosing creativity as part of problem solving both in terms of the process of generating ideas, and in terms of making the decision to utilize creativity as a natural part of their problem-solving repertoire.

Teaching to use creativity in learning and problem solving (see Makel, 2009; Renzulli, 1992) are really at the heart of the matter with regard to the issue of educational creativity. As mentioned above, many teachers would argue that creativity is something that is nice, but not nearly so critical as developing reading comprehension skills or the

ability to solve word problems in mathematics. But, if creativity can be shown to be a critical element in the development of those skills, then it will earn a seat at the table with most educators. Stemler, Elliott, Grigorenko, and Sternberg (2006) provided a practical approach to incorporating creativity along with practical and analytical skills in teaching. We believe that when creativity is seen as a central cognitive process in education, and not an ancillary one, then we will see it encouraged and valued.

Teaching creativity is one thing. Teaching creatively is a whole other kettle of fish. A third idea for consideration is teaching creatively. As discussed, educators tend to think of creativity, especially in their own teaching, as trying something new and different, even if the idea is taken entirely from the work of someone else. If one were to walk into a classroom in the middle of the school year and see it functioning effectively, with students happily and productively engaged in learning, one can be certain that that classroom did not spring up overnight. It reflects the efforts of the teacher, possibly based on several years of experience, to develop a positively functioning classroom, and it almost certainly took a lot of work in that given year. Teachers are often loath to engage in activities that might disrupt the smooth functioning and positive ethos that exists in a classroom in order to be creative in their teaching.

So what does that mean for the notion of creative teaching? Here, we might argue, we need to think again about what we mean by teaching creatively. We can return to the biology bucks teacher at the beginning of the chapter, and reconsider the notion of creative teaching. The first time he used biology bucks, we think it is clear that he was teaching creatively. But what about the second time? Or the tenth time? What about teachers who are always bringing new ideas to the classroom, but they are never their own ideas? Such teachers certainly seem to be creative, or at least to be teaching creatively. When a teacher brings ideas to the classroom in terms of how classroom learning is realized, or when he or she comes up with an alternative explanation, or a second or third metaphor or example, we need a definition of *creative teaching* that can accommodate such events. We need a conceptual breakthrough on the order of a "teaching mini-c" to accommodate this situation and bridge the education/creativity researcher gap.

Perhaps the notion of valuing creativity comes into play at this point; we thus segue into a fourth area of overlap that appears promising to us. Teachers who are looking for new and different ways to teach, and who encourage creativity in the classroom, who value creativity in their own work and in the work of their children, are teaching creatively. The concept of valuing creativity seems somewhat esoteric. But Sternberg has demonstrated how one might make valuing creativity concrete and consequential. The Rainbow Project (Sternberg, 2004; Sternberg & Rainbow Project Collaborators, 2006) uses measures of creative and practical intelligence, components of Successful Intelligence, to predict college performance from college admissions measures. This approach has been applied successfully to admissions decisions at Tufts University, where Sternberg is Dean of Arts and Sciences. But valuing creativity does not have to occur in so broad a context as college admissions. It can occur in a one-to-one setting, such as talking to a child about ideas for a science fair project. Such a conversation sends a simple, but clear message: "We're sitting down and talking about this, so it is important (even if your kid sister came up with a far better idea than either of us)."

Those are four ideas that struck us as we worked our way back and forth between the research literature and teachers at the chalk-face. What might happen if some of these powerful ideas can successfully be brought to education? If creativity is valued at a highly selective and prestigious university, then perhaps it can be important in an elementary school. If it can be shown to be an important component of successful problem solving, then perhaps it should be more prominent in the curriculum. If it can be

shown to be capable of being taught, encouraged, enhanced, and developed, then perhaps it will be taught, enhanced, encouraged, and developed. If it improves life in classrooms and the success of children, then teachers will embrace it. All of which brings us to a research agenda for educational creativity.

Educational Creativity: A Research Agenda

In working on this chapter, we reviewed a number of studies related to education and creativity. Some of them bemoaned the lack of activity in this area, whereas others earnestly addressed the issue. In thinking about education and creativity, we noticed that some of the work we read seems particularly exciting and useful to us. We see three basic areas where some good work has been done, and we believe a lot more can be done in order to bring creativity to what we probably all believe is its "rightful" place in education.

Defining Creativity and Bringing It to the Classroom and to Children

What does creativity look like in a 7-year-old? How is that different from what it looks like in a 15-year-old, or in an adult? Is creativity something that can be taught and learned, or is it more a developmental phenomenon that can be enhanced and encouraged, but perhaps not taught directly? Educators need to understand creativity in order to embrace it. Those who work with little children need to know the activities that help children become more creative (Eckoff & Urbach, 2008) – but so do teachers of high school calculus. This begins with a clear understanding of what creativity is, how we can find it in students, and how it develops over the life span. Plucker, Beghetto, and Dow (2004) fundamentally made this same argument; our approach is somewhat different from theirs, but this is the type of discussion, debate, and exploration that needs to occur within the field.

262 JEFFREY K. SMITH AND LISA F. SMITH

Establishing the Utility of Creativity as a Central Component of Academic Growth

If creativity is a central component of the educational enterprise, if it leads to developing abilities in problem solving, creative writing, interpreting data, and employing the scientific process, then it ought not be too difficult to demonstrate that empirically. Instructional interventions, both short term and long term, can be evaluated for effectiveness. There are extant models for this type of research (O'Hara & Sternberg, 2000–2001; Sternberg & Grigorenko, 2007; Sternberg, Torff, & Grigorenko, 1998). This sort of work is arduous, involving the cooperation of school districts and teachers, as well as careful observation of the implementation of programs, but the payoffs can be substantial.

Demonstrating the Effectiveness of Approaches to Use Creativity, to Enhance and Encourage It

What should teachers do in order to teach creativity, or to enhance it, or to combine it with other abilities to produce meaningful learning? What are the characteristics of highly effective approaches? This research is not asking, "Can this be done?" but rather "How can it *best* be done?" There is some good work in this area (e.g., Fasko, 2000–2001; Jeffrey & Craft, 2004; Murdoch & Keller-Mathers, 2008), but there needs to be much more. In the absence of solid research guiding practice, the programs that we will see in schools will be the ones that have been promoted most heavily through marketing. Additionally, it is important for us to understand how students can use creative approaches across subject areas, or to question if this is possible (e.g., Kaufman & Baer, 2004; Smith 2008). Are methods that are effective with younger students also effective with older students? Do approaches have to change as students become more sophisticated in their intellectual abilities? Our research efforts must address not only basic research questions, but also the practical questions that affect the lives of teachers and students.

Concluding Remarks

At some level, education is a zero sum game; there are only so many hours in the day, so many things that can be included in the curriculum, so many ways a teacher can expend energy and focus attention. Time spent on topic or skill X means time not spent on topic or skill Y. This brings us to the compelling simple question: *Would we value educational creativity if we knew how to do it?* Florida (2002, 2005) argued that it is fundamentally the road to the future for us as a society. Sternberg (2002) made the case that creativity is a key ingredient in having a successful life. Creativity lies behind the major accomplishments of humankind – as well as the ability to make the connection between a clock and a multiplication problem, or how to reward students for contributing to the workings of a biology class, or how to keep warm in the winter. It's better to be creative than to not be. It solves problems, makes life more interesting, and is useful in schools. Creativity and education are natural allies; as educational psychologists, we just need to make that simple reality more apparent.

References

Amabile, T. (1979). Effects of external evaluation on artistic creativity. *Journal of Personality and Social Psychology*, 37, 221–233.

Amabile, T. M. (1986). The personality of creativity. *Creative Living*, 15(3), 12–16.

Amabile, T. M. (1996). *Creativity in context: Update to the social psychology of creativity*. Boulder, CO: Westview.

Atchley, R. A., Keeney, M., & Burgess, C. (1999). Cerebral hemispheric mechanisms linking ambiguous word meaning retrieval and creativity. *Brain & Cognition*, 40, 479–499.

Barron, F. (1969). *Creative person and creative process*. New York: Holt, Rinehart, & Winston.

Beghetto, R. A., & Kaufman, J. C. (2007). Toward a broader conception of creativity: A case for "mini-c" creativity. *Psychology of Aesthetics, Creativity, and the Arts*, 1, 73–79.

Bloom, B. S. (1956). *Taxonomy of educational objectives, Handbook I: The cognitive domain*. New York: David McKay.

Craft, A. (2005). *Creativity in schools: Tensions and dilemmas*. London: Routledge.

Cropley, A., & Cropley, D. (2008). Resolving the paradoxes of creativity: An extended phase model. *Cambridge Journal of Education*, 38, 355–373.

Csikszentmihalyi, M. (1996). *Creativity: Flow and the psychology of discovery and invention*. New York: HarperCollins.

Davis, G. A. (1982). A model for teaching for creative development. *Roeper Review*, 5(2), 27–29.

de Bono, E. (1992). *Serious creativity: Using the power of lateral thinking to create new ideas*. Toronto: HarperCollins.

Duckworth, E. (1972). The having of wonderful ideas. *Harvard Educational Review*, 42, 217–231.

Eckoff, A., & Urbach, J. (2008). Understanding imaginative thinking during childhood: Sociocultural conceptions of creativity and imaginative thought. *Early Childhood Education Journal*, 36, 179–185.

Edwards, S. M. (2001). The technology paradox: Efficiency versus creativity. *Creativity Research Journal*, 13, 221–228.

Fasko, D. Jr., (2000–2001). Education and creativity. *Creativity Research Journal*, 13, 317–327.

Feldman, D. H., & Benjamin, A. C. (2006). Creativity and education: An American retrospective. *Cambridge Journal of Education*, 36, 319–336.

Florida, R. (2002). *The rise of the creative class: And how it's transforming work, leisure, community, and everyday life*. New York: Basic Books.

Florida, R. (2005). *The flight of the creative class: The new global competition for talent*. New York: HarperBusiness.

Gardner, H. (1983). *Frames of mind*. New York: Basic Books.

Gardner, H. (1993). *Creative minds*. New York: Basic Books.

Getzels, J., & Jackson, P. (1962). *Creativity and intelligence: Explorations with gifted students*. New York: Wiley.

Guilford, J. P. (1950). Creativity. *American Psychologist*, 5, 444–454.

Guilford, J. P. (1975). Varieties of creative giftedness, their measurement and development. *Gifted Child Quarterly*, 16, 175–184, 239–243.

Guilford, J. P. (1985). The structure-of-intellect model. In B. B. Wolman (Ed.), *Handbook of intelligence: Theories, measurements, and applications* (pp. 225–266). New York: Wiley.

Jeffrey, B., & Craft, A. (2004). Teaching creatively and teaching for creativity. *Educational Studies*, 30(1), 77–87.

Kaufman, J. C., & Baer, J. (2004). Sure, I'm creative – but not in mathematics: Self-reported creativity in diverse domains. *Empirical Studies of the Arts*, 22, 143–155.

Kaufman, J. C., & Beghetto, R. A. (2009). Beyond big and little: The four c model of creativity. *Review of General Psychology*, 13, 1–12.

Kaufman, J. C., & Sternberg, R. J. (2007, July/August). Resource review: Creativity. *Change*, 39, 55–58.

Makel, M. C. (2009). Help us creativity researchers, you're our only hope. *Psychology of Aesthetics, Creativity, and the Arts*, 3, 38–42.

Murdoch, M. C., & Keller-Mathers, S. (2008). Teaching and learning creativity with the Torrance Incubation Model: A research and practice update. *The International Journal of Creativity & Problem Solving*, 18(2), 11–33.

O'Hara, L. A., & Sternberg, R. J. (2000–2001). It doesn't hurt to ask: Effects of instructions to be creative, practical, or analytical on essay-writing performance and their interaction with students' thinking styles. *Creativity Research Journal*, 13, 197–210.

Plucker, J. A., Beghetto, R. A., & Dow, G. T. (2004). Why isn't creativity more important to educational psychologists? Potentials, pitfalls, and future directions in creativity research. *Educational Psychologist*, 39, 83–96.

Renzulli, J. S. (1992). A general theory for the development of creative productivity through the pursuit of ideal acts of learning. *Gifted Child Quarterly*, 36, 170–182.

Richards, R. (2007). Everyday creativity: Our hidden potential. In R. Richards (Ed.), *Everyday creativity and new views of human nature: Psychological, social and spiritual perspectives* (pp. 3–22). Washington, DC: American Psychological Association.

Runco, M. A. (1992). Children's divergent thinking and creative ideations. *Developmental Review*, 12, 233–264.

Runco, M. A. (1996). Personal creativity: Definition and developmental issues. *New Directions in Child Development*, 72(Summer), 3–30.

Runco, M. A. (2003). Education for creative potential. *Scandinavian Journal of Educational Research*, 47, 317–324.

Runco, M. A. (2004). Creativity. *Annual Review of Psychology*, 55, 657–687.

Stemler, S. E., Elliott, J. G., Grigorenko, E. L., & Sternberg, R. J. (2006). There's more to teaching than instruction: Seven strategies for dealing with the practical side of teaching. *Educational Studies*, 32(1), 101–118.

Silberman, C. E. (Ed.). (1973). *The open classroom reader*. New York: Random House.

Simonton, D. K. (1994). *Greatness*. New York: Guilford.

Smith, L. F. (2008). The art of science and the science of art. *International Journal of Creativity, and Problem Solving*, 18(2), 101–113.

Sternberg, R. J. (Ed.). (1999). *Handbook of creativity*. New York: Cambridge University Press.

Sternberg, R. J. (2000). Creativity is a decision. In A. L. Costa (Ed.), *Teaching for intelligence II*. Arlington Heights, IL: Skylight Training and Publishing.

Sternberg, R. J. (2002). Raising the achievement of all students: Teaching for successful intelligence. *Educational Psychology Review*, 14, 383–393.

Sternberg, R. J. (2003). Creative thinking in the classroom. *Scandinavian Journal of Educational Research*, 47, 325–338.

Sternberg, R. J. (2004). Theory-based university admissions testing for a new millennium. *Educational Psychologist*, 39, 185–198.

Sternberg, R. J. (2006). The nature of creativity. *Creativity Research Journal*, 18, 87–98.

Sternberg, R. J., & Grigorenko, E. L. (2000–2001). Guilford's structure of intellect model and model of creativity: Contributions and limitations. *Creativity Research Journal*, 13, 309–316.

Sternberg, R. J., & Grigorenko, E. L. (2004). Successful intelligence in the classroom. *Theory into Practice*, 43, 274–280.

Sternberg, R. J., & Grigorenko, E. L. (2007). *Teaching for successful intelligence* (2nd ed.). Thousand Oaks, CA: Corwin Press.

Sternberg, R. J., & The Rainbow Project Collaborators. (2006). The Rainbow Project: Enhancing the SAT through assessment of analytical, practical, and creative skills. *Intelligence*, 34, 321–350.

Sternberg, R. J., Torff, B., & Grigorenko, E. L. (1998). Teaching triarchically improves school achievement. *Journal of Educational Psychology*, 90, 374–384.

Thurstone, L. L. (1938). Primary mental abilities. *Psychometric Monographs*, 1.

Torrance, E. P. (1966). *Torrance tests of creative thinking: Technical-norms manual*. Lexington MA: Personnel Press.

Torrance, E. P. (1972). Can we teach children to think creatively? *Journal of Creative Behavior*, 6, 114–143.

Torrance, E. P. (1981). Creative teaching makes a difference. In J. C. Gowan, J. Khatena, & E. P. Torrance (Eds.), *Creativity: Its educational implications* (2nd ed., pp. 99–108). Dubuque, IA: Kendall/Hunt.

Wallas, G. (1926). *The art of thought*. New York: Harcourt Brace.

Weisberg, R. W. (1993). *Creativity: Beyond the myth of genius*. Freeman: New York.

CHAPTER 14

Cross-Cultural Perspectives on Creativity

Todd Lubart

Creativity is a contextually embedded phenomenon. It involves a person or group of people who operate within a context. This context has many levels and facets. It is possible to distinguish the physical and social characteristics of an environment. Within the social environment, there are several levels ranging from the family, school, and work-organizational setting, to the local community and regional environment, to the national or transnational level. Culture can be defined as "an historically transmitted pattern of meanings embodied in symbols, a system of inherited conceptions expressed in symbolic forms by means of which men communicate, perpetuate, and develop their knowledge about and attitudes toward life" (Geertz, 1973, p. 89). In the recent GLOBE international research program, House and Javidan (2004) defined culture as "shared motives, values, beliefs, identities, and interpretations or meanings of significant events that result from common experiences of members of collectives and are transmitted across age generations" (p. 15).

In this chapter, culture will be examined mainly at the national level. For example, French culture can be operationalized, for the current work, as the composite traditions, beliefs, values and preferred ways of behaving in contemporary France. Of course, French culture is not confined within the borders of modern France. French culture can be found to varying degrees in many parts of the world. French culture, which has been evolving for thousands of years, involves a way of seeing the world, including a shared lifestyle and language. French culture is part of European culture, which together with some other cultural regions can be viewed as part of the "Western" world. Of course, contemporary French culture is somewhat different from its historical versions (such as French culture in the times of Louis XIV). Modern French culture is also influenced by its current geographical, economic, and political situation. (France is currently a Republic with representative government, and part of the European Union, rather than an isolated monarchy.) Finally, it is worth noting that French culture is not a homogeneous entity. Indeed, some cultural patterns in southern France are quite different from those in northern, western, or eastern France. Finally, Parisians claim to have a specific subculture. This example illustrates some of the complexities involved in capturing the "culture" variable in order to study its impact on creativity. The same observations could be made concerning other cultural settings, such as the United States, in which we may refer to "American culture," although many regional and other subcultures exist.

Culture is a pervasive, omnipresent part of human living conditions. It is so connected with everyday behavioral patterns that we tend to take it for granted. Often, we do not even realize the impact of culture. To take a hypothetical case, if a person lives in a world in which all objects are round, the person may not even realize that this feature of the environment influences how they live. Of course, a brief trip to another planet for which all objects are square may offer some insights, perhaps producing "culture shock" when the usual ways of acting in a round world are employed in a square world. Given the variations in cultural context that exist, an enhanced understanding of creativity may be gained by comparing and contrasting creativity in different cultures. This chapter does not seek to provide a comprehensive review of all relevant studies on the topic. Rather, the goal is to raise key issues, highlight major trends, and provide illustrations of research findings. In this way, this chapter offers a complementary view to previous syntheses on creativity and culture (see Lubart, 1990, 1999; Ludwig, 1992; Niu & Sternberg, 2002; Rudowicz, 2003, Westwood & Low, 2003).

In this chapter, three main topics concerning culture and creativity will be examined. First, cultural differences may exist in the conception of creativity. Does "creativity" mean the same thing in different cultural settings? Recent research based on people's conceptions of creativity, including implicit and explicit definitions of creativity, descriptions of creative people, and evaluations of creative productions will be highlighted. Second, a large number of cross-cultural studies have focused on certain dimensions, such as individualism–collectivism, on which societies vary. Are these cultural dimensions related to differences in creativity? Finally, there is increasing interest in the impact of exposure to multiple cultures as a source of creativity. Research on multicultural experiences will be reviewed.

Conceptions of Creativity across Culture

The conception of creativity includes its defining features as well as associated characteristics. For example, in psychology, Western researchers' definitions of creativity tend to focus on a capacity to produce work (ideas or productions of all kinds) that is both novel and adaptive or useful given the task or situational parameters. According to this conception, central features are production, originality, and adaptiveness. It is worth examining whether these same defining features hold across all cultural settings. Of course, the investigation needs to be conducted in the most unbiased way possible so that researchers based in a Western approach do not see everything through their own perspective. In this respect, it was noted several times in Kaufman and Sternberg's (2006) *International Handbook of Creativity* that research on creativity in various parts of the world has often been dominated by Western paradigms.

Several methods allow conceptions of creativity to be examined. First, it is possible to ask people in different cultural settings to define creativity in their own culturally appropriate way. Second, people can nominate examples of "creativity" in their cultural context, and the common features can be examined. Third, people can indicate the individual or social variables that characterize creative people or creative accomplishments. Finally, people may be asked to judge a set of work, and their evaluations of creativity can provide insight into the criteria that they use implicitly.

One goal of research on conceptions of creativity is to define the concept. A second goal, as mentioned earlier, is to identify characteristics associated with creativity. These include, for example, the fields of endeavor in which creativity is valued in a culture, the categories of people who are expected to be creative, and the way that creative activities are organized.

Defining Features

Research evidence suggests that there may be some universal components of creativity. The most obvious one is the notion of novelty or originality. However, novelty is itself context dependent. What is novel in one society may not be novel in another. Furthermore, the degree of novelty is relevant. As an extreme case, some authors have argued that a vast number of sentences uttered in everyday conversations are novel combinations of words. In this view, nearly everyone engages in some creative activity every day. However, for others this kind of novelty is not sufficient and would be disregarded. Thus, it is possible to distinguish the issue of what is novel (content) from how much novelty has been expressed (degree). The degree of novelty leads to an important definitional issue concerning the fundamental nature of the novelty. Is the conceptual model one of rupture with the past, and thus of a radical, categorically new and different idea? Or, rather, is the model one of progressive improvement, modification, and adaptation (see Puccio & Chimento, 2001)? In this case, the cutoff for deciding that an idea or other form of production is creative will be less strict. It has been suggested that a high level of novelty, with conceptual rupture, may be the underlying view in some cultures, in particular Western ones, and the more gradual concept of continuing levels of novelty, working off of an existing idea may characterize other cultures, perhaps Eastern ones. For example, Li (1997) compared Chinese ink-brush painting and modern Western painting. Chinese ink-brush painting was viewed as a "vertical" domain in which some elements are essential in each work, and certain aspects can be modified (such as using humor concerning a theme). In contrast, modern West-ern painting is a horizontal domain with novelty allowed, supposedly, on all aspects. Thus, novelty can occur "in all directions" in modern Western painting but only in certain directions in Chinese ink-brush paintings. Different processes of creating may be associated with these kinds of novelty. Thus, there seems to be a general reference to novelty across cultural definitions of creativity, but the meaning of this novelty and the way to achieve it may vary substantially.

The second main definitional component of creativity that seems to be cross-culturally recognized is adaptive value. The term *value* is used here to cover the notions of usefulness, constraint satisfaction, adaptiveness, appropriateness, effectiveness, and relevance within the context in which the novelty is generated. It is clear that across various domains of endeavor, the relative weight of novelty versus adaptive value can vary. For example, in the artistic field, novelty is perhaps more highly valued than adaptiveness, whereas in engineering, the trend may be inverted. Thus, to the extent that a cultural group or society values creativity in some sectors of activity more than others, the definition of creativity may reflect this strategic choice. Beyond this domain-related variation in the importance of adaptive value, variations can occur in the importance placed generally on usefulness. If utilitarianism is highly valued in a cultural context, the adaptiveness component of creativity will have a relative importance with respect to the novelty component. Paletz and Peng (2008) explored the relative weights of novelty and appropriateness in judgments of creativity by university students in China, Japan, and United States; scenarios concerning creative productions in which novelty and appropriateness varied showed that both novelty and appropriateness influenced judgments in all three cultural samples, but the American and Japanese groups were particularly sensitive to variations in appropriateness.

Finally, the notion of adaptive value has another facet, which is the societal utility of the creative act. This trend appears most clearly in studies of creativity in Asian and

African settings; creativity involves novelty that contributes positively to society (Mpofu, Myambo, Mogaji, Mashego, & Khaleefa, 2006; Niu & Kaufman, 2005). Some debate on novel thinking and productions, such as inventions for evil purposes (the dark side of creativity), may not necessarily be classified as creative acts in all cultures because they lack moral validity. In Kenya, creative storytelling, according to Gacheru, Opiyo, and Smutny (1999), should be both imaginative and provide an ethical message.

A few cross-cultural studies have examined agreement on creativity ratings of productions, such as drawings, evaluated by judges from different cultures, in particular United States and China (Chen et al., 2002; Niu & Sternberg, 2001; Rostan, Pariser, & Gruber, 2002). For example, Niu and Sternberg (2001) had Chinese and American graduate students in psychology rate collage and drawing productions made by Chinese and American college students. High levels of agreement were observed between Chinese and American judges. Chen et al. (2002) had American and Chinese college students make drawings based on geometric figures (triangle, rectangle, circle). These drawings were evaluated by American and Chinese undergraduate judges, who had not produced drawings and were blind to the origin of each drawing. The overall correlation between the judges from different cultures was .97, indicating a nearly perfect level of interjudge agreement on the relative creativity of the productions. Of course, it can be argued that these studies optimized the conditions for cross-cultural agreement because the tasks used relatively neutral stimuli, familiar in both cultures; moreover, judges were from relatively similar groups (university students) and were blind to the cultural origin of each production.

Associated Characteristics

Product versus Process Orientation

The outcome of a creative act is a production, which can be evaluated as more or less novel, original, and adaptive. The creative act, or creative process, refers to the sequence of events, including mental events that lead to the production. Some cultures, particularly modern Western cultures, focus on the production itself, with relatively less attention paid to the way the creator achieved the outcome. When the process is considered, it is typically viewed as a linear sequence of events that moves the individual from a known starting point to a new place in the field, which is ideally as far as possible from the starting point. This view can be contrasted with an "Eastern" perspective, in which the key to creativity is the process more than the result. The creative process is cyclic, nonlinear, and enlightenment oriented. It involves connecting to a larger reality, reconfiguring or rediscovering existing elements. In this way, respecting traditions is not alien to creating, because the creative act involves finding new interpretations of existing elements, giving new breath to old ideas and practices. In this line, Westwood and Low (2003) cited the examples of creativity in a Hindu perspective, in which traditional truths are revealed in a new way, and classic Chinese visual art, in which a well-known topic represented with a certain style is explored in a new way.

Gender Differences

As Ludwig (1992) noted, various gender-related differences can be observed for creativity as we look across cultures. In certain traditional societies, men may show their creativity in woodcraft, sculpture, and medicinal-healing practices, whereas women may express their creativity in basket weaving, making clothing, embroidery, rugs, or pottery (see, e.g., Oral, 2006; Shostak, 1993). In some cultures, one gender group may be allowed access to fields involving creative work, with the other gender group denied access. Kim (2007) argued that Asian cultures based on Confucianism have long fostered inequality between men and women, with a woman traditionally being expected to show high levels of obedience, which is not conducive to creative work. Of course, creative work is not inherently gender typed. Gender differences seem often to be related to social status, and as different kinds of work in society vary in social status, creativity becomes gender related. Recent trends suggest that the gender-related organization of creativity may be decreasing given the numerous changes in modern societies.

Individual or Collective Forms

In some cultural contexts, the individual creator is the focus of attention, whereas in other cultures, creativity is mainly a collective act, often situated at the group level. For example, a contrast can be made in the musical domain between a focus on creative composition being driven by individual composers or by musical groups. In traditional Balinese society, for example, Colligan (1983) observed that musical creativity is an essentially collective task accomplished by musical groups rather than by individual musicians. Sawyer (2006) described another example of habitual collective (dyadic) creativity in traditional societies, in which a shaman, based on a vision from a possession state, would work with a carver to realize a spiritual mask for ceremonial use. The position that a culture adopts on the individualistic nature of creativity is hypothesized to be related to the individualism–collectivism dimension of cultural variation, which will be described in more detail in the section "Culture Influences the Amount of Creativity."

Domains

Several authors have observed that some cultures channel creativity into certain domains more than others (Lubart, 1990, 1999; Ludwig, 1992). Creativity may, for example, be recognized, valued, and promoted in the visual arts or technical inventions more than in religious or political spheres (Mpofu et al., 2006). As culture is often intertwined with religion, it has been noted that Islamic societies appear to foster artistic creativity in particular in nonrepresentational styles (such as geometric designs, decorative works, calligraphy) as well as in verbal creativity such as poetry, literary compositions, storytelling, and folk songs (Khaleefa, Erdos, Ashria, 1996; Ludwig, 1992, Mpofu et al. 2006; Oral, 2006). Other reports indicate that in Turkey scientific and technological creativity are highly valued, and in Latin America there is emphasis on creativity in business and advertising (Rudowicz, 2003). In studies comparing Hong Kong Chinese to North Americans, Rudowicz and Hui (1998) found that respondents in Hong Kong nominated businessmen, fashion designers, and politicians as most creative, followed by film directors, actors, singers and architects, with artists and writers less often nominated. Cheung and Yue (2007) examined which Chinese creators were the most well known and valued by high school and university students; they found that scientific creators and to some extent politicians were most nominated, with creative entertainers also particularly valued in Hong Kong. Other studies indicated that creative accomplishments in domains with a strong social impact were most valued by Chinese participants (see Niu & Kaufman, 2005).

Big-C, little-c

The distinction between eminent cases of creativity, Big-C creativity, and everyday acts of creativity, little-c creativity, can be examined across cultures. In some cultural settings, everyone can be creative. In others, it is an exclusive ability, reserved for a few exceptional people. It is interesting to note that in the Polish language, the word tworczosc refers to eminent creativity marked by distinguished achievements, whereas kreatywnosc refers to everyday creativity, conceived as a personal trait (Necka, Grohman, & Slabosz, 2006).

Of course, a range of creativity may be recognized in nearly every culture, even if the prototype of a creative person or group varies. It seems that numerous Western societies recognize everyday creativity but highlight and glorify the eminent cases of creativity, such as Einstein, Marie Curie, Bach,

Michelangelo, and Sylvia Plath. Montuori and Purser (1995) raised the possibility of the "Lone Genius Myth"; cultures that focus on eminent cases of creativity tend to highlight the individual characteristics of these special people, reducing the perceived contribution of their environment. This tendency was hypothesized to be related to a culture's position on the individualism-collectivism dimension.

In contrast, according to some reports in other cultures, everyone is naturally creative in all activities of life, such that the question itself of nominating creative people is odd and often meets with no response. For example, the !Kung San are a tribal group living in the Kalahari Desert who engage in creative activities such as bead weaving, storytelling, and music performance; when Shostak (1993) asked who were the most creative people, respondents would often list everyone engaged in the activity. Mpofu et al. (2006) reported on a study with people from Arab and sub-Saharan Africa, representing 28 linguistic groups. They found that the concept of creativity was often expressed as a commonplace ability intertwined with resourcefulness, intelligence, wisdom, talent, originality, and inventiveness. In their sample, more than two-thirds of the sub-Saharan and Arab Africans described themselves as involved in creative activities in their daily life. On the extreme side of little-c creativity, the possibility of creativity at the personal level – in creative acts of self-development that yield no tangible production – can be mentioned. This personal creativity, a form of self-actualization or individual self-development, is valued in some cultures more than others.

Characteristics of Creative People

Numerous studies have been conducted on folk conceptions of creative people in diverse cultural settings. People's implicit "theories" of the key features of creative people examined in United States, Britain, Brazil, Argentina, Cuba, China, Korea, Singapore, India, Romania, and other locations show that essentially the same cognitive skills (ability to make connections, ask questions, use imagination, think flexibly, experiment with ideas), personality characteristics (e.g., independence, self-confidence, assertiveness), and motivational attributes (e.g., high energy, ambition, enthusiasm) are cited across cultures (see Kaufman & Sternberg, 2006; Rudowicz, 2003). This basic finding holds for studies conducted with university students and adults from the general population describing creative people, as well as parents and teachers describing creative children. However, some cross-cultural differences were found.

First, some characteristics are mentioned in one culture but not others. For example, "sense of humor" and "aesthetic" or "artistic orientation" are present in North American conceptions but not in Chinese ones (Mainland China, Hong Kong, and Taiwan) (Rudowicz, 2003). In contrast, collectivistic features of creative people, such as "inspires people," "makes a contribution to the progress of society," and "is appreciated by others" are mentioned by Hong Kong Chinese but not by North Americans. Some differences in characteristics of creative people were also observed within each culture, such as in Rudowicz and Yue's (2000) study of undergraduates from Beijing, Guangzhou, Taipei, and Hong Kong, with the characteristic of "enjoying life" cited by the Taipei sample but not the others. Finally, some cultures may emphasize a subset of characteristics. For example, Korean conceptions appear to focus on cognitive characteristics more than on personality and motivational ones (Lim & Plucker, 2001).

Third, some characteristics attributed to creative people are not necessarily viewed positively. Studies with Chinese teachers suggest that nonconformity, expressiveness, and assertiveness are seen as characteristics of creative students, but are viewed negatively in terms of rebelliousness, being opinionated, and being self-centered (see Chan & Chan, 1999). Lim and Plucker (2001) report a similar finding with a Korean sample in which creative people are characterized by a set of deviant features – being indifferent to others' opinions, being headstrong, making conflicts in working groups, being rude, or being abnormal.

Fourth, the extent to which creativity is distinguished from related concepts, such as intelligence or wisdom, may vary according to cultural context. For example, some studies with North American samples suggest that creativity can be well distinguished from related concepts; other research in Asia or Africa suggests that the concepts are more intertwined in laypeople's conceptions (Chan & Chan, 1999).

Culture Influences the Amount of Creativity

The issue of whether one culture fosters creativity more than another has often been raised. This question concerns both the quantity of creative production in a given culture and the quality or greatness of the productions. Simonton (1999), using the historiometric approach, has greatly contributed to comparisons of creativity within and across cultural centers during long historical periods. Effects of political fragmentation, turmoil and war, ideological diversity, and economic circumstances, for example, have been found. The current issue – comparing contemporary cultures in terms of creative production – has been attempted; typically, samples from two different cultures, such as students from United States and from China, complete the same experimental creative thinking task, and then their productions are compared. These productions may be responses to divergent thinking tests, drawings, collages, or other kinds of work. Of course, there are some important methodological issues, such as the appropriateness of the "creativity" task in each culture as a valid measure of creativity.

Presuming that the creativity measure is equally valid (which is difficult to certify), several studies have shown that one cultural group outperforms another. The next step is to investigate why these differences were observed. In some cases there may be several variables confounded in the "cul-

ture" variable. For example, it is important that the two contrasting cultural groups do not differ on age, socioeconomic status, education level, access to technology, and other variables. If these potential confounds are controlled, the remaining differences observed stem, it is argued, from cultural characteristics.

Some studies comparing creative performance in "Westerners" (notably people from the United States) with "Easterners" (Asians in Japan, Hong Kong, Taiwan and Singapore) have found results favoring samples from the United States (for examples of studies using divergent-thinking tests, see Saeki, Fan, & Van Dusen, 2001, which compares American and Asian samples; Kharkhurin & Motalleebi, 2008, compare American, Russian, and Iranian samples). Niu and Sternberg (2001) compared artistic creativity in American (Yale University) and Chinese (Peking University) students using a collage-making and an alien-drawing tasks. The productions were evaluated by American and Chinese graduate students in psychology. The results indicated that the American students received higher scores on creativity than Chinese students, according to both American and Chinese judges (who were blind to the cultural origin of each drawing). Of course, the findings are not always in favor of U.S. samples. In studies showing an advantage for a Japanese or Chinese sample, the argument that the task taps a specific domain enhanced by a particular kind of education in the culture showing good results is typically evoked, to avoid countering the logic of the main cultural dimension argument (Niu & Sternberg, 2002, 2003).

In terms of the psychological bases of cultural effects, a few main dimensions have guided cross-cultural studies in past decades (Hoftstede, 1980; Schwartz, 1994, 1999; Triandis, 1994). The dimensions proposed by Hofstede in his landmark study of people working at IBM across the world are among the most known and researched, with the following four dimensions proposed: individualism–collectivism, power distance, masculinity–femininity, uncertainty avoidance–uncertainty acceptance. Recently, the GLOBE study of cultural dimensions relevant to professional contexts and leadership in organizations was conducted. In the GLOBE study, House, Hanges, Javidan, Dorfman, and Gupta (2000) investigated, in 62 societies, the dimensions of Assertiveness, Future Orientation (planning, investing in the future, delaying gratification), Gender Egalitarianism, Human Orientation (fairness, altruism), Institutional Collectivism (encourage collective distribution of resources and action), In-group Collectivism (pride, loyalty, cohesiveness of the group), Performance Orientation, Power Distance, and Uncertainty Avoidance. Several of these dimensions continue in line with Hofstede's work, whereas others propose new avenues that seem relevant to cross-cultural comparisons. The GLOBE study focused on leadership, so there is a large potential for future research on creativity based on these dimensions.

It is worth noting that cultures, studied at the societal levels, can be described by profiles of scores on these GLOBE dimensions. When examined together, the nine dimensions across 62 societies allow cultural clusters to be identified. There are 10 clusters: Anglo cultures (e.g., Australia, England, USA); Latin Europe (e.g., France, Portugal, Spain, Italy); Nordic Europe (e.g., Finland, Sweden); Germanic Europe (e.g., Germany, Netherlands); Southern Asia (e.g., India, Indonesia, Philippines); Eastern Europe (e.g., Greece, Russia); Latin America (e.g., Argentina, Colombia, Mexico); sub-Saharan Africa (Nigeria, Zimbabwe); Middle East/Arab (e.g., Egypt, Morocco, Qatar); and Confucian Asia (China, South Korea, Japan). These clusters could serve as a basis for future investigations on creativity.

Work related to creativity has centered on individualism–collectivism, uncertainty avoidance, and power distance (Hofstede, 2001; Rank, Pace, & Frese, 2004). Individualism–collectivism characterizes the strength and cohesion of bonds between people, with people looking after themselves in individualist societies and looking after the larger societal unit to which they belong in collectivist societies. Power distance refers to the extent to which power and authority are expected and accepted to be distributed unequally in a society. Uncertainty avoidance concerns the extent to which people feel uncomfortable or threatened by unknown, uncertain situations.

In general, collectivism, high levels of uncertainty avoidance and high power distance (hierarchical structure) are negatively related to national levels of inventiveness (Hofstede, 2001). Shane (1992, 1993) examined national rates of innovation in 33 countries, based on per-capita number of patents, and found an advantage for societies with low uncertainty acceptance, low power distance, and high individualism. An acceptance of uncertainty (low uncertainty avoidance) may foster tolerance for risk and change. Individualism is associated with autonomy, independence (defining one's self as unique from the group), and freedom. Ng (2003) provides empirical evidence for a model in which cultural individualism–collectivism influences self-construal as independent or interdependent on others, and this self-concept in turn influences creativity and conformity tendencies. Lack of power, characteristic of nonhierarchical societies, fosters enhanced interactions and communication between people at different status levels, such as superiors and subordinates. Finally, hierarchical societies do not tend to embrace change because of the potential redistribution of power that might go against vested interests.

Thus, the classic argument is that cultures showing the creativity-compatible profile on certain dimensions (individualism, etc.) will favor the development and expression of creativity. People from these cultures should show higher performance on laboratory creativity tasks, more creative productions (e.g., more patents for inventions), and greater levels of creativity (e.g., Nobel Prize winners). It is worth noting, however, the simple effects of cultural dimensions. Phases of creative and innovative processes may relate differentially to these cultural dimensions. For example, low power distance, individualism, and low uncertainty avoidance may foster creativity, but hinder idea implementation. Hofstede (2001) suggested collecting ideas in certain cultural contexts (e.g., weak uncertainty avoidance, with tolerance for deviant ideas and unpredictable situations) and refining them in others (strong uncertainty avoidance, senses of detail and precision). In a similar vein, Rank et al. (2004) noted that Schwartz's value dimension of conservatism versus intellectual autonomy is relevant to creativity. Valuing intellectual autonomy is positive for generating ideas but may hinder implementation and acceptance of creative ideas.

Shane, Venkataraman, and MacMillan (1995) examined national culture and preferences for innovation-championing strategies in 30 countries, with 1,228 professionals from four different industries. Innovation champions are those who promote the new ideas and help to overcome resistance to these ideas in organizational contexts. In this study, innovation was defined as any idea that is new to an organization (administrative, technological, product, process, and so forth). Questionnaires were used to measure the perceived effectiveness of various innovation-championing strategies. The results show that high uncertainty avoidance is related to preferences for idea champions to work within existing organizational rules and procedures to promote the ideas. For high power-distance contexts, effective innovation champions focus on gaining the approval of important authority figures, whereas in low power-distance contexts, innovation champions can seek to build a broad base of people who see value in an innovation. Finally, collectivism was associated with the strategy of getting people from different organizational departments to see the benefits of an innovation, and thereby build consensus for the new idea.

Another potential effect of cultural variability on dimensions such as uncertainty avoidance or individualism is the impact on the role of creativity-related personality traits at the level of individuals. For exam-

ple, in a culture that shows high uncertainty avoidance as a general societal characteristic, natural variability of individuals on tolerance of ambiguity and risk taking, personality traits considered important for creativity and related to uncertainty avoidance, exists. It is reasonable to hypothesize that individual differences of tolerance for ambiguity or risk taking will have an enhanced importance in this cultural context because the baseline cultural contribution is low. In contrast, in a culture that shows low uncertainty avoidance, individual differences in ambiguity tolerance and risk taking will have relatively less importance in predicting differences in people's creative output. Every individual benefits from the cultural context, and other variables that distinguish individuals will become the discriminating factors. The same line of argument can be developed concerning individualism-collectivism. This dimension is related to individual differences regarding individuality, self-expression, and conformity. Thus, in a highly individualist cultural setting, the relative importance of individual differences concerning conformity will be low compared to other variables relevant to creativity (such as ambiguity tolerance). In contrast, in a collectivist culture, given the baseline, individual differences regarding conformity will play a relatively important role in determining people's creative output.

Cultural "Gestalt"

The simple impact of one or another cultural dimension, such as individualism-collectivism, needs to be nuanced by the fact that these dimensions occur always as part of a larger cultural pattern, in which the effect of one dimension may be modified in the context of other factors. For example, Chinese culture is complex and can not be reduced to being simply "collectivist" (Lau, Hui, & Ng, 2004). Several authors have called attention to a set of features characterizing modern Asian society that may in combination inhibit creativity, at least in terms of Western views. Ng (2001, 2004) highlights how the Confucian tradition of learning focuses on education as the acquisition of correct knowledge, the text as the authoritarian source of knowledge, and the teacher as a repository of knowledge, which must be respected. In addition, there is, of course, a high value placed on collectivism, avoiding conflict, showing obedience, and respecting social norms. Finally, there is a competitive academic system based on social recognition and bringing honor to one's family. In his books *Why Asians are Less Creative than Westerners* and *Liberating the Creative Spirit in Asian Students*, Ng suggests that this combination of cultural features leads to difficulties for thinking in new ways (which involves disrespect for tradition and existing knowledge) and engaging a divergent mode of thought, thereby differentiating one's ideas from those of others. Rudowicz (2003) provides a literature review on Asian culture; she observes that parental attitudes and child-rearing practices focused on filial piety, respecting a teacher's authority, adhering to expectations for respect and obedience, and respecting existing knowledge and tradition provide a cultural context that is not conducive to creativity. Kim (2007) argues that the four principles of Confucianism that inhibit creativity – emphasis on education through rote learning, the family system (obedience), hierarchical social structure, and benevolence (self-restraint, emotional control, humility) – all impact negatively on originality. Some research suggests that creativity can be enhanced in such cultural settings through instructions and exercises (Kim, 2005; Ng 2004; Niu & Sternberg, 2003; see also Basadur, Pringle, & Kirkland, 2002, for a study in South America). Also, some work has suggested that certain features of Asian cultures, notably Chinese and Japanese cultures, may foster creativity (Lau et al., 2004; Westwood & Low, 2003). For example, collectivist values may foster, via processes involving compromise, incremental innovations (as opposed to radical innovations), with people working together

toward creativity in a collective interest. Exploring another facet of culture, Hofstede and Bond (1988) proposed a dimension of long-term versus short-term orientation. Long-term orientation, characteristic of Asian cultures, fosters perseverance and effective goal-setting practice, both of which are relevant to creativity (Westwood & Low). Also, creativity at the group level, which is often the operational unit in the workplace, may be enhanced by collectivistic identification with group goals, less social loafing by individual members of groups, and higher perseverance at the group level in the face of obstacles encountered during a task. To the extent that the group sets a goal to be creative, the collectivist culture may allow group members to cooperate efficiently to reach the goal. It is interesting to note, in this regard, that several ministries of education in Asian societies have set goals to promote creativity in schools (e.g., China, Taiwan, Singapore; see Ho & Rainbow, 2008).

Multicultural Experiences

A line of research has been developing in recent decades concerning the influence of exposure to several cultures. This work concerns effects of short-term stays in a foreign culture, as well as long-term exposure in a multicultural society, living near to contrasting cultural centers, or living in bilingual or multilingual contexts. Multicultural experiences may involve time spent living abroad, interactions with people from diverse nationalities and ethnic groups, exposure to foreign languages, immigration experiences, and exposure to other cultures via educational experiences. In general, the basic hypothesis is that exposure to multiple cultures and/or multiple languages is beneficial for creativity. This exposure enhances knowledge and provides contrasts with typical modes of thought and action that help people overcome their cultural habits. Multicultural experiences may foster openness to new ideas. Leung, Maddux, Galinsky, and Chiu (2008) suggested that multicultural experience can provide exposure and knowledge concerning diverse ideas, allow multiple interpretations of the same object, "destabilize" routine knowledge structures, promote a tendency to seek information from unfamiliar sources, and foster syntheses of diverse ideas.

The earliest studies set their focus on the potential advantages of bilingualism for creativity, generally using divergent-thinking tests. The hypothesis that language influences thought and that exposure to more than one linguistic system will open up possibilities to view the world alternatively has been proposed. Findings tend to show higher divergent-thinking performance for bilinguals compared to monolinguals (see Ricciardelli, 1992; Simonton, 2008). In a recent example of this kind of research using a divergent-thinking test and a structured imagination test, Kharkhurin (2009) compared Farsi-English bilinguals living in the United Arab Emirates and Farsi monolinguals living in Iran. Bilingualism was related to higher originality scores for the divergent-thinking test and the tendency to break away from standard category properties in the structured-imagination task. Kharjhurin (2008), in another study, compared Russian-English bilingual immigrants and English monolingual native speakers and found that bilinguals showed enhanced performance compared to monolinguals, with effects of age of bilingual acquisition and exposure time to the new culture.

Of course, these studies illustrate a few of the potential complications with studies of bilingual populations: Bilinguals may live in a completely different cultural context than monolinguals; they may be part of a subculture within a larger cultural context; and they may be immigrants who integrated a new cultural context. Furthermore, they may be part of a minority group. These parameters yield a number of potential confounds (such as minority status), leading to a difficulty in isolating the "pure" effect of bilingualism. Additionally, there are various degrees or types of bilingualism.

Once confounds associated with bilingualism are taken into account, to the extent that they can be controlled, bilingualism is hypothesized to facilitate creativity because of the specific "double coding" of concepts in memory, with each language providing nuances on the same concept. The alternative lexical coding schemes can facilitate associations and conceptual blends. Another facilitative effect of bilingualism is enhanced mental flexibility, which is perhaps develops as bilinguals need to move from one language to another in their daily life (see Simonton, 2008, for a review of this literature).

In addition to effects of exposure to multiple languages, research on societies' geopolitical situation, generally using historiometric data on creative output of societies over centuries, have shown that societies located near contrasting cultural centers, or at the crossroads of cultural exchange, tend to show higher creative output (Simonton, 1984). Data show also that societies characterized by political fragmentation (i.e., societies comprising multiple political entities or parties) tend to have higher rates of creative activity (Simonton, 1984, 1999). Therivel (1995) contrasted societies with unified power (one party, "insular" societies) with those having a division of power. A historical ethno-psychological approach suggests that exposure to multiple sources of power is beneficial, allowing an expanded worldview and less conformity pressure.

Some recent studies have focused directly on multicultural exposure. Leung et al. (2008) reported on a series of studies that indicate that exposure to multiple cultures can be beneficial for creativity. For example, in one experimental study, people who saw simultaneously stimuli from two cultures (American and Chinese) wrote more creative stories than those exposed to stimuli from only one culture. These same participants, tested one week later, showed a continuing effect of the multicultural experience on a different, creative analogy generation task. In other studies, positive links were found between creative-idea generation, using tasks such as generating ideas for unconventional gifts, and a questionnaire of multicultural life experiences.

Conclusion

Culture is omnipresent, and for this very reason its impact is often underestimated. Culture provides the bedrock, the deep psychological structure in which all human activity occurs. For complex activities with social facets, such as creativity, the importance of understanding the influence of culture is particularly important. Culture influences both the production of "creative" work and its reception, recognition, and diffusion. Culture influences the who, what, and why of creativity; it influences they way creativity is expressed and the degree to which it is expressed. In this chapter, findings from several cultural contexts were cited as illustrations of the different ways in which culture may influence creativity. First, it was argued that culture influences the definition and conceptual boundaries of creativity, although there is some evidence for similarities across cultures on key components of creativity. Second, research on basic cultural dimensions on which societies vary was overviewed and the implications for creativity were developed. Third, the impact of exposure to several cultures – multiculturalism – was discussed, with research suggesting a positive impact on creativity.

References

Basadur, M., Pringle, P., & Kirkland, D. (2002). Crossing cultures: Training effects on the divergent thionine attitudes of Spanish-speaking South American managers. *Creativity Research Journal*, 14(3–4), 395–408.

Chan, D., & Chan, L.-K. (1999). Implicit theories of creativity: Teacher's perception of student characteristics in Hong Kong. *Creativity Research Journal*, 12(3), 185–195.

Chen, C., Kasof, J. Himsel, A. J., Greenberger, E., Dong, Q., & Xue, G. (2002). Creativity in drawings of geometric shapes: A cross-cultural examination with the consensual assessment technique. *Journal of Cross-Cultural Psychology*, 33, 171–187.

Cheung, C.-K., & Yue, X. D. (2007). Which Chinese creators are famous and why: Views from Hong Kong and Mainland Chinese students. *Journal of Creative Behavior*, 41(3), 177–195.

Colligan, J. (1983). Musical creativity and social rules in four cultures. *Creative Child and Adult Quaterly*, 8(1), 39–47.

Gacheru, M., Opiyo, M., & Smutny, J. F. (1999). Children's creative thinking in Kenya. *Childhood Education*, 75(6), 346–349.

Geertz, C. (1973). *The interpretation of cultures*. New York: Basic Books.

Ho, D. Y. F., & Rainbow, T. H. H. (2008). Knowledge is a dangerous thing: Authority relations, ideological conservatism, and creativity in Confucian heritage cultures. *Journal for the Theory of Social Behaviour*, 38(1), 69–85.

Hofstede, G. (1980). *Culture's consequences: International differences in work-related values*. Beverly Hills, CA: Sage.

Hofstede, G. (2001). *Culture's consequences: Comparing values, behaviors, institutions and organizations across nations*. Thousand Oaks, CA: Sage.

Hofstede, G., & Bond, M. H. (1988). The Confucious connection: From cultural roots to economic growth. *Organisational Dynamics*, 17, 4–21.

House, R. J., Hanges, P. J., Javidan, M., Dorfman, P. W., & Gupta, V. (Eds.). (2004). *Culture, leadership and organizations: The GLOBE study of 62 societies*. Thousand Oaks, CA: Sage.

House, R. J., & Javidan, M. (2004). Overview of GLOBE. In R. J. House, P. J. Hanges, M. Javian, P. Dorfman, & V. Gupta (Eds.), *Leadership, culture and organizations: The GLOBE study of 62 societies* (pp. 9–28). Thousand Oaks, CA: Sage

Kaufman, J. C., & Sternberg, R. J. (2006). *The international handbook of creativity*. New York: Cambridge University Press.

Khaleeefa, O. H., Erdos, G., & Ashria, I. H. (1996). Creativity in an indigenous Afro-Arab Islamic culture: The case of Sudan. *Journal of Creative Behavior*, 30, 268–283.

Kharkhurin, A. V. (2008). The effects of linguistic proficiency, age of second language acquisition, and length of exposure to a new cultural environment on bilinguals' divergent thinking. *Bilingualism: Language and Cognition*, 11(2), 225–243.

Kharkhurin, A. V. (2009). The role of bilingualism in creative performance on divergent thinking and Invented Aliens creativity tests. *Journal of Creative Behavior*, 43(1), 59–71.

Kharkhurin, A. V., & Motalleebi, S. N. S. (2008). The impact of culture on the creative potential of American, Russian an Iranian college students. *Creativity Research Journal*, 20(4), 404–411.

Kim, K. H. (2005). Learning from each other: Creativity in East Asian and American education. *Creativity Research Journal*, 17(4), 337–347.

Kim, K. H. (2007). Exploring the interactions between Asian culture (Confucianism) and creativity. *Journal of Creative Behavior*, 41(1), 28–53.

Lau, S., Hui, A. N. N., & Ng, G. Y. C. (Ed.). (2004). *Creativity: When East meets West*. Singapore: World Scientific.

Leung, A. K., Maddux, W. W., Galinsky, A. D., & Chiu, C. (2008). Multicultural experience enhances creativity. *American Psychologist*, 63(3), 169–181.

Li, J. (1997). Creativity in horizontal and vertical domains. *Creativity Research Journal*, 10(2–3), 107–132.

Lim, W., &, Plucker, J. A. (2001). Creativity through a lens of social resposibility: Implicit theories of creativity with Korean samples. *Journal of Creative Behavior*, 35(2), 115–130.

Lubart, T. I. (1990). Creativity and cross-cultural variation. *International Journal of Psychology*, 25(1), 39–59.

Lubart, T. I. (1999). Creativity across cultures. In R. J. Sternberg (Ed.), *Handbook of creativity* (pp. 339–350). New York: Cambridge University Press.

Ludwig, A. M. (1992). Culture and creativity. *American Journal of Psychotherapy*, 46(3), 454–469.

Montuori, A., & Purser, R. E. (1995). Deconstructing the lone Genius myth: Toward a contextual view of creativity. *Journal of Humanistic Psychology*, 35(3), 69–111.

Mpofu, E., Myambo, K., Mogaji, A. A., Mashego, T-A., & Khaleefa, O. H. (2006). African perspectives on creativity. In J. C. Kaufman, & R. J. Sternberg (Eds.), *The international handbook of creativity* (pp. 456–489). New York: Cambridge University Press.

Necka, E., Grohman, M., & Slabosz, A. (2006). Creativity studies in Poland. In J. C. Kaufman & R. J. Sternberg (Eds.), *The international handbook of creativity* (pp. 270–306). New York: Cambridge University Press.

Ng, A. K. (2001). *Why Asians are less creative than Westerners*. Singapore: Prentice-Hall.

Ng, A. K. (2003). A cultural model of creative and conforming behavior. *Creativity Research Journal*, 15(2–3), 223–233.

Ng, A. K. (2004). *Liberating the creative spirit in Asian students*. Singapore: Prentice-Hall.

Niu, W., & Kaufman, J. C. (2005) Creativity in troubled times: Factors associated with recognitions of Chinese literary creativity in the 20th century. *Journal of Creative Behavior*, 39(1), 57–67.

Niu, W., & Sternberg, R. J. (2001). Cultural influences on artistic creativity and its evaluation. *International Journal of Psychology*, 36(4), 225–241.

Niu, W., & Sternberg, R. J. (2002). Contemporary studies on the concept of creativity: The East and the West. *Journal of Creative Behavior*, 36, 269–288.

Niu, W., & Sternberg, R. J. (2003). Societal and school influence on students' creativity. *Psychology in the schools*, 40, 103–114.

Oral, G. (2006) Creativity in Turkey and Turkish-speaking countries. In J. C. Kaufman & R. J. Sternberg (Eds.), *The international handbook of creativity* (pp. 337–373). New York: Cambridge University Press.

Paletz, S. B. F., & Peng, K. (2008). Implicit theories of creativity across cultures: Novelty and appropriateness in two product domains. *Journal of Cross-Cultural Psychology*, 39(3), 286–302.

Puccio, G., & Chimento, M. D. (2001). Implicit theories of creativity: Laypersons' perceptions of the creativity of adaptors and innovators. *Perceptual and Motor Skills*, 92, 675–681.

Rank, J., Pace, V. L., & Frese, M. (2004). Three avenues for future research on creativity, innovation, and intiative. *Applied Psychology: An Interantional Review*, 53(4), 518–528.

Ricciardelli, L. A. (1992). Creativity and bilingualism. *Journal of Creative Behavior*, 26, 242–254.

Rostan, S. M., Pariser, D., & Gruber, H. E. (2002). A cross-cultural study of the development of artistic talent, creativity and giftedness. *High Ability Studies*, 13(2), 125–155.

Rudowicz, E. (2003). Creativity and culture: A two-way interaction. *Scandinavian Journal of Educational Research*, 47(3), 273–290.

Rudowicz, E., & Hui, A. (1998). Hong Kong people's views of creativity. *Gifted Education International*, 13(2), 159–174.

Rudowicz, E., & Yue, X.-D. (2000). Concepts of creativity: Similarities and differences among Mainland, Hong Kong and Taiwanese Chinese. *Journal of Creative Behavior*, 34(3), 175–192.

Saeki, N., Fan, X., & Van, L. (2001). *A comparative study of creative thionine of American and
Japanese college students*. 35(1), 24–36.

Sawyer, R. K. (2006). *Explaining creativity: The
science of human innovation*. New York:
Oxford University Press.

Schwartz, S. H. (1994). Are there universal
aspects in the structure and contents of human
values? *Journal of Social Issues*, 50(4), 19–45.

Schwartz, S. H. (1999). A theory of cultural values and some implications for work. *Applied
Psychology*, 48, 23–47.

Shane, S. (1992). Why do some societies invent
more than others? *Journal of Business Venturing*, 7(1), 29–47.

Shane, S. (1993). Cultural influences on national
rates of innovation. *Journal of Business Venturing*, 8(1), 59–73.

Shane, S., Venkataraman, S., & MacMillan,
I. (1995). Cultural differences in innovation
championing strategies. *Journal of Management*, 21(5), 931–952.

Shostak, M. (1993). The creative individual in
the world of the !Kung San. In S. Lavie,

K. Narrayan, & R. Ronaldo (Eds.). *Cre-
ativity/anthropology* (pp. 54–69). Ithaca, NY:
Cornell University Press.

Simonton, D. K. (1984). *Genius, creativity and
leadership*. Cambridge, MA: Harvard University Press.

Simonton, D. K. (1999). Creativity from a
historiometric perspective. In R. J. Sternberg (Ed.), *Handbook of creativity* (pp.
116–133). New York: Cambridge University
Press.

Simonton, D. K. (2008). Bilingualism and creativity. In J. Altarriba & R. R. Heredia (Eds.), *An
introduction to bilingualism: Principles and processes* (pp. 147–166). Mahwah, NJ: Erlbaum.

Therivel, W. A. (1995). Long-term effect of
power on creativity. *Creativity Research Journal*, 8(2), 173–192.

Triandis, H. T. (1994). *Culture and social
behaviour*. New York: McGraw-Hill.

Westwood, R., & Low, D. R. (2003). The multicultural muse: Culture, creativity and innovation. *International Journal of Cross Cultural
Management*, 3(2), 235–259.

CHAPTER 15

Evolutionary Approaches to Creativity

Liane Gabora and Scott Barry Kaufman

1. Introduction

Many species engage in acts that could be called creative (J.C. Kaufman & A.B. Kaufman, 2004). However, human creativity is unique in that it has completely transformed the planet we live on. We build skyscrapers, play breathtaking cello sonatas, send ourselves into space, and even decode our own DNA. Given that the anatomy of the human brain is not so different from that of the great apes, what enables us to be so creative? Recent collaborations at the frontier of anthropology, archaeology, psychology, and cognitive science are culminating in speculative but increasingly sophisticated efforts to piece together an answer to this question. Examining the skeletons of our ancestors gives cues as to the anatomical constraints that hindered or enabled various kinds of creative expression. Relics of the past have much to tell us about the thoughts, beliefs, and creative abilities of the people who invented and used them. How the spectacular creativity of humans came about is the first topic addressed in this chapter.

Studies at the intersection of creativity and evolution are not limited to investigations into the biological evolution of a highly creative species. Creative ideas themselves might be said to evolve through culture. Human creativity is distinctive because of the adaptive and open-ended manner in which change accumulates. Inventions build on previous ones in ways that enhance their utility or aesthetic appeal, or make them applicable in different situations. There is no a priori limit to how a creative idea might unfold over time. A cartoon character may inspire the name and logo for a hockey team (the Mighty Ducks), which might in turn inspire toys, cereal shapes, cigarette lighter designs, or for that matter work its way into an academic book chapter. It is this proclivity to take an idea and make it our own, or "put our own spin on it," that makes creative ideas appear to evolve. The next section of this chapter investigates in what sense creative ideas evolve through culture.

Finally, we address the question of *why* creativity evolved. What forces supported the evolution of creativity? Does being creative help us live longer, or attract mates?

Do creative projects sometimes *interfere* with survival and reproductive fitness; are there nonbiological factors that compel us to create? This is a third topic addressed in this chapter.

2. The Birth of Human Creativity

Looking at an artifact that was fashioned thousands or millions of years ago is an awe-inspiring experience because it gives us a glimpse into the lives and worldviews of our earliest ancestors. To be sure, creative works disintegrate. The farther back in time we look for signs of creativity, the fewer creative works of that time remain with us today. But by corroborating theory and data from different fields, we are on our way toward putting together a coherent picture of how and when the creative abilities of humans arose.

We begin this section by examining the archaeological evidence for the earliest indications of human creativity, and the anthropological evidence for concurrent changes in the size and shape of the cranial cavity. We then examine various hypotheses that have been put forward to explain these data.

2.1 *The Earliest Evidence of Human Creativity:* Homo habilis

It is generally agreed that ancestral humans started diverging from ancestral apes approximately 6 million years ago. The first Homo lineage, *Homo habilis*, appeared approximately 2.4 million years ago in the Lower Paleolithic. The earliest known human inventions, referred to as *Oldowan* artifacts (after Olduvai Gorge, Tanzania, where they were first found), are widely attributed to *Homo habilis* (Semaw et al., 1997), although it is possible that they were also used by late australopithecines (de Beaune, 2004). They were simple, mostly single faced stone tools, pointed at one end (M.D. Leakey, 1971). These tools were most likely used to split fruits and nuts (de Beaune, 2004), although some of the more recent ones have sharp edges, and are found

with cut-marked bones, suggesting that they were used to sharpen wood implements and butcher small game (Bunn & Kroll, 1986; M.D. Leakey, 1971).

These early tools were functional but simple and unspecialized; by our standards they were not very creative. Feist (2008) refers to the minds of these early hominids as *pre-representational*, suggesting that hominids at this time were not capable of forming representations that deviated from their concrete sensory perceptions; their experience was tied to the present moment. Similarly, Mithen (1996) refers to minds at this time as possessing *generalized intelligence*, reflecting his belief that domain general learning mechanisms, such as Pavlovian conditioning and implicit learning (e.g., A.S. Reber, 1993), predominated.

Nevertheless, the early tools of this period mark a momentous breakthrough for our species. Today we are accustomed to seeing everywhere the outcomes of what began as a spark of insight in someone's mind, but when the world consisted solely of naturally formed objects, the capacity to imagine something and turn it into a reality may well have seemed almost magical. As de Baune (2004) puts it, "the moment when a hominin . . . produced a cutting tool by using a thrusting percussion . . . marks a break between our predecessors and the specifically human" (p. 142).

2.2 *The Adaptive Larger-Brained* Homo erectus

Homo habilis persisted from approximately 2.4 to 1.5 million years ago. Approximately 1.8 million years ago, *Homo erectus* appeared, followed by *Homo ergaster, archaic Homo sapiens*, and *Homo neanderthalensis*. The size of the *Homo erectus* brain was approximately 1,000 cc, about 25% larger than that of *Homo habilis*, and 75% of the cranial capacity of modern humans (Aiello, 1996; Lewin, 1999; Ruff, Trinkaus, & Holliday, 1997). *Homo erectus* exhibit many indications of enhanced ability to creatively adapt to the environment to meet the demands of survival, including sophisticated, task-specific stone hand axes, complex stable seasonal habitats, and long-distance hunting strategies involving large game. By 1.6 million years ago, *Homo erectus* had dispersed as far as Southeast Asia, indicating the ability to adjust lifestyle to vastly different climates (Antón & Swisher, 2004; Cachel & Harris, 1995; Swisher et al., 1994; Walker & Leakey, 1993). In Africa, West Asia, and Europe, by 1.4 million years ago *Homo erectus* developed the Aschulean hand axe (Asfaw et al., 1992), a do-it-all tool that may even have had some function as a social status symbol (Kohn & Mithen, 1999). These symmetrical biface stone tools probably required several stages of production, bifacial knapping, and considerable skill and spatial ability to achieve their final form.

Though the anatomical capacity for language was present by this time (Wynn, 1998), verbal communication is thought to have been limited to (at best) presyntactical protolanguage (Dunbar, 1996). Thought during this time period was most likely only first order; the capacity for thinking about thinking (i.e., metacognition) had not yet developed.

2.3 *Possible Explanations for the Onset of Human Creativity*

It has been suggested that these early archaeological finds do not reflect any underlying biological change but were simply a response to climactic change (Richerson & Boyd, 2000). However, given the significant increase in cranial capacity, it seems parsimonious to posit that this dramatic encephalization allowed a more sophisticated mode of cognitive functioning and is thus at least partly responsible for the appearance of cultural artifacts (and the beginnings of an archaeological record).

There are multiple versions of the hypothesis that the onset of the archaeological record reflects an underlying cognitive transition. One suggestion is that the appearance of archaeological novelty is due to the onset of the capacity to imitate (Dugatkin, 2001), or the onset of a *theory of mind* – the capacity to reason about the men-

tal states of others (Premack & Woodruff, 1978). However, other species possess a theory of mind (Heyes, 1998) and imitate (Byrne & Russon, 1998; Darwin, 1871), yet they do not compare to hominids with respect to creativity. Moreover, although these hypotheses may explain how new ideas, once in place, spread from one individual to another, they are inadequate as an explanation of the enhanced capacity for coming up with new ideas in the first place.

Yet another proposal is that *Homo* underwent a transition at this time from an *episodic mode* of cognitive functioning to a *mimetic mode* (Donald, 1991). The episodic mind of *Homo habilis* was sensitive to the significance of episodes, and it could encode them in memory and coordinate appropriate responses. But it could not voluntarily access them independent of cues. The enlarged cranial capacity of *Homo erectus* enabled it to acquire a mimetic form of cognition, characterized by possession of what Donald (1991) refers to as a "self-triggered recall and rehearsal loop," or SRRL. The SRRL enabled hominids to voluntarily access memories independent of cues and thereby act out events that occurred in the past, or that could occur in the future (indeed the term *mimetic* is derived from the word "mime"). Thus not only could the mimetic mind temporarily escape the here and now, but through gesture it could bring about a similar escape in other minds. The SRRL also enabled hominids to engage in a stream of thought, such that attention is directed away from the external world toward one's internal model of it, and one thought or idea evokes another, revised version of it, which evokes yet another, and so forth recursively. Finally, the SRRL enabled the capacity to evaluate and improve motor acts through repetition or rehearsal, and adapt them to new situations, resulting in more refined artifacts and survival tactics.

It seems reasonable that a larger brain might be more likely to engage in self-triggered recall and rehearsal, but Donald's scenario becomes even more plausible when considered in light of the structure and dynamics of associative memory (Gabora,

2003, 2010). We know that neurons are sensitive to *microfeatures* – primitive attributes of a stimulus, such as a sound of a particular pitch, or a line of a particular orientation (Churchland & Sejnowski, 1992; Smolensky, 1988). Episodes etched in memory are *distributed* across a bundle or cell assembly of these neurons, and likewise, each neuron participates in the encoding of many episodes. Finally, memory is *content addressable* such that similar stimuli activate and get encoded in overlapping distributions of neurons. It seems reasonable that brain enlargement entails a transition from a more coarse-grained to a more fine-grained memory, such that episodes are encoded in more detail. This means there are more ways in which distributions can overlap, and thus more routes by which one can evoke another, providing an anatomical basis for self-triggered recall and rehearsal, and the forging of creative connections. The enhanced ability to make connections would in turn have paved the way for a more integrated internal model of the world, or worldview.

3. Over a Million Years of Creative Stasis

The hand axe persisted as the almost exclusive tool of choice for over a million years, spreading by 500,000 years ago into Europe, where was it used until about 200,000 years ago. Indeed during this period not only is there almost no change in tool design, but little evidence of creative insight of any kind, with the exception of the first solid evidence for controlled use of fire some 800,000 years ago in the Levant (Goren-Inbar et al., 2004).

3.1 *A Second Increase in Brain Size*

Between 600,000 and 150,000 years ago there was a second spurt in brain enlargement (Aiello 1996; Ruff et al., 1997). But although *anatomically* modern humans had arrived, *behavioral* modernity had not. It would make our story simple if the increase in brain size coincided with the burst of creativity in the Middle/Upper Paleolithic (Bickerton,

1990; Mithen, 1998), to be discussed in the next section. It does correspond with the revolutionary advancement of the Levallois flake, which came into prominence approximately 250,000 years ago in the Neanderthal line. But although one sees in the artifacts of this time the germ of modern-day representational thought, it is clear that cognitive processes are still primarily first order – tied to concrete sensory experience – rather than second order – derivative, or abstract. R. Leakey (1984) writes of anatomically modern human populations in the Middle East with little in the way of culture, and concludes that "the link between anatomy and behavior therefore seems to break" (p. 95).

It may be that this second spurt in brain size exerted an impact on expressions of creativity that leave little trace in the archaeological record, such as finding ways of manipulating competitors for purposes of survival and reproduction (Baron-Cohen, 1995; Byre & Whiten, 1988; Dunbar, 1996; Humphrey, 1976; Whiten, 1991; Whiten & Byrne, 1997; Wilson, Near, & Miller, 1996). However it is possible that what we see in the archaeological record really does reflect what was happening at the time, i.e. that there really was a rift between anatomical and behavioral modernity. We will return to this mystery after examining how the spectacular creativity of modern humans came about.

4. The Creative Minds of Modern Humans

The European archaeological record indicates that a truly unparalleled cultural transition occurred between 60,000 and 30,000 years ago at the onset of the Upper Paleolithic (Bar-Yosef et al., 1986; Klein, 1989a; Mellars, 1973, 1989a, 1989b; Soffer, 1994; Stringer & Gamble, 1993). Considering it "evidence of the modern human mind at work," Richard Leakey (1984, pp. 93–94) describes the Upper Paleolithic as "unlike previous eras, when stasis dominated, . . . [with] change being measured in millennia rather than hundreds of millennia." Similarly, Mithen (1996) refers to the Upper Paleolithic as the "big bang" of human culture, exhibiting more innovation than in the previous 6 million years of human evolution. At this time that we see the more-or-less simultaneous appearance of traits considered diagnostic of behavioral modernity. It marks the beginning of a more organized, strategic, season-specific style of hunting involving specific animals at specific sites, elaborate burial sites indicative of ritual and religion, evidence of dance, magic, and totemism, the colonization of Australia, and replacement of Levallois tool technology by blade cores in the Near East. In Europe, complex hearths and many forms of art appeared, including naturalistic cave paintings of animals, decorated tools and pottery, bone and antler tools with engraved designs, ivory statues of animals and sea shells, and personal decoration such as beads, pendants, and perforated animal teeth, many of which may have been used to indicate social status (White, 1989a, 1989b). Indeed, White (1982, p. 176) also writes of a "total restructuring of social relations." What is perhaps most impressive about this period is not the novelty of any particular artifact but that the overall pattern of cultural change is cumulative; more recent artifacts resemble older ones but have modifications that enhance their appearance or functionality. This appears to be uniquely human (Donald, 1998) and it has been referred to as the *ratchet effect* (Tomasello, 1999).

Despite a lack of any overall increase in cranial capacity, there was a significant increase in the size of the prefrontal cortex – and particularly the orbitofrontal region (Deacon, 1997; Dunbar, 1993; Jerison, 1973; Krasnegor, Lyon, & Goldman-Rakic, 1997; Rumbaugh, 1997), and it was likely a time of major neural reorganization (Henshilwood, d'Errico, Vanhaeren, van Niekerk, & Jacobs, 2004; Klein, 1999; Pinker, 2002). These brain changes may have given rise to what Feist (2008) refers to as "meta-representational thought," or the ability to reflect on representations and think about thinking. Along similar lines, Dennett (1976) suggests that an important transition in the evolution of *Homo sapiens* is from first-order intentionality to second-order intentionality. A first-order intentional system has beliefs and desires but cannot reflect on those beliefs and desires, whereas second-order intentional system has beliefs and desires about the beliefs and desires of themselves and others.

Whether this period was a genuine revolution culminating in behavioral modernity is hotly debated because claims to this effect are based on the European Paleolithic record, and largely exclude the African record (Henshilwood & Marean, 2003; McBrearty & Brooks, 2000). Indeed, most of the artifacts associated with a rapid transition to behavioral modernity between 40,000 and 50,000 years ago in Europe are found in the African Middle Stone Age tens of thousands of years earlier. These include blades and microliths, bone tools, specialized hunting, long-distance trade, art and decoration (McBrearty & Brooks, 2000), the Berekhat Ram figurine from Israel (d'Errico & Nowell, 2000), and an anthropomorphic figurine of quartzite from the Middle Ascheulian (ca. 400 ka) site of Tan-tan in Morocco (Bednarik, 2003). Moreover, gradualist models of the evolution of behavioral modernity well before the Upper Paleolithic find some support in archaeological data (Bahn, 1991; Harrold, 1992; Henshilwood & Marean, 2003; White, 1993; White et al., 2003). If modern human behaviors were indeed gradually assembled as early as 250,000 to 300,000 years ago, as McBrearty and Brooks (2000) argue, it pushes the transition into alignment with the most recent spurt in human brain enlargement. However, the traditional and probably currently dominant view is that behaviorally modern humans appeared in Africa approximately 50,000 years ago, and spread throughout in Europe, replacing others who had not achieved behavioral modernity, including the Neanderthals (e.g., Ambrose, 1998; Gamble, 1994; Klein, 2003; Stringer & Gamble, 1993). From this point onward, anatomically and behaviorally modern *Homo sapiens* were the only living hominids.

4.1 *Cognitive Explanations*

Whether one believes the change happened gradually or suddenly, it is accepted that the Middle/Upper Paleolithic was a period of unprecedented creativity. How and why did it occur? What kind of cognitive processes were involved? We now review the most popular hypotheses for what kind of biologically evolved cognitive advantages gave rise to behavioral modernity at this time.

4.1.1 ADVENT OF SYNTACTIC LANGUAGE

It has been suggested that humans underwent at this time a transition from a predominantly gestural to a vocal form of communication (Corballis, 2002). Although owing to the ambiguity of the archaeological evidence we may never know exactly when language began (Bednarik, 1992, p. 30; Davidson & Noble, 1989), most scholars agree that although earlier Homo and even Neanderthals may have been capable of primitive protolanguage, the grammatical and syntactic aspects of language emerged near the beginning of the Upper Paleolithic (Aiello & Dunbar, 1993; Bickerton, 1990, 1996; Dunbar, 1993, 1996; Tomasello, 1999). Carstairs-McCarthy (1999) presents a modified version of this proposal, suggesting that although some form of syntax was present in the earliest languages, most of the later elaboration, including recursive embedding of syntactic structure, emerged in the Upper Paleolithic. Syntax enabled language to become general purpose and put to use in a variety of situations. It enhanced not just the ability to communicate with others, spread ideas from one individual to the next, and collaborate on creative projects (thereby speeding up cultural innovation), but also the ability to think things through precisely for oneself and manipulate ideas in a controlled, deliberate fashion (Reboul, 2007).

4.1.2 SYMBOLIC REASONING

Another suggestion is that the creativity of the Middle/Upper Paleolithic was due to the emergence of an ability to internally represent complex, abstract, internally coherent systems of meaning, including sym-

bols and the *causal relationships* amongst them (Deacon, 1997). According to Deacon, we shifted from *iconic representation*, in which the representation physically resembles what it 'stands for', to *indexical representation*, in which the representation implies or 'points' to the thing it stands for, to *symbolic representation*, in which there is no similarity or implied relationship between the representation and what it stands for. Deacon claims that the onset of symbol use colored our existence by making us view objects and people in terms of the roles they could play in stories, and the point or meaning they could potentially have, or participate in.

4.1.3 COGNITIVE FLUIDITY

It is undoubtedly the case that symbolic representation plays a fundamental role in the mental life of modern humans. Others however believe that the transition from iconic to indexical to symbolic representation was a secondary consequence of onset of the intuitive, divergent, associative processes by which we unearth *relationships of correlation* (or roughly, similarity), such as through the discovery of analogies. Fauconnier and Turner (2002) propose that the exceptional creativity of the Middle/Upper Paleolithic was due to the onset of the capacity to blend concepts, which facilitated analogy formation and the weaving of experiences into stories and parables. A similar explanation is put forward by Mithen (1996), drawing on the evolutionary psychologist's notion of massive modularity (Buss, 1999/2004; Cosmides & Tooby, 1992; Dunbar et al., 1994; Rozin, 1976; for an extensive critique see Buller, 2005). Mithen suggests that the creativity of the modern mind arose through the onset of *cognitive fluidity*, resulting in the *connecting* of what were previously encapsulated (functionally isolated) brain modules devoted to natural history, technology, social processes, and language. This he claims gave us the ability to map, explore, and transform conceptual spaces, referring to Boden's (1990) definition of a conceptual space as a "style of thinking – in music, sculpture, choreography, chemistry, etc." Sperber (1994) proposes that the connecting of modules involved a special module, the "module of meta-representation" (MMR) which contains "concepts of concepts," and enabled cross-domain thinking, and particularly analogies and metaphors.

Note that the notion of modules amounts to an explicit high-level compartmentalization of the brain for different tasks. However, this kind of division of labor – and the ensuing creativity – would emerge unavoidably as the brain got larger *without* explicit high-level compartmentalization, owing to the sparse, distributed, content-addressable manner in which neurons encode information (Gabora, 2003, 2010). As noted earlier, neurons are tuned to respond to different microfeatures, and there is a systematic relationship between the content of a stimulus and the distributed set of neurons that respond to it, such that neurons that respond to similar microfeatures tend to be near one another. Thus, as the brain got larger, the number of neurons increased, and the brain accordingly responded to more microfeatures, so items could be encoded in more detail. Neighboring neurons tended to respond to microfeatures that were more similar, and distant neurons tended to respond to microfeatures that were more different. Therefore there were more ways in which distributed representations could overlap and creative connections could be made. Thus a weak modularity of sorts emerges naturally at the neuronal level without any explicit high-level compartmentalization going on, and it need not necessarily correspond to how humans carve up the world, that is, to categories such as natural history, technology, and so forth. Moreover, explicit connecting of modules is not necessary for creative connections to be made; all that is necessary is that the relevant domains be simultaneously accessible.

4.1.4 CONTEXTUAL FOCUS
The above proposals for what kind of cognitive change could have led to the Upper Paleolithic transition stress different

aspects of cognitive modernity. Acknowledging a possible seed of truth in each of them, we begin to converge toward a common (if more complex) view. Conceptual blending is characteristic of *divergent* or associative *thought*, which tends to be automatic, intuitive, and diffuse. This is quite different from *convergent* or *analytical thought*, which tends to be logical, and controlled. It is widely believed that the modern mind engages in both (Arieti, 1976; Ashby & Ell, 2002; Freud, 1949; Guilford, 1950; James, 1890/1950; Johnson-Laird, 1983; Kris, 1952; Neisser, 1963; Piaget, 1926; Rips, 2001; Sloman, 1996; Stanovich & West, 2000; Werner, 1948; Wundt, 1896). This is sometimes referred to as the dual-process theory of human cognition (Chaiken & Trope, 1999; Evans & Frankish, 2009) and it is consistent with current theories of creative cognition (Finke, Ward, & Smith, 1992; Gabora, 2002, 2010; Smith, Ward, & Finke, 1995; Ward, Smith, & Finke, 1999). Divergent processes are hypothesized to occur during idea generation, whereas convergent processes predominate during the refinement, implementation, and testing of an idea. It has been proposed that the Paleolithic transition reflects a mutation to the gene(s) involved in the fine-tuning of the biochemical mechanisms underlying the capacity to shift between these modes, depending on the situation, by varying the specificity of the activated cognitive receptive field (Gabora, 2003, 2010; for similar ideas see Howard-Jones & Murray, 2003; Martindale, 1995). This is referred to as *contextual focus*[1] because it requires the ability to focus or defocus attention in response to the context or situation one is in. Defocused attention, by diffusely activating a broad region of memory, is conducive to divergent thought; it enables obscure (but potentially relevant) aspects of the situation to come into play. Focused attention is conducive to convergent thought; memory activation is constrained enough to hone in and perform

1 In neural net terms, contextual focus amounts to the capacity to spontaneously and subconsciously vary the shape of the activation function, flat for divergent thought and spiky for analytical.

logical mental operations on the most clearly relevant aspects. Thus in an analytic mode of thought the concept *giant* might only activate the notion of large size, whereas in an associative mode the giants of fairytales might come to mind. Once it was possible to shrink or expand the field of attention, and thereby tailor one's mode of thought to the demands of the current situation, tasks requiring either convergent thought (e.g., mathematical derivation), divergent thought (e.g., poetry), or both (e.g., technological invention) could be carried out more effectively. When the individual is fixated or stuck, and progress is not forthcoming, defocusing attention enables the individual to enter a more divergent mode of thought, and working memory expands to include peripherally related elements of the situation. This continues until a potential solution is glimpsed, at which point attention becomes more focused and thought becomes more convergent, as befits the fine-tuning and manifestation of the creative work.

Thus the onset of contextual focus would have enabled the hominid to adapt ideas to new contexts or combine them in new ways through divergent thought, and to fine-tune these strange new combinations through convergent thought. In this way the fruits of one mode of thought provide the ingredients for the other, culminating in a more fine-grained internal model of the world.

4.1.1 SHIFTING BETWEEN IMPLICIT AND EXPLICIT THOUGHT

In a similar vein, it has been proposed that cognitive fluidity enabled hominids to move not just 'horizontally' between domains (as Mithen [1996] suggests), but also 'vertically' between implicit and explicit modes of thought (Feist, 2008). Implicit and explicit cognition map roughly onto divergent and convergent modes of thought. While *explicit cognition* is equated with advanced abilities such as planning, reasoning, and hypothesis-guided deduction, *implicit cognition* is associated with the ability to automatically detect complex regularities, contingencies, and covariances in our environment (e.g., A.S. Reber, 1993). Implicit cognition plays

a significant role in structuring our perceptions and behavior (Berry & Broadbent, 1988; Cleeremans & Jiménez, 2002; Hassin, Uleman, & Bargh, 2005; S.B. Kaufman, 2007; Lewicki, Czyzewska, & Hoffman, 1987; Lewicki & Hill, 1987; McGeorge & Burton, 1990; A.S. Reber, 1967, 1993; P.J. Reber & Kotovsky, 1997; Squire & Frambach, 1990). It is thought to be useful for making broad associations and arriving at creative ideas, and believed to be a fundamental aspect of our humanness (Bowers, Farvolden, & Mermigis, 1995; S.B. Kaufman, 2008, in press).

It may be that the fruits of associative or implicit processes come to awareness only once they have been honed into a form that is sufficiently well defined that we can mentally operate on them, or on symbolic representations of them. Then the executive functions associated with explicit cognition use this information to produce thought and behavior that is more complex than could have resulted from either associative/implicit or analytic/explicit processes alone. A contributing factor to the emergence of the ability to shift between these modes of thought may have been the expansion of the prefrontal cortex, and the associated executive functions and enhanced working memory[2] capacity that came with the expansion. Enhanced working memory allowed humans more control over their focus of attention so as to maintain task goals in the presence of interference. Indeed, individual differences in working memory are strongly related to fluid intelligence among modern humans (Conway, Jarrold, Kane, Miyake, & Towse, 2007; Engle, Tuholski, Laughlin, & Conway, 1999; Kane, Hambrick, & Conway, 2005; S.B. Kaufman, DeYoung, Gray, Brown, & Mackintosh, 2009).

4.2 The Multi-Layered Mind and a Return to the Lag between Anatomical and Behavioral Modernity

Several researchers emphasize that the modern human mind consists of various "kinds of

---

2   Working memory is the ability to maintain, update, and manipulate information in an active state.

minds" layered on top of one another (A.S. Reber, 1989, 1993; A.S. Reber & Allen, 2000; Dennett, 1995, 1996). According to these accounts, these multiple minds are continuously operative, giving rise to many internal and external conflicts amongst members of our species, as well as contributing to our most distinctly human intellectual and creative accomplishments. Arthur Reber proposes that implicit cognition is evolutionarily older than explicit cognition. It may stem from the oldest parts of the brain and in its crudest form be involved in the execution of behavior patterns that are prewired, reflexive, and tied to survival-related goals, while our later-evolving explicit capacities for reflection and deliberate reasoning may allow us to override strictly survival-related goals (Stanovich, 2005).

Alternatively, it may be that more brain tissue simultaneously allowed for not *just* the onset of explicit reasoning but also a qualitatively different kind of implicit processing, one in which the detection of gradations of similarity paves the way for cognitive flexibility. Let us return briefly to the question of why the burst of creativity in the Upper Paleolithic occurred well after the second rapid increase in brain size approximately 500,000 years ago. A larger brain provided more room for episodes to be encoded, and particularly more association cortex for connections between episodes to be made, but it is not necessarily the case that this increased brain mass could straightaway be optimally navigated. There is no reason to expect that information from different domains (whether strongly modular or weakly modular) would immediately be compatible enough to coexist in a stream of thought, as in the production of a metaphor. It is reasonable that it took time for the anatomically modern brain to fine-tune how its components "talk" to each other such that different items could be blended together or recursively revised and recoded in a coordinated manner (Gabora, 2003). Only then could the full potential of the large brain be realized. Thus the bottleneck may not have been sufficient brain size but sufficient sophistication in the *use of*

the memory already available, through contextual focus, or shifting between implicit and explicit thought. It is worth noting that other periods of revolutionary innovation, such as the Holocene transition to agriculture and the modern Industrial Revolution, occurred long after the biological changes that made them cognitively possible.

4.3 "Recent" Creative Breakthroughs

Of course the story of how human creativity evolved does not end with the arrival of anatomical and behavioral modernity. The end of the ice age approximately 10,000 to 12,000 years ago witnessed the beginnings of agriculture and the invention of the wheel. Written languages developed around 5,000 to 6,000 years ago, and approximately 4,000 years ago astronomy and mathematics appear on the scene. We see the expression of philosophical ideas around 2,500 years ago, invention of the printing press 1,000 years ago, and the modern scientific method about 500 years ago. And the past 100 years have yielded a technological explosion that has completely altered the daily routines of humans (as well as other species), the consequences of which remain to be seen.

5. Creativity and Cultural Evolution

We have examined how the *capacity* for creativity evolved over millions of years. In this section we explore the possibility that creative ideas *themselves* evolve through culture, in the sense that they exhibit "descent with modification," or incremental adaptation to the constraints of their environment. (A related idea is that the creative process not at the cultural level but within the mind of one individual is Darwinian; this is discussed in Chapter 9, this volume.)

5.1 Creative Cultural Change as a Darwinian Process

It has been proposed that the process by which creative ideas change over time as they pass from person to person can be described in Darwinian terms (Aunger, 2000; Blackmore, 1999; Boyd & Richerson, 1985; Cavalli-Sforza & Feldman, 1981; Dawkins, 1975; Durham, 1991). This approach is sometimes referred to as "dual inheritance theory," the idea being that we inherit cultural as well as biological information, and the units of cultural information are sometimes referred to as "memes." The rationale is clear; since natural selection is useful for explaining the astonishing creativity of nature, perhaps it is also useful for explaining the astonishing creativity of human culture. There are many parallels between the two. Clearly, new inventions build on existing ones, but it isn't just the *cumulative* nature of human creativity that is reminiscent of biological evolution. Cumulative change is after all rather easy to come by; in the days of taping music, each time a tape was copied it became cumulatively more scratched. The creativity of human cultures is reminiscent of biological evolution because of the *adaptive and open-ended manner* in which change accumulates. New inventions don't just build on old ones, they do so in ways that meet our needs and appeal to our tastes, and as in biological evolution there is no limit to how any particular invention or creative work may inspire or influence other creative works. Moreover, culture generates phenomena observed in biological evolution, such as drift[3] and niches[4] (Bentley et al., 2004; Gabora, 1995, 1997). A theory that encompasses the two would put us on the road to uniting the social sciences with the biological sciences.

In order to see how Darwinian theory might be applied to the evolution of creativity ideas in culture, let us examine what kind of process natural selection can describe, and how it works. The paradox faced by Darwin and his contemporaries was the following: How does biological change accumulate when traits acquired over an organism's lifetime are obliterated? For example, a rat whose tail is cut off does not give birth to rats with cut-off tails; the rat lineage loses this trait. Note that this kind of continual "backtracking" to an earlier state (e.g., in the above example, the state of having a full tail) is unique to biology; if, for example, an asteroid crashes into a planet, the planet cannot revert to the state of having not had the asteroid crash into it.[5]

Darwin's genius was to explain how living things adapt over time despite the fact that new modifications keep getting discarded, by looking from the level of the individual to the level of the *population* of interbreeding individuals. He realized that individuals who are better equipped to survive in their given environment tend to leave more offspring (be "selected"). Thus, although their *acquired* traits are discarded, their *inherited* traits (loosely speaking, the traits they were born with) are more abundant in the next generation. Over generations this can lead to substantial change in the distribution of traits across the population as a whole. Natural selection was not put forth to explain how biological novelty originates. It assumes random variation of heritable traits, and provides an explanation for population-level change in the *distribution* of variants.

We now ask: Can natural selection similarly explain the process by which creative ideas evolve through culture? A first thing that can be noted is that the problem for

3 Drift refers to changes in the relative frequencies of variants through random sampling from a finite population. It is the reason why variation is reduced in reproductively isolated populations such as those living on a small island. Drift has been shown to occur in a culture context with respect to such things as baby names and dog breed preferences (Bentley et al., 2004; Madsen et al., 1999; Neiman, 1995). In a computer model of cultural evolution, the smaller the society of artificial agents, the lower the cultural diversity (Gabora, 1995).
4 Just as the biological evolution of rabbits created niches for species that eat them and parasitize their guts, the cultural evolution of cars created niches for seat belts and gas stations (Gabora, 1997, 1998).

5 Although Darwin observed that this was the case, he did not know why. We now know that the reason acquired traits are not inherited in biology is that organisms replicate using a template – a self-assembly code that is both actively transcribed to produce a new individual, and passively copied to ensure that the new individual can itself reproduce.

which natural selection was put forward as a solution does not exist with respect to culture (Gabora, 2008). That is, there is no sense in which the components of creative ideas cyclically accumulate and then get discarded at the interface between one generation and the next. For example, unlike the chopped off tail which does not get transmitted to offspring, once someone invented the spout on a teapot, teapots could forever after have spouts. One might ask if Darwin's solution is nevertheless applicable; might processes outside of biology evolve through selection even if selection was originally advanced as a solution to a paradox that is unique to biology? The problem is that since acquired change can accumulate orders of magnitude faster than inherited change, if it is *not* getting regularly discarded, it quickly overwhelms the population-level mechanism of change identified by Darwin. This is particularly the case with respect to creative ideas since they do not originate through random processes – or even processes prone to canceling one another out – but through strategic or implicit, intuitive processes, making use of the associative structure of memory.

Darwinian approaches to culture posit that the basic units of this second Darwinian process are discrete elements of culture that pass from one person to another intact except for random change akin to mutation that arises through copying error or biased transmission (preferential copying of high-status individuals). Copying error and biased transmission are sources of change that take place at the time an idea spreads from one individual to another, which creativity researchers tend to view as a relatively minor source of creative change compared with cognitive processes such as imagining, planning, analogizing, concept combination, and so forth. The reason that Darwinian theories of culture focus on sources of change that occur when an idea spreads from one individual to another is not accidental; it stems from the fact that natural selection is of explanatory value only to the extent that there is negligible trans-

mission of acquired characteristics. This is the case in biology, as we saw with the cut-off tail example; change acquired during an individual's lifetime is not generally passed on to its offspring. As another example, you didn't inherit your mother's tattoo – something she acquired between the time she was born and the time she transmitted genetic material to the next generation.

However, few scholars accept that there is negligible transmission of acquired characteristics in culture. The cultural equivalent of the individual is the creative idea. A new "generation" begins when this idea is transmitted from person A to person B, and lasts until the idea is transmitted from person B to person C. Any changes to an idea between the time B learned it and the time B expressed it are "acquired characteristics." If B mulls the idea over or puts it into her own terms or adapts it to her own framework, the process by which this idea changes cannot be explained by natural selection, because as mentioned earlier, this kind of 'intragenerational' change quickly drowns out the slower intergenerational mechanism of change identified by Darwin; it "swamps the phylogenetic signal." The Darwinian perspective on culture therefore leads to a view of the human condition as "meme hosts," passive imitators and transmitters of prepackaged units of culture, which evolve as separate lineages. To the extent that these lineages "contaminate one another" – that is, to the extent that we actively and creatively transform elements of culture in ways that reflect our own internal models of the world, altering or combining them to suit our needs, perspectives, or aesthetic sensibilities – natural selection cannot explain cultural change. It has been argued that due to this "lack-of-inheritance-of-acquired-characteristics" problem, not just the evolution of creative ideas (Gabora, 2005) and the evolution of culture (Gabora, 2004, 2008), but the evolution of early life itself (Gabora, 2006; Vetsigian et al., 2006), and even of many features of modern life (e.g. Jablonka & Lamb, 2005; Kauffman, 1993; Newman & Müller, 1999; Schwartz, 1999), cannot be described by Darwin's theory of natural selection.

5.2 *A Non-Darwinian Theory of How Creative Ideas Evolve*

If creative ideas do not evolve through selection, how do they evolve? One possibility is that the evolution of creative ideas through culture is more akin to the evolution of the earliest biological life forms than to present-day DNA-based life (Gabora, 2000, 2004, 2008). Recent work suggests that early life emerged and replicated through a self-organized process referred to as *autocatalysis*, in which a set of molecules catalyze (speed up) the reactions that generate other molecules in the set, until as a whole they self-replicate (Kauffman, 1993). Such a structure is said to be *autopoietic*, or *self-regenerating*, because the whole is reconstituted through the interactions of the parts (Maturana & Varela, 1980). These earliest precursors of life evolved not through natural selection at the level of the population, like present-day life, but communal exchange of innovation at the individual level (Gabora, 2006; Vetsigian, Woese, & Goldenfeld, 2006). Since replication of these pre-DNA life forms occurred through regeneration of catalytic molecules rather than (as with present-day life) by using a genetic self-assembly code, acquired traits were inherited. In other words, their evolution was, like that of culture, Lamarckian.

This has led to the suggestion that worldviews evolve through culture, through the same non-Darwinian process as the earliest forms of life evolved, and creative products such as tools and dances and architectural plans are external manifestations of this process; they reflect the states of the particular worldviews that generate them. The idea is that like these early life forms, worldviews evolve not through natural selection, but through self-organization and communal exchange of innovations. One does not accumulate elements of culture transmitted from others like items on a grocery list, but hones them into a unique tapestry of understanding, a worldview, which like these early

life forms is autopoietic in that the whole emerges through interactions amongst the parts. It is *self-mending* in the sense that, just as injury to the body spontaneously evokes physiological changes that bring about healing, events that are problematic or surprising or evoke cognitive dissonance spontaneously evokes streams of thought that attempt to solve the problem or reconcile the dissonance (Gabora, 2008). Thus, according to this view it is not chance, mutation-like processes that propel creativity, but the self-organizing, self-mending nature of a worldview.

6. Why Did Creativity Evolve?

We have discussed how human creativity evolved, and in what sense creative ideas can be said to evolve. We now address a fundamental question: *Why* did human creativity evolve?

6.1 *Creativity as Evolutionary Spandrels*

Some forms of creativity enhance survival and thus reproductive fitness. For example, the invention of weapons most likely evolved as a creative response to a need for protection from enemies and predators. For other forms of creative expression, however, such as art and music, the link to survival and reproduction is not so clear-cut. Why do we bother?

One possibility is that art, music, humor, fiction, religion, and philosophy are not real adaptations, but evolutionary spandrels: side-effects of abilities that evolved for other purposes (Pinker, 1997; see also Carroll, 1995; Gabora, 2003; J.C. Kaufman, Lee, Baer, & Lee, 2007; McBrearty & Brooks, 2000). Pinker likens these forms of creativity to cheesecake and pornography – cultural inventions that stimulate our senses in novel ways but do not improve our biological fitness.

The "spandrels" explanation assumes that what drives creativity is biological selection forces operating at the individual level, and there is some empirical support for this.

Some forms of human creativity, such as art and music, indeed demonstrate the features of a naturally selected adaptation (Dissanayake, 1988, 1992). First, many forms of creativity are ubiquitous. Although styles differ, every culture creates works of art and music. Second, many forms of creativity are pleasurable for both the artist and the audience, and evolutionarily adaptive behaviors are usually pleasurable. Third, many forms of human creativity require considerable time and effort. The fact that creativity is costly is suggestive of a selective pressure at work.

6.2 Group Bonding

Even if creativity is at least in part driven by individual-level biological selection forces, other forces may also be at work. Natural selection is believed to operate at multiple levels, including gene-level selection, individual-level survival selection, individual-level sexual selection, kin selection, and group selection. Although there is evidence from archaeology, anthropology, and ethnography that individual-level survival selection plays a key role in human creativity, other levels may have an impact as well. For example, some anthropologists view the function of forms of creativity such as art and music as strengthening a group's social cohesion. For music in particular, Mithen (2006) presents evidence that the melodious vocalizations by our earliest ancestors played an important role in creating and manipulating social relationships through their impact on emotional states.

6.3 Sexual Selection

Miller (2000a) argues that group-bonding accounts of creativity ignore the possible role of sexual selection in shaping creative behavior, and cannot account for the sexual attractiveness of various forms of creativity. This idea has its roots in Darwin, who once said, "It appears probable that the progenitors of man, either the males or females or both sexes, before acquiring the power of expressing mutual love in articulate language, endeavored to charm each other with musical notes and rhythm" (Darwin, 1871, p. 880).

According to the sexual-selection account, there is competition to mate with individuals who exhibit creative traits that are (in theory) metabolically expensive, hard to maintain, not easily counterfeited, and highly sensitive to genetic mutation because they are the most reliable indicators of genetic fitness. In recent years, Miller (1998, 2000a, 2000b, 2001; J.C. Kaufman et al., 2007) has developed and popularized this theory. He argues that sexual selection played a much greater role than natural selection in shaping the most distinctively human aspects of our minds, including storytelling, art, music, sports, dance, humor, kindness, and leadership. He contends that these creative behaviors are the result of complex psychological adaptations whose primary functions were to attract mates, yielding reproductive rather than survival benefits. Miller notes that cultural displays of human creativity satisfy these requirements. According to this account, cultural displays are the result of efforts to broadcast courtship displays to recipients: "art evolved, at least originally, to attract sexual partners by playing upon their senses and displaying one's fitness" (Miller, 2000a, p. 267).

Along similar lines, Marek Kohn and Steven Mithen (Kohn, 1999; Kohn & Mithen, 1999) propose what they refer to as the "sexy-hand axe hypothesis." According to this hypothesis, sexual-selection pressures may have caused men to produce symmetric hand axes as a reliable indicator of cognitive, behavioral, and physiological fitness. As Mithen (1996) notes, symmetrical hand axes are often attractive to the modern eye, but require a huge investment in time and energy to make – a burden that makes it hard to explain their evolution in terms of strictly practical, survival purposes. Since hand axes may be viewed as the first aesthetic artifacts in the archeological record, these products may indeed be the first evidence of sexual selection shaping the emergence of art.

Although it is conceivable that sexual selection plays some role in the evolution of ornamental or aesthetic forms of creativity, such as art, music, dance, and humor, it is less conceivable that it plays a role in the evolution of forms of creativity with direct survival benefits, such as technological advances (Feist, 2001). Moreover, to make the argument convincing it would be necessary to show that creative people are indeed considered more attractive, and have greater reproductive success. Although there is some evidence that intelligent and creative individuals are considered more attractive and have more sexual partners (Buss, 1989; Griskevicius, Cialdini, & Kenrick, 2006; Nettle & Clegg, 2006; Prokosch et al., 2009), there is also evidence that creative people tend to be less likely to marry and, when they do, have fewer children (Harrison, Moore, & Rucker, 1985), a factor that surely also impacts their reproductive success. Moreover time spent on creative projects may be time taken away from mating and child rearing.

Mithen (2006) presents evidence that the musicality of our ancestors and relatives did in fact have considerable survival value as a means of communicating emotions, intentions, information, and facilitating cooperation, and thus sexual selection may well not be the sole or primary selective pressure for musicality. Additionally, he notes that although it may appear at first blush that creative men have more short-term sexual partners because of their creativity, their attractiveness may be more the combination of good looks, style, and an antiestablishment persona.

Perhaps the most reasonable conclusion is that sexual selection may have helped ramp up the evolution of creativity, exaggerating certain forms, or making them not so purely functional but also ornamental.

6.4 Non-biological Explanations for Creativity

If culture constitutes a second form of evolution, it may also exert pressures on us that differ from, or even counter, those exerted on us by our biology. The drive to create is often compared with the drive to procreate, and evolutionary forces may be at the genesis of both. In other words, we may be tinkered with by two evolutionary forces, one that prompts us to act in ways that foster the proliferation of our biological lineage, and one that prompts us to act in ways that foster the proliferation of our cultural lineage. For example, it has been suggested that we exhibit a cultural form of altruism, such that we are kind not only to those with whom we share genes but with whom we share ideas and values (Gabora, 1997). By contributing to the well-being of those who share our cultural makeup, we aid the proliferation of our "cultural selves." Similarly, when we are in the throes of creative obsession, it may be that cultural forces are compelling us to give all we have to our ideas, much as biological forces compel us to provide for our children.

Note that all of the theories discussed so far in this section attempt to explain why humans are creative at all, but even with these same pressures operating we would not be particularly creative if we did not live in a richly fascinating world that *affords* creativity. Rosch (1975) provides evidence that we form concepts in such a way as to internally mirror the correlational structure of the external world. Similarly, much creativity is inspired by the goal of understanding, explaining, and mastering the world we live in. Thus the beauty and intricacy of our ideas, and how they unfold over time, reflects in part the beauty and intricacy of our world, not just the world we actually live in, but the potential worlds *suggested by* the world we live in, and the fact that as our internal models of the world – our worldviews – change, so does this halo of potential worlds. Indeed one could say that human creativity evolves by compelling susceptible individuals (those whose minds are poised to solve particular creatively challenging problems or engage in creative tasks) to temporarily put aside concerns associated with survival of the "biological self," and to reach into this "halo of possibility," rework familiar narratives, or juxtapose familiar objects and reconceptualize their interrelationships, and thereby hone a more nuanced "cultural self." In sum, the creative process is compelling and our creative achievements unfold with breathtaking speed and complexity in part because we are fortunate enough to live in a world that offers infinite possibilities for exploring not just the realm of "what is" but the realm of "what could be."

7. Conclusions

This chapter addressed a number of questions that lie at the foundation of who we are and what makes human life meaningful. Why does no other species remotely approach the degree of cultural complexity of humans? How did humans become so good at generating ideas and adapting them to new situations? Why are humans driven to create? Do creative ideas evolve in the same sense as biological life – through natural selection – or by some other means?

We began with a brief tour of the history of *Homo sapiens*, starting 6 million years ago when we began diverging from our ancestral apes. The earliest signs of creativity are simple stone tools, thought to be made by *Homo habilis*, just over 2 million years ago. Although primitive, they marked a momentous breakthrough: the arrival of a species that would eventually refashion to its liking an entire planet. With the arrival of *Homo erectus* roughly 1.8 million years ago, there was a dramatic enlargement in cranial capacity coinciding with solid evidence of creative thinking: task-specific stone hand axes, complex stable seasonal habitats, and signs of coordinated, long-distance hunting. It has been proposed that the larger brain allowed items encoded in memory to be more fine grained, which facilitated the forging of creative connections between them, and paved the way for self-triggered thought, rehearsal and refinement of skills, and thus the ability mentally to go beyond "what is" to "what could be."

Another rapid increase in cranial capacity occurred between 600,000 and 150,000 years ago. It preceded by some hundreds of thousands of years the sudden flourishing of creativity between 60,000 and 30,000 years ago in the Middle/Upper Paleolithic, which is associated with the beginnings of art, science, politics, religion, and probably syntactical language. The time lag suggests that behavioral modernity arose owing not to new brain parts or increased memory but a more sophisticated way of *using* memory. This may have involved the onset of symbolic thinking, cognitive fluidity, and the capacity to shift between convergent and divergent or explicit and implicit modes of thought. Also, the emergence of metacognition enabled our ancestors to reflect on and even override their own nature.

This chapter also reviewed efforts to understand the role of creativity in not just biological but also cultural evolution. Some have investigated the intriguing possibility that the cultural evolution of ideas and inventions occurs through a Darwinian process akin to natural selection. A problem faced by Darwinian approaches is that natural selection is inapplicable to the extent that there is inheritance of acquired traits, and so such an approach is inappropriate to the extent that individuals actively shape ideas and adapt them to their own needs and aesthetic tastes. They can account for creative change that occurs during transmission (e.g., owing to biased transmission or copying error), but not for change that occurs because of thinking through how something could work. Nevertheless, ideas clearly exhibit phenomena observed in biological evolution, such as adaptation, niches, and drift. If they do not evolve through selection, how might they evolve? It was noted that the self-organized, self-regenerating autocatalytic structures widely believed to be the earliest forms of life did not evolve through natural selection either, but through communal exchange of innovations. It has been proposed that what evolves through culture is individuals' internal models of the world, or worldviews, and that like early life they are self-organized and self-regenerating. Worldviews evolve not through 'survival of the fittest' but through 'transformation of all' (the fit and the less fit), as new elements get incorporated, reflected upon, and adapted to new circumstances. Because no self-assembly code (such as the genetic code) is involved, their evolution is Lamarckian; acquired characteristics are inherited.

Finally, this chapter addressed the question of *why* creativity evolved. Some propose that creativity emerged as an evolutionary spandrel, that it promoted group bonding, or that sexual selection played an important role in shaping aesthetic/ornamental forms of creativity. Another possible answer derives from the theory that culture constitutes a second form of evolution, and that our thought and behavior are shaped by *two* distinct evolutionary forces. Just as the drive to procreate ensures that at least some of us make a dent in our biological lineage, the drive to create may enable us to make a dent in our cultural lineage. This second deeply embedded way of exerting a meaningful impact on the world and thereby feeling part of something larger than oneself may well come to be important as our planet becomes increasingly overpopulated. Thus, by understanding the evolutionary origins of human creativity, we gain perspective on pressing issues of today and are in a better position to use our creativity to direct the future course of our species and our planet.

Acknowledgments

This work was funded in part by grants to the first author from the *Social Sciences and Humanities Research Council of Canada* and the GOA program of the Free University of Brussels, Belgium.

References

Aiello, L. C. (1996). Hominine preadaptations for language and cognition. In P. Mellars & K. Gibson (Eds.), *Modeling the early human mind* (pp. 89–99). Cambridge: McDonald Institute Monographs.

Aiello, L. C., & Dunbar, R. (1993). Neocortex size, group size, and the evolution of language. *Current Anthropology, 34*, 184–193.

Aiello, L. C., & Wheeler, P. (1995). The Expensive-tissue hypothesis: The brain and the digestive system in human and primate evolution. *Current Anthropology, 3*, 199–221.

Ambrose, S. H. (1998.) Chronology of the later stone age and food production in East Africa. *Journal of Archaeological Science, 25*, 377–92.

Antón, S. C., & Swisher, C. C. (2004). Early dispersals of homo from Africa. *Annual Review of Anthropology, 33*, 271–296.

Arieti, S. (1976). *Creativity: The magic synthesis.* New York: Basic Books.

Asfaw, B., Beyene, Y., Suwa G., Walter, R. C., White, T. D., Woldegabriel, G., et al. (1992). The earliest acheulean from Konso-Gardula. *Nature, 360*, 732–735.

Ashby, F. G., & Ell, S. W. (2002). Single versus multiple systems of learning and memory. In J. Wixted & H. Pashler (Eds.), *Stevens' handbook of experimental psychology: Vol. 4. Methodology in experimental psychology.* New York: Wiley.

Aunger, R. (2000). *Darwinizing culture.* Oxford: Oxford University Press.

Bahn, P. G. (1991). Pleistocene images outside Europe. *Proceedings of the Prehistoric Society, 57*, 99–102.

Bahn, P. G. (1998). Neanderthals emancipated. *Nature, 394*, 719–721.

Baron-Cohen, S. (1995). *Mindblindness: An essay on autism and theory of mind.* Cambridge, MA: MIT Press.

Bar-Yosef, O., Vandermeersch, B., Arensburg, B., Goldberg, P., & Laville, H. (1986). New data on the origin of modern man in the Levant. *Current Anthropology, 27*, 63–64.

Bednarik, R. G. (1992). Paleoart and archaeological myths. *Cambridge Archaeological Journal, 2*, 27–57.

Bednarik, R. G. (2003). A figurine from the African Acheulian. *Current Anthropology, 44*, 405–413.

Bentley, R. A., Hahn, M. W., & Shennan, S. J. (2004). Random drift and culture change. *Proceedings of the Royal Society: Biology, 271*, 1443–1450.

Berry, D. C., & Broadbent, D. E. (1988). Interactive tasks and the implicit-explicit distinction. *British Journal of Psychology, 79*, 251–272.

Bickerton, D. (1990). *Language and species.* Chicago: Chicago University Press.

Bickerton, D. (1996). *Language and human behavior*. London: UCL Press.

Blackmore, S. J. (1999). *The meme machine*. Oxford: Oxford University Press.

Boden, M. (1990). *The creative mind: Myths and mechanisms*. Grand Bay, NB: Cardinal.

Bowers, K. S., Farvolden, P., & Mermigis, L. (1995). Intuitive antecedents of insight. In S. M. Smith, T. B. Ward, & R. A. Finke (Eds.), *The creative cognition approach* (pp. 27–52). Cambridge, MA: MIT Press.

Boyd, R., & Richerson, P. (1985). *Culture and the evolutionary process*. Chicago: University of Chicago Press.

Boyd, R., & Richerson, P. (1996). Why culture is common, but cultural evolution is rare. *Proceedings of the British Academy*, 88, 77–93.

Buller, D. J. (2005). *Adapting minds*. Cambridge: MIT Press.

Bunn, H. T., & Kroll, E. M. (1986). Systematic butchery by plio/pleistocene hominids at Olduvai Gorge, Tanzania. *Current Anthropology*, 27, 431–452

Buss, D. M. (1989). Sex differences in human mate preferences: Evolutionary hypotheses tested in 37 cultures. *Behavioral and Brain Sciences*, 12, 1–49.

Buss, D. M. (1994). *The evolution of desire: Strategies of human mating*. New York: Basic Books.

Buss, D. M. (1999/2004). *Evolutionary psychology: The new science of the mind*. Boston: Pearson.

Byrne, R. W., & Russon, A. (1998). Learning by imitation: A hierarchical approach. *Behavioral and Brain Sciences*, 21, 667–721.

Byre, R. W., & Whiten, A. (1988). *Machiavellian intelligence: Social expertise and the evolution of intellect in monkeys, apes, and humans*. Oxford: Clarendon Press.

Cachel, S., & Harris, J. W. K. (1995). Ranging patterns, land-use and subsistence in homoerectus from the perspective of evolutionary ecology. In J. R. F. Bower & S. Sartono (Eds.), *Evolution and ecology of homoerectus* (pp. 51–66). Leiden: Pithecanthropus Centennial Foundation.

Carey, S., & Spelke, E. (1994). Domain specific knowledge and conceptual change. In L. A. Hirschfeld & S. A. Gelman (Eds.), *Mapping the mind: Domain specificity in cognition and culture* (pp. 169–201). Cambridge, UK: Cambridge University Press.

Carstairs-McCarthy, A. (1999). *The origins of complex language*. Oxford: Oxford University Press.

Carroll, J. (1995). *Evolution and literary theory*. Columbia: University of Missouri Press.

Cavalli-Sforza, L. L., & Feldman, M. W. (1981). *Cultural transmission and evolution: A quantitative approach*. Princeton, NJ: Princeton University Press.

Chaiken, S., & Trope, Y. (1999). *Dual-process theories in social psychology*. New York: Guilford.

Churchland, P. S. & Sejnowski, T. (1992). *The Computational Brain*. Cambridge MA: MIT Press.

Cleeremans, A., & Jiménez, L. (2002). Implicit learning and consciousness: A graded, dynamic perspective. In R. M. French & A. Cleeremans (Eds.), *Implicit learning and consciousness* (pp. 1–40). Hove, UK: Psychology Press.

Conway, A. R. A., Jarrold, C., Kane, M. J., Miyake, A., & Towse, J. N. (2007). *Variation in working memory*. New York: Oxford University Press.

Cosmides, L., & Tooby, J. (1992). Cognitive adaptations for social exchange. In J. Barkow, L. Cosmides, & J. Tooby (Eds.), *The adapted mind* (pp. 163–228). New York: Oxford University Press.

Corballis, M. (2002). *From hand to mouth: The origins of language*. Princeton, NJ: Princeton University Press.

Darwin, C. (1871). *The descent of man, and selection in relation to sex* (2 vols.). London, UK: John Murray.

Dasgupta, S. (2004). Is creativity a Darwinian process? *Creativity Research Journal*, 16, 403–413.

Davidson, I., & Noble, W. (1989) The archaeology of perception: Traces of depiction and language. *Current Anthropology*, 30(2), 125–155.

Dawkins, R. (1975). *The selfish gene*. Oxford: Oxford University Press.

Deacon, T. W. (1997). *The symbolic species*. New York: W. W. Norton.

de Beaune, S. A. (2004). The invention of technology: Prehistory and cognition. *Current Anthropology*, 45, 139–162.

Dennett, D. (1976). Conditions of personhood. In A. Rorty (Ed.), *The identities of persons* (pp. 175–197). Berkeley: University of California Press.

Dennett, D. (1995). *Darwin's dangerous idea: Evolution and the meaning of life*. New York: Simon & Schuster.

Dennett, D. (1996). *Kinds of minds*. Basic Books.

D'Errico, F., & Nowell, A. (2000). A new look at the berekhat ram figurine: Implications for the origins of symbolism. *Cambridge Archaeological Journal*, 10, 123–167.

Dissanayake, W. (1988). *Communication theory: The Asian perspective*. Singapore: Asian Mass Communication Research and Information Centre.

Dissanayake, E. (1992). *Homo aestheticus: Where art comes from and why*. Seattle: University of Washington Press.

Donald, M. (1991). *Origins of the modern mind: Three stages in the evolution of culture and cognition*. Cambridge, MA: Harvard University Press.

Donald, M. (1998). Hominid enculturation and cognitive evolution. In C. Renfrew & C. Scarre (Eds.), *Cognition and material culture: The archaeology of symbolic storage* (pp. 7–17). Cambridge: McDonald Institute Monographs.

Dugatkin, L. A. (2001). *Imitation factor: Imitation in animals and the origin of human culture*. New York: Free Press.

Dunbar, R. (1993). Coevolution of neocortical size, group size, and language in humans. *Behavioral and Brain Sciences*, 16(4), 681–735.

Dunbar, R. (1996). *Grooming, gossip, and the evolution of language*. London, UK: Faber & Faber.

Evans, J., & Frankish, K. (Eds.). (2009). *In two minds: Dual processes and beyond*. New York: Oxford University Press.

Durham, W. (1991). *Coevolution: Genes, culture, and human diversity*. Stanford, CA: Stanford University Press.

Engle, R. W., Tuholski, S. W., Laughlin, J. E., & Conway, A. R. A. (1999). Working memory, short-term memory and general fluid intelligence: A latent variable approach. *Journal of Experimental Psychology: General*, 128, 309–331.

Evans, J., & Frankish, K. (2009). *In two minds: Dual processes and beyond*. New York: Oxford University Press.

Eysenck, H. J. (1995). *Genius: The natural history of creativity*. Cambridge, England: Cambridge University Press.

Fauconnier, G., & Turner, M. (2002). *The way we think: Conceptual blending and the mind's hidden complexities*. New York: Basic Books.

Feist, G. (2001). Natural and sexual selection in the evolutionary of creativity. *Bulletin of Psychology and the Arts*, 2, 11–16.

Feist, G. (2008). *The psychology of science and the origins of the scientific mind*. New Haven, CT: Yale University Press.

Finke, R. A., Ward, T. B., & Smith, S. M. (1992). *Creative cognition: Theory, research, and applications*. Cambridge, MA: The MIT Press.

Fodor, J. (1983). *The modularity of mind*. Cambridge, MA: MIT Press.

Fracchia, J., & Lewontin, R. C. (1999). Does culture evolve? *History and Theory*, 38, 52–78.

Freud, S. (1949). *An outline of psychoanalysis*. New York: Norton.

Gabora, L. (1995). Meme and variations: A computer model of cultural evolution. In L. Nadel & D. Stein (Eds.), *Lectures in complex systems* (pp. 471–486). Reading MA: Addison-Wesley.

Gabora, L. (1996). A day in the life of a meme. *Philosophica*, 57, 901–938.

Gabora, L. (2000). Conceptual closure: Weaving memories into an interconnected worldview. In G. Van de Vijver & J. Chandler (Eds.), *Closure: Emergent organizations and their dynamics*. New York: Annals of the New York Academy of Sciences.

Gabora, L. (2002). Cognitive mechanisms underlying the creative process. In T. Hewett & T. Kavanagh (Eds.), *Proceedings of the fourth international conference on creativity and cognition* (pp. 126–133). Loughborough, UK: Loughborough University Press.

Gabora, L. (2003). Contextual focus: A tentative cognitive explanation for the cultural transition of the middle/upper Paleolithic. In R. Alterman & D. Hirsch (Eds.), *Proceedings of the 25th Annual Meeting of the Cognitive Science Society*, Boston, MA. Hillsdale, NJ: Erlbaum.

Gabora, L. (2004). Ideas are not replicators but minds are. *Biology & Philosophy*, 19(1), 127–143.

Gabora, L. (2005). Creative thought as a non-Darwinian evolutionary process. *Journal of Creative Behavior*, 39(4), 65–87.

Gabora, L. (2006). Self-other organization: Why early life did not evolve through natural selection. *Journal of Theoretical Biology*, 241(3), 443–450.

Gabora, L. (2008). The cultural evolution of socially situated cognition. *Cognitive Systems Research*, 9(1–2), 104–113.

Gabora, L. (2010). Revenge of the "neurds": Characterizing creative thought in terms of the structure and dynamics of human memory. *Creativity Research Journal*, 22(1), 1–13.

Gamble, C. (1994). *Timewalkers: The prehistory of global colonization*. Cambridge, MA: Harvard University Press.

Gardner, H. (1983). *Frames of mind: The theory of multiple intelligences*. New York: Basic Books.

Gardner, H. (1999). *Intelligence reframed: Multiple intelligences for the 21st century*. New York: Basic Books.

Geary, D. C., & Huffman, K. J. (2002). Brain and cognitive evolution: Forms of modularity and functions of mind. *Psychological Bulletin*, 128, 667–698.

Gelman, R., & Brenneman, L. (1994). First principles can support both universal and culture specific learning about number and music. In L. A. Hirschfeld & S. A. Gelman (Eds.), *Mapping the mind: Domain specificity in cognition and culture* (pp. 369–391). New York: Cambridge University Press.

Gopnik, A., Meltzoff, A. N., & Kuhl, P. K. (1999). *The scientist in the crib: Minds, brains, and how children learn*. New York: William Morrow.

Goren-Inbar, N., Alperson, N., Kislev, M. E., Simchoni, O. Melamed., Y., Ben-Nun, A., et al. (2004). Evidence of Hominin control of fire at Gesher Benot Ya'aqov, Israel. *Science*, 304, 725–727.

Griskevicius, V., Cialdini, R. B., & Kenrick, D. T. (2006). Peacocks, Picasso, and parental investment: The effects of romantic motives on creativity. *Journal of Personality and Social Psychology*, 91, 63–76.

Guilford, P. J. (1950). Creativity. *American Psychologist*, 5, 444–454.

Harrison, A., Moore, M., & Rucker, M. (1985). Further evidence on career and family compatibility among eminent women and men. *Archivo di Psicologia, Neurologia Psichiatria*, 46, 140–155.

Harrold, F. (1992). Paleolithic archaeology, ancient behavior, and the transition to modern Homo. In G. Bräuer & F. Smith (Eds.), *Continuity or replacement: Controversies in homo sapiens evolution* (pp. 219–30). Rotterdam: Balkema.

Hassin, R. R., Uleman, J. S., & Bargh, J. A. (2005). *The new unconscious*. New York: Oxford University Press.

Henshilwood, C., d'Errico, F., Vanhaeren, M., van Niekerk, K., & Jacobs, Z. (2004). Middle stone age shell beads from South Africa. *Science*, 304, 404.

Henshilwood, C. S., & Marean, C. W. (2003). The origin of modern human behavior. *Current Anthropology*, 44, 627–651

Heyes, C. M. (1998). Theory of mind in nonhuman primates. *Behavioral and Brain Sciences*, 211, 104–134.

Howard-Jones, P. A., & Murray, S. (2003). Ideational productivity, focus of attention, and context. *Creativity Research Journal*, 15(2&3), 153–166.

Humphrey, N. (1976). The social function of intellect. In P. P. G. Bateson & R. A. Hinde (Eds.), *Growing points in ethology* (pp. 303–317). Cambridge, UK: Cambridge University Press.

Jablonka, E., & Lamb, M. (2005). *Evolution in four dimensions: Genetic, epigenetic, behavioural and symbolic variation in the history of life*. Cambridge, MA: MIT Press.

James, W. (1890/1950). *The principles of psychology*. New York: Dover.

Jerison, H. J. (1973). *Evolution of the brain and intelligence*. New York: Academic Press.

Johnson-Laird, P. N. (1983). *Mental models*. Cambridge, MA: Harvard University Press.

Kane, M. J., Hambrick, D. Z., & Conway, A. R. A. (2005). Working memory capacity and fluid intelligence are strongly related constructs: Comment on Ackerman, Beier, and Boyle. *Psychological Bulletin*, 131, 66–71.

Karmiloff-Smith, A. (1992). *Beyond modularity: A developmental perspective on cognitive science*. Cambridge, MA: MIT Press.

Kauffman, S. (1993). *Origins of order*. New York: Oxford University Press.

Kaufman, J. C., Lee, J., Baer, J., & Lee, S. (2007). Captions, consistency, creativity and the consensual assessment technique: New evidence of reliability. *Thinking Skills and Creativity*, 2(2), 96–106.

Kaufman, J. C., & Kaufman, A. B. (2004). Applying a creativity framework to animal cognition. *New Ideas in Psychology*, 22, 143–155.

Kaufman, S. B. (2007). Commentary: Investigating the role of domain general mechanisms in the acquisition of domain specific expertise. *High Ability Studies*, 18, 71–73.

Kaufman, S. B. (2008). Commentary: Intuition and creative cognition. *Periodicals of Implicit Cognition*, 1, 5–6.

Kaufman, S. B. (in press). Intelligence and the cognitive unconscious. To appear in R. J. Sternberg & S. B. Kaufman (Eds.), *The Cambridge handbook of intelligence*. Cambridge, UK: Cambridge University Press.

Kaufman, S. B., Kozbelt, A., Bromley, M. L., & Miller, G. F. (2008). The role of creativity and humor in human mate selection. In G. Geher & G. Miller (Eds.), *Mating intelligence: Sex, relationships, and the mind's reproductive system* (pp. 227–263). Mahwah, NJ: Erlbaum.

Kaufman, S. B., DeYoung, C. G., Gray, J. R., Brown, J., & Mackintosh, N. (2009, July/August). Associative learning predicts intelligence above and beyond working memory and processing speed. *Intelligence*, 37, 374–382.

Klein, R. G. (1989a). Biological and behavioral perspectives on modern human origins in South Africa. In P. Mellars & C. Stringe (Eds.), *The human revolution*. Edinburgh: Edinburgh University Press.

Klein, R. G. (1989b). *The human career*. Chicago: University of Chicago Press.

Klein, R. G. (1989). *The human career: Human biological and cultural origins*. Chicago: University of Chicago Press.

Klein, R. G. (2003). Whither the Neanderthals? *Science*, 299, 1525–1527.

Kohn, M. (1999). A race apart. *Index on Censorship*, 28(3), 79.

Kohn, M., & Mithen, S. (1999). Handaxes: Products of sexual selection? *Antiquity*, 73, 281.

Krasnegor, N., Lyon, G. R., & Goldman-Rakic, P. S. (1997). *Prefrontal cortex: Evolution, development, and behavioral neuroscience*. Baltimore: Brooke Publishing.

Kris, E. (1952). *Psychoanalytic explorations in art*. New York: International Universities Press.

Leakey, M. D. (1971). *Olduvai gorge: Excavations in beds I and II, 1960–1963*. Cambridge: Cambridge University Press.

Leakey, R. (1984). *The origins of humankind*. New York: Science Masters Basic Books.

Lewicki, P., & Hill, T. (1987). Unconscious processes as explanation of behaviour in cognitive, personality, and social psychology. *Personality and Social Psychology Bulletin*, 13, 355–362.

Lewicki, P., Czyzewska, M., & Hoffman, H. (1987). Unconscious acquisition of complex procedural knowledge. *Journal of Experimental Psychology: Learning, Memory, and Cognition*, 13, 523–530.

Madsen, M., Lipo, C., & Cannon, M. (1999). Fitness and reproductive trade-offs in uncertain environments: Explaining the evolution of cultural elaboration. *Journal of Anthropological Archaeology*, 18, 251–281.

Martindale, C. (1995). Creativity and connectionism. In S. M. Smith, T. B. Ward, & R. A. Finke (Eds.), *The creative cognition approach* (pp. 249–268). Cambridge MA: MIT Press.

Maturana, R. H., & Varela, F. J. (1980). *Autopoiesis and cognition: The realization of the living*. New York: Springer.

McBrearty, S., & Brooks, A. S. (2000). The revolution that wasn't a new interpretation of the origin of modern human behavior. *Journal of Human Evolution*, 39, 453–563.

McGeorge, P., & Burton, M. A. (1990). Semantic processing in an incidental learning task. *Quarterly Journal of Experimental Psychology A: Human Experimental Psychology*, 42, 597–609.

Mellars, P. (1973). The character of the middle-upper transition in South-West France. In C. Renfrew (Ed.), *The explanation of culture change* (pp. 255–276). London: Duckworth.

Mellars, P. (1989a). Technological changes in the middle-upper Paleolithic transition: Economic, social, and cognitive perspectives. In P. Mellars & C. Stringer (Eds.), *The human revolution* (pp. 338–365). Edinburgh: Edinburgh University Press.

Mellars, P. (1989b). Major issues in the emergence of modern humans. *Current Anthropology*, 30, 349–385.

Mesoudi, A., Whiten, A., & Laland, K. (2004). Toward a unified science of cultural evolution. *Evolution*, 58(1), 1–11.

Miller, G. F. (1998). How mate choice shaped human nature: A review of sexual selection and human evolution. In C. B. Crawford & D. L. Krebs (Eds.), *Handbook of evolutionary psychology: Ideas, issues, and applications* (pp. 87–129). Mahwah, NJ: Erlbaum.

Miller, G. F. (2000a). *The mating mind: How sexual choice shaped the evolution of human nature*. London: Vintage.

Miller, G. F. (2000b). Mental traits as fitness indicators: Expanding evolutionary psychology's adaptationism. In D. LeCroy & P. Moller (Eds.), *Evolutionary perspectives on human reproductive behavior* (pp. 62–74). New York: New York Academy of Sciences.

Miller, G. F. (2001). Aesthetic fitness: How sexual selection shaped artistic virtuosity as a fitness indicator and aesthetic preferences as mate choice criteria. *Bulletin of Psychology and the Arts*, 2, 20–25.

Mithen, S. (1996). *The prehistory of the mind: The cognitive origins of art and science*. London, UK: Thames and Hudson.

Mithen, S. (Ed.). (1998). *Creativity in human evolution and prehistory*. London: Routledge.

Mithen, S. (2006). *The singing Neanderthals: The origins of music, language, mind, and body.* London: Weidenfeld and Nicolson.

Neiman, F. D. (1995). Stylistic variation in evolutionary perspective. *American Antiquity*, 60, 7–36.

Neisser, U. (1963). The multiplicity of thought. *British Journal of Psychology*, 54, 1–14.

Newman, S. A., & Müller, G. B. (1999). Morphological evolution: Epigenetic mechanisms. In Nature Publishing Group (Ed.) *Embryonic encyclopedia of life sciences* (pp. 1–6). London: Nature Publishing Group.

Nettle, D., & Clegg, H. (2006). Schizotypy, creativity and mating success in humans. *Proceedings of the Royal Society of London*, 273, 611–615.

Parker, S. T., & McKinney, M. L. (1999). *Origins of intelligence.* Baltimore, MD: Johns Hopkins University Press.

Piaget, J. (1926). *The language and thought of the child.* Kent, UK: Harcourt Brace.

Pinker, S. (1997). *How the mind works.* New York: Norton.

Pinker, S. (2002). *The blank slate: The modern denial of human nature.* New York: Viking.

Premack, D., & Woodruff, G. (1978). Does the chimpanzee have a theory of mind? *Behavioral and Brain Sciences*, 1, 515–526.

Prokosch, M. D., Coss, R. G., Scheib, J. E., & Blozis, S. A. (2009). Intelligence and mate choice: Intelligent men are always appealing. *Evolution and Human Behavior*, 30, 11–20.

Reber, A. S. (1967). Implicit learning of artificial grammars. *Journal of Verbal Learning and Verbal Behavior*, 6, 855–863.

Reber, A. S. (1989). Implicit learning and tacit knowledge. *Journal of Experimental Psychology: General*, 118, 219–235.

Reber, A. S. (1993). *Implicit learning and tacit knowledge: An essay on the cognitive unconscious.* New York: Oxford Psychology Series.

Reber, A. S., & Allen, R. (2000). Individual differences in implicit learning: Implications for the evolution of consciousness. In R. G. Kunzendorf & B. Wallace (Eds.), *Individual differences in conscious experience* (pp. 228–247). Philadelphia: John Benjamins Publishing Company.

Reber, P. J., & Kotovsky, K. (1997). Implicit learning in problem solving: The role of working memory capacity. *Journal of Experimental Psychology: General*, 162, 178–203.

Reboul, A. (2007). Does the Gricean distinction between natural and non-natural meaning exhaustively account for all instances of communication? *Pragmatics & Cognition*, 15(2), 253–276.

Richerson, P., & Boyd, R. (1998). The evolution of human ultrasociality. In I. Eibl-Eibesfeldt & F. K. Salter (Eds.), *Indoctrinability, ideology, and warfare; evolutionary perspectives* (pp. 71–95). New York: Berghahn Books.

Richerson, P., & Boyd, R. (2000). Climate, culture, and the evolution of cognition. In C. Heyes & L. Huber (Eds.), *Evolution of cognition* (pp. 329–346). Cambridge, MA: MIT Press.

Rips, L. (2001). Necessity and natural categories. *Psychological Bulletin*, 127(6), 827–852.

Rosch, R. H. (1975). Cognitive reference points. *Cognitive Psychology*, 7, 532–47.

Rozin, P. (1976). The evolution of intelligence and access to the cognitive unconscious. In J. M. Sprague & A. N. Epstein (Eds.), *Progress in psychobiology and physiological psychology* (pp. 245–280). New York: Academic Press.

Ruff, C., Trinkaus, E., & Holliday, T. (1997). Body mass and encephalization in Pleistocene Homo. *Nature*, 387, 173–176.

Rumbaugh, D. M. (1997). Competence, cortex, and primate models: A comparative primate perspective. In N. A. Krasnegor, G. R. Lyon, & P. S. Goldman-Rakic (Eds.), *Development of the prefrontal cortex: Evolution, neurobiology, and behavior* (pp. 117–139). Baltimore: Paul.

Schwartz, J. H. (1999). *Sudden origins.* New York: Wiley.

Semaw, S., Renne, P., Harris, J. W. K., Feibel, C. S., Bernor, R. L., Fesseha, N., et al. (1997). 2.5-million-year-old stone tools from Gona, Ethiopia. *Nature*, 385, 333–336.

Sloman, S. (1996). The empirical case for two systems of reasoning. *Psychological Bulletin*, 9(1), 3–22.

Smith, W. M., Ward, T. B., & Finke, R. A. (1995). *The creative cognition approach.* Cambridge, MA: The MIT Press.

Smolensky, P. (1988). On the proper treatment of connectionism. *Behavioral and Brain Sciences*, 11, 1–43.

Soffer, O. (1994). Ancestral lifeways in Eurasia – The middle and upper Paleolithic records. In M. Nitecki & D. Nitecki (Eds.), *Origins of anatomically modern humans* (pp. 101–119). New York: Plenum Press.

Sperber, D. (1994). The modularity of thought and the epidemiology of representations. In L. A. Hirshfield & S. A. Gelman (Eds.), *Mapping the mind: domain specificity in cognition and culture* (pp. 39–67). Cambridge, UK: Cambridge University Press.

Squire, L. R., & Frambach, M. (1990). Cognitive skill learning in amnesia. *Psychobiology*, 18, 109–117.

Stanovich, K. E. (2005). *The robot's rebellion: Finding meaning in the age of Darwin.* Chicago: University of Chicago Press.

Stanovich, K. E., & West, R. F. (2000). Individual differences in reasoning: Implications for the rationality debate? *Behavioral and Brain Sciences*, 23, 645–726.

Sternberg, R. J. (1998). Cognitive mechanisms in human creativity: Is variation blind or sighted? *Journal of Creative Behavior*, 32, 159–176.

Sternberg, R. J. (2000). Cognition: The holey grail of general intelligence. *Science*, 289, 399–401.

Stringer, C., & Gamble, C. (1993). *In search of the Neanderthals.* London: Thames and Hudson.

Swisher, C. C., Curtis, G. H., Jacob, T., Getty, A. G., Suprijo, A., & Widiasmoro, S. (1994). Age of the earliest known hominids in Java, Indonesia. *Science*, 263, 118–21.

Thagard, P. (1980). Against evolutionary epistemology. In P. D. Asquith & R. N. Giere (Eds.), *PSA 1980* (pp. 187–96). East Lansing, MI: Philosophy of Science Association.

Tomasello, M. (1999). *The cultural origins of human cognition.* Cambridge, MA: Harvard University Press.

Vetsigian, K., Woese, C., & Goldenfeld, N. (2006). Collective evolution and the genetic code. *Proceedings of the New York Academy of Science USA*, 103, 10696–10701.

Walker, A. C., & Leakey, R. E. (1993). *The Nariokotome Homo erectus skeleton.* Cambridge, MA: Harvard University Press.

Ward, T. B., Smith, S. M., & Finke, R. A. (1999). Creative cognition. In R. J. Sternberg (Eds.), *Handbook of creativity* (pp. 189–213). Cambridge, MA: Cambridge University Press.

Watts, D. J., & Strogatz, S. H. (1998). Collective dynamics of small-world networks. *Nature*, 392, 440–442.

Weisberg, R. W. (2000). An edifice built on sand? [Review of Origins of Genius: Darwinian Perspectives on Creativity, D. K. Simonton]. *Contemporary Psychology: APA Review of Books*, 45, 589–593.

Weisberg, R. W. (2004). On structure in the creative process: A quantitative case-study of the creation of Picasso's Guernica. *Empirical Studies of the Arts*, 22, 23–54.

Weisberg, R. W., & Hass, R. (2007). We are all partly right: Comment on "The creative process in Picasso's Guernica sketches: Monotonic improvements versus nonmonotonic variants." *Creativity Research Journal*, 19(4), 345–360.

Werner, H. (1948). *Comparative psychology of mental development.* New York: International Universities Press.

White, R. (1982). Rethinking the middle/upper Paleolithic transition. *Current Anthropology*, 23, 169–189.

White, R. (1989a). Production complexity and standardization in early Aurignacian bead and pendant manufacture: Evolutionary implications. In P. Mellars & C. Stringer (Eds.), *The human revolution: Behavioral and biological perspectives on the origins of modern humans* (pp. 366–90). Cambridge: Cambridge University Press.

White, R. (1989b). Toward a contextual understanding of the earliest body ornaments. In E. Trinkhaus (Eds.)*The emergence of modern humans: Biocultural adaptations in the later Pleistocene* (pp. 211–231). Cambridge: Cambridge University Press.

White, R. (1993). Technological and social dimensions of 'Aurignacian-age' body ornaments across Europe. In H. Knecht, A. Pike-Tay, & R. White (Eds.), *Before Lascaux: The complex record of the early upper Paleolithic* (pp. 277–299). New York: CRC Press.

White, T., Asfaw, B., Degusta, D., Gilbert, H., Richards, G. D., Suwa, G., et al. (2003). Pleistocene Homo sapiens from middle awash, Ethiopia. *Nature*, 423, 742–747.

Whiten, A. (Eds.). (1991). *Natural theories of mind.* Oxford, UK: Basil Blackwell.

Whiten, A., & Byrne, R. (1997). *Machiavellian intelligence II: Extensions and evaluations.* Cambridge, UK: Cambridge University Press.

Wilson, D. S., Near, D., & Miller, R. R. (1996). Machiavellianism: A synthesis of the evolutionary and psychological literatures. *Psychological Bulletin*, 119, 285–299.

Wundt, W. (1896). *Lectures on human and animal psychology.* New York: MacMillan.

Wynn, T. (1998). Did Homo erectus speak? *Cambridge Archaeological Journal*, 8, 78–81.

CHAPTER 16

Functional Creativity

"Products" and the Generation of Effective Novelty

David Cropley and Arthur Cropley

Functional Creativity: "Products" and the Generation of Effective Novelty

The successful launching of Sputnik I in October 1957 marked the beginning of the modern creativity era. Following this, the Western world was judged to have been beaten in the first event in the space race by what was then the Soviet Union, and this defeat was attributed to the lack of creativity of the West's *engineers*. Thus, the modern era did not start with concern about what probably springs most readily to mind when creativity is mentioned – the production of works of art and the formulation of new systems of thought about topics such as the meaning of existence – but with concern about more down-to-earth issues of technology and design. What was seen as vitally necessary was novel, useful, *practical products* – "product" meaning not only physical objects (regrettably often weapons) including machines, appliances, or structures such as bridges and buildings, but also processes, production and distribution systems, and services – which

would make the West prosperous and safe.

Creativity in this sense can be contrasted with the spiritual or aesthetic view expressed in an extreme form in the art for art's sake movement in nineteenth-century Paris: As the novelist Theophile Gautier put it in the preface to his novel *Mademoiselle de Maupin*, published in 1836, "Nothing is truly beautiful unless it is *useless*" [italics added]. Horenstein (2002, p. 2) put the opposite point of view: Practical, useful creativity involves "devices or systems that *perform tasks or solve problems*" [emphasis added]. Burghardt (1995, p. 4) made the distinction even more explicit: He saw engineering and technological creativity as "creativity *with a purpose*" [emphasis added], whereas creativity in fine art and the like is "creativity with *no functional purpose*" [emphasis added]. D. H. Cropley and A. J. Cropley (2005, p. 171) used the term *functional creativity* to differentiate novel, useful creativity (which Horenstein and Burghardt, among others, were emphasizing) from that which is merely aesthetic.

In this chapter, we focus on observable, concrete, useful products. In particular, we are interested in the question of where functionally creative products come from and the steps through which they come into existence. Our position is that they derive from existing knowledge and that they are achieved by means of systematic hard work. We will analyze this hard work by means of a phase model, which divides the emergence of a solution (product) into a series of steps, each of which is characterized by intermediate products both qualitatively and quantitatively different from products in other phases. A phase approach also helps understand apparently "paradoxical" (A. J. Cropley, 1997) aspects of creative processes – namely, personal characteristics and favorable environmental conditions – and offers insights into how to foster functional creativity in the classroom.

The Shift in Focus

It is clear that early twentieth-century writers were thoroughly aware of the importance of useful, practical products in creativity, that is, of functional creativity. Prindle (1906) and Rossman (1931), for instance, studied patented inventions. Early post-Sputnik writers such as Clifford (1958) and Gordon (1961) also concentrated on functional products. In fact, interest in socially useful creativity goes back to the ancient world – the Chinese Emperor Han Wu-di, who reigned until 87 BCE, was intensely interested in finding innovative thinkers and giving them high rank in the civil service, and he reformed the method of selection of mandarins to achieve this. Both Francis Bacon (1604/1909) and René Descartes (1644/1991), two of the founders of modern science, saw scientific creativity as involving the harnessing of the forces of nature *for the betterment of the human condition.*

Interestingly, and not insignificantly, the position just attributed to Bacon and Descartes is very close to modern definitions of the discipline of engineering. For example, the U.S. Accreditation Board for Engineering and Technology (ABET) has defined engineering as

the profession in which a knowledge of the mathematical and natural sciences gained by study, experience, and practice is applied with judgment to develop ways to utilize economically, the materials and forces of nature for the benefit of mankind.

However, in the early post-Sputnik years the creativity discussion soon came to be dominated by psychologists and educators (e.g., Barron, 1969; Getzels & Jackson, 1962; Guilford, 1950, 1967; Torrance, 1962, 1963, 1965), largely as a result of the seminal paper of Guilford (1950), the most momentous scholarly event of the modern creativity era. When politicians, engineers, and educators cast about for an explanation of the Western world's defeat in the space race by the Soviet Union, Guilford's work offered just what was needed – a psychological concept for understanding both what engineers lacked (skills in divergent thinking), as well as what was needed to rectify the situation (more appropriate education). Indeed, in the United States it was the "National Defense *Education* Act" [emphasis added] of 1958 (NDEA; U.S. Congress, Public Law 85–864) that represented the first legislative reaction to this "crisis."

Researchers began to look at creativity from the point of view of the "four Ps" – Person, Product, Process, and Press (e.g., Barron, 1955; Rhodes, 1961, p. 305) to denote the pressure exerted by the environment, in particular education – and there was thus a tendency in the early years to focus on psychological/educational topics: creative thinking (Process; e.g., Guilford), the creative personality (Person), and the best classroom environment for fostering such thinking (Press; e.g., Torrance). Theoretical discussions of creativity were also heavily influenced by humanistic psychologists (e.g., Maslow, 1973; May, 1976; Rogers, 1961), who saw its value as lying in its beneficial effects on self-actualization and similar aspects of individual well-being (Person). The result was that fostering creativity in the classroom came to be seen as a matter of offering conditions that would foster personal growth.

Although perhaps being useful in that they cast light on thinking processes and personal properties, products that are merely a means to the end of studying person and process and not a focus of interest in themselves may involve what Cattell and Butcher (1968, p. 271) called "pseudo-creativity" (novelty deriving only from nonconformity, lack of discipline, blind rejection of what already exists and simply letting oneself go), or "quasi-creativity" (Heinelt, 1974), which has many of the elements of genuine creativity – such as a high level of fantasy – but only a tenuous connection with reality, that is, a lack of practical usefulness. An example would be the novelty generated in daydreams. Of course, fostering personal growth is a highly desirable classroom goal, but reduction of creativity to a process leading to increased individual well-being runs the risk of making its main purpose that of the "glorification of individuals" (Boden, 1994a, p. 4).

The Neglected *P*

Although in his seminal paper (1950) Guilford himself argued that creativity must lead to something useful, and MacKinnon (1978, p. 187) described the study of products as the "bedrock" of creativity research, it quickly became apparent that defining creative products is difficult. In any case, since children rarely achieve highly acclaimed products, the fourth P (Product) came to be relatively neglected in educational discussions, or to be trivialized by focusing on activities such as cutting up egg cartons and pasting them back together in unusual shapes. Some early post-Sputnik writers (e.g., A. J. Cropley, 1967) went so far as specifically to recommend ignoring products and focusing on person, process, and press.

Authors like Amabile (1985) and Csikszentmihalyi (1988) began to make the point that public acclaim is the best way of determining whether a product is creative – if people who know about an area agree that a product is creative, then it is; if they do not, then it is not. As Csikszentmihalyi (1999) put it, creativity involves a "novel variation" in a domain of practice that *experts in the domain* regard as worth incorporating into it. In other words, a product's creativity is as much dependent on the properties of the environment as on its own qualities. Even products that achieve public acclaim must conform to the norms or fashions of a society or an era, the competence of judges to make a judgment, or their openness or tolerance.

In Georgian England, for instance, Shakespeare's plays were regarded as indecent and had to be edited to make them respectable – in 1818 Dr. Thomas Bowdler published the *Family Shakespeare*, in which he removed expressions that could not with propriety be read aloud in the family circle. He "bowdlerized" Shakespeare, as we would say nowadays. In the field of music the compositions of J. S. Bach were not widely known in his own lifetime (Bach was known primarily as an accomplished organist), and it was not until almost one hundred years after his death that his compositions began to receive wide acclaim. He is now seen as one of the greatest composers of all time.

The example of the French mathematician Evariste Galois is also very instructive in this context. He made a major and highly creative contribution to group theory, now known as "Galois theory" (Rothman, 1982), but his work was initially adjudged to be meaningless because mathematicians at the time of his death in 1832 could not see the logic of his conclusions – his work was too creative for the experts of his time. It was not until several years later, after the mathematical knowledge of the experts had caught up with Galois's thinking, that the outstanding creativity of his work was recognized. It can be mentioned in passing that Alfred Einstein's dissertation was rejected by the *Technische Hochschule* in Zurich because the examiners could not follow his arguments. He wrote the papers that led to the theories of relativity at home in the evenings, while working as a patent clerk in the day! The experts in the domain literally advised him not to give up his day job!

In any event, practically applicable, physically useful products came to receive less attention than at the time of the initial burst of enthusiasm for engineering creativity that had immediately followed Sputnik I. Emphasis was transferred to the other Ps, especially cognitive processes favorable for creativity (such as divergent thinking), and personal properties that encouraged people to be creative (such as daring, unconventionality, or ego strength). Where the P for Product was studied it was often because products were seen as helpful in investigating the other Ps, especially thinking processes and personal properties. Plucker and Renzulli (1999), for instance, summarized a substantial number of research studies that involved products (as against, for instance, test scores). However, the interest of these authors was in psychological testing, and they saw the study of products as a response to a "perceived need for external criteria to which researchers could compare other methods of measuring creativity" (p. 44). The "other methods" mainly involved creative thinking (Process) or personal properties (Person), products thus being little more than a tool for looking at these.

The Importance of Functionally Creative Products

Of course, products are only the visible tip of an iceberg that reflects the operation of other less readily observable Ps such as motivation (e.g., willingness to take risks), personal properties (e.g., self-confidence), or social factors (e.g., tolerance/rejection of deviation from the conventional). We do not wish to adopt a neo-Watsonian (e.g., Watson, 1913) or black-box (e.g., Skinner, 1950) position and ignore mental phenomena (such as aspects of Person or Process) because they are not directly observable, whereas products are. However, we do take the view that useful, novel products that solve concrete problems in real life should be studied *in their own right*. There are ample reasons for adopting this position.

For instance, economic theory suggests that returns on investments in rich countries should have been lower during the second half of the twentieth century than during the first half, because the stock of capital was rising faster than the workforce. However, the fact is that they were considerably higher. How was this possible? The decisive factor that defeated the law of diminishing returns and added greatly to an explosion of human material welfare was the *addition to the system of new knowledge and technology*, that is, creativity. In fact, at the turn of the century creative products were accounting for more than half of economic growth (*The Economist Technology Quarterly*, 2002, p. 13). Buzan (2007, p. vii) stated that "it is a globally accepted awareness that right now any individual, company or country wishing to survive in the twenty-first century must develop the brain's seemingly infinite capacity to create and to innovate." He also drew attention to initiatives in various countries to "raise the level of national creativity" as a means for ensuring growth. Florida (2004) tied the strength of the world's largest economy, the United States, directly to creativity by attributing its success to its openness to new ideas and its ability to attract creative people to work within its environment.

In addition to its value to society in business, production, and technology, functional creativity is also important in helping find ways of dealing with human issues that are, among others, demographic (e.g., aging of the population, changing family patterns), social (e.g., inequality, adaptation of labor migrants and refugees), environmental (e.g., global warming, gene-modified crops), and political (e.g., terrorism, achieving fairness in international relations). The fear is that societies will stagnate, even deteriorate, not only technologically and economically but also socially, politically, and civilly, unless their leaders and thinkers find creative ways of dealing with issues of the kind just mentioned.

The global financial crisis that began to make its impact felt in mid-2008 is an example of a situation where generation of effectively novel, concrete solutions is of the greatest importance. This means that discussions of creativity should not be restricted to fostering the development of fully self-realized individuals dreaming of truth and beauty and giving expression to their thoughts in aesthetic products that promote their own freedom and well-being but hardly relate to concrete real-world problems. Rather, discussions of creativity should look closely also at the generation of functionally creative products. A simple example of functional creativity addressing a concrete, real-world problem is seen in the solution that the package delivery company UPS developed to cut its operating costs. Simply by using navigation software to route its vehicles in such a way that left-hand turns are avoided, thus reducing time spent waiting at intersections for an opportunity to turn across on-coming traffic, UPS has reportedly saved millions of dollars worth of fuel. This solution is highly practical, novel, and elegant, not only saving the company in question money, but also dramatically reducing its carbon emissions.

Where Do Functionally Creative Products Come From?

A pleasingly romantic idea is that useful, creative products spring fully formed into an inventor's head as a result of inspiration or intuition, and without the bother of effort. For instance, in 1881 Henri Poincaré, the French mathematician now remembered as one of the most creative mathematicians of all time, was about to enter a bus for a sightseeing trip during a fact finding tour. He was not thinking about mathematics at all. Suddenly, the Fuchsian functions (nowadays known as "automorphic functions") came unexpectedly into his head (for a more detailed discussion see Miller, 1992). Refinements of the equations came later in a second burst while he was having a relaxing walk by the sea. Similar anecdotes such as that of August Kekulé's discovery of the benzene ring in a daydream (see Ghiselin, 1955) also seem to support this idea of effortless creativity.

A related idea is that usefully novel products come into existence by chance. There are many examples of apparently lucky combinations of events that led to acknowledged creative solutions (see Rosenman, 1988). For instance, Pasteur, Fleming, Roentgen, Becquerel, Edison, Galvani, and Nobel all described chance events that led them to breakthroughs. A typical anecdote is that of James Goodyear's accidental discovery of the process of vulcanization when he spilled sulfur and raw rubber onto a hot stove. Another often cited example is that of the French physicist Antoine Henri Becquerel. In 1896, while studying properties of minerals that had been exposed to the newly discovered x-rays, Becquerel happened to leave a photographic plate and a container with uranium compounds in it in a drawer of his desk (Nobel Foundation, 1967). Upon opening the drawer some time later, he noticed to his surprise that the photographic plate had fogged. This unexpected event piqued his curiosity. Instead of throwing the "ruined" plate away he began to study it intensively. He eventually concluded that the uranium compounds had emitted some kind of rays similar to x-rays, apparently without any source of energy, and that these unknown rays were responsible for the fogging. He was able to confirm that the mystery rays emanated from the uranium compounds and that they differed qualitatively from x-rays. After initially being called "Becquerel rays," the newly discovered radiation subsequently became known as "radioactivity" and led Becquerel to a Nobel Prize for Physics in 1903.

Some writers really do seem to suggest that the main way of achieving effective novelty is to stumble on it more or less by accident. Without advocating blind guessing, Sir Harold Kroto (1996 Nobel Prize for Chemistry) drew attention to the importance of being open for the unexpected or for something that you were not actually seeking at the moment of discovery: "If it interests you ... explore it, because something unexpected often turns up, *just when you least expect it*" (Frängsmyr, 1997; emphasis added). Numbers of writers from differing societies and with different scientific backgrounds emphasize the role of luck in creativity. The German physicist Ernst Mach (1905, p. 293) referred to "die Rolle des Zufalls bei Erfindungen und Entdeckungen" [the role of chance in inventions and discoveries], the French philosopher of aesthetics Paul Souriau concluded (1881) that "le principe de l'invention est le hasard" [the basis of creativity is chance], and the Scottish philosopher and educator Alexander Bain acknowledged (1868, p. 196) the importance of hard work in creativity but saw this work as "energy put forth . . . on the chance of making lucky hits."

Austin (1978) identified four kinds of happy chance that might lead to creativity: *blind chance* (the individual creator plays no role except that of being there at the relevant moment); *serendipity* (a person stumbles on something novel and effective when not actually looking for it); the *luck of the diligent* (a hardworking person finds in an unexpected setting something that is being sought – Diaz de Chumaceiro, 1999, p. 228, called this *"pseudo-serendipity"* since in genuine serendipity the person would not be looking for what was found); *self-induced luck* (special qualifications of a person – such as knowledge, close attention to detail, or willingness to work long hours – create the circumstances for a lucky breakthrough). Case studies suggest, however, that genuinely creative people enjoy a combination of all four kinds of luck, which raises the question of whether it is a matter of luck at all, since at least the luck of the diligent and also self-induced luck clearly contain elements of hard work, general and specialized knowledge, and the like.

Despite anecdotes such as those about Poincaré, Becquerel, Kekulé, or Goodyear, it does not seem plausible that useful novel products emerge spontaneously without any preparation. Poincaré, for instance, was one of the most learned mathematicians of his time; Goodyear worked on the problem of vulcanization for much of his life; and Kekulé had withdrawn to the quiet forest setting where he came on the idea of the benzene ring in order to be able

to give his undivided attention to a matter he had been working on for a considerable time. Becquerel could not have capitalized on the opportunity chance presented had he not possessed, among other things, the general knowledge that permitted him to realize that the fogging was unusual and important, the specific knowledge that told him that some kind of radiation had caused the phenomenon, and the research skills that enabled him to clarify the whole situation. Indeed, had Becquerel not already been engaged in relevant research, the uranium compounds and the photographic plate would not have found themselves in the drawer together in the first place: Thus, he could be said not only to have been able to profit from chance because of, among other things, his knowledge and skills, but in fact to have created his own lucky chance!

Weisberg (1993) presented a number of case studies of famous instances of the generation of useful, novel products that demonstrate the importance of years of hard preparatory work and do not support the idea of effortless or out-of-the blue creativity, as attractive as that idea is. In fact, Gardner (1993) formulated the "10-year rule": An apprenticeship of at least 10 years is necessary for acquiring the foundation necessary for creativity. Of what, then, does this foundation consist? Although it is a popular rather than scholarly publication, Gladwell's (2008) discussion of people who are "outliers" makes an important point in this context: He argues that one of the crucial factors in achieving outstanding success in all areas is *long hours of practice*. His estimate is that 10,000 hours are needed in more or less any field.

Existing Knowledge as the Basis of Functional Creativity

Despite the fact that some writers (e.g., Hausman, 1984) have argued that true creativity is always so novel that it is unprecedented, and thus has no connection to anything that went before, others such as

Bailin (1988) have concluded that creative products are always conceived by both the creative person and external observers in terms of *existing knowledge*. This idea was well established before the beginning of the modern era: Rossman's (1931) study of inventors, for instance, concluded that they "manipulate the symbols of... *past experience*" (p. 82; italics added). He also showed that they combined "*known* movements" (p. 77; italics added), adding to a mix of ideas until a happy combination was found.

Indeed, it is clear that many novel ideas are based on what already exists, even if existing knowledge is transferred to a field quite different from the one in which it is already known. In the early 1700s, it had been known for many hundreds of years that organic fibers would form a kind of interlocking mat (i.e., paper) when separated and suspended in water. In Europe, old rags were used as the source of fiber – an expensive source because the raw materials had already been subjected to substantial refining and manufacturing. The French entomologist, René de Réaumur, noticed that certain wasps, nowadays known as the "paper" wasp, chewed up wood, digested it, regurgitated it, and used the resulting material to build their nests. The material dried out to form a paper-like substance. Réaumur realized that, in fact, *chemical* processes in the wasps' stomachs were making paper out of raw wood, in contrast to human papermaking, in which *physical* processes were applied to already expensively processed plant fibers. Réaumur proposed transferring the wasps' chemical approach to human papermaking and thus invented modern papermaking techniques (although it must be admitted that he never succeeded in getting the process to work properly).

In fact, the Canadian Intellectual Property Office reported (http://strategis.gc.ca/sc_mrksv/cipo/patents/pat_gd_protect-e.html#sec2) that 90% of new patents are improvements of existing patents. Even many of the innovations introduced by America's most distinguished inventor, Thomas Alva Edison, were improvements on existing technology or ideas. Edison worked with a large staff of engineers and technicians who constantly improved their own existing ideas: For instance, over the course of time they took out more than 100 patents for the electric light bulb alone. Indeed, in an aphorism that was printed in *Harper's Monthly* in 1932 (Josephson, 1959, p. 97), Edison concluded that "genius is 1% inspiration, 99% perspiration," thus coming down squarely on the side of hard work and knowledge rather than inspiration, intuition, luck, chance, or any other form of "out-of-the-blue" creativity.

Lubart (2000–2001) made perhaps the strongest statement linking knowledge and creativity. He suggested that there may well be no difference between the *processes* of divergent and convergent thinking. Differences in outcome may not depend on the process at all but on "the quality of the material (e.g., knowledge)" (p. 301). This idea has been put in more formal terms by Boden (1994b), who uses the language of artificial intelligence. The more "structural features" of a domain are represented in a person's mind (the more the person knows about the domain), the more creative the person has the potential to be.

A number of authors have examined the processes through which existing knowledge is transformed into effectively novel, useful products. Sternberg, Kaufman, and Pretz (2002) introduced the useful idea of creativity as "propelling a field" and suggested a number of ways in which this can occur:

1. *Conceptual replication* (the known is transferred to a new setting);
2. *Redefinition* (the known is seen in a new way);
3. *Forward incrementation* (the known is extended in an existing direction);
4. *Advance forward incrementation* (the known is extended in an existing direction but goes beyond what is currently tolerable);
5. *Redirection* (the known is extended in a new direction);
6. *Reconstruction and redirection* (new life is breathed into an approach previously abandoned);

7. *Reinitiation* (thinking begins at a radically different point from the current one and takes off in a new direction).

Of these, only the last involves something quite new. All the others are based on modifying what already exists.

Savransky (2000) too discussed the processes through which existing knowledge is used to develop effective novelty: He argued that inventive solutions to problems always involve a change in what already exists and suggested six ways in which this can occur. Slightly modified for present purposes, generating effective novelty involves, according to Savransky, one or more of the following:

1. *Improvement* (improvement or perfection of both quality and quantity of what already exists);
2. *Diagnostics* (search for and elimination of shortcomings in what already exists);
3. *Trimming* (reduction of costs associated with existing solutions);
4. *Analogy* (new use of known processes and systems);
5. *Synthesis* (generation of new mixtures of existing elements);
6. *Genesis* (generation of fundamentally new solutions).

As was the case with Sternberg's list, only the last of these involves bringing into existence something fundamentally new.

The Russian researcher Altshuller (1988) also emphasized the role of the already known in his procedure for developing creative products – known as TRIZ (a transliteration of the Russian acronym for "Theory of inventive problem solving"). This procedure is based on an analysis of thousands of successful patent applications, that is, on effective novelty that is already known. It argues that all engineering systems display the same systematic patterns of change: Creativity is the result of development of what already exists according to these trends. TRIZ identifies these systematic processes of novelty generation so that people working with a new problem can apply them to derive their own novel solutions.

"Darwinian" vs. "non-Darwinian" Models of Production of Useful Novelty

How do effectively novel products emerge from existing knowledge? In essence there are two competing views on this matter: the "Darwinian" and the "non-Darwinian" approaches (e.g., Dasgupta, 2004). Some writers argue that novel ideas evolve through what Sternberg and Davidson (1999) called *haphazard recombinations*. According to this evolutionary or Darwinian view of creativity (e.g., Campbell, 1960), a process of blind variation generates novelty, and selective retention leads to preservation of effective elements of the novelty, thus yielding useful, practical creativity. Simonton (1988) refined this approach through what he called the *chance configuration* model. He concluded – somewhat adapted for present purposes – that generation of effective novelty starts with acquisition of a large number of pieces of information, memories, ideas, and concepts. Unfettered associations are then made, more or less randomly or blindly, until a happy combination occurs by chance, a combination that is just what is needed to solve the problem in question – a configuration.

In its extreme form, the blind-variation-and-survival-of-whatever-proves-effective approach to creativity interprets generation of effective novelty in a way similar to Charles Darwin's position on the origin of species. Indeed, Simonton (1999) made this link explicit by referring to "the origins of genius" in the title of his 1999 book. Dasgupta (2004) pointed out that more formal discussions use the term *evolutionary epistemology* to describe this model of creativity. However, in reviewing a number of relevant empirical studies, Howe, McWilliam, and Cross (2005) showed that many researchers deny that creativity involves working more or less blindly through ideas until something good suddenly pops up. They emphasized, instead, systematic heuristic processes such as set-breaking or construction of neural networks.

Although our focus here is on functional creativity, there are concrete examples of the deliberate use of chance combinations in aesthetic creativity, as paradoxical as that sounds. In aleatoric music, or aleatory, first identified by Werner Meyer-Eppler at the Darmstadt Summer School in the early 1950s, notes are combined in a random manner, for example, in Stockhausen's *Klavierstück XI*. Aleatoric music leaves either some component of the musical composition to chance or leaves elements of the performance to the discretion of the performer. The origins of this musical form can even be linked to Mozart, who is thought to have indulged in the so-called *musikalische Würfelspiele* (musical dice games) popular at the time. These games involved creating sequences of music whose variations were selected literally by the throw of a dice. The general form of *chance music* is also linked to John Cage, who used a variety of methods, including coin tossing, to compose some works.

The Process of Generation of Functional Creativity

Gestalt psychologists (e.g., Vinacke, 1953; Wertheimer, 1945) argued that effectively new products emerge in a person's mind whole and complete. By contrast, Arieti (1976) supported the idea of a series of steps. In phenomenological studies in which they reflected introspectively on their own creativity, nineteenth-century writers (e.g., Alexander Bain, Hermann Helmholtz, Henri Poincaré – see Sawyer et al., 2003, p. 22) had already identified and named various stages in the emergence of a creative product. Hadamard (1945), also reflecting on his own creative work as a mathematician, argued for four phases, *Preparation, Incubation, Illumination,* and "*Precising.*"

A relevant early empirical investigation more in the modern mold was that of Prindle (1906). He studied inventors and concluded that every invention is the result of *a series of small steps*, each step advancing the development of the invention by a small amount by adding something on to what had already been achieved. The product of one step creates a new jumping off point for the next step, and so on, in a process of *continuous invention*. Rossman (1931) also studied inventors. He too concluded that the emergence of a new invention involved a series of steps, but he went further by identifying seven such steps: *Becoming aware of a problem, Analyzing the problem, Surveying available information, Formulating candidate solutions, Analyzing the candidate solutions, Identifying one as a new idea,* and *Testing the new idea in order to ascertain its usefulness.* Osborn (1953) too argued for a seven-step creativity process involving *Orientation, Preparation, Analysis, Ideation, Incubation, Synthesis,* and *Evaluation.*

Later models (see also below) differ from Prindle's approach in that they visualize phases in which the work of the phase yields not simply an increase in the level of refinement of the product; rather, the work in each phase is qualitatively different from the work in the previous phase – a different *kind* of activity is carried out in each phase. The most widely accepted modern phase approach, that of Wallas (1926), reflects this view. Initially he suggested that there are seven phases: *Encounter* (a problem or challenge is identified), *Preparation* (information is gathered), *Concentration* (an effort is made to solve the problem), *Incubation* (ideas churn in the person's head), *Illumination* (what seems to be a solution becomes apparent), *Verification* (the individual checks out the apparent solution), and *Persuasion* (the individual attempts to convince others that the product really does solve the problem). Barron (1988) supported the idea of a four-stage model. Using the metaphor of giving birth, he identified the phases of *Conception, Gestation, Parturition,* and *Bringing up the baby.* Nowadays Wallas's model is also usually reduced to four phases: *Preparation, Incubation, Illumination,* and *Verification.* More recently, Koberg and Bagnall (1991) proposed the "universal traveler" model of creativity, which reverted to seven steps or phases: *Accepting the challenge, Analyzing, Defining, Ideating, Selecting, Implementing,* and *Evaluating.*

We regard a seven-phase model as most appropriate. At the very beginning, before *Incubation* (or in Barron's terms *Gestation*), there must be (a) *Preparation* (familiarity with a field is acquired – as Csikszentmihalyi [1996] put it, it is not possible to be creative in a field to which you have not been exposed), and (b) *Activation* (problem awareness develops). At the other end of the sequence, after *Verification* (in Hadamard's terms *Precising*, in Barron's terms *Bringing up the baby*, in those of Koberg and Bagnall *Selection*) come (c) *Communication*, when the result of the creative process is made available to other people, and (d) *Validation*, the final phase in which the external environment applies – or withholds – the label "creative."

There are substantial discussions in recent literature supporting the importance of the four elements to which we have given particular emphasis in the phase model just outlined: (a) achieving familiarity with a field (*Preparation*), (b) developing problem awareness (*Activation*), (c) making results known to other people (*Communication*), and (d) gaining acceptance by others (*Validation*). A. J. Cropley and D. H. Cropley (2008) listed Albert, Amabile, Campbell, Chi, Feldhusen, Gardner, Gruber, Mednick, Simonton, and Weisberg as examples of writers who give a prominent place to acquiring familiarity with the field, that is, to *Preparation*. However, it should be born in mind that, as Gardner (1993, p. 52) pointed out, there may be "tension between creativity and expertise." For instance, working successfully in an area over a long period of time (i.e., becoming an expert) can provide a knowledge base that can be manipulated to yield effective novelty, but it can also result in a vested interest in maintaining the *status quo*. By rendering their lifetime's work irrelevant, radical new solutions to old and intractable problems may threaten the self-image and the social status of experts who have labored long on a particular problem. The result may be that they resist *Activation*. Other processes that can lead to a negative correlation between creativity and expertise are cognitive in nature

(e.g., sets, functional fixity, and confirmation bias). Mumford and Gustafson (1988) and Martinson (1995), among others, suggested that the relationship between level of preexisting knowledge and creativity is U-shaped: Both very high (great expertise) and very low (ignorance) levels of preexisting knowledge may inhibit *Activation*. *Preparation* thus has its pitfalls.

From almost the beginning of modern interest in creativity, some writers have emphasized the importance of recognizing that there is a problem (e.g., Rossman, 1931). Guilford himself referred to the importance of "sensitivity to problems" (1950, p. 449). Einstein (in Miller, 1992) described how his dissatisfaction with existing theories of thermodynamics led him to develop the theories of relativity. In the case of creativity, it seems that more is required than simply recognizing obvious problems; more important is finding your own problem or defining the problem in your own way (e.g., Torrance, 1965). Jay and Perkins (1997) and Mumford, Baughman, Threlfall, Supinski, and Costanza (e.g., 1996) identified problem "construction" as a key step in generating novel solutions. Mumford and Moertl (2003) described two case studies of innovation in social systems (management practice and student selection for admission to university) and concluded that both innovations were driven by "intense dissatisfaction" (p. 262) with the status quo. Thus, there is widespread support for positing a phase of *Activation*.

Nonetheless, Unsworth (2001) showed that the relationship between problem definition and functional creativity is complex. She distinguished between creativity where (a) a person solves a problem defined by other people at the other people's behest (what she called "responsive" creativity), (b) a person solves a self-discovered problem to satisfy other people's demands ("expected" creativity), (c) a person is self-motivated but the problem is defined externally ("contributory" creativity), and finally, (d) a person solves self-defined problems for his or her own personal satisfaction ("proactive" creativity).

Turning to the final two phases, Dasgupta (2004, p. 406) summarized the need for *Communication* very aptly: To be judged creative, a product must reach a sufficient state of "maturity" or completeness to be "manifested publicly." Of course, communication involves different tools, skills, and products in different fields. In the case of a scientist, it might be a series of papers in which experiments are written up, whereas in technology it might be a set of plans or an artifact. We see such public manifestation of a mature functional product as the second-last phase. This idea is by no means new. At the very beginning of the modern era Torrance (1966, p. 6), for instance, defined creativity as including "*communicating* the results" (italics added).

As Csikszentmihalyi (e.g., 1999) has stated strongly, products achieve the status of creativity only when they are judged by external authorities to be worth incorporating into the field – in the case of functional products this might mean being manufactured and marketed to the public or being adopted in production or administrative systems. In other words, not only is *Communication* necessary, but the approval of others, such as accountants or production or marketing executives, is as well. We call this final step of obtaining such approval "*Validation*." In the phase of *Generation* (what Wallas called "*Incubation*"), numerous possible solutions may be generated, yielding several "candidate" solutions that are checked out in *Verification* and perhaps reduced to only one candidate, then passed on to others in the phase of *Communication*. In aesthetic creativity these others are experts in the domain in question (e.g., Csikszentmihalyi, 1999) such as art, music, or literature critics, but in the case of functional creativity they are more likely to be managers or financial or marketing people, as well as customers or consumers, or those who foot the bill such as the company financing the construction of a building or a bridge. When such "others" accept a candidate solution (they "validate" it), it ceases to be a candidate and becomes a validated solution – a functionally creative product.

There are also problems with Wallas's term *Incubation*. The metaphor he used implies ideas working in a person's head until a solution springs forth fully formed, in the way a chicken hatches from an egg in an incubator as a fully formed if immature bird. We have just argued against such an essentially Darwinian approach and prefer to talk about a phase of *Generation*. Thus, we argue for a model with the following seven phases: *Preparation, Activation, Generation, Illumination, Verification, Communication,* and *Validation*. We are not suggesting here that such a phase model is an exact and concrete description of the process of the emergence of functionally creative products. In fact, Glover, Ronning, and Reynolds (1989) showed that many famous creators are unaware of or deny any such step-by-step procedure in their own creativity.

In practice, production of an effectively novel product may not follow a linear pathway involving always starting at *Preparation* and moving in order through the other phases to eventual *Validation*. The process can be broken off in any phase – for instance, when the phase in question fails to yield the raw material needed for the next phase. If *Generation* yielded nothing, for instance, there could not be an *Illumination*, and without *Illumination* nothing could be subjected to *Verification*. Without *Preparation* (heavily dependent on acquisition of knowledge), the process would not even begin. On the other hand, the process can begin part way through, such as when knowledge and problem awareness obtained at some earlier date, possibly years before, serve as the raw material for *Generation*, apparently without any *Preparation* or *Activation*. The phases can also interact with each other. For example, additional information gathered in the phase of *Verification* could indicate the necessity of a return to the *Preparation* phase, leading to a new *Illumination*, and so on. This interaction among the phases has been described in greater detail by Shaw (1989), who referred to "loops," giving each loop a name. To take several examples, the "Arieti-loop" involves the interaction between *Preparation* and *Incubation*, the

Table 16.1: The Core Psychological/Educational Products of the Seven Phases

Phase	Core Product
Preparation	A varied stock of general and specific knowledge
Activation	Awareness of problems in what exists which emerges from the knowledge obtained in the phase of *Preparation*
Generation	A stock of candidate solutions to the problem(s) identified in the phase of *Activation*. These may be generated with minimal concern about usefulness
Illumination	One or more promising solution from among the candidates produced in *Generation*
Verification	A promising solution (it seems to do what it is supposed to do) from among those identified in the phase of *Illumination*.
Communication	A candidate solution which is "mature" enough to be proposed to other people. Often only a single mature solution emerges from candidates generated in earlier phases
Validation	A solution that has been communicated to "experts in the domain" and received positive (or negative) feedback from them

"Vinacke-loop" that between *Incubation* and *Illumination*, and the "Lalas-loop" links *Illumination* and *Verification*.

An example of how complex looping may be is to be seen in the example of Evariste Galois already mentioned. In 1832, the young Frenchman was killed at the age of 20 in a duel so uneven that he knew he was doomed (Rothman, 1982). He left a body of mathematical writings on which he worked even on the night before his death (i.e., he went to great lengths to try to *communicate* the results of his work – his level of *activation* was high). Because of the obvious importance that he had attached to them, these writings were examined after his death, and the ideas in them pronounced to be worthless (they were denied *validation*). They were judged to be novel, to be sure, but Galois had not successfully *communicated* their value. He himself was aware of this, as he indicated in his notes that more detail was needed to flesh out his arguments – unfortunately, he did not have time to do this.

It was only after the passage of several years, during which mathematics advanced enough for the importance of Galois's work to become apparent, that their creativity was recognized. In other words, it was only after the external world was well enough *pre-*pared and had reached a sufficient level of problem awareness (*activation*) that *validation* occurred. Thus, not only may the phases of *Illumination* and *Verification*, on the one hand, and *Communication* and, finally, *Validation*, on the other, be separated by years, but the process may be restarted with a return to *Preparation* and *Activation*, with the crucial new *Preparation* and *Activation* perhaps carried out by people different from the original creative individual.

Table 16.1 summarizes what we call the "core products" of each phase. They are referred to as "core" products because we do not wish to imply that they are the only results of a particular phase; they do, however, encapsulate the essence of the phase and form the most important result of this phase. For instance, a rich and varied fund of general and specific knowledge is the core product of the phase of *Preparation*, although it is perfectly imaginable that people may acquire knowledge in other phases too.

Of course, the process described in Table 16.1 may stall – perhaps because no novelty is generated, a promising candidate solution cannot be verified, external judges do not accept it as effectively novel, and so on. Thus, Table 16.1 depicts the ideal case where a successful, useful, novel product emerges.

A further complication must be mentioned briefly here, although space does not permit discussing it in great detail. As Csikszentmihalyi (2006), among others, argued, different phases may draw on different psychological resources (processes and personal properties). According to Table 16.1, if we take, let us say, the phase of *Preparation*, we see that the core product of the phase is factual knowledge, and this requires mainly convergent thinking. In the phase of *Activation*, on the other hand, the core product is problem awareness, and what is crucial is not convergent but divergent thinking. Turning to the phase of *Generation*, we see that the core product is a stock of candidate solutions, and their generation requires flexibility, lack of concern about conventional opinions, and low drive for closure, whereas in the phase of *Communication* the individual must make a public commitment to a single "mature" solution (closure is required) and "sell" this solution (be very concerned about what others think).

The crucial point is that apparently contradictory aspects of the other Ps (Process, Person, Press) are needed for generation of functionally creative products. However, the phase model shows that contradictory aspects are not needed in the same phase of the process. As creative people move through the phases on their way to a validated product, they alternate between poles such as divergent versus convergent thinking, or openness versus a drive for closure, according to the kind of product the particular phase requires. Facaoaru (1985) demonstrated empirically that creative engineers were able to move back and forth between apparently conflicting cognitive and noncognitive processes such as divergent and convergent thinking. Martindale (1989, p. 228) gave the name "oscillation" to this process of moving backwards and forwards from one pole of a paradox to the other in the course of generation and exploitation of effective novelty. According to Koberg and Bagnall (1991, p. 38), it involves "alternating psycho-behavioral waves." But, as the phase approach emphasizes, this fluctuation is systematic, not arbitrary.

A Pedagogy for Functional Creativity

The importance to society of generation of useful practical products in technology, business, administration, production and delivery systems, and so on strongly implies that vigorous attempts need to be made to foster their production, especially in school-level and higher education. However, when D. H. Cropley and A. J. Cropley (2005) reviewed findings on fostering creativity in engineering education in the United States of America, they concluded that there is little support for creative students. It is true that there has been some effort in recent years to encourage creativity in colleges and universities. For instance, in 1990 the National Science Foundation (NSF) established the Engineering Coalition of Schools for Excellence and Leadership (ECSEL). This has the goal of transforming undergraduate engineering education. However, a review of current practice throughout higher education in the United States conducted 10 years later (Fasko, 2000–2001) indicated that deliberate training in creativity is rare.

The problem is not confined to the United States of America. Although the European Union has established programs bearing the names of famous innovators such as SOCRATES or LEONARDO, it is astonishing that in the guidelines for the development of education in the community, concepts like "innovation" or "creativity" simply do not exist. To take a second example, at least until recently the Max Planck Institute for Human Development, Germany's leading research institute for the development of talent in research in the social sciences, had never supported a project on the topics of creativity or innovation. In a personal letter dated April 26, 2006, the office of the President of the Max Planck Society confirmed that the organization does not see creativity as a significant area of research.

At the school level, recent curriculum guidelines (e.g., International Technology Education Association, 2000) give great emphasis to the role of design in technology education. Indeed, as Mawson (2003) pointed out, the design process is now well-established as a key element in such education. However, Mawson went on to argue that, despite this, *current paradigms for teaching design are flawed* and an alternative pedagogy is needed. In a comprehensive review, Lewis (2005) turned to psychological research on creativity for ideas on what is needed. According to him, technology education nowadays (as well as art education, physical education, and music education, among others) needs to promote more than simply knowledge of materials and mastery of special technical skills such as correct use of tools or instruments. It needs to go beyond these to pursue "more subjective and elusive goals" (p. 35). Among these he includes "creative insight" (p. 35).

According to Lewis, teaching of design is "almost ideally suited to uncovering dimensions of the creative potential of children that would remain hidden in much of the rest of the curriculum" (p. 43). The special property of design is what Lewis called its "open-endedness" (p. 43): Students must produce a tangible product, but design problems are ill structured, answers are not defined in advance, and the pathway to the solution is open. These are precisely the conditions that A. J. Cropley (2005) identified as most favorable for creativity, which offers cause for optimism about the chances of fostering it in technology education.

Nonetheless, Lewis (2005, p. 44) came to a negative but in our view moderate conclusion:

> There are indications in the literature that we still have some way to go before creativity becomes a more central feature of the teaching of design in the United States and elsewhere. [italics added].

Lewis drew up a list of what is required, and included the following as the very first items:

(a) implications for design/problem-solving *pedagogy* and
(b) implications for *assessment*.

We will look briefly at these two issues in the reverse order: How can you tell if a product is creative, and how can you teach students to generate more creative products?

In looking at assessment, D. H. Cropley and A. J. Cropley (2005) and A. J. Cropley (2005) suggested "indicators" of the functional creativity of students' solutions to design problems such as "Design and build a wheeled vehicle powered by the energy stored in a mousetrap," or "Design and build a device capable of lowering an uncooked egg from a height of at least 1 meter, without using any ropes, chains, wheels or pulleys," and gave an example of its application. The arguments presented above suggest that a creativity-oriented pedagogy focused on fostering the generation of functionally creative products needs to encourage students to build up a fund of knowledge (*Preparation*), encourage and train them to identify problems (*Activation*), teach them to generate novelty (*Generation*), help them recognize possible solutions (*Illumination*), show them how to evaluate candidate solutions (*Verification*), encourage them to make verified solutions available to other people (*Communication*), and help them deal with feedback from the external world (*Validation*).

A more detailed presentation of our own work here would go beyond the limits of a handbook chapter. However, A. J. Cropley and D. H. Cropley (2008) uses a phase approach as the analytic tool to give a more comprehensive presentation of the general principles involved by comparing and contrasting mathematics teaching in Japan, on the one hand, and in the USA and Germany, on the other. Finally, D. H. Cropley and A. J. Cropley (2009), gives more concrete details of a specific class on engineering innovation based on a phase approach.

References

Altshuller, G. S. (1988). *Creativity as an exact science*. New York: Gordon and Breach.

Amabile, T. (1985). Motivation and creativity: Effects of motivational orientation on creative writers. *Journal of Personality and Social Psychology*, 48, 393–399.

Arieti, S. (1976). *Creativity: The magical synthesis.* New York: Basic Books.

Austin, J. H. (1978). *Chase, chance, and creativity.* New York: Columbia University Press.

Bacon, F. (1899). *Advancement of learning and Novum Organum.* New York: The Colonial Press. (Original work published 1604)

Bailin, S. (1988). *Achieving extraordinary ends: An essay on creativity.* Dordrecht: Kluwer.

Bain, A. (1868). *The senses and the intellect* (3rd ed.). London: Longman Green.

Barron, F. X. (1955). The disposition towards originality. *Journal of Abnormal and Social Psychology*, 51, 478–485.

Barron, F. (1969). *Creative person and creative process.* New York: Holt, Rinehart & Winston.

Barron, F. (1988). Putting creativity to work. In R. J. Sternberg (Ed.), *The nature of creativity* (pp. 76–98). Cambridge: Cambridge University Press.

Boden, M. A. (1994a). Introduction. In M. A. Boden (Ed.), *Dimensions of creativity* (pp. 1–8). Cambridge, MA: MIT Press.

Boden, M. A. (1994b). What is creativity? In M. A. Boden (Ed.), *Dimensions of creativity* (pp. 75–118). Cambridge, MA: MIT Press.

Burghardt, M. D. (1995). *Introduction to the engineering profession* (2nd ed.). New York: Addison-Wesley.

Buzan, A. (2007). Foreword. In S. C. Lundin & J. Tan (Eds.), *CATS: The nine lives of innovation* (pp. v–viii). Spring Hill, Queensland: Management Press.

Campbell, D. T. (1960). Blind variation and selective survival as a general strategy in knowledge processes. In M. C. Yovits & S. Cameron (Eds.), *Self-organizing systems* (pp. 205–231). New York: Pergamon.

Canadian Intellectual Property Office. (2007). What can you patent? Retrieved from http://strategis.gc.ca/sc_mrksv/cipo/patents/pat_gd_protect-e.html#sec2 on November 20, 2007.

Cattell, R. B., & Butcher, H. J. (1968). *The prediction of achievement and creativity.* New York: Bobbs-Merrill.

Clifford, P. I. (1958). Emotional contacts with the external world manifested by selected groups of highly creative chemists and mathematicians. *Perceptual and Motor Skills*, Monograph Supplement No 1, 8, 3–26.

Cropley, A. J. (1967). *Creativity.* London: Longmans.

Cropley, A. J. (1997). Creativity: A bundle of paradoxes. *Gifted and Talented International*, 12, 8–14.

Cropley, A. J. (2005). *Creativity and problem-solving: Implications for classroom assessment* (24th Vernon-Wall Lecture, Glasgow, 6th November 2004). Leicester: British Psychological Society.

Cropley, A. J., & Cropley, D. H. (2008). Resolving the paradoxes of creativity: An extended phase model. *Cambridge Journal of Education*, 38, 355–373.

Cropley, D. H., & Cropley, A. J. (2005). Engineering creativity: A systems concept of functional creativity. In J. C. Kaufman & J. Baer (Eds.), *Faces of the muse: How people think, work and act creatively in diverse domains* (pp. 169–185). Hillsdale, NJ: Erlbaum.

Cropley, D. H., & Cropley, A. J. (2009, August). Recognizing and fostering creativity in design education, *International Journal of Technology and Design Education*, DOI 10.1007/s10798-009-9089-5, online.

Csikszentmihalyi, M. (1988). Society, culture, and person: A system view of creativity. In R. J. Sternberg (Ed.), *The nature of creativity* (pp. 325–339). New York: Cambridge University Press.

Csikszentmihalyi, M. (1996). *Creativity: Flow and the psychology of discovery and invention.* New York: HarperCollins.

Csikszentmihalyi, M. (1999). Implications of a systems perspective for the study of creativity. In R. J. Sternberg (Ed.), *Handbook of creativity* (pp. 313–335). Cambridge: Cambridge University Press.

Csikszentmihalyi, M. (2006). Foreword: Developing creativity. In N. Jackson, M. Oliver, M. Shaw, & J. Wisdom (Eds.), *Developing creativity in higher education: An imaginative curriculum* (pp. xviii–xx). London: Routledge.

Dasgupta, S. (2004). Is creativity a Darwinian process? *Creativity Research Journal*, 16, 403–414.

Descartes, R. (1991). *Principles of philosophy* (V. R. Miller & R. P. Miller, Trans.). Boston: Kluwer. (Original work published 1644)

Diaz de Chumaceiro, C. L. (1999). Research on career paths: Serendipity and its analog. *Creativity Research Journal*, 12, 227–229.

Economist Technology Quarterly. (September 21, 2002). *Thanksgiving for innovation* (pp. 13–14).

Facaoaru, C. (1985). *Kreativität in Wissenschaft und Technik* [Creativity in science and technology]. Bern: Huber.

Fasko, D. (2000–2001). Education and creativity. *Creativity Research Journal*, 13, 317–328.

Florida, R. (2004). America's looming creativity crisis. *Harvard Business Review*, 82(10), 122–136.

Frängsmyr, T. (Ed.). (1997). *Les Prix Nobel. The Nobel Prizes 1996*. Stockholm: Nobel Foundation.

Gardner, H. (1993). *Creating minds*. New York: Basic Books.

Getzels, J. W., & Jackson, P. W. (1962). *Creativity and intelligence*. New York: Wiley.

Ghiselin, B. (1955). *The creative process*. New York: Mentor Books.

Gladwell, M. (2008). *Outliers*. New York: Little Brown.

Glover, J. A., Ronning, R. R., & Reynolds, C. R. (Eds.). (1989). *Handbook of creativity*. New York: Plenum.

Gordon, W. J. (1961). *Synectics*. New York: Harper.

Guilford, J. P. (1950). Creativity. *American Psychologist*, 5, 444–454.

Guilford, J. P. (1967). *The nature of human intelligence*. New York: McGraw-Hill.

Hadamard, J. (1945). *The psychology of invention in the mathematical field*. New York: Dover.

Hausman, C. R. (1984). *A discourse on novelty and creation*. Albany: State University of New York Press.

Heinelt, G. (1974). *Kreative lehrer/kreative schueler* [Creative teachers/creative students]. Freiburg: Herder.

Horenstein, M. N. (2002). *Design concepts for engineers* (2nd ed.). Upper Saddle River, NJ: Prentice-Hall.

Howe, C., McWilliam, D., & Cross, G. (2005). Chance favours only the prepared mind: Cogitation and the delayed effects of peer collaboration. *British Journal of Psychology*, 96, 67–93.

International Technology Education Association. (2000). *Standards for technological literacy – Content for the study of technology*. Reston, VA: Author.

Jay, E. S., & Perkins, D. N. (1997). Problem finding: The search for mechanisms. In M. A. Runco (Ed.), *The creativity research handbook* (Vol. 1, pp. 257–294). Cresskill, NJ: Hampton Press.

Josephson, M. (1959). *Edison: A biography*. New York: Wiley.

Koberg, D., & Bagnall, J. (1991). *The universal traveler: A soft systems guide to creativity, problem solving and the process of reaching goals*. Menlo Park, CA: Crisp Publications Inc.

Lewis, T. (2005). Creativity – A framework for the design/problem solving discourse in technology education. *Journal of Technology Education*, 17, 35–52.

Lubart, T. (2000–2001). Models of the creative process: Past, present and future. *Creativity Research Journal*, 13, 295–308.

Mach, E. (1905). *Erkenntnis und Erratum. Skizzen zur Psychologie der Forschung* [Knowledge and error. Sketches of the psychology of research]. Leipzig: Johann Ambrosius Barth.

MacKinnon, D. W. (1978). *In search of human effectiveness: Identifying and developing creativity*. Buffalo, NY: Creative Education Foundation.

Martindale, C. (1989). Personality, situation, and creativity. In J. A. Glover, R. R. Ronning, & C. R. Reynolds (Eds.), *Handbook of creativity* (pp. 211–228). New York: Plenum.

Martinson, O. (1995). Cognitive styles and experience in solving insight problems: Replication and extension. *Creativity Research Journal*, 8, 291–298.

Maslow, A. H. (1973). Creativity in self-actualizing people. In A. Rothenberg & C. R. Hausman (Eds.), *The creative question* (pp. 86–92). Durham, NC: Duke University Press.

Mawson, B. (2003). Beyond "The Design Process": An alternative pedagogy for technology education. *International Journal of Technology and Design Education*, 13, 117–128.

May, R. (1976). *The courage to create*. New York: Bantam.

McMullan, W. E. (1978). Creative individuals: Paradoxical personages. *Journal of Creative Behavior*, 10, 265–275.

Miller, A. I. (1992). Scientific creativity: A comparative study of Henri Poincaré and Albert Einstein. *Creativity Research Journal*, 5, 385–418.

Mumford, M. D., Baughman, W. A., Threlfall, K. V., Supinski, E. P., & Costanza, D. P. (1996). Process-based measures of creative problem-solving skills: I. Problem construction. *Creativity Research Journal*, 9, 63–76.

Mumford, M. D., & Gustafson, S. B. (1988). Creativity syndrome: Integration, application and innovation. *Psychological Bulletin*, 103, 27–43.

Mumford, M. D., & Moertl, P. (2003). Cases of social innovation: Lessons from two innovations in the 20th Century. *Creativity Research Journal*, 13, 261–266.

Nobel Foundation. (1967). *Nobel lectures, Physics 1901–1927*. Amsterdam: Elsevier.

Osborn, A. (1953). *Applied imagination*. New York: Scribners.

Plucker, J. A., & Renzulli, J. S. (1999). Psychometric approaches to the study of human creativity. In R. J. Sternberg (Ed.), *Handbook of creativity* (pp. 35–61). New York: Cambridge University Press.

Prindle, E. J. (1906). The art of inventing. *Transactions of the American Institute for Engineering Education*, 25, 519–547.

Rhodes, H. (1961). An analysis of creativity. *Phi Delta Kappan*, 42, 305–310.

Rogers, C. R. (1961). *On becoming a person*. Boston: Houghton Mifflin.

Rosenman, M. F. (1988). Serendipity and scientific discovery. *Journal of Creative Behavior*, 22, 132–138.

Rossman, J. (1931). *The psychology of the inventor: A study of the patentee*. Washington: Inventors' Publishing.

Rothman, A. (1982). Genius and biographers: the fictionalization of Evariste Galois. *American Mathematical Monthly*, 89(2), 84–106.

Savransky, S. D. (2000). *Engineering of creativity*. Boca Raton, FL: CRC Press.

Sawyer, R. K., John-Steiner, V., Moran, S., Sternberg, R. J., Feldman, D. H., Gardner, H., et al. (2003). *Creativity and development*. New York: Oxford University Press.

Shaw, M. P. (1989). The Eureka process: A structure for the creative experience in science and engineering. *Creativity Research Journal*, 2, 286–298.

Simonton, D. K. (1988). *Scientific genius: A psychology of science*. New York: Cambridge University Press.

Simonton, D. K. (1999). *Origins of genius: Darwinian perspectives of creativity*. New York: Oxford University Press.

Skinner, B. F. (1950). Are theories of learning necessary? *Psychological Review*, 57, 193–216.

Souriau, P. (1881). *Théorie de l'invention* [A theory of invention]. Paris: Hachette.

Sternberg, R. J., & Davidson, J. E. (1999). Intuition. In M. A. Runco & S. R. Pritzker (Eds.), *Encyclopedia of creativity* (Vol. 2, pp. 57–69). San Diego: Academic Press.

Sternberg, R. J., Kaufman, J. C., & Pretz, J. E. (2002). *The creativity conundrum: A propulsion model of kinds of creative contributions*. New York: Psychology Press.

Torrance, E. P. (1962). *Guiding creative talent*. Englewood Cliffs, NJ: Prentice Hall.

Torrance, E. P. (1963). *Education and the creative potential*. Minneapolis: University of Minnesota Press.

Torrance, E. P. (1965). *The Minnesota studies of creative thinking: Widening horizons in creativity*. New York: Wiley.

Torrance, E. P. (1966). *The Torrance Tests of Creative Thinking – Norms, technical manual*. Princeton, NJ: Personnel Press.

Unsworth, K. L. (2001). Unpacking creativity. *Academy of Management Review*, 26, 286–297.

U.S. Congress. (1958). *National Defense Education Act of 1958*, P.L. 85–864. 85th Congress, September 2. Washington, DC: GPO.

Vinacke, W. E. (1953). *The psychology of thinking*. New York: McGraw Hill.

Wallas, G. (1926). *The art of thought*. New York: Harcourt Brace.

Watson, J. B. (1913). Psychology as the behaviorist views it. *Psychological Review*, 20, 158–177.

Weisberg, R. W. (1993). *Creativity: Beyond the myth of genius*. New York: W.H. Freeman.

Weisberg, R. (2003). Case studies of innovation: Ordinary thinking, extraordinary outcomes. In L. V. Shavinina (Ed.), *International handbook on innovation* (pp. 204–247). Oxford: Elsevier.

Wertheimer, M. (1945). *Productive thinking*. New York: Harper.

Section III

CONTEMPORARY DEBATES

CHAPTER 17

Is Creativity Domain Specific?

John Baer

In its 20-year history, the *Creativity Research Journal* has invited and published just one set of Point-Counterpoint articles. Those two articles debated the evidence for and against the domain specificity of creativity (Baer, 1998; Plucker, 1998). Whether creativity is a general, domain-transcending set of skills, aptitudes, traits, propensities, and motivations that can be productively deployed in any domain – or, conversely, whether the skills, aptitudes, traits, propensities, and motivations that lead to creative performance vary from domain to domain – is a key question in creativity research and theory.

Some have questioned whether the domain specificity and generality problem is an important, useful, or potentially productive one. For example, Sternberg (2005) wrote that "the problem of the domain specificity versus domain generality is not productive," at least as currently conceptualized (p. 305). As I will argue in this chapter, the answer to this generality-specificity question is in all likelihood one that finds some kind of middle ground; as Sternberg said later in the same paragraph, it is prob-

able that "things are neither wholly domain general nor wholly domain specific." So it is not all one or the other, nor is it even clear what definition(s) of domains will best capture the substantial differences in creativity across domains that research has uncovered. The lack of clarity about domains is a key issue in Sternberg's argument, which suggests that we "cannot talk about domain specificity until we have a theory of domains" (p. 305), whether that be in the study of creativity or of any other area or psychology. But the fact that this is neither a winner-take-all contest nor one in which all the players have been clearly identified does not make it an unimportant one. Like nature-nurture questions, in which the answer is almost always that (a) both matter and (b) the exact kinds of contributions made by heredity and by environment in shaping particular behaviors are often not well known, a lack of complete clarity does not mean that efforts to determine the right mixture are unimportant. Partialling out the effects of environments and heredity on some traits, illnesses, or skills can help us determined what kinds of interventions it might be most effective to try or what kinds of questions it might be most productive to ask and to research (even though in doing so we may not yet be able to specify the exact genes or environmental factors causing those differences). In the same way, a better understanding of the different contributions of domain-specific and domain-general factors to creative performance can help us better understand, assess, and nurture creativity. Such an understanding can also guide us to ask more productive research question and build more useful theories (as Sternberg himself seemed to acknowledge in his recent book, *Creativity: From Potential to Realization* [Sternberg, Grigorenko, & Singer, 2004], which like this chapter focuses on the domain generality-specificity question).

Common usage would suggest that creativity is domain general. When referring to someone as "skillful" or "knowledgeable," it is common to specify some limited range of skill or knowledge (e.g., a skillful cook or plumber or writer, or someone knowledgeable about sports or politics or Russian history). People rarely expect others (or themselves) to be skillful or knowledgeable across the board. Such wide-ranging talent or knowledge is sufficiently unexpected that in the case of someone whom one believes to be knowledgeable or skilled in many diverse arenas, one is likely to note how unusual this is by referring to that person as a Renaissance person. But people often refer to others (or themselves) as "creative" without specifying particular areas or limitations to one's creativity. The implicit assumption is that a creative person has some skills, aptitudes, traits, propensities, and motivations that lend themselves to creative performance in whatever activities one undertakes. Creativity is thought of more in the way that intelligence is generally conceptualized, as a general ability that will affect performance in significant ways in almost any endeavor. As Feist (2004) wrote:

> It is a very appealing, and ultimately firmly American, notion that a creative person could be creative in any domain he or she chose. All the person would have to do would be to decide where to apply her or his talents and efforts, practice or train a lot, and voila, you have creative achievement. On this view, talent trumps domain and it really is somewhat arbitrary in which domain the creative achievement is expressed. Indeed, we often refer to people as "creative" not as "a creative artist" or "creative biologist." (p. 57)

Feist (2004) contested this view, however, arguing "that this is a rather naïve and ultimately false position and that creative talent is in fact domain specific. . . . There are some generalized mental strategies and heuristics that do cut across domains, but creativity and talent are usually not among the domain-general skills" (p. 57).

This is a relatively new position, but one that has a growing number of adherents. The psychologist who is commonly credited with putting creativity into (or back into) psychology's agenda, Joy Guilford (1950, 1956, 1967; Guilford & Hoepfner, 1971), also argued for a less holistic approach to creativity, but not one bounded in any way by content domains or fields of inquiry. His model of the intellect, of which creativity was a key component, was composed of many discrete (and, he believed, measurable) interacting abilities, but his model was nonetheless virtually silent on the question of domains. There were different skills that led to creative performance, but these skills could, one might assume, be used in many domains where creative performance was possible; there was an implicit "assumption of content generality" (Plucker, 1998, p. 178). If there were domains, they were only very broadly defined ones such as his five kinds of contents (visual, auditory, symbolic, semantic, and behavioral).

The most widely used measures of creativity, the Torrance Tests of Creative Thinking (TTCT), are based on Guilford's model (Kim, 2006). Although they measure only one component of that model, divergent thinking, they claim to predict creative performance generally (Plucker, 1998). The Torrance tests have two forms, the TTCT-Verbal and the TTCT-Figural. The

TTCT-Verbal consists of five activities: ask-and-guess, product improvement, unusual uses, unusual questions, and just suppose. The TTCT-Figural consists of three activities: picture construction, picture completion, and repeated figures of lines or circles. This division might seem to suggest a distinction between these two types of creativity, but the two domain-based forms are just viewed as different ways to measure the same underlying (and general) construct (Torrance, 1966, 1974, 1990, 1998; Torrance & Ball, 1984). Domains don't matter in most commonly used methods of creativity assessment; the special something that leads to creativity, as assessed by divergent-thinking tests (or even the Remote Associates Test; Mednick, 1962; Mednick & Mednick, 1967), is assumed to be the same in all domains.

In this chapter I will briefly review the evidence for domain generality and domain specificity, noting how those favoring one view or the other tend to look for different kinds of evidence to support their views. These varying kinds of evidence may point to different understandings of what it means to be creative. I will also discuss some red-herring kinds of evidence that often confuse people when thinking about these issues. At the end of the chapter I will look at new theories that attempt to integrate both models into a single, overarching theory of creativity.

By way of full disclosure, it is important to note that I have not been a dispassionate bystander to this debate. I have been an active participant (and even authored one of the two Point-Counterpoint articles mentioned in the first paragraph of this chapter, arguing the case for domain specificity). I have attempted in this chapter to be as evenhanded as possible in my presentation of both sides of this debate, but as Kuhn (1979) warned us, there is often no neutral ground from which competing theories can be judged or even described. Successive theories are "incommensurable...in the sense that the referents of some of the terms which occur in both are a function of the theory within which those terms appear. There is

no neutral language into which both the theories and the relevant data may be translated for purposes of comparison" (Kuhn, 1979, p. 540), and one can therefore not think in terms of two competing theories at the same time, but only, at best, switch back and forth between them. So just as one can see only, in any single moment, either a vase or a profile in the vase-profile gestalt found in almost every introductory psychology textbook, theories of domain specificity and generality may be incommensurable: Perhaps one can at best switch between two such opposing points of view but never see both theories through a single set of lenses. The differences of course are not so great as between, say, Copernican and Ptolemaic worldviews, but in fact such deep revolutions as the Ptolemaic are quite rare; McMullin (1998) showed that most revolutions are "shallow" (p. 122), requiring modification of only small parts of the "disciplinary matrix" that Kuhn (1970), in his Postscript to *The Structure of Scientific Revolutions*, suggests are needed to hold together a field of study. But the differences are nonetheless quite real, and within this limited region of creativity's disciplinary matrix, the distinctions between viewpoints, meanings, and assumptions of domain-general and domain-specific theories can be at times vertiginous, and defenders of conflicting theories can easily fail to understand each other's arguments as a result. "The premises and values shared by the two parties to a debate over paradigms are not sufficiently extensive for that" (Kuhn, 1970, p. 94).

Arguments and Evidence for Domain Generality and Domain Specificity

How is one to choose between competing theories? Philosophers of science are not in agreement about what makes a theory a scientific theory or what kinds of evidence should cause us to favor one theory over another (Curd & Cover, 1998a), but Popperian falsificationism (Popper, 1959, 1963) has probably been the most influential theory among working scientists (Curd

& Cover, 1998b). Popper argued that a scientific theory must make explicit predictions. Any theory that does not make such predictions cannot be falsified, and such an unfalsifiable theory is not scientific. It seems appropriate that the dispute about the domain specificity of creativity should be held to this standard. So what different predictions do the two sides of this debate make? One creativity researcher, Ivcevic (2007), summarized how these predictions should differ:

> Domain generality would be supported by high intercorrelations among different creative behaviors and a common set of psychological descriptors for those behaviors, while domain specificity would be supported by relatively low correlations among different behaviors, and a diverging set of psychological descriptors of those behaviors. (p. 272)

This is a good summary of what the opposing views would predict, but its is not as specific as one would like, making it possible for different theorists (a) to look for very different kinds of relevant behaviors and psychological descriptors (e.g., should one look at creative products in different domains made by the same people, such as poems or collages, or at personality traits of more and less creative people in different domains?) and (b) to interpret the same outcome in different ways (e.g., is a correlation between products in different domains of .2 or .3 – accounting for 4% to 9% of the variance – enough to make the case for domain generality; or, conversely, are these correlations so low that they should count as evidence of domain specificity?). And then there are questions relating to the difference between Big-C, domain-altering, genius-level creativity versus everyday, garden-variety, little-c creativity. Does the expectation of "high intercorrelations among different creative behaviors" under domain generality mean that Big-C creators would be expected to show extraordinary levels of creativity in several fields, or does this expectation apply only to little-c creativity? Or perhaps domain generality would mean that

Big-C creators should show Big-C creativity in just one or a few fields along with much higher-than-expected little-c creativity in other fields (assuming that Big-C and little-c creativity operate by the same processes but at different levels, which is itself a somewhat controversial argument)?

Space limitations make it impossible to list every study that provides evidence regarding the domain specificity or generality of creativity, and readers looking for that kind of detail should consider some recent books on this topic (e.g., Baer, 1993; Kaufman & Baer, 2005a; Sternberg, Grigorenko, & Singer, 2004). The approach I will take here is to examine the kinds of evidence most commonly used in arguments for and against domain specificity.

Evidence for Domain Specificity

Arguments for domain specificity tend to look for evidence in the creativity of artifacts produced by subjects in different domains. The basic argument runs as follows: If creativity is a domain-general skill, then it should influence creativity on virtually any task one undertakes. Other things will of course be important (e.g., specialized domain skills and knowledge, interest in a specific domain, and availability of domain-specific tools), and these will also influence the level of creative performance in a given domain, but if creativity is domain-general, then *on average*, people who are more creative than most people in one domain should be more creative in other domains as well. This parallels the primary argument for the existence of g in the intelligence literature.

Domain generality of creativity thus predicts, at a modest to high level, positive correlations among the creativity ratings of artifacts produced by subjects in different domains. Domain specificity predicts the opposite: low or nonexistent levels of correlation among creative products produced by subjects in different domains. Advocates of domain specificity in the area of creativity who accept a general intelligence factor (g) and who believe that intelligence is one factor influencing creative performance would predict a low level of correlation among the creative products produced by subjects in different domains (and to the extent that IQ tests measure *g*, the degree of influence of *g* on creative performance would be measurable by those tests, and that impact could then be statistically removed by partialling out variance attributable to *g*). This is the position of most who have argued for domain specificity. There are also other candidates for general creativity-relevant factors that might contribute to domain generality, such as motivation and conscientiousness. Motivation can of course be domain specific (e.g., someone who finds astronomy fascinating might not have similar motivation to study history or dance), but motivation might also be a general, domain-transcending attribute, one that would influence one's performance in any domain. To the extent that one acknowledges any general factors, one would expect to see higher correlations among the creativity ratings of products produced by subjects in different domains. Advocates of domain specificity who do *not* accept any general factors (like intelligence, motivation, or conscientiousness) that might impact creative performance across domains would predict zero or random correlations among those ratings.

This would seem to lead to a rather simple test. All we need to do is find out if people who are more creative in domain X are also more creative in domains Y and Z; that is, are there in fact "high intercorrelations among different creative behaviors" (Ivcevic, 2007, p. 272), as domain generality predicts? Assessment of creativity is difficult, unfortunately, and most of the methods commonly used have approached creativity rather indirectly, via skills or behaviors or traits theoretically linked to creativity, rather than assessing creative products themselves. The most common measures of creativity are divergent-thinking tests, but these are not helpful in the generality-specificity debate for at least two reasons: (1) they assume domain generality, and therefore all the standard divergent-thinking

tests report only domain-general scores, and (2) even if specially constructed, domain-specific divergent-thinking tests were created (which is quite possible; in fact, Torrance [1966, 1974] himself made a step in this direction with his verbal and figural forms of the TTCT, although he believed they were both testing a single, domain-general skill), such tests are at best measures of a skill or set of skills – divergent-thinking skills – that although theoretically linked to creativity are nonetheless, at most, just one aspect of creativity, and therefore not actually a measure of creativity itself. (Even assuming creativity to be domain general and that divergent thinking is a component of creativity, calling divergent thinking tests creativity tests would be rather like calling tests of one's ability to recall strings of random numbers intelligence tests. At most these would be but one part of a larger general factor.) Personality and trait theories of creativity also most often assume domain generality, and once again these are not measures of creative performance but rather things that are either theoretically or empirically linked to creativity (Kaufman, Plucker, & Baer, 2008). So none of these standard methods of creativity assessment is appropriately free of theoretical bias, and none measures actual creativity, only some limited range of its surrogates that are believed to be correlated with creativity.

There is one method of creativity assessment that does seem well-suited to test the domain specificity question, however: the Consensual Assessment Technique (CAT), originally developed by Teresa Amabile (1982, 1983, 1996) and further developed by others (e.g., Baer, Kaufman, & Gentile, 2004; Hennessey et al., 2008; Kaufman et al., 2008). The CAT has sometimes been called the "Gold Standard" of creativity assessment (Carson, 2006) because (a) it is based on evaluations of actual creative performances or artifacts, and therefore a measure of the actual creativity of those products, not just of things believed to be related in some way to creativity, (b) it is not linked to or dependent for its validity on any particular theory of creativity, and (c) it uses essentially the

Table 17.1: Correlations Among Creativity Ratings

Task	Poetry	Story	Word Problem	Equation
Poetry	–	.23	.31*	−.14
Story		–	.20	−.03
Word Problem			–	−.20

$N = 50$; * $p < .05$, two-tailed

same method for assessing creativity as is used in most domains in the "real world." The CAT asks experts to rate the creativity of products in a domain in comparison to one another, in the same way that, say, the Academy Awards ask experts in the field to rate movies, actors, and directors, or Nobel Prize committees in different fields rate the work of practitioners in their fields. The CAT is certainly not perfect (neither, one could argue, are the judgments of Nobel Prize Committees!), but it is perhaps the best available method to assess real-world creativity.

The CAT is based on this idea that the best measure of the creativity of a work of art, a theory, or any other artifact is the combined assessment of experts in that field. Whether one is selecting a poem for a prestigious award or judging the creativity of a fifth grader's collage, one doesn't score it by following some checklist or applying a general creativity-assessment rubric. The best judgments of the creativity of such artifacts that can be produced – imperfect though these may be – are the combined opinions of experts in the field. That's what most prize committees do (which is why only the opinions of a few experts matter when choosing, say, the winner of the Fields Medal in mathematics – the opinions of the rest of us just don't count). The CAT uses essentially the same procedure to judge the creativity of more everyday creations. (Kaufman, Plucker, & Baer, 2008. pp. 54–55)

Experts rate the creativity of a set of artifacts by comparing them to one another. They are given no other instruction – it is important that they use their own expert sense of what is creative in a domain – and work independently. Interrater reliability is quite good,

generally in the .80 to .90 range (Amabile 1982, 1983, 1996; Baer, 1993; Baer, Kaufman, & Gentile, 2004; Kaufman, Plucker et al., 2008).

CAT and CAT-like assessments of the creativity of subjects in diverse domains have been conducted, and the result is generally quite low intercorrelations among the creativity ratings of different artifacts produced by the same subjects. For example, Baer (1993) asked 50 eighth-grade students to create a poem, a story, a mathematical word problem, and an interesting equation (in which students were asked to create a mathematical equality that they considered especially interesting; see Baer, 1993, pp. 49–52 for more complete details on the tasks). Of six correlations, three were positive and three were negative, with a mean correlation of .06 and with just one of the six reaching statistical significance (Table 17.1).

When variance attributable to math and verbal standardized test scores is removed there are again three positive and three negative correlations, with a mean correlation of −.05, and the only statistically significant correlation is a negative one (Table 17.2).

These results, and similar results with adults, fifth-grade students, fourth-grade students, and second-grade students, led Baer to conclude that the seven studies he reported of this kind "make a strong case for an absence of any significant effects of general creative-thinking skills on the performance of a wide range of subjects on a variety of creativity-relevant tasks" (1993, p. 67).

Similar results have been obtained in other studies. Ruscio, Whitney, and Amabile (1998) asked undergraduate subjects to complete three tasks (structure building,

Table 17.2: Partial Correlations Among Creativity Ratings

Task	Poetry	Story	Word Problem	Equation
Poetry	–	−.01	.19	−.14
Story		–	.05	.07
Word Problem			–	−.45[*]

$N = 50$; * $p < .01$, two-tailed

collage making, and poetry writing) and found little evidence of general creativity (correlations of 0.18, 0.09. and −0.02). Of these, only one – the correlation between structure building and collage making, which had a correlation of .18, accounting for a little more than three per cent of the total variance – reached the .05 level of statistical significance. These two tasks were both from the same domain or general thematic area (for discussion of different levels of domain, see the section "*Evidence for domain generality*"); for one task the instructions were to "build an aesthetically appealing structure that's at least fifteen inches tall" (p. 248), and for the other task the instructions were to "make a collage out of the materials you see in front of you" (p. 249). So to the degree that this study showed any commonality among the creative performances of subjects on different tasks, it was found only between tasks in the same general area. Correlations of measures of creative performance across domains were totally absent. Similarly, in a study using expert raters to assess the creativity of elementary school children's art, Runco (1989) found low correlations (median r = 18) among the different kinds of works of art produced by his subjects. Even within the same broadly defined domain of art, there was only a modest degree of generality across different tasks.

Conti, Coon, and Amabile (1996) offered evidence to support Amabile's (1983) componential model of creativity, which posits both domain-specific and creativity-general skills that influence creative performance. (These two kinds of factors are in addition to a third factor, task motivation, which has been Amabile's primary interest and focus

of study; see Amabile, 1983, 1996.) Conti, Coon, and Amabile's study was actually a re-analysis of data gathered in three different studies after it was found that some subjects had participated in two or all three of these studies, and therefore correlations among their creative performances on a number of different tasks in two domains could be computed. There were a total of four story-writing tasks (using different prompts) and three art activities. The intercorrelations among the story-writing creativity ratings were both high and statistically significant, suggesting that these measures were largely measures of the same domain-based ability. Intercorrelations among the three stories written as part of one study ranged from .43 to .87, confirming the prediction that "creativity measures taken within the same context and domain should be strongly positively related" (p. 387). Correlations with creativity ratings of these stories and stories written at a different time and under different experimental constraints were as expected somewhat lower; "as predicted, creativity measures within the same domain are substantially intercorrelated, although not as strongly as those taken within the same experimental context" (p. 387).[1] Correlations among the ratings of the art-related tasks were also positive, but not as strong.

---

1 These domain-based creative-writing abilities have been shown to be fairly consistent over time, however. Working with much younger subjects, Baer (1994) found fairly robust long-term stability using essentially the same short story-writing task with a one-year interval between testing. The story-writing creativity of 9-year-old participants correlated .58 with the story-writing creativity of the same participants one year later, which is not far off the .60 to .80 stability coefficients found for IQ test scores at this age (Kogan, 1983).

Unlike the writing tasks, which were all very similar (all required subjects to write a short story based on a prompt), "here the tasks were substantially different, stretching the definition of 'domain' somewhat. Nonetheless, drawing and collage creativity are highly correlated, and painting and collage creativity are moderately correlated" (p. 387).

These correlations show that creativity on different tasks in the same domain are highly correlated, and the more closely related the tasks are, the higher the correlations, but they tell us nothing about the question of domain specificity or generality. It is the cross-domain correlations that speak to the generality-specificity question. Of the 13 correlations of this kind, 8 were positive, 4 were negative, and 1 was zero. None of these correlations was statistically significant, which means they provided *no* substantive evidence at all for domain generality. The mean of these 13 correlations was .109, which would account for barely more than one percent of the variance. Conti, Coon, and Amabile (1996) argued that this is evidence for domain specificity, but it is certainly the weakest imaginable evidence. Their acknowledgment that some of these correlations "show no consistent pattern" (p. 387, describing the comparison of the results of Studies 2 and 3) seems an apt description of all the cross-domain comparisons. (If measures of g showed levels of consistency across skills hypothesized to be part of general intelligence that were in this range – if the component skills that make up IQ tests had only tiny and statistically insignificant correlations with one another, as Conti, Coon, and Amabile reported for cross-domain creativity ratings – it seems likely that g would have no adherents at all. And given Baer's [1993] finding that standardized test scores had low but statistically significant correlations with most CAT-measured creativity ratings, it seems likely that even the very small amount of shared variance that Conti, Coon, and Amabile reported was likely due to intelligence, not to a domain-general creativity factor.)

One recent study did find evidence of domain generality across artifacts in different domains. Chen, Himsel, Kasof, Greenberger, and Dmitreiva (2006) reported that in contrast to the many studies that had shown no evidence of domain generality, theirs was "*the first study* to our knowledge that provides reasonable psychometric evidence" (p. 195; italics added) for the domain generality of creativity. Subjects were 159 undergraduates, who produced a number of products in different domains. A principal-components analysis resulted in three factors that generally corresponded to the domains of artistic, verbal, and mathematical creativity, which were the three kinds of tasks subjects performed. Using these they created three summary scores of subjects' verbal, artistic, and mathematical creativity. They submitted these scores to a factor analysis and extracted a single factor that accounted for 45% and 52% of the variance in two subject groups. These results are different, as the authors noted, from all previous research of this kind. Unfortunately, the authors did not follow the required procedures for the CAT, because they replaced expert raters with "trained undergraduate research assistants" (p. 186). Use of expert judges is the very basis for the CAT's validity claims, and the substitution of novices is not supported either (a) by Amabile's (1982, 1983, 1996) original work on the CAT, where she wrote that "it would be a mistake to conclude that everyone (or even every psychology graduate student) can be considered an appropriate judge" and "the best guideline is to use judges who have at least some formal training and experience in the target domain" (Amabile, 1996, p. 72) or (b) by more recent work comparing the ratings of novices (college students like the ones used by Chen et al.) with experts. In the domains of poetry (Kaufman, Baer, Cole, & Sexton, 2008) and short stories (Kaufman, Baer, & Cole, 2009), experts' creativity ratings and the creativity ratings of undergraduates were *not* sufficiently correlated to allow the replacement of expert judges by novices (and these studies used two of the task domains employed by Chen et al., whose subjects created two poems and one story). There is no research to date on the use of novice judges for art and mathematical creativity tasks, but without data showing that expert raters in a domain can be reliably replaced by novices, ratings provided by those novices cannot be considered valid. Thus in what they claimed was the first study to provide reasonable psychometric evidence for domain generality of creativity, the raw data used is unfortunately not valid data (Chen et al.).

Available evidence to date from the many studies that have looked at actual creative products in search of the "high intercorrelations among different creative behaviors" (Ivcevic, 2007, p. 272) that would demonstrate domain generality have for the most part come up empty-handed. What these studies have typically found is either low or essentially random correlations. This research has been challenged, however, by Kogan (1994), who argued that limited sample size and restriction of range may have limited the size of the observed correlations in some of Baer's (1991, 1993) early studies. For example, in the study reported above of 50 eighth-graders' creativity in four different tasks, all participants were in the upper quartile academically. A partial replication of that study was therefore conducted, this time with the entire eighth grade (N = 128) of a middle school with an academically diverse population (Baer, 1994). Just two tasks, poetry writing and story writing, were used; these two had one of the highest correlations (.23) reported in the earlier study, which might be expected because they come from the same general thematic area of writing (although from different domains within that field). In the 1994 replication, this correlation actually dropped slightly (to .19), suggesting that the design of the earlier study had not prejudiced the results.

There is also a question of the reliability of the assessments used, which is an issue with any assessment technique. Low reliability would artificially reduce the observable intercorrelations. CAT-rated assessments of creativity are basically single-item tests (although of course the "single item" is not a brief response like a multiple-choice answer but rather a complete product, such as a short story or a collage, which provides a much richer assessment even though there is but a single thing to judge; similarly, comparisons of novels submitted for a contest such as the Booker Prize or of films for a Directors' Guild Award also involve single-item tests – each novel or film being a single item – but these are especially rich single-item test materials!). Like any assessment, CAT assessments are not perfectly reliable. A correction for attenuation can be used to estimate the extent to which observed correlations are attenuated by measurement error (Cohen & Cohen, 1983; Nunnally, 1978). To the extent that measurements are unreliable, correlations between those measures will be lessened, and an estimate can be made of what the correlation would have been if perfectly reliable measures had been used. There is some controversy about when this should be applied (Cohen & Cohen, 1983; Nunnally, 1978), but even if used, it makes little difference in the data presented above regarding intercorrelations across domains. The impact of this correction increases with the unreliability of the measures, and as the reliabilities for the most part are quite good (typically in the .80 to .90 range), the impact is small. The magnitude of the effect also increases with the size of the correlation, however. This means that the much higher correlations found among creativity ratings of artifacts in the same general thematic area or domain increase more when corrected for attenuation than the very low or nonexistent correlations of creativity ratings across domains. The effect on the interpretation of the results is minimal; the changes produce slightly larger positive and slightly larger negative correlations. There is little change in the overall pattern, or in the general conclusion that there is little evidence of the influence of general creative-thinking skills such as divergent thinking. Baer (1993) reported corrections for attenuation in all seven of the studies he presented. Here are all the changes based on correction for attenuation for the study of eighth-grade students reported above:

Tests	Change from	to
Poetry – Story	.23	.26
Poetry – Word problem	.31	.38
Poetry – Equation	−.14	−.16
Story – Word problem	.20	.24
Story – Equation	−.03	−.03
Word problem – Equation	−.20	−.24

One different but related kind of study has also supported the domain specificity of creativity. Baer (1994a, 1996) has shown that when creativity training is targeted at improving divergent-thinking skills in a particular domain (or even a particular subdomain), it is creativity in that area alone that shows an increase in subsequent testing. Creativity ratings on tasks in other domains or subdomains is not affected by domain-specific creativity training.

In all of these assessments, creative performance is assessed in the here-and-now; the CAT is more like an achievement test than an aptitude test, and its goal is not to predict future performance but simply to measure current levels of creativity. Subjects with more experience in a particular domain are likely to evidence more creativity in that domain, because domain-specific prior knowledge and experience are part of what one needs to be creative, even under domain generality (which argues that there are significant domain-general factors that influence creative performance across all domains, but also acknowledges some domain-specific factors like content knowledge or skills). One might worry that domain-specific differences in subjects' prior knowledge and experience could undermine the use of the CAT to test for domain generality, so it's important to explain why that is not a problem.

The developer of the CAT, Teresa Amabile (1983, 1996), used fairly common tasks, like collage making and storytelling, that required little formal training because her main interest was in changes resulting from different motivational constraints, although

she understood that training and experience would still influence creative performance even with these familiar tasks. One wouldn't want to assess subjects' creativity in a domain that is totally unfamiliar to them (e.g., asking everyone to write a concerto, or to write a *haiku* in Japanese) because that would result in few or no subjects producing anything. But as long as all subjects have some experience in the domain, she didn't think the fact that some subjects might have more knowledge and experience would be a problem. The goal is not to assess some hidden, possibly innate but undeveloped creative ability. The focus is on current levels of creative performance, not what subjects *might* have done (or might be able to do) with proper training.

Let me illustrate this distinction with a quote from Lady Catherine de Bourgh in *Pride and Prejudice* (Austen, 1813/2006), who made an amusing appeal of this kind that tried to shift the focus from achievement to aptitude when she argued that if she and her daughter had only had musical training, they would have been quite proficient.

> There are few people in England, I suppose, who have more true enjoyment of music than myself, or a better natural taste. If I had ever learnt, I should have been a great proficient. And so would Anne, if her health had allowed her to apply. I am confident that she would have performed delightfully. (p. 195)

Perhaps Lady Catherine and Anne *might* have hidden musical talent that training could have brought forth (although one doubts that this would have been part of Austen's backstory!), but in the meantime, neither is very proficient (or creative) musically. Similarly (and like the assessments made by almost all award committees, most of which use a process very similar to the CAT), what the CAT assesses is what someone can do now, with the skills, knowledge, interests, motivations, and so forth that they bring to a particular task at a particular point in time. These may change as one gains more experience, skills, or knowledge in a field. (Research in fact has shown that CAT ratings in a given domain are fairly stable over time – subjects whose work has received CAT-based ratings in a domain tend to receive similar ratings when tested using a different task in the same domain a year later – and these ratings therefore do predict future creative performance on particular kinds of tasks, such as writing stories or poems, rather well [Baer, 1994c]. But these ratings have also been shown to change substantially with domain-specific training, although only in the domain where training has occurred [Baer, 1994c, 1996]. It should also be noted that, unlike divergent-thinking tests, it is impossible to game CAT measures. Simply knowing how a divergent-thinking test will be scored makes it possible to increase one's score quite easily, and with just a little training, divergent-thinking test scores can be inflated significantly [Baer, 1997]. This is not true with CAT ratings.)

As far as using CAT ratings to test for domain generality, it's possible that one might find more domain generality if all subjects had similar levels of training and knowledge in all fields (which is why using fairly young children with similar educational backgrounds and using common tasks with which everyone has at least some experience may be the best way to conduct these tests, although then one gets complaints like Kogan's about restriction of range). But if creativity is a domain-general skill, then it should still tend to enhance creativity in *all* areas (just as a rising tide will lift all boats, large and small), so even when using adult subjects with widely varying expertise in the domains in question, domain generality would still predict significant positive correlations across domains. That is *not* what research has found, however, with either children or adults. The observed correlations simply don't support much in the way of domain generality.

There is also interesting evidence for domain specificity in the cognitive functioning of other primates.[2] Cheney and Seyfarth

(2007), for example, noted that discrepancies in the kinds of things animals seem able to learn are both frequent and yet surprising. For example, vervet monkeys, for whom pythons often lie in wait, seem unable to attend to the very obvious (to humans) trails that pythons leave. "When crossing open ground, pythons lay distinct, wide, straight tracks that cannot be mistaken for those of any other snake. Local humans recognize them easily, and it is relatively easy to find a concealed python by following its track" (p. 128). Nonetheless – and despite the fact that vervet monkeys regularly fall prey to pythons – vervets "seem unable to recognize that a fresh python track signals danger.... The vervets' ignorance of python tracks was striking.... The association between a fresh track and a python was as statistically reliable as the association between two vervets in the same family who groom each other at high rates, but evidently more difficult for the vervets to learn" (p. 128). This and other evidence led them to conclude that vervet monkeys' knowledge of their social companions is impressive, whereas their knowledge of some ecological relations is "underwhelming" (p. 130). Cheney and Seyfarth (2007) provide many additional examples that show that such "'attentive biases' are common among animals" (p. 129; see also Cheney & Seyfarth, 1985, 1990) and demonstrate very different and seemingly nontransferable abilities in different domains.

Such evidence of domain specificity among other primates does not, of course, provide evidence that creativity in humans is domain specific. There are also many commonalities observable in primate behavior, skills that clearly are domain general (e.g., vision is not limited to particular classes of objects). It does suggest, however, that brains do often operate in a domain-general fashion – that brains are not simply general-purpose computing machines, equally applicable to any kind of cognitive task, in the manner that behaviorists of another era once viewed learning.[3] Comparative cognition

2 I will not try to discuss here animal *creativity* per se; for such a discussion, see Kaufman and Kaufman (2004).

3 Many more modern behaviorists continue to argue that the kinds of animal learning discussed here

observations such as those of Cheney and Seyfarth (1985, 1990, 2007) do at least make clear that fairly rigid domain-specific cognitive functioning can and does occur, even when considering cognitive operations that on the surface appear quite similar (as in the example with vervet monkeys, which involved nothing more than simple association learning).

Although evidence of the importance of domains in creative performance is rather well established, domain-specificity theorists have not reached complete consensus on what the primary domains might be. Feist (2004) proposed seven "domains of mind": social-emotional, physics, natural history, language, mathematics, art, and music. These are somewhat similar to Gardner's (1999) well-known eight intelligences (language, logical-mathematical, interpersonal, intrapersonal, spatial, natural history, bodily-kinesthetic, and musical). Feist also catalogued six other, somewhat similar, domain inventories and has provided evidence that his seven domains of mind are fairly universal. At the end of this chapter I present a hierarchical model that includes both domain-general and domain-specific features, with empirically derived domains that are also similar to Feist's.

Evidence for Domain Generality

In his Point-Counterpoint article supporting domain generality of creativity, Plucker (1998) noted that

> the idea that cognitive abilities, particularly creative ones, are content general is currently much maligned: Creativity and other thinking skills applied within certain content areas are widely believed to be independent of creativity

are the result of simple associations. Schusterman and Kastak (1993, 1998; Kastak & Schusterman, 2002) present laboratory evidence for fairly simple associationistic principles that might guide the social learning of primates. Researchers working in more ecologically valid contexts, however, find the results of such studies unconvincing. See Cheney and Seyfarth (2007) for a review of this evidence and argument.

> and thinking skills applied in other content areas.... [One] could reasonably assume that the debate is settled in favor of content specificity. (p. 179)

He argued, however, that it depends on the kind of evidence one looks at. Arguments for domain generality generally do not look at creative performances, but instead typically focus on psychometric and personality data.

> The conclusions of researchers using the CAT are almost always that creativity is predominantly task or content specific... [but] researchers utilizing traditional psychometric methods usually conclude that creativity is predominantly content general. (p. 181)

Plucker (1998) agreed with proponents of domain specificity that "researchers approaching creativity (especially divergent thinking) from a psychometric perspective over the past 50 years have worked under the assumption that creativity is content general (e.g., Guilford, 1967; Torrance, 1974)" and that divergent-thinking tests like the TTCT assume that performance on any particular divergent-thinking task is *not* "specific only to the task or content area addressed in a particular divergent-thinking test" (p. 179). Tests that assume content generality can be valid only to the extent that creativity is content general and cannot, therefore, provide evidence in the generality-specificity debate.

The kinds of psychometric data most commonly used to argue for content generality are creativity checklists. Plucker (1998) wrote that "performance assessments produce evidence of task specificity, and creativity checklists and other traditional assessments suggest that creativity is content general" (p. 180). Lubart and Guignard (2004) came to a similar conclusion, writing that "performance-based evaluations provide results favoring a domain-specific view, whereas self-report inventories lead to a more general-oriented conception of creativity" (p. 53). As an example of this, Plucker (1998) cited a study by Runco (1987) that used students' self-reported levels of creativity in seven performance domains:

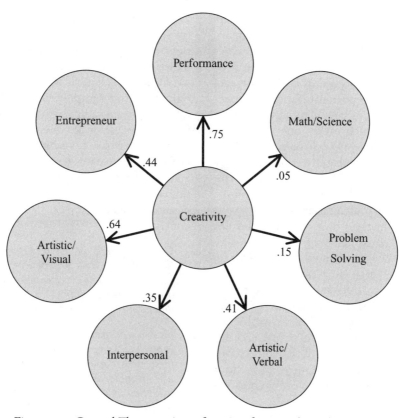

Figure 17.1. General Thematic Areas from Kaufman, Cole, and Baer (2009)

Runco (1987) compared students' creativity checklist responses to quality ratings of the students' creativity (scored using a technique not unlike the CAT). The students' checklist scores provided evidence of content generality, and the quality ratings suggested content specificity.

Self-report scales like the one Runco (1987) used and Plucker (1998) cited are an important source of evidence for generality in creativity, and they do tend to support at least a modest degree of domain generality. For example, Hocevar (1976) found "low to moderate" (p. 869) correlations (ranging from .17 to .76) among self-report indexes of creativity in various domains for college students. In a study in which several thousand subjects self-reported their own creativity in 56 domains, Kaufman, Cole, and Baer (2009) found both an overarching general factor and seven more specific areas of creative performance. Here are the seven factors and

their relationship with (standardized loadings on) a general creativity factor:

Self-report data may be a problematic source of information, however. Although Hocevar (1981) claimed that such self-report scales were "perhaps the most easily defensible way to identify creative talent" (p. 455), others have questioned the validity of self-report scales, both in creativity research and more generally (Azar, 1997; Brown, 1989; Rowe, 1997). The problems of self-report data in arenas with much higher stakes than most creativity research can be both large and troubling. In one medical study, "doctors self-reported their hand-washing rate at 73 percent, whereas when these same doctors were observed, their actual rate was a paltry 9 percent" (Dubner & Levitt, 2006). It is perhaps not surprising that people will sometimes misrepresent themselves when doing so is likely to benefit them in some tangible way, but people have also been shown to self-report erroneously – and to flat out lie – in astonishingly large numbers even when it can result in significant financial *loss*, apparently just to make themselves look better (Dubner, 2008).

Brown (1989) argued that in assessing creativity, "self-report data and retrospective case histories are generally unverifiable" (p. 29), which makes one hesitant to rely very heavily on such data, and there is evidence that such self-report data may be invalid measures of creativity. Kaufman, Evans, and Baer (in press), for example, reported that fourth-grade students' self-assessments of their own creativity did not match the assessments of experts in any of the four domains tested (math, science, writing, and art). It wasn't simply that the students tended to inflate their self-assessments. Their self-assessments actually bore no relationship whatsoever to the ratings experts made of their actual creative products (although none of the correlations was statistically significant, three of the four were negative and the mean of the four correlation was – 0.075).

Self-rated creativity may be suspect, but there are ways to get around the validity problem associated with creativity self-ratings. For example, studies of creative people who have achieved some level of eminence eliminate the need for such self-ratings (although studies of such creators still typically use self-ratings of personality, where even eminent creators may not be experts). In these studies, the creativity of such successful artists and scientists has been judged by the gatekeepers of their respective domains to have contributed significantly to their fields, and we therefore are not dependent on how these highly creative people might rate their own accomplishments. Similarly, people working in a field (whether creatively or not) can be clearly identified as such using objective measures (such as profession or college major) that do not require subjects to rate their own creativity in any way. These data can be used to show interest in a domain and as at least rough indicators of domain-based creativity.

Feist (1998, 1999) subjected 50-years worth of this kind of research – including any published research that looked at possible connections between creativity and personality – to a meta-analytic review. He included any study that looked at personality traits of scientists and artists, requiring only that the sample show some special talent or interest in science (including the social sciences) or art. He conducted three comparisons: scientists with nonscientists, more-creative versus less-creative scientists, and artists versus nonartists. He found both domain-based differences and similarities across domains. Here is a summary of his conclusions:

> Creative people in art and science tend to be open to new experiences, less conventional and less conscientious, more self-confident, self accepting, driven, ambitious, dominant, hostile, and impulsive.

> Creative people in art and science do not share the same unique personality profiles: Artists are more affective, emotionally unstable, as well as less socialized and accepting of group norms, whereas scientists are more conscientious. (p. 290)

Feist noted that from the observed correlations one cannot infer causation; that is, one cannot know whether the observed shared personality traits lead to creative behavior in both domains, or if (conversely) creativity in either domain leads to some similar personality traits. This can be easily understood by considering such traits as self-confidence, ambition, and dominance, all of which were traits shared by more creative scientists and artists. These might be traits that promote creativity – one could certainly make sense of such a claim – but one could as easily see how these traits might be the *result* of (rather than the cause of) creativity. People who are creative (even if their creativity were limited to a single domain) might be expected to be more self-confident, ambitious, and dominant. The fact that one could make sense of a causal arrow going in either direction does not allow one to know which is cause and which is effect (or even if these traits covary with no causal connection).

It is also not clear if the shared personality traits are shared across domains.

More creative artists and scientists both tend to be open to new experiences, but is this a general trait or a domain-specific one? Are artists open to the same kinds of new experiences as scientists, or might openness to experience mean openness to *certain kinds* of experiences (perhaps those in a particular domain or general thematic area)? Similarly, more-creative people may be more highly motivated (more ambitious, more driven) than their less-creative counterparts. As Mlodinow (2008) suggested, "successful people in every field are almost universally members of a certain set – the set of people who don't give up" (p. 11). This may well result in higher levels of creative performance, but even if the causal arrow does go in that direction (which seems reasonable), is motivation a common, domain-general resource, or is it specific to a domain? Might a creative novelist refuse to give up when it comes to improving her writing, but give up easily when it comes to playing tennis, solving math exercises, or arguing with her accountant? Recall Feist's (2004) suggestion that if domain generality were true, "a creative person could be creative in any domain he or she chose" (p. 57). Was Picasso's interest and talent in art simply accidental; might he instead have chosen biology as a career and been equally creative? Or might his motivation, and his openness to new ideas, have had a much more limited focus that did not encompass biology (and/or mathematics, engineering, physics, drama, cooking, etc.)?

Despite these caveats, personality measures provide support for at least a modest degree of domain generality, in contrast to the performance measures of creativity that almost universally support domain specificity. Self-report measures of creativity also provide support for domain generality (and for domain specificity as well). In the next section, I will discuss how these conflicting viewpoints might profitably be combined into a hierarchical model of creativity, but first I need to set aside some red-herring arguments for specificity and generality that are simple, seductive, and dangerously wrong.

Red-herring evidence: Why neither the presence nor absence of creative genius in multiple fields tells us anything about the domain generality or specificity of creativity.

When people first encounter the concept of domain specificity of creativity, many ask about polymaths like da Vinci. If creativity is domain specific, they ask, how could one person be so creative in more than one domain? Many others have just the opposite response: Domain specificity, they think, explains why there are so few people like da Vinci who have made contributions at the highest levels in multiple fields. But this isn't just a question of seeing a half-full or half-empty glass. It is more a matter of seeing a glass that isn't really there.

People like da Vinci are certainly interesting, but they tell us nothing about the domain specificity or generality of creativity. Here's an analogy: Someone can have a high IQ and also be a good high jumper, and yet these can remain distinct domains with distinct underlying abilities required for success. Being creative in two domains doesn't demonstrate that creativity is domain general any more than a smart high jumper demonstrates that high jumping and intelligence rely on the same basic substrate of abilities. If creativity is domain specific, then one would *expect* some people to be highly creative in more than one domain. Domain specificity doesn't predict that people will be creative in only a single domain. It says only that because the underlying skills/knowledge/talent/whatever underlying creativity in different domains are different, creativity in one domain does not predict creativity in other domains. Assuming that such domain-based creativity-relevant talents are randomly distributed, one would *expect* a few people to be creative in many domains, some people to be creative in several domains, and some others to be creative in few domains or none, based on a normal distribution of unrelated abilities. So the presence of a few da Vincis does not disprove domain specificity. It is *exactly* what domain specificity predicts.

But what about the opposing argument, that the scarcity of multidomain creative genius proves domain specificity? If creativity is domain general and a person has a lot of it – enough to be highly creative in any domain – then in everything one does, isn't it reasonable to except similar levels of creativity? Conversely, if one lacks creativity in any area, then under domain generality isn't it reasonable to expect low levels of creativity in everything one does? But most genius-level creators are *not* immensely creative outside the one domain in which they show excellence, and even the da Vincis do not produce remarkable accomplishments in *every* field. (Even da Vinci is not remembered for creative genius in such areas as philosophy, chemistry, animal husbandry, or psychology.)

Explaining the hole in this *Why wasn't Emily Dickinson a great painter and chemist?* argument is just a little more complicated than the *How could da Vinci be accomplished in so many fields?* argument. There is in creativity research something called the "ten-year rule" (Hayes, 1989). This "rule" argues that it takes many years of preparation before "even the most noteworthy and 'talented' individuals" (Weisberg, 1999, p. 230) can reach the levels of knowledge and skill necessary to produce groundbreaking work in any domain. As Gruber and Davis (1988) wrote, "Perhaps the single most reliable finding in our studies is that creative work takes a long time" (p. 264). These long years of intense preparation must be spent in "deliberate practice and the development of expert performance" (Weisberg, 1999, p. 233). So if it takes ten years just to *prepare* one's self for the kind of paradigm-shifting creative work that may one day come to be called a work of genius, it should come as little surprise that few people manage to reach the highest levels of creative accomplishment in a dozen or more fields in a single lifetime.

It is worth noting that Simonton (2006) has recently challenged the ten-year rule by showing that the greatest geniuses typically spend less time in domain knowledge acquisition before exhibiting their remarkable

creativity than their less creative peers. But he also has shown that the greatest geniuses produce the greatest quantity of work – his "equal-odds rule" claims that "quality should be a probabilistic consequence of quantity" (2006, p. 54) – which also limits the likelihood of creative genius in multiple fields. There just may not be enough time to produce a sufficiently large quantity of works in multiple domains.

It's certainly true that many highly creative people have other creative interests outside the field in which they have become famous, as Root-Bernstein and Root-Bernstein (2004) have noted. But the fact that, say, Woody Allen is both a brilliant filmmaker and fairly good musician isn't evidence for domain generality. This is impressive, but if one is arguing for the domain generality of creativity, one must ask why has he been able to be a highly creative filmmaker but only a middling musician, despite working diligently in both fields, being knowledgeable in both fields, and having access to all the tools he would need to succeed in both fields? Domain generality predicts he could use his creativity wherever he chose to apply it. But like a high-IQ student who might like to be a better high jumper but finds she simply can't transfer the skills that lead to high test scores to jumping higher, Woody Allen somehow couldn't simply transfer his creativity from one domain to another. (And these are just two domains; should we also expect Allen to be a creative chef, engineer, or human relations expert?)

Domain specificity argues that we should *expect* to find a few high-IQ high jumpers and a few creative filmmakers who are also good musicians; we just shouldn't expect to find a general correlation between the two skills. These examples do nothing to disprove domain specificity. Similarly, the many geniuses who failed to find even modest success in other fields do not disprove domain generality, because most geniuses commit to one field and are simply unable to give as much attention and effort and time to any other pursuit. As Georgia O'Keeffe once told Joni Mitchell, "I would have liked to have been a painter and a musician, but you can't do both." Mitchell replied, "Oh, yes, you *can!*" (Weller, 2008, p. 427), based perhaps on her own prodigious output as a musician and as a painter. But being highly creative in just two domains is indeed extraordinary, and it is almost impossible to find an example of anyone being creative at the very highest level in three or more domains. In the final analysis, the single or multiple talents of the most talented people simply don't tell us much, one way or the other, about the question of domain generality or specificity.

A Hierarchical Model That Includes Both Domain-General and Domain-Specific Elements

There are theories of creativity that include both domain-general and domain-specific elements, such as Amabile's (1983, 1996) componential model, which was introduced in the first section of the chapter. Amabile's primary research interest when proposing this model was with the third component, motivation, and she therefore did little work elaborating on the other two components. Here is how she conceptualized these two components:

> Domain-relevant skills *are the basic skills that lead to competent performance in a given domain, such as writing or drawing. This component includes factual knowledge, special skills, and talents.* Creativity-relevant skills *are those skills that contribute to creative performance across domains and include cognitive style, working style, and divergent thinking abilities.* (Conti, Coon, & Amabile, 1996, p. 385)

Although she has on occasion defended these aspects of her model, Amabile has not specified what the domains are or how they might relate to each other or to domain-general creativity-relevant skills.

Kaufman and Baer (Baer & Kaufman, 2005; Kaufman & Baer, 2004, 2005b) proposed a hierarchical model of creativity that includes both domain-general and domain-specific elements. There are four levels in this hierarchy:

- *Initial Requirements* are completely domain-general factors that influence creative performance to some degree across all domains (e.g., intelligence).
- *General Thematic Areas* are broadly defined fields or areas that include many related domains, such as Artistic/Verbal, Artistic/Visual, and Math/Science. The seven General Thematic Areas that they have identified are depicted in Figure 17.1.
- *Domains* lie within larger General Thematic Areas and refer to a more limited range of creative activities. For example, in the General Thematic Area of Artistic/Verbal one would find subdomains such as poetry, fiction, and playwriting.
- *Micro-domains* refer to more specific tasks within domains. As examples, Kaufman and Baer (2005b) suggested that "studying fruit flies intensively for five years may help one develop creative theories in one of biology's Micro-Domains but be of little use in another; and practicing on a 12-string guitar may help one perform creatively in some Micro-Domains of the music world but not others." (p. 326)

Whether it is Kaufman and Baer's APT Model[4] or some future hierarchical model, this kind of fusion is perhaps the most likely eventual resolution of the

4 APT is an abbreviation for Amusement Park Theoretical Model. "The APT Model is based on the metaphor a large amusement park. In an amusement park there are initial requirements (e.g., a ticket) that apply to all areas of the park. Similarly, there are initial requirements that, to varying degrees, are necessary to creative performance in all domains (e.g., intelligence, motivation). Amusement parks also have *general thematic areas* (e.g., at Disney World one might select among EPCOT, the Magic Kingdom, the Animal Kingdom, and Disney-MGM Studios), just as there are several different general areas in which someone could be creative (e.g., the arts, science). Once in one type of park, there are sections (e.g., Fantasyland, Tomorrowland), just as there are *domains* of creativity within larger *general thematic areas* (e.g., physics and biology are domains in the *general thematic area* of science). These domains in turn can be subdivided into *micro-domains* (e.g., in Fantasyland one might visit Cinderella's Castle or It's a Small World; in the domain of psychology, one might specialize in cognitive psychology or social psychology)" (Kaufman, Cole, & Baer, 2009, p. 120).

domain-specificity question. The exact number of levels is perhaps somewhat arbitrary, but the key insight – that the talents, knowledge, skills, motivations, traits, propensities, and so forth that underlie creative performance (a) vary depending on the kind of work one is undertaking, (b) are similar across related field or kinds of creative work, and (c) become progressively dissimilar as one moves to increasingly disparate fields of endeavor – is able to incorporate the research findings of researchers and theorists from both the domain-specific and domain-general camps. As such, it may transcend their differences in a way that brings together their ideas while losing none of the key insights of either group.

References

Amabile, T. M. (1982). Social psychology of creativity: A consensual assessment technique. *Journal of Personality and Social Psychology*, 43, 997–1013.

Amabile, T. M. (1983). *The social psychology of creativity*. New York: Springer-Verlag.

Amabile, T. M. (1996). *Creativity in context: Update to the social psychology of creativity*. Boulder, CO: Westview.

Austen, J. (2008). *Pride and prejudice*. New York: Simon and Schuster. (Original work published 1813)

Azar, B. (1997, January). Poor recall mars research and treatment. *APA Monitor*, 28, 1, 29.

Baer, J. (1991). Generality of creativity across performance domains. *Creativity Research Journal*, 4, 23–39.

Baer, J. (1993). *Divergent thinking and creativity: A task-specific approach*. Hillsdale, NJ: Erlbaum.

Baer, J. (1994a). Divergent thinking is not a general trait: A multi-domain training experiment. *Creativity Research Journal*, 7, 35–46.

Baer, J. (1994b). Generality of creativity across performance domains: A replication. *Perceptual and Motor Skills*, 79, 1217–1218.

Baer, J. (1994c). Performance assessments of creativity: Do they have long-term stability? *Roeper Review*, 7(1), 7–11.

Baer, J. (1996). The effects of task-specific divergent-thinking training. *Journal of Creative Behavior*, 30, 183–187.

Baer, J. (1997). *Creative teachers, creative students*. Boston: Allyn and Bacon.

Baer, J. (1998). The case for domain specificity in creativity. *Creativity Research Journal*, 11, 173–177.

Baer, J., & Kaufman, J. C. (2005). Bridging generality and specificity: The Amusement Park Theoretical (APT) model of creativity. *Roeper Review*, 27, 158–163.

Baer, J., Kaufman, J. C., & Gentile, C. A. (2004). Extension of the consensual assessment technique to nonparallel creative products. *Creativity Research Journal*, 16, 113–117.

Brown, R. T. (1989). Creativity: What are we to measure? In J. A. Glover, R. R. Ronning, & C. R. Reynolds (Eds.), *Handbook of creativity* (pp. 3–32). New York: Plenum.

Carson, S. (2006). Creativity and Mental Illness. Invitational Panel Discussion Hosted by Yale's Mind Matters Consortium, New Haven, CT, April 19, 2006.

Chen, C., Himsel, A., Kasof, J., Greenberger, E., & Dmitreiva, J. (2006). Boundless creativity: Evidence for domain generality of individual differences in creativity. *Journal of Creative Behavior*, 40, 179–199.

Cheney, D. L., & Seyfarth, R. M. (1985). Social and non-social knowledge in vervet monkeys. *Philosophic Transactions of the Royal Society London B*, 308. 187–201.

Cheney, D. L., & Seyfarth, R. M. (1990). *How monkeys see the world*. Chicago: University of Chicago Press.

Cheney, D. L., & Seyfarth, R. M. (2007). *Baboon metaphysics*. Chicago: University of Chicago Press.

Cohen, J., & Cohen, P. (1983). *Applied multiple regression/correlation analysis for the behavioral sciences* (2nd ed.). Hillsdale, NJ: Erlbaum.

Conti, R., Coon, H., & Amabile, T. M. (1996). Evidence to support the componential model of creativity: Secondary analyses of three studies. *Creativity Research Journal*, 9, 385–389.

Curd, M., & Cover, J. A. (Eds.). (1998a). *Philosophy of science: The central issues*. New York: Norton.

Curd, M., & Cover, J. A. (1998b). Science and pseudoscience: Introduction. In M. Curd & J. A. Cover (Eds.), *Philosophy of science: The central issues* (pp. 1–2). New York: Norton.

Dubner, S. J. (2008). Why do you lie? The perils of self-reporting. *New York Times*, Retrieved February 22, 2010 from http://freakonomics.blogs.nytimes.com/2008/06/23/

why-do-you-lie-the-perils-of-self-reporting/
?hp.

Dubner, S. J., & Levitt, S. D. (2006). The petri-dish screen saver. *New York Times*, September 24, 2006. Retrieved February 22, 2010 from http://www.nytimes.com/2006/09/24/magazine/24wwln_freak.html.

Feist, G. J. (1998). A meta-analysis of personality in scientific and artistic creativity. *Personality and Social Psychology Review*, 1998, 290–309.

Feist, G. J. (1999). The influence of personality on artistic and scientific creativity. In R. J. Sternberg (Ed.), *Handbook of human creativity* (pp. 273–296). New York: Cambridge University Press.

Feist, G. J. (2004). The evolved fluid specificity of human creative talent. In R. J. Sternberg, E. L. Grigorenko, & J. L. Singer (Eds.), *Creativity: From potential to realization* (pp. 57–82). Washington, DC: American Psychological Association.

Gardner, H. (1999). *Intelligence reframed: Multiple Intelligences for the 21st century*. New York: Basic Books.

Gruber, H. E., & Davis, S. N. (1988). Inching our way up Mt. Olympus: The evolving-systems approach to creative thinking. In R. J. Sternberg (Ed.), *The nature of creativity* (pp. 243–270). New York: Cambridge University Press.

Guilford, J. P. (1950). Creativity. *American Psychologist*, 5, 444–454.

Guilford, J. P. (1956). The structure of intellect. *Psychological Bulletin*, 53, 267–293.

Guilford, J. P. (1967). *The nature of human intelligence*. New York: McGraw-Hill.

Guilford, J. P., & Hoepfner, R. (1971). *The analysis of intelligence*. New York: McGraw-Hill.

Hayes, J. R. (1989). Cognitive processes in creativity. In J. A. Glover, R. R. Ronning, & C. R. Reynolds (Eds.), *Handbook of creativity* (pp. 135–146). New York: Plenum Press.

Hennessey, B. A., Kim, G, Guomin, Z., & Weiwei, S. (2008). A multi-cultural approach to the application of the consensual assessment technique. *International Journal of Creativity and Problem Solving*, 18(2), 87–100.

Hocevar, D. (1976). Dimensionality of creativity. *Psychological Reports*, 39, 869–870.

Hocevar, D. (1981). Measurement of creativity: Review and critique. *Journal of Personality Assessment*, 45, 450–464.

Ivcevic, Z. (2007). Artistic and everyday creativity: An act-frequency approach. *Journal of Creative Behavior*, 41, 271–290.

Kastak, C. R., & Schusterman, R. J. (2002). Sea lions and equivalence: Expanding classes by exclusion. *Journal of Experimental Analysis of Behavior*, 78(3), 449–465.

Kaufman, J. C., & Baer, J. (2004). The Amusement Park Theoretical (APT) model of creativity. *The Korean Journal of Thinking & Problem Solving*, 14(2), 15–25.

Kaufman, J. C., & Baer, J. (Eds.). (2005a). *Creativity across domains: Faces of the muse*. Hillsdale, NJ: Erlbaum.

Kaufman, J. C., & Baer, J. (2005b). The amusement park theory of creativity. In J. C. Kaufman & J. Baer (Eds.), *Creativity across domains: Faces of the muse* (pp. 321–328). Hillsdale, NJ: Erlbaum.

Kaufman, J. C., Baer, J., & Cole, J. C. (2009). Expertise, domains, and the Consensual Assessment Technique. *Journal of Creative Behavior*, 43, 223–233.

Kaufman, J. C., Baer, J., Cole, J. C., & Sexton, J. D. (2008). A comparison of expert and nonexpert raters using the Consensual Assessment Technique. *Creativity Research Journal*, 20, 171–178.

Kaufman, J. C., Cole, J. C., & Baer, J. (2009). The construct of creativity: Structural model for self-reported creativity ratings. *Journal of Creative Behavior*, 43, 119–132.

Kaufman, J. C., Evans, K. L., & Baer, J. (in press). The American Idol Effect: Are students good judges of their creativity across domains? *Empirical Studies of the Arts*.

Kaufman, J. C., Kaufman, A. B. (2004). Applying a creativity framework to animal cognition. *New Ideas in Psychology*, 22, 143–155.

Kaufman, J. C., Plucker, J. A., & Baer, J. (2008). *Essentials of creativity assessment*. New York: Wiley.

Kim, K. H. (2006). Can we trust creativity tests? A review of the Torrance Tests of Creative Thinking (TTCT). *Creativity Research Journal*, 18, 3–14.

Kogan, N. (1983). Stylistic variation in childhood and adolescence: Creativity, metaphor, and cognitive styles. In P. H. Mussen (Ed.), *Handbook of child psychology: Vol. 3. Cognitive development* (4th ed., pp. 628–706). New York: Wiley.

Kogan, N. (1994). Diverging from divergent thinking [Review of *Creativity and divergent thinking: A task-specific approach]. Contemporary Psychology*, 39, 291–291.

Kuhn, T. S. (1970). *The structure of scientific revolutions* (2nd. ed.). Chicago: University of Chicago Press.

Kuhn, T. S. (1979). Metaphor in science. In A. Orotny (Ed.), *Metaphor and thought* (2nd. ed., pp. 533–560). Cambridge, MA: Cambridge University Press.

Lubart, T., & Guignard, J.-H. (2004). The generality-specificity of creativity: A multivariant approach. In R. J. Sternberg, E. L. Grigorenko, & J. L. Singer (Eds.), *Creativity: From potential to realization* (pp. 43–56). Washington, DC: American Psychological Association.

McMullin, E. (1998). Rationality and paradigm change in science. In M. Curd & J. A. Cover (Eds.), *Philosophy of science: The central issues* (pp. 119–138). New York: Norton.

Mednick, S. A. (1962). The associative basis of the creative process. *Psychological Review*, 69, 220–232.

Mednick, S. A., & Mednick, M. T. (1967). *Examiner's manual: Remote Associates Test*. Boston: Houghton-Mifflin.

Mlodinow, L. (2008). *The drunkard's walk: How randomness rules our lives*. New York: Pantheon Books,

Nunnally, J. C. (1978). *Psychometric theory* (2nd ed.). New York: McGraw-Hill.

Plucker, J. A. (1998). Beware of simple conclusions: The case for the content generality of creativity. *Creativity Research Journal*, 11, 179–182.

Plucker, J. A. (2005). The (relatively) generalist view of creativity. In J. C. Kaufman & J. Baer (Eds.), *Creativity across domains: Faces of the muse* (pp. 307–312). Hillsdale, NJ: Erlbaum.

Popper, K. R. (1959). *The logic of scientific discovery*. New York: Basic Books.

Popper, K. R. (1963). *Conjectures and refutations*. London: Routledge & Kegan Paul.

Root-Bernstein, R., & Root-Bernstein, M. (2004). Artistic scientists and scientific artists: The link between polymathy and creativity. In R. J. Sternberg, E. L. Grigorenko, & J. L. Singer (Eds.), *Creativity: From potential to realization* (pp. 127–152). Washington, DC: American Psychological Association.

Rowe, P. (1997, January). The science of self-report. *APS Observer*, 10(3), 35–38.

Runco, M. A. (1987). The generality of creative performance in gifted and nongifted children. *Gifted Child Quarterly*, 331, 121–125.

Runco, M. A. (1989). The creativity of children's art. *Child Study Journal*, 19, 177–190.

Ruscio, J., Whitney, D. M., & Amabile, T. M. (1998). Looking inside the fishbowl of creativity: Verbal and behavioral predictors of creative performance. *Creativity Research Journal*, 11, 243–263.

Schusterman, R. J., & Kastak, D. A. (1993). A California sea lion (Zalophus californianus) is capable of forming equivalence relations. *Psychological Record*, 43, 823–839.

Schusterman, R. J., & Kastak, D. A. (1998). Functional equivalence in a California sea lion: Relevance to animal social and communicative interactions. *Animal Behavior*, 55, 1087–1095.

Simonton, D. K. (2006). Creative genius, knowledge, and reason. In J. C. Kaufman & J. Baer (Eds.), *Creativity across domains: Faces of the muse* (pp. 43–59) Hillsdale, NJ: Erlbaum.

Sternberg, R. J. (2005). The domain generality versus domain specificity debate: How should it be posed? In J. C. Kaufman & J. Baer (Eds.), *Creativity across domains: Faces of the muse* (pp. 299–306). Hillsdale, NJ: Erlbaum.

Sternberg, R. J., Grigorenko, E. L., & Singer, J. L. (2004). *Creativity: From potential to realization*. Washington, DC: American Psychological Association.

Torrance, E. P. (1966). *The Torrance Tests of Creative Thinking – Norms-Technical Manual Research Edition – Verbal Tests, Forms A and B – Figural Tests, Forms A and B*. Princeton, NJ: Personnel Press.

Torrance, E. P. (1974). *The Torrance Tests of Creative Thinking – Norms-Technical Manual Research Edition – Verbal Tests, Forms A and B – Figural Tests, Forms A and B*. Princeton, NJ: Personnel Press.

Torrance, E. P. (1990). *The Torrance Tests of Creative Thinking Norms-Technical Manual Figural (Streamlined) Forms A & B*. Bensenville, IL: Scholastic Testing Service, Inc.

Torrance, E. P. (1998). *The Torrance Tests of Creative Thinking Norms-Technical Manual Figural (Streamlined) Forms A & B*. Bensenville, IL: Scholastic Testing Service, Inc.

Torrance, E. P., & Ball, O. E. (1984). *The Torrance Tests of Creative Thinking Streamlined (revised) manual, Figural A and B*. Bensenville, IL: Scholastic Testing Service, Inc.

Weisberg, R. W. (1999). Creativity and knowledge: A challenge to theories. In R. J. Sternberg (Ed.), *Handbook of creativity* (pp. 226–250). New York: Cambridge University Press.

Weller, S. (2008). *Girls like us: Carle King, Joni Mitchell, Carly Simon – and the journey of a generation*. New York: Atria Books.

CHAPTER 18

The Creativity-Motivation Connection

Beth A. Hennessey

From the earliest days of the study of psychology, researchers and theorists have been fascinated by creative behavior. For well over half a century, discussions about creativity have been intertwined with questions of task motivation. In his explorations of the life and work of geniuses of the caliber of da Vinci and Michelangelo, Freud (see Pope, 2005) argued strongly that it was a deficiency in the lives of these individuals, or perhaps even deficiencies in their basic psychological make-up, that drove their creativity. According to this view, everything about motivation and creativity could be framed in terms of a deficit model. At its core, Freudian theory explained a single-minded dedication to one's craft in terms of the displacement of repressed needs.

Expanding on this psychoanalytic view, White (1959) associated motivational orientation with ego processes, and Erikson (1968) set out to reduce the concept of task motivation to the status of a defense, an often futile attempt to repair damage and fill voids caused by difficult experiences that happened early in life. Like the psychoanalytic approach, this reductionist view, described in detail by Ochese (1990), portrayed the creative person as troubled and driven by primarily negative forces. Although the early days of the psychological study of creative behavior might have been better served by a more positive psychological approach, these theorists did much to solidify the theoretical link between task motivation and creative performance; and in so doing, they laid important groundwork for what has now emerged as a rich and fruitful research tradition.

Psychologists have long been concerned with and puzzled by behaviors such as exploration and challenge seeking that have no clear external reinforcements. As early as 1926, investigators like Cox were already theorizing about the importance of internal sources of motivation as they predicted that a young person who was intellectually brilliant but not especially motivated would not be as likely as his less brilliant but highly motivated counterpart to go on to make important creative contributions (see Cox, 1983). Slowly, theorists began to view high levels of task motivation and the human capacity to become lost in a project or problem as central to the creative process. Kohut (1966) analyzed creativity and the motivation that drives it as a positive transformation of narcissism. Hebb (1955) and Berlyne (1960) proposed that the activities or questions most likely to capture and keep our attention are those that present an optimal level of novelty. And White (1959) and Harter (1978) suggested that a sense of competence and mastery are central components of the motivation behind creative behavior.

The bifurcation of motivational orientation into intrinsic and extrinsic components was driven initially by the work of social psychologist Fritz Heider, who in 1958 was already exploring individuals' explanations for their own and others' behavior. The founder of the modern field of social cognition, Heider proposed an Attribution Theory designed to specify the circumstances under which behavior will be attributed to an individual's disposition (e.g., personality traits, personal motives, or attitudes) or to situational variables (e.g., external pressures, social norms, peer pressure, or environmental factors). Heider was the first to make the argument that when attempting to make sense of our own or another's behavior, we tend to overemphasize internal, dispositional causes over external causes – this phenomenon later became known as the "fundamental attribution error" (Ross, 1977).

The use of the terms *intrinsic* and *extrinsic* began to appear with some regularity in the motivation literature around 1970; and today, the intrinsic/extrinsic distinction tends to dominate discussions of the association between motivation and creative behavior. Pioneering theorists in this area were DeCharms (1968), Deci (1971), and Lepper and colleagues (Lepper, Greene, & Nisbett, 1973), who placed their emphasis on a sense of control: When a person perceives her task engagement as externally controlled, she is extrinsically rather than intrinsically motivated. Most contemporary theorists define extrinsic motivation as the motivation to do something for some exter-

nal goal, a goal outside the task itself. Intrinsic motivation, on the other hand, is seen as the motivation to engage in an activity for its own sake, for the sheer pleasure and enjoyment of the task. Persons who approach an activity, question, or problem with an intrinsic motivational orientation are usually propelled by a sense of curiosity. In addition, they feel a certain degree of competence, believe that their involvement is free of external control, and have a sense that they are playing rather than working (Hennessey, 2003, 2004). Taken together, intrinsic and extrinsic motivational orientations have been shown to play a major role in determining whether a creative product will be produced or a creative solution to a problem will be generated. Motivational orientation marks the dividing line between what a creative individual is capable of doing and what he or she actually will do in a given situation (see Amabile, 1990, 1996).

Two Basic Forms of Investigation

Investigations of and theorizing about the interface between motivation and creative performance have taken one of two basic forms. Some research and modeling in this area has viewed creativity and motivational orientation as relatively enduring and stable traits. For example, case studies of creative geniuses typically assume that these individuals are likely to exhibit high levels of intrinsic motivation and creativity across time and in a variety of situations. Assessments of creativity coming out of this personality psychology perspective tend to resemble IQ or achievement tests in that they have been specifically constructed to highlight individual differences. The most widely used measure of creativity in this genre, the Torrance Tests of Creative Thinking (Torrance, 1990), has been demonstrated both to discriminate between individuals and to show acceptable levels of test-retest reliability (Treffinger, 1985; TTCT-figural manual of 1990). Similarly, a few other paper-and-pencil assessments such as the Kirton

Adaptation Inventory (KAI) (Kirton, 1982), The Guilford Unusual Uses Test (Guilford, Merrifield, & Wilson, 1958) and the Wallach-Kogan Test of Creative Potential (Wallach & Wing, 1969) have also been shown to yield relatively stable trait-like measures of creative ability and problem-solving style.

Some motivational theorists and researchers have explored the possibility that motivational orientation can also be construed as a stable individual-difference variable. Early on in this research tradition, Bem's seminal work on self-perception (1967, 1972) assessed the extent to which individuals' intrinsic and extrinsic motivational orientations were strong and salient to them as well as the extent to which persons differed from one another in these motivational orientations. DeCharm's (1968; deCharm, Carpenter, & Kuperman, 1965) early studies of motivation and personal causation revealed that some persons reported that they often felt like pawns of authority, and that these same individuals tended to be primarily extrinsically motivated. On the other hand, persons who were more likely to feel like they were the origins of their own behavior tended to be driven by perceptions of self-investment and were most often intrinsic in their motivational orientation. And Deci and Ryan (1985a) also found individual differences in enduring motivational orientations.

More recently, empirical investigations of creativity in business (e.g., Amabile, 1988, 1990; Dewett, 2007; Shin & Zhou, 2007) have also shown the utility of operationalizing motivational orientation as being relatively trait-like and stable across time. And, in fact, investigations utilizing measures such as the Work Preference Inventory (WPI) (Amabile, Hill, Hennessey, & Tighe, 1994), Harter's self-report Scale of Intrinsic versus Extrinsic Orientation in the Classroom (Harter, 1981; Harter & Jackson, 1992) and the Interest/Enjoyment subscale of the Intrinsic Motivation Inventory (IMI) (Ryan, 1982; Tsigilis & Theodosiou, 2003) have all yielded data arguing for such stability in populations of elementary-school children,

high schoolers, college students, and working adults. In addition, a longitudinal investigation spanning the middle-elementary through high-school years (Gottfried, Fleming, & Gottfried, 2001) showed continuity of levels between academic intrinsic motivation and individual differences in creativity. In sum, there is some empirical research to suggest that both motivational orientation and creativity can be conceptualized as fairly stable individual-difference variables. However, the bulk of the literature linking motivation and creativity has taken the opposite approach – operationalizing creative behavior and the intrinsic motivation that drives it as the result of fleeting and situation-specific states.

Investigators who take a social-psychological approach to the study of the interface between creativity and motivation, rather than a personality approach, strive to control for and, as much as possible, eliminate the impact of individual differences in their research designs. In other words, they seek to find measures of creativity and motivation that minimize within-group variability in order to detect more global between-group differences produced by the direct experimental manipulations of social and environmental factors. In these investigations, individual differences constitute the error variance, rather than the primary outcome variable. Researchers in this category are not interested in whether a particular child or adult is likely to evince on a consistent basis greater levels of creativity or intrinsic or extrinsic motivation than the majority of their peers. Rather, they conceptualize creativity not as a relatively enduring and stable *trait*, but as the result of a transitory *state* determined in large part by motivational orientation, which is itself determined by the presence or absence of environmental factors, such as the offer of reward or the expectation of an impending evaluation. What these investigators seek are measurement tools that deemphasize individual differences between study participants. They need measures of creativity that allow for considerable flexibility and novelty of response and that do not depend heavily on the level of an individual's skills or the range of her experience.

Empirical Investigations of the Social Psychology of Creativity

A second approach and theoretical orientation, the social-psychological study of the impact of extrinsic constraints on motivation, has a long and well-established tradition. One of the first published studies of this type (Deci, 1971) focused on the undermining effects of expected reward and was soon supplemented by other papers reporting similar decreases in intrinsic task motivation subsequent to the offer of reward (Deci, 1972; Kruglanski, Friedman, & Zeevi, 1971). In 1973, Lepper, Greene, and Nisbett expanded on this research paradigm when they set out to examine the effects of reward on both motivational orientation and quality of performance. These researchers found that, for preschoolers who initially displayed a high level of intrinsic interest in drawing with magic markers, working for an expected "Good Player Award" significantly decreased their interest in and enjoyment of the task. When compared with an unexpected reward group and a control (no reward) group, the children who had made drawings for the experimenters in order to receive a Good Player Award spent significantly less time using the markers during subsequent free-play periods than did their nonrewarded peers. Moreover, this undermining of interest persisted for at least a week beyond the initial experimental session; and, importantly, the globally assessed "quality" of the drawings produced under expected reward conditions was found to be significantly lower than that of the unexpected reward or control groups.

Although this study was probably *the first* to demonstrate empirically the deleterious effects of expected reward on both intrinsic task motivation and quality of performance, speculations about the impact of extrinsic constraints on performance were not new. As early as 1954, Carl Rogers had talked about the "conditions for creativity" and the importance of setting up situations of what he called "psychological safety and freedom." Yet, the Lepper et al. (1973) exploration of the negative effects of reward captured the attention of researchers and theorists alike, and this 1973 so-called "Magic Marker" study was quick to spawn a variety of empirical investigations of reward contingencies and their impact on performance, most especially creativity (e.g., Garbarino, 1975; Greene & Lepper, 1974; Loveland & Olley, 1979; McGraw & McCullers, 1979; Pittman, Emery, & Boggiano, 1982; Shapira, 1976). In a series of three experimental studies, Amabile, Hennessey, and Grossman (1986) even showed a negative impact of contracted-for reward when the reward was delivered *prior* to task engagement. In fact, one study in this series served to demonstrate that if it is described to subjects as a reward, an experimental task can *itself* serve to undermine subsequent motivation and creativity of performance.

Much of this research focusing on the effects of expected reward used a protocol that asked study participants to produce some sort of real-world, tangible product that was then rated for creativity and a variety of other dimensions using the Consensual Assessment Technique (CAT) (Amabile, 1982b; Hennessey & Amabile, 1999) or a similar product assessment procedure. And although, over the years, experimental approaches have become increasingly complex, the basic message has remained the same. Hundreds of published investigations have revealed that the promise of a reward made contingent on task engagement often serves to undermine intrinsic task motivation and qualitative aspects of performance, including creativity (for a more complete review of the literature, see Amabile, 1996, Deci, Koestner, & Ryan, 2001; Hennessey, 2000, 2003; Hennessey & Amabile, 1988). This effect is so robust that it has been found to occur across a wide age range, with everyone from preschoolers to seasoned business professionals and retired R&D scientists experiencing essentially the same negative consequences.

Importantly, reward has not been the only extrinsic constraint to be manipulated experimentally. Amabile, DeJong, and Lepper (1976) identified a negative impact of time limits on subsequent task motivation; and investigators expanding their focus to include the impact of competition have found that the expectation that one's work will be judged and compared to products produced by others may well be the most deleterious extrinsic constraint of all. Perhaps because situations of competition often combine aspects of other "killers" of motivation and creativity, including expected reward and expected evaluation, situations of competition have been shown to undermine severely the task interest and performance of persons across the age spectrum. In one study, Amabile (1982a) presented data showing that competitive elements were especially harmful to children's intrinsic task motivation and creativity on an artistic activity; and Amabile, Goldfarb, and Brackfield (1990) reported similar findings for college students.

Proposed Cognitively-Based Mechanisms

More than 30 years of empirical investigations reveal that environmental constraints, including expected reward, expected evaluation, and competition, can be powerful killers of intrinsic task motivation and creativity of performance. As a result of these compelling data, the Intrinsic Motivation Principle of Creativity was born: Intrinsic motivation is conducive to creativity, and extrinsic motivation is almost always detrimental (Amabile, 1983, 1996). In its earlier incarnations, this proposed relation between motivational orientation and creativity of performance was advanced as a tentative research hypothesis. But social psychologists seeking to better understand the psychosocial factors that promote creativity have now gathered so much unequivocal research evidence that this proposition has been elevated to the status of an undisputed principle.

But why is intrinsic motivation so crucial for creative performance? In the face of an expected reward, evaluation, or other extrinsic constraint, the goal is to "play it safe" – to generate a suitable idea or solve a problem as quickly and efficiently as possible. The most straightforward path to a solution is likely to be chosen, as most of us, young children and professionals alike, will avoid taking risks that might result in a less than acceptable outcome. For a creative idea or solution to be generated, however, it is often necessary to temporarily "step away" from environmental constraints (Newell, Shaw, & Simon, 1962), to become immersed in the problem itself, to suspend judgment, to experiment with alternative pathways, and to direct attention toward the more seemingly incidental aspects of the task. The more focused an individual is on a promised reward or evaluation, the less likely it is that these alternative paths will be explored. This tendency to avoid potential pitfalls and opt instead for a safe albeit mediocre solution appears to capture the thought processes and behavior of the majority of persons who approach an open-ended, "creativity-type" task with an expectation of reward or impending evaluation.

Yet empirical investigations of the impact of extrinsic constraints on motivation and qualitative aspects of performance have become increasingly finely tuned over the years. Researchers now have a far more sophisticated and nuanced understanding of reward and evaluation effects and are quick to point out that not all extrinsic contingencies can be expected to have the same deleterious impact. Theorists now understand that the type of task presented to study participants can, in large part, drive their experimental results; and investigations reveal that under certain specific conditions, the delivery of a competence-affirming evaluation or reward or the expectation of an impending evaluation can sometimes increase levels of extrinsic motivation without having any negative impact on intrinsic motivation or performance. In fact, some forms of evaluation and reward expectation can actually enhance creativity of performance. These complex effects are demonstrated in several publications (e.g., Harackiewicz, Abrahams, & Wageman, 1991; Jussim, Soffin, Brown, Ley, & Kohlhepp, 1992).

To complicate things even further, so-called "immunization techniques" incorporating intrinsic motivation training have been shown to successfully counteract the negative effects of expected reward on children. In the first of these research attempts (Hennessey, Amabile, & Martinage, 1989, Study 1), elementary-school students were randomly assigned to intrinsic-motivation-focus or control groups and met with an experimenter over two consecutive days to view videos and engage in directed discussion. The tapes shown to students in the intrinsic-motivation-focus condition depicted two 11-year-olds talking with an adult about various aspects of their school-work. Scripts for this condition were constructed so as to help children focus on the intrinsically interesting, fun, and playful aspects of a task. Ways to make even the most routine assignment exciting were suggested, and participants were helped to distance themselves from socially imposed extrinsic constraints, such as rewards. Tapes shown to students in the control condition featured the same two young actors talking about some of their favorite things.

Following this training procedure, all students met individually with a second experimenter for testing. Half the children in each training condition (intrinsic motivation and control) were told that they could take two pictures with an instant camera only if they promised to tell a story later for the experimenter. For children in the no-reward conditions, this picture taking was presented simply as the first of two "things to do."

This design crossed presentation of reward with type of training received. It was expected that only participants who had been purposefully instructed in ways to overcome the usual deleterious effects of extrinsic constraints would maintain baseline levels of intrinsic motivation and creativity in situations of expected reward (i.e., they would be immunized against the effects

of extrinsic constraints). The data from this initial investigation not only confirmed these expectations but indicated that the training intervention had much more of an influence than expected. Intrinsic-motivation-trained children tended to report higher levels of intrinsic task motivation on a paper-and-pencil assessment than did children in the control (no-training) condition; and it was also found that the offer of reward actually augmented the creativity of children who had undergone intrinsic motivation training. This additive effect of intrinsic and extrinsic motivation was quite robust. In fact, the creativity of children who received intrinsic motivation training and expected a reward was significantly higher than that of any other design group.

In our initial discussion of these immunization study results, my colleagues and I conjectured that the reward may have heightened their already positive feelings about the tasks they were doing. Two follow-up investigations of these immunization techniques (Hennessey, Amabile, & Martinage, 1989, Study 2; Hennessey & Zbikowski, 1993) were subsequently carried out. Each was designed as a conceptual replication of Study 1. Essentially the same experimental design was employed; and it was again the children who had received immunization training and who were expecting a reward who produced the most creative products. Yet, in these subsequent two studies, the effect of intrinsic motivation training was far less dramatic. In Study 2, statistical comparisons revealed that the creativity of those children receiving intrinsic motivation training and expecting a reward for their performance was significantly different from both the no-training/reward and no-training/no-reward groups. In Study 3, although children assigned to the intrinsic-motivation-training/reward condition again produced the most creative products, their performance was only significantly different from that of the no-training/reward group.

The results of Studies 2 and 3 indicated that we cannot expect that children exposed to intrinsic motivation training and offered a reward for their performance will always

BETH A. HENNESSEY

demonstrate unusually high levels of creativity. We can expect, however, that these children will be able to maintain baseline levels of intrinsic motivation and creativity under reward conditions. In fact, in a subsequent empirical replication of these immunization techniques (Gerrard, Poteat, & Ironsmith, 1996), teacher judges again gave the highest creativity ratings to products produced by elementary school students who had been randomly assigned to an intrinsic-motivation-training/reward condition.

What is it about this immunization procedure that allows children to maintain their creativity even when they expect a reward? It appears that training sessions designed to help them learn to deemphasize extrinsic incentives and concentrate instead on their own intrinsic interest and task enjoyment really do pay off. Even in the face of a highly salient, expected reward, elementary-school children who have been "immunized" have been repeatedly shown to be able to maintain a positive, intrinsically motivated outlook. They approach the experimental tasks with a playfulness and a willingness to take risks that many researchers believe are crucial to creativity – elements that, in the absence of immunization training, are easily undermined by expected reward or other extrinsic constraints (Amabile, 1983a, 1996; Barron, 1968; Campbell, 1960; Crutchfield, 1962; Dansky & Silverman, 1975; Lieberman, 1965; Stein, 1974).

Evidence from nonexperimental "field" studies coupled with observations of and interviews with persons who rely on their creativity for their life's work echo these "immunization" results. Although many "killers" of motivation and creativity that have been isolated experimentally have also been found to be detrimental in the work world, these negative effects have not proven universal. For some individuals, certain extrinsic motivators have been shown to have either no effect or even a positive effect on task interest and creativity of performance. For example, in an investigation of commissioned and noncommissioned works done by professional artists,

the extrinsic incentive of a commission was seen by some study participants as a highly controlling constraint; and the creativity of their work plummeted. Yet for those who viewed the commission as an opportunity to achieve recognition or a confirmation of their competence by respected others, creativity was enhanced (Amabile, Phillips, & Collins, 1993).

How can these individual differences in response to extrinsic constraints be explained? Data on these professional artists and the children taking part in the immunization studies parallel nicely earlier work exploring the relevance of self-perception processes to motivational orientation. What we have come to understand is that most of the time, the majority of us are not all that in touch with our own motivations. We do not always know why it is that we do the things we do, and we often apply to our own behavior the same rubrics we use for making sense of the actions of others. More specifically, in situations where both a plausible intrinsic and extrinsic explanation for an action are available, we tend to dismiss the internal cause in favor of the external cause. Some social psychologists have referred to this process as the "discounting principle" (see, e.g., Kelley, 1973). Other theorists propose a related explanation termed the "over-justification" hypothesis, a formulation derived from the attribution theories of Bem (1972), Kelley (1967, 1973) and deCharms (1968). According to this model, when a behavior is over-justified (when there exists both a possible internal and external cause for one's own or another's behavior), each of us will tend to overlook the internal cause (the presence of intrinsic task motivation) in favor of the external cause (a reward or evaluation was at stake). In effect, we discount the excess justification for explaining why we ourselves or someone else has done something.

Early work carried out by Deci, Ryan, and colleagues (Deci, 1975; Deci, Cascio, & Krusell, 1975; Deci & Ryan, 1985a), supplemented these discounting and over-justification models with what these researchers termed Cognitive Evaluation Theory (CET). This formulation also proposed that when individuals who are initially intrinsically motivated to perform an activity are promised an extrinsic reward, they are prompted to ask themselves why they are engaging in the activity in the first place. This self-evaluation eventually leads them to assume that the more salient of the two possible reasons for task engagement, the fact that a reward has been offered, is driving their behavior, and a reduction of intrinsic motivation is the result. Moreover, Deci, Ryan, and their co-investigators found that if this person is later asked to engage in the same activity in the absence of extrinsic reward, overall intrinsic task motivation will remain low.

Importantly, whatever the terminology employed, this cognitive evaluation process, this over-justification or discounting, is not inevitable. In situations where our own (or another's) intrinsic task interest is especially salient, we may not opt for an extrinsic explanation of behavior. As early as 1972, Bem suggested that individuals' internal attitudes and states would be most subject to external influences when those initial internal states were vague or ambiguous. And in a 1981 investigation carried out by Fazio, the negative impact of expected reward was mitigated in young children for whom initial intrinsic interest in the target activity had been made salient to them. In other words, it may not be the expectation of a reward or an evaluation per se that undermines intrinsic motivation; rather, it may be the individual's interpretation of that reward or evaluation and his or her role in the reward/evaluation process that in large part determine whether task motivation will be undermined, enhanced, or remain unchanged.

Whereas rewards and evaluations are most often experienced as externally controlling, they can under some circumstances serve to heighten feelings of competence or support autonomy. In the words of Vallerand, Pelletier, and Koestner (2008), "being criticized by a teacher with whom

one connects is not the same as being criticized by a teacher we do not like" (p. 258).

Building on the research program that resulted in their CET, Deci and Ryan have for over two decades carried out important work in an effort to consolidate and formalize what, in the minds of many, had become a comparatively narrow and disjointed approach to the study of the mechanisms underlying the formation of task motivation. The result of this work has been the formulation of Self-Determination Theory (SDT) (Deci & Ryan, 1985a, 1985b, 1996, 2000, 2008), a conceptual refinement of the earlier CET model. Self-Determination Theory concentrates on innate psychological needs and the degree to which persons are able to satisfy these basic needs as they pursue and attain their valued goals. Integrating a variety of literatures, this model offers an ambitious and insightful synthesis of what up until recently had been a conglomeration of related but distinct motivational approaches (including areas of intrinsic motivation and internalization). SDT places the focus on causality orientations, or characteristic ways that each of us develops for understanding and orienting to inputs. More specifically, Deci and Ryan have hypothesized that individuals vary in the degree to which they exhibit three such orientations ("autonomy," "control," and "impersonal"), and they have argued that these individual differences have important implications for a variety of motivationally involved processes. Within this SDT framework, extrinsic motivation (termed "controlled motivation" by Deci and Ryan) is not seen as the simple absence of intrinsic motivation (termed "autonomous motivation"). Instead, motivational orientation is viewed as a highly complex and multilayered continuum. Self-determination theory both explains specific motivational phenomena and provides a framework for integrating these understandings and formulating additional hypotheses.

Amabile's (1993) model of "motivational synergy" was also constructed in an attempt to apply a systems perspective to the interface between motivation and environment. Amabile has proposed that expected rewards (or evaluations) can sometimes serve as "synergistic extrinsic motivators." In other words, rather than detract from initial interest, they can, under certain specific circumstances, combine in an *additive* fashion with intrinsic motivation and actually enhance task enjoyment and involvement. Importantly, this synergistic effect has been found to occur only under circumstances in which initial task intrinsic motivation was especially strong and salient. For the elementary-school students who had undergone intrinsic motivation training, their enjoyment of school-related work was exactly that. In each of the three immunization investigations, the data showed that children in the intrinsic motivation training condition scored significantly higher than did their nontrained peers on a questionnaire tapping motivation for learning (Hennessey, Amabile, & Martinage, 1989, Study 2; Hennessey & Zbikowski, 1993). And interviews with the professional artists whose creativity thrived when they were working for a commission also tended to evidence especially high levels of intrinsic motivation for their craft (Amabile, Phillips, & Collins, 1993).

The Role of Affect and Individual Differences

In addition to cognitive processes, affect too may play a pivotal role in determining whether an anticipated reward, evaluation, or other extrinsic constraint will serve to undermine or enhance intrinsic motivation and creativity. And although the over-justification and discounting models have proven useful for understanding the negative effects of reward and evaluation in adults, they have failed to explain adequately why young children have also been observed to suffer decreases in intrinsic motivation and creativity. Simply stated, children under the age of 7 or 8 years lack the cognitive capabilities necessary for weighing multiple sufficient causes and employ-

ing discounting (see Shultz, Butkowsky, Pearce, & Shanfield, 1975; Smith, 1975). In fact, some studies have indicated that many young children seem to employ an additive algorithm and interpret the expectation of reward as an *augmentation* of intrinsic interest (see DiVitto & McArthur, 1978; Morgan, 1981). How is it that, when working for a reward, young children frequently demonstrate decreases in intrinsic motivation and creativity of performance, yet they seem cognitively incapable of engaging in the thought processes that underlie the over-justification and/or discounting paradigms?

One possible answer to this puzzle is that the reduction in intrinsic interest in young children (and perhaps all of us) is driven primarily by the learned expectation that rewards, evaluation, time limits, and competitive elements are usually paired with activities that need to be done, activities that are often not fun and sometimes even aversive. The undermining of intrinsic interest may result as much from emotion or affect as it does from thoughts or cognitive analysis. Children may learn to react negatively to a task as "work" when their behavior is controlled by socially imposed factors (such as rewards), and they may react positively to a task as "play" when there are no constraints imposed. Negative affect resulting from socially learned stereotypes or scripts of work (see Lepper et al., 1982; Morgan, 1981; Ransen, 1980) may be what leads to decrements in intrinsic interest (see Hennessey, 1999).

In fact, a review of the literature reveals that contemporary views of intrinsic motivation frequently include an affective component. One group of theorists, for example, has concentrated their attention on the relation between positive affect and intrinsic motivation (e.g., Isen & Reeve, 2005). Others have focused specifically on the affective components of interest and excitement (e.g., Izard, 1977). Some researchers have presented data emphasizing the link between intrinsic motivation and feelings of happiness, surprise, and fun (Pretty & Seligman, 1983; Reeve, Cole, & Olson, 1986). And the prolific and influential work of

Csikszentmihalyi (1997; Csikszentmihalyi, Abuhamdeh, & Nakamura, 2005; Nakamura & Csikszentmihalyi, 2003) has brought to light the elation that can result from deep task involvement. As described by Csikszentmihalyi, the truly intrinsic motivational state is characterized by a sense of "flow" and "optimal experience." For the majority of persons, flow is not an everyday occurrence, but when it does come, it brings with it feelings of intense concentration and deep enjoyment – feelings that transport the individual into a new reality of "previously undreamed-of states of consciousness" (1990, p. 74). Taken together, these scholarly explorations make a strong argument for the connection between motivational orientation and emotion, with Izard (1991) arguing that like motivation, emotions too can function as both traits and states.

In addition to affective components, individual-difference variables may also play an important role in the mediation of environmental effects. Deci and Ryan (1985a) offered evidence that variability in response to extrinsic constraints may stem, at least in part, from enduring differences in motivational orientation. Cheek and Stahl (1986) reported that when informed that they would receive evaluative feedback, shy subjects performed significantly less creatively than did those who were not shy. And gender too may play an important role in determining the impact of expected evaluation. In two studies in which children were segregated by gender and asked to make collages under competitive or noncompetitive conditions, the detrimental effects of competitive evaluation were found to apply to girls but not to boys (Conti, Collins, & Picariello, 2001). In fact, in both of these investigations, boys appeared to demonstrate *higher* levels of artistic creativity under competitive conditions. Work carried out by Baer (1997, 1998) showed similar interactions between gender and motivational condition. The expectation of reward or evaluation lowered the creativity of middle school girls but not that of boys. And the creativity of second grade boys, but not girls,

was significantly increased by the expectation of evaluation. In addition, when Conti and Amabile (1995) examined the creativity of computer science students, they found that participants' skill levels mediated the impact of evaluation. In situations where study participants had virtually no previous experience or training in the domain being tapped, evaluations appeared to serve not as killers of intrinsic task motivation but as much-needed sources of information and validation. Low-skill students wrote more creative programs when expecting an evaluation, and higher-skill students wrote better programs in the no-evaluation condition. Similar effects were found by Pollak (1992) in a study in which advanced art students were asked to produce a drawing; and Hill, Amabile, Coon, and Whitney (1994) also reported a skill-level-evaluation interaction pattern.

Immunization? Affect? Gender? Individual differences in skill level, and shyness? The more we know, the more we realize we need to know.

Hydraulic or Additive?

Researchers have found it all too easy to undermine intrinsic motivation and creativity of performance with the imposition of extrinsic constraints. For the majority of persons in the majority of situations, intrinsic motivation has proven to be a most delicate and fleeting entity. The Intrinsic Motivation Principle of Creativity (IMP) (Amabile, 1983, 1996) rests on the assumption that intrinsic and extrinsic sources of motivation can be expected to work in opposition to one another. This model, which can be likened to a hydraulic water pump, predicts that when the "flow" of intrinsic motivation is decreased, the level of extrinsic motivation will necessarily be increased. This implicit assumption is in evidence throughout the literature that laid the basis for the social psychology of creativity (see, e.g., Lepper & Greene, 1978). Indeed, many researchers and theorists have operationally defined intrinsically motivated behaviors as those that occur in the absence of extrinsic motivators (e.g., Deci, 1971; Lepper, Greene, & Nisbett, 1973). Yet as the investigations reviewed above reveal, over time we have come to understand that the relation between environmental constraints, motivational orientation, and creativity of performance is not nearly as straightforward as we once believed. As outlined by Deci and Ryan in their Self-Determination Theory (1985a, 1985b, 1996, 2000), extrinsic motivation must be understood as far more than the simple absence of intrinsic motivation; and researchers continue to uncover violations of the IMP hydraulic model.

How can we predict whether an individual's motivation and creativity of performance will be undermined, enhanced, or remain relatively impervious to the imposition of a reward, an evaluation, or other extrinsic constraint? Importantly, each of the hallmarks of intrinsic motivation outlined earlier focuses on the individual's inner psychological state. Whether prompted by just the right amount of novelty, feelings of competence, or a sense of control, an intrinsically motivated orientation comes about as the result of an internal, entirely individualized and especially complex process.

Although a single formulation or theory accounting for all the various potential motivational reactions to environmental factors has yet to be advanced, in recent years, some researchers have added to our understanding with the introduction of what they term Expectancy-Value Theory (Eccles, 1983; Eccles, Wigfield, & Schiefele, 1998). According to this model, the offer of a reward or the promise of an evaluation can, under specific circumstances, cause the individual to place increased value on performance, leading to deeper task involvement and interest. And whereas many of the investigators subscribing to this view have tended to focus on the self-regulation of behavior rather than intrinsic motivation per se, others have worked to bridge the intrinsic-motivation and expectancy-value approaches with a focus on the individual's phenomenological experience while working toward a goal.

In an exploration of the role played by affect in the regulation of behavior, Sansone and Harackiewicz (1996) contended that we must think about intrinsic or extrinsic motivation not only as an end-state but as a process. In other words, although outcome-derived motivation resulting from the promise of a reward or an evaluation may pull one into an activity, a self-regulated, process-derived motivation (e.g., cognitive and affective absorption in the task) may be necessary to maintain performance over time. Sansone and Harackiewicz believe that this self-regulation of behavior requires that the individual actively maintain both internal and external sources of motivation. If a task is to be brought to successful completion, expectancy and valuation processes must be oriented at compatible outcomes. In other words, like Amabile, they have argued that extrinsic incentives and task motivation must combine in a synergistic, additive, or complementary fashion.

This melding of the these two goal types – the individual's own goals for task engagement and the incentives imposed within the environment – is critical to the self-regulatory process. External intervention has, under certain circumstances, proven effective in helping some persons to make this match and change their phenomenological experience from neutral or negative to a more positive state. And some individuals have, themselves, been found to take the steps necessary to transform a task into something they feel more positive about performing (Sansone & Harackiewicz, 1996). For example, research reveals that study participants given a choice about task engagement can perceive their receipt of a reward as a kind of "bonus" rather than a controlling extrinsic constraint. In one instance, college students who believed that they had freely chosen to take part in a research study and who had been offered a reward for their participation were the most creative and most intrinsically motivated of any group, including a no-reward "control" condition (Amabile, Hennessey, & Grossman, 1986, Study 3).

Intrigued by these findings, researchers have gone on to discover an *additive* effect of intrinsic and extrinsic motivation in a variety of circumstances. They now understand that the powerful undermining impact of expected reward is most likely to occur when what have come to be termed "task-contingent" rewards have been promised. Task-contingent rewards are rewards made conditional simply on task completion. The impact of so-called "performance-contingent" rewards promised and delivered only if a certain level of competency or proficiency is reached is less straightforward.

Under certain specific circumstances, in fact, the informational value implicit in performance-contingent rewards has been shown to *augment* feelings of self-efficacy, intrinsic task interest, and qualitative aspects of performance. For example, a field study conducted by Pallak, Costomiris, Sroka, and Pittman (1982) showed that, for children attending schools where competence-affirming rewards were regularly employed, the promise of a "good-player award" was interpreted as conveying supportive information and increased student intrinsic motivation. However, these same good player awards were perceived as being controlling, and thus decreased intrinsic motivation, when promised to children in schools where such informational incentives were not typically used (see also Deci & Ryan 1985a; Harackiewicz, Manderlink, & Sansone, 1984).

To reiterate, an astounding number of careful empirical investigations have shown that for the majority of persons in the majority of situations, the imposition of extrinsic constraints, including expected reward, is highly likely to have a negative impact on both intrinsic task motivation and creativity of performance. Yet researchers continue to uncover important and not entirely infrequent exceptions to this rule. And one group of investigators, most notably Eisenberger, Cameron, and colleagues (Cameron & Pierce 1994; Eisenberger & Cameron, 1996, 1998; Eisenberger & Selbst, 1994), have long contended that creativity can be easily *increased* by the use of rewards.

Clashing Views

These researchers and theorists who represent the behaviorist view maintain that any detrimental effects of reward occur only under limited conditions that can be easily avoided. More specifically, they have offered a simple "diffusion of attention" or "competing response" model to explain the many deleterious effects of expected reward reported in the literature. In other words, individuals who are promised a reward are portrayed as being distracted by their excitement about a soon-to-be-delivered prize or gift. Intrinsic motivation and enjoyment of the task at hand are thought to be directly blocked by the competing response of reward anticipation, and study participants are believed to rush through their work rather than make their best effort.

Importantly, researchers representing a social-psychological perspective take an opposing view and point out that although this diffusion-of-attention or competing-response hypothesis may account for the undermining impact of reward under some specific circumstances, the undermining effects of task-contingent reward have been seen even when the reward was delivered *before* the target task was attempted (Amabile, Hennessey, & Grossman, 1986). In addition, they maintain that diffusion of attention fails to explain longer-term negative consequences of reward contingencies; and they argue that it also can not account for the fact that when subjects perceive they have no choice but to perform a task, the promise and receipt of reward does not lead to negative effects.

This debate over the impact of reward on motivational orientation and creativity of performance first surfaced in the literature in the mid-1990s, prompting researchers and theorists on both sides to publish a series of heated commentaries, critiques, and replies (see Eisenberger & Cameron, 1996, 1998; Hennessey & Amabile, 1998; Lepper, 1998; Sansone & Harackiewicz, 1998). In the main, this controversy has been healthy for the field in that it has motivated researchers to examine more closely the details surrounding reward types and the operationalization of and measurement of creativity. For example, rewards that convey competence information may not undermine intrinsic motivation (and creativity of performance) as much as rewards that convey only controlling information. When compared with no-reward controls, persons receiving informational rewards have under certain circumstances been shown to experience enhanced intrinsic motivation (Deci & Ryan 1985a; Harackiewicz, Manderlink, & Sansone, 1984). In many of the "token economy" experiments cited by Eisenberger and Cameron (1996, 1998), study participants were provided with just this sort of continuous information about their performance as they were promised and received contingent rewards over long periods of time.

Differences in the measurement and operationalization of creativity may also play a part in determining study results. In many investigations demonstrating creativity enhancement after the promise of reward, creativity was assessed in terms of scores on a standard paper-and-pencil creativity test. Such tests equate creativity with simple statistical infrequency of response; and although such measures might be legitimately viewed as tapping originality or divergent thinking, they do not adequately capture the elements of creativity as it is generally defined in the literature: novelty combined with appropriateness, value, or usefulness. Moreover, standardized tests of creativity have been specifically designed to assess creativity as a relatively enduring personal trait. Social-psychological studies of the interface between creativity and motivation, on the other hand, see creativity as a very much fleeting and situation-specific state. In addition, intrinsic motivation theorists have long emphasized that it makes sense to expect an undermining of intrinsic motivation only when the target task is initially intrinsically interesting to study participants. If there is no intrinsic interest to begin with, there obviously can be no decrease in intrinsic motivation after rewards are promised and delivered. Innate levels of interest in the target creativity task

mark one crucial difference between empirical studies showing negative and positive effects of reward.

Importantly, the overwhelming majority of tasks used in studies conducted by researchers influenced by the behavior modification perspective have had relatively clear and straightforward paths to solution. Moreover, in many of these investigations, subjects were purposefully told to be creative and in some cases they were instructed as to exactly what kinds of responses would be given high creativity ratings. Work carried out by O'Hara and Sternberg (2001) has explored whether such directives to "be creative" will act as goals and promote creativity or be perceived as constraints and undermine creativity. Specific instructions to be creative, practical, or analytical resulted in college students demonstrating higher levels of performance in each of these three areas, relative to the performance of a no-instruction group. Probing further, these investigators found that persons who preferred to play with their own ideas showed higher levels of creative thinking when not given any specific instructions, whereas persons who preferred to analyze and evaluate their own ideas showed lower levels of creative thinking in the absence of specific instructions.

More recent publications authored by Eisenberger, Cameron, and colleagues have continued to argue for the *positive* impact of expected reward on task interest and creative performance. Over time, these theorists have come to explore the possible mechanisms behind what they view as a reward's enhancing effects. One series of studies argued that creativity might be increased when levels of extrinsic motivation or perceived self-determination (and therefore intrinsic motivation) are enhanced (Eisenberger & Rhoades, 2001; Eisenberger, Rhoades, & Cameron, 1999). These authors have also examined the interplay between explicit training in creativity and the expectation of reward. In one such investigation, they presented data indicating that because training in divergent thinking can convey a task administrator's desire for creative performance, sixth graders were likely to generalize this discrimination to new tasks administered by other individuals and perform creatively when motivated by the promise of reward (Eisenberger, Haskins, & Gambleton, 1999).

The debate continues. Eisenberger and co-authors have contended that the failure to come to agreement about the effects of reward should not be blamed on any great complexity of research findings, but instead rests in the clash between romantic and behaviorist worldviews about basic human nature (Eisenberger & Shanock, 2003). As research paradigms and the theories and models they generate become increasingly nuanced, it can be expected that this rift between the two philosophical camps may, in fact, narrow. In the meantime, like their behaviorist counterparts, researchers and theorists taking a social-psychological approach to the investigation of the impact of expected reward and other environmental constraints have made good progress in expanding their investigative paradigms and research "lens."

A Sampling of Recent Investigations

A review of the literature in this area reveals few recent investigations modeled after the original basic experimental paradigm contrasting the creative behavior and motivation of persons randomly assigned to constraint and no-constraint conditions. In a paper published 10 years ago, Joussemet and Koestner (1999) examined the effect of expected rewards on the creativity of young girls. This research design was expanded to also include an exploration of the possibility that the impact of the reward contingency might transfer to a subsequent no-reward situation. All study participants (ages 4 to 17 years) completed a training task requiring divergent thinking (generating themes for an upcoming gymnastics gala) followed by an artistic transfer task. Half the children were promised a reward for their completion of the idea generation task. Importantly, this reward contingency was in effect only during this training task phase. Results showed that expected reward led younger children to generate less appropriate themes on the training task; and after receiving a reward, girls of all ages tended to draw pictures that were judged to be less creative in the transfer task. This study is representative of a small but growing body of studies seeking to expand our understanding of the relation between environmental factors, motivational orientation, and creativity of performance.

Researchers interested in the impact of the environment on creativity have turned their attention to a variety of new and exciting questions. In many respects, it might be argued that these investigators have succeeded in putting the "social" back into the study of the social psychology of creativity. Rather than attempt to construct a "one-size-fits-all" model of the impact of extrinsic constraints on intrinsic motivation and creativity of performance, more recent studies have tended to explore individual-difference variables and to measure more directly the cognitive, affective, and emotional impacts of a variety of factors in the creator's environment.

Isen and Reeve (2005) carried out two experiments showing that positive affect not only fosters intrinsic motivation and enjoyment of novel and challenging tasks but also promotes extrinsic motivation and responsible work behavior in situations where less interesting tasks need to get done. Reporting data that appear to contradict the Isen and Reeve findings, Kaufmann and Vosburg (1997) carried out two studies designed to investigate the influence of affective state on actual creative problem-solving behavior. Study I focused on adolescents, and revealed that positive mood led to significantly poorer creative problem-solving performance, whereas no significant effects of positive or negative mood states were found for analytic problem-solving tasks by comparison. In this initial investigation, study participants' naturally occurring mood states were assessed. In Study II, involving adults ranging in age from 19 to 41 years, mood state was experimentally manipulated. Results paralleled those reported in the first investigation. In the induced mood conditions, negative mood significantly facilitated creative problem solving relative to induced neutral mood, which led to better performance than the control condition. The poorest performance was seen in the positive-mood condition.

Following up on these initial studies, Kaufmann (2003) provided additional evidence showing that under certain routine conditions, positive mood can impair creativity, whereas negative and neutral moods can sometimes promote insight and solutions to problems. These authors then went on to present a new theory of the effect of mood states on creative problem solving, criticizing the prevailing notion that there is an unconditional positive and causal link between positive mood and creative behavior.

Friedman, Förster, and Denzler (2007) offered a motivationally based account for the influence of mood on creative generation. Positive moods were proposed to signal to individuals that they are safe, motivating them to take advantage of this presumed safety by seeking stimulation and incentives (i.e., having fun). Negative moods were proposed to signal to individuals that there are problems at hand, motivating them to solve these problems. Findings from three experiments at least partially supported the prediction that positive and negative moods should enhance effort on creative generation tasks construed as compatible with the motivational orientations they elicit. Specifically, positive moods were observed to enhance effort on tasks construed as fun and silly, whereas negative moods tended to bolster effort on tasks construed as serious and important.

Turning their attention to another individual difference variable, a construct they termed "general causality orientation," King and Gurland (2007) expanded the examination of motivational orientation to include the *experience* of creating a product. Reasoning that how people feel during a task is indicative of their type of motivation (intrinsic vs. extrinsic), they set out to examine the possible interactive effects of causality orientation (operationalized here as a "trait" variable with the anchors autonomous vs. control oriented) coupled with an environmental factor – expected evaluation – on college students' creative performance on a collage-making task. A significant main effect of evaluation was found, such that across both causality orientations, subjects expecting an evaluation of their collages felt less competent at the task than did those who did not expect an evaluation. Among men only, evaluation condition interacted with autonomy orientation to significantly affect both creativity and novelty of idea. Low levels of autonomy orientation had no effect in the no-evaluation condition but was associated with lower ratings of collage creativity and novelty of idea in the evaluation condition.

One final example of the innovation and broadening of scope being demonstrated in the recent creativity/motivation literature comes from a study published by Shalley and Perry-Smith in 2001. This laboratory-based investigation examined the independent and joint effects of expected evaluation and modeling on study participants' creativity on job-related problems. Manipulating the controlling and informational aspects of a promised evaluation, these researchers presented college students with either no example, a standard example, or an especially creative example of a solution to a management problem. Study participants showed significantly higher levels of creativity and intrinsic motivation when they anticipated an informational rather than a controlling evaluation. In addition, those students given a highly creative example earned higher creative performance scores than those given no example. The lowest levels of intrinsic motivation and creativity were shown by students who had both been led to expect a controlling evaluation and who had been shown a standard problem solution.

Where Do We Go From Here?

Clearly, the infusion of elements such as individual-difference variables and the modeling of problem solutions coupled with the fine-tuning of reward or evaluation manipulations and an examination of possible interaction effects have already done a lot to expand our appreciation of the interface between environment, motivation, and creative behavior. Yet there is much that we still do not understand. Whenever I set out to design a new empirical investigation or to construct a review or chapter such as this, I begin with an electronic search of the data bases in an attempt to catch up on the latest trends and findings. Invariably, I am struck by a consistent and almost seemingly intentional segregation in the literature. Generally speaking, investigators and theorists interested in promoting creativity and motivation in the schools or in the workplace fail to incorporate or even acknowledge theorizing and research stemming from a less applied and more theoretical, laboratory-based perspective. By the same token, a recent monograph I authored as part of the NRCG/T series on the topic of developing creativity in gifted children (Hennessey, 2004) underscored the failure of mainstream academic psychology to "cross-pollinate" with work being done in the gifted and talented educational community. As a result, these two research traditions have for many years followed two separate but parallel trajectories – arriving at many of the same understandings about the origins and promotion of creativity but failing to benefit from the other's findings and expertise. How much more fruitful their efforts might have been had these two camps joined forces. (And it is not too late!)

Similarly, a careful review of the motivation literature reveals almost a complete rift between the social-psychological research and theorizing reviewed in this chapter and work being done on what has come to be termed Achievement Goal Theory. Like Expectancy-Value Theory, Self-Determination Theory, and the modeling being done within the framework of a social psychology of creativity, Achievement Goal Theory (see E. Anderman & Wolters, 2006; Meece, Anderman, & Anderman, 2006; Pintrich, 2000) is based on a social-cognitive view of motivation. More than 25 years of research and theorizing has positioned this approach as an especially prominent and influential theory of motivation (E. Anderman & Wolters, 2006; Pintrich, 2000). Yet this influence has been almost entirely restricted to work carried out in classroom settings. Achievement Goal Theory has served as an especially important tool in the analysis of the impact of different classroom structures and school environments on student motivation and learning. Instead of emphasizing ability perceptions and causal attributions, Achievement Goal Theory focuses on the types of goals pursued in achievement situations, most especially goals involving the development and demonstration of competence (Maehr & Nicholls, 1980; Nicholls, 1984).

Earlier applications of Achievement Goal Theory contrasted learning versus performance goals (Dweck & Elliott, 1983), task-involved versus ego-involved goals (Nicholls, 1984), and mastery versus ability-focused goals (Ames, 1992; Ames & Archer, 1988). More recent work has tended to subsume these categories into a more general mastery-versus-performance dichotomy. A mastery goal orientation is operationalized in terms of developing one's own abilities, mastering a new skill, and rising to a challenge. Success is measured in terms of self-improvement, and the individual is seen as deriving satisfaction from the inherent qualities of the task itself. A performance goal orientation, on the other hand, focuses the individual on doing better than others or surpassing normative performance standards.

The parallels between these mastery/performance goal orientations and the operationalizations of intrinsic and extrinsic motivation are obvious. So too are the similarities in the behavioral outcomes reported in the two literatures. Researchers working from an Achievement Goal Theory perspective have reported a number of achievement-related patterns that are established by the mastery or performance goal orientation; and the patterns that come with a mastery orientation read very much like a list of attitudes and behaviors associated with high levels of creative performance. At all grade levels, students who focus on mastery goals persist at difficult tasks (Elliott & Dweck, 1988; Stipek & Kowalski, 1989), show high levels of task involvement (Harackiewicz, Barron, Tauer, Carter, & Elliott, 2000), effort, and persistence (Grant & Dweck, 2003; Miller, Greene, Montalvo, Ravindran, & Nichols, 1996; Wolters, 2004), and report enhanced feelings of self-efficacy (Meece, Blumenfeld, & Hoyle, 1988; Midgley et al., 1998; Roeser, Midgley, & Urdan, 1996; Wolters, 2004).

Not only has Achievement Goal Theory proven useful for categorizing individual differences in student motivation, but it has also provided researchers with a valuable framework for analyzing the impact of classroom environment on student motivation and learning outcomes. For example, researchers have examined how educators create varying classroom goal structures with their use of instructional, evaluation, and grouping techniques. Students who believe that their teachers emphasize effort and understanding are more likely to adopt mastery-oriented goals. By the same token, students are more likely to take on a performance orientation when they perceive that their school is focused on competition for grades and comparisons of students' ability levels.

Again, the parallels between this body of work and the scholarship on the social psychology of creativity are many. Yet even the most comprehensive reviews of Achievement Goal Theory (see especially Meece, Anderman, & Anderman, 2006) fail to reference this complementary body of literature. And the same can be said as to the failure of scholars on the other side to recognize and reference the important work being done on Goal Theory. One exception to this rule comes in the form of a 2000 volume edited by Sansone and Harackiewicz. This book brings together thoughtful papers written by leading scholars in the heretofore almost entirely separate areas of experimental social psychology, educational psychology, industrial psychology, and mainstream motivational theory. Although individual authors make few attempts to incorporate the work of colleagues with theoretical perspectives very different from their own, a careful reading does allow for at least the beginnings of a more integrated and comprehensive perspective.

Another unusual but fruitful attempt at integrating what have grown up as entirely separate research approaches comes in the form of an empirical research report authored in 2006 by Vansteenkiste, Lens, and Deci. This paper, which melds the approaches taken by Achievement Goal Theorists and those who subscribe to Self-Determination Theory, is a prime example of the fruitful insights that can result from a combination of theoretical viewpoints. Researchers representing these and other distinct theoretical trajectories stand to learn a lot from one another. For example, it was only fairly recently that theorists adopting an Achievement Goal Theory approach came to consider the possibility that not all performance goals are created equal. They now appreciate the distinction between performance-approach and performance-avoidance goals and understand that these two goal types may have distinct motivational consequences. And researchers and theorists trained in experimental social psychology came slowly to the realization that the effect of extrinsic rewards on intrinsic motivation is not universal but depends on many factors, including how rewards are defined and operationalized. Tangible rewards, such as monetary payment, tend to have a more deleterious effect on intrinsic motivation than do less tangible rewards, such as verbal praise.

There are numerous parallels such as this, far too many to mention; and opportunities for a cross-pollination of ideas across the literatures and research traditions abound. It is possible, for example, that the long-identified but yet to be entirely understood creative "slump" that occurs around the fifth-grade year (Torrance, 1968) could be explained by two findings coming from the Achievement Goal Theory literature. One research outcome showed that elementary-school teachers reported using instructional practices that emphasize mastery goals more than did middle-school teachers who tended to work to promote performance goals (Midgley, Anderman, & Hicks, 1995). Another finding (E. Anderman & Hicks, 1999) revealed that as students transition to middle school, they become increasingly likely to show strong affective responses (both positive and negative) to classroom routines and teacher behaviors. And a third, longitudinal study (L. Anderman & Anderman, 1999) found that personal mastery goals decreased and personal performance goals increased as students moved from elementary to middle school.

Results from some studies reported in the Achievement Goal Theory literature also underscore the important role played by students' perceptions of their learning situations, and researchers working within this tradition have recently called for an examination of the phenomenology – or what they term the "functional significance" – of the classroom and school experience that can be assessed only from the learners' perspective (McCombs, 2003; Meece, Herman, & McCombs, 2003). The parallel here, of course, is that researchers and theorists adopting a social-psychological perspective have also recently come to understand that it is an individual's idiosyncratic interpretation of a reward or evaluation contingency and not the reward or evaluation itself that will determine whether intrinsic motivation (and creativity) will be enhanced, undermined, or remain relatively unchanged.

By their very nature, the study of complicated constructs like motivation and creativity, with all of their implications and applications, will always be messy and especially challenging. If we are to understand more fully the interface between environment, motivation, and creativity of performance, we must work to develop more precise definitions and operationalizations of goals, motivational orientation, rewards, and the like. And we must also strive to understand the impact of the environment from each individual's own, unique perspective. As evidenced by the research and theories summarized in this chapter, we have made great headway in many of these areas. A melding of what have remained up until this point parallel but isolated research traditions, models, and findings is one obvious important next step.

References

Amabile, T. M. (1982a). Children's artistic creativity: Detrimental effects of competition in a field setting. *Personality and Social Psychology Bulletin*, 8, 573–578.

Amabile, T. M. (1982b). Social psychology of creativity: A consensual assessment technique. *Journal of Personality and Social Psychology*, 43, 997–1013.

Amabile, T. M. (1983). The social psychology of creativity: A componential conceptualization. *Journal of Personality and Social Psychology*, 45, 357–376.

Amabile, T. M. (1988). A model of creativity and innovation in organizations. In B. M. Staw & L. L. Cummings (Eds.), *Research in organizational behavior* (Vol. 10, pp. 123–167). Greenwich, CT: JAI Press.

Amabile, T. M. (1990). Within you, without you: The social psychology of creativity, and beyond. In M. A. Runco & R. S. Albert (Eds.), *Theories of creativity* (pp. 61–91). Newbury Park, CA: Sage.

Amabile, T. M. (1993). Motivational synergy: Toward new conceptualizations of intrinsic and extrinsic motivation in the workplace. *Human Resource Management Review*, 3, 185–201.

Amabile, T. M. (1996) *Creativity in context*. Boulder, CO: Westview.

Amabile, T. M., DeJong, W., & Lepper, M. R. (1976). Effects of externally imposed deadlines on subsequent intrinsic motivation. *Journal of Personality and Social Psychology*, 34, 92–98.

Amabile, T. M., Goldfarb, P., & Brackfield, S. C. (1990). Social influences on creativity: Evaluation, coaction, and surveillance. *Creativity Research Journal*, 3, 6–21.

Amabile, T. M., Hennessey, B. A., & Grossman, B. S. (1986). Social influences on creativity: The effects of contracted-for reward. *Journal of Personality and Social Psychology*, 50, 14–23.

Amabile, T. M., Hill, K. G., Hennessey, B. A., & Tighe, E. M. (1994). The Work Preference Inventory: Assessing intrinsic and extrinsic motivational orientations. *Journal of Personality and Social Psychology*, 66, 950–967.

Amabile, T. M., Phillips, E. D., & Collins, M. A. (1993). *Creativity by contract: Social influences on the creativity of professional artists.* Unpublished manuscript.

Ames, C. (1992). Classrooms: Goals, structures, and student motivation. *Journal of Educational Psychology, 84,* 261–271.

Ames, C., & Archer, J. (1988). Achievement goals in the classroom: Students' learning strategies and motivation processes. *Journal of Educational Psychology, 80,* 260–267.

Anderman, E. M., & Hicks, L. (1999). Classroom goal orientation, school belonging and social goals as predictors of students' positive and negative affect following the transition to middle school. *Journal of Research and Development in Education, 32,* 89–103.

Anderman, E. M., & Wolters, C. (2006). Goals, values and affects: Influences on student motivation. In P. Alexander & P. Winne (Eds.), *Handbook of educational psychology* (2nd ed., pp. 369–390). New York: Simon & Schuster.

Anderman, L. H., & Anderman, E. M. (1999). Social predictors of changes in students' achievement goal orientations. *Contemporary Educational Psychology, 24,* 21–37.

Barron, F. (1968). *Creativity and personal freedom.* New York: Van Nostrand.

Baer, J. (1997). Gender differences in the effects of anticipated evaluation on creativity. *Creativity Research Journal, 10,* 25–31.

Baer, J. (1998). Gender differences in the effects of extrinsic motivation on creativity. *Journal of Creative Behavior, 32,* 18–37.

Bem, D. J. (1967). Self-perception: An alternative interpretation of cognitive dissonance phenomena. *Psychological Review, 74,* 183–200.

Bem, D. (1972). Self-perception theory. In L. Berkowitz (Ed.), *Advances in experimental social psychology* (Vol. 6, pp. 1–62). New York: Academic Press.

Berlyne, D. E. (1960). *Conflict, arousal, and curiosity.* New York: McGraw-Hill.

Cameron, J., & Pierce, W. D. (1994). Reinforcement, reward, and intrinsic motivation: A meta-analysis. *Review of Educational Research, 64,* 363–423.

Campbell, D. (1960). Blind variation and selective retention in creative thought as in other knowledge processes. *Psychological Review, 67,* 380–400.

Cheek, J. M., & Stahl, S. (1986). Shyness and verbal creativity. *Journal of Research in Personality, 20,* 51–61.

Conti, R., & Amabile, T. M. (1995). *Problem solving among computer science students: the effects of skill, evaluation expectation and personality on solution quality.* Paper presented at the Annual Meeting of the Eastern Psychological Association, Boston.

Conti, R., Collins, M., & Picariello, M. (2001). The impact of competition on intrinsic motivation and creativity: Considering gender, gender segregation, and gender role orientation. *Personality and Individual Differences, 30,* 1273–1289.

Cox, C. M. (1983). The early mental traits of three hundred geniuses. In R. S. Albert (Ed.), *Genius and eminence* (pp. 46–51). Oxford: Pergamon. (Original work published 1926)

Crutchfield, R. (1962). Conformity and creative thinking. In H. Gruber, G. Terrell, & M. Wertheimer (Eds.), *Contemporary approaches to creative thinking* (pp. 120-140). New York: Atherton Press.

Csikszentmihalyi, M. (1990). *Flow: The psychology of optimal experience.* New York: Harper and Row.

Csikszentmihalyi, M. (1997). *Creativity: Flow and the psychology of discovery and invention.* New York: HarperCollins.

Cskiszentmihalyi, M., Abuhamdeh, S., & Nakamura, J. (2005). Flow. In A. J. Elliot & C. S. Dweck (Eds.), *Handbook of competence and motivation* (pp. 598–608). New York: Guilford Publications.

Dansky, J., & Silverman, I. (1975). Play: A general facilitator of fluency. *Developmental Psychology, 11,* 104.

deCharms, R. (1968). *Personal causation: The internal affective determinants of behavior.* New York: Academic Press.

deCharms, R., Carpenter, V., & Kuperman, A. (1965). The "origin-pawn" variable in person perception. *Sociometery, 28,* 241–258.

Deci, E. L. (1971). Effects of externally mediated rewards on intrinsic motivation. *Journal of Personality and Social Psychology, 18,* 105–115.

Deci, E. L. (1972). Intrinsic motivation, extrinsic reinforcement, and inequity. *Journal of Personality and Social Psychology, 22,* 113–120.

Deci, E. L. (1975). *Intrinsic motivation.* New York: Plenum.

Deci, E. L., Cascio, W. F., & Krussel, J. (1975). Cognitive evaluation theory and some comments on the Calder and Staw critique. *Journal of Personality and Social Psychology, 31,* 81–85.

Deci, E. L., Koestner, R., & Ryan, R. M. (2001). Extrinsic rewards and intrinsic motivation in education: Reconsidered once again. *Review of Educational Research, 71,* 1–27.

Deci, E. L., & Ryan, R. M. (1985a). *Intrinsic motivation and self-determination in human behavior.* New York: Plenum.

Deci, E. L., & Ryan, R. M. (1985b). The General Causality Orientations Scale: Self-determination in personality. *Journal of Research in Personality, 19,* 109–134.

Deci, E. L., & Ryan, R. M. (1996). *Why we do what we do: Understanding self-motivation.* New York: Penguin.

Deci, E. L., & Ryan, R. M. (2000). The what and why of goal pursuits: Human needs and the self-determination of behavior. *Psychological Inquiry, 11,* 227–268.

Deci, E. L., & Ryan, R. M. (2008). Self-determination theory: A macrotheory of human motivation, development, and health. *Canadian Psychology/Psychologie canadienne, 49,* 182–185.

Dewett, T. (2007). Linking intrinsic motivation, risk taking, and employee creativity in an R&D environment. *R&D Management, 37,* 197–208.

DiVitto, B., & McArthur, L. Z. (1978). Developmental differences in the use of distinctiveness, consensus, and consistency information for making causal attributions. *Developmental Psychology, 14,* 474–482.

Dweck, C. S., & Elliott, S. (1983). Achievement motivation. In P. Mussen (Ed.), *Handbook of child psychology: Socialization, personality, and social development* (Vol. 4, pp. 643–691). New York: Wiley.

Eccles, J. S. (1983). Expectancies, values, and academic choice: Origins and changes. In J. Spence (Ed.), *Achievement and achievement motivation* (pp. 87–134). San Francisco: Freeman.

Eccles, J. S., Wigfield, A., & Schiefele, U. (1998). Motivation to succeed. In W. Damon & N. Eisenberg (Eds.), *Handbook of child psychology: Volume 3. Social, emotional, and personality development* (5th ed., pp. 1017–1095). New York: Wiley.

Eisenberger, R., & Cameron, J. (1996). Detrimental effects of reward: Reality of myth? *American Psychologist, 51,* 1153–1166.

Eisenberger, R., & Cameron, J. (1998). Rewards, intrinsic interest and creativity: New findings. *American Psychologist, 53,* 676–679.

Eisenberger, R, Haskins, F., & Gambleton, P. (1999). Promised reward and creativity: Effects of prior experience. *Journal of Experimental Social Psychology, 35,* 308–325.

Eisenberger, R., & Rhoades, L. (2001). Incremental effects of reward on creativity. *Journal of Personality and Social Psychology, 81,* 728–741.

Eisenberger, R., Rhoades, L., & Cameron, J. (1999). Does pay for performance increase or decrease perceived self-determination and intrinsic motivation? *Journal of Personality and Social Psychology, 77,* 1026–1040.

Eisenberger, R., & Selbst, M. (1994). Does reward increase or decrease creativity? *Journal of Personality and Social Psychology, 66,* 1116–1127.

Eisenberger, R., & Shanock, L. (2003). Rewards, intrinsic motivation, and creativity: A case study of conceptual and methodological isolation. *Creativity Research Journal, 15,* 121–130.

Elliott, E. S., & Dweck, C. S. (1988). Goals: An approach to motivation and achievement. *Journal of Personality and Social Psychology, 54,* 5–12.

Erikson, E. (1968). *Identity: Youth and crisis.* New York: Norton.

Fazio, R. H. (1981). On the self-perception explanation of the overjustification effect: The role of salience of initial attitude. *Journal of Experimental Social Psychology, 17,* 417–426.

Friedman, R. S., Förster, J., & Denzler, M. (2007). Interactive effects of mood and task framing on creative generation. *Creativity Research Journal, 19,* 141–162.

Garbarino, J. (1975). The impact of anticipated reward upon cross-age tutoring. *Journal of Personality and Social Psychology, 32,* 421–428.

Gerrard, L. E., Poteat, M., & Ironsmith, M. (1996). Promoting children's creativity: Effects of competition, self-esteem, and immunization. *Creativity Research Journal, 9,* 339–346.

Gottfried, A. E., Fleming, J. S., & Gottfried, A. W. (2001). Continuity of academic intrinsic motivation from childhood through late adolescence: A longitudinal study. *Journal of Educational Psychology, 93,* 3–13.

Grant, H., & Dweck, C. S. (2003). Clarifying achievement goals and their impact. *Journal of Personality and Social Psychology, 85,* 541–553.

Greenberg, J. R., & Mitchell, S. A. (1983). *Object relations in psychoanalytic theory.* Cambridge, MA: Harvard University Press.

Greene, D., & Lepper, M. (1974). Effects of extrinsic rewards on children's subsequent interest. *Child Development, 45,* 1141–1145.

Guilford, J. P., Merrifield, P. R., & Wilson, R. C. (1958). *Unusual Uses Test.* Orange, CA: Sheridan Psychological Services.

Harackiewicz, J. M., Abrahams, S., & Wageman, R. (1991). Performance evaluation and intrinsic motivation: The effects of evaluative focus, rewards and achievement orientation. *Journal of Personality and Social Psychology*, 63, 1015–1029.

Harackiewicz, J. M., Barron, K. E., Tauer, J. M., Carter, S. M., & Elliott, A. J. (2000). Short-term and long-term consequences of achievement goals: Predicting interest and performance over time. *Journal of Educational Psychology*, 92, 316–330.

Harackiewicz, J., Manderlink, G., & Sansone, C. (1984). Rewarding pinball wizardry: The effects of evaluation on intrinsic interest. *Journal of Personality and Social Psychology*, 47, 287–300.

Harter, S. (1978). Effectance motivation reconsidered: Toward a developmental model. *Human Development*, 21, 34–64.

Harter, S. (1981). A new self-report scale of intrinsic versus extrinsic orientation in the classroom: Motivational and informational components. *Developmental Psychology*, 17, 300–312.

Harter, S., & Jackson, B. K. (1992). Trait vs nontrait conceptualizations of intrinsic/extrinsic motivational orientation. *Motivation and Emotion*, 16, 209–230.

Hebb, D. O. (1955). Drives and the CNS. *Psychological Review*, 62, 243–254.

Heider, F. (1958). *The psychology of interpersonal relations*. New York: Wiley.

Hennessey, B. A. (1999). Intrinsic motivation, affect and creativity. In S. Russ (Ed.), *Affect, creative experience and psychological adjustment* (pp. 77–90). Philadelphia, PA: Taylor & Francis.

Hennessey, B. A. (2000). Rewards and creativity. In C. Sansone & J. Harackiewicz (Eds.), *Intrinsic and extrinsic motivation: The search for optimal motivation and performance* (pp. 55–78). New York: Academic Press.

Hennessey, B. A. (2003). The social psychology of creativity. *Scandinavian Journal of Educational Psychology*, 47, 253–271.

Hennessey, B. A. (2004). *Developing creativity in gifted children: The central importance of motivation and classroom climate* (RM04202). The National Research Center on the Gifted and Talented *Senior Scholar Series*. Storrs, CT: NRC/GT, University of Connecticut.

Hennessey, B. A., & Amabile, T. M. (1998). Reward, intrinsic motivation, and creativity. *American Psychologist*, 53, 674–675.

Hennessey, B. A., & Amabile, T. M. (1999). Consensual assessment. In M. Runco & S. Pritzker (Eds.), *Encyclopedia of creativity* (pp. 347–359). New York: Academic Press.

Hennessey, B. A., Amabile, T. M., & Martinage, M. (1989). Immunizing children against the negative effects of reward. *Contemporary Educational Psychology*, 14, 212–227.

Hennessey, B. A., & Zbikowski, S. (1993). Immunizing children against the negative effects of reward: A further examination of intrinsic motivation training techniques. *Creativity Research Journal*, 6, 297–307.

Hill, K., Amabile, T. M., Coon H. M., & Whitney, D. (1994). *Testing the componential model of creativity*. Unpublished manuscript.

Isen, A. M., & Reeve J. M. (2005). The influence of positive affect on intrinsic and extrinsic motivation: Facilitating enjoyment of play, responsible work behavior, and self-control. *Motivation and Emotion*, 29, 297–325.

Izard, C. (1977). *Human emotions*. New York: Plenum.

Izard, C. E. (1991). *The psychology of emotions*. New York: Plenum.

Izard, C. (2000). Affect. In A. E. Kazdin (Ed.), *Encyclopedia of psychology* (Vol. 4, pp. 332–333). Washington, DC: American Psychological Association.

Joussemet, M., & Koestner, R. (1999). Effect of expected rewards on children's creativity. *Creativity Research Journal*, 12, 231–239.

Jussim, L. S., Soffin, S., Brown, R., Ley, J., & Kohlhepp, K. (1992). Understanding reactions to feedback by integrating ideas from symbolic interactionism and cognitive evaluation theory. *Journal of Personality and Social Psychology*, 62, 402–421.

Kaufmann, G. (2003). The effect of mood on creativity in the innovative process. In L. V. Shavinina (Ed.), *The international handbook on innovation* (pp. 191–203). New York: Elsevier Science.

Kaufmann, G., & Vosburg, S. K. (1997). Paradoxical mood effects on creative problem-solving. *Cognition and Emotion*, 11, 151–170.

Kelley, H. (1967). Attribution theory in social psychology. In D. Levine (Ed.), *Nebraska symposium on motivation* (Vol. 15, pp. 192–240). Lincoln: University of Nebraska.

Kelley, H. (1973). The processes of causal attribution. *American Psychologist*, 28, 107–128.

King, L., & Gurland, S. T. (2007). Creativity and experience of a creative task: Person and environment effects. *Journal of Research in Personality, 41,* 1252–1259.

Kirton, M. J. (1982). *Kirton Adaptation-Innovation Inventory (KAI) manual* (Research Ed.). Hertfordshire, England: Occupational Research Centre.

Kohut, H. (1966). Forms and transformations of narcissism. *Journal of the American Psychoanalytic Association, 14,* 243–272.

Kruglanski, A. W., Friedman, I., & Zeevi, G. (1971). The effects of extrinsic incentive on some qualitative aspects of task performance. *Journal of Personality, 39,* 606–617.

Lepper, M. R. (1998). A whole much less than the sum of its parts: A comment on Eisenberger and Cameron. *American Psychologist, 53,* 675–676.

Lepper, M. R., & Greene, D. (Eds.). (1978). *The hidden costs of reward.* Hillsdale, NJ: Erlbaum.

Lepper, M., Greene, D., & Nisbett, R. (1973). Undermining children's intrinsic interest with extrinsic rewards: A test of the "overjustification" hypothesis. *Journal of Personality and Social Psychology, 28,* 129–137.

Lepper, M., Sagotsky, G., Dafoe, J. L., & Greene, D. (1982). Consequences of superfluous social constraints: Effects on young children's social inferences and subsequent intrinsic motivation. *Journal of Personality and Social Psychology, 42,* 51–65.

Lieberman, J. N. (1965). Playfulness and divergent thinking: an investigation of their relationship at the kindergarten level. *Journal of Genetic Psychology, 107,* 219–224.

Loveland, K. K., & Olley, J. (1979). The effect of external reward on interest and quality of task performance in children of high and low intrinsic motivation. *Child Development, 50,* 1207–1210.

Maehr, M. L., & Nicholls, J. G. (1980). Culture and achievement motivation. A second look. In N. Warren (Ed.), *Studies in cross-cultural psychology* (Vol. 2, pp. 221–267). London: Academic Press.

McCombs, B. L. (2003). Applying educational psychology's knowledge base in educational reform: From research to application to policy. In W. M. Reynolds & G. E. Miller (Eds.), *Contemporary handbook of psychology: Vol 7. Educational psychology* (pp. 583–607). New York: Wiley.

McGraw, K., & McCullers, J. (1979). Evidence of a detrimental effect of extrinsic incentives on breaking a mental set. *Journal of Experimental Social Psychology, 15,* 285–294.

Meece, J. L., Anderman, E. M., & Anderman, L. H. (2006). Classroom goal structure, student motivation, and academic achievement. *Annual Review of Psychology, 57,* 487–503.

Meece, J. L., Blumenfeld, P., Hoyle, R. (1988). Students' goals orientations and cognitive engagement in classroom activities. *Journal of Educational Psychology, 80,* 514–523.

Meece, J. L., Herman, P., & McCombs, B. (2003). Relations of learner-centered teaching practices to adolescents' achievement goals. *International Journal of Educational Research, 39,* 457–475.

Midgley, C., Anderman, E. M., & Hicks, L. (1995). Differences between elementary and middle school teachers and students: A goal theory approach. *Journal of Early Adolescence, 15,* 90–113.

Midgley, C., Kaplan, A., Middleton, M., Maehr, M. L., Urdan, T., Hicks Anderman, L., et al. (1998). The development and validation of scales assessing students' achievement goal orientations. *Contemporary Educational Psychology, 23,* 113–131.

Miller, R. B., Greene, B. A., Montalvo, G. P., Ravindran, B., & Nichols, J. D. (1996). Engagement in academic work: The role of learning goals, future consequences, pleasing others and perceived ability. *Contemporary Educational Psychology, 21,* 388–422.

Morgan, M. (1981). The overjustification effect: a developmental test of self-perception interpretations. *Journal of Personality and Social Psychology, 40,* 809–821.

Nakamura, J., & Csikszentmihalyi, M. (2003). The motivational sources of creativity as viewed from the paradigm of positive psychology. In L. G. Aspinwall & U. M. Staudinger (Eds.), *A psychology of human strengths: Fundamental questions and future directions for positive psychology* (pp. 257–269). Washington, DC: American Psychological Association.

Newell, A., Shaw, J., & Simon, H. (1962). The processes of creative thinking. In H. Gruber, G. Terrell, & M. Wertheimer (Eds.), *Contemporary approaches to creative thinking* (pp. 63–119). New York: Atherton.

Nicholls, J. G. (1984). Achievement motivation: Conceptions of ability, subjective experience, task choice, and performance. *Psychological Review, 91,* 328–346.

Ochese, R. A. 1990. *Before the gates of excellence: The determinants of creative genius*. Cambridge, UK: Cambridge University Press.

O'Hara, L. A., & Sternberg, R. J. (2001). It doesn't hurt to ask: Effects of instructions to be creative, practical or analytical on essay-writing performance and their interaction with students' thinking styles. *Creativity Research Journal*, 13, 197–210.

Pallak, S. R., Costomiris, S., Sroka, S., & Pittman, T. S. (1982). School experience, reward characteristics, and intrinsic motivation. *Child Development*, 53, 1382–139.

Pintrich, P. R. (2000). The role of goal orientation in self-regulated learning. In M. Boekaerts, P. R. Pintrich, & M. Zeidner (Eds.), *Handbook of self-regulation* (pp. 452–502). San Diego: Academic Press.

Pittman, T. S., Emery, J., & Boggiano, A. K. (1982). Intrinsic and extrinsic motivational orientations: Reward-induced changes in preference for complexity. *Journal of Personality and Social Psychology*, 42, 789–797.

Pollak, S. (1992). *The effects of motivational orientation and constraint on the creativity of the artist*. Unpublished manuscript.

Pope, R. (2005). *Creativity: Theory, history, practice*. New York: Routledge.

Pretty, G., & Seligman, C. (1983). Affect and the overjustification effect. *Journal of Personality and Social Psychology*, 46, 1241–1253.

Ransen, D. (1980). The mediation of reward-induced motivation decrements in early and middle childhood: A template matching approach. *Journal of Personality and Social Psychology*, 35, 49–55.

Reeve, J., Cole, S., & Olson, B. (1986). Adding excitement to intrinsic motivation research. *Journal of Social Behavior and Personality*, 1, 349–363.

Roeser, R. W., Midgley, C. M., & Urdan, T. C. (1996). Perceptions of the school psychological environment and early adolescents' psychological and behavioral functioning in school: The mediating role of goals and belonging. *Journal of Educational Psychology*, 88, 408–422.

Rogers, C. R. (1954). Towards a theory of creativity. *ETC: A Review of General Semantics*, 11, 249–260.

Ross, L. (1977). The intuitive psychologist and his shortcomings: Distortions in the attribution process. In L. Berkowitz (Ed.), *Advances in experimental social psychology* (Vol. 10, pp. 173–220). New York: Academic Press.

Ryan, R. M. (1982). Control and information in the intrapersonal sphere: An extension of cognitive evaluation theory. *Journal of Personality and Social Psychology*, 43, 450–461.

Sansone, C., & Harackiewicz, J. M. (1996). "I don't feel like it": The function of interest in self-regulation. In L. Martin & A. Tesser (Eds.), *Striving and feeling: Interactions among goals, affect, and self-regulation* (pp. 203–228). Mahwah, NJ: Erlbaum.

Sansone, C., & Harackiewicz, J. M. (1998). "Reality" is complicated. *American Psychologist*, 53, 673–674.

Sansone, C., & Harackiewicz, J. (Eds.). (2000). *The search for optimal motivation and performance*. San Diego CA: Academic Press.

Shalley, C. E., & Perry-Smith, J. E. (2001). Effects of social-psychological factors on creative performance: The role of informational and controlling expected evaluation and modeling experience. *Organizational Behavior and Human Decision Processes*, 84, 1–22.

Shapira, Z. (1976). Expectancy determinants of intrinsically motivated behavior. *Journal of Personality and Social Psychology*, 39, 1235–1244.

Shin, S., & Zhou, J. (2007). When is educational specialization heterogeneity related to creativity in research and development teams? Transformational leadership as a moderator. *Journal of Applied Psychology*, 92, 1709–21.

Shultz, T., Butkowsky, I., Pearce, J., & Shanfield, H. (1975). The development of schemes for the attribution of multiple psychological causes. *Developmental Psychology*, 11, 502–510.

Smith, M. C. (1975). Children's use of the multiple sufficient cause schema in social perception. *Journal of Personality and Social Psychology*, 32, 737–747.

Stein, M. I. (1974). *Stimulating creativity* (Vols. 1–2). New York: Academic Press.

Stipek, D. J., & Kowalski, P. S. (1989). Learned helplessness in task-orienting versus performance-orienting testing conditions. *Journal of Educational Psychology*, 81, 384–391.

Torrance, E. P. (1968). A longitudinal examination of the fourth grade slump in creativity. *Gifted Child Quarterly*, 12, 195–199.

Torrance, E. P. (1990). *The Torrance Tests of Creative Thinking Norms-Technical Manual Figural (Streamlined) Forms A & B*. Bensenville, IL: Scholastic Testing Service.

Treffinger, D. J. (1985). Review of the Torrance Tests of Creative Thinking. In J. V. Mitchell

Jr. (Ed.), *The ninth mental measurements yearbook* (pp. 1632–1634). Lincoln: Buros Institute of Mental Measurements, University of Nebraska.

Tsigilis, N., & Theodosiou, A. (2003). Temporal stability of the Intrinsic Motivation Inventory. *Perceptual and Motor Skills, 97*, 271–280.

Vallerand, R. J., Pelletier, L. G., & Koestner, R. (2008). Reflections on self-determination theory. *Canadian Psychology/Psychologie Canadienne, 49*, 257–262.

Vansteenkiste, M., Lens, W., & Deci, E. L. (2006). Intrinsic versus extrinsic goal contents in self-determination theory: Another look at the quality of academic motivation. *Educational Psychologist, 41*, 19–3

Wallach, M. A., & Wing, C. W. (1969). *The talented student: A validation of the creativity-intelligence distinction.* New York: Holt, Rinehart, & Winston.

White, R. (1959). Motivation reconsidered: The concept of competence. *Psychological Review, 66*, 297–333.

Wolters, C. A. (2004). Advancing achievement goal theory: Using goal structures and goal orientations to predict students' motivation, cognition, and achievement. *Journal of Educational Psychology, 96*, 236–250.

CHAPTER 19

Individual and Group Creativity

R. Keith Sawyer

Creativity researchers are scientists who study how new things are created by human beings. We seek to answer a basic research question: What is the best scientific explanation of how new things are created? In addition to this basic research question, creativity researchers also seek to answer an applied question: How can we use these explanations to provide advice to people, groups, and organizations about how to increase their ability to generate new and useful things?

The evidence resulting from this scientific exploration could lead us to conclude that the best explanations of creativity are couched in the language of psychology: Creativity might be best explained in terms of properties and laws about people's mental states, personality traits, and behaviors. However, there is a second possible outcome to this research project: The scientific study of how new things emerge could instead conclude that the emergence of new things is best explained in terms of groups, or in terms of social and cultural context. These two possibilities might combine to lead to a third possible outcome: The best scientific

explanation of creativity might be hybrid, incorporating properties of both individuals and groups. This is the issue I address in this chapter: What is the proper *level of analysis* at which to explain how new things are created?

I review several influential arguments in favor of both individual explanation and collective explanation. These arguments have a long history in the philosophy of the social sciences and in sociological theory, and they have been applied to a wide range of psychological and social phenomena, including economic behavior, social evolution, and social and cognitive development. Building on these arguments, I present a framework, *collaborative emergence*, that combines both individual and collective explanation. I apply this framework to analyze two empirical examples of group creativity – an improvisational performance and a work team. My discussion of these examples demonstrates how the framework of collaborative emergence can be used to determine the relative benefits of individual-level explanation and group-level explanation when examining any specific case of creativity. I conclude by arguing that the best scientific explanations of creativity will involve multiple levels of analysis: They will incorporate properties and laws associated with individuals and with groups. I provide some guidelines for how to proceed, drawing on how other scientific disciplines approach these same issues regarding levels of analysis and scientific explanation.

1. Scientific Explanation

As creativity researchers, we want to explain the emergence of new things from human activity. Explanations are attempts to account for *why* things happen – singular events or regular, repeatable patterns. The things of interest to creativity researchers are specific instances of new things emerging, or regular repeatable patterns of new things emerging. In the philosophy of science, there is a long history of discussion surrounding scientific explanation; I briefly describe two influential positions: the deductive-nomological (DN) or covering-law approach (Hempel, 1965), and the mechanistic approach (Bechtel & Richardson, 1993; Hedström & Swedberg, 1998).

In the covering-law approach, a phenomenon is said to be explained when salient properties of the event are shown to be consequences of general laws, in combination with known antecedent conditions. A strength of the covering-law approach is that laws both explain *and* predict; once a law is discovered, it can be used both to explain past phenomena and also to predict when similar phenomena will occur in the future.

Covering-law models have always been problematic in the social sciences – including in psychology – primarily because of difficulty translating the notion of "law" to social reality. Try to think of a creativity law: It's hard to identify a lawful relation that is supported by creativity research, one that both explains and predicts. One possible candidate is the widely reproduced finding that brainstorming groups have fewer ideas than nominal groups composed of the same

number of solitary individuals (Paulus & Nijstad, 2003), a law that holds at the group level of analysis rather than the psychological level. But is this a law, in the same sense as the ideal gas law (pressure equals temperature times density)? The problem is that candidates for psychological and social laws always have exceptions. On average, brainstorming groups have fewer ideas than nominal groups, but there could occasionally be an unusual brainstorming group that proved to be an exception. Laws with exceptions are problematic in the DN approach, and this is why there is a history of debate concerning whether psychological or social laws exist at all. Philosophers of social science have taken various positions on the status of these laws (Beed & Beed, 2000; Blau, 1983; Giddens, 1984; Kincaid, 1990; Little, 1993; McIntyre, 1996). Much of this discussion centers on what constitutes a law: Must it be invariant and universal, or can it admit of some exceptions? Even the strongest advocates of lawful explanation admit that there are no exceptionless laws outside of the natural sciences.

In the last decade or so, philosophers of biology (Bechtel & Richardson, 1993; Craver, 2007; Machamer, Darden, & Craver, 2000) and philosophers of social science (Elster, 1989; Hedström & Swedberg, 1998) have begun to develop a new approach to explanation that is based on causal mechanisms rather than laws. In the mechanism approach, a phenomenon is said to be explained when the realizing mechanism that gave rise to the phenomenon is sufficiently described. A mechanistic explanation of an event traces the causal processes and interactions leading up to that event, and it also describes the processes and interactions that make up the event. Rather than a covering-law explanation in terms of laws and regularities, a mechanism approach provides explanations by postulating the processes constituted by the operation of mechanisms that generate the observed phenomenon. A mechanist would argue that the brainstorming law I proposed above, although it describes an observed regularity, is not an explanation of the observed phenomenon. A mechanist would attempt to explain the regularity by identifying individual mental processes of the participants, and the interactional processes among the participants, that ultimately resulted in the total number of ideas generated by the group. This fundamentally reductionist approach is called *methodological individualism*: It attempts to explain an observed group-level regularity in terms of mental states and actions of the individual members of the group.

2. Mechanisms and Emergence

Many systems in nature contain hundreds, thousands, or millions of components, all of which interact in dense, overlapping networks. Many such systems are *chaotic*, highly nonlinear and essentially impossible to explain and predict from mechanisms and laws. The atmosphere is a chaotic system, and this makes weather prediction difficult. Weather forecasts are not derived from mechanisms and laws relating individual molecules in the atmosphere, but instead from historical trends. But in some systems, a relatively simple higher-level order emerges from quite complex lower-level processes. Such systems manifest many features that make them difficult to explain using a reductionist approach that would first analyze and explain the components, and then the components' interactions, to derive an explanation of the higher-level pattern. Complexity scientists have long invoked the human brain as a prototypical example of a complex system (Bechtel & Richardson, 1993). It is this complexity that enables the human mind to generate novelty. More recently, complexity scientists have argued that many social systems are complex systems that share many systemic properties with other complex systems, including the human mind (Sawyer, 2005). This raises the possibility that complex social systems could generate novelty (cf. the concept of "distributed creativity," (Sawyer & DeZutter, 2009). If so, a complete scientific explanation of creativity would have to include detailed accounts of both psychological and social mechanisms.

In my empirical work, I study mechanisms of *collaborative emergence* in small groups (Sawyer 2003b). Group behavior must be thought of as emergent in those cases where there is not a structured plan guiding the group, and where there is no leader who directs the group. Examples of collaborative emergence include everyday conversation, small-group collaborations, brainstorming sessions, and discussion seminars. All of these phenomena are *improvisational*, because there is no director and no guiding script. Consequently, as an ideal type of collaborative emergence, I have conducted several studies of creative improvisational performances, including jazz, improvisational theater, and children's fantasy play (Sawyer, 1997, 2003a, 2003b). Example 1 presents an example of collaborative emergence drawn from my study of improvisational theater (Sawyer, 2003b). After completing these studies, I began to apply the ideal type explanation, that emerged from analyzing these groups, to study a broader range of group creative phenomena, including project teams, study groups, classroom discussions, and leadership teams. Example 2 presents an example of collaborative emergence in a work team.

The transcript in Example 1 is taken from a performance from Spring 1993, by the Chicago theater group, Jazz Freddy (Sawyer, 2003b, pp. 193–194). On this night, the group asked the audience for an event and a location. The suggestions taken were "The Olympics" (the event) and "A convent" (the location). The group then proceeded to perform for almost an hour, with an intermission halfway through the performance. Figure 1 represents the first 2.5 minutes of the performance. Note that the actors do not use props; all actions described are mimed.

EXAMPLE 1
Lights up. MAN carries a chair to front stage right and sits facing audience. He mimes working at a desk – takes a cap off of a pen, opens a book, starts to make underlining motions as he studies the page. He stops to rub his eyes. He then turns the page, and underlines some more. The other

actors watch intently from the sides of the stage; the audience is completely quiet. After about 20 seconds, WOMAN stands up from her position at the opposite side of the stage, and walks over to MAN, miming the act of carrying something in both hands, held in front of her:

1	WOMAN:	Here are those papers.	Puts down the "papers."
2	(2 second pause)		She remains standing.
3	MAN:	Thanks	Looks up to face WOMAN
		(2 second pause)	
4		I really appreciate your doing those copies for me.	
5	*A second man, MAN 2, approaches from stage left, also carrying "papers," and stops next to WOMAN.*		
6	MAN 2:	Here are those papers.	Puts down the papers.
7	MAN	Thanks a lot,	Still facing the two
8		You guys have really been great. (2 second pause)	
9		I'm gonna stop booking for now	Closes book on desk.
10	WOMAN:	//OK//	
11	MAN 2:	//Sure// (1 second pause)	
12		I'm gonna go get some more papers.	
13	MAN:	Alright (1 second pause)	He stands up
14		Thanks a lot, I appreciate it.	
15	MAN 2:	You're welcome. (1 second pause)	
16		We mean it.	
17	*(As he says this, MAN 2 touches WOMAN's arm; woman reaches up her other hand to grasp his hand; they stand holding hands.)*		
18	MAN:	Thanks for being in my corner.	
19	MAN 2:	We always will be.	

This improvisational theater dialogue displays the essential characteristics of collaborative emergence. First, note the many pauses between turns, more frequent and longer than a typical conversation. The actors do this to leave space for everyone to contribute equally, and to wait for inspiration to emerge collectively from the group. Improv theater has an egalitarian ethos; there is no group leader, and actors frown on actors who try to control a scene too much.

The second feature to notice is the relative *lack of specificity*. After 2.5 minutes, it is hard to understand what is going on. This is intentional; the actors leave many things unresolved, knowing that the group will eventually collectively begin to make sense of these unfolding dialogues. In these early stages, the actors are actually trying to generate complexity and ambiguity, because they know from experience that the complexity of information leads to greater group creativity later in the performance.

The third feature of this dialogue is *moment to moment contingency*: At any moment, the scene can take a wide range of different directions, and no single actor's action ever fixes the future flow of the performance. Unlimited options are available at the beginning of the scene, of course. MAN could have chosen a different activity; or another actor might have entered the scene first. The determination of who will begin the scene is itself emergent from the split-second decisions of all 10 actors. Likewise, any of the nine remaining actors could have entered the scene next, during the 20-second period when all of them were watching him "study." The ensemble does not choose which actors will be in a scene, nor their order. A different actor may have been just a split-second away from deciding to stand up, but WOMAN made the first move.

At line 1, WOMAN could have chosen a wide range of activities and utterances. Improv actors are taught that everything introduced by a fellow actor must be accepted, and then elaborated – the "Yes, And" rule. Thus WOMAN must accept everything MAN has done nonverbally – and it is fairly clear to this largely college-educated audience that he is studying. By saying "Here are those papers" she provides several new pieces of information – she implies that the man's activity is part of a larger project; that there is a group of individuals (at least two) participating collaboratively in the effort. She also suggests that not only are books involved, but "papers" as well. This is not surprising; but neither would hundreds of other possible actions have been any more surprising. For example, she could have said "Joe! What are you doing in my neighborhood coffee shop?" suggesting a casual friendship and a public location. She could have said "Staying late again today, eh?" suggesting a collegial office encounter between peers. She could have established a status relationship by saying, for example, "Don't forget to take care of that Johnson report before you leave."

Likewise, in his response at lines 3 and 4, MAN has hundreds of possible actions that would have seemed equally coherent and plausible. At line 4, MAN suggests an asymmetrical status relationship, by proposing that WOMAN has done the copies for him. It would have been just as dramatically coherent for MAN to take on a subordinate relationship; for example, he could have said "I can't believe you're giving me more work, it's already 8pm!" Or he could have hinted at a conspiratorial scenario: "I can't believe you managed to get those papers! Who did you pay off?" The contingency that is present at each line of dialogue multiplies from turn to turn, resulting in combinatorial complexity of possible scenes. This is a classic property of complex dynamical systems – their rapidly expanding combinatorial possibility.

A fourth feature of this dialogue is *retroactive meaning*: No single actor can know the real meaning of his or her own utterance until the other actors have responded. The meaning of each line is retroactively determined by the collective flow of the dialogue. For example, WOMAN's line 2, "Here are those papers," could have been treated as either the command of a supervisor, or the report of a subordinate. The complete meaning is dependent on the flow of the subsequent dialogue. And not only these two actors are involved; all 10 actors are involved, because the entire group collaboratively determines – through their actions *and* nonactions – which actors will enter a scene. Because meaning is retroactively determined, any one actor's intentions and goals have limited explanatory power.

By line 19, a few dramatic elements are starting to emerge. MAN and MAN 2 seem to be coworkers, yet MAN's repeated "Thanks" also seems to imply that MAN 2 and WOMAN are helping him out of friendship, or that they are going beyond the call of duty. This seems to be a high-pressure situation, one that involves working late, a large volume of work already done, and still more to be done; and a possible "us against them" mentality. All of these dramatic elements are *emergent* – they have emerged from the collective interaction and creative contributions of all three actors. No single actor has determined the direction of the scene.

By the intermission, 30 minutes later, Jazz Freddy had created two completely independent plot lines, one inspired by each of the two audience suggestions. The Olympics plot was about a baseball team training for the Olympics, and John had become an umpire who wasn't very good and probably needed glasses. The second plot took place at a convent, where nuns were staying up late playing cards and spray-painting graffiti on the religious murals. In the second act, the actors managed to weave these two plots together. The baseball games get ugly as the team becomes filled with hate for their opponents, and the play ends with several of the female baseball players quitting the sport to join the convent. Note how little of this could have been predicted after reading the initial dialogue in Example 1; this unpredictability is characteristic of collaborative emergence.

Example 2 presents a second example of collaborative emergence, this time drawn from a creative work team. This is a transcript of a meeting of ten artists and writers working on the Cartoon Network's cartoon "Samurai Jack." Although the meetings are led by the cartoon's creator, Genndy Tartakovsky, he does not direct the course of the meeting; instead, he fosters a spirit of participatory collaboration designed to encourage new ideas to emerge from the group's conversation. In Example 2, a writer named Andy has come up with the seed of an idea for a new episode. Whenever one of the others speaks up I have simply indicated "Artist":

EXAMPLE 2
Story meeting of the Samurai Jack team (from Wilkinson, 2002):

Andy   We're looking to do the story we talked about, where Jack gets infected with a virus and it takes over his arm. Then it would slowly take over his whole body. Then half of him becomes evil, and he's going to fight himself.

Tartakovsky   How do we set it up?

Artist   Could he have battled Aku, and Aku has a cold, and he sneezes on him?

Tartakovsky   (nods) It's almost like we're at the end of another show with a great fight. Except this one starts with a battle. And he's fighting these robots, and Aku's commanding them. It's cold and drafty, and Aku starts sneezing, and says, "Oy, I've got to get some chicken soup."

Artist   Oy?

Artist   How do we get it out that he's infected?

Artist   We had talked about him showing a guy his face. And it's half in shadow.

Artist   He becomes Aku.

Artist   He becomes *Jaku*.

Artist   The more evil he becomes, the more erratic his body is.

Artist   Maybe somebody's getting robbed, he saves him, and the guy thanks him, and he's walking away, and in Jack's other hand is the guy's watch.

Artist   Do we need to find somebody to summon him? Is there a psychic battle with himself?

Artist   Or a fight in his head? I was thinking, he knows a place to cleanse himself – a monastery. And the monks help him.

Artist   The B story is no one's trusting Jack – they see him and they run.

Tartakovsky   It's always stronger if Jack can help himself. I like the image of Jack as Aku with one eye. I like it half and half. The more I think about it, the body of the show is him fighting himself.

Artist   He realizes he'd better get out of the city before he hurts someone, so he travels to a village.

Tartakovsky   I still want to keep it real simple, though.

Artist   At the monastery, they tie him up so he can't do any harm.

Tartakovsky   Does Aku know that Jack has what he has?

Artist   No, he's too sick.

As with staged theater improvisations, in Example 2 no one is in charge, and no one creates any more than anyone else. Even though the discussion started with Andy's idea, he said nothing after getting it started. And even though Tartakovsky is the group leader, he does not dominate the group. The cartoon that is eventually produced, a collective creation of ten people, collaboratively emerges from the group's dialogue. This is a common mode of operation for the creative teams that generate movies, videogames, music videos, and television shows (Pritzker & Runco, 1997; Sawyer, 2007).

Examples 1 and 2 demonstrate how collaborative emergence results from the interactions of individuals. But although group creativity emerges from individual creative acts, these phenomena are difficult to understand by simply analyzing the members of the group individually. Explanations focused on the mental states and behaviors of individual actors cannot provide a complete explanation of how the final performance emerges from the group. For example, because meaning is retroactively determined, an actor's intentions when forming an utterance are not explanatorily relevant to how that utterance contributes to the scene. Also in brainstorming groups (Sawyer, 2007) and in work teams like Example 2, one person's idea is often transformed and reinterpreted by the ensuing thought process of the group. Because of moment-to-moment contingency, no one act meaningfully explains or predicts what happens next.

Many philosophers of mind use emergentist concepts to argue that the mind is emergent from, but not reducible to, the biological brain (Sawyer, 2002a). It could be the case that the psychology of creativity would ultimately reduce to neuroscience. If this comes to pass, the *Cambridge Handbook of Creativity* in the year 2050 might look very different from today's. But owing to emergence, it could also be the case that neuroscience could never fully explain mental processes of ideation; that a science of creativity would always of necessity involve an irreducibly psychological level of analysis. Using a similarly structured argument, many sociological theorists use emergence to argue that collective phenomena are collaboratively created by individuals, yet are not reducible to individual action (Sawyer, 2005). These accounts argue that although only individuals exist, collectives possess emergent properties that are irreducibly complex and thus cannot be reduced to individual properties. These arguments likewise provide grounds to claim that some creative processes and outcomes could require social-group level explanations and are not be reducible to individual psychological explanation.

How could one determine whether or not a given psychological phenomenon was reducible to neurobiological explanation? Likewise, how could one determine whether or not a given social phenomenon was reducible to individual psychological explanation? To answer this question, I have developed an account of emergence that I call *nonreductive individualism* (NRI) (Sawyer, 2005). Some emergent social properties may be real – and necessarily figure in scientific explanations, just like real properties at any other level of analysis (including at the psychological level). A presentation of this account is beyond the scope of this chapter; but in the following section, I draw on this account to help answer the question: Which instances of creativity are likely to require both individual- and group-level explanations?

3. Characteristics of Collaborative Emergence

Ultimately, the determination of whether or not the emergence of something new can be explained at the individual psychological level of analysis, or whether the complete explanation requires group-level properties, laws, and mechanisms, is an empirical question that must be resolved anew with each instance of creativity. However, there is a large body of research in complexity science, and on emergence more generally, that has identified the characteristics of systems that are more likely to be irreducible to scientific explanations solely in terms of the component parts of the system. Creative outputs from social systems that have the following characteristics are more likely to require group-level accounts:

1. Unpredictability
2. Non-reducibility to models of participating agents
3. Processual intersubjectivity
4. Individual agency and creative potential on the part of individual agents
5. The cost of explanation

1. *Unpredictability*

Almost all emergentists argue for the unpredictability of complex emergent system behavior from laws at the lower level. In the improv theater transcript in Example 1, no actor knows what is going to happen next. At each point in the improvisation, the actor can choose from a wide range of moves to propel the dramatic frame forward. Each turn is unpredictable and novel, accumulating to result in a collaboratively created, novel performance. No actor knows how his turn will be interpreted by the others; each turn gains its final meaning only from the ensuing flow of discourse. Thus, the actor's intention does not fully constrain the eventual dramatic meaning of the turn; each turn of dialogue, although spoken by a single actor, eventually takes on a dramatic meaning that is determined by a collaborative, emergent process.

2. *Not Reducible to Models of Component Parts*

Bechtel and Richardson (1993) argue that emergent systems do not demonstrate any of the characteristics of reducible systems: direct localization, near decomposability, functional and physical independence of units, and linearity. The discipline of psychology often implicitly accepts a version of reductionism that is referred to as *methodological individualism* because it assumes that all properties of group behavior can be reduced to, and ultimately derived from, properties of individuals (Lukes, 1977).

These assumptions lead psychologists to consider creativity – even when it emerges from collaborating groups or complex organizations – to ultimately be a property of human minds, thus requiring psychological explanation. The main threads of creativity research within psychology have all been individualistic: for example, cognitive scientific theories of analogical thinking or conceptual combination; or personality trait researchers' measures of "divergent thinking" or "stylistic preferences." These approaches are methodologically individualist in holding that creativity involves human agency, intentionality, decision making, and problem solving, and that social groups themselves cannot be explanatorily relevant to creativity (except in how they impinge on individuals).

Individualist psychology does not provide very helpful explanations of collaboratively emergent phenomena such as improvisational theater. An actor's intention for an utterance is not necessarily the eventual meaning of the utterance; in the above transcript, the actors purposely generate utterances with ambiguous interpretations, knowing that the other actors will later attribute more specific meanings to them. Likewise, no single actor can decide the direction that the scene will take; decision

making, if it can be said to exist at all, is a collective social process.

3. *Intersubjectivity*

One possible non-emergence account of Example 1 would be to claim that the first MAN to enter the stage established the activity of studying, and everything that the other actors do simply followed from that. But this cannot be correct; I have suggested a few of the alternative possibilities that were available at each line of dialogue. Nonetheless, this claim gets at an important truth of improvisation: Once properties of the dramatic scene are established, they become collective property, and constrain all of the actors. MAN does in fact establish the act of studying (or "working"), and this act constrains MAN 2 and WOMAN. Throughout the one-hour performance, there is an ever-changing dramatic *emergent* – a shared understanding of what has been established and what is going on – and the actors' future creativity has to proceed within the frame established by this emergent drama. But this constraining shared frame is itself an emergent social product; it is ever-changing, created in a bottom-up fashion from the actions of individual actors, yet once created, it constrains and influences the later actions of those individuals in a top-down fashion.

Traditionally, intersubjectivity is defined as a state of overlapping, symmetrical mental representations; two or more people are said to "have intersubjectivity" when their mental representations of the situation are in agreement. This traditional view is implicitly reductionist, because intersubjectivity is reduced to individual subjectivities and their additive relations. In other words, intersubjectivity, and hence all collective activity, is regarded as a simple sum of individual mental states (Matusov, 1996, p. 26).

The traditional account of intersubjectivity is inadequate to describe collaborative emergence, because there are many social interactions where participants do not share mental representations, such as disputes, arguments, and debates. In fact, even when there is no overt disagreement, it is unlikely that participants would have identical mental representations of what is going on. In the improv-theater transcript of Example 1, there is a high degree of ambiguity at each dialogue turn. Although each actor may have a rather different interpretation of what is going on and where the scene might be going, they can nonetheless proceed to collectively create a coherent dramatic frame. The key question about intersubjectivity is not how agents come to share identical representations, but rather how a coherent interaction can proceed even when they do not.

The traditional account of intersubjectivity does not leave room for novelty or for emergence, because it stresses the reproductive aspects of interaction – in interaction, I recreate something within your mental state, and you recreate something that was within mine. This view does not account for how something new could be created by group interaction. To properly represent collaborative emergence, we need to think of intersubjectivity as, following Matusov (1996), "a process of coordination of individual contributions to joint activity rather than as a state of agreement" (p. 34).

4. Creativity of the Components

Many complex systems in nature generate novelty even though they are composed of noncreative components. The human brain is a complex system, and its components are neurons; individual neurons are not creative under even the broadest definitions of creativity. In complex systems with noncreative components, the moment-to-moment contingency of the process of emergence is quite limited. Consequently, components can simply be designed to be prepared for all foreseeable emergents – like a computer program, or a detailed workflow diagram. In contrast, in collaborative emergence the degree of unpredictability of the interaction crosses a threshold at which the individuals must engage in cre-

ative behavior if they are to participate at all. A member of the Samurai-Jack writing team cannot predict how the final cartoon will shape up; the potential creative trajectories are innumerable. Thus, collaborative emergence requires individual agency and creative potential on the part of individual participants.

A complete scientific explanation of mental creativity might not require that neurobiological components be explicitly represented in the explanation; most psychologists who study creativity do not couch their explanations in terms of neuroscience. However, because the components of social systems are themselves creative individuals, a complete scientific explanation of social creativity is likely to involve psychological components.

5. The Cost of Explanation

Von Neumann, one of the founders of computer science, was the first to suggest that for complex systems, the simplest description of a complex system might be its simulation (von Neumann, 1949/1966, pp. 31–41, 47). For such systems, one cannot deduce all of its properties from the description of its mechanism; rather, the simulation must be run to determine its properties. Such arguments have become increasingly widespread in complexity science.

These insights have complex implications for psychological attempts to explain group creativity. First, they raise the possibility that for the creativity of groups and organizations, the only potential psychological "explanation" would be to develop a simulation of the mechanism that realized the group-level emergent behavior – the individuals in the group or organization, all of their psychological processes, and their interactions – and then to run the simulation. Second and more problematic, running and then analyzing the simulation might be less efficient than explanation in terms of group-level properties and laws. (This is why we still use the ideal gas law, even though statistical mechanics has provided us with a reductionist account of the mechanisms that realize the law.)

Dupré (1993) noted that reductionist work in the human sciences can give us good lower-level theories of *how* systems do what they do, but not exactly *what* those systems do. Lower-level mechanisms do not make predictions about how the system will change over time; to address these dynamic questions we may need to use the higher level, even when we already have a good mechanistic understanding of the realizing system (Godfrey-Smith, 1999, p. 177). Higher-level properties may be ineliminable because they provide the lowest-cost and highest-benefit descriptions of the regularities in the phenomena at that level (Wimsatt, 1976). If so, there are grounds for the retention of causal explanations at the higher level.

4. Types of Emergent Novelty

What is new? What is the exact nature of the novelty that emerges from a person, a group, or an organization? Methodological individualists, including most psychologists, claim that groups do not really create, because, after all, their creations are just composed of the creative ideas of their members. Why do we need to examine collaborative emergence, if all of the action is in individual minds?

Reductionists of various sorts have used such arguments to accuse emergentists of being nonscientific for more than 100 years. In the 1890s, the French sociologist Emile Durkheim had to defend his argument for a social level of analysis against individualist critics who accused him of positing a mysterious sociological substance, a "group mind" (Durkheim, 1895; Sawyer, 2005). In the 1920s, advocates of emergent evolution had to repeatedly and explicitly deny that they were vitalists (the belief that living things contained some additional substance in addition to physical matter); they held that their position was compatible with a thoroughly materialistic ontology, while at the same time extending beyond reductionist materialism (Morgan, 1923; Wheeler, 1928). Like their counterparts in the 1920s, today's emergent thinkers go to extremes to avoid associations with spooky, mysterious vitalism, coining terms like "emergent mechanism" (Bechtel & Richardson, 1993) or "emergentist materialism" (Bunge, 1977).

Emergent thinking often veers dangerously close to *dualist ontology*: if you claim that an emergent group creation has an ontological status distinct from the ideas of the members of the group, then you seem to be claiming that there is some entity or substance in addition to the material world. And if you deny that this is your claim, the materialist can accuse you of just being a confused, hypocritical materialist. The goal of most emergent thinkers, from Durkheim through the 1920s to today, is to navigate these difficulties and to establish a middle ground between reductionist individualism and reifying group properties. The difficulty arises because in creative multileveled systems, higher-level emergents seem to take on causal properties, and thus take on what seems to be an ontological status independent of the components. But where does this emergent property come from, if not from the lower-level interactions? What is the ontological status of these emergents?

In part, the ontological confusion results from the difference between emergent *process* and emergent *product* (Sawyer, 2003a). We usually think of creativity as resulting in a *product* – a painting, a scientific journal article – that has its own physical existence, apart from the creator, a product that can be copied and disseminated, taking on a life of its own. Something now exists that did not exist before the emergent process generated it. Although generated by an emergent process (either conceived of as being within the brain, or as being a social process), the end product is ontologically distinct from that process.

Yet many emergent systems do not generate ostensible products. To take a simple physical example, a volume of a gas inside a container generates the emergent property "pressure," but that pressure is not itself a product that results from the molecules in interaction. When the container is removed and the molecules dissipate, the "pressure" no longer exists. An improv theater performance is ephemeral in the same way as the pressure of a gas. After it is over, nothing remains but the memories of those who were present during the performance. Of course, in recent decades modern recording technology has made it possible to "productize" improvisational performances, but nonetheless most improvisations are not recorded (whether jazz, improv theater, or ritualized oral performance), and the participants perform with the intention of making the process work for that moment, not with the intention of generating a product to be viewed again. A language like English is emergent and collaboratively created, but it does not have an independent physical existence. Of course, several hundred years ago, technologies of printing, publishing, and systems of national standardization resulted in the publication of dictionaries and style guides that attempt to capture this emergent process in ostensible product form. But just as with improvised performance, this recording occurs after the emergence has occurred and does not change the processual essence of the emergence itself.

Keeping these thoughts in mind, I describe three types of emergent novelty:

1. Novel products
2. Collaborative emergence
3. Historical or evolutionary emergence

The latter two forms of emergence do not generate ostensible products. This discussion raises several fruitful questions for future research: Are there fundamental ontological differences between product-generating emergence, and non-product-generating emergence? Do these differences affect the decomposability or reducibility of such systems?

Type 1. Novel Products

In traditional creative domains, like the arts and sciences, an *ostensible product* is created. These creative disciplines require manipulation of some set of physical and/or conceptual objects that exist apart from the individual creator. The result of the creative process is an object with an existence independent of the creator. These products, in turn, influence the future creative acts of all members of the discipline upon viewing, analysis, and internalization.

Type 2. Collaborative Emergence

Some emergent processes are ephemeral; once an improv performance is over, there is nothing left. But the emergent nonetheless has top-down effects. In an improv theater performance, at every moment of the performance, the *emergent* – the collaboratively created dramatic frame – is a socially shared emergent entity, which constrains the next dramatic action.

The school of psychology known as *sociocultural psychology* has begun to focus on these types of emergent social processes (Rogoff, 1998; Sawyer, 2002b). One of its distinguishing features is its rejection of reductionist methods, and its attempt to explore emergent group phenomena. Socioculturalists argue that many phenomena of interest cannot be explained through reductionist analysis, because they emerge from group interaction. Sociocultural approaches include the lines of research called social constructivism, activity theory, computer supported collaborative work (CSCW; Stahl, 2006), and situated cognition (Robbins & Aydede, 2008). All of these approaches share a top-down view of human behavior and hold that social groups are emergent phenomena that cannot be understood by analyzing the individual members of the group. These researchers argue that reductionist analysis won't help us understand social groups – families, peers on the playground, or classrooms – because the analyst can't predict characteristics of the higher level from properties of a lower level.

A collaborative emergent is not a final end product; it is a constantly changing ephemeral property of the interaction, which in turn influences the emergent processes that are generating it. This results in both top-down and bottom-up processes; the emergent is initially created with bottom-up dialogic processes, but immediately it takes on constraining, or top-down, characteristics. In complex multilayered systems, top-down and bottom-up processes are always simultaneous and bidirectional.

Type 3. Historical Emergence

The emergence of a new molecule, new species, or new sensory organ falls into this category. As Morgan (1933) pointed out, some of these emergents can be retrospectively viewed as deterministic. For example, water is emergent from hydrogen and oxygen, and according to Morgan the properties of water could not be predicted from those of hydrogen and oxygen *before the first occurrence of water*; but after the first time, we can formulate laws with predictive power. Evolutionary biologists generally hold that we cannot predict which species would evolve at time t, even knowing fully the traits of existing species and the features of the environment at time t-1 (Gould, 1989).

Also in this category is the emergence of cultural and historical novelty – a political revolution, a new Creole language. Social entities like money, systems of exchange, and language are not individual creations but are emergent from complex social systems. Language is perhaps the prototype example of an emergent, collective product that is stable over time, although it is not represented by a product (until perhaps the advent of literacy). These types of emergence also involve processes of type-2 emergence, in complex and poorly understood ways (see Sawyer, 2005, Chapter 10).

In economics, the classic emergent is the commodity price (Arrow, 1994). Arrow argued that price formation cannot be explained with individualistic models, writing "What individual has chosen prices? In the formal theory, at least, no one. They are determined on (not by) social institutions known as markets" (p. 4). Arrow concluded that macrolevel social variables – which are emergent and unpredictable from individual behavior – are essential to studying all social systems.

5. Ratio of Novelty to Preexisting Structure

In emergent systems, the final state is the accumulation of hundreds or thousands of tiny emergent steps. This is the classical view of how new species emerge in evolutionary biology. From an evolutionary perspective, if there is to be continuity and novelty in evolution, "the viable novelty at each emergence must be very small indeed.... Novelties such as life and mind... are of such magnitude that we can regard them only as representing the final accumulative stages of a very long series of minimal emergences" (Wheeler, 1928, p. 24).

Incremental emergence is also characteristic of collaborative emergence. At each dialogue turn, an actor can modify the emergent only a small amount; after all, that has to be the case if it is to be collaborative. Is one turn the analog of one creative product in science? Is the course of a 5-minute scene more like the history of a scientific paradigm? These questions have rarely been addressed.

The incrementalist view is compatible with fields like the history of science, or the sociology of art – which take the position that each advance is only a tiny step forward in a larger historical story. In contrast, psychologists and cognitive scientists tend to think in terms of the ultimate endproduct of emergent novelty. A higher-level historical or sociological view generally reveals that there is a great deal of stability and structure to creative social systems (defined above the level of the individual) and that each emergent novelty is a rather small modification to the system.

6. Conclusion

In this chapter, I have drawn on well-established concepts in the philosophy of science to present a framework to help us think about the relation between individual and group creativity. This framework, collaborative emergence, does not argue for one or another form of explanation for any particular observed phenomenon. However, it suggests that it is an empirical question whether a specific instance of creativity is best described in terms of individual mental processes, or in terms of the social interactions of groups of individuals. It cannot be known a priori whether or not a given creation can be scientifically explained solely in terms of properties and laws about individuals. Drawing on theories of explanation and on complexity science, I presented several features of complex systems that are likely to lead them to require explanations that incorporate higher-level properties and laws.

Even if one cannot explain a creation using only psychological concepts and laws, creativity researchers might still be able to develop scientific explanations using concepts and laws of sociology, perhaps in combination with individual concepts and laws. In most scientific disciplines, it is uncontroversial that scientific explanation might include systems and mechanisms at higher levels of analysis (Wight, 2004). After all, individual properties such as creative insights and conceptual combinations are themselves realized in the lower-level substrate of neurons and their synaptic connections; on what grounds would a psychologist hold that mental properties should be allowed in a scientific explanation, but not social properties (Sawyer 2002a)?

Creativity research should be an interdisciplinary endeavor, bringing together scientists who are experts in multiple levels of analysis – neurons, mental states, groups, and organizations. Prominent creativity researchers including Mike Csikszentmihalyi and Howard Gardner have advocated for a "systems approach" that combines individualist perspectives with analyses of the social organization of creative fields, and the symbolic structure of creative domains. I have called this the *sociocultural* approach (Sawyer, 2006). If creative groups generate emergent phenomena that cannot be fully explained using the laws and concepts of individualist psychology, a full explanation of creativity will of necessity incorporate group-level laws and concepts. An interdisciplinary science of creativity has the potential to provide a more complete scientific explanation of how new things emerge from human activity.

References

Arrow, K. J. (1994). Methodological individualism and social knowledge. *The American Economic Review*, 84(2), 1–9. (Originally presented as the Richard T. Ely lecture at the American Economics Association, Boston, MA, January 3–5, 1994)

Bechtel, W., & Richardson, R. C. (1993). *Discovering complexity: Decomposition and localization as strategies in scientific research*. Princeton, NJ: Princeton University Press.

Beed, C., & Beed, C. (2000). Is the case for social science laws strengthening? *Journal for the Theory of Social Behaviour*, 30(2), 131–153.

Blau, P. M. (1983). Comments on the prospects for a nomothetic theory of social structure. *Journal for the Theory of Social Behaviour*, 13(3), 265–271.

Bunge, M. (1977). Commentary: Emergence and the mind. *Neuroscience*, 2, 501–509.

Craver, C. (2007). *Explaining the brain: Mechanisms and the mosaic unity of neuroscience*. New York: Oxford University Press.

Dupré, J. (1993). *The disorder of things: Metaphysical foundations of the disunity of science*. Cambridge, MA: Harvard University Press.

Durkheim, E. (1895/1964). *The rules of sociological method*. New York: Free Press. (Originally published as *Les règles de la méthode sociologique*, Paris: Alcan, 1895)

Elster, J. (1989). *Nuts and bolts for the social sciences*. New York: Cambridge University Press.

Giddens, A. (1984). *The constitution of society: Outline of the theory of structuration*. Berkeley: University of California Press.

Godfrey-Smith, P. (1999). Procrustes probably: Comments on Sober's "Physicalism from a probabilistic point of view." *Philosophical Studies*, 95(1–2), 175–181.

Gould, S. J. (1989). *Wonderful life: The Burgess Shale and the nature of history*. New York: W. W. Norton.

Hedström, P., & Swedberg, R. (Eds.). (1998). *Social mechanisms: An analytical approach to social theory*. New York: Cambridge University Press.

Hempel, C. G. (1965). *Aspects of scientific explanation and other essays in the philosophy of science*. New York: Free Press.

Kincaid, H. (1990). Defending laws in the social sciences. *Philosophy of the Social Sciences*, 20(1), 56–83.

Little, D. (1993). On the scope and limits of generalization in the social sciences. *Synthese*, 97(2), 183–207.

Lukes, S. (1977). Methodological individualism reconsidered. In S. Lukes (Ed.), *Essays in social theory* (pp. 177–186). New York: Columbia University Press.

Machamer, P., Darden, L., & Craver, C. F. (2000). Thinking about mechanisms. *Philosophy of Science*, 67, 1–25.

Matusov, E. (1996). Intersubjectivity without agreement. *Mind, Culture, and Activity*, 3(1), 25–45.

McIntyre, L. C. (1996). *Laws and explanation in the social sciences: Defending a science of human behavior*. Boulder, CO: Westview.

Morgan, C. L. (1923). *Emergent evolution*. London: Williams and Norgate. (Originally presented as the 1922 Gifford lectures at the University of St. Andrews)

Morgan, C. L. (1933). *The emergence of novelty*. London: Williams & Norgate Ltd.

von Neumann, J. (1949/1966). Theory and organization of complicated automata. In A. W. Burks (Ed.), *Theory of self-reproducing automata* (pp. 29–87). Urbana: University of Illinois Press. (Originally presented as five

lectures delivered at the University of Illinois in December 1949)

Paulus, P. B., & Nijstad, B. A. (2003). *Group creativity: Innovation through collaboration*. New York: Oxford University Press.

Pritzker, S., & Runco, M. A. (1997). The creative decision-making process in group situation comedy writing. In R. K. Sawyer (Ed.), *Creativity in performance* (pp. 115–141). Norwood, NJ: Ablex.

Robbins, P., & Aydede, M. (Eds.). (2008). *The Cambridge handbook of situated cognition*. New York: Cambridge University Press.

Rogoff, B. (1998). Cognition as a collaborative process. In D. Kuhn & R. S. Siegler (Eds.), *Handbook of child psychology: Vol. 2. Cognition, perception, and language* (5th ed., pp. 679–744). New York: Wiley.

Sawyer, R. K. (1997). Improvisational theater: An ethnotheory of conversational practice. In R. K. Sawyer (Ed.), *Creativity in performance* (pp. 171–193). Greenwich, CT: Ablex.

Sawyer, R. K. (2002a). Emergence in psychology: Lessons from the history of nonreductionist science. *Human Development*, 45, 2–28.

Sawyer, R. K. (2002b). Unresolved tensions in sociocultural theory: Analogies with contemporary sociological debates. *Culture & Psychology*, 8(3), 283–305.

Sawyer, R. K. (2003a). *Group creativity: Music, theater, collaboration*. Mahwah, NJ: Erlbaum.

Sawyer, R. K. (2003b). *Improvised dialogues: Emergence and creativity in conversation*. Westport, CT: Greenwood.

Sawyer, R. K. (2005). *Social emergence: Societies as complex systems*. New York: Cambridge University Press.

Sawyer, R. K. (2006). *Explaining creativity: The science of human innovation*. New York: Oxford University Press.

Sawyer, R. K. (2007). *Group genius: The creative power of collaboration*. New York: Basic Books.

Sawyer, R. K., & DeZutter, S. (2009). Distributed creativity: How collective creations emerge from collaboration. *Psychology of Aesthetics, Creativity, and the Arts*, 3(2), 81–92.

Stahl, G. (2006). *Group cognition: Computer support for building collaborative knowledge*. Cambridge, MA: MIT Press.

Wheeler, W. M. (1928). *Emergent evolution and the development of societies*. New York: Norton. (Portions originally presented at the symposium on emergence held in Cambridge, MA, September 14, 1926)

Wight, C. (2004). Theorizing the mechanisms of conceptual and semiotic space. *Philosophy of the Social Sciences*, 34(2), 283–299.

Wilkinson, A. (2002, May 27). Moody toons: The king of the cartoon network. *The New Yorker*, 76–81.

Wimsatt, W. C. (1976). Reductionism, levels of organization, and the mind-body problem. In G. G. Globus, G. Maxwell, & I. Slavodnik (Eds.), *Consciousness and the brain* (pp. 199–267). New York: Plenum.

CHAPTER 20

Creativity and Mental Illness

Paul J. Silvia and James C. Kaufman

Few scientific topics arouse vocal conflict and strong passions among creativity researchers, but the link between mental health and creativity is one of them. Are creative people more likely to suffer from mental health disorders? Are people with psychological disorders more likely to be creative? And if so, how and why does this happen? It is hard to tiptoe around this controversial topic: Recent books and reviews have taken bold and sometimes contradictory positions, such as that creativity and mental illness are absolutely unrelated (Schlesinger, 2009), basically unrelated (Sawyer, 2006; Weisberg, 2006), or deeply entwined (Kottler, 2005; Nettle, 2002).

This research area is one of the few scientific domains driven by popular books and the cultural imagination. The world has at least one too many movies about tortured painters, narcissistic architects, depressed poets, and drug-addicted musicians. Perhaps it is hard to find dramatic incident in a movie about a photographer who gets a BFA degree in Studio Art, attends graduate school to refine her skills, and then spends decades honing her craft and reputation. If pop culture is our guide, there are no great writers who write for a few hours in the morning and then spend the afternoon playing tennis and drinking martinis (Talese, 2006).

What does research show about creativity and mental illness? If we can set aside our strong feelings and cultural prejudices, what does the evidence tell us? Recent writings have exhaustively reviewed past research (Kaufman, 2009; Weisberg, 2006) and appraised the field's thorny methodological issues (Schlesinger, 2009). Instead of beginning this chapter with a review of the studies, we will instead start with a conceptual groundwork for thinking about the problem before discussing some of the landmark findings. This area needs more research, but we hope to motivate future research that avoids the problems that have beset this complicated and controversial topic.

Conceptual and Methodological Issues

The Dark Art of Case Studies

In the study of creativity and mental illness, researchers want to have their case studies but eat them, too. It is standard in this field to bemoan the problems with case studies and to criticize books that have used such studies exclusively. At the same time, many researchers smuggle case studies through the back door, particularly when they hold up particular creators as compelling examples or counterexamples. Someone who believes that American writers tend to be troubled, for example, might discuss John Cheever, William Faulkner, and F. Scott Fitzgerald, three writers who struggled with alcoholism. But someone who believes that writers tend to be resilient, resourceful, and healthy might discuss Toni Morrison, Gay Talese, and Tom Wolfe, three living legends who seem to be doing just fine.

We agree that case-study methods have problems, but the problems are perhaps not what people think they are. The standard criticism of case studies, of course, concerns generality: It's hard to know how well conclusions based on one person apply to another person. The generality criticism is sound, but it isn't the main problem with case-study methods as applied to creativity and mental health. In fact, it's immaterial, for this topic, that case studies involve a single participant. After all, some of the most incisive research in creativity has involved only one participant, such as Simonton's (1989, 1997, 2004) analyses of Shakespeare or Kozbelt's analyses of Mozart (Kozbelt, 2005) and Beethoven (Kozbelt, 2007). The problem is research design, not sample size. In a "one-shot case study" design (Campbell & Stanley, 1966), one person or sample is assessed once – and that's it. As Campbell and Stanley (1966) claim, "securing scientific evidence involves making at least one comparison" (p. 6). Without comparison, contrast, or covariance, we can't draw scientific conclusions from our observations.

The problem of generality is not generality across people; the bigger problem is generality across judges. In Cronbach's generalizability model, variance is partitioned into facets (Cronbach, 1982; Cronbach, Gleser, Nanda, & Rajaratnam, 1972). Participants, the objects of study, are one source of variance; other interesting sources include fac-

tors such as time of assessment, types of methods, assessment location, raters and judges, and their interactions. The hard question, we think, is whether case studies of creativity and mental illness generalize across judges – the people conducting the case analysis. Typically, one researcher picks the creator to analyze, appraises the creator's mental health, assesses the person's creative accomplishments, and makes inferences about the how the symptoms relate to the accomplishments. The one-shot case study thus has only one participant and one judge – as a result, the judge and participant are confounded.

As an illustration of the single-judge problem, we can consider the case of William Saroyan (Balakian, 1998; Lee & Gifford, 1984; Legget, 2002). Saroyan is one of the few writers to become an adjective (the Saroyanesque style) and to succeed in several literary domains: He won an Academy Award (for *The Human Comedy*) and a National Drama Critics Circle Award (for *The Time of Your Life*), and he published several landmark works of short fiction (*My Name is Aram, The Daring Young Man on the Flying Trapeze*) and memoir (*Places Where I've Done Time, Obituaries*). A psychologist could conclude that Saroyan's life shows signs of hypomania. Ebullient, extraverted, gregarious, and grandiose, Saroyan published his best-known work early in his career. He eventually struggled with alcoholism and gambling – two common problems associated with the mania spectrum – and never regained his literary fame. In this case analysis, Saroyan was a classic creative burn-out: His manic symptoms caused early success and later failure.

Another judge, however, might draw different conclusions. Saroyan had an explosive early career, publishing award-winning plays and screenplays and several acclaimed books. His struggles with gambling and alcoholism clearly damaged his relationships and derailed his career, leading to a period of inferior creative work. But Saroyan, unlike many other writers, overcame his addictions and returned to writing. Deciding to avoid the genres and themes that made him famous – short stories and plays – Saroyan turned in the 1960s to literary non-fiction, an emerging genre in American writing. For his remaining years, he published a diverse range of memoir, criticism, and essays. Saroyan is particularly remembered for his wide-ranging and experimental contributions to the practice of memoir, such as memoir expressed via descriptions of places, friends' obituaries, letters to infamous people, and impressionistic diaries. Some of his best writing was published in this period; his final book, *Obituaries*, was nominated for an American Book Award. In this case analysis, Saroyan showed psychological resilience: He overcame his problems, reinvented himself as a writer, and achieved success in a new literary domain.

What can we conclude from a case analysis of William Saroyan? Not much, we think. Qualitative case studies are interesting in the way that all works of biography and memoir are interesting, but they have no scientific value for tackling the complicated problem of creativity and mental health. If one person can pick the subject, choose the standard for diagnosing symptoms, assess all of the variables, and draw the conclusions, then the method is simply too impressionistic and subjective. Did Saroyan's ebullience and grandiosity rise to the level of clinically relevant mania, or was he merely an energetic and eccentric person? Did his struggles with alcoholism reflect an underlying vulnerability, or was he merely one of millions of people who struggle with substance abuse?

A Domain-Specific Stereotype?

Many writers have suggested that people have a "mad-genius stereotype" (Kaufman, Bromley, & Cole, 2006; Plucker, Beghetto, & Dow, 2004). Like other stereotypes, the belief that creative people are likely to be mentally ill is an exaggerated, overly general belief about a class of people. Although we are reluctant to say that there is nothing to this stereotype – it's an empirical question – there are certainly good reasons to agree that such a stereotype exists.

The mad-genius stereotype is curiously specific: It appears for only some disorders and for some creative domains. Regarding disorders, the stereotype primarily involves mood disorders (depression, anxiety, social anxiety, and the bipolar family of disorders), thought disorders (the schizophrenia spectrum of disorders), and substance abuse (alcoholism and illicit substance abuse). We rarely hear about creativity being associated with disorders such as caffeine addiction, frotteurism, trichotillomania, and animal phobias. Regarding creative domains, the stereotype primarily involves the fine arts (painting, photography, music performance, and composition) and creative writing.

To see the other side of the mad-genius stereotype, we can explore the creative domains that it excludes. It is rare to see the stereotype applied to mechanical engineers, bond analysts, historians, real-estate developers, international economists, or landscape architects. The landmark innovators in these fields made powerful creative contributions to their domains, but the lay public is unlikely to apply a mad-genius stereotype to them. For example, in the 1950s, mechanical engineers at Carl Hansen, a Danish furniture company, invented a high-speed process for carving and lathing teak, a dense and difficult wood. This invention enabled the teak revolution in Danish furniture design and afforded some of the century's seminal designs, such as the sculptural chairs of Finn Juhl. How did this creative breakthrough happen? Did the engineers stay up all night, half-mad and consumed by demons, furiously scribbling geometric blueprints for lathing blades and guides?

As another example, creative business models enable companies to create what investors call a "wide moat," a massive advantage that staves off competitors. "You can't just beat your rivals by the old rules," wrote Jack and Suzy Welch (2008); "to grow, you have to invent a new game and beat them at that, too." The world of business has many examples of corporate innovation. John Bogle, for example, invented an innovative corporate structure for the

Vanguard Group, an investment and advisory corporation. By inverting the relationship between a company and its mutual funds, he enabled the company to offer bargain-basement advisory fees and accumulate a trillion dollars of assets under management. If his autobiography is any guide, Bogle arrived at his invention over years of incremental thought (Bogle, 1999), not from a burst of manic insight or a collision of aberrant, schizotypal thoughts.

It's hard to say where the mad-genius stereotype comes from. Weisberg (2006) suggests that it dates to the Greeks' belief in Muses, in which inspiration comes from deities seizing control of one's thoughts. Simonton (1994) traces the connection back to Aristotle. Plucker et al. (2004) suggest that the stereotype persists because it is comforting to the unaccomplished – it establishes a "weirdness" about creative people. In any case, the presence of this cultural stereotype requires researchers to be particularly cautious. Many hypotheses about creativity and mental illness may feel intuitive, compelling, and sensible simply because they fit a prevailing cultural model.

Regardless of the stereotype's origins, it is worth considering what people mean by mental health and illness. In a typical pathology model, and in everyday discourse about this topic, people view mental illness as the presence of impairing symptoms that may rise to the level of a clinical diagnosis. In short, people have a mental disorder. As odd as it sounds, we wonder if people who do creative work in the face of a mental disorder should be viewed as being mentally ill. Consider, for example, creators who do important work despite disastrous childhoods, chronic symptoms, and difficult addictions. Such creators are stronger and healthier than creators who face none of these barriers to creative work; they have demonstrated high resilience. From this perspective, there is much more to mental health than the mere presence of a diagnosis. The ability to cope with and learn from problems and to grow in the face of adversity are hallmarks of healthy functioning.

But resilience is apparent only in the face of adversity, so many seemingly healthy people are merely lucky and untested (Ryff & Singer, 2003; Tedeschi & Calhoun, 2004).

What Does Mental Health or Illness Do?

Why would creativity and mental illness covary? What would such a relationship mean? The mad-genius stereotype proposes that creative people tend to have problems, but the meaning, direction, and nature of such an effect is obscure. There are a few possibilities. The first, of course, is that mental illness causes creativity: Some disorders foster, enable, or provoke creative thought and accomplishment. In this sense, achievement springs forth from anguish and pain, as befits the romantic stereotype of the mad genius. Research on schizotypy and the schizophrenia spectrum is an example of this implied direction. For the most part, researchers have suggested that the diverse, loosely associated pattern of thought fosters creative ideas (e.g., Batey & Furnham, 2008).

A second possibility is that creativity brings about mental illness. Doing important work is hard. Gay Talese (2006), for example, described writing books as "like driving a truck at night without headlights, losing your way along the road, and spending a decade in a ditch" (p. 75). This causal direction is less intuitive, but some researchers have suggested that it deserves serious consideration (e.g., Weisberg, 2006). One mechanism, perhaps, involves an accumulation of risk factors as a result of a creative lifestyle. For example, anyone who devotes years to a solitary, low-paying domain can have a lifestyle with several risk factors for mental illness, such as low socioeconomic status, low social support, and poor access to mental health services. Similarly, high levels of creative accomplishment put people at risk for intense criticism and rejection. Sherwood Anderson, for example, appeared to enter a depressive period in the late 1920s and early 1930s (Rideout, 2006). Although one could view this as support for a mad-genius stereotype, one could also view it as a natural human response to rejection and failure. After hailing his early work from early 1920s, critics turned against Anderson. Several of his books were ridiculed by prominent intellectuals in major outlets, including a nasty book-length appraisal by Cleveland Chase. How many people could handle a blistering condemnation of their life's creative work with resilience and good humor?

A third possibility – one that deserves much more attention, in our opinion – is that creativity and mental illness merely co-occur. Third variables – such as childhood experiences, socioeconomic status, peer groups, and normal personality traits – cause both creativity and mental illness, thereby creating a spurious covariance between them. Few studies have controlled for potential confounding variables, so it is hard to know if a relationship is robust. Consider, for example, the trait of sensation seeking. People high in sensation seeking are more likely to use and abuse alcohol and illicit drugs, to have friends with similar patterns of drug use and abuse, to enjoy risky and unconventional activities, to behave impulsively, and to pick unconventional occupations (Zuckerman, 1994, 2006). It wouldn't be surprising to find experimental artists with substance abuse problems, given that sensation seeking predicts both variables.

The "third variable problem" strikes us as a big issue for the study of creativity and mental illness. Few studies have assessed and controlled for potential confounds, so it is hard to know if relationships between mental health and creativity are robust. A good example is a study of schizotypy and creativity by Miller and Tal (2007). They assessed positive and negative schizotypy, verbal and visual divergent thinking, and dimensions of normal personality. Schizotypy predicted creative performance at the zero-order level, but only before controlling for normal personality. Openness to experience and fluid intelligence washed out schizotypy's effects. The incremental validity of mental health

symptoms deserves more attention in future work.

Conditional Probabilities and the Fallacy of the Inverse

Imagine that a research group recruited a sample of accomplished architects, painters, and writers along with a sample of adults with no creative accomplishments. After assessing the presence of clinical disorders, the researchers found that the creative groups had higher rates of mental health problems. Based on the evidence, they concluded that people with mental illnesses are more likely to be creative. Is this conclusion appropriate?

No, actually. This conclusion involves a common fallacy known as the *fallacy of the inverse*, a confusion of conditional probabilities. (Bayesian psychologists and the researchers who love them will recognize this classic problem.) Unlike simple probabilities, conditional probabilities express the likelihood of an event given something else. For example, the probability that someone is a man, given that the person has a beard, is expressed as $p(\text{man} \mid \text{beard})$; the probability that someone has a beard, given that the person is a man, is expressed as $p(\text{beard} \mid \text{man})$. The fallacy of the inverse occurs when people confuse the two probabilities. For example, if someone has a beard, the probability of being a man is quite high; but if someone is a man, the probability of having a beard is relatively low.

In creativity research, researchers commonly confuse two conditional probabilities: $p(\text{mentally ill} \mid \text{creative})$ and $p(\text{creative} \mid \text{mentally ill})$. In the first, the question is "What is the probability of a mental illness given that someone is creative?"; in the second, the question is "What is the probability of being creative given that someone has a mental illness?" Theoretically, it is possible for the two probabilities to oppose each other. For example, a study of schizophrenia may find that adults with a diagnosis of schizophrenia have more creative accomplishments than people with no clinical disorder. This finding is "if disordered, then more creative." A study of creative accomplishment, however, may find that adults who are highly accomplished in creative domains are less likely to be schizophrenic than people with no creative accomplishments. This finding is "if creative, then less disordered."

Recognizing the difference between the conditional probabilities can clarify much of the confusion in the literature on creativity and mental illness. (We won't name names, but the fallacy of the inverse is widespread in this research area.) Another virtue is that it allows researchers to apply Bayes' theorem, the bane of undergraduates enrolled in Judgment and Decision Making classes, to model the probabilistic relationships between creativity and mental illness. For example, we can apply Bayes' theorem to compute $p(\text{creative} \mid \text{ill})$, the probability that someone is creative given that he or she has a mental illness. The equation is solved as follows:

$$
\begin{aligned}
p(\text{creative} \mid \text{ill}) \\
= p(\text{ill} \mid \text{creative})\,p(\text{creative})/ \\
p(\text{ill} \mid \text{creative})\,p(\text{creative}) \\
+ p(\text{ill} \mid \text{uncreative})\,p(\text{uncreative})
\end{aligned}
$$

These probabilities are unknown, which says something about the state of the research literature, so we will use invented values for the sake of example. Although we made them up, the values are not unrealistic. In our example, we will assume the following:

$p(\text{creative}) = .05$	(The probability that someone is creatively accomplished, also known as the *base rate* of creativity.)
$p(\text{uncreative}) = .95$	(The probability that someone is not creatively accomplished.)
$p(\text{ill} \mid \text{creative}) = .30$	(The probability that someone is mentally ill, given that he or she is creative. This fictional value is deliberately high.)
$p(\text{ill} \mid \text{uncreative}) = .20$	(The probability that someone is mentally ill, given that he or she is not creative.)

Note that we set up these fictional values to favor a link between creativity and mental illness: The first conditional probability is higher than the second. Plugging in the numbers yields the following: $p(\text{creative} \mid \text{ill}) = (.30)(.05) / (.30)(.05) + (.20)(.95)$.

Crunching the numbers yields a probability of .073, so there is only a 7.3% chance (based on our fictional inputs) that someone is creative if he or she has a mental illness. Note that this value is low despite the fairly high $p(\text{ill} \mid \text{creative})$ value of .30. If the base rate of creativity is low, which it must be, then $p(\text{creative} \mid \text{ill})$ won't be much higher than the base rate unless the relationship between creativity and mental illness is quite high – that is, unless $p(\text{ill} \mid \text{creative})$ is much higher than $p(\text{ill} \mid \text{uncreative})$.

We can rerun this example by presuming that there is no link. To do so, we can set both $p(\text{ill} \mid \text{creative})$ and $p(\text{ill} \mid \text{uncreative})$ to .20. In this case, $p(\text{creative} \mid \text{ill})$ is .05, which is simply the base rate of creativity. Stated differently, the base rate of creativity is the best estimate that someone is creative if mental illness is unrelated to creativity. For symmetry, we can rerun the example by presuming that creative people are less likely to be mentally ill. For this example, we can simply reverse the values of .30 and .20. In this case, $p(\text{creative} \mid \text{ill})$ is around .034, which is lower than the base rate of creativity.

Playing around with Bayes' theorem is illuminating – even our fictional data offer food for thought. Our examples show that the chance that someone is creative given that he or she is mentally ill, $p(\text{creative} \mid \text{ill})$, will always be small so long as (1) the base rate of creativity is low and (2) the link between creativity and mental health is not huge. Researchers on all sides of this controversy would agree with the first point, and most researchers would probably agree that the creativity–mental health effect size is probably small or moderate instead of large. As a result, researchers should expect only low rates of creativity in samples of people with mental illnesses.

As we noted earlier, many researchers have staked extreme positions on the debate over a creativity–mental illness link. But this link can take two conditional forms: Creative people may tend to be mentally ill, or mentally ill people may tend to be creative. Both claims might be true or false; furthermore, only one of the two could be true. When the fallacy of the inverse is recognized, creativity researchers on different sides of this debate suddenly have more to argue about.

A Selected Review of Research

Studying Creative People

Certainly, the most straightforward way to study the mental illness–creativity connection is to test creative people and see if their rates of mental illness are higher than the norm. One place to start would be by testing noted or eminent creators. Frank Barron and his colleagues at the Institute of Personality Assessment and Research (IPAR) studied architects, scientists, mathematicians, entrepreneurs, and writers, among others. Most creators scored higher on the pathology-related scales of the MMPI (e.g., Barron, 1965, 1969, 1995; see also Richards, 2006).

Perhaps the most well-known single empirical study on this topic was conducted by Andreasen (1987), who used structured interviews to analyze 30 creative writers, 30 matched controls, and first-degree relatives of each group. The writers had a higher rate of mental illness, with a particular tendency toward bipolar and other affective disorders. The writers' first-degree relatives were more likely to both be creative and have affective disorders. This study is often used as a cornerstone for demonstrating a connection between creative writing and mental illness. It is worth pointing out, however, that there have been several critiques of the methodology (Lindauer, 1994; Rothenberg, 1990, 1995; Schlesinger, 2003). Rothenberg (1990), for example, argues that Andreasen's control group was not well-matched to the writers chosen; the creative group was comprised of faculty members from the creative writing department, whereas the control group

had a wide mix of people. Andreasen was the sole interviewer, with no corroborating opinions about the mental health of the writers.

Most of the other studies of living, eminent people have also been conducted on writers. Jamison (1989) interviewed 47 British artists and writers and found that a significantly higher percentage of them suffered from some form of mental illness, particularly from affective disorders (such as bipolar), than would be expected from population rates. Ludwig (1994) studied 59 female writers and 59 matched controls, and found that the writers were more likely to have mental illness, including mood disorders (including bipolar) and general anxieties. Staltaro (2003) looked at 43 published poets and found that approximately one-third had a history of at least one psychiatric condition and more than half had been in therapy (this is notably higher than population rates). But poets did not score significantly higher than the norm on a measure of current depression. Nettle (2006) examined poets, mathematicians, visual artists, and average people, finding higher levels of schizotypy in poets and visual artists and lower levels in mathematicians. Another study that found domain-based differences was Rawlings and Locarnini (2008), who gave measures of subclinical psychosis and autism to artists and scientists. In the artist group, creativity was linked to schizotypy and hypomania. In the scientist group, these connections were not found; however, a slight connection was found between creativity and autistic tendencies. The relationship between schizotypy and creativity, however, is not uncontested. Miller and Tal (2007) found that although both openness to experience and intelligence predicted creativity, schizotypy did not.

Other studies have examined creative traits in everyday people and "lesser" subclinical disorders, such as hypomania (Furnham et al., 2008) and schizotypy (Abraham & Windmann, 2008; Karimi, Windmann, Güntürkün, & Abraham 2007; Nettle, 2006). Hypomania, as Furnham et al.

(2008) and Lloyd-Evans, Batey, and Furnham (2006) argue, is a disorder that is related to bipolar depression – there are periods of elevated mood, but these are less intense and shorter – yet it does not necessarily lead to a diagnosis of "mentally ill." People with minor hypomania may be more creative, whereas people with extreme bipolar disorder may be less creative (see also Richards & Kinney, 1990). Similarly, there are several studies on schizotypy, a disorder that is closer to a personality trait than a mental illness (Kwapil, Barrantes-Vidal, & Silvia, 2008). Symptoms of schizotypy, which includes some components of psychoticism, are similar to creativity, such as unusual and sudden thoughts. Burch, Pavelis, Hemsley, and Corr (2006) found visual artists to be higher on both schizotypy and creativity than nonartists.

Another methodology is psychological autopsies, in which a creative person's symptoms are assessed based on life details, such as suicide attempts or hospitalizations. There are a few problems with this technique. Some argue it is unscientific, in part because any diagnosis is given by the researcher, who knows the hypothesis of the study (e.g., Schlesinger, 2003). In other words, in many cases the same person is planning the study, developing the hypothesis, choosing the sample, and deciding if these people have a mental illness. A related but more conservative approach is traditional historiometric research, in which one reads biographies of eminent people and takes note of important life events (marriages, winning prizes, or a personal trauma).

Some studies that have used psychological autopsies include Wills's (2003) investigation of jazz musicians (musicians showed higher rates of psychopathology), Post's (1994) study of 291 eminent men (visual artists and writers suffered from more personality disorders), and Post's (1996) replication with 100 writers (higher rates of affective disorders). Other studies are more traditionally historiometric, looking at life events without necessarily doing a full psychiatric analysis. Perhaps the most extensive historiometric study was conducted by Ludwig (1995), who investigated over 1,000 eminent individuals who were the subjects of major biographies written between 1960 and 1990. Among many other discoveries, he found a higher incidence of mental illness among people in artistic professions (e.g., writing, art, and theater) than in nonartistic professions (e.g., business, politics, and science), similar to Nettle's (2006) work. In another study, Ludwig (1998) found that visual artists with a more emotive style were more likely to suffer from depression and other disorders than artists with more formal styles.

This line of research may indicate that the issue of domains is more important than the issue of creativity. For example, female poets were significantly more likely to suffer from mental illness (as measured by suicide attempts, hospitalizations, or specific periods of depression that warranted discussion in a brief biography) than other types of women writers (fiction writers, playwrights, and nonfiction writers) and male writers (fiction writers, poets, playwrights, and nonfiction writers; Kaufman, 2001). An additional study looked only at women and compared poets with journalists, politicians, actresses, novelists, and visual artists. Again, poets were significantly more likely to have mental illness than any other group (Kaufman, 2001). This finding was dubbed the "Sylvia Plath Effect."

Other studies have also explored writers. Kaufman (2005) studied 826 writers from Eastern Europe from the fourth century to the present day. He found ·that poets were significantly more likely to suffer from mental illness than any other type of writer (fiction writer, playwright, nonfiction writer). Similarly, Thomas and Duke (2007) found that eminent poets showed significantly more cognitive distortion than fiction writers; they hypothesized that poets were more apt to accept depressive thinking. Stirman and Pennebaker (2001) found that suicidal poets were likely to use words associated with the self (as opposed to the collective) in their poetry, as opposed to nonsuicidal poets. The authors of the study suggested that this tendency revealed an inward focus and lack of social integration. Forgeard (2008) examined the linguistic patterns of eminent writers who were either bipolar, unipolar, or neither; bipolar writers used more death-related words than unipolar, whereas unipolar writers were less likely to use self-related words than the controls. Her findings are somewhat consistent with Stirman and Pennebaker in that unipolar depressives are less likely to commit suicide than bipolar depressives (who used more self-associated words). Djikic, Oatley, and Peterson (2006) explored linguistic patterns of creative writers and physicists; the writers used more emotion-related words and specifically more negative-emotion words (i.e., related to anger, anxiety, or depression). This finding doesn't necessarily mean that writers feel these emotions more, just that they are more likely to use these words.

Studying People with Mental Illnesses

A different approach is to study people with mental illness and see if they are creative. Richards, Kinney, Lunde, Benet, and Merzel (1988) looked at 17 people with manic depression, 16 people with severe mood swings (cyclothymes), 11 normal first-degree relatives, and 33 controls. They found higher creativity levels (as measured by a Lifetime Creativity Scale) in the 33 people with mental illness and their relatives, as compared to the controls. Kinney, Richards, Lowing, LeBlanc, and Zimbalist (2001) tested adults who were born to schizophrenic parents and adopted by nonschizophrenic parents and compared them to adults born to and adopted by nonschizophrenic parents. They found that people with schizophrenia-spectrum disorders were more creative than those without the disorder, but the presence of schizophrenia in biological parents didn't affect creativity.

Keefe and Magaro (1980) gave measures of divergent thinking to 10 paranoid schizophrenics, 10 nonparanoid schizophrenics, 10 nonpsychotic psychiatric patients, and 10 controls. The nonparanoid schizophrenics had higher divergent-thinking scores than the other three groups. Wadeson (1980) found that bipolar patients going through depression and unipolar depressive patients had similar painting styles, with fewer colors; bipolar patients in a manic stage used more colors and were more expressive. Strong et al. (2007) studied creativity and personality in bipolar and unipolar depressives, as well as controls from creative and non-creative disciplines. They found two distinct factors: One was strongly based in neuroticism and mood disorders (cyclothymia and dysthymia), whereas the other was comprised mostly of openness to experience and creativity. Although both factors were related to self-report measures of creativity, neither factor was related to scores on the Torrance Tests.

It is also interesting, incidentally, to note that Ghadirian, Gregoire, and Kosmidis (2001) studied a total of 44 psychiatric patients with and without bipolar illness and found no difference between the two groups in creative abilities. Eisenman (1990) tested 37 individuals with schizophrenia, manic depression, or psychotic depression, and found them to be *less* creative than controls. Rubenstein (2008) examined the divergent-thinking scores of psychiatric inpatients who had a diagnosis of either schizophrenia, major depression, anxiety, or one of several personality disorders (narcissistic, borderline, or schizoid). The schizophrenic patients had significantly and substantially lower ideational fluency scores (the number of responses) than the other groups; the groups didn't differ in ideational originality (the number of unique responses).

Looking Ahead to Future Work

Subclinical Spectrum Models

One valuable direction for future research is to explore the full spectrum of disordered symptoms, not just the extreme, clinically interesting levels (Schuldberg,

2000–2001). Dimensional models of mental illness propose that disorders usually appear as a dimension of adjustment, not as exclusive *normal–disordered* classes. People can thus be located on a spectrum instead of being classified as disordered or healthy (Widiger & Lowe, 2007). One example is schizotypy, which represents a subclinical risk for schizophrenia-spectrum disorders (Kwapil et al., 2008). Most people at risk for schizophrenia will not develop the disorder, but they nevertheless will exhibit some of the symptoms, mannerisms, and features of people with schizophrenia. Similarly, social phobia can be thought of as the extreme end of a continuum that contains milder social anxiety, common social fears, and normal shyness (McNeil, 2001).

Because it is easier to recruit nonclinical samples, researchers can expand the range of variables they assess and recruit larger samples. With many measures and a big sample, researchers can then analyze latent-variable relationships between creativity and symptoms (Silvia & Kimbrel, 2009). By modeling variance due to measurement, latent-variable models afford better estimates of the true effect sizes (Skrondal & Rabe-Hesketh, 2004).

When studying dimensions of psychopathology, researchers should control for dimensions of normal personality, such as well-known traits (e.g., the Big Five) and abilities (e.g., fluid and crystallized intelligence). Symptom dimensions might not offer anything beyond the widely studied and well-understood dimensions of individual differences. It's possible that many dimensions of psychopathology won't add to our prediction of creativity – they may lack incremental validity – but only research will tell.

Clinical Samples

A second valuable direction is to study clinical samples. This strategy, perhaps, is a hedge: Although many clinical researchers endorse a dimensional model of disorders, many others endorse categorical models of disorders. The psychology of creativity needn't take a side in this conflict – it is fruitful for us to study both subclinical and clinical samples. It is likely, too, that some effects will appear only when extreme levels of a trait are sampled, particularly when a relationship is nonlinear.

It is particularly important for future research with clinical samples to take care with conditional probabilities. As we noted earlier, there is a big difference between claiming "If people are creative, then they're probably mentally ill" and "If people are mentally ill, then they're probably creative." Research that samples creative people and assesses mental illness affords very different conclusions than research that samples the mentally ill and assesses creativity.

By exploring both clinical and subclinical samples, researchers can appraise whether creativity differs across levels of impairment. People with subclinical trait levels may be more creative but, at the same time, people with the full-blown disorder may not be, owing to greater impairment. For example, research on the schizophrenia spectrum suggests that subclinical schizotypal traits in normally functioning adults are related to creativity (e.g., Batey & Furnham, 2008; Burch et al., 2006) but that full-blown schizophrenia is not (e.g., Rubenstein, 2008).

Levels of Creativity

In our selective review, we found enormous variability in the definition and assessment of creativity. When creativity is the independent variable, it has been quantified based on creative eminence or scores on creativity tests. When creativity is the outcome, it has been quantified as the quality of creative products, divergent-thinking scores, lifetime creative achievements, everyday creative behaviors, or levels of traits relevant to creativity. Certainly, the kinds of conclusions one could make will differ based on how creativity was operationalized. In future research, researchers should cast a broad net: It's worth including divergent-thinking tasks (Silvia et al., 2008), measures of everyday creativity (Batey & Furnham, 2008), creative achievement inventories (Carson, Peterson, & Higgins, 2005), and scales that assess goals and self-beliefs related to creativity (Kaufman & Baer, 2004). The relations between different facets of creativity are themselves interesting, and a broad approach to creativity assessment will make it easier to find the boundaries of any effects. For example, it is possible that some aspects of mental illness foster creative ways of thinking (e.g., divergent thinking) but not creative accomplishments, which take sustained effort and training.

Quantitative Synthesis

Meta-analysis is a useful tool for bringing order to large, diverse literatures. To date, creativity research has not had the benefit of meta-analytic integration. Excellent exceptions are recent studies by Kim, who has examined the relationship between intelligence and divergent thinking (Kim, 2006) and between divergent thinking and creative accomplishment (Kim, 2008). A good meta-analysis can isolate the signal in a noisy literature, summarize what has been found, and provide guidance for future research. In a fractious research area, meta-analysis can integrate findings more objectively – strong feelings and opinions have a greater influence on subjective literature reviews than meta-analyses, although meta-analytic methods, like all methods, have room for subtle biases. More than any other area of creativity research, the study of creativity and mental health needs a comprehensive meta-analysis.

Conclusion

The study of creativity and madness can drive creativity researchers to madness. This problem evokes strong feelings, which can cloud the research literature and stunt the growth of future research. In this chapter, we sought to bring some methodological and conceptual clarity to this sprawling literature. We think this problem is stated too abstractly – it is impossible to answer a question as broad as "Is creativity related to mental illness?" There are many mental disorders (e.g., personality disorders, thought disorders, mood disorders), many domains of creative accomplishment (e.g., writing, music performance, education, leadership), and many levels of creativity (e.g., little-c vs. Big-C; see Kaufman & Beghetto, 2009). To get a foothold into this area, researchers should frame the problem more concretely. In particular, recognizing the different conditional relationships – "if creative, then mentally ill" versus "if mentally ill, then creative" – is important to avoiding confusion about the proper conclusions that can be made from past research.

Research to date, in our view, is consistent with the view that some domains of creativity are associated with some forms of mental illness. We think "associated with" is about as strong of a conclusion as the literature can support. Some domains, particularly creative writing, have some reliable links with some kinds of disordered symptoms and behavior. Similarly, some subclinical traits, such as schizotypy, have some reliable links with some kinds of creative behavior, such as the visual arts. Much more work is needed to understand the boundaries of these relationships and the incremental validity of clinical symptoms over and above normal dimensions of personality.

Future work, in our view, should pursue different parts of the creativity–mental illness problem. Some research should study clinical samples; other research should study samples of accomplished creators in different domains; and yet other research should study the spectrum of clinical symptoms and creative achievement. Over time, these strands can be brought together via quantitative synthesis, such as meta-analysis. By building a rich, diverse, and high-quality research literature, researchers can set the stage for quantitative integrations, such as large-scale meta-analyses, which will ground this thorny problem in scientific evidence instead of cultural stereotypes or personal prejudices.

References

Abraham, A., & Windmann, S. (2008). Selective information processing advantages in creative cognition as a function of schizotypy. *Creativity Research Journal*, 20, 1–6.

Andreasen, N. C. (1987) Creativity and mental illness: Prevalence rates in writers and their first-degree relatives. *American Journal of Psychiatry*, 144, 1288–1292.

Balakian, N. (1998). *The world of William Saroyan.* Lewisburg, PA: Bucknell University Press.

Barron, F. (1965). The psychology of creativity. In T. Newcomb (Ed.), *New directions in psychology* (Vol. 2, pp. 3–134). New York: Holt, Rinehart & Winston.

Barron, F. (1969). *Creative person and creative process.* New York: Holt, Rinehart & Winston.

Barron, F. (1995). *No rootless flower: An ecology of creativity.* Cresskill, NJ: Hampton Press.

Batey, M., & Furnham, A. (2008). The relationship between measures of creativity and schizotypy. *Personality and Individual Differences*, 45, 816–821.

Bogle, J. C. (1999). *Common sense on mutual funds: New imperatives for the intelligent investor.* New York: Wiley.

Burch, G., Pavelis, C., Hemsley, D., & Corr, P. (2006). Schizotypy and creativity in visual artists. *British Journal of Psychology*, 97, 177–190.

Campbell, D. T., & Stanley, J. C. (1966). *Experimental and quasi-experimental designs for research.* Boston: Houghton Mifflin.

Carson, S. H., Peterson, J. B., & Higgins, D. M. (2005). Reliability, validity, and factor structure of the Creative Achievement Questionnaire. *Creativity Research Journal*, 17, 37–50.

Cronbach, L. J. (1982). *Designing evaluations of educational and social programs.* San Francisco: Jossey-Bass.

Cronbach, L. J., Gleser, G. C., Nanda, H., & Rajaratnam, N. (1972). *The dependability of behavioral measurements: Theory of generalizability for scores and profiles.* New York: Wiley.

Djikic, M., Oatley, K., & Peterson, J, B. (2006). The bitter-sweet labor of emoting: The linguistic comparison of writers and physicists. *Creativity Research Journal*, 18, 191–197.

Eisenman, R. (1990). Creativity, preference for complexity, and physical and mental illness. *Creativity Research Journal*, 3, 231–236.

Forgeard, M. (2008). Linguistic styles of eminent writers suffering from unipolar and bipolar mood disorder. *Creativity Research Journal*, 20, 81–92.

Furnham, A., Batey, M., Anand, K., & Manfield, J. (2008). Personality, hypomania, intelligence and creativity. *Personality and Individual Differences*, 44, 1060–1069.

Ghadirian, A., Gregoire, P., & Kosmidis, H. (2001). Creativity and the evolution of psychopathologies. *Creativity Research Journal*, 13, 145–148.

Jamison, K. R. (1989). Mood disorders and patterns of creativity in British writers and artists. *Psychiatry*, 52, 125–134.

Karimi, Z., Windmann, S., Güntürkün, O., & Abraham, A. (2007). Insight problem solving in individuals with high versus low schizotypy. *Journal of Research in Personality*, 41, 473–480.

Kaufman, J. C. (2001). Genius, lunatics, and poets: Mental illness in prize-winning authors. *Imagination, Cognition, and Personality*, 20, 305–314.

Kaufman, J. C. (2005). The door that leads into madness: Eastern European poets and mental illness. *Creativity Research Journal*, 17, 99–103.

Kaufman, J. C. (2009). *Creativity 101.* New York: Springer.

Kaufman, J. C., & Baer, J. (2004). Sure, I'm creative – but not in mathematics! Self-reported creativity in diverse domains. *Empirical Studies of the Arts*, 22, 143–155.

Kaufman, J. C., & Beghetto, R. (2009). Beyond big and little: The four c model of creativity. *Review of General Psychology*, 13, 1–12.

Kaufman, J. C., Bromley, M. L., & Cole, J. C. (2006). Insane, poetic, lovable: Creativity and endorsement of the "Mad Genius" stereotype. *Imagination, Cognition, and Personality*, 26, 149–161.

Keefe, J. A., & Magaro, P. A. (1980). Creativity and schizophrenia: An equivalence of cognitive processing. *Journal of Abnormal Psychology*, 89, 390–398.

Kim, K. H. (2006). Can only intelligent people be creative? A meta-analysis. *Journal of Secondary Gifted Education*, 16, 57–66.

Kim, K. H. (2008). Meta-analyses of the relationship of creative achievement to both IQ and divergent thinking test scores. *Journal of Creative Behavior*, 42, 106–130.

Kinney, D. K., Richards, R., Lowing, P. A., LeBlanc, D., & Zimbalist, M. E. (2001). Creativity in offspring of schizophrenic and control parents: An adoption study. *Creativity Research Journal*, 13, 17–25.

Kottler, J. (2005). *Divine madness*. San Francisco: Jossey-Bass.

Kozbelt, A. (2005). Factors affecting aesthetic success and improvement in creativity: A case study of the musical genres of Mozart. *Psychology of Music*, 33, 235–255.

Kozbelt, A. (2007). A quantitative analysis of Beethoven as self-critic: Implications for psychological theories of musical creativity. *Psychology of Music*, 35, 144–168.

Kwapil, T. R., Barrantes-Vidal, N., & Silvia, P. J. (2008). The dimensional structure of the Wisconsin schizotypy scales: Factor identification and construct validity. *Schizophrenia Bulletin*, 34, 444–457.

Lee, L., & Gifford, B. (1984). *Saroyan: A biography*. New York: Harper & Row.

Legget, J. (2002). *A daring young man: A biography of William Saroyan*. New York: Knopf.

Lindauer, M. S. (1994). Are creative writers mad? An empirical perspective. In B. M. Rieger (Ed.), *Dionysus in literature: Essays on literary madness*. Bowling Green, OH: Bowling Green State University Popular Press.

Lloyd-Evans, R., Batey, M., & Furnham, A. (2006). Bipolar disorder and creativity: Investigating a possible link. *Advances in Psychology Research*, 40, 11–142.

Ludwig, A. M. (1994). Mental illness and creative activity in female writers. *The American Journal of Psychiatry*, 151, 1650–1656.

Ludwig, A. M. (1995). *The price of greatness*. New York: Guilford.

Ludwig, A. M. (1998). Method and madness in the arts and sciences. *Creativity Research Journal*, 11, 93–101.

McNeil, D. W. (2001). Terminology and evolution of constructs in social anxiety and social phobia. In S. G. Hofmann & P. Marten (Eds.), *From social anxiety to social phobia* (pp. 8–19). Boston: Allyn & Bacon.

Miller, G. F., & Tal, I. R. (2007). Schizotypy versus openness and intelligence as predictors of creativity. *Schizophrenia Research*, 93, 317–324.

Nettle, D. (2002). *Strong imagination*. Oxford: Oxford University Press.

Nettle, D. (2006). Psychological profiles of professional actors. *Personality and Individual Differences*, 40, 375–383.

Plucker, J., Beghetto, R. A., & Dow, G. (2004). Why isn't creativity more important to educational psychologists? Potential, pitfalls, and future directions in creativity research. *Educational Psychologist*, 39, 83–96.

Post, F. (1994). Creativity and psychopathology: A study of 291 world-famous men. *British Journal of Psychiatry*, 165, 22–34.

Post, F. (1996). Verbal creativity, depression and alcoholism: An investigation of one hundred American and British writers. *British Journal of Psychiatry*, 168, 545–555.

Rawlings, D., & Locarnini, A. (2008). Dimensional schizotypy, autism, and unusual word associations in artists and scientists. *Journal of Research in Personality*, 42, 465–471.

Richards, R. (2006). Frank Barron and the study of creativity: A voice that lives on. *Journal of Humanistic Psychology*, 46, 352–370.

Richards, R., & Kinney, D. K. (1990). Mood swings and creativity. *Creativity Research Journal*, 3, 202–217.

Richards, R. L., Kinney, D. K., Lunde, I., Benet, M., & Merzel, A. P. C. (1988). Creativity in manic-depressives, cyclothemes, their normal relatives, and control subjects. *Journal of Abnormal Psychology*, 97, 281–288.

Rideout, W. B. (2006). *Sherwood Anderson: A writer in America* (2 vols.). Madison: University of Wisconsin.

Rothenberg, A. (1990). *Creativity and madness: New findings and old stereotypes*. Baltimore, MD: The Johns Hopkins University Press.

Rothenberg, A. (1995). Creativity and mental illness. *American Journal of Psychiatry*, 152, 815–816.

Rubenstein, G. (2008). Are schizophrenic patients necessarily creative? A comparative study between three groups of psychiatric inpatients. *Personality and Individual Differences*, 45, 806–810.

Ryff, C. D., & Singer, B. (2003). Flourishing under fire: Resilience as a prototype of challenged thriving. In C. L. M. Keyes & J. Haidt (Eds.), *Flourishing: Positive psychology and the life well-lived* (pp. 15–36). Washington, DC: American Psychological Association.

Sawyer, R. K. (2006). *Explaining creativity: The science of human innovation*. Oxford: Oxford University Press.

Schlesinger, J. (2003). Issues in creativity and madness, part three: Who cares? *Ethical Human Sciences & Services*, 5, 149–152.

Schlesinger, J. (2009). Creative mythconceptions: A closer look at the evidence for the "mad genius" hypothesis. *Psychology of Aesthetics, Creativity, and the Arts*, 3, 62–72.

Schuldberg, D. (2000–2001). Six subclinical spectrum traits in normal creativity. *Creativity Research Journal*, 13, 5–16.

Silvia, P. J., & Kimbrel, N. A. (2009). *A dimensional analysis of creativity and mental illness: Do anxiety and depression symptoms predict creative cognition, creative accomplishments, and creative self-concepts?* Unpublished manuscript.

Silvia, P. J., Winterstein, B. P., Willse, J. T., Barona, C. M., Cram, J. T., Hess, K. I., et al. (2008). Assessing creativity with divergent thinking tasks: Exploring the reliability and validity of new subjective scoring methods. *Psychology of Aesthetics, Creativity, and the Arts, 2,* 68–85.

Simonton, D. K. (1989). Shakespeare's sonnets: A case for and of single-case historiometry. *Journal of Personality, 57,* 695–721.

Simonton, D. K. (1994). *Greatness: Who makes history and why.* New York: Guilford.

Simonton, D. K. (1997). Imagery, style, and content in thirty-seven Shakespeare plays. *Empirical Studies of the Arts, 15,* 15–20.

Simonton, D. K. (2004). Thematic content and political context in Shakespeare's dramatic output, with implications for authorship and chronology controversies. *Empirical Studies of the Arts, 22,* 201–213.

Skrondal, A., & Rabe-Hesketh, S. (2004). *Generalized latent variable modeling: Multilevel, longitudinal, and structural equation models.* Boca Raton, FL: Chapman & Hall/CRC.

Staltaro, S. O. (2003). *Contemporary American poets, poetry writing, and depression.* Unpublished doctoral dissertation, Alliant International University at Fresno.

Stirman, S. W., & Pennebaker, J. W. (2001). Word use in the poetry of suicidal and non-suicidal poets. *Psychosomatic Medicine, 63,* 517–523.

Strong, C. M., Nowakowska, C., Santosa, C. M., Wang, P. W., Kraemer, H. C., & Ketter, T. A. (2007). Temperament-creativity relationships in mood disorder patients, healthy controls and highly creative individuals. *Journal of Affective Disorders, 100,* 41–48.

Talese, G. (2006). *A writer's life.* New York: Knopf.

Tedeschi, R. G., & Calhoun, L. G. (2004). Posttraumatic growth: Conceptual foundations and empirical evidence. *Psychological Inquiry, 15,* 1–18.

Thomas, K., & Duke, M. P. (2007). Depressed writing: Cognitive distortions in the works of depressed and non-depressed poets and writers. *Psychology of Aesthetics, Creativity, and the Arts, 1,* 204–218.

Wadeson, H. (1980). *Art psychotherapy.* New York: Wiley.

Weisberg, R. W. (2006). *Creativity: Understanding innovation in problem solving, science, invention, and the arts.* Hoboken, NJ: Wiley.

Welch, J., & Welch, S. (2008, November 4). Barack Obama's victory: Three lessons for business. *BusinessWeek.* Retrieved February 28, 2010 from http://www.businessweek.com/magazine/content/08_46/b4108000836030.htm?chan=top+news_top+news+index+-+temp_top+story.

Widiger, T. A., & Lowe, J. R. (2007). Five-factor model assessment of personality disorder. *Journal of Personality Assessment, 89,* 16–29.

Wills, G. I. (2003). A personality study of musicians working in the popular field. *Personality and Individual Differences, 5,* 359–360.

Zuckerman, M. (1994). *Behavioral expressions and biosocial bases of sensation seeking.* New York: Cambridge University Press.

Zuckerman, M. (2006). *Sensation seeking and risky behavior.* Washington, DC: American Psychological Association.

CHAPTER 21

The Relationship between Creativity and Intelligence

Kyung Hee Kim, Bonnie Cramond, and Joyce VanTassel-Baska

The Relationship between Creativity and Intelligence

Researchers have long pondered the relationship between intelligence and creativity, and practitioners have wondered about the importance of each construct in respect to what should be emphasized in schools to develop high level abilities. This chapter lays out what we know about each construct from research and how the two constructs relate to each other. It examines claims that intelligence and creativity are interrelated as well as claims suggesting they are separate constructs based on meta-analytic findings. Genetics research is also reviewed noting the prevalent view of the power of the environment impacting genetic potential. Research on intelligence testing is presented noting the relationship of IQ to life success and failure and national/cultural well-being and dominance. The savant syndrome is also discussed as an anomaly of intelligence. We also review creativity research on personality, the creative process, and its products. The chapter further explores evidence suggesting that creativity development for all

students may be an important strategy for world societies to promote as they wish to elevate their quality of life.

What Is Intelligence?

Intelligence is an ability to understand complex ideas, to adapt to the environment, to learn from experience, and to engage in reasoning to overcome obstacles (Neisser, 1996). Intelligence reflects an individual's capacities, shaped by experience and learning, and is often operationally defined by schools as the cognitive abilities that are measured by an IQ test. Thus, IQ is a measure of intelligence and is an acceptable proxy for intelligence, although it is not the same as intelligence. One of the differences between intelligence and IQ is that the latter is limited by what is measured, whereas, in a pure form, intelligence is complex and multidimensional.

Genetic Influences on Intelligence

Research has been focused on whether there is a difference in intelligence in terms of genetic factors. The nature–nurture controversy continues to wage, with different researchers concluding different degrees of impact from genetics or environment. However, a series of studies by Plomin (1999) and his colleagues of twins reared apart (cf. Petrill et al., 2004; Plomin, DeFries, McClearn, & McGuffin, 2001; Plomin, Fulker, Corley, & DeFries, 1997; Plomin & Spinath, 2004) has led him to conclude the following things about the heritability of intelligence. First, genetic influence increases rather than decreases during development. This seems counterintuitive, but Plomin explains it as due to the tendency of individuals to select and shape their environments to fit their genetic predispositions. Thus, an intense, bookish child may grow up to be an intense, solitary researcher because she selects highly academic and solitary activities and is able to do so more and more as she matures. Second, environmental influences that are shared by family members tend to decline until they are insignificant by the time individuals reach adolescence. In fact, van Leeuwen, van den Berg, and Boomsma (2008) concluded that environmental factors influencing IQ are not shared among siblings because each individual's environmental influences that matter are internalized differently. This relates to Plomin's third point, that even environmental factors are mediated by genetics. In other words, not only do individuals experience and internalize environmental factors differently depending on their genetic makeup, but their genetic tendencies also affect how the world reacts to and treats them. Fourth, genetic effects are broad rather than specific. The same genes are responsible for several cognitive abilities, giving credence to the concept of a general intellectual factor. And, fifth, the specific genes that are related to intellectual abilities are beginning to be identified through the Human Genome Project (Plomin & Spinath, 2004), although the research is still in its early stages. Ultimately, Plomin has recognized the mutual influences of genetics and environment, but he has argued that it is difficult to separate the two for study (Plomin & Price, 2003).

Thus, although individual differences in IQ are strongly attributed to genetic differences, the environmental effects of education over time have shown the capacity to raise IQ scores by at least 10 points (Finkel & Pedersen, 2001). Further, some researchers have observed that environmental factors may be more or less important depending on the level of intelligence. It has been noted that environment seems to be more influential for low-IQ individuals than high-IQ individuals (Finkel & Pedersen, 2001; Jensen, 1970). Also, Plomin and Petrill (1997) advised that the etiology of intelligence may be different for low- and high-IQ individuals.

Plomin's assertions have not gone unanswered by those who take a different view. A series of responses by environmental psychologists in the March 1994 issue of *Social Development* argued for a much stronger emphasis on environment (Brofenbrenner & Ceci, 1994; Hoffman, 1994; McCall, 1994; Wachs, 1994), and Plomin responding in the same issue largely agreed (Plomin, 1994). All agreed that both nature and nurture impact development and behavior, they just did not necessarily agree on degree and cause. Further, Turkheimer, Haley, Waldron, D'Onofrio, and Gottesman (2003) suggested that the heritability of IQ varies with social class. They found that 60% of the variance in IQ is accounted for by the shared environment, and the contribution of genes is close to zero in low-SES families, whereas the result is the reverse in high-SES families. More recently, Richardson and Norgate (2006) took exception to many of the conclusions drawn from twin studies, such as those that informed Plomin and his colleagues, citing problems with methods as well as assumptions. They argued that the studies do not convincingly show that genetic and environmental influences are additive and that either genetics or environment can be shown to have independent influence on development. In addition, they argued that twin studies do not meet the conditions of random-effects design, and thus they violate the assumptions of the statistics used to substantiate them. Moore (2006) further argued that the studies are flawed in assuming causation from correlations. Some studies have indicated that an enriched environment can actually enhance brain development, and thus intelligence. Diamond (1988) was able to synthesize almost 30 years of research to show that a stimulating environment has a physiological effect on the brain. Similarly, Greenough, Black, and Wallace (1987) reviewed studies about the effects of environmental stimulation on the brain, effectively arguing that stimulating experiences impact neural growth and synapse connections.

The extreme view for the preeminence of environmental effects over genetics on intelligence was proposed by the behaviorists, such as Skinner and Watson, but few psychologists take such a limited view any more. As Eysenck (1998) observed in his chapter entitled "Nature and nurture: The great partnership," "no serious scientists will argue for one or the other being singly responsible for human or animal behaviour. Both are always involved and interact in complex ways" (p. 47). Likewise, Halpern (1997) argued for a psychobiological model of intelligence in which the causes and effects of heredity and environment are circular (p. 1097).

The Role of Intelligence in Economic Productivity

Much research has been done regarding possible effects of intelligence. It has been reported that the economic prosperity of both individuals and nations is related to their IQs. Jensen (1998) reported a positive relationship between one's childhood IQ and adult income. Murray (1998) also reported a positive relationship between one's adolescent IQ and early adult income. Not just individuals' intelligence, but countries' average intelligence is also the subject of research. Lynn and Vanhanen (2002) reported a positive relationship between average IQs among 185 countries and their economic prosperity measured by gross domestic product per capita (GDP/c), although there have been criticisms of this

work. The cognitive level of a nation measured by international student assessment studies such as the International Evaluation of Educational Achievement-Reading (IEA-Reading), the Trends in International Mathematics and Science Study (TIMSS), the Program for International Student Assessment (PISA), and the Progress in International Reading Literacy study (PIRLS) have been found to have a positive relationship with GDP (Rindermann, 2008; Wittmann & Hunt, 2008).

However, the effects of IQ on academic achievement are mediated by personality and learning approaches (Chamorro-Premuzic & Furnham, 2008). One's beliefs about the nature of intelligence affects motivation and achievement such that holding entity theory beliefs (e.g., that ability is stable and cannot be changed) was found to have a detrimental impact on academic achievement when compared to holding an incremental theory by which one believes that ability is malleable and can be developed (Cury, Fonseca, Zahn, & Elliot, 2008; Good, Aronson, & Inzlicht, 2003; Thompson & Musket, 2005).

One of the most widely used tests for making high-stakes decisions about educational opportunities, placements, and diagnoses is the Scholastic Aptitude Test (SAT), now called the Scholastic Assessment Test. Studies have shown the usefulness of the SAT as a predictor of success in college performance (e.g., Bridgeman, McCamley-jenkins, & Ervin, 2000), especially for early-college academic performance (Kuncel, Hezlett, & Ones, 2001). Other studies have shown the efficacy of this test for finding younger students who reason extraordinarily well in verbal and mathematical areas and who demonstrate higher evidence of creative productivity in professional domains than less able counterparts and comparison groups who were not so identified over 30 years later (Webb, Lubinski, & Benbow, 2007). Shorter-term academic growth patterns have been noted as well for students who receive advanced instruction, based on their SAT scores in the middle school years (Olszewski-Kubilius, 2006). IQ scores have also been found to be highly correlated to both the American College Test (ACT) and the SAT. The ACT is designed to be curriculum-based and to measure the preparedness of a student for more advanced education, whereas the SAT has traditionally been seen as a specific aptitude measure to assess verbal and mathematical reasoning abilities, especially when used with younger populations. Further, even though the ACT is used in college admissions decisions as an alternative to the SAT, it is not an aptitude test or an IQ test according to the ACT Newsroom (2010). However, because of the high correlations with IQ test scores, the ACT (Koenig, Frey, & Detterman, 2008) and the SAT (Frey & Detterman, 2004) appear to be good proxy measures of intelligence. Consequently, it can be said that colleges are making admission decisions based on a student's demonstrated achievement or aptitude, which is related to their IQ. Further, both the SAT I and SAT II results are found to be related to family income and parental education, favoring Caucasian and Asian students but disfavoring African-American, Hispanic, and Native American students (Kobrin, Camara, & Milewski, 2002). Studies suggesting that the SAT is biased against minority groups and not a strong prediction of college grades have led to its reduced use and change in format to a more achievement-oriented measure.

Gordon (1997) suggested that life outcomes can be traced to extreme levels of IQ scores, noting that higher education, higher income, and prestigious career choices favor high-IQ individuals, whereas crime, poverty, and unemployment relate to low-IQ individuals. However, it should be noted that other variables contribute strongly as well to life circumstance.

Environmental Impacts on Intelligence

After re-examining the Lynn and Vanhanen's (2002) data set, Wittmann and Hunt (2008) question Lynn and Vanhanen's conclusion that intelligence causes a nation's well-being. Rather, Wittmann and Hunt

suggested that, first, intelligence produces wealth; next, wealthier nations can provide better schools, health, and stable living conditions for students; and finally, these things improve cognitive competence. Ceci (1991; Ceci & Williams, 1997) also argued that education can improve childhood IQ through schooling, especially during early preschool and school years so that children can develop long-term positive attitudes toward learning. They also argued that early strategies to guide learning, parental and family attitudes about supporting education, and parents' and children's expectations for academic achievement are inculcated during this period. Further, Dickens and Flynn (2001) demonstrated how IQ can be improved by intellectual challenges. They explained that very large environmental effects can arise from iterative processes in which a small improvement leads to more challenge, which leads to further improvement resulting in higher challenges, which leads to even further improvement, and so on. In addition, Turkheimer et al. (2003) found that heritability of IQ depends on SES.

There is confusion about whether intelligence is decreasing or increasing. Genotypic intelligence has been defined as the genetic makeup of intelligence, and phenotypic intelligence is that which is demonstrated and can be measured by intelligence tests (Retherford & Sewell, 1988). There is evidence that phenotypic intelligence has been increasing. Flynn (1984) documented that IQs based on the test norms of the Stanford-Binet and Wechsler tests have increased in the United States over the decades of the last century. Flynn (2007) also documented the worldwide increase in IQs during the past century. He reported that IQs on the Raven's Matrices and on the Similarities subtest of the Wechsler Intelligence Scale for Children (WISC) have gained by about 25 points, and the IQs on the WISC Arithmetic, Information, and Vocabulary subtests have gained by about 3, which he indicated might be due to reduced inbreeding, improved nutrition, or increased affluence.

On the other hand, there is evidence that genotypic intelligence is decreasing. Galton (1869) warned earlier about the possibility that British people's as well as other developed nations' intelligence might decrease. Recently, Teasdale and Owen (2008) found that IQs are decreasing in highly developed countries. Herrnstein and Murray (1994) showed that nations' intelligence is decreasing by reporting that women with an average IQ of 111 had 1.6 children, whereas women with an average IQ of 81 had 2.6 children. Zajonc (1976, 1983, 2001a, 2001b) found negative relationships between intelligence and both family size and birth order. He explained that the smaller the number of children in the family, the greater attention they can get from their parents. Moreover, older siblings teach younger siblings, and this teaching role enhances the intelligence of older siblings starting at age 12, plus or minus 2 years (Zajonc, 2001a). Both Lentz (1927) and Cattell (1937) also showed the negative relationship between intelligence and family size, which has been known as dysgenic fertility. Dysgenic fertility has been confirmed in the United States (Lynn, 1996; Lynn & Van Court, 2004; Rodgers, Cleveland, Van den Oord, & Rowe, 2000; Vining, 1982, 1995) as well as in England, Scotland, and Greece (Lynn, 1996). Further, Shatz (2008) also reported a negative relationship between national IQ and national indicators of fertility in his cross-national study.

Teasdale and Owen (2008) reported that most of the recent findings of the Flynn Effect for the phenotypic intelligence are from developed countries from the last century. They concluded that there is little evidence that the trend has continued in this century; moreover, they observed a decline in scores in a population of Danish males. Based on this conclusion and observation, they predicted that IQ scores will decrease and that the Flynn Effect is now almost at an end. In fact, Lynn and Harvey (2008) found that the increase of the world's phenotypic IQ has more than compensated for the decrease of the world's genotypic IQ between 1950 and 2000. Therefore, Shatz (2008) concluded that the environmental improvements responsible for the Flynn Effect are likely to diminish, and if dysgenic fertility continues, then phenotypic intelligence will begin to decrease.

The Special Case of Savants: An Intelligence Anomaly

The real mystery of intelligence, and how little we know about it, is suggested by the idiosyncratic talents of individuals with Savant Syndrome. These individuals, whose condition was popularized by the 1988 movie *Rain Man*, have simultaneously extreme abilities and disabilities. Treffert and Wallace (2004) described savants as possessing "astonishing islands of ability and brilliance that stand in jarring juxtaposition to their overall mental handicap" (p. 3).

Peek, who was a model for the savant character in the movie *Rain Man*, has amassed great quantities of knowledge through his prolific reading and incredible powers of memory, and he has the savant ability to name days of the week for any calendar date. However, he lacks the ability to do the most basic self-care (bathing, shaving, brushing his teeth) and is perplexed by metaphors and other abstractions (Peek, 2007).

Even savants, similar in that they have amazing discrepancies in abilities, are dissimilar in the nature and degree of their functioning. Most have some type of autism or other developmental disorder (Treffert & Wallace, 2004). Unlike Kim Peek, Daniel Tammet is a very highly functioning savant who lives independently and has learned to respond socially (Tammet, 2007). Diagnosed with Asperger's Syndrome, a high-functioning type of autism, Tammet's remarkable abilities include being able to recite pi to more than 5,000 decimal places. The special abilities of savants are restricted to a few areas that seem to require extreme focus and memory skills; most commonly they have restricted abilities in music, art, calendar calculating, mathematics, and mechanical or spatial skills (Treffert, 2010, p. 3).

The existence of Savant Syndrome would be intriguing, but perhaps unworthy of widespread interest, if it merely reflected on the relatively few individuals so diagnosed. However, the nature and expression of savant abilities provide a way to view intelligence and brain functioning, especially in the light of their connection, or lack thereof, to creativity. Although almost exclusively restricted to right-hemisphere functions, they are primarily nonsymbolic and restricted to memory and motor functions (Treffert & Wallace, 2006). Therefore, the skills that they exhibit are performance and reproduction, not original creation and interpretation, the hallmarks of creativity.

What Is Creativity?

An idea or product must be original to be considered creative, and at the same time, originality must be defined within a particular sociocultural group (Simonton, 1999) because what may be original in one society or culture may be common in other societies or cultures. What is original could be a breakthrough that causes a paradigm shift in a field or an important synthesis of existing thought in various forms (VanTassel-Baska, 1998). Moreover, the idea or product that is original cannot be considered as creative unless it has social value and appropriateness (Runco, 1993). Thus, creativity is the ability to produce work that is both original and appropriate or useful (Barron, 1988; 1995; MacKinnon, 1962) as judged by the culture at a given point in time, not by the originator (Simonton, 1999).

What are the conditions for creative productivity? According to Rhodes (1961), there are four Ps to explain the multifaceted construct of creativity – Person, Process, Product, and Press. Person includes cognitive abilities, biological traits, biographical traits, and personalogical traits; Process describes the mental processes operative in creating ideas, which include preparation, incubation, illumination, and verification (Wallas, 1926); Product includes ideas expressed in the form of language or craft; Press includes the relationship between a person and his

or her environment (Rhodes, 1961). Creative products are the outcome of creative processes engaged in by creative persons, which is supported by creative press. Torrance (1988) started with research on the creative process and then asked what kind of person one must be to engage in the creative process successfully; what kind of environments (Press) will facilitate it; and what kinds of creative products will result from successful operation of the creative processes. More current creativity researchers have focused strongly on the environmental contexts that are conducive to creativity (Amabile, Schatzel, Moneta, & Kramer, 2004), the quality of the products that are created (Simonton, 1999), and the role of cultural acceptance of the innovation (Csikszentmihalyi, 2000).

The Lack of Consensus about the Relationship between Creativity and Intelligence

Research on the relationship between creativity and intelligence has been a topic of interest to researchers for a long time, but there has been no clear consensus among the researchers yet. Guilford (1967) was the first researcher to develop a taxonomy of human abilities, called the Structure of Intellect (SOI), in which creative thinking was prominently featured as a part of intellectual functioning. He argued that traditional intelligence tests do not sufficiently measure creative abilities, and he hypothesized that creative individuals possess divergent thinking abilities including idea production, fluency, flexibility, and originality. Many studies (e.g., Getzels & Jackson, 1958; Torrance, 1977a; Furnham & Bachtiar, 2008; Furnham & Chamorro-Premuzic, 2006) have been conducted illustrating that creativity and intelligence have low correlations; that is, a highly intelligent person is not necessarily highly creative. Further, Guilford's (1967) theories spawned an array of divergent-thinking or creativity tests such as the Torrance Tests of Creative Thinking, Wallach and Kogan Divergent Thinking Tasks, and the Guilford Divergent Thinking Tasks.

They also spawned research that correlate scores on these divergent-thinking tests with creative potential. However, in general, creativity tests do not carry political weight compared to IQ tests: Creativity tests are sometimes used for identifying gifted students for programs, but the impact of creativity scores on the decision counts less than that of IQ (Kaufman & Baer, 2006).

Cattell and Horn (Cattell, 1943, 1971; Horn & Cattell, 1966) did not separate the two concepts of creativity and intelligence and divided intelligence into crystallized intelligence (gC) and fluid intelligence (gF). According to Cattell, (1943, 1971), gC is the ability to use skills, knowledge, and experience, and to gain, retain, structure, and conceptualize information, which can be measured by tests of general knowledge and verbal comprehension, whereas gF is the ability to draw inferences and understand the relationships of concepts, which can be measured by tests of abstract reasoning. Cattell (1971) argued that creative performance is determined first by one's gF and then by one's personality factors. Later, Furnham, Batey, Anand, and Manfield (2008) found that gF is specifically related to more divergent-thinking fluency than self-rated creativity or the inventory of creative behaviors.

Recently, Cattell-Horn's gC and gF theory has been combined with Caroll's (1993) Three-Stratum Theory, which is called the Cattell-Horn-Carroll (CHC) theory. There are some differences between the Cattell-Horn's and the Caroll's theories, including the presence (for Caroll's, but not for Cattell-Horn's) of a g factor or a general intellectual factor. However, the CHC theory has emerged as the consensus psychometric-based models for understanding the structure of human intelligence (McGrew, 2009) and is the intelligence theory that is most used in IQ tests (Kaufman, 2009). The CHC theory consists of the 16 different broad abilities (McGrew, 2009): Ga (auditory processing), Gc (comprehension knowledge; the breadth and depth of a person's accumulated knowledge of a culture and the ability to use that knowledge

to solve problems), Gf (fluid reasoning; the ability to solve novel problems), Gh (tactile abilities), Gk (kinesthetic abilities), Gkn (general [domain-specific] knowledge), Glr (long-term storage and retrieval), Go (olfactory abilities), Gp (psychomotor abilities), Gps (psychomotor speed), Gq (quantitative knowledge), Grw (reading and writing), Gs (processing speed), Gsm (short-term memory), Gt (reaction and decision speed), and Gv (visual processing). Although the CHC theory does not specify creativity, creativity seems to be a primary component of its Gf (Kaufman, 2009).

In 1993, Gardner focused on the idea of eminence, which requires sustained creative productivity over time. He analyzed the lives of seven eminent creative individuals of the twentieth century, each of whom specialized in one of his multiple intelligences. Gardner (1995) has argued that intelligence is a multifaceted collection of eight distinct intelligences and that creativity is the highest level of application of these intelligences.

Renzulli's (1986) three-ring conception of giftedness suggested that giftedness is at the intersection of above-average ability (intelligence), creativity, and task commitment, in which creativity and intelligence are components of giftedness. On the contrary, Sternberg and Lubart's (1991) investment theory of creativity suggested that intelligence is a subset of creativity and that there are six elements that combine to form creativity: intelligence, knowledge, thinking styles, personality, motivation, and environment. Both of these models value creativity as the more relevant concept to giftedness.

Many researchers in the field (e.g., Barron, 1961; Guilford, 1967; MacKinnon, 1961, 1967; Simonton, 1994) agree with the "threshold theory," which assumes that above an IQ score of 120 there is no correlation between measured creativity and intelligence. The threshold theory agrees with the assertion that creativity and intelligence are separate constructs above a minimum level of IQ 120. However, there have been only a few studies that systematically investigated the threshold theory, and results are inconclusive (Runco, 1991). Kim's meta-analysis (2005) found that the relationship between creativity and intelligence is negligible at any IQ level, which undermines the threshold theory and supports the underlying belief that creativity and intelligence are separate constructs. The threshold theory was further investigated using structural-equation modeling but was not supported (Preckel, Holling, & Wiese, 2006). Moreover, Park, Lubinski, and Benbow (2007) found that the threshold theory is not supported by their data either.

Kim (2005) found that the relationship between creativity and intelligence among younger children was weaker than for any other age groups, which might be because of little educational influence over the use of their cognitive abilities. Some studies (e.g., Iscoe & Pierce-Jones, 1964, Wallach & Kogan, 1965) indicated that the correlations between creativity and IQ measures are significantly increased when creativity tests are administered as serious tests rather than as a fun activity, especially for kindergarten or children in the early elementary years. In fact, Kim's (2005) meta-analysis found that scores on the Wallach and Kogan Divergent Thinking Tasks had a weaker relationship to intelligence than any other creativity tests had, which might be because the Wallach and Kogan Divergent Thinking Tasks are administered as non-testlike and untimed, a common and positive aspect of creativity testing. Therefore, Kaufman and Baer (2003) concluded that creativity tests are often administered as serious tests under a timed condition, which may have led to poor convergent validity among creativity test scores and poor discriminant validity between creativity test scores and IQ test scores.

The Role of Personality

According to Silvia (2008), personality variables confound correlations between intelligence and creativity, suggesting that personality may be a part of the creative process. Personality variables such as openness to experience predict both IQ (DeYoung,

Peterson, & Higgins, 2005) and creativity (Feist, 1998). Openness to experience is found to be the most influential factor on intelligence (Furnham & Thomas, 2004; Furnham & Chamorro-Premuzic, 2006), especially on gC and is even more strongly related to creativity (McCarthy, 1987; Miller & Tal, 2007). However, according to Furnham and Chamorro-Premuzic (2006), openness to experience is positively related to gF but not related to general intelligence. Harris (2001) also reported that openness was related to intelligence; however, creativity was a subscale of the intelligence factor in his study.

Neuroticism as related to anxiety, hostility, and depression are found to be negatively related to intelligence (Ackerman & Heggestad, 1997). Neuroticism is also negatively related to scientific creativity but positively related to artistic creativity (Götz & Götz, 1979).

Agreeableness in personality traits such as trust, modesty, and compliance is found not to be related to intelligence (Ackerman & Heggestad, 1997). Conscientiousness is found to be weakly related to intelligence (Zeidner & Matthews, 2000) but negatively related to creativity (Furnham & Chamorro-Premuzic, 2006).

Feist's (1998) meta-analysis reported that creative people tend to be autonomous and introverted, open to new experiences, norm-doubting, self-confident, self-accepting, driven, ambitious, dominant, hostile, and impulsive. After an extensive literature review, Batey and Furnham (2006) found that the most common personality traits that are related to creativity are confidence, independence, and openness to new ideas. Eminent creators have had a certain level of knowledge to advance in a field, although there is a curvilinear relationship between knowledge and creativity, which indicates that too much knowledge leads to entrenchment and an inability to conceive of the field in a radically different light (Batey & Furnham, 2006; Sternberg & Lubart, 1995).

Feist (1998) found that openness to experience and extraversion are the characteristics that most strongly distinguish

THE RELATIONSHIP BETWEEN CREATIVITY AND INTELLIGENCE

creative from noncreative scientists. In addition, he found that conscientiousness, conventionality, and closed-mindedness tend to be negatively related to being a creative scientist. Extraversion was found to be strongly related to four measures of creativity (Furnham & Bachtiar, 2008); Guilford's (1967) unusual uses divergent thinking test, the biographical inventory of creative behaviors (see Batey, 2007), a self-rated measure of creativity (see Batey, 2007), and the Barron-Welsh Art Scale (Welsh, 1987).

Creativity and Intelligence: Studies of Brain Activity

Modern technologies have allowed researchers to gain information about brain processing that was not possible before. Specifically, electroencephalography (EEG) is used for measuring electrical activity produced by the brain using electrodes on the scalp to indicate levels of brain activity. Thus, an EEG may be used to show differences in brain activity in different stages of wakefulness or active problem solving. The other new technology is functional magnetic resonance imaging (fMRI), which measures changes in blood flow related to brain activity, showing the areas of the brain that are activated during certain tasks.

Different patterns of EEG are produced between divergent-thinking tasks and convergent-thinking tasks (Fink & Neubauer, 2006; Jaušovec, 2000; Mölle, Marshall, Wolf, Fehm, & Born, 1999; Razoumnikova, 2000): Creative problem-solving tasks produce synchronization of alpha activity, typical of wakeful relaxation, whereas convergent tasks produce desynchronization of alpha activity (Fink & Neubauer, 2006). Higher EEG complexity is documented when divergent-thinking tasks are being administered to subjects as opposed to convergent thinking tasks (Mölle et al., 1999). The highly creative group showed more decoupling of brain areas, whereas the highly intelligent showed a more intense cooperation between brain areas

when resting (Jaušovec & Jaušovec, 2000). Jaušovec (2000) found that, when engaged in creative problem solving, the highly creative showed less mental activity than the less creative, and the highly creative showed more cooperation between brain regions than the highly intelligent.

Through the combined use of fMRI and EEG, Jung-Beeman and colleagues (cf. Jung-Beeman et al., 2004) scanned people's brains while they solved different types of puzzles. They found that the combined use of these technologies gave them both good spatial information (fMRI) and good temporal information (EEG) to understand what was happening in the brain, when and where, during problem solving that requires insight. Thus, they have been able to observe what parts of the brain are activated during different stages of problem solving and when solving problems with insight, where the answer suddenly seems to appear out of nowhere, versus solving problems through systematic analysis. Most strikingly, the brain measurement technologies show that when solving insight problems, an individual's realization of a solution is preceded by a burst of brain activity. In fact, 300 milliseconds before a participant communicates the answer, the EEG registers a spike of gamma rhythm — the highest electrical frequency of the brain. Also, the anterior superior temporal gyrus (aSTG), a small area on the surface of the right hemisphere, becomes unusually active in the second before the insight. Such brain information illustrates physiological differences in methods of problem solving that may be related to differences between creativity and intelligence.

Distinctions between Creativity and Intelligence

Highly creative individuals may or may not be the same as highly intelligent individuals. Compared with highly intelligent individuals, highly creative individuals have distinctive characteristics conducive to originating creative ideas or products. Some of these characteristics are conducive to having difficulties in traditional school settings. Many highly creative students have trouble in traditional school environments (Cramond, 1995; Amabile, 1989). Sixty percent of 400 eminent people had serious school problems (Goertzel & Goertzel, 1960). Torrance (Gowan, Khatena, & Torrance, 1979) referred to highly creative students as "creatively handicapped" because their creativity may make their achievement in traditional classrooms difficult, although creativity can be an asset in their lives. The energy of Thomas Edison and Nikola Tesla got them into trouble in childhood but helped them when working the long hours on their creative tasks (Cramond, 1995). Virginia Woolf and Samuel Taylor Coleridge were well known as being constant talkers in childhood, which is a characteristic of creative individuals and is often a problem in school, but their verbal ability was an asset to their creative tasks of writing (Cramond & Kim, 2007). When highly creative students are forced into traditional school environments, they routinely become troublesome to teachers, disruptive in the classroom, and resent the constraining structure of the classroom, excessive rules and regulations, and the press for conformity.

Teachers often prefer students who are achievers and teacher pleasers rather than disruptive or unconventional creative students (Davis & Rimm, 1994; Rudowicz, 2003; Rudowicz & Yue, 2000; Scott, 1999), even among the teachers who value creativity (Hunsaker, 1994; Westby & Dawson, 1995). Many teachers see creative children as a source of interference and disruption (Scott, 1999), and thus teachers' judgment of their favorite students is negatively related with creativity, and they may tend to devalue their students' creative behaviors even when they highly value creativity (Westby & Dawson, 1995). Similarly, Hunsaker (1994) found that teachers' observations for nomination for a gifted program focused more on classroom performance than on creativity, even when teachers proclaim that they highly value the construct of creativity. Many teachers prefer students with a high IQ to students who are both

highly creative and intelligent (Anderson, 1961). Teachers rate students with high IQs as more desirable, better known, or understood, and more studious than students with high creativity (Torrance, 1962).

Using the checklist that Torrance (1975) created to assess attitudes toward creative children, Singh (1987) found that parents did not respond favorably to the personality characteristics of creative children. However, such perceptions can vary with time and place. In 1984, Douglas, Jenkins-Friedman, and Tollefson found that teachers' views of creative personality characteristics had changed from those that Torrance had measured 20 years earlier. They found that teachers who completed the Ideal Child Checklist were more likely to value independence, courage, sincerity, and personal initiative than had the teachers in the earlier study who indicated that they favored more conforming and socially acceptable behaviors. In Eastern societies, the top-ranked traits for an ideal student were honest, self-disciplined, responsible, and respectful of parents; these characteristics were followed by diligent, unselfish, humble, and obedient (e.g., Rudowicz, 2003; Rudowicz & Yue, 2000).

Teachers' views are important in that teachers have the power to promote students' creativity directly through using creative-thinking strategies, by encouraging intrinsic motivation, and by providing opportunities for choice and discovery as well as imagination and fantasy (Schacter, Thum, & Zifkin, 2006). Fostering creativity should not be just for high-IQ students, but for every student. Russo (2004) found that high-IQ students were not different from regular students in creativity scores at either pretest or posttest after 6 months of the Future Problem Solving program, and both high-IQ students and regular students benefit from creativity and problem-solving skills training.

The Value-Added Aspect of Creativity

Because achievement tests in school settings assess rote knowledge and skills and do not measure higher-level executive functions including abstract thinking, creative thinking, and problem solving (Delis et al., 2007; Gardner, 1993; Sternberg, 1985), it is important to consider value-added assessment approaches that do provide data on how students process information at high levels. Sternberg, Grigorenko, and Jarvin, (2006) argued that one important goal for future study should be creating standardized tests that reduce ethnic group differences but still maintain test validity. Sternberg and his Rainbow Project collaborators (2006) have argued that analytical abilities are necessary but not sufficient for college success, and that creative and practical skills are needed for success in school and life. Therefore, based on his triarchic theory of successful intelligence, Sternberg et al. (2006) developed a supplementary assessment for analytical, practical, and creative skills to augment the role of the SAT in predicting students' college success. They found that the measure enhanced predictive validity for college GPA and substantially reduced ethnic group differences compared to high school GPA and the SAT.

This indicates that adding assessments for practical and creative skills to traditional analytical skills can be effective in predicting college success and can be fairer to students from diverse cultures. Creativity assessment allows students to respond from their own knowledge rather than from predetermined knowledge and is, therefore, potentially fairer to students from diverse cultures, especially when the assessment minimizes verbal components (Jellen & Urban, 1989; Torrance, 1977b; Voss, 1998). Evidence from data collected statewide on the effects of the Georgia multiple criteria rule for identifying students (Georgia Department of Education, 2010) supports the effectiveness of adding creativity assessments for identifying gifted students, especially those from underserved populations (Williams, 2000). The addition of a creativity assessment as an option to meet the standards for identification has been very helpful in identifying students from underserved populations (Krisel & Cowan, 1997).

The Future Primacy of the Concept of Creativity

A society in which independence, ownership, and democracy are encouraged is beneficial to individuals' intrinsic motivation and thus creativity (Amabile, 1996). Florida (2002) concluded that the key to any country's prosperity is its ability to attract creative people. DiPietro (2004) reported positive relationships among the creativity index from the World Economic Forum (2000), the IQ from Lynn and Vanhanen's report (2002), and the freedom index on political rights and on civil liberties. DiPietro explained that although high IQ enables a country to be capable of creativity, the extent of freedom on political rights and on civil liberties in a country determines the degree to which creativity is not confined and, therefore, has the opportunity to flourish. It takes time to change a society into one that encourages creativity. However, even when micro environments such as classroom settings, teaching styles, and assessments are changed into ones that encourage creativity and intrinsic motivation, students' creativity can be improved (Dineen & Niu, 2008). This situation carries positive implications for the role of creativity in schools if teachers and other educators are willing to open up the curriculum and instructional process to ensure that creative challenge is the rule and not the exception.

References

Ackerman, P. L., & Heggestad, E. D. (1997). Intelligence, personality, and interests: Evidence for overlapping traits. *Psychological Bulletin*, 121(2), 219.

ACT newsroom. (2010). Retrieved March 2, 2010 from http://www.act.org/news/aapfacts.html

Amabile, T. M. (1989). *Growing up creative: Nurturing a lifetime of creativity*. Williston, VT: Crown House Publishing Limited.

Amabile, T. M. (1996). *Creativity in context: Update to "The social psychology of creativity."* Boulder, CO: Westview Press.

Amabile, T., Schatzel, E., Moneta, G., & Kramer, S. (2004). Leader behaviors and the work environment for creativity: Perceived leader support. *Leadership Quarterly, 15,* 5–32.

Anderson, K. E. (1961). *Research on the academically talented student.* Washington, DC: National Education Association Project on the Academically Talented Student.

Barron, F. (1961). Creative vision and expression in writing and painting. In D. W. MacKinnon (Ed.), *The creative person* (pp. 237–251). Berkeley: Institute of Personality Assessment Research, University of California.

Barron, F. (1988). Putting creativity to work. In R. J. Sternberg (Ed.), *The nature of creativity* (pp. 76–98). New York: Cambridge University Press.

Barron, F. (1995). The disposition toward originality. *Journal of Abnormal and Social Psychology, 51,* 478–485.

Baruch, I., Hemsley, D. R., & Gray, J. A. (1988a). Differential performance of acute and chronic schizophrenics in a latent inhibition task. *Journal of Nervous and Mental Disease, 176,* 598–606.

Baruch, I., Hemsley, D. R., & Gray, J. A. (1988b). Latent inhibition and "psychotic proneness" in normal subjects. *Personality and Individual Differences, 9,* 777–783.

Batey, M. D. (2007). *A psychometric investigation of everyday creativity.* Unpublished doctoral thesis, University of London, U.K.

Batey, M., & Furnham, A. (2006). Creativity, intelligence, and personality: A critical review of the scattered literature. *Genetic, Social, and General Psychology Monographs, 132,* 355–429.

Bridgeman, B., McCamley-Jenkins, L., & Ervin, N. (2000). *Predictions of freshman grade-point average from the revised and recentered SAT I: Reasoning test.* New York: College Entrance Examination Board College Board Report No. 2000–1.

Brofenbrenner, U., & Ceci, S. J. (1994). Toward a more developmental behavioral genetics. *Social Development, 3,* 64–65.

Cantor, J. M., Blanchard, R., Robichaud, L. K., & Christensen, B. K. (2005). Quantitative reanalysis of aggregate data on IQ in sexual offenders. *Psychological Bulletin, 131,* 555–568.

Carroll, J. B. (1993). *Human cognitive abilities: A survey of factor-analytical studies.* New York: Cambridge University Press.

Carson, S. H., Peterson, J. B., & Higgins, D. M. (2003). Decreased latent inhibition is associated with increased creative achievement in high-functioning individuals. *Journal of Personality and Social Psychology, 85,* 499–506.

Cattell, R. B. (1937). *The fight for our national intelligence.* London: King.

Cattell, R. B. (1943). The measurement of adult intelligence. *Psychological Bulletin, 40,* 153–193.

Cattell, R. B. (1971). *Abilities, their structure, growth and action.* Boston, MA: Houghton Mifflin.

Ceci, S. J. (1991). How much does schooling influence general intelligence and its cognitive components? *Developmental Psychology, 27*(5), 703.

Ceci, S. J., & Williams, W. M. (1997). Schooling, intelligence, and income. *American Psychologist, 52*(10), 1051.

Chamorro-Premuzic, T., & Furnham, A. (2008). Personality, intelligence and approaches to learning as predictors of academic performance. *Personality and Individual Differences, 44,* 1596–1603.

Cheney, M. (1981). *Tesla: Man out of time.* New York: Prentice-Hall.

Cheung, G. W., & Rensvold, R. B. (2000). Assessing extreme and acquiescence response sets in cross-cultural research using structural equations modeling. *Journal of Cross-Cultural Psychology, 31,* 187–212.

Corballis, M. C., Hattie, J., & Fletcher, R. (2008). Handedness and intellectual achievement: An even-handed look. *Neuropsychologia, 46,* 374–378.

Coyle, T. R. (2003). Corrigendum to IQ, the worst performance rule, and Spearman's law: A reanalysis and extension. *Intelligence, 31*(6), 473–489.

Cramond, B. (1995). *The coincidence of attention deficit hyperactivity disorder and creativity* (RBDM 9508). Storrs: The National Research Center on the Gifted and Talented, University of Connecticut.

Cramond, B., & Kim, K. H. (2007). The role of creativity tools and measures in assessing potential and growth. In J. VanTassel-Baska (Ed.), *Critical issues in equity and excellence in gifted education series: Alternative assessment with gifted and talented students* (pp. 203–225). Waco, TX: Prufrock Press.

Crow, T. J., Crow, L. R., Done, D. J., & Leask, S. (1998). Relative hand skill predicts academic ability: Global deficits at the point of hemispheric indecision. *Neuropsychologia, 36,* 1275–1282.

Csikszentmihalyi, M. (2000). Happiness, flow, and economic equality. *American Psychologist*, 55(10), 1163–1164.

Cury, F., Fonseca, D. D., Zahn, I., & Elliot, A. (2008). Implicit theories and IQ test performance: A sequential meditational analysis. *Journal of Experimental Social Psychology*, 44, 783–791.

Dandy, J., & Nettelbeck, T. (2002). Research note: A cross-cultural study of parents' academic standards and educational aspirations for their children. *Educational Psychology: An International Journal of Experimental Educational Psychology*, 22(5), 621–27.

Davis, G. A., & Rimm, S. B. (1994). *Education of the gifted and talented* (3rd ed.). Needham Heights, MA: Allyn and Bacon.

Delis, D. C., Lansing, A., Houston, W. S., Wetter, S., Han, S. D., Jacobson, M., et al. (2007). Creativity lost: The importance of testing higher-level executive functions in school-age children and adolescents. *Journal of Psychoeducational Assessment*, 25, 29–40.

DeYoung, C. G., Peterson, J. B., & Higgins, D. M. (2005). Sources of openness/intellect: Neuropsychological correlates of the fifth factor of personality. *Journal of Personality*, 73, 825–858.

Diamond, M. (1988). *Enriching the brain*. New York: Free Press/Simon and Schuster.

Dickens, W. T., & Flynn, J. R. (2001). Heritability estimates versus large environmental effects: The IQ paradox resolved. *Psychological Review*, 108(2), 346.

Dineen, R., & Niu, W. (2008). The effectiveness of Western creative teaching methods in China: An action research project. *Psychology of Aesthetics, Creativity, and the Arts*, 2, 42–52.

DiPietro, M. (2004). Bayesian randomized responses as a class project. *American Statistician*, 58(4), 303–309.

Douglas, M., Jenkins-Friedman, R., & Tollefson, N. (1984). A new criterion for the "ideal" child? *Gifted Child Quarterly*, 28, 31–36.

Eysenck, H. J. (1998). *Intelligence: A new look*. Piscataway, NJ: Transaction Publishers, Rutgers University.

Feist, G. J. (1998). A meta-analysis of personality in scientific and artistic creativity. *Personality and Social Psychology Review*, 2, 290–309.

Fink, A., & Neubauer, A. C. (2006). EEG alpha oscillations during the performance of verbal creativity tasks: Differential effects of sex and verbal intelligence. *International Journal of Psychophysiology*, 62, 46–53.

Finkel, D., & Pedersen, N. L. (2001). Sources of environmental influence on cognitive abilities in adulthood. In E. L. Grigorenko, & R. J. Sternberg (Eds.), *Family environment and intellectual functioning: A life-span perspective* (pp. 173–194). Mahwah, NJ: Erlbaum.

Florida, R. (2002). The economic geography of talent. *Annals of the Association of American Geographers*, 92(4), 743–755.

Flynn, J. R. (1984). The mean IQ of Americans-Massive gains 1932 to 1978. *Psychological Bulletin*, 95, 29–51.

Flynn, J. R. (1998). WAIS-III and WISC II IQ gains in the United States from 1972–1995. *Perceptual & Motor Skills*, 86(3), 1231.

Flynn, J. R. (2007). *What is intelligence? Beyond the Flynn Effect*. New York: Cambridge University Press.

Frey, M. C., & Detterman, D. K. (2004). Scholastic assessment or g? The relationship between the SAT and general cognitive ability. *Psychological Science*, 15, 373–378.

Furnham, A. B., & Bachtiar, V. (2008). Personality and intelligence as predictors of creativity. *Personality & individual differences*, 45(7), 613–617.

Furnham, A., Batey, M., Anand, K., & Manfield, J. (2008). Personality, hypomania, intelligence and creativity. *Personality & individual differences*, 44(5), 1060–1069.

Furnham, A., & Chamorro-Premuzic, T. (2006). Personality, intelligence and general knowledge. *Learning & Individual Differences*, 16(1), 79–90.

Furnham, A., & Thomas, C. (2004). Parents' gender and personality and estimates of their own and their children's intelligence. *Personality & Individual Differences*, 37(5), 887–903.

Galton, F. (1869). *Hereditary genius*. London: Macmillan.

Gardner, H. (1993). *Frames of mind: The theory of multiple intelligences*. New York: Basic Books.

Gardner, H. (1995). Reflections on multiple intelligences: Myths and messages. *Phi Delta Kappan*, 77(3), p. 200–203, 206–209.

Genovese, J. E. C. (2008). Head size correlates with IQ in a sample of Hooton's criminal data. *Personality and Individual Differences*, 44, 129–139.

Georgia Department of Education. (2010). *Resource manual for gifted education services*. Retrieved March 4, 2010 from http://public.doe.k12.ga.us/DMGetDocument.aspx/gifted_regulations.pdf?p=4BE1EECF99CD36

4EA5554055463F1FBB77B0B70FECF5942E12E1
23FE4810FFF53501CAAE8CB828386A1B54D8
AFDA9790&Type=D.

Getzels, J. W., & Jackson, P. W. (1958). The meaning of "Giftedness" – An examination of an expanding concept. *Phi Delta Kappan*, 40, 75–77.

Goertzel, M. G., & Goertzel, V. H. (1960). Intellectual and emotional climate in families producing eminence. *Gifted Child Quarterly*, 4, 59–60.

Good, C., Aronson, J., & Inzlicht, M. (2003). Improving adolescents' standardized test performance: An intervention to reduce the effects of stereotype threat. *Applied Developmental Psychology*, 24, 645–662.

Gordon, R. A. (1997). Everyday life as an intelligence test: Effects of intelligence and intelligence context. *Intelligence*, 24(1), 203.

Götz, K. O., & Götz, K. (1979). Personality characteristics of professional artists. *Perceptual & Motor Skills*, 49, 327–334.

Gowan, J. C., Khatena, J., & Torrance, E. P. (1979). *Educating the ablest – a book of readings on the education of gifted children*. Itasca: Peacock.

Greenough, W. T., Black, J. E., & Wallace, C. S. (1987). Experience and brain development. *Child Development*, 58, 539–559.

Guilford, J. P. (1967). *The nature of human intelligence*. New York: McGraw-Hill.

Halpern, D. F. (1997). Sex differences in intelligence: Implications for education. *American Psychologist*, 52, 1091–1102.

Harris, C. R. (2001). Fostering creativity in the Asian-Pacific child K-8: Identification, strategies, implications. In M. D. Lynch & C. R. Harris (Eds.), *Fostering creativity in children, K-8: Theory and practice* (pp. 101–112). Needham Heights, MA: Allyn and Bacon.

Herrnstein, R. J., & Murray, C. (1994). *The Bell Curve: Intelligence and class structure in American life*. New York: Free Press.

Hoffman, L.W. (1994). A proof and a disproof questioned. *Social Development*, 3, 60–63.

Horn, J. L., & Cattell, R. B. (1966). Refinement and test of the theory of fluid and crystallized intelligence. *Journal of Educational Psychology*, 57, 253–270.

Hunsaker, S. L. (1994). Adjustments to traditional procedures for identifying underserved students: Successes and failures. *Exceptional Children*, 61(1), 72–76.

Iscoe, I., & Pierce-Jones, J. (1964). Divergent thinking, age, and intelligence in white and Negro children. *Child Development*, 35, 785–798.

Jaušovec, N. (2000). Differences in cognitive processes between gifted, intelligence, creative, and average individuals while solving complex problems: An EEG study. *Intelligence*, 28, 213–237.

Jaušovec, N., & Jaušovec, K. (2000). Differences in resting EEG related to ability. *Brain Topography*, 12, 229–240.

Jellen, H., & Urban, K. (1989). Assessing creative potential world-wide: The first cross-cultural application of the Test for Creative Thinking – Drawing Production (TCT-DP). *Gifted Education International*, 6, 78–86

Jensen, A. R. (1970). IQ's of identical twins reared apart. *Behavior Genetics*, 1, 133–148.

Jensen, A. R. (1998). *The g factor*. Westport, CT: Praeger.

Jung-Beeman, M., Bowden, E.M., Haberman, J., Frymiare, J. L., Arambel-Liu, S., Greenblatt, S. R., Reber, P. J., & Kounios, J. (2004) Neural Activity When People Solve Verbal Problems with Insight. *PLoS Biology*, 2, 500–510: e97. doi:10.1371/journal.pbio.0020097.

Kammrath, L. K., & Dweck, C. (2006). Voicing conflict: Preferred conflict strategies among incremental and entity theorists. *Personality & Social Psychology Bulletin*, 32, 1497–1508.

Kanazawa, S. (2004). General intelligence as a domain-specific adaptation. *Psychological Review*, 111, 512–523.

Kanazawa, S. (2008). Temperature and evolutionary novelty as forces behind the evolution of general intelligence. *Intelligence*, 36, 99–108.

Kaufman, J. C. (2009). *Creativity 101*. New York: Springer.

Kaufman, J. C., & Baer, J. (2003). Do we really want to avoid Denny's?: The perils of defying the crowd. *High Ability Studies*, 14(2), 149–150.

Kaufman, J. C., & Baer, J. (2006). Intelligence testing with Torrance. *Creativity Research Journal*, 18, 99–102.

Kim, K. H. (2005). Can only intelligent people be creative? A Meta-Analysis. *Journal of Secondary Gifted Education*, 16, 57–66.

Kobrin, J. L., Camara, W. J., & Milewski, G. B. (2002). *The utility of the SAT I and SAT II admissions decisions in California and the nation*. New York: College Entrance Examination Board.

Koenig, K. A., Frey, M. C., & Detterman, D. K. (2008). ACT and general cognitive ability. *Intelligence*, 36, 153–160.

Krisel, S. C., & Cowan, R. S. (1997). Georgia's journey toward multiple-criteria identification of gifted students, *Roeper Review*, 20(2), A1–A3.

Kuncel, N. R., Hezlett, S. A., & Ones, D. S. (2001). A comprehensive meta-analysis of the predictive validity of the Graduate Record Examinations. *Psychological Bulletin* 127(1), 162.

Lentz, T. F. (1927). The relation of IQ to size of family. *Journal of Educational Psychology*, 18, 486–496.

Levine, S. Z. (2008). Using intelligence to predict subsequent contacts with the criminal justice system for sex offences. *Personality and Individual Differences*, 44, 453–463.

Lubart, T. I. (1990). Creativity and cross-cultural variation. *International Journal of Psychology*, 25, 39–59.

Lynn, R. (1991). The evolution of race differences in intelligence. *Mankind Quarterly*, 32, 99–173.

Lynn, R. (1996). *Genetic deterioration in modern populations*. Westport, CT: Praeger.

Lynn, R. (2008). *The global bell curve: Race, IQ and inequality worldwide*. Augusta, GA: Washington Summit.

Lynn, R., & Harvey, J. (2008). The decline of the world's IQ. *Intelligence*, 36, 112–120.

Lynn, R., & Van Court, M. (2004). New evidence of dysgenic fertility for intelligence in the United States. *Intelligence*, 32, 193–201.

Lynn, R., & Vanhanen, T. (2002). *IQ and the wealth of nations*. Westport, CT: Praeger.

MacKinnon, D. W. (1961). Creativity in architects. In D. W. MacKinnon (Ed.), *The creative person* (pp. 291–320). Berkeley: Institute of Personality Assessment Research, University of California.

MacKinnon, D. W. (1962). The nature and nurture of creative talent. *American Psychologist*, 17, 484–495.

MacKinnon, D. W. (1967). Educating for creativity: A modern myth? In P. Heist (Ed.), *Education for creativity* (pp. 1–20). Berkeley, CA: Center for Research and Development in Higher Education.

McCall, R. B. (1994). Advice to the new social genetics: Lessons partly learned from the genetics of mental development. *Social Development*, 3, 54–59.

McCarthy, J. M. (1987). A response to the regular education/special education initiative. *Learning Disabilities Focus*, 2(2), 75–77.

McGrew, K. S. (2009). CHC theory and the human cognitive abilities project: Standing on the shoulders of the giants of psychometric intelligence research. *Intelligence*, 37, 1–10.

Meisenberg, G., Lawless, E., Lambert, E., & Newton, A. (2006). The social ecology of intelligence on a Caribbean island. *Mankind Quarterly*, 46, 395–433.

Meisenberg, G., & Williams, A. (2008). Are acquiescent and extreme response styles related to low intelligence and education? *Personality and Individual Differences*, 44, 1539–1550.

Messick, S., & Frederiksen, N. (1958). Ability, acquiescence, and "authoritarianism." *Psychological Reports*, 4, 687–697.

Miller, G. F., & Tal, I. R. (2007). Schizotypy versus openness and intelligence as predictors of creativity. *Schizophrenia Research*, 93(1–3), 317–324.

Mölle, M., Marshall, L., Wolf, B., Fehm, H. L., & Born, J. (1999). EEG complexity and performance measures of creative thinking. *Psychophysiology*, 36, 95–104.

Moore, D. S. (2006). A very little bit of knowledge: Re-evaluating the meaning of the heritability of IQ. *Human Development*, 49, 347–353.

Murray, C. (1998). *Income, inequality, and IQ*. Washington, DC: American Enterprise Institute.

Neisser, U. (1996). Intelligence: Knowns and unknowns. *American Psychologist*, 51(2), 77–101.

Nettelbeck, T., & Wilson, C. (2005). Intelligence and IQ: What teachers should know. *Educational Psychology*, 25(6), 609–630.

Olszewski-Kubilius, P. (2006). Addressing the achievement gap between minority and non-minority children. *Gifted Child Today*, 29(2), 28–37.

Park, G., Lubinski, D., & Benbow, C. P. (2007). Contrasting intellectual patterns predict creativity in the arts and sciences: Tracking intellectually precocious youth over 25 years. *Psychological Science*, 18, 948–952.

Peek, F. (2007). *The life and message of the real rain man: The journey of a mega-savant*. Port Chester, NY: National Professional Resources.

Petrill, S. A., Lipton, P. A., Hewitt, J. K., Plomin, R., Cherny, S. S., Corley, R., & DeFries, J.C.(2004). Genetic and environmental contributions to general cognitive ability through the first 16 years of life. *Developmental Psychology*, 40, 805–812.

Peterson, J. B., & Carson, S. (2000). Latent inhibition and openness to experience in a high-achieving student population. *Personality and Individual Differences, 28*, 323–332.

Peterson, J. B., Smith, K. W., & Carson, S. (2000). Openness and extraversion are associated with reduced latent inhibition: Replication and commentary. *Personality and Individual Differences, 33*, 1137–1147.

Plomin, R. (1994). Response to commentaries. *Social Development, 3*, 71–76.

Plomin, R. (1999). Genetic research on general cognitive ability as a model for mild mental retardation. *International Review of Psychiatry, 11*, 34–46.

Plomin, R., DeFries, J. C., McClearn, G. E., & McGuffin, P. (2001). *Behavioral genetics* (4th ed.). New York: Worth Publishers.

Plomin, R., Fulker, D. W., Corley, R., DeFries, J. S. (1997). Nature, nurture, and cognitive development from 1 to 16 years: A parent-offspring adoption study. *Psychological Science, 8*, 442–447.

Plomin, R., & Petrill, S. A. (1997). Genetics and intelligence: What's new? *Intelligence, 24*, 53–77.

Plomin, R., & Price, T. S. (2003). The relationship between genetics and intelligence. In N. Colangelo & G. Davis (Eds.) *Handbook of gifted education* (3rd ed., pp. 113–123) Boston: Allyn & Bacon.

Plomin, R., & Spinath, F. M. (2004). Intelligence: Genetics, genes, and genomics. *Personality and Social Psychology, 86*, 112–129.

Preckel, F., Holling, H., & Wiese, M. (2006). Relationship of intelligence and creativity in gifted and non-gifted students: An investigation of threshold theory. *Personality and Individual Differences, 40*, 159–170.

Ratcliff, R., Schmiedek, F., & McKoon, G. (2008). A diffusion model explanation of the worst performance rule for reaction time and IQ. *Intelligence, 36*(1), 10–17.

Razoumnikova, O. M. (2000). Functional organization of different brain areas during convergent and divergent thinking: An EEG investigation. *Cognitive Brain Research, 10*, 11–18.

Renzulli, J. S. (1986). The three-ring conception of giftedness: A developmental model for creative productivity. In R. J. Sternberg & J. E. Davidson (Eds.), *Conceptions of giftedness* (pp. 332–357). New York: Cambridge University Press.

Retherford, R. D., & Sewell, W. H. (1988). Intelligence and family size reconsidered. *Social Biology, 35*, 1–40.

Rhodes, M. (1961). An analysis of creativity. *Phi Delta Kappan, 42*, 305–310.

Richardson, K., & Norgate, S. H. (2006). A critical analysis of IQ studies of adopted children. *Human Development, 49*, 319–335.

Rindermann, H. (2008). Relevance of education and intelligence at the national level for the economic welfare of people. *Intelligence, 36*, 127–142.

Rindermann, H., & Neubauer, A. C. (2004). Processing speed, intelligence, creativity, and school performance: Testing of causal hypothesis using structural equation models. *Intelligence, 32*(6), 573–589.

Rodgers, J., Cleveland, H., Van Den Oord, E., & Rowe, D. (2000). Resolving the debate over birth order, family size, and intelligence. *American Psychologist, 55*, 599–612.

Rudowicz, E. (2003). Creativity and culture: A two way interaction. *Scandinavian Journal of Educational Research, 47*, 273–190.

Rudowicz, E., & Yue, X.-D. (2000). Compatibility of Chinese and creative personalities. *Creativity Research Journal, 14*, 387–394.

Runco, M. A. (1991). *Divergent thinking*. Norwood, NJ: Ablex.

Runco, M. A. (1993). Operant theories of insight, originality, and creativity. *American Behavioral Scientists, 37*, 54–67.

Rushton, J. P. (1995). *Race, evolution, and behavior: A life history perspective*. New Brunswick, NJ: Transaction.

Rushton, J. P. (2008). Testing the genetic hypothesis of group mean IQ differences in South Africa: Racial admixture and cross-situational consistency. *Personality and Individual Differences, 44*, 768–776.

Russo, C. F. (2004). A comparative study of creativity and cognitive problem-solving strategies of high-IQ and average students, *Gifted Child Quarterly, 48*, 179–190.

Schacter, J., Thum, Y. M., & Zifkin, D. (2006). How much does creative teaching enhance elementary school students' achievement. *Journal of Creative Behavior, 40*(1), 47–72.

Scott, C. L. (1999). Teachers' biases toward creative children. *Creativity Research Journal, 12*, 321–328.

Shatz, M. S. (2008). IQ and fertility: A cross-national study. *Intelligence, 36*, 109–111.

Sheppard, L. D., & Vernon, P. A. (2008). Intelligence and speed of information-processing: A review of 50 years of research. *Personality and Individual Differences, 44*, 535–551.

Silvia, P. J. (2008). Another look at creativity and intelligence: Exploring higher-order models and probable confounds. *Personality and Individual Differences, 44*, 1012–1021.

Simonton, D. K. (1994). *Greatness: Who makes history and why.* New York: Guilford.

Simonton, D. K. (1999). *Origins of genius: Darwinian perspective on creativity.* New York: Oxford University Press.

Singh, R. P. (1987). Parental perception about creative children. *Creative Child and Adult Quarterly, 12,* 39–42.

Sternberg, R. J. (1985). *Beyond IQ: A triarchic theory of human intelligence.* New York: Cambridge University Press.

Sternberg, R. J., Grigorenko, E. L., & Jarvin, L. (2006). Identification of the gifted in the new millennium: Two assessments for ability testing and for the broad identification of gifted students. *KEDI Journal of Educational Policy, 3*(2), 7–27.

Sternberg, R. J., & Lubart, T. I. (1991). An investment theory of creativity and its development. *Human Development, 34,* 1–32.

Sternberg, R. J., & Lubart, T. I. (1995). *Defying the crowd: Cultivating creativity in a culture of conformity.* New York: Free Press.

Tammet, D. (2007). *Born on a blue day: Inside the extraordinary mind of an autistic savant.* New York: Free Press.

Teasdale, T. W., & Owen, D. R. (2008). Secular declines in cognitive test scores: A reversal of the Flynn Effect. *Intelligence, 36,* 121–126.

Thompson, T., & Musket, S. (2005). Does priming for mastery goals improve the performance of students with an entity view of ability? *British Journal of Educational Psychology, 75,* 391–409.

Torrance, E. P. (1962). *Guiding creative talent.* Englewood Cliffs, NJ: Prentice-Hall.

Torrance, E. P. (1975). Assessing children, teachers, and parents against the ideal child criterion. *Gifted Child Quarterly, 19,* 130–139.

Torrance, E. P. (1977a). *Creativity in the classroom.* Washington, DC: National Education Association.

Torrance, E. P. (1977b). *Discovery and nurturance of giftedness in the culturally different.* Reston, VA: Council for Exceptional Children.

Torrance, E. P. (1988). The nature of creativity as manifest in its testing. In R. J. Sternberg (Ed.), *The nature of creativity* (pp. 43–75). New York: Cambridge University Press.

Treffert, D. A. (2010). Savant syndrome: An extraordinary condition. A synopsis: Past, present, future. Retrieved March 2, 2010 from http://www.wisconsinmedicalsociety.org/system/files/savant_article.pdf.

Treffert, D. A., & Wallace, G. L. (January, 2004). Islands of genius. *Scientific American,* No. 31, pp. 2–6. Retrieved May 17, 2009, from http://www.scientificamerican.com/article.cfm?id=islands-of-genius.

Turkheimer, E., Haley, A., Waldron, M., D'Onofrio, B., & Gottesman, I. I. (2003). Socioeconomic status modifies heritability of IQ in young children. *Psychological Science, 14,* 623–628.

van Leeuwen, M., van den Berg, S. M., & Boomsma, D. I. (2008). A twin-family study of general IQ. *Learning and Individual Differences, 18,* 76–88.

VanTassel-Baska, J. (1998). The development of academic talent. *Phi Delta Kappan, 79*(10), 760.

Vernon, P. A., Wickett, J. C., Bazana, P. G., & Stelmack, R. M. (2000). The neuropsychology and psychophysiology of human intelligence. In R. J. Sternberg (Ed.), *Handbook of intelligence* (pp. 245–264). Cambridge, UK: Cambridge University Press.

Vining, D. R. (1982). On the possibility of the reemergence of a dysgenic trend with respect to intelligence in American fertility differentials. *Intelligence, 6,* 241–264.

Vining, D. R. (1995). On the possibility of the reemergence of a dysgenic trend with respect to intelligence in American fertility differentials: An update. *Personality and Individual Differences, 19,* 259–263.

Voss, D. H. (1998). Determining test fairness and differential validity of scores for the Torrance Tests of Creative Thinking for kindergarten students. (Doctoral dissertation, Texas Tech University, 1997). *Dissertation Abstracts International, 58*/10, 3828.

Wachs, T. D. (1994). Genetics, nurture, and social development: An alternative viewpoint. *Social Development, 3,* 66–70.

Wallach, M. A., & Kogan, N. (1965). A new look at the creativity-intelligence distinction. *Journal of Personality, 33*(3), 348–369.

Wallas, G. (1926). *The art of thought.* New York: Harcourt Brace.

Webb, R. M., Lubinski, D., & Benbow, C. P. (2007). Spatial ability: A neglected dimension in talent searches for intellectually precocious youth. *Journal of Educational Psychology, 99*(2), 397–420.

Welsh, G. S. (1987). *Manual for the Barron-Welsh Art Scale.* Redwood City, CA: Mind Garden.

Westby, E., & Dawson, V. L. (1995). Creativity: Asset or burden in the classroom? *Creativity Research Journal,* 8, 1–10.

Williams, E. (2000). *The history of the evolution of gifted identification procedures in Georgia.* (Doctoral dissertation, University of Georgia, 2000). *Dissertation Abstracts International,* 160, 153.

Wittmann, W., & Hunt, E. (2008). National intelligence and national prosperity. *Intelligence,* 36, 1–9.

Zajonc, R. B. (1976). Family configuration and intelligence. *Science,* 192, 227–236.

Zajonc, R. B. (1983). Validating the confluence model. *Psychological Review,* 93, 457–480.

Zajonc, R. B. (2001a). The family dynamics of intellectual development. *American Psychologist,* 56, 490–496.

Zajonc, R. B. (2001b). Birth-order debate resolved? *American Psychologist,* 56, 522–523.

Zeidner, M., & Matthews, G. (2000). Personality and intelligence. In R. J. Sternberg (Ed.), *Handbook of human intelligence* (2nd ed., pp. 581–610). Cambridge, UK: Cambridge University Press.

CHAPTER 22

Divergent Thinking, Creativity, and Ideation

Mark A. Runco

Introduction

There is probably as much research on divergent thinking (DT) as any other single topic in creative studies. That research has been produced over more than six decades, although of course there have been a number of innovations during that time. This chapter summarizes the research on DT and identifies innovations in testing and theories of DT. The importance of DT is implied by the amount of research that has been devoted to it over the years and by the large number of practical applications of the research. Indeed, DT applies to education, organizations, and even the natural environment (*everyday creativity*) as well as anything in the field of creative studies. There are misunderstandings, the most notable that tests of DT measure creativity, which they do not. It is important to refute such misunderstandings, which is another objective of this chapter.

The coverage of this chapter is broader than may be obvious with the label *divergent thinking*. That is because many assessments used in the scientific literature are

in fact focused on the same thing (ideas) but not called tests of DT. This is true of most research employing *ill-defined* problems (e.g., Mumford, Reiter-Palmon, & Redmond, 1994), as well as those using *idea-generation* tasks (e.g., Kaufmann & Vosburg, 2002; Pannells & Claxton, 2008; Sosik, Kahai, & Avolio, 1998; Ward, Patterson, & Sifonis, 2004). The best overarching label for all such assessments and the focus of the relevant theories and tests is probably *ideation*. That should not be taken to imply that DT describes only the generation of ideas. Decisions, judgments, and evaluations are also inherent in the ideation that is indicative of creative potential. Additionally, generalizations across ideational research findings may not generalize to all open-ended tests. Quite the contrary. The research reviewed herein indicates that generalizations of this sort are rarely warranted. There are, for example, differences among (a) subtests in batteries of tests (Wallach & Kogan, 1965), (b) verbal and figural tests (Richardson, 1986; Runco & Albert, 1985), (c) tests given with different instructions (Harrington, 1975; Runco, 1986), (d) tests with abstract or concrete tasks (Runco et al., 2000), (e) untimed tests and those with time limits (Mednick, 1962; Runco, 1985), and (f) the various indices and scores (fluency, originality, flexibility, appropriateness, creativity, quality) obtained from tests of ideation (Guilford, 1968; Runco & Charles, 1993; Torrance, 1995). This is just a sample of what the research on DT has confirmed and what is reviewed below. This chapter examines what is suggested about (a) ideation by the research on DT, and (b) creative thinking by research on ideation, including the research on DT.

The focus on ideation underscores the role of DT in much of what we do in the natural environment. Admittedly, many actions are based on routine and are quite often *mindless* (Langer, 1989). Mindlessness might intimate that we are lazy or careless, at least some of the time, but actually there are advantages to this kind of selective attention and allocation of resources. The fact that we can sometimes rely on routine or habit provides us with the capacity to focus when we need to and relax when we do not. Additionally, we do frequently adapt, cope, and process new information in a mindful and active manner as we negotiate daily events and demands. That is when we are the most likely to produce new – and potentially original – ideas. For this reason, the research on DT, to the extent that it contributes to our understanding of ideation more generally than just creative ideation, is a useful topic even outside of creative studies. Creativity is a good thing, and new ideas are useful things to produce. The research on DT is one of the more useful ways to study ideas, and therefore creative potential, as well as our more general everyday problem solving.

This chapter offers a comprehensive review of the research on DT and summarizes the various innovations, debates, theories, and misunderstandings about it. It presents the most realistic view of DT, which is that DT offers an objective perspective on certain kinds of creative potential. DT is not a synonym for creativity but is useful for research on creative potential

and the creative thinking that occurs in the natural environment. Research on DT has many attractions, including the fact that it provides information about both process and product, and it is quite practical. The role of ideas in process and product perspectives is reviewed in the next section. Psychometric research is then examined, as is the research connecting ideas to enhancement efforts, development, health, and domain differences.

Ideation as Process, Ideas as Products

One attractive feature of research on DT is that it offers information about both creative product and the creative process. *Product* and *process* are both facets of the framework that is very frequently used to organize creative studies (Rhodes, 1961; Runco, 2007). Rhodes initially proposed the four P's after examining diverse definitions of creativity. He identified four strands and used alliterative labels for them: person, products, places, and processes. Simonton (1995) later added *persuasion*, based on the idea that creative people change the way others think. Runco recently proposed a hierarchical modification with *creative potential* and *creative performance* at the highest level. The former includes personality research and research on creative environments and places. Personality and places are related to creative performance but do not guarantee it. They can contribute to the fulfillment of potential. With certain personality characteristics (as well as attitudes and values), a person is more likely to perform creatively than when supporting traits, attitudes, and values are lacking. Similarly, certain environments (Amabile, 1990; Harrington, Block, & Block, 1987; McCoy, 2000) are conducive to creativity, though not absolute assurances of it, and other environments tend to inhibit creative performances.

Research on creative performance, in contrast to research on creative potential, looks to products and persuasion. Attributional theory (Kasof, 1995) exemplifies this research in that it assumes that creativity is a social judgment based on actual manifest actions and accomplishments. Similarly, systems theories, which describe how an individual may change a field and perhaps eventually an entire domain (Csikszentmihalyi, 1990), also assume actual performance. This hierarchical theory has the advantage of including perspectives that have been developed since the original framework (Rhodes, 1961) and it allows predictions about how potential can be translated into actual performance and creative accomplishment. Ideation is described by both process theories and product theories, and in fact, it may need to be targeted in any effort to translate mere potential into actual performance.

The idea of DT as process is clear in Guilford's (1968) seminal Structure of Intellect (SOI) model. Guilford described the process by which ideas are produced and distinguished thinking that moves in divergent directions (and may therefore be original) from that which converges (and usually leads only to convention). Certainly, both divergent and convergent thinking play a role in creative performances (A. Cropley, 2006; Runco, 1991), but for now, the point is that Guilford was not merely interested in the qualities of the ideas and solutions generated. He was interested in the intellectual processes that lead to divergent or convergent ideas.

Mednick's (1962) associative theory is sometimes cited as further rationale for DT, and it too focuses on processes. Mednick seemed to prefer his own Remote Associates Test, but his theory describes the process by which an individual moves from idea to idea. One idea leads to another, for Mednick, because they are associated somehow. One idea may be acoustically similar to another idea, for example, so the individual thinks of "duck" right after "truck." Ideas are also sometimes connected via function or experiential proximity. The generation of ideas is, then, a matter of associations, with ideas chained together, one after another. Mednick's explanations for associations are quite

useful for understanding DT. Perhaps most significant is that more original ideas are usually produced late in flow of ideation. Mednick explained this well with his idea of *remote associates*. These are ideas found late in an associative chain. They are far removed from the starting point, and hence remote. They are also the most likely to be original.

The importance of DT, as topic in this volume and in the entire field of creative studies, is reinforced further by the fact that a surprisingly large number of the major issues and questions about creativity have been studied, at one time or another, in research involving ideation. This is not to say that the research on ideation, nor the research specifically on DT, gives a comprehensive picture of the creativity literature. Yet something can be learned about that literature by merely reading the research on DT. It has been used in studies of the so-called "mad-genius controversy," for example, as well as investigations of creativity's relationship with health. It has played an instrumental role in the debate about the domain specificity versus generality of creativity, and in the controversy about creativity being blind rather than intentional, a function of chance rather than directed. This chapter cites each of these, as well as research on DT and aging, motivation, affect, play, problem finding, memory information and knowledge, culture, and various manifestations of a dark side to creativity (e.g., lying, disruptive behavior).

The practicality of DT is reinforced by the fact that it can be used not only as a dependent measure in research but also as part of educational and enhancement methods. Various enhancement efforts are reviewed below. Even more broadly, it is very easy to adapt most tests of DT such that they are exercises for individuals to practice ideation, originality, fluency, and flexibility. In a sense, if a teacher or facilitator takes this approach, and uses DT to exercise the mind, the benefit is a fairly general capacity to produce original ideas. There is also the message – that it is a good thing to generate many ideas when faced with the problem.

Apparently, some people have a tendency toward satisficing, which means that they put in a minimal amount of effort when solving problems. They probably do not produce many ideas when satisficing and the idea of DT suggests that there would be a benefit to being more fluent and considering a larger number of ideas.

Mistakes can be made when using DT for practice and exercise. Brainstorming, for example, is often misused. It is essentially a kind of group DT. When brainstorming a group of people is asked to produce as many ideas as possible for an assigned topic. They are told to (a) postpone judgment, (b) focus on quantity of ideas (fluency) and not quality of ideas, and (c) use each other's ideas as springboards for one's own thinking. But brainstorming does not work well. If a facilitator's, manager's, or teacher's intent is to exercise originality or creativity, he or she should not encourage brainstorming. Individuals tend to be more fluent and original when they work alone in so-called nominal groups than when they work with other individuals (Rickards & DeCock, in press). When in groups, *social loafing* is likely, and when working in a group, the most original ideas tend to be risky precisely because they are original. They are risky in the sense that an individual is taking a chance by sharing something that other people may not understand or appreciate. In fact, Rubenson and Runco (1995) described how there is a linear function that describes the number of individuals involved in a group and the likelihood of being original: When working alone, originality is most likely; when working in a dyad with one other individual, being original is slightly less likely because there is a small amount of the risk defined above; and every time the group increases, the risk increases, and the probability of being original decreases. It certainly is easier to be conventional and take no risks, knowing that your ideas are just like other people's ideas, but creativity requires original and unconventional thinking, and this means that ideas shared may be criticized or misunderstood. There is, then, a risk when thinking in an original and divergent fashion.

A Brief History

These concerns about brainstorming may come as a surprise. They certainly do exemplify the dialectical history of DT research. When theories of DT were first published there was great enthusiasm, in part because tests of DT provided an alternative to IQ tests, which were at that point being severely criticized. At the same time, the Zeitgeist was such that there was a growing interest in creativity. This enthusiasm was unrealistic. The assumption was that DT was an index of all creativity and DT tests were considered valid indicators of actual creative performance (cf. Wallach, 1970). In the 1960s and 1970s, the pendulum went to the other extreme, when research demonstrated that DT test scores demonstrated only moderate or perhaps even low predictive validity. Validity coefficients eventually improved, in part because of innovations in test administration. More will be said about these improvements in the testing and psychometric sections of this chapter. For now, the point is that the pendulum has found a moderate position, with tests of DT clearly not perfect indicators of actual creative performance, yet providing useful information about an individual's potential to produce original ideas, and therefore about the potential for creative problem solving. It is a shame when even today DT tests are sometimes criticized, but only the unimpressive research from the 1960s, 1970s, or 1980s is cited. The picture of DT painted by research in the past 20 years is more balanced, realistic, and accurate. DT provides useful estimates of the potential for creative problem solving (Chand & Runco, 1992; Diakidoy, Constantinos, & Constantinou, 2001; Livne & Milgram, 2006; Walczyk et al., 2008). Note "estimates" and "potential" in that claim.

Structure of Intellect

Empirical efforts focused on DT are usually said to have started with J. P. Guilford's (1950) seminal Presidential Address to the

American Psychological Association. (The address was actually given in 1949 but was not published until 1950.) The claim that creativity research started with Guilford is not very accurate, given the empirical efforts that predated Guilford's address. These efforts include Patrick's (1935, 1937, 1938, 1941) various investigations of artists and other creative groups and, of more relevance, Alfred Binet's inclusion of a task requiring ideation in his seminal work on intelligence and the IQ (Binet & Simon, 1905). Without a doubt, Guilford's SOI model was a huge step forward, and perhaps the most comprehensive model of creative thinking yet published.[1] Creativity and even DT were, however, being studied before Guilford by Binet, Patrick, and others.

Guilford (1950, 1968) referred to *divergent production*. This label follows from the SOI model. In one version of the model, it covers four types of *content* (semantic, symbolic, figural, and behavioral), five distinct *operations* (convergent production, divergent production, cognition, evaluation, and memory), and six different possible *products* (units, classes, relations, systems, transformations, and implications). As Bachelor and Michael (1991) expressed it, "an ability is described as one type of psychological operation processing one type of content (input) to generate one form of product (output)" (p. 160). Early on the SOI contained fewer than 100 "cells," but soon Guilford soon identified others and mostly used the model with 120 cells. In his last publication, Guilford (1986) suggested that there were 180 distinct abilities in the SOI.

Research on SOI did not end with Guilford's death. Bachelor and Michael (1991),

for example, reanalyzed data originally collected by Guilford. (Michael was one of Guilford's students). These represented 53 tests that had been administered to over 400 officers in the U.S. Air Force. Bachelor and Michael were initially interested in testing the reliability of higher order factors. Such higher order factors are constructed from factor scores rather than raw data. In other words, some sort of factor analysis is done with raw data, and then the factor scores are themselves factor analyzed to determine if there is a parsimonious explanation and reliable higher order factors. Bachelor and Michael concluded that a "relatively objective oblique exploratory factor analysis technique" confirmed the reliability of the same four factors Guilford himself had found and associated with creativity. This is striking because Horn (1970) reported factor analyses which brought Guilford's work into question. Bachelor and Michael employed Pro-Max analytic techniques to support Guilford, so apparently the analytic approach dramatically influences the reliability of the SOI factors.

The four factors uncovered by Bachelor and Michael represented ideational fluency, word fluency, sensitivity to problems, and the flexibility of closure. The last apparently represents a transformation or redefinition capacity. Bachelor and Michael (1991, p. 157) concluded,

> although substantial support was found for higher order factors models which distinguished among five types of psychological operations and at three kinds of test content, statistical indicators of closeness of fit suggested that a mixed model of both first-order and higher order factors was required to describe creativity thinking, perhaps within some form of hierarchical ordering. In addition to recognition of divergent production as a key component of creative endeavor, it appeared that a higher order convergent production factor involving primarily semantic and symbolic transformations constituted a dimension of potential importance to the creative thinking of mathematicians, scientists, engineers, and inventors. It was hypothesized that in creative thinking a

---

1 The concept of "creativity" has had very different meanings though history. Hence DT and other current topics (e.g., domain differences) have much longer histories than is usually acknowledged, although perhaps with different labels and wording. Interestingly, theories of DT and the concept of domain specificity are somewhat at odds. The former tend to assume that creativity is a reflection of a general and universal process, whereas the latter emphasizes specificity and differences among domains and processes.

variety of psychological operations within a dynamic, interactive system is employed almost simultaneously in a forward and backward manner.

This conclusion is entirely compatible with the idea of *recursion* as an important part of the creative process, and with the recognition that both convergent and DT are involved in actual creativity (Basadur & Runco, 1993; A. Cropley, 2006; Runco, 2003). Incidentally, the idea of orthogonal abilities or factors mentioned in the quotation from Bachelor and Michael indicates merely that the factors were orthogonal in a statistical sense, or even more simply, relatively independent and uncorrelated with one another. This is worth noting because many criticisms directed at Guilford's work, including Horn and Knapp (1973), focused on his choice of rotation and related methods.

Torrance Tests of Creative Thinking

Torrance (1963, 1965, 1995) is best known for developing the most commonly used measure of DT, the Torrance Tests of Creative Thinking (TTCT), but his extensive research exemplifies what was proposed above about DT being applicable to a very large range of issues and topics in creativity research. Consider, for instance, the test called "Ask and Guess." It presents an examinee with a picture and asks, "The next three tasks will give you a chance to see how good you are at asking questions to find out things that you do not know and at making guesses about possible causes and consequences of events. Look at the picture. What is happening? What can you tell for sure? What do you need to know to understand about what is happening, what caused it to happen, and what will be the result?" This task can be used with very young children. Note also that it may tap *problem finding*. That is a very important part of creativity (Jay & Perkins, 1997; Runco, 1994); not all creativity involves only problem *solving*. Guilford's sensitivity to problems, mentioned earlier, also relates to problem finding. Some say

that problem finding is more important than problem solving (e.g., Getzels, 1975).

Torrance had much to say about the conditions that support DT. Some of these apply directly to the test setting, but some are more generally applicable to any situation that is intended to facilitate creative thinking. Consider the instructions given with the DT task, *Guessing Causes*: "list as many possible causes as you can of the action shown in the picture. You may use things that might have happened just before the event in the picture or something that happened a long time ago and made the event happen. Make as many guesses as you can. Do not be afraid to guess." This task reveals

subjects' ability to formulate hypotheses concerning cause and effect. The number of relevant responses produced by a subject yields one measure of ideational fluency. The number of shifts in thinking or number of different categories of questions, causes or consequences gives one measure of flexibility. The statistical and frequency of these questions, causes or consequences or extent to which the response represents a mentally departure from the obvious and commonplace gives one measure of originality. The detail and specificity incorporated into questions and hypotheses provide one measure of ability to elaborate. (Torrance, 1995, p. 88)

That is quoted in its entirety because it defines the four most commonly used indices of DT: ideational fluency, flexibility, originality, and elaboration. In the 1984 version of the TTCT he described how 13 specific *creative strengths* could be identified in DT. These included Emotional Expressiveness, Internal Visualization, and Richness of Imagery. Torrance suggested that these strengths most accurately represent the breadth of creativity demonstrated in an individual's ideation. *Guessing Causes* also suggests that there are particular applications of DT, in this case to scientific thinking. Several others have developed tests specifically ideation and diverted thinking within the domain of science (Hu, Shi, Han,

Wang, & Adey, 2010). Other domain-specific DT are explored later in this chapter.

Torrance (1995) expressed concern about the social conditions that may facilitate or inhibit DT and creative performance. Very disturbing was his report that educators tend to prefer children with traditional intelligence and high IQs over highly creative students. This may not be much of a surprise because he also cited support for the disappointing tendency of school administrators to prefer "less creative teachers to be more creative ones" (p. 13). Furthermore,

> just as the highly creative child causes classroom problems, the highly creative teacher generates problems for the school administrator. To be creative is to be unpredictable and the unpredictable always makes us uneasy. We like to be able to predict things because we feel safer, more secure, more in control of things. The uneasiness and uncertainty of the administrator may find expression and feelings and even actions of hostility towards a creative teacher. Furthermore, resentment reflected in the recommendation and ratings received from other administrators concerning candidates is likely to influence one's own recommendations and ratings.

Also worthy of note is Torrance's longitudinal study, begun in the 1950s and which included tests of DT. It was this longitudinal investigation that uncovered the fourth-grade slump in creative thinking (Torrance, 1965). Follow-up reports from it are still being produced, the most recent a 50-year assessment that found the TTCT predicted achievement in public and personal creative domains, with predictive validity coefficients exceeding .30.

Torrance developed one DT test (e.g., Action in Movement) just for very young children who do not yet have reading and writing skills. Moran, Milgram, Sawyers, and Fu (1983) also described a method for assessing the DT of preschool children, but they relied on three-dimensional (3-D) stimuli and asked the children to talk about all of the things that each stimulus could be. This is essentially a 3-D version of the questions that are posed to older children in paper-and-pencil tests. Thus a child above, say, third or fourth grade, who has experience with tests and working independently, might be given one of the following tests of DT:

Instances: Name all of the triangular things you can think of. List things that fly in the air.
Uses: List as many uses for a tire as you can. List uses for a toothbrush.
Similarities: How are a desk and a table alike? How are a rock and a plant alike?

With preschool children, on the other hand, it is best to provide them with 3-D tangible objects, such as a square piece of Styrofoam, and then simply ask them to talk about what it could be or how it could be used. There are idiosyncrasies in the Torrance tests. Although Torrance complimented the idea of a *permissive testing environment* (Wallach & Kogan, 1965) and sometimes used what have since become known as *explicit instructions* (Harrington, 1975; Runco, 1986), he also sometimes timed examinees. This is controversial because time limits can distract examinees and keep them from being maximally original (Koestler, 1964). One example of explicit instructions included in the Torrance tests asks for "unusual or provocative questions about common objects such as ice, grass, apples or mountains" (Torrance, 1995). Research comparing explicit and standard instructions is reviewed later in this chapter.

Modes of Thinking in Young Children

Wallach and Kogan (1965) were cited just above on the value of a permissive testing environment. This was initially based on their extensive study of the DT of fifth-grade students. Wallach and Wing (1969) presented a replication with high school students. In both cases, the DT battery contained three verbal tests (Instances, Similarities, and Uses) and two figural tests (Line Meanings and Pattern Meanings). As is true of the Performance Tests from the Wechsler

Intelligence Scale for Children (WISC), the figural tests cannot be considered nonverbal, hence the label figural (or "visual"). They do rely on nonverbal stimuli but directions and responses are verbal, so it is certainly not a nonverbal test. Recall the examples given above with the Instances test asking examinees to name all of the things that they can think of that are triangular, or things that they can think of that fly. The Uses test asks examinees to list as many uses as they can think of for a tire or toothbrush. Similarities asks examinees to list similarities between a desk and table or pickle and banana. The difference between the two figural tests is that Pattern Meanings contains stimuli that are regular, coherent, and largely symmetrical rather than just showing a line in some arrangement on the page.

Line meanings would probably be considered more abstract than Pattern Meanings. This is a potentially importance difference, especially if associative theory (Mednick, 1962) is again applied. That is because associative theory describes how ideas are found, with the most original (and therefore potentially creative ones) well removed from initial idea or stimulus. If that stimulus is abstract, the associations will move in that direction. This kind of influence of DT task stimuli has been noted many times over. In addition to differences between verbal and figural stimuli (Richardson, 1986; Runco & Albert, 1985), there are differences between hypothetical and realistic DT tasks, with originality more likely with the latter than the former. There are educational implications of differences among various DT tasks. If people are accustomed to academic (convergent thinking) tests for example, they might first be given verbal tests, and only later be given highly abstract tasks. According to operant theory, this is essentially a kind of *fading*, where support is gradually removed until individuals emit the appropriate behavior on their own, without support. In the case of DT, that appropriate behavior is original ideation.

Wallach and Kogan (1965) created a permissive testing environment by emphasizing that the DT tasks were games, not tests, that all ideas were worthwhile, not just correct ones, that spelling did not matter, and so on. Wallach and Kogan also told examinees that "the more ideas, the better," which implies that fluency was the objective. On the one hand, a focus on fluency is reasonable, given that originality and flexibility often follow directly from fluency (Hocevar, 1979, 1980). Subsequent research has demonstrated that there are also benefits to explicit instructions for originality or flexibility (Harrington, 1975; Runco, 1986). Such maximal scores tend to be the most reliable, and after all, originality is the index that is the most closely tied to creativity, so it should be maximized. Interestingly, explicit instructions to be flexible do not lead to high originality (Runco, 1985). This is one piece of evidence supporting the separation of the various DT indices. If they were interdependent instead of separate, changes in one would be accompanied by changes in the other, which was not the case. Later in this chapter the debate over that separation is explored in more detail.

Innovations in Testing DT

DT tests take many forms. Batteries developed by Guilford (1968), Torrance (1995), and Wallach and Kogan (1965) have been mentioned, but there are a number of alternatives. Williams (1980), for example, published the Creativity Assessment Package (CAP), intended to estimate fluency, flexibility, originality, elaboration, and titles scores. It does so by providing examinees with a series of frames on which they can draw. Fluency is based on the number of frames used by an examinee. Originality is defined in terms of how often an examinee draws things outside a frame. Abedi (2002; Auzmendi, Villa, & Abedi, 1996) developed a multiple-choice paper-and-pencil test of DT, the Abedi-Schumaker Creativity Test, as a brief alternative to the TTCT. Abedi (2002) and Auzmendi et al. (1996) offered a modicum of psychometric support for this new test based on a Spanish translation and two criteria of creative performance, including teachers' evaluations. They also provided yet more support for the independence of the various indices (fluency, originality, flexibility, and elaboration) of DT.

The Test for Creative Thinking–Drawing Product (TCT-DP) was designed to test DT in a culturally fair fashion (Urban, 1991; Urban & Jellen, 1996). To that end it contains only five figural fragments (e.g., a curved line, a right angle) within one large frame, and then a small frame outside of the larger one. It is, then, a nonverbal test that uses only simple, presumably universally recognizable figures. Examinees are told that some artist began working but stopped and that examinees should continue working on the incomplete drawing. Their work is rated for (a) Continuations, any use or extension of the six fragments; (b) Completions, any additions to these fragments; (c) New elements, new figures, symbols, or elements; (d) Connections made with a line; (e) Connections made to produce a theme, any figure that contributes to the compositional theme; (f) Boundary breaking, nonaccidental drawing outside the frame but not using the small open square; (g) Perspective, three-dimensional elements; (h) Humor and affect; (i) Unconventionality as apparent in manipulation of the material, surreal or abstract drawings, signs or symbols, or nonstereotypical figures. Although judges must be employed and it is not an entirely objective test, interrater reliability after training judges range from .74 to .90 (Dollinger, Urban, & James, 2004, pp. 38–39).

Milgram and Milgram (1976) developed a domain-specific DT test battery, which they called the Tel Aviv Creativity Test. This is scored for the number of ideas that are both unusual and of high quality. The Tel Aviv test has been translated into seven languages (Milgram, Dunn, & Price, 1993). Practically speaking, it is one of the best for preschool and similarly young children (Moran et al., 1983) although it can also be used with adolescents and adults (Milgram & Hong, 1999). A fair amount of validity and reliability information is available (Milgram & Hong, 1999; Milgram & Rabkin, 1980).

Some DT tests go beyond problem solving. The premise is that creative thinking may involve problem solving, but sometimes it is more self-expressive or proactive, and as such is not a reaction to a problem (Runco, 2007). Other times ideation occurs before a problem is ready to be solved. This kind of ideation represents a kind of *problem finding*, although a more accurate label may be problem *identification* or problem *generation*, depending on the particular task or situation. Problem identification is necessary before cognitive resources are deployed, but a problem can be identified and yet not defined in a way that allows progress. *Problem definition* may therefore be necessary after problem identification.

Theories of problem finding and problem definition led to the development of DT tests, which are useful for assessing the ideation that occurs before problem solving. The relevant DT tests are best viewed as measures of *problem generation.* Wakefield (1989) initiated research along these lines when he administered figural DT tasks to a group of children, and then also asked them to design a figure before generating ideas for what it could represent. Runco and Okuda (1988) extended this line of work with a group of adolescents and three verbal divergent-thinking tests: Uses, Instances, and Similarities. Each test consisted of three presented problems and one discovered problem. In the *presented problems*, students were given tasks such as, "Name all the things you can think of which are square." The *discovered problems* asked the subjects first to define a task, and then to provide solutions to it. Each of the presented and discovered items was scored for the number of distinct ideas. Contrasts indicated that the adolescents generated significantly more responses to the discovered problems than to the presented problems. Additionally, discovered problems elicited highly reliable scores that were more highly correlated with criteria of creative performance. Support for the distinctiveness of the problem-finding component of creative performance was given by results of a hierarchical regression analysis.

Another kind of DT test is highly realistic. Realistic DT questions ask examinees about specific issues at home, school, work, or perhaps with other persons. Such realistic tests are attractive in part because, in general, the more closely the contents of a test (or the tasks therein) resemble behaviors used the natural environment, the more valid the test is likely to be. In other words, when test questions are realistic, performances are more indicative of what occurs in the natural environment. Not surprisingly, realistic tasks are used fairly regularly. Meline (1976) had questions such as "How would you get people to quit smoking?" Getzels and Smilansky (1983) asked about school regulations, student cliques, and homework.

Okuda, Runco, and Berger (1991) compared (a) realistic versus standard DT tests, and (b) problem-generation versus problem-solving DT tests, in terms of predictive validity. The participants in this research were elementary school children. The criterion of performance was a check list, not unlike that used by Holland (1961) in his work on extracurricular achievement, and used many times since (Hocevar, 1979; Milgram & Milgram, 1978; Runco, 1986; Wallach & Wing, 1969). Okuda et al. found that the variance explained by the realistic problem generation tasks was statistically significant above and beyond (i.e., after controlling) that provided by the other tests. They were indeed the most accurate predictors of the creative activities described by the check list criteria.

This work with realistic DT tests and tests of problem generation is notable in part because of the psychometric improvements. In his review of creativity measures, Hocevar (1981) reported that, in studies where significant positive correlations between standard DT tasks and other measures of creativity had been reported, the coefficients rarely exceeded .30. Similar findings were reported by Rotter, Langland, and Berger (1971) and Wallach (1983). In the research

with realistic and problem-generation DT tests, the correlations between the real-world problem-finding task and the creative activities were all much higher (average $r = .49$). In fact, one investigation found a canonical predictive validity coefficient in excess of .70 (Chand & Runco, 1992).

The Abbreviated Torrance Test for Adults (ATTA; Torrance, Clements, & Goff, 1989) is also used with regularity. It contains three items from the long form of the TTCT and provides a "creative ability" score that represents a composite of fluency, flexibility, originality, and elaboration. Care must be taken with the composite. Torrance (1995) himself expressed concern over adding the individual scores together, although at one point he stated that such a composite might be indicative of overall energy for creative thinking.

Some of the older DT tests have been used in new ways. Byrne, Shipman, and Mumford (in press) for example, used Guilford's Seeing Problems test (Berger, Guilford, & Christensen, 1957; Kettner, Guilford, & Christensen, 1959; Merrifield, Guilford, Christensen, & Frick, 1961; Wilson, Guilford, Christensen, & Lewis, 1954) in order to assess *forecasting*. As implied by its title, Seeing Problems requires that examinees list potential problems with a common object, such as a tree or hammer. Even more than is the case with Ask and Guess, mentioned earlier, Seeing Problems would appear to be relevant to theories of problem finding and problem definition (Csikszentmihalyi & Getzels, 1970; Runco, 1994). Still, Byrne et al. (in press) defined forecasting a bit more generally such that it included solution implementation and not just problem definition.

Evaluation of Ideas

These ideas about solution implementation and problem finding collaborating with DT suggest that ideation does not operate in isolation. It is, for example, most likely when the individual is interested or motivated. Both declarative and procedural knowledge may also come into play, and some sort of evaluation of ideas must also be involved for creative problem solving. Otherwise there is no way to insure that ideas are in fact effective and useful. Various models of the creative process therefore put DT and ideation into a larger context, such that they work with motivation, knowledge, problem finding, and idea evaluation. The two-tier model, presented in Figure 22.1, describes motivation and knowledge as influences on the problem-generation, ideation, and evaluation process.

The inclusion of an evaluative component may seem to be at odds with the idea of DT. Evaluations may imply convergent thinking. The reason the judgments about ideas are called evaluative is, however, precisely to separate them from the convergent thinking that is denoted by *critical thinking*. Critical thinking focuses on what is wrong or missing; evaluative thinking allows recognition of what is original and creative. It is actually valuative and evaluative. It is also statistically independent of critical thinking (Runco & Smith, 1992).

Several techniques have been developed to assess individual differences in these evaluative abilities (Runco, 1986; Runco & Smith, 1992; Runco & Vega, 1990). Usually ideas are elicited with DT tasks and then judged according to some relevant criterion. They might be judged for creativity, originality, appropriateness, or even popularity. The last of these has been tested with the assumption that (a) it might be the most operational and therefore easiest to judge ("how many other people will think of this idea?") and that (b) it is the opposite of originality and therefore creativity. If something is popular in the sense of being commonplace, it is not original in the sense of being novel. Creativity requires originality. Various investigations have confirmed that evaluative abilities can be reliably assessed and are related only moderately to DT. This is precisely what you would expect since experience with DT probably provides practice at evaluation. Runco and Smith added that intra- and interpersonal evaluations are not strongly related, so accurately judging one's own ideas is no guarantee that ideas given by others will be accurately judged. Runco and Vega reported that experience with children increased the accuracy of evaluations given by adults. Curiously, no differences between teachers and nonteachers were found.

Runco (1991) noted that several predictable biases may occur if an individual looks back at his or her own *associative histories* and evaluates ideas. The individual may see that he or she has generated a number of similar ideas or solutions, for example, and hence when evaluating any of them the conclusion is that none is very original, and therefore none is very creative. But this is based on the fact that the individual has had several similar ideas and none of them appears to be novel or unique. Other people examining the same ideas may think them quite original and creative. That is because a judge or audience does not have the associative history available and therefore does not realize that a number of similar ideas were proposed. Runco (2003) used this to explain why intra- and interpersonal evaluations of ideas are so often discrepant (Runco, 1989; Runco & Smith, 1992; Runco & Vega, 1990).

This line of research reinforces the view that research on DT provides information about both processes and products. The latter, be they inventions, paintings, novels, poems, performances, compositions, patents, or ideas, can be counted; reliability is easy to check; objectivity is admirable; and there is no ambiguity about whether or not the person has the wherewithal, motivation, and persistence to actually complete and publicize his or her work. When products are examined, that is all in the past. Performance is a done deal. DT tests offer this kind of product information, although the products are merely ideas. They are not tangible products but they can be counted and studied. In fact, the quality and quantify of the ideas can be objectively determined. Ideas can be examined for their fluency, originality, flexibility, and so on, and it is fairly easy to check reliability, just as was the case with other more tangible products. Certainly, there may be a gap between what ideas are considered and what ideas are actually recorded. Only the latter can be used in product types of analyses. This is another way of saying that there is a difference between potential and actual performance. Still, it is possible to examine the DT and ideas of individuals who are not yet productive in any socially impressive fashion. In that light, ideas and DT are useful in studies of *everyday creativity* (Runco & Richards, 1998).

Groborz and Necka (2003) examined the role of cognitive control (estimated by the Stroop test) in the evaluation of ideas. DT was assessed with the Drawing Production Test (Urban & Jellen, 1996). Groborz and Necka concluded that accurate evaluations are associated with general cognitive control such that, the more the control, the more accurate the evaluation.

Psychometric Issues

The research on ideational evaluation helps fill in what would otherwise be missing in the creative process. Ideation does not work in isolation. Still, even with a more complete theory of the creative process, the research on DT, problem generation, and ideation evaluation must be empirically validated. For this reason, a large portion of the research on DT is psychometric; it focuses on the tasks and assessment. It is not intended to test any particular hypothesis about development, education, health, or the like, but is instead focused on one kind of validity (e.g., predictive, discriminant, incremental) or reliability. Such psychometric work is very different from hypothesis testing and relies on continuous scales for both validity and reliability (Anastasi, 1982; Nunnally, 1978) rather than on probability levels (.05 or .01). The psychometric efforts indicate that DT tests are imperfect. Yet no test is perfect. All tests focus on samples of behavior and only provide estimates.

This is why the best definition of DT is that tests of it represent *estimates of the potential for creative thinking and problem solving*. There is no guarantee that an individual who does well on a test of DT will do extraordinarily creative things in the natural environ-

ment any more than there is a guarantee that someone with a very high GPA will do great things after graduating from high school, college, or graduate school. In fact, the largest predictive validity coefficients using tests of DT as predictors and various actual creative performance indicators as criteria are equivalent or may even exceed typical predictive validity coefficients from IQ tests. Still, a fairly wide range of predictions has been found for both DT and IQ tests, and both of them can provide useful information. The following section of this chapter examines some of the psychometric issues that are most relevant to DT tests.

An enormous amount of research has examined the *predictive validity* of DT tests. Carson, Peterson, and Higgins (2005), for example, reported a predictive validity coefficient of .47 between DT and their own Creative Achievement Questionnaire (CAQ). The CAQ is a self-report that asks about 10 different domains of creativity. Carson et al. found it to be reliable and related to art projects (collages) and a standardized measure of creative personality, as well as DT. The CAQ also showed good discriminant validity in (low) correlations with IQ. This is all useful information, given how difficult it is to find a good criterion for creativity (Shapiro, 1970).

One of the best ways to determine predictive validity is longitudinally. Torrance himself initiated that longitudinal investigation in 1957–1958 in the context of the fourth-grade slump. The most recent follow-up (Runco, Millar, Acar, & Cramond, 2010) supported the use of the TTCT, with coefficients in excess of .30. These analyses used DT data from the initial stages of the longitudinal study, collected in the late 1950s, and correlated them with criterion data collected 50 years later! At least as impressive was Plucker's (1999) re-analysis of Torrance's longitudinal data. Plucker used structural-equation modeling techniques and discovered that nearly 50% of the variability creative achievement indicators for adults could be predicted from DT. Most impressive was that DT explained approximately three times the variance in creativity achievement as did IQ scores.

Other investigations of predictive validity of DT have been presented by Milgram and Milgram (1978), Hocevar (1980), Runco (1986), and Ward, Kogan, and Pankove (1972). Keep in mind that most of these investigations report only moderate validity for DT. The difference in those with moderate and those with impressive predictive validities seems to be in the criteria used. The more the criteria are connected to ideation, the higher the validity. When criteria representing creative accomplishments that depend on resources, domain-specific skills, and things in addition to simply the generation of ideas are used, predictive validities are approximately .30; but when a measure of ideational activity is used, they jump dramatically.

Silvia (2008) also published a re-analysis, only he used data from Wallach and Kogan's (1965) classic study and his concern was *discriminant validity*. Wallach and Kogan reported very low correlations (mean r = .09) between various measures of intelligence (including academic aptitude) and various measures of creative potential. Silvia used latent-variable analysis and found only slightly larger correlations (approximately .20). In his case, these correlations used latent variables representing fluency and originality and not the DT scores themselves. Clearly, intelligence and DT are far from redundant. Recall here that much of the work summarized earlier in this chapter (e.g., Getzels & Jackson, 1962; Wallach & Kogan, 1965) is relevant to discriminant validity.

Something must be said at this point about the *threshold hypothesis* (Guilford, 1968; Kim, 2002; Runco & Albert, 1985). This hypothesis posits that the relationship of DT (or any index of creativity) is related to general intelligence, but only up to a moderate level. That is the threshold that led to the label, the threshold hypothesis. Beyond this level, DT and general intelligence are unrelated. Hence, some IQ is necessary for creative thinking, but high IQ (e.g., above 120) is not at all necessary.

Statistically, the threshold implies a curvilinear relationship between "g" and DT. This can confuse tests of discriminant validity, for if they sample high ability individuals, DT and "g" are independent of one another, but if the sample represents only low-ability participants, there might be a moderate or even strong correlation between IQ and DT and an apparent lack of discriminant validity. The relationship between general ability and DT is also influenced by the testing environment (Wallach & Kogan, 1965), such that the separation is clear only when examinees are allowed to play with ideas and told not to treat DT tasks as tests.

Another kind of discriminant validity involves the various indices of DT (e.g., fluency, originality, flexibility, and elaboration). On the one hand, three lines of investigation bring the discrimination of the various indices into question. First are the factor analyses of DT test scores that often uncover only one factor. Then there are multitrait/multimethod comparisons that suggest that scores within any one method (i.e., one test) are more highly correlated than indices (traits) across tests. And there are the simple product moment correlations, which also suggest redundancy, especially between fluency and originality, and between fluency and flexibility. For these three reasons it has been said that fluency might be used alone. After all, it predicts originality and flexibility.

The use of only one index of DT is unfortunate on several grounds. First and least important, if only one index were to be used for some reason, fluency is probably not the best one. As noted above, originality is more strongly tied to creativity than is fluency, so if one index were to be used alone, it should probably be originality. Additionally, there is experimental evidence that the indices are independent and represent independent processes. Runco (1985), for example, demonstrated that explicit instructions to be flexible do not necessarily lead to high originality scores, and this fact suggests a kind of operational independence. Similarly, when explicitly directed to be original, fluency scores tend to drop (Harrington,

1975; Runco, 1986). A change in one index, in one direction, accompanied by a change in the opposite direction in another index, would not occur if they were interdependent. In addition, the correlations between fluency and originality or fluency and flexibility are large but not perfect. Hence, there is unique variance, even if it is smaller than that which is shared. Finally, regression techniques have removed variance shared by fluency and originality, allowing the reliability of the unique variance of originality (or flexibility) to be examined (Hocevar, 1980; Runco & Albert, 1985). The unique variance of originality is reliable, at least in some tests and individuals, at moderate or high levels of talent.

Actually, there is also a practical reason to continue to use at least three indices of DT. This is the benefit to educators and individuals who need to interpret DT test scores. They will have more information if they have all three indices or scores and can examine them together as a kind of profile. Otherwise they are really just looking at ideational productivity, something which is quite limited and far from equivalent to creative potential.

Developmental research on DT supports the use of several indices of DT as well. That research shows that the various indicators have different trajectories through the life span. The different trajectories support the independence of the indices. If they were interdependent, they would probably develop at the same rate, but they do not. There is, for instance, the fourth-grade slump mentioned above (Torrance, 1965), and it is the most obvious in originality but not obvious in the other indices of DT There is also a tendency for flexibility, in particular, to suffer late in life (Guilford, 1970). This is no surprise if you think about what Chown (1960) referred to as "age and the rigidities," or the general tendency for adults to increasingly rely on routine and habit. The fourth-grade slump and the slump in flexibility late in life are two examples of the way that the various indicators of DT change in idiosyncratic ways. They do not all increase or decrease at the same time. The differences

in increases and decreases in turn, imply that they provide unique information which would be lost if only one indicator, such as fluency, were used. Incidentally, the fourth-grade slump was replicated with various samples, but it is probably not universal. Raina (1975) did not find it in children from India. Nonetheless, it did seem to plague perhaps 50% or even 60% of the students in the United States and in several other countries.

Other indices of DT have been proposed. Milgram (1990) argued that it is best to score DT tests for nonoverlapping originality and commonness scores, and Bachelor and Michael (1991), Guilford (1968), Feldman, Marrinan, and Hartfeldt (1972), and Jackson and Messick (1965) recognized a transformational capacity. In their investigation of transformation, Feldman et al. (1972) asked judges to examine ideas elicited by the TTCT and to look for three things: first, the degree to which an idea could "stimulate thinking and reflection about the possibilities generated by the response," second, "break the constraints of the situation," and third, cause the judges "to accommodate their thinking to the 'new reality' generated by the response" (p. 336).

Bachelor and Michael's (1991) view of transformation was tied to the possibility of redefining a situation and "flexibility of closure" (p. 165). Bachelor and Michael (p. 170) emphasized the importance of transformation.

> *Deserving almost a special status among the six elements in the SOI dimension of products, transformations are extremely important in the types of tasks that mathematicians, scientists, engineers, and inventors frequently have to achieve in arriving at unique solutions to problems appearing in a highly altered and often foreign context.*

As would be expected (Michael having been a student of Guilford's), a parallel perspective can be found in Guilford (1983).

There is surprisingly little research on the actual or literal divergence of ideas elicited by DT tests. Divergence is at the heart of the concept, but it is not necessarily involved in any particular index of DT. Originality and flexibility may result from divergence of thought, but they may also result from nondivergent pathways, as is the case when remote associates are original and varied (Mednick, 1962; Milgram & Milgram, 1978; Runco, 1985). Remote associates may be quite removed from an initial problem state, and they are often quite original, but they may be associated with that initial state in a linear fashion.

The idea of divergence was suggested by the research of Bossomaier, Harr, Knittel, and Snyder (2009). They used semantic networks to understand DT and then proposed an algorithm to calculate a creativity quotient (CQ) to use when testing DT. Semantic networks allow for an actual divergence.

Ideational Pools

Runco and Mraz (1992) introduced a new technique for scoring DT tests. Instead of scoring each idea as original or flexible, and instead of counting each individual idea and adding all of them together for a fluency score, the total ideational output of an individual was considered all at once. They called the compilations *ideational pools*. Scoring all ideas at once was justified by the fact that it could save an enormous of time, and, more importantly, it would provide those doing the scoring with much more information than the traditional method. After all, if scores are determined one idea at a time, judges only have that one idea to work with. But if the entire ideational output is being examined, the judge has everything there is from the examinee. He or she can see how many ideas were given and get a feeling for how original and varied they might be. Runco and Mraz also decided to ask judges to score ideational pools for creativity and not just the typical fluency, originality, and flexibility. A Q-sort method was adapted whereby the ideational pools of 24 adolescents were rated by 30 college students. Results supported the reliability of the method, especially in interrater agreement, with intraclass coefficients in excess of .90, but a bit less in inter-item consistency, with alphas of approximately .62. There was a hint of bias in that correlations between ratings of creativity and ratings of intelligence were above .50, thus bringing discriminant validity into question. Still, this lack of discriminant validity might be circumvented by providing the judges with explicit definitions of both intelligence and creativity. Amabile (1990) suggested that judges not be given definitions, but it has been done in the past (Runco, 1989) with good results and might improve ratings of ideational pools. In fact, findings from Rossman and Gollob (1975) imply that judges might also be given background information about examinees to make the best possible judgment.

Runco and Charles (1993) used ideational pools in their investigation of how the originality of ideas was related to the appropriateness of ideas. This relationship was of interest because creativity is usually defined such that both originality and appropriateness are required. Originality may be called uniqueness, novelty, or unusualness, and appropriateness may be called effectiveness, fit, or practicality. Whatever the label, creative things do require some sort of originality and some sort of appropriateness (Albert, 1975; Bruner, 1962; Khandwalla, 1993; MacKinnon, 1963; Rothenberg & Hausman, 1976). The method using ideational pools allowed an empirical test of how originality and appropriateness are related to one another.

Runco and Charles (1993) addressed these questions by systematically arranging the cards to be used in a Q-sort, such that some contained primarily original ideas (determined objectively from earlier samples), some contained primarily appropriate ideas, and some contained a combination of the two. This manipulation was in contrast to the earlier work of Runco and Mraz (1992); they relied on actual ideational pools rather than manipulating the contents to insure high or low originality or appropriateness, as was done in the work of Runco and Charles.

Appropriateness was surprisingly difficult to operationalize. Runco and Charles accomplished it by relying on tasks that

allowed solutions that were clearly effective or ineffective, fitting or unfitting. They
were, however, forced to rely on very literal definitions of fitting. To this end, they
used the DT task, "list as many square
things as you can," and then used responses
that were literally square. This meant that
only responses describing things with four
and only four sides, each of which was
equal, things that were two dimensional
rather than 3-D, and things that were literally rather than metaphorically square ("my
dad's music" or "a meal"), were deemed
appropriate.

Judges were asked to sort cards containing
the ideational pools for originality, appropriateness, or creativity (counterbalancing the
order with which they did each of these).
When the arrangements of pools were quantified, as has been done in Q-sort methodology, results indicated that the judges' ratings
agreed very well with objective ratings, for
both originality and appropriateness. Contrary to theoretical expectations, appropriateness ratings were inversely related to originality ratings. Additionally, the only ratings
that were associated with creativity were the
originality ratings. It appeared that when
unoriginal ideas were being judged, their
appropriateness actually lowered ratings of
creativity. Very likely, the limited and literal
definition of appropriateness had an impact
on these findings.

Domains and Special Populations

There are numerous modifications of DT
tasks for special populations or domains.
Some of these tasks were designed for particular cultures or languages (e.g., Chan,
Cheung, Lau, Wu, Kwong, & Li, 2000–
2001; Milgram et al., 1993), others for
the assessment of DT within a particular
domain.

Goldschmidt and Tatsa (2005) used tests
of DT with architecture and design students. Interestingly, they calculated two special ideational scores. The first, "composite
score," reflected ideas that captured two or
more different styles or topics or designs

in one idea. The second, "critical ideas,"
was calculated by examining the students'
identification of the elements that were
most important (or critical) for a particular
design. That is, of course, similar to the evaluative scores used by Runco (1991; Runco &
Smith, 1992) in his studies of the interplay of
DT and evaluative thinking.

Hu and Adey (2002) developed a test of
scientific creativity for use with secondary
school students. Although intriguing, this
measure was validated only in England, and
was quite short, with only seven items. The
length is an important limitation of Hu and
Adey's measure, as short tests are not as reliable as long tests (because errors of measurement are not numerous enough fully to
cancel out). Hu and Adey had one question
from a Uses test, for example, and another
to tap the capacity to ask good scientific
questions. A third was adapted from *Product Improvements* ("*how could a hammer be
improved?*"). A fourth is similar to Torrance's
test called *Just Suppose task* (e.g., "*suppose
the earth was entirely covered with water –
how would things be different?*"). One task
was not really justified by Hu and Adey
("draw as many possible methods for dividing a square into four equal pieces") and
another was much more complicated and
time consuming than all others combined
("design an apple picking machine"). Hu
and Adey validated the test only by comparing students of different ages (the older
students received the highest scores) and by
comparing three "bands" of students who
had previously been rated by teachers in
terms of scientific ability. There was, then,
no attempt to validate the test against criteria of scientific potential. A better validated but more focused test of scientific potential was developed by Hu et al.
(2010). It was called Formulating Hypotheses and allowed students to do just that.
The fluency, originality, and flexibility of
the hypotheses can be determined, as is
the case with any DT test. Other domain
specific DT tests have been developed
for mathematics (Livne & Milgram, 2000;
Mann, 2009) and physics (Diakidoy et al.,
2001).

Walczyk et al. (2008) examined lying with particular DT tests. This may sound like a test of malevolent creativity (D. Cropley, Kaufman, & Cropley, 2008) or even of the dark side of creativity (McLaren, 2003; Runco, 1993), but as Walczyk et al. noted, lying is not necessarily immoral or malevolent. They described how lying "is a ubiquitous expedient for achieving social goals such as fostering harmony, sparing the feelings of friends, concealing wrongdoing, or exploiting others" (p. 328). To examine the predicted relationship, they developed 18 social dilemmas, each of which allowed for deception to be a reasonable path to resolution. Analyses of responses given by 81 college students suggested that creative liars tend to have high DT.

James and Asmus (2000) examined the relationship between personality and creative potential, but they did so within artistic and social domains and hypothesized that cognitive skill (DT) would mediate the impact of personality on creative performance. This hypothesis was supported by their empirical findings, at least for the cognitive capacity to generate original ideas, which did in fact mediate as expected. In fact, there was also an indication of an interaction between personality and cognitive capacity in analyses of predictive validity.

Joussemet and Koestner (1999) looked to the domain of gymnastics and examined the impact of expected reward. Practice DT tasks required that the female gymnasts (4–17 years of age) generate themes for a gymnastics gala. Approximately half were in a reward condition, the other half, in a no-reward condition. The impact of practice was determined by administering different (figural) DT tasks. Importantly, actual rewards were only given during the practice sessions; hence the expectation of reward. Joussemet and Koestner asked judges to rate the responses but also calculated originality scores from the rare (unusual) ideas. All participants were less original when rewards were expected. There were some age effects, with the younger participants tending toward less appropriate themes, at least in the ratings from the judges. Perhaps judges are better able to determine things like appropriateness, while originality can be found via rarity and the unusualness of ideas.

Ziv and Keydar (2009) tested DT in her investigation of music and the preferences for complexity. Participants in this research listened to music after two DT tasks had been administered. Not surprisingly, Ziv and Keydar found differences in the impact of the different pieces of music, but there was an overarching relationship for DT to be associated with a preference for more complex music. A fair amount of earlier research has also supported the role of preference for complexity in creative efforts (Barron, 1995; Eisenman, 1980).

Scratchley and Hakstian (2000–2001) tested both personality and cognitive capacity in their work on managerial creativity. Openness to experience and DT were both correlated with "creative management performances" of actual managers. Discriminant validity was also suggested by the fact that general intelligence had lower relationships with creative potential than did DT and openness. In fact, when DT was statistically controlled, there was no relationship at all between general intelligence and managerial creative performance. DT, on the other hand, remained statistically significant as a predictor even when general intelligence was controlled. Not surprisingly, the most accurate predictions of managerial creative performance took both DT and openness into account.

Jung (2000–2001) looked specifically at leadership and DT. In particular, Jung examined transformational and transactional leadership practices while individuals worked in groups. Transactional leadership is characterized by supervisors who set goals and then reward behaviors that move the group toward those goals. Transformational leadership is characterized by discussion of different points of view, intellectual exchanges, and collective action. Jung found that individuals in transformational groups had higher DT than those in transactional groups. Nominal groups (composed of individuals working alone) also had higher DT than the transactional groups, but this relationship was also expected, given the typical advantage of nominal groups (Rickards & DeCock, in press; Runco, 2007).

Sosik et al. (1998) also looked to transformational leadership but also examined the impact of working on a computer. They manipulated the level of transformational leadership and the identification (or anonymity) of participants. This is an important point because anonymity may support DT and originality for reasons that are similar to what was just noted: It is easy to be weird and unconventional when there is no risk of being identified (Rubenson & Runco, 1995). In fact, Barron (1993) once referred to creativity as *controlled weirdness*! Sosik et al. reported that transformational groups had high originality and elaboration scores on the DT tasks. Contrasts indicated that groups with varied levels of anonymity differed in their flexibility scores from the DT tasks. The positive impact of transformational leadership might seem to be at odds with the results of Scratchley and Hakstian (2000–2001), but the methodologies of the two studies make comparisons difficult. This is especially true, given the role of the computer in the research of Sosik et al. Note that their findings reinforce the conclusion offered above that it is useful to take several DT indicators into account rather than relying entirely on fluency or any one index of DT.

Before moving to the next section, a parallel line of work should be cited. This research does not look at DT within domains but does assume a kind of specialization. Hudson (1968) initiated work along these lines he compared divergers and convergers. More recently, Brophy (2001) compared individuals tending toward divergent thinking, convergent thinking, or a combination of both. Basadur (1994) summarized evidence of similar relationships between DT and various cognitive styles.

Criteria of Creativity

The criterion problem was recognized very early in creative studies (Shapiro, 1970).

Runco (2007) suggested that it is a particular problem for studies of DT. Too often the criteria used to validate DT focus on behaviors and activities that are removed from ideation, if they are related at all, even though DT focuses on ideas. As mentioned above, DT is sometimes misunderstood. Tests of DT are not tests of creativity. They are instead tests of ideation, and in particular fluency, originality, and flexibility with ideas. It makes no sense to validate them against creative performances that are removed from ideation. The creative activity and achievement check lists cited several times in this chapter are useful and reliable criteria of some kinds of creative talent, but they assess only socially recognized products and performances. Socially recognized products and performances can be quite different from more personal kinds of creativity. They are also not entirely appropriate criteria for studies of the predictive validity of DT tests.

Runco et al. (2000) developed a criterion specifically for investigations of the predictive validity of DT. It is a self-report, known as the Ideational Behavior Scale, that asks about ideation occurring in the natural environment. (To insure a unique label, the author's name was added, so it is the RIBS.) Items include, "I come up with an idea or solution other people have never thought of," "I am able to think about things intensely for many hours," and "I often have trouble sleeping at night, because so many ideas keep popping into my head." Runco et al. (2000) reported interitem reliabilities in excess of .91. Discriminant validity is also good, with a correlation of .11 between the RIBS and GPA. Both U.S. and Korean individuals had completed the RIBS, but Runco et al. (2000) found no significant differences between them. More is said about culture and group differences later in this chapter.

The RIBS was also used in a test of the two-tiered model of the creative process (Chand & Runco, 1992), which was described earlier. The unique measure in that investigation focused on *discretionary time on task* (D-TOT). It was assessed by determining precisely how much time examinees put into their divergent thinking when at liberty to decide for themselves. In a sense, the two-tiered model was not unambiguously supported because the interaction between motivation (time on task) and DT predicted ideational behaviors only when abstract (not realistic) tests of DT were used. Still, time on task was related to DT, and the RIBS, and of most importance for the present purposes, DT and the RIBS are significantly correlated.

Runco et al. (2000) acknowledged that most of the relationships among time, DT, and ideational behavior (the RIBS) could be moderated by attitude. Indeed, certain attitudes have proven to be critical for DT (Basadur, 1994; Basadur & Runco, 1993). Basadur (1994) pointed specifically to *Openness to Divergence* and *Premature Closure*, the former a support for DT and the latter a potential inhibitor. He developed a 14-item self-report, which assesses each and has reported a number of investigations supporting their association with DT.

Enhancement of Ideation

Not surprisingly, given the omnipresence of technology in today's society, computer training for DT has been examined. Benedek, Fink, and Neubauer (2006), for example, compared two computer-based DT enhancement programs. One focused on verbal DT and the other on "functional DT." Training was fairly extensive, consisting of nine sessions and, within each session, practice with eight different DT exercises. Ideational fluency clearly responded to the training, even with general intelligence controlled. Originality did not. Findings like this support the separation of fluency and originality (also see Runco, 1985) and are not at all surprising, given that originality requires some acumen, judgment, and often an aesthetic sensibility.

The most direct method for increasing DT and original thinking focuses on *explicit instructions*. Harrington (1975) compared standard and one kind of explicit instructions ("be creative … creative ideas

are both original and worthwhile"). Sure enough, the explicit instructions led to higher originality scores than the inexplicit standard instructions. Harrington explained the findings in terms of task perception. Runco (1986) extended this line of work by testing the impact of explicit instructions with both nongifted and gifted children. He replicated the earlier findings but discovered that the improvements were the most dramatic for the nongifted individuals. This might seem like marginal returns, and indeed, Runco (1986) proposed that the gifted individuals may have been strategic about the DT even before they were told how to be creative.

Keep in mind that even standard instructions are designed to encourage DT. Without them, examinees tend to treat DT tasks as tests that are more convergent than divergent (Wallach & Kogan, 1965). Standard instructions highlight the fact that DT tasks are not typical academic tests and that examinees should not think about only one answer, nor about only the answer that a teacher or supervisor might expect. They are told not to worry about spelling or points or grades, and they are usually told to take their time and perhaps even to treat the tasks as games rather than as tests. When these kinds of instructions are not given, scores on DT tests are much too highly correlated with tests of convergent thinking, suggesting that examinees tend to use their convergent-thinking skills unless explicitly told to think divergently.

Runco and Okuda (1988) used explicit instructions to test the relationship between fluency, originality, and flexibility. They expected originality and flexibility to be particularly strongly related, the assumption being that flexible ideation leads to original ideas. Surprisingly, results indicated that flexibility and originality were unrelated. This pattern was suggested by the flexibility scores in the originality condition, and the originality scores in the flexibility instructional condition. Most important were the originality scores, which were low when the participants were asked to be flexible in their ideation. Participants had been given strategies for proposing flexible ideas, but these did not lead to highly original ideas.

Chand and Runco (1992) compared the impact of explicit and standard instructions on two realistic DT tests and two problem-generation tests. The latter asked participants to generate problems and then choose one, and only then to generate solutions. The realistic tasks directed examinees to problems that they might encounter in the natural environment, including those at work or school. Analyses confirmed that realistic tests differ from standard tasks; there was a significant Test X Instruction interaction. At least as important was that the predictive validity of the DT tests was much higher than that obtained with standard instructions. In fact, the validity coefficient was .70 (a canonical Rc)! When standard instructions were administered, the canonical coefficient was much smaller and nonsignificant. Incidentally, one drawback of problem-generation tasks is that originality cannot be objectively determined (i.e., in terms of statistical infrequency). That is because each examinee is solving his or her own problems, so ideas cannot be compared to one another.

Explicit instructions may provide the *conceptual* or *procedural* information that is included in the two-tiered model of the creative process as well. The former might include definitions of originality or creativity, for example, and the latter know-how and procedures for finding creative or original ideas (e.g., "give ideas that no one else will think of"). Runco, Illies, and Reiter-Palmon (2005) reported that procedural instructions had a more dramatic impact on DT than did conceptual instructions. This was particular obvious in originality scores.

Runco, Illies, and Eisenman (2005) used explicit instructions with the creativity and appropriateness of ideas, as well as originality. The scoring criteria for appropriateness were in some ways similar to those used in the earlier research of Runco and Charles (1993) and, before that, by Guilford, Wilson, and Christiansen (1952) with their "social institutions test." Appropriate ideas were defined as (a) feasible, (b) successful in solving the problem at hand, and (c) not viewed as inappropriate by other people (e.g., they were not illegal). Ideas that did not address the main objective implied by the problem were deemed inappropriate, as were those that were dangerous, harmful to others or to living things, or which cost the individual his or her job or standing. Solutions that described impossible acts (e.g., being in two places at once) were deemed inappropriate. Kelder, McNamara, Carlson, and Lynn (1991) had demonstrated that judges can reliably judge appropriateness.

Runco, Illies, and Eisenman (2005) used realistic and standard DT tasks but four different kinds of instructions, asking the participants to generate (a) as many ideas as they could, (b) only creative ideas, (c) only original ideas, or (d) only appropriate ideas. Significantly, the standard tasks tended to elicit higher originality and flexibility scores than did the realistic tasks. The realistic tasks elicited higher appropriateness scores. Not surprisingly, these differences varied from one instructional group to the other. The appropriateness and originality scores shared very little (7%) of their variance.

Houtz, Jambor, Cifone, and Lewis (1989) took a slightly different approach and compared explicit instructions that asked for as many unique ideas as possible ("give ideas that no one would think of") with those asking for as many common ideas as possible ("give ideas that everyone else would think of"). The results revealed that the boys given directions calling for common ideas outperformed the boys given directions for unique ideas, with exactly the opposite effect for girls. Houtz et al. attributed this finding to the possibility that the directions to "think of only [sic] ideas that everyone else will also think of" may be inconsistent with the typical male thinking pattern. They suggested that boys may have a shorter list of such ideas because they tend to think in an individualistic fashion. Girls, on the other hand, may have a larger base of both common and novel ideas as a result of their own cultural stereotypical role development. Admittedly, these sex differences are not entirely consistent with the broader literature on creativity and gender (Runco, Cramond, & Pagnani, in press).

Clapham (1997) took a broader view of enhancement and compared training that focused completely on ideation with training that depended on a lecture on the value of creativity, goal setting, and self-talk. Interestingly, both forms of training were effective, at least in that each had DT scores in excess of those from a control group. The inclusion of values is notable and consistent with several other studies in the broader creativity literature (Joy, 2008; Kasof, Chen, Himsel, & Greenberger, 2007).

Not all enhancement involves (and is limited to) college students. One training effort was directed at managers in midsized firms. They received DT tasks before and after training, as well as Basadur's measure of problem solving style which categorized them as *generator, conceptualizer, optimizer,* or *implementor.* Their attitudes and evaluative accuracy was also assessed. The training provided (a) detailed information about all stages of the creative problem solving process (see Basadur, 1994) and (b) opportunities for practice. Comparisons of pre- and posttraining confirmed significant improvements in the evaluative accuracy of the managers. They were much better, after training, at recognizing original ideas. They were also more original. Some of the improvement seems to have been moderated by the preference for ideation attitude, which makes great sense given suggestions that attitude is the most sensitive and malleable of the influences on creative performances (Davis & Subkoviak, 1975).

Support for training efficacy is also provided by Ma's (2009) meta-analysis. He confirmed the effectiveness of enhancement efforts and was able to show that, across studies, verbal DT seemed to be the easiest of all ideation to enhance. This meta-analysis was not, however, focused on DT but covered all enhancement efforts. Still, this is probably a sound conclusion given that (a) most training will need to include a verbal

component since that is how people, including facilitators, communicate, and (b) the meta-analysis included 111 empirical investigations and 2013 effect sizes. The unweighted grand mean of these was .69, which is quite sizeable.

Influences on DT

The psychometric research reviewed above confirms that DT is a meaningful indicator of the potential for ideation and originality. The research specifically on the testing environment and the impact of instructions further confirms that DT is influenced by a variety of factors in the immediate environment. Not surprisingly, it is also influenced by more remote and long-term factors, including family background, personality, motivation, and affect. It is also associated with health, certain biological variables, and culture, though here, bidirectionality is quite possible. DT may be influenced by these things, but it in turn also has a potential influence on them.

Family Background

Family structure is related to various personality traits, including conventionality and its antithesis, rebellion, so it is no surprise that there is research also tying it to DT. Family structure is not easy to investigate, however, because families are (a) private entities, (b) far from static, and (c) quite complicated. Even family structure is complex in that it involves the number of persons, the number of children ("sibsize"), the ages among family members (and "age gaps"), the sex of the members, and so on. Given this complexity, it is no surprise that research results are themselves not clear-cut. Lichtenwalner and Maxwell (1969) reported that first born and only children had the highest DT scores, but they had used only one test of DT and only fluency scores. Still, Eisenman and Schussel (1970) reported much the same with a different sample. Eisenman (1964) and Staffieri and

Bassett (1970) had previously that first born individuals had lower scores. Datta (1968) and Wilks and Thompson (1979) found no relationship between birth order and creativity. Runco and Bahelda (1986) collected DT data from a moderately large group and found that only children had the highest scores. Differences between eldest, middle, and youngest children were not statistically significant (Radio Gaynor & Runco, 1992).

The parents are of course also likely influences on DT. Runco and Albert (1985) reported a canonical correlation of .55 between parents' and children's DT scores. They also found parental personality to be an influence, with a canonical correlation of .53 between DT test scores and various traits from the California Psychological Scale (also see Fu, Moran, Sawyers, & Milgram, 1983).

Noble, Runco, and Ozkaragoz (1993) also found significant intrafamilial correlations but differences among three groups: One represented families with a history of alcoholism (the father was a recovered alcoholic); another represented families with histories of alcoholism but no current alcoholism; and there was additionally a control group. As was the case in Runco and Albert (1985), the correlations were strongest between fathers and their sons. Additionally, the two samples with a family history of alcoholism had lower DT test scores. Additional research, not using DT but focusing on creativity and alcoholism, was presented by Rothenberg (1990), Lang, Verret, and Watt (1984), and Andreason (1987).

Health

The research on families with histories of alcoholism brings us to the topic of DT and health. There are many different questions in the creativity literature about health. It is important to keep in mind that these questions involve various directions of effect, with health either the causal agent or the result of creative tendencies.

Schubert (1988) reported that high scores on several of Guilford's DT tests were asso-

ciated with low anxiety, hysteria, paranoia, psychasthenia, schizophrenia, social introversion, and repression, as indexed by the MMPI. The first and last of these associations may be the most interesting. The first suggests that it may be adaptive to generate alternatives and produce ideas. Coping might, in that light, depend on our capacity to find alternatives. The finding about repression is contrary to reports that creative persons have access to a range of different levels of consciousness and modes of thought (including immature and even primitive; Torrance, 1995). Schubert also reported that the DT scores were negatively related to responsibility. He suggested that the relationship with responsibility allowed the individual to resist social pressure. Such avoidance of social pressure certainly makes sense, given the unconventional tendencies of creative persons.

The association of DT and coping has been explored in studies of stress. The premise here is that stress is a failure to adapt. With this in mind, Carson et al. (2005) administered two stress tests (a hassles scale and the events-change scale) and two sets of DT tasks to a group of students. The DT tasks required both problem generation and problem solving. Both kinds of DT were correlated with coping, although only modestly. Smith and Van der Meer (1990) also explored the possibility that creative potentials support coping and adaptation.

The relationship of DT to insomnia was examined by Healy and Runco (2007). This relationship was examined in part because the persistence that so often characterizes creative persons (Gruber, 1993) could interfere with sleep. Healy and Runco cited several earlier studies on insomnia and overactive minds. They also cited a theory that insomnia is a result of problem solving and, in particular, reappraisals of problems. To test the various possibilities, Healy and Runco administered DT tests to 60 gifted children and compared scores to sleep patterns. Results confirmed that those with the highest scores reported the most disturbances while trying to sleep.

DT has also proven to be useful in studies of the suicide ideation that very likely always precedes actual suicide attempts. The thought of suicide, or suicide as an option, must be considered before an effort is made (Dixon, Heppner, & Anderson, 1991; McLeavey, Daly, Murray, & O'Riordan, 1987; Orbach, Bar-Joseph, & Dror, 1990; Patsiokas, Clum, & Luscomb, 1979; Schotte & Clum, 1987). Flexibility from the DT tests was expected to be the best predictor of suicidal ideation, given its tie to coping and adaptability. Actual results indicated that the interaction of stress and DT was related to suicidal ideation (Rc = .69, $p < .001$). Problem-generation tasks seemed to be the best of the DT test scores for this prediction. Most important was a significant interaction in the prediction equations, which indicated that suicidal ideation was accurately predicted from (a) high fluency with problem generation, and (b) low flexibility with problem solving. This is easy to interpret because it indicates that people who consider suicide may see many problems but very few alternatives. The lack of alternatives is not just in their number, however, but in their variety (i.e., low flexibility). The prediction offered by this interaction was as high as any previous prediction of suicidal ideation. Typically, depression had been viewed as the most accurate predictor of suicide ideation, but apparently a better prediction might be constructed from that combination of DT.

Cox and Leon (1999) administered several tests of DT in their examination of schizotypy. Importantly, schizotypy is not necessarily psychopathological. Like mood swings, there are subclinical tendencies among a large segment of the population. Cox and Leon did emphasize that "schizotypal traits and symptoms provide a framework for understanding an individual's proneness to psychosis" (p. 25). With this view in mind, they measured various perceptual tendencies and several relevant personal traits, along with DT, in a nonclinical sample. One manifestation of schizotypy (anhedonia) was correlated with DT test scores. One other manifestation of schizo-typy (psychoticism) was correlated with their measure of creative personality and with perceptual tendencies. Eysenck (1995) also reported associations between ideation and subclinical levels of psychosis. He suggested that the relationship is a result of *over-inclusive thinking* tendencies. These tendencies lead the individual to vague and pliable conceptual boundaries, so things that often do not belong in particular categories are in fact included, giving these persons very atypical patterns of thought.

DT and Affect

Butcher and Niec (2005) examined the possibility that *affect regulation* is functionally related to creative potential. They observed 6- to 10-year-old children engaged in fantasy play and asked parents to complete measures of affect regulation and creativity. Interestingly, Butcher and Niec found that lower levels of DT and creative potential from the parents' reports were both related to the disruptive behaviors of the children. They also found that this relationship was mediated by affect regulation. Creative potential was unrelated to negative affect.

Russ and Schafer (2000) used a "puppet play task" (which is part of Russ' *Affect in Play Scale*) and administered the Uses DT test and a questionnaire about emotional memories to school-aged children. Affect in play was significantly related to both fluency and originality on the Uses task, and interestingly, negative affect seemed to provide a benefit, at least for DT. Emotion in memory was also associated with affect in play.

Kaufmann and Vosburg (2002; Vosburg, 1998) reported several studies to test the relationship of creative problem solving (CPS) to mood. They argued that previous research ignored a critical variable, namely, the type of task used to assess CPS. Most important in task is degree of constraint. This is an issue with all DT testing, because the tests are open-ended but to varying degrees. Vosburg (1998) assessed mood with a self-report and reported "a perfect, theoretically predicted rank order between positive mood and degree of solution constraint measured by the DT indices" (p. 315). The quantity of ideas (fluency) was indeed related to positive mood while the quality of ideas was not. This supported predictions made by Weisberg (1994) that only fluency of ideas benefits from positive mood and that the quality of ideas would not.

Kaufmann and Vosburg (2002) extended this line of work in a comparison of moods at different stages of the creative process. Unlike in the earlier study, they manipulated mood by asking participants to view brief video (cf. Hoppe & Kyle, 1990). Some saw happy situations, some sad, and some neutral. Four DT tasks were administered, with scores computed for work done within four-minute intervals. Analyses confirmed that the highest number of ideas was produced early in the problem solving process when people were in a positive mood. Negative mood was associated with higher ideation later in the process.

Clapham (2001) examined the relationships of affect, information exposure, and DT. Four experimental conditions were compared: negative affect, positive affect, diverse information, and a control. The Velten procedure was used for the affect conditions. It presents participants with statements that are intended to convey either depression or elation. The control group received instructions for correct word processing. DT was measured with the TTCT. Statistical comparisons indicated that information contributed to DT but mood did not. There may be, then, differences in relationships that reflect the methodology used.

Pannells and Claxton (2008) examined one particular affective state, namely happiness, and its relationship with DT. Happiness was assessed with the Oxford Happiness Inventory, and ideation with the RIBS. No actual DT test was administered. Recall here that the RIBS is essentially a survey allowing self-report of how frequently a person generates ideas. Results indicated that happiness was associated with frequency of ideation.

Biology

Even with numerous indications that affect manipulations and enhancement efforts (e.g., explicit instructions) can alter DT, surely DT depends on both nature and nurture. Biological perspectives on DT are, however, few and fairly recent. Still, there is at least one point of agreement. It involves the neurotransmitter dopamine.

Schmajuk, Aziz, and Bates (2009) drew from classical conditioning and recent theories of attention and associative processes in an attempt to explain why persons with manifest creative talents "show improved (a) DT (fluency and originality), (b) performance in remote associations tests, and (c) problem solving; but impaired (d) latent inhibition and (e) generalization (overinclusion)" (p. 92). They were not alone in looking to latent inhibition as relevant to creative thinking. Eysenck (1997) also emphasized it. He defined it as follows:

> Latent inhibition is defined by an experimental paradigm which requires, as a minimum, a two-stage procedure. The first stage involves stimulus pre-exposure, i.e. the to-be-CS (conditioned stimulus) is exhibited without being followed by any unconditioned stimulus (UCS); this leads theoretically to the CS acquiring a negative salience, i.e. it signals a lack of consequences, and thus acquires inhibitory properties. The second stage is one of acquisition, i.e. the CS is now followed by an UCS, and acquires the property of initiating the UC response (UCR). Latent inhibition (LI) is shown by increasing difficulties of acquiring this property, as compared with lack of pre-exposure.

Schmajuk et al. (2009) predicted that the attention to novelty of creative persons might be associated with the release of dopamine in the brain's nucleus accumbens. (This is a cluster of neurons in the front-most section of the brain. It is often assigned a role in pleasure and laughter, as well as fear and addiction. The last of these is intriguing because creativity is sometimes associated with perseverance, almost as if there is an addiction-like focus on an intrinsically motivated topic.) Schmajuk et al.'s hypothesis about dopamine release is certainly a testable hypothesis. It is also quite consistent with several other observations, including Eysenck's (1997).

The recent research on the genetic basis of DT also looks to dopamine (Reuter et al., 2005; Runco, Noble et al., 2010). Reuters et al. found evidence that DT was associated with dopamine reception (DRD2 and DRD4) and not dopamine release. Runco et al. examined at the same two dopamine genes (as well as four others) but found only an association with fluency and not with originality or flexibility scores from DT tests (both verbal and figural). They concluded that the genes (and the propensity for dopamine reception) were not really associated with creativity per se but only with the capacity to generate ideas. Creativity certainly involves more than fluency, and yet dopamine reception was only related to ideational fluency.

The biology of DT has been examined with other methodologies. Jausovec and Bakracevic (1995), for example, examined the relationship of creativity and brain function by measuring heart rate (HR) and Feelings of Warmth (FOW). They reported that different kinds of problems were associated with different HR and FOW. DT problems were characterized by fairly irregular HR, for example, especially in insight problems where there was a regular HR and then sudden change. FOW measures, obtained by asking individuals to "think aloud" while working on various kinds of problems, produced parallel findings. FOW ratings were also irregular for DT tasks. Khandwalla (1993) also had great success with think aloud procedures and DT.

Sensory capacity has also been tied to creativity and DT. This should come as no surprise, given early theories of creativity. They often recognized that creative capacities were related to physical processes and sensitivities (e.g., Stein, 1953). Additionally, sensory processes may determine the qualities of information and associations that are available when people are thinking divergently. With this in mind, Harland

and Coren (2001) examined the color discrimination ability, visual acuity, pure tone hearing, and stereopsis of 1,461 individuals. They reported that "individuals with moderate deficits in visual acuity and stereopsis . . . performed significantly worse. Performance of those with moderate color discrimination or auditory deficits . . . was indistinguishable from those without such deficits" (p. 385). Harland and Coren postulated that "poor visual acuity and stereopsis may reduce success in DT tasks because the effectiveness of imagery in achieving novel solutions is reduced when stored images are lacking in details" (p. 385).

Marijuana, Alcohol, and Ritalin

The research on marijuana and DT assumes a chemical influence on the latter. Bourassa and Vaugeois (2001) compared novice and regular users after randomly distributing them into one of three experimental conditions: placebo, marijuana, or no marijuana. Bourassa and Vaugeois found that there was no relationship with DT among the novices, and the DT of the regular users decreased.

Much the same logic applies to alcohol use. Norlander and Gustafson (1998), for example, examined the DT of intoxicated persons. They used Wallas's (1926) four-stage theory of creativity and expected different effects in the different stages. Participants were 21 writers who were compared with a matched group of nonwriters. Norlander and Gustafson found that persons receiving alcohol had lower flexibility scores than a placebo group, but higher originality scores compared to a control group (no alcohol or placebo). There were no differences between the writers and the nonwriters in terms of the impact of alcohol. The difference between the placebo and control groups is important because one view of alcohol is that it only feels like it enhances DT but that this merely reflects inhibited discrimination and judgment and not increased ideation or originality.

A related study examined DT and Ritalin. Although this is not related to substance abuse – at least aside from instances where it is given to children with ADHD without accurate diagnosis or due cause – the investigations summarized above concerning marijuana and alcohol also focused on relationships with DT and not abuse. In any case, the work of Swartwood, Swartwood, and Farrell (2003) on Ritalin and DT rounds out the picture of what might be called chemicals and DT. They tested the hypothesis that flexibility would be particularly reactive to Ritalin by administering several tests of DT, a Card Sorting Test, and a standardized measure of ADHD. Symptoms of ADHD were significantly lower with the Ritalin (MPH administration), but only ideational elaboration from the DT tests decreased with the medication.

Culture and Multicultural Experience

The research on culture and DT is at least as extensive as that on the biology of DT. Chan et al. (2000–2001) and Cheung, Lau, Chan, and Wu (2004), for instance, reported several empirical studies of the DT of Chinese students. This work has practical importance in their publishing norms for DT, with the assumption that those norms differ from what are available for students in the United States or elsewhere around the world. Rudowicz, Lok, and Kitto (1995) had previously noted that the images and objects in a translated version of the TTCT were "culturally bound" and therefore not generalizable across cultures.

Cultural differences specifically involving the East and West are most often explained with the dichotomy between collectivist and individualistic cultures, the former a common label for Asian cultures and the latter of Western cultures (cf. Ng, 2005; Rudowicz, 2003; Runco, 2001, 2004, 2007). Where there is a tendency toward *collectivism* and its corollaries (e.g., harmony, conventionality), originality and therefore creativity may very well suffer. The world continues to change and different cultures may be sharing more and more. Also, generalizations are always dubious, and this is true across cultures.

There may be general tendencies within one culture or another, but very likely those are only indications of central tendency and certainly do describe everyone in that culture. Of course, this is how norms are best used, as indices of central tendency.

Research has also compared Western groups. Milgram and Rabkin (1980), for example, found more DT among Israeli and U.S. students than among those from the USSR. She pointed to differences in dogmatism to explain these differences. More recently, Kharkhurin and Motalleebi (2008) reported that Russian and American students had higher DT scores on the Abbreviated TTCT than did Iranian students, at least in terms of originality and "abilities to consider a problem from different perspectives" (p. 404). Kharkhurin and Motalleebi suggested that this pattern of results might reflect cultural values and that Iranian students might not associate originality with creativity. A related point could be added to this: It may be that the students differed in the quantitative indices but not in the qualities of their ideas (cf. Dudek & Verreault, 1989; Khandwalla, 1993).

Multicultural experiences have also been studied. This is especially intriguing because of the idea that creativity can benefit from multiple knowledge structures (Hunter, Bedell-Avers, Hunsicker, Mumford, & Ligon, 2008), cultural marginality (Gardner & Wolf, 1988; Runco, 2007), and access to multiple perspectives (Runco, 1999; Westwood & Low, 2003). To examine multicultural experience, Leung and Chiu (2008) administered a test of DT along with a test of nonprototypical exemplar retrieval. The last of these assessments indicates the ease with which original ideas and memories are retrieved from long-term memory. The tasks were administered to a group of European American undergraduates. Statistical comparisons indicated that the extent of the multicultural experience was associated with high scores on both indicators of creative potential, but only when individuals also had measurable openness to experience. Without such openness, multicultural experience had no benefit. This makes perfect sense. Experience without the right attitude and state of mind is usually not influential. "You can lead a horse to water," as they say, "but you can't make it drink."

Conclusions

DT tests are probably the most commonly administered paper-and-pencil tests of creative potential. Reliabilities and validities of these tests vary and seem to depend on the stimuli and questions contained in a particular test, the scoring procedures used, and the administration and setting. Clearly, performance on tests of DT tests does not guarantee actual creative performance and accomplishment in the natural environment. Still, when used appropriately, these tests do provide useful estimates of the potential for creative problem solving and for the ideation that is so useful in the natural environment.

This chapter suggests that there is a good balance of basic and applied research on DT. Much of the research has been conducted in controlled settings and is adequately rigorous, at least by the standards and conventions of the behavioral sciences. Generalizations must be drawn very carefully, yet there are clear implications for education, development, psychometrics, and our understanding of human cognition, or at least ideation. Recall also that memory, information usage, attention, and a few other cognitive processes have been tied to DT. In fact, as noted earlier, the research on DT covers a huge amount of ground. Various forms of exceptionality were involved in the research reviewed in this chapter, as were different psychopathologies, affect, and health. Domain differences were reported, as were age and cultural differences.

Something should be said about the unit of measurement in tests of DT. That unit is *the idea*. This may sound like an amorphous, ambiguous, and perhaps ephemeral kind of cognition, and perhaps a psychological construct without clear referent or physical basis. Neuropsychological research may soon find a physical basis of ideation, most likely at the point where a coherence

of thought is suggested by a change in electrical activity. Yet even without a clear neurochemical basis, the idea is a useful unit of measurement. It may seem to be ambiguous, but actually it is much like other psychological constructs used in the cognitive sciences. Consider the *bit* of information used in the cognitive sciences. It too does not yet have a clear neurochemical basis and varies from person to person, as is the case with ideas.

One implication of the research on DT is that it is influenced by both immediate and remote experiences and factors. The immediate environment can, for example, influence ideation, as can the much more distal and remote experiences from childhood or cultural background. These influences on ideation suggest that it is possible to manipulate ideation such that originality and creativity are probable.

An even more concrete implication follows from the psychometric research: Evidence suggests that more than one index of DT (e.g., fluency, originality, flexibility) should be included in research and practice. These indices are moderately independent and may each convey unique and useful information. Findings such as these in turn indicate that when studying ideation and DT, it is vital to consult recent research. That should be a given, but DT theories and methods have evolved over the years and what was suggested 30 and 40 years ago may no longer apply. Reviews such as those found in this *Handbook* are useful in that they allow us to determine what findings replicate and which have been modified by empirical research.

References

Abedi, J. (2002). A latent-variable modeling approach to assessing reliability and validity of a creativity instrument. *Creativity Research Journal*, 14, 267–276.

Albert, R. S. (1975). Toward a behavioral definition of genius. *American Psychologist*, 30, 140–151.

Amabile, T. M. (1990). Within you, without you: The social psychology of creativity, and beyond. In M. A. Runco & R. S. Albert (Eds.), *Theories of creativity* (Rev. ed.). Cresskill, NJ: Hampton Press.

Anastasi, A. (1982). *Psychological testing* (5th ed.). New York: MacMillan.

Andreasen, N. (1987). Creativity and mental illness. *American Journal of Psychiatry, 144,* 1288–1292.

Auzmendi, E., Villa, A., & Abedi, J. (1996). Reliability and validity of a newly constructed multiple-choice creativity instrument. *Creativity Research Journal, 9,* 89–95.

Bachelor, P., & Michael, W. B. (1991). Higher order factors of creativity within Guilford's structure-of-intellect model: A re-analysis of a fifty-three variable data base. *Creativity Research Journal, 4,* 157–175.

Barron, F. (1993). Controllable oddness as a resource in creativity. *Psychological Inquiry, 4,* 182–184.

Barron, F. (1995). *No rootless flower: An ecology of creativity.* Cresskill, NJ: Hampton Press.

Basadur, M. (1994). *Managing the creative process in organizations. Problem finding, problem solving, and creativity.* Westport, CT: Ablex.

Basadur, M., & Runco, M. A. (1993). Assessing ideational and evaluative skills and creative styles and attitudes. *Creativity and Innovation Management, 2,* 166–173.

Benedek, M., Fink, A., & Neubauer, A. (2006). Enhancement of Ideational Fluency by Means of Computer-Based Training. *Creativity Research Journal, 18,* 317–328.

Berger, R., Guilford, J., & Christensen, P. (1957). A factor-analytic study of planning abilities. *Psychological Monographs, 71.*

Binet, A., & Simon, T. (1905). The development of intelligence in children. *L'Annee Psychologique, 11,* 163–191.

Bossomaier, T., Harr, M., Knittel, A., & Snyder, A. (2009). A semantic network approach to the creativity quotient (CQ). *Creativity Research Journal, 21,* 64–71.

Bourassa, M., & Vaugeois, P. (2001). Effects of marijuana use on divergent thinking. *Creativity Research Journal, 13,* 411–416.

Brophy, D. (2001). Comparing the attributes, activities, and performance of divergent, convergent, and combination thinkers. *Creativity Research Journal, 13,* 439–455.

Bruner, J. (1962). The conditions of creativity. In J. Bruner (Ed.), *On knowing: Essays for the left hand.* Cambridge, MA: Harvard University Press.

Butcher, J. L., & Niec, L. N. (2005). Disruptive behaviors and creativity in childhood: The importance of affect regulation. *Creativity Research Journal, 17,* 181–193.

Byrne, C. L., Shipman, A. S., & Mumford, M. D. (in press). The effects of forecasting on creative problem-solving: An experimental study. *Creativity Research Journal.*

Carson, S., Peterson, J., & Higgins, D. (2005). Reliability, Validity, and Factor Structure of the Creative Achievement Questionnaire. *Creativity Research Journal, 17,* 37–50.

Chan, D. W., Cheung, P., Lau, S., Wu, W. Y. H., Kwong, J. M. L., & Li, W. (2000–2001). Assessing ideational fluency in primary students in Hong Kong. *Creativity Research Journal, 13,* 359–365.

Chand, I., & Runco, M. A. (1992). Problem finding skills as components in the creative process. *Personality and Individual Differences, 14,* 155.

Cheung, P. C., Lau, S., Chan, D. W., & Wu, W. Y. H. (2004). Creative potential of school children in Hong Kong: Norms of the Wallach Kogan Creativity Tests and their implications. *Creativity Research Journal, 16,* 69–78.

Chown, S. (1960). A factor analysis of the Wesley Rigidity Inventory: Its relationship to age and nonverbal intelligence. *The Journal of Abnormal and Social Psychology, 61,* 491–494.

Clapham, M. M. (1997). Ideational skills training: A key element in creativity training programs. *Creativity Research Journal, 10,* 33–44.

Clapham, M. M. (2001). The effects of affect manipulation and information exposure on divergent thinking. *Creativity Research Journal, 13,* 335–350.

Cox, A., & Leon, J. (1999). Negative schizotypal traits in the relation of creativity to psychopathology. *Creativity Research Journal, 12,* 25–36.

Cropley, A. J. (2006). In praise of convergent thinking. *Creativity Research Journal, 18,* 391–404.

Cropley, D. H., Kaufman, J. C., & Cropley, A. J. (2008). Malevolent creativity: A functional model of creativity in terrorism and crime. *Creativity Research Journal, 20,* 105–115.

Csikszentmihalyi, M. (1990). The domain of creativity. In M. A. Runco & R. S. Albert (Eds.), *Theories of creativity* (pp. 190–212). Newbury Park, CA: Sage.

Csikszentmihalyi, M., & Getzels, J. (1970). Concern for discovery: An attitudinal component of creative production. *Journal of Personality*, 38, 91–105.

Datta, L. (1968). Birth order and potential scientific creativity. *Sociometry*, 31, 76–88.

Davis, G. A., & Subkoviak, M. J. (1975). Multidimensional analysis of a personality-based test of creative potential. *Journal of Educational Measurement*, 12, 37–43.

Diakidoy, I.-A. K., Constantinos, P., & Constantinou, C. P. (2001). Creativity in physics: Response fluency and task specificity. *Creativity Research Journal*, 13, 401–410.

Dixon, W., Heppner, P., & Anderson, W. (1991). Problem solving appraisal, stress, hopelessness, and suicide ideation in a college population. *Journal of Counseling Psychology*, 38, 51–56.

Dollinger, S. J., Urban, K. K., & James, T. A. (2004). Creativity and openness: Further validation of two creative product measures. *Creativity Research Journal*, 16, 35–47.

Dudek, S. Z., & Verreault, R. (1989). The creative thinking and ego functioning of children. *Creativity Research Journal*, 2, 64–99.

Eisenman, R. (1964). Birth order and artistic creativity. *Journal of Individual Psychology*, 20, 183–185.

Eisenman, R. (1980). Effective manipulation by psychopaths. *Corrective & Social Psychiatry & Journal of Behavior Technology, Methods & Therapy*, 26, 116–118.

Eisenman, R., & Schussel, N. R. (1970). Creativity, birth order, and preference for symmetry. *Journal of Con-suiting and Clinical Psychology*, 34, 275–280.

Eysenck, H. J. (1995). *Genius: The natural history of creativity*. New York: Cambridge University Press.

Eysenck, H. J. (1997). Creativity and personality. In M. A. Runco (Ed.), *The creativity research handbook* (Vol. 1, pp. 41–66). Cresskill, NJ: Hampton Press.

Feldman, D. H., Marrinan, B. M., & Hartfeldt, S. D. (1972). Transformational power as a possible index of creativity. *Psychological Reports*, 30, 335–338.

Fu, V. R., Moran, III, J. D., Sawyers, J. K., & Milgram, R. M. (1983). Parental influence on creativity in preschool children. *Journal of Genetic Psychology*, 143, 289.

Gardner, H., & Wolf, C. (1988). The fruits of asynchrony: A psychological examination of creativity. *Adolescent Psychiatry*, 15, 96–120.

Getzels, J. W. (1975). Problem finding and the inventiveness of solutions. *Journal of Creative Behavior*, 9, 12–18.

Getzels, J. W., & Jackson, P. (1962). *Creativity and intelligence: Explorations with gifted students*. Oxford, England: Wiley.

Getzels, J. W., & Smilansky, J. (1983). Individual differences in pupil perceptions of school problems. *British Journal of Educational Psychology*, 53, 307–316.

Goldschmidt, G., & Tatsa, D. (2005). How good are good ideas? Correlates of design creativity. *Design Studies*, 26, 593–611.

Groborz, M., & Necka, E. (2003). Creativity and cognitive control: Explorations of generation and evaluation skills. *Creativity Research Journal*, 15, 183–197.

Gruber, H. (1993). Creativity in the moral domain: Ought implies can implies create. *Creativity Research Journal*, 6, 3–15.

Guilford, J. P. (1950). Creativity. *American Psychologist*, 5, 444–454.

Guilford, J. P. (1968). *Intelligence, creativity and their educational implications*. San Diego: Knapp.

Guilford, J. P. (1970). Creativity: Retrospect and prospect. *Journal of Creative Behavior*, 5, 77–87.

Guilford, J. P. (1983). Transformation abilities or functions. *Journal of Creative Behavior*, 17, 75–83.

Guilford, J. P. (1986). *Creative talents: Their nature, uses and development*. Buffalo, NY: Bearly.

Guilford, J. P., Wilson, R. C., & Christiansen, P. R. (1952). *A factor-analytic study of creative thinking: II. Administration of tests and analysis of results*. (Psychological Laboratory Rep., No. 8). Los Angeles: University of Southern California.

Harland, R., & Coren, S. (2001). Individual differences in divergent thinking as a function of variations in sensory status. *Creativity Research Journal*, 13, 385–391.

Harrington, D. M. (1975). Effects of explicit instructions to be creative on the psychological meaning of divergent test scores. *Journal of Personality*, 43, 434–454.

Harrington, D. M., Block, J. H., & Block, J. (1987). Testing aspects of Carl Rogers' theory of creative environments: Child rearing antecedents of creative potential in young adolescents. *Journal of Personality and Social Psychology*, 52, 851–856.

Healey, D., & Runco, M. A. (2007). Could creativity be associated with insomnia? *Creativity Research Journal*, 18, 39–43.

Hocevar, D. (1979). Ideational fluency as a confounding factor in the measurement of originality. *Journal of Educational Psychology*, 71, 191–196.

Hocevar, D. (1980). Intelligence, divergent thinking, and creativity. *Intelligence*, 4, 25–40.

Hocevar, D. (1981). Measurement of creativity: Review and critique. *Journal of Personality Assessment*, 45, 450–464.

Holland, J. L. (1961). Creative and academic achievement among talented adolescents. *Journal of Educational Psychology*, 52, 136–147.

Hoppe, K., & Kyle, N. (1990). Dual brain, creativity, and health. *Creativity Research Journal*, 3, 150–157.

Horn, J. (1970). Review of J. P. Guilford's "The nature of human intelligence." *Psychometrics*, 35, 273–277.

Horn, J. L., & Knapp, J. R. (1973). On the subjective character of the empirical base of Guilford's structure-of-intellect model. *Psychological Bulletin*, 80, 33–43.

Houtz, J. C., Jambor, S. D., Cifone, A., & Lewis, C. D. (1989). Locus of evaluation control, task directions, and type of problem effects on creativity. *Creativity Research Journal*, 2, 118–125.

Hu, W., & Adey, P. (2002). A scientific creativity test for secondary school students. *International Journal of Science Education*, 24, 389–403.

Hu, W., Shi, Q. Z., Han, Q., Wang, X., & Adey, P. (2010). Creative scientific problem finding and its developmental trend. *Creativity Research Journal*, 22, 46–52.

Hudson, L. (1968). *Contrary imaginations*. London: Penguin.

Hunter, S., Bedell-Avers, K., Hunsicker, C., Mumford, M., & Ligon, G. (2008). Applying multiple knowledge structures in creative thought: Effects on idea generation and problem-solving. *Creativity Research Journal*, 20, 137–154.

Jackson, P. W., & Messick, S. (1965). The person, the product, and the response: Conceptual problems in the assessment of creativity. *Journal of Personality*, 33, 309–329.

James, K., & Asmus, C. (2000). Personality, cognitive skills, and creativity in different life domains. *Creativity Research Journal*, 13, 149–159.

Jausovec, N., & Bakracevic, K. (1995). What can heart rate tell us about the creative process? *Creativity Research Journal*, 8, 11–24.

Jay, E., & Perkins, D. (1997). Creativity's compass: A review of problem finding. In M. A. Runco (Ed.), *Creativity research handbook* (Vol. 1, pp. 257–293). Cresskill, NJ: Hampton Press.

Joussemet, M., & Koestner, R. (1999). Effect of expected rewards on children's creativity. *Creativity Research Journal*, 12, 231–239.

Joy, S. P. (2008). Personality and creativity in art and writing: Innovation motivation, psychoticism, and (mal)adjustment. *Creativity Research Journal*, 20, 262–277.

Jung, D. (2000–2001). Transformational and transactional leadership and their effects on creativity in groups. *Creativity Research Journal*, 13, 185–195.

Kasof, J. (1995). Explaining creativity: The attributional perspective. *Creativity Research Journal*, 8, 311–366.

Kasof, J., Chen, C., Himsel, A., & Greenberger, E. (2007). Values and creativity. *Creativity Research Journal*, 19, 105–122.

Kaufmann, G., & Vosburg, S. K. (2002). The effects of mood on early and late idea production. *Creativity Research Journal*, 14, 317–330.

Kelder, L. R., McNamara, J. R., Carlson, B., & Lynn, S. J. (1991). Perceptions of physical punishment. *Journal of Interpersonal Violence*, 6, 432–445.

Kettner, N., Guilford, J., & Christensen, P. (1959). A factor-analytic study across the domains of reasoning, creativity, and evaluation. *Psychological Monographs*, 73(9, Whole No. 479),

Khandwalla, N. (1993). An exploratory study of divergent thinking through protocol analysis. *Creativity Research Journal*, 6, 241–260.

Kharkhurin, A., & Motalleebi, S. (2008). The impact of culture on the creative potential of American, Russian, and Iranian college students. *Creativity Research Journal*, 20, 404–411.

Kim, Y. (2002). Satisficing and fairness in ultimatum bargaining game experiments. *Risk, Decision & Policy*, 7, 235–247.

Koestler, A. (1964). *The act of creation*. New York: Macmillan.

Lang, A. R., Verret, L. D., & Watt, C. (1984). Drinking and creativity: Objective and subjective effects. Addictive and subjective effects. *Addictive Behaviors*, 9, 395–399.

Langer, E. (1989). *Mindfulness*. Reading, MA: Addison-Wesley.

Leung, A., & Chiu, C. (2008). Interactive effects of multicultural experiences and openness to experience on creative potential. *Creativity Research Journal, 20,* 376–382.

Lichtenwalner, J. S., & Maxwell, J. W. (1969). The relationship of birth order and socioeconomic status to the creativity of preschool children. *Child Development, 40,* 1241–1247.

Livne, N., & Milgram, R. (2000). Assessing four levels of creative mathematical ability in Israeli adolescents utilizing out-of-school activities: A circular three-stage technique. *Roeper Review, 22,* 111–116.

Livne, N., & Milgram, R. (2006). Academic versus creative abilities in mathematics: Two components of the same construct? *Creativity Research Journal, 18,* 199–212.

Ma, H. H. (2009). The effect size of variables associated with creativity: A meta-analysis. *Creativity Research Journal, 21,* 30–42.

MacKinnon, D. W. (1963). Creativity and images of the self. In R. W. White (Ed.), *The study of lives* (pp. 251–278). New York: Atherton Press.

Mann, E. (2009). The search for mathematical creativity: Identifying creative potential in middle school students. *Creativity Research Journal, 21,* 1–11.

McCoy, J. (2000, September). The creative work environment: The relationship of the physical environment and creative teamwork at a state agency. *A case study. Dissertation Abstracts International Section A, 61.*

McLaren, R. B. (2003). Tackling the intractable: An interdisciplinary exploration of the moral proclivity. *Creativity Research Journal, 15,* 15–24.

McLeavey, B., Daly, R., Murray, C., & O'Riordan, J. (1987). Interpersonal problem-solving deficits in self-poisoning patients. *Suicide and Life-Threatening Behavior, 17,* 33–49.

Mednick, S. A. (1962). The associative basis of the creative process. *Psychological Review, 69,* 220–232.

Meline, C. W. (1976). Does the medium matter? *Journal of Communication, 26,* 81–89.

Merrifield, P., Guilford, J., Christensen, P., & Frick, J. (1961). Interrelationships between certain abilities and certain traits of motivation and temperament. *Journal of General Psychology, 65,* 57–74.

Milgram, R. M. (1990). Creativity: An idea whose time has come and gone? In M. A. Runco & R. S. Albert (Eds.), *Theories of creativity* (pp. 215–233). Newbury Park, CA: Sage.

Milgram, R. M., Dunn, R., & Price, G. E. (Eds.). (1993). *Teaching and counseling gifted and talented adolescents: An international learning style perspective.* New York: Praeger.

Milgram, R. M., & Hong, E. (1999). Creative out-of-school activities in intellectually gifted adolescents as predictors of their life accomplishment in young adults: A longitudinal study. *Creativity Research Journal, 12,* 77–87.

Milgram, R. M., & Milgram, N. (1976). Creative thinking and creative performance in Israeli students. *Journal of Educational Psychology, 68,* 255–258.

Milgram, R. M., & Milgram, N. (1978). Quality and quantity of creative thinking in children and adolescents. *Child Development, 49,* 385–388.

Milgram, R. M., & Rabkin, L. (1980). Developmental test of Mednick's associative hierarchies of original thinking. *Developmental Psychology, 16,* 157–158.

Moran, J. D., Milgram, R. M., Sawyers, J. K., & Fu, V. R. (1983). Stimulus specificity in the measurement of original thinking in preschool children. *Journal of Psychology, 4,* 99–105.

Mumford, M. D., Reiter-Palmon, R., & Redmond, M. R. (1994). Problem construction and cognition: Applying problem representations in ill-defined domains. In M. A. Runco (Ed.), *Problem finding, problem solving, and creativity* (pp. 3–39). Norwood, NJ: Ablex.

Ng, R. (2005). Cognitive therapy supervision–A pilot study. *Hong Kong Journal of Psychiatry, 15,* 122–126.

Noble, E. P., Runco, M. A., & Ozkaragoz, T. Z. (1993). Creativity in alcoholic and non-alcoholic families. *Alcohol, 10,* 317–322.

Norlander, T., & Gustafson, R. (1998). Effects of alcohol on a divergent figural fluency test during the illumination phase of the creative process. *Creativity Research Journal, 11,* 265–274.

Nunnally, J. C. (1978). *Psychometric theory.* New York: McGraw-Hill.

Okuda, S. M., Runco, M. A., & Berger, D. E. (1991). Creativity and the finding and solving of real-world problems. *Journal of Psychoeducational Assessment, 9,* 45–53.

Orbach, I., Bar-Joseph, H., & Dror, N. (1990). Styles of problem solving in suicidal individuals. *Suicide and Life-Threatening Behavior, 20,* 56–64.

Pannells, T., & Claxton, A. (2008). Happiness, creative ideation, and locus of control. *Creativity Research Journal, 20,* 67–71.

Patrick, C. (1935). Creative thought in poets. *Archives of Psychology, 26,* 1–74.

Patrick, C. (1937). Creative thought in artists. *Journal of Psychology*, 5, 35–73.

Patrick, C. (1938). Scientific thought. *Journal of Psychology*, 5, 55–83.

Patrick, C. (1941). Whole and part relationship in creative thought. *American Journal of Psychology*, 54, 128–131.

Patsiokas, A. T., Clum, G. A., & Luscomb, R., L. (1979). Cognitive characteristics of suicide attempters. *Journal of Consulting and Clinical Psychology*, 3, 478–484.

Plucker, J. A. (1999). Is the proof in the pudding? Reanalyses of Torrance's (1958 to Present) longitudinal data. *Creativity Research Journal*, 12, 103–114.

Radio Gaynor, J., & Runco, M. (1992). Family size, birth-order, age-interval, and the creativity of children. *Journal of Creative Behavior*, 26, 108–118.

Raina, M. K. (1975). Parental perception about ideal child: A cross-cultural study. *Journal of Marriage & Family*, 37, 229–232.

Reuter, M., Panksepp, J., Schnabel, N., Kellerhoff, P., Kempel, P., & Henning, J. (2005). Personality and Biological Markers of Creativity. *European Journal of Personality*, 19, 83–95.

Rhodes, M. (1961). An analysis of creativity. *Phi Delta Kappan*, 42, 305–310.

Richardson, A. G. (1986). Two factors of creativity. *Perceptual and Motor Skills*, 63, 379–384.

Rickards, T., & DeCock, C. (in press). Understanding organizational creativity: Toward a multi-paradigmatic approach. In M. A. Runco (Ed.), *Creativity research handbook* (vol. 3). Cresskill, NJ: Hampton Press.

Rossman, B., & Gollob, H. (1975). Comparison of social judgments of creativity and intelligence. *Journal of Personality and Social Psychology*, 31, 271–281.

Rothenberg, A. (1990). Creativity, mental health, and alcoholism. *Creativity Research Journal*, 3, 179–201.

Rothenberg, A., & Hausman, C. R. (Eds.). (1976). *The creativity question*. Durham, NC: Duke University Press.

Rotter, D. M., Langland, L., & Berger, D. (1971). The validity of tests of creative thinking in seven year old children. *Gifted Child Quarterly*, 16, 273–278.

Rubenson, D. L., & Runco, M. A. (1995). The psychoeconomic view of creative work in groups and organizations. *Creativity and Innovation Management*, 4, 232–241.

Rudowicz, E. (2003). Creativity and culture: A two way interaction. *Scandinavian Journal of Educational Research*, 47, 273–290.

Rudowicz, E., Lok, D., & Kitto, J. (1995). Use of the Torrance Test of Creative Thinking in an exploratory study of creativity in Hong Kong primary school children: A cross cultural comparison. *Journal of Psychology*, 30, 417–430.

Runco, M. A. (1985). Reliability and convergent validity of ideational flexibility as a function of academic achievement. *Perceptual and Motor Skills*, 61, 1075–1081.

Runco, M. A. (1986). Maximal performance on divergent thinking tests by gifted, talented, and nongifted children. *Psychology in the Schools*, 23, 308–315.

Runco, M. A. (1989). Parents' and teachers' ratings of the creativity of children. *Journal of Social Behavior and Personality*, 4, 73–83.

Runco, M. A. (1991). The evaluative, valuative, and divergent thinking of children. *Journal of Creative Behavior*, 25, 311–319.

Runco, M. A. (1993). Moral creativity: Intentional and unconventional. *Creativity Research Journal*, 6, 17–28.

Runco, M. A. (Ed.). (1994). *Problem finding, problem solving, and creativity*. Norwood, NJ: Ablex.

Runco, M. A. (1999). *Perspective*. In M. A. Runco & S. Pritzker (Eds.), *Encyclopedia of creativity* (pp. 373–376). San Diego, CA: Academic Press.

Runco, M. A. (2001). Foreword: The intersection of creativity and culture. In N. A. Kwang (Ed.), *Why Asians are less creative than Westerners*. Singapore: Prentice-Hall.

Runco, M. A. (2003). Idea evaluation, divergent thinking, and creativity. In M. A. Runco (Ed.), *Critical creative processes* (pp. 69–94). Cresskill, NJ: Hampton Press.

Runco, M. A. (2004). Personal creativity and culture. In L. Sing, A. N. N. Hui, & G. C. Ng (Eds.), *Creativity: When East meets West* (pp. 9–21). Singapore: World Scientific.

Runco, M. A. (2007). A hierarchical framework for the study of creativity. *New Horizons in Education*, 55, 1–9.

Runco, M. A., & Albert, R. S. (1985). The reliability and validity of ideational originality in the divergent thinking of academically gifted and nongifted children. *Educational and Psychological Measurement*, 45, 483–501.

Runco, M., & Bahleda, M. (1986). Implicit theories of artistic, scientific, and everyday creativity. *Journal of Creative Behavior*, 20, 93–98.

Runco, M. A., & Charles, R. (1993). Judgments of originality and appropriateness as predictors of creativity. *Personality and Individual Differences*, 15, 537–546.

Runco, M. A., Cramond, B., & Pagnani, A. (in press). Sex differences in creative potential and creative performance. In D. McCreary (Ed.), *Handbook of gender research in psychology*. New York: Springer.

Runco, M. A., Illies, J. J., & Eisenman, R. (2005). Creativity, originality, and appropriateness: What do explicit instructions tell us about their relationships? *Journal of Creative Behavior*, 39, 137–148.

Runco, M. A., Illies, J. J., & Reiter-Palmon, R. (2005). Explicit instructions to be creative and original: A comparison of strategies and criteria as targets with three types of divergent thinking tests. *Korean Journal of Thinking and Problem Solving*, 15, 5–15.

Runco, M. A., Millar, G., Acar, S., & Cramond, B. (2010). Torrance Tests of Creative Thinking as Predictors of Personal and Public Achievement: A Fifty Year Follow-Up. Submitted for publication.

Runco, M., & Mraz, W. (1992). Scoring divergent thinking tests using total ideational output and a creativity index. *Educational and Psychological Measurement*, 52, 213–221.

Runco, M. A., Noble, E. P., Reiter-Palmon, R., Acar, S., Ritchie, T., & Yurkovich, J. M. (2010). The Genetic Basis of Creativity and Ideational Fluency. Submitted for publication.

Runco, M. A., & Okuda, S. M. (1988). Problem discovery, divergent thinking, and the creative process. *Journal of Youth and Adolescence*, 17, 211–220.

Runco, M. A., Plucker, J. A., & Lim, W. (2000). Development and psychometric integrity of a measure of ideational behavior. *Creativity Research Journal*, 13, 393–400.

Runco, M., & Richards, R. (1998). *Everyday creativity, eminent creativity, and health*. Norwood, NJ: Ablex.

Runco, M., & Smith, W. (1992). Interpersonal and intrapersonal evaluations of creative ideas. *Personality and Individual Differences*, 13, 295–302.

Runco, M., & Vega, L. (1990). Evaluating the creativity of children's ideas. *Journal of Social Behavior & Personality*, 5, 439–452.

Russ, S. W., & Schafer, E. D. (2000). Affect in fantasy play, emotion in memories, and divergent thinking. *Creativity Research Journal*, 18, 347–354.

Schmajuk, N., Aziz, D., & Bates, M. (2009). Attentional-associative interactions in creativity. *Creativity Research Journal*, 21, 92–103.

Schotte, D., & Clum, G. (1987). Problem solving skills in suicidal psychiatric patients. *Journal of Consulting and Clinical Psychology*, 1, 49–54.

Schubert, D. S. P. (1988). Creativity and the ability to cope. In F. Flach (Ed.), *The creative mind* (pp. 97–114). New York: Bearly Ltd.

Scratchley, L., & Hakstian, A. (2000–2001). The measurement and prediction of managerial creativity. *Creativity Research Journal*, 13, 367–384.

Shapiro, R. J. (1970). The criterion problem. In P. E. Vernon (Ed.), *Creativity* (pp. 257–269). New York: Penguin.

Silvia, P. J. (2008). Creativity and intelligence revisited: A latent variable analysis of Wallach and Kogan (1965). *Creativity Research Journal*, 20, 34–39.

Simonton, D. K. (1995). Exceptional personal influence: An integrative paradigm. *Creativity Research Journal*, 8, 371–376.

Smith, G., & Van der Meer, G. (1990). Creativity in old age. *Creativity Research Journal*, 3, 249–264.

Sosik, J. J., Kahai, S. S., & Avolio, B. J. (1998). Transformational leadership and dimensions of creativity: Motivating idea generation in computer-mediated groups. *Creativity Research Journal*, 11, 111–121.

Staffieri, J. R., & Bassett, J. E. (1970). Birth order and perception of facial expressions. *Perceptual and Motor Skills*, 30, 606.

Stein, M. I. (1953). Creativity and culture. *Journal of Psychology*, 36, 31–32.

Swartwood, M., Swartwood, J., & Farrell, J. (2003). Stimulant treatment of ADHD: Effects on creativity and flexibility in problem solving. *Creativity Research Journal*, 15, 417–419.

Torrance, E. P. (1963). *Education and the creative potential*. Minneapolis: University of Minnesota Press.

Torrance, E. P. (1965). *The Minnesota studies of creative thinking: Widening horizons in creativity*. New York: Wiley.

Torrance, E. P. (1995). Insights about creativity: Questioned, rejected, ridiculed, ignored. *Educational Psychology Review*, 7, 313.

Torrance, E. P., Clements, C. B., & Goff, K. (1989). Mind-body learning among the elderly: Arts, Fitness, Incubation. *Educational Forum*, 54, 123–133.

Urban, K. K. (1991). On the development of creativity in children. *Creativity Research Journal*, 4, 177–191.

Urban, K. K., & Jellen, H. G. (1996). *Test for Creative Thinking Drawing Production (TCT-DP)*. Lisse, Netherlands: Swets and Zeitlinger.

Vosburg, S. K. (1998). Mood and the quantity and quality of ideas. *Creativity Research Journal*, 11, 315–324.

Wakefield, J. F. (1989). Creativity and cognition: Implications for arts education. *Creativity Research Journal*, 2, 51–63.

Walczyk, J. J., Runco, M. A., Tripp, S. M., & Smith, C. E. (2008). The creativity of lying: Divergent thinking and ideational correlates of the resolution of social dilemmas. *Creativity Research Journal*, 20, 328–342.

Wallach, M. A. (1970). Creativity. In P. Mussen (Ed.), *Carmichael's handbook of child psychology* (pp. 1211–1272). New York: Wiley.

Wallach, M. A. (1983). What do tests tell us about talent? In R. S. Albert (Ed.), *Genius and eminence* (pp. 99–113). Oxford: Pergamon.

Wallach, M. A., & Kogan, N. (1965). *Modes of thinking in young children*. New York: Holt, Rinehart & Winston.

Wallach, M. A., & Wing, C. (1969). *The talented student*. New York: Holt, Rinehart & Winston.

Wallas, G. (1926). *The art of thought*. New York: Harcourt Brace & World.

Ward, W. C., Kogan, N., & Pankove, E. (1972). Incentive effects in children's creativity. *Child Development*, 43, 669–676.

Ward, T. B., Patterson, M. J., & Sifonis, C. M. (2004). The role of specificity and abstraction in creative idea generation. *Creativity Research Journal*, 16, 1–9.

Weisberg, R. W. (1994). Genius and madness? A quasi experimental test of the hypothesis that manic depression increases creativity. *Psychological Science*, 5, 361–367.

Westwood, R., & Low, D. R. (2003). The multicultural muse: Culture, creativity, and innovation. *International Journal of Cross Cultural Management*, 3, 235–259.

Wilks, L., & Thompson, P. (1979). Birth order and creativity in young children. *Psychological Reports*, 45, 443–449.

Williams, F. (1980). *Creativity assessment packet: Manual*. East Aurora, NY: DOK Publishers.

Wilson, R. L., Guilford, J. P., Christensen, P. R., & Lewis, D. J. (1954). A factor analytic study of divergent thinking abilities. *Psychometrica*, 19, 297–311.

Ziv, N., & Keydar, E. (2009). The relationship between creative potential, aesthetic response to music, and musical preferences. *Creativity Research Journal*, 21, 125–133.

CHAPTER 23

Creativity in the Classroom

Ronald A. Beghetto

Creativity occupies somewhat of a conflicted position in many classrooms. Although psychologists have long viewed the identification and development of creative potential as a key educational goal (Guilford, 1950; Vygotsky, 1967/2004), realizing this goal has presented a challenge for creativity researchers and educators (Plucker, Beghetto, & Dow, 2004).

The purpose of this chapter is to provide an overview of the conflicted nature of creativity in the classroom. Researchers have explored related issues in college-level classrooms (e.g., Halpern, in press; Plucker & Dow, in press) and international settings (e.g., Kaufman & Sternberg, 2006; Tan, 2007); however, this chapter focuses on creativity in conventional K–12 classrooms typically found in the United States. The chapter opens with a brief discussion of creativity as a mainstream curricular goal. Next, a variety of common barriers to creativity in the classroom are discussed along with considerations for how creativity researchers might help address these barriers. The chapter closes by highlighting key directions for future research.

Creativity as Curricular Goal

Life in the twenty-first century is marked by great uncertainty; this, in part, is due to unprecedented social, economic, and global changes. Although it is difficult to predict what the future might hold, one thing is clear: Students will need to be better equipped to successfully navigate the increasingly complex and ill-defined nature of life in the twenty-first century (Wells & Claxton, 2002).

Establishing a common curricular goal of developing the creative competence of children is one way to help prepare students for an uncertain future. Psychologists have long recognized the importance of this goal. For instance, Lev Vygotsky, the highly influential Russian psychologist, argued that

> we should emphasize the particular importance of cultivating creativity in school-age children. The entire future of humanity will be attained through the creative imagination; orientation to the future, behavior based on the future and derived from this future, is the most important function

of the imagination. To the extent that the main educational objective of teaching is guidance of school children's behavior so as to prepare them for the future, development and exercise of the imagination should be one of the main forces enlisted for the attainment of this goal. (Vygotsky, 1967/2004)

J. P. Guilford (1950), in his presidential address to the American Psychological Association, also stressed the importance of developing the creative potential of school-age children. His emphasis on school-age children was underwritten by persistent concerns about the potential for creative thinking to be "seriously discouraged" (p. 448) in schools and classrooms.

Less than a decade after Guilford's address, E. P. Torrance offered further evidence in validation of these concerns. Summarizing findings from some of his earliest empirical work, Torrance (1959) reported, "we have seen many indications in our testing of first and second grade children that many with apparently impoverished imaginations seemed to have been subjected to concerted efforts to eliminate fantasy from their thinking too early" (p. 313). Torrance went on to document, in a series of longitudinal studies, what he called a "fourth-grade slump" in the divergent thinking of approximately half of the children he studied (Torrance, 1968).

Importantly, many of those students later rebounded from this slump and subsequent studies (e.g., Claxton, Pannells, & Rhoads, 2005) have found a variety of patterns in the development of divergent thought across grade and age levels (see Kaufman, Plucker, & Baer, 2008, for a discussion). There are at least two important points for creativity researchers to consider when interpreting the somewhat mixed findings on creativity development in schools and classrooms.

First, and perhaps most important, the schooling experience does not necessarily suppress student creativity. And even for those who have experienced a slump, Torrance himself demonstrated that students can be helped to recover from creativity-stifling experiences (Torrance, 1970; Torrance & Gupta, 1964). This is good news for proponents of creativity in schools and classrooms because it demonstrates that the suppression of student creativity is by no means a hopeless situation. Second, the issue is not whether the schooling experience impacts the development of students' creative potential, but rather how creativity researchers might help educators support (rather than suppress) students' creative potential. Creativity researchers working primarily in the area of gifted education have made the most strides in this area. Even so, nurturing creative potential is often still viewed as separate from the mainstream academic curriculum and reserved only for the select few – those fortunate enough to be classified as "gifted" or "talented." Consequently a very small proportion of students are typically afforded systematic opportunities to develop their creative potential in schools and classrooms. Moreover, this inequity is particularly pronounced for culturally diverse students who historically have been underrepresented in U.S. gifted education programs (Ford & Grantham, 2003; USDE, 1993).

Creativity and the Curriculum: Important but Separate

Identifying creative potential in youngsters gained a great deal of momentum following Sidney Marland's (1972) landmark report to the U.S. Congress on the education of gifted and talented students – which specifically mentioned "creative and productive thinking" as one of six possible indicators of giftedness. Marland, who was U.S. Commissioner of Education at the time, reported on a study commissioned by the U.S. Congress aimed at exploring whether high ability students were be appropriately educated in U.S. schools. The report is perhaps best known for its broad (at least, at the time) definition of giftedness and also for making a strong argument in favor of a specialized (or separate) education for students who exhibited high potential or achievement.

In the decades following the publication of that report, a variety of programs and curricula aimed at identifying and nurturing creative potential in youngsters were adopted in gifted education programs. Although gifted educators clearly see the importance of nurturing creativity, many still conceptualize creativity and academic learning as separate curricular goals (Beghetto & Kaufman, 2009).

For instance, Renzulli (2005) defined two types of giftedness: "schoolhouse giftedness" and "creative-productive giftedness." Similarly, Callahan and Miller (2005), have described an "academic" and "innovative" path in their Child-Responsive model of giftedness (noting that there is sometimes an overlap in these paths). Although it may be helpful to make this distinction when attempting to tailor instruction to students' demonstrated potential, this separation can reinforce the belief that nurturing creativity is something that can (and perhaps should) be addressed outside of the mainstream academic curriculum.

Consequently, mainstream teachers may mistakenly believe that identifying and nurturing creativity is not part of their curricular responsibility (because it will be address in gifted and talented programs, after school programs, or other extracurricular activities). This may also be why educational policy makers have often failed to include the development of creativity in their mandates to improve public education (consider, for instance, the No Child Left Behind Act of 2001).

A New Trend in Educational Policy?

Although educational policymakers have traditionally neglected creativity, there is evidence that a new trend is developing (mostly in countries outside of the United States). Craft (2007), for instance, has reported that starting in the 1990s, policymakers from around the globe (e.g., Australia, Canada, England, Hong Kong, China, Singapore, and the Middle East) have started to enact policy initiatives aimed at developing students' creative potential – viewing such efforts as an investment in their students' and country's future. Within the United States, scholars (most notably Florida, 2004) have made similar arguments linking creativity with economic and cultural prosperity. Given the growing turbulence and uncertainness of the global economy in the twenty-first century, such arguments may soon catch the attention of educational policymakers in the United States.

Although it may seem encouraging that policymakers are starting to recognize the importance of including creativity in the mainstream curriculum, Anna Craft and her colleagues (Craft, 2005; Craft, Gardner, & Claxton, 2008) have raised concerns about the market-based motivations that often drive such policy initiatives. Craft (in press), for instance, has argued that a globalized market approach to creativity in education – based on Western capitalist individualism – can have potentially destructive and ethically questionable ecological and cultural consequences.

Moreover, it is somewhat difficult to discern what *exactly* creativity-in-education policy initiatives might mean for supporting creativity in schools and classrooms. Clearly, a "creativity mandate" from external policymakers will do little to help address long-standing barriers to creativity in the classroom. In fact, adding a creativity mandate may only serve to exacerbate several of these barriers. This is because externally imposed educational mandates often fail to take into consideration the realities of classroom teaching and create a situation in which teachers feel overwhelmed and caught between seemingly contradictory demands (Ingersoll, 2003). Mandating that teachers add creativity to their curriculum may only increase the feelings of being overwhelmed and do nothing to address the more fundamental barriers to creativity in the classroom. A seemingly more fruitful approach would be for creativity researchers to become more directly involved in helping teachers become aware of and begin addressing common barriers (discussed in the next section) to meaningfully including creativity in their own classrooms.

Barriers to Creativity in the Classroom

Researchers have identified a host of barriers that can suppress creativity in the classroom, including convergent teaching practices; teachers' attitudes and beliefs about creativity; the motivational environment; and students' own creativity-related beliefs. Each of these barriers will be discussed in the sections that follow.

CONVERGENT TEACHING PRACTICES
A good place to start when examining barriers to classroom creativity is with the most easily observable: the way teachers teach. Researchers who have looked in classrooms have described what has become an iconic, "disturbingly familiar" (Oakes & Lipton, 2007) image: an individual teacher, standing in front of rows of students, transmitting factual bits of information to be copied and recited (Sirotnik, 1983). It is an image of classroom teaching that – in more than 200 years of schooling – hasn't changed much (Cuban, 1993).

Goodlad (2004), describing results from a massive, multiyear (extending from the late 1970s through the early 1980s) study of more than 1,000 elementary and secondary classrooms, illustrates the starkness of this approach:

> We observed that, on average, about 75% of class time was spent on instruction and that nearly 70% of this was "talk" – usually teacher to students. Teachers out-talked the entire class of students by a ratio of about three to one.... These findings are so consistent in the schools of our sample that I have difficulty assuming that things are much different in schools elsewhere... the bulk of this teacher talk was instructing in the sense of telling. Barely 5% of this instructional time was deigned to create students' anticipation of needing to respond. Not even 1% required some kind of open response involving reasoning or perhaps an opinion from students. (p. 229)

Underwriting this convergent approach to teaching is a pattern of talk that has been called the "IRE pattern" (Mehan, 1979), which stands for *Initiate, Respond,* and *Evaluate*. IRE is the "default option" (Cazden, 2001) used by teachers and is (tacitly) taught in the interactions between teachers and students. In fact, the IRE pattern has been observed in some of the earliest schooling and preschool experiences of youngsters (Cazden, 2001). Consequently, by the time most students complete their first few years of formal schooling they come to learn their "role" in this pattern of talk: Wait for the teacher to ask a question, quickly raise your hand, quietly wait until the teacher calls on you (or calls on someone who raised their hand before you), share your response (usually by trying to match your response with what you think the teacher expects to hear), and wait for the teacher to tell you if your answer is appropriate, correct, or acceptable.

The IRE pattern, as convergent as it is, does have some appropriate uses in the classroom (Cazden, 2001). For instance, it can be useful for quickly reviewing information or checking students' ability to recall factual information. However, when this approach comes to dominate classroom talk, teaching becomes akin to a game of "intellectual hide-and-seek" (Beghetto, 2007a) in which teachers hold all the answers and student success is contingent on correctly guessing what is held in the minds of teachers. This, in turn, affords little or no opportunity for students to explore and express their own ideas, interpretations, and insights. Students soon get the message: Unexpected or otherwise creative responses are not welcome in the classroom.

Suppression of Creative Expression

Given the prevalence of teacher-dominated, convergent teaching approaches, it should come as no surprise that researchers have found that many teachers come to view unexpected student ideas as disruptive. For instance, Beghetto (2007b) found that even prospective teachers generally preferred expected ideas (over unexpected or unique ideas). The most frequent explanation offered by prospective teachers who held a low preference for unique or unexpected student ideas was that such ideas represented a potential – and in some cases, intentional – distraction. Experienced teachers have also been observed to habitually dismiss unexpected student ideas, expressing concerns about going off-task: "some teachers mentioned fear of chaos, others a need to stick with the plan, others a personal need for order" (Kennedy, 2005, p. 264).

When teachers view unexpected ideas as disruptive and habitually dismiss them, they are seriously undermining opportunities for students to share and develop potentially creative ideas. Of course, an unexpected idea is not necessarily a creative idea. However, in the context of the classroom, a potentially creative idea may first appear as an unexpected idea (Beghetto, 2009a). In this way, unexpected ideas can serve as a signifier of creative potential and should at least be explored or followed up on by teachers (rather than simply dismissed).

Proponents of creativity in the classroom have held longstanding concerns about such creativity suppressing practices. For instance, Guilford (1950) noted more than 50 years ago that

> we frequently hear the charge that under present-day mass-education methods, the development of creativity personality is seriously discouraged. The child is under pressure to conform for the sake of economy and for the sake of satisfying prescribed standards. . . . We are told, also, that the emphasis upon memorization of facts sets the wrong kind of goal for the student. (p. 448)

Importantly, the concern is not with standards, memorization, or the learning of facts, per say. In fact, Guilford made a point of emphasizing that "no creative person can get along without previous experience or facts" and that creators "never create in a vacuum or with a vacuum" (p. 448). Rather, the concern is directed at the undue *emphasis* that teachers often place on the acquisition of facts, which suggested

to Guilford (and many after him) a confusion of educational objectives, belying teachers' espoused desires to teach students to think broadly and creatively.

Factors beyond the Individual Teacher

It is important to note that the ubiquity of highly convergent teaching practices strongly suggests that there are factors beyond the individual teacher that result in the reproduction of these practices across time, place, and person. One such factor is the role played by teachers' own prior schooling experiences. Consider the average number of hours spent in school by a prospective teacher who has completed 12 years of schooling: slightly less than 13,000 hours.[1] Now consider that experts in a domain – expert musicians, for instance – typically have spent 10,000 or more hours of practice (Krampe & Ericsson, 1996). The amount of time prospective teachers have spent in school might also be thought of as a form of practice – not necessarily for developing expertise in teaching or learning – but rather for developing an expertise in the schooling experience.

Dan Lortie (1975), a sociologist of education who studied the schooling process and the development of teachers, described the prior schooling experiences of teachers as an "apprenticeship of observation." This apprenticeship has a profound influence on prospective teachers' instructional beliefs, knowledge, and practice. Consequently, by the time prospective teachers have entered their teacher preparation programs, they have already developed robust beliefs, images, and assumptions about teaching (Pajares, 1992; Richardson, 2003). Evidence of carryover effects have been found in a variety of prospective teachers' beliefs, including everything from beliefs about classroom assessment (Beghetto, 2005b), motivational beliefs about students (Beghetto, 2007c), and the

---

1 This average is based on the average school year lasting 180 days at approximately 6 hours per day spent in school during those days.

importance and perceived ability to support student creativity in the classroom (Beghetto, 2006a). Left unchecked, images and beliefs from prospective teachers' prior schooling experiences can carry over into their own classrooms (Borko & Putnam, 1996; Calderhead & Robson, 1991).

Given the potentially profound influence that factors – such as teachers' own prior schooling experience – can have on instructional beliefs and practices, it is important for creativity researchers to resist the temptation to demonize teachers for practices that they may have inherited or have felt pressured to adopt. Of course, this doesn't mean that such practices should be ignored or excused. Rather, creativity researchers need to include such factors in their research on teacher behaviors and practices. By doing so they will have a much richer context from which they can interpret and attempt to address potentially problematic beliefs, behaviors, and assumptions about creativity in the classroom. One such factor that needs to be taken into consideration, given its potential to reinforce or exacerbate convergent teaching practices, is externally imposed accountability mandates.

Accountability Mandates and Creativity

Accountability mandates, such as the No Child Left Behind Act of 2001, have placed increased pressure on teachers to conform to externally imposed standards. This, in turn, has increased the urgency of concerns raised by proponents of creativity in schools. Eisner (2002), for instance, has expressed his concern that students' creative imagination can easily "dry up under the relentless impact of 'serious' academic schooling" (p. 5). By "serious," Eisner means an emphasis on "facticity, correctness, linearity, concreteness" (p. 189). Again, like Guilford 50 years earlier, the concern is not that students are being required to learn factual knowledge, but rather that far too many students are "being taught to do little more than recall and recognize" (Sternberg, 2004, p. 68).

A core component of the accountability mandates in the United States has been the increased use of externally mandated, fact-based tests. It should come as little surprise, then, that the increased use of this type of testing makes it more likely for teachers to use an approach to teaching that mirrors the convergent nature of such tests. As Darling-Hammond and Rustique-Forrester (2005) have explained, the predominant use of fact-based tests "drives" instruction in ways that mirror the content, types of thinking, and representation of knowledge on those tests.

Standardized testing becomes a barrier for creativity when teachers feel pressured to believe that preparing students for such tests is their most important pedagogical goal. McNeil (2000), for instance, reports – in her book-length study on schools facing imposed standardization mandates – that teachers' most immediate response was to narrow the scope and quality of course content and, in turn, distance students from more meaningful and active learning of that content. This convergent impact was most profoundly felt, according to McNeil (2000), by students who attended schools in low-income and predominately ethnic- and racial-minority neighborhoods – exacerbating longstanding inequalities in the opportunities and access to quality education afforded to traditionally underserved students.

Sawyer (2004) has also reported that efforts aimed at standardized teaching have resulted in increased numbers of schools – particularly those labeled as "underperforming" and in urban districts adopting "teacher-proof" or scripted curricula. These scripted curricula encourage teachers to read – word-for-word – from instructional scripts rather than "rely either on [their own] creative potential or their subject matter expertise" (Sawyer, 2004, p. 12). Although the use of scripted curricula might offer some (superficial level of) assurance for educational leaders and policy makers that teachers – particularly those who are inexperienced – are covering required content, it represents a worse-case scenario for proponents of creativity in the classroom.

"Both/And" vs. "Either/Or"

Creativity stands little chance in classroom where teaching and learning are (literally) scripted. Of course, it doesn't have to be this way. Scripted curricula represent the most extreme form of convergent teaching, completely separating learning from the development of creative thinking. A much more complimentary view is also possible. Rather than view teaching as developing *either* academic knowledge *or* creative potential, teachers can develop *both* creative potential *and* students' knowledge of academic subject matter.

Guilford (1950), among others, recognized the link between creativity and learning, noting that "a creative act is an instance of learning" and that a "comprehensive learning theory must take into account both insight and creative activity" (p. 446). Vygotsky (1967/2004) also recognized this connection, describing a "double, mutual dependence" (p. 17) between the creative imagination and learning experiences. That is, the creative imagination both depends on knowledge and experience, and, at the same time, creative thought can serve as the means by which a students' learning experience can be broadened. In this view, learning and the development of creative potential play complementary and reciprocal roles.

Encouraging creative thinking while learning not only enlivens what is learned but can also deepen student understanding. This is because, in order for students to develop an understanding of what they are learning, they need to go beyond simple memorization and recall of facts and be able to come up with their own unique examples, uses, and applications of that information. In order for this to happen, expectations for novel yet appropriate applications of learning need to be included in classroom assessments of student learning.

Classroom Assessment and Creativity

Classroom assessment practices can have a profound influence on creativity in the classroom. This is because assessments signal to students what is *really* valued and important. Indeed, Guilford (1950) cautioned, "Let us remember ... the kinds of examinations we give really set the objectives for the students, no matter what objectives we may have stated" (p. 448). Guilford's admonition is important to keep in mind for the use of assessments in general and how creativity is assessed in schools and classrooms in particular.

With respect to the more general implications of assessment use, regardless of how teachers encourage their students to share their creativity, unless teachers also include expectations for creativity in their assignments and assessments, then the message is quite clear: Creativity really doesn't matter. Of course, simply including expectations for creativity in an assignment doesn't guarantee that original or creative thought will be recognized and rewarded.

Consider the somewhat humorous incident related by Guilford (1950). As the story goes, a university teacher told his students that their term paper grades would be based on the amount of originality shown. One student, who was very concerned about receiving high marks in the class, submitted a paper that was "essentially a stringing together of her transcribed [verbatim] lecture notes, in which the professor's pet ideas were given prominent place" – her paper received an "A" with the added note, "This is one of the most original papers I have ever read" (p. 448).

As the above anecdote helps illustrate, assessing student creativity is often easier said then done. As with all assessments, when it comes to assessing creativity, what you assess is essentially what you get. If classroom assessments are too focused on convergent thought, then students will quickly get the message that this is what matters most. This is why many creativity researchers have stressed the importance of carefully considering how educators might better assess creativity in schools and classrooms.

There are a vast array of creativity assessment methods and techniques available (see Kaufman, Plucker, & Baer, 2008, and Plucker & Makel, this volume), including, but certainly not limited to divergent-thinking tests (e.g., Torrance Tests of Creative Thinking, Torrance, 1998), self-report measures and checklists (e.g., Creative Self-Efficacy, Beghetto, 2006b; Tierney & Farmer, 2002; Group Inventory for Finding Creative Talent, Rimm, 1980), teacher ratings of students (e.g., Scales for Rating the Behavioral Characteristics of Superior Students, Renzulli, Smith, White, Callahan, & Hartman, 1976), and instruments designed to evaluate the creativity of products (e.g., Creative Product Semantic Scale, O'Quin & Besemer, 1989; Consensual Assessment Technique, Amabile 1996).

In many cases, these measures and techniques are most useful for research purposes or, in some instance, making placement decisions for gifted and talented programs. When it comes to using creativity assessments for placement decisions, Cramond (1994), for instance, has stressed the importance of using "any and all methods available to ascertain where children's strengths lie" (p. 70). This view is in alignment with Hunsaker and Callahan's (1995) caution that educators should avoid relying on "one-quick-test approaches to assessing the creativity of students" (p. 110).

Although classroom teachers need to be aware of these issues, as some of their own students will likely be tested for placement in gifted and talented programs, in most cases teachers need support in developing creativity assessments within their own curriculum to be used with all students.

Research in this area is limited; however, recent work on curriculum based measures of creativity is quite promising. Elena Grigorenko and her colleagues, for instance, have demonstrated how teaching and assessing student creativity can be "naturally integrated into teaching and assessing domain-specific knowledge" (Grigorenko, Jarvin, Tan, & Sternberg, 2008, p. 304). This work

has illustrated how the inclusion of curriculum based measures of creativity can be used to monitor and support creative thinking proficiency in specific subject areas (like reading, math, and science). Of course, in order for curriculum based measures of creativity to take root in the classroom, problematic beliefs and attitudes about creativity need to be addressed.

PROBLEMATIC ATTITUDES AND BELIEFS ABOUT CREATIVITY

Creativity researchers have identified a variety of problematic beliefs and attitudes about creativity that reinforce and are reinforced by convergent approaches to teaching. How teachers conceptualize the "ideal student" is a prime example. Torrance (1963) was one of the earliest creativity researchers to document how teachers typically view the ideal student as compliant and conforming. In more recent years, researchers have reported similar findings, documenting that teachers have been found to associate creativity with nonconformity, impulsivity, and disruptive behavior (Chan & Chan, 1999; Dawson, 1997; Scott, 1999). Of course not all teachers have been found to view creative students unfavorably (Runco, Johnson, & Bear, 1993; Thomas & Burke, 1981). Still, in the context of highly convergent approaches to teaching, it makes sense that teachers would view conformity and compliance as "ideal."

Interestingly, creativity researchers have also found that many teachers who value compliance and conformity still claim to value and have respect for student creativity (Aljughaiman & Mowrer-Reynolds, 2005; Westby & Dawson, 1995). How might teachers claim to respect student creativity and, at the same time, value traits of compliance and conformity? In considering these paradoxical findings, Runco (2007), somewhat with tongue in cheek, explained, "No doubt [teachers] do respect creativity, in the abstract, but not when faced with a classroom with 30 energetic children!"

These generally mixed and somewhat paradoxical findings about teachers' attitudes and beliefs about creativity have suggested to some researchers that teachers, like many people, may not have a clear understanding of creativity (Plucker et al., 2004). Confusion about the nature of creativity can be a key roadblock for teachers who might otherwise want to support the creative potential of their students. In fact, this confusion can underwrite a variety of problematic beliefs and biases about creativity, including originality bias, Big-C bias, and product bias.

Originality Bias

A common area of confusion for educators is equating creativity with originality. This is not surprising given that originality is the most widely recognized attribute of creativity (Runco, 2004). Creativity researchers are in general agreement, however, that originality, although necessary for creativity, is not sufficient. For instance, Plucker and colleagues (2004) found that the most common attributes found in published descriptions of creativity included some combination of originality, uniqueness, or novelty *and* socially determined fit, appropriateness, or usefulness.

Recognizing that creativity involves a combination of originality and appropriateness can help teachers see how constraints are not antithetical to creativity, but rather play a necessary role for creative expression (see also Stokes, 2006). Without some level of constraints placed on originality, there would be no way to "distinguish eccentric or schizophrenic thought from creative thought" (Feist, 1998, p. 290). This is one reason why some creativity researchers (e.g., Csikszentmihalyi, 1988; Runco, 2003) have even described unchecked originality as dangerous. Runco (2003) states that "the danger is that an individual can forget that there is a distinction between reality in the environment and reality in one's own thoughts" (p. 30).

Constraints also provide necessary boundaries for considering whether and how an original idea, product, or contribution is appropriate and therefore creative. Without recognizing the important and necessary role that constraints play in creativity,

it is easy to understand how teachers might come to associate creativity with negative forms of deviance (e.g., disruptions, off-task behavior, and curricular chaos) and feel that it has no legitimate place in their classroom (Plucker et al., 2004).

Big-C Bias

Often, when people think of creativity, iconic or legendary creators come to mind (Mozart, Picasso, Gandhi, Dickinson). This is not too surprising – given the attention such creators have received in the professional literature and popular forms of media. This emphasis on creative eminence can have the unfortunate consequence of reinforcing a Big-C (or legendary) creativity bias, in which teachers come to believe that the only creativity that matters is at the most eminent levels. However, creativity scholars (e.g., Cohen, 1989; Stein, 1953) have argued that Big-C creativity represents only the far end of the creativity continuum and have distinguished between different levels of creative magnitude, ranging from more subjective (smaller-c levels) to more objective (Larger-C) levels of creativity (Beghetto & Kaufman, 2007; Csikszentmihalyi, 1996, 1998; Stein, 1953).

Recently, Kaufman and Beghetto (2009) proposed a Four C Model of Creativity that provided categories for this continuum. These categories include, from largest to smallest, *Big*-C or legendary creativity (e.g., the revolutionary "stride piano" style of jazz great Fats Waller); *Pro*-C or non-eminent, professional creativity (e.g., the jazz piano of a professional musician who makes her living playing in clubs and social events); *little-c* or everyday creativity (e.g., the passable jazz piano of a jazz enthusiast who plays for family and friends); and *mini-c* or interpretive creativity (e.g., the new and personally meaningful insight of a youngster who is learning how to combine "riffs" when playing jazz piano). To the extent that teachers fail to recognize the importance of smaller-c levels of creativity in their classrooms, they might mistakenly believe that creativity is an extremely rare trait of highly gifted youngsters (as opposed to a gift possessed by all students) and feel that nurturing creative potential and talent is a job better suited for gifted education (rather than all) teachers.

Product Bias

Another popular misconception held by teachers is the belief that creativity requires the production of a tangible product. This misconception or "product bias" (Runco, 2007) may be common for the simple reason that products are easier to recognize and evaluate than the more subjective, internal constructions of smaller-c creativity. However, focusing only on creative end-products runs the risk of overlooking the creative potential of individuals who have not yet "impressed some qualified audience" (Runco, 2005, p. 616).

Consequently, a teacher might applaud the creativity of a small group of eighth-grade students who produced an original *i-movie* (which they used to illustrate the process of photosynthesis); yet that same teacher may fail to recognize the creative potential of another group of students (who needed more support to take their ideas from potential to product). The argument for recognizing potential is meant not to equate undemonstrated potential with actual accomplishments, but rather to help educators recognize that part of their role is to draw out and support the development of students' potential.

MOTIVATIONAL MESSAGES OF
THE CLASSROOM
In addition to beliefs and attitudes, teachers' use of common motivational strategies can also undermine student creativity. Consider, for instance, the common practice of displaying only the "best" work on the classroom walls. Many teachers use this strategy in an effort to motivate their students to work hard and, in turn, enjoy the rewards of social recognition. Although such practices can, indeed, motivate some students to strive to take intellectual risks and express their creativity, it can also have the unintended and directly opposite effect.

Extrinsic Motivators and Creativity

Creativity researchers, most notably Teresa Amabile and her colleagues (see Amabile, 1996; Collins & Amabile, 1999; Hennessey, this volume), have provided compelling evidence that helps explain why such practices might suppress student creativity. This line of research has demonstrated that creativity generally flourishes under conditions that support intrinsic motivation (signified by enjoyment, interest, involvement, and focus on personally challenging tasks) and can suffer under conditions that stress extrinsic motivators (such as promising rewards or incentives for creative work), competitions, social comparisons, and expectations of judgments from others. Indeed, concerns about comparisons to others and evaluation pressures can cause anxiety that undermines students' willingness and capacity for creative expression (Collins & Amabile, 1999; Runco, 2003; Tighe, Picariello, & Amabile 2003).

Other researchers (Clifford, 1991; Harter, 1978; Wallach & Kogan, 1965) have also documented how the nature of learning tasks can influence students' willingness to take the intellectual risks necessary for creative expression. For instance, Clifford and Chou (1991) found that when Taiwanese fourth graders were prompted to believe that they were playing a game ("play a game to practice your thinking skills") versus demonstrating their ability on a school-like task ("take a test to show how good your thinking skills are"), students in the game-like conditions were significantly more likely to take intellectual risks (by selecting more challenging tasks). This, of course, is not to say that teachers should never use tasks and activities for evaluative purposes. Rather, teachers need to be aware of the potential for such tasks to undermine creativity and thereby make clear to students when tasks are "not being graded" as well as minimize the "test-like" and competitive features of learning activities.

At the same time, it is important for teachers to recognize that some students can and will be motivated by creative competitions. Amabile (1996), for instance, has explained that although win–lose competitions seem to undermine creativity, there is evidence that competitions can have a positive effect for some individuals and work teams. The key is for teachers to become aware of the potential for competitions and assessments to suppress creativity.

In addition to competitions, rewards and incentives can also suppress creativity. Indeed, teachers, like many people, may feel that using rewards and incentives is a positive and productive strategy for encouraging students to engage in and complete tasks and activities. Although there is evidence that rewards can, in some cases, have a positive influence on creative performance (Eisenberger & Cameron, 1998; Eisenberger & Shanock, 2003), there is also compelling evidence highlighting how rewards can suppress creativity. Collins and Amabile (1999), for instance, have reported that using rewards and incentives to motivate students can actually divide students' attention and take away from the requisite concentration, risk taking, and task involvement necessary for creative expression.

Given these somewhat mixed results, it is probably unwise (and unrealistic) to request that teachers completely eliminate rewards and competitions in schools and classrooms. Rather, it is more useful for creativity researchers to help teachers become actively aware of and carefully monitor the motivational messages they are sending in their classroom. In this way teachers can better protect (or at least attempt to counterbalance) the creativity suppressing potential of extrinsic motivators.

Protecting Creativity

One way that creativity researchers have helped teachers protect student creativity from extrinsic motivators is the "immunization" approach – developed by Beth Hennessey and her colleagues (Hennessey, Amabile, & Martinage, 1989; Hennessey & Zbikowski, 1993; Hennessey, this volume). This approach involves "immunizing"

(providing intrinsic motivation training to) students in an effort protect them from the negative consequences of reward expectations. The inoculation procedure includes having students watch a video of age-related peers who are discussing academic tasks and who are also focused on the intrinsically motivating – interesting, fun, and exciting – aspects of those tasks. The intrinsic features of the task are emphasized in an effort to reduce the salience of extrinsic motivators. Results of this work, although somewhat mixed (see Gerrard, Poteat, & Ironsmith, 1996), have provided some evidence that creativity can be protected in the face of potentially creativity-suppressing motivators, such as rewards (Hennessey et al., 1989; Hennessey & Zbikowski, 1993).

STUDENTS' SELF-BELIEFS

Students' self-beliefs also play an important role in determining whether students' creativity will be expressed (or suppressed) in the classroom. Although self-beliefs are susceptible to bias and inaccuracy (Dunning, Health, & Suls, 2004), such beliefs provide students with the confidence necessary to share and develop their ideas. As Bandura (1997) has noted, "above all, innovativeness requires an unshakeable sense of efficacy to persist in creative endeavors" (p. 239). This sense of efficacy, referred to as "creative self-efficacy" (Beghetto, 2006b; Tierney & Farmer, 2002) represents an extension of the more general construct of "self-efficacy" (Bandura, 1997).

Creative Self-Efficacy

Creative self-efficacy is a self-judgment of one's imaginative ability and perceived competence in generating novel and adaptive ideas, solutions, and behaviors. Such beliefs have been linked with a variety of positive beliefs and outcomes, including students' motivational beliefs and academic aspirations (Beghetto, 2006b), creativity ratings from supervisors (Tierney & Farmer, 2002), teachers' ratings of creative expression in elementary math and science learning (Beghetto, Kaufman, & Baxter, 2010), and students' willingness to take intellectual risks in the classroom (Beghetto, 2009b),

Intellectual Risk Taking

The link between creative self-efficacy beliefs and intellectual risk taking is particularly important. Bandura (1997), for instance, has reported how healthy self-efficacy beliefs can help individuals frame risks as challenging opportunities (rather than threats), influence willingness to take risks, and sustain one's effort in the face of challenges. Bandura has also noted how healthy creative self-efficacy beliefs are essential for creative productivity.

> The history of innovation vividly documents that premature abandonment of advantageous ventures because of early failures and discouraging setbacks would have deprived societies of the major advances they enjoy in virtually every aspect of life. It was Edison's unshakeable belief in his inventive efficacy that illuminated our environment and spawned the recording and movie industries, just to mention a few of his wondrous creations. (p. 456)

With respect to the classroom, students' willingness to take intellectual risks – in the form of sharing novel ideas and insights, raising new questions, and attempting to do and try new things – is no less important. Such behaviors are "risky" because they involve uncertainty (Byrnes, 1998) – and place students at risk of making mistakes, appearing less competent, or feeling inferior to others. These concerns are very real for students (Dweck, 1999) and, in the absence of a supportive classroom environment, can underwrite conforming and risk-avoidant behaviors in the classroom.

Supportive Feedback and Healthy Self-Beliefs

One of the most direct and potentially influential ways that teachers can support the development of students' creative self-efficacy beliefs is to provide informative feedback on their creative potential and ability. Indeed, positive efficacy beliefs have been found to be associated with supportive feedback (Bandura, 1997; Tierney & Farmer, 2002). In a recent classroom-based study (Beghetto, 2006b), for instance, positive teacher feedback was found to be the strongest unique predictor of middle and secondary students' self-beliefs about their own creativity.

Of course, meaningful creative accomplishment requires much more than simply having received positive feedback about one's own creative ability. Indeed, without the requisite domain-relevant knowledge, skills, resources, support, and sustained effort, no amount of self-belief in one's creative ability will result in creative accomplishment. Still, it is important to not overlook the role that teachers can play in helping students develops *healthy* self-efficacy beliefs. Healthy is meant here in the sense that the feedback provided will help students calibrate their beliefs – challenging themselves to go beyond their current level of competence, yet at the same time not be too excessive (Bandura, 1997).

The cultivation of healthy self-beliefs has important short- and long-term consequences for the development of students' creativity. In the short run, students need to have enough confidence in their ideas to be willing to share them and make them available to feedback. By doing so, students can learn how to clarify, strengthen, and when necessary abandon ideas (in pursuit of more viable ideas). In the long run, healthy self-beliefs can help sustain students as they put forth the sustained effort necessary to develop domain relevant knowledge and skills, seek out supports and resources, and face the obstacles and set-backs inherent in most any creative endeavor.

Future Directions

Throughout this chapter it has been argued that creativity occupies a conflicted space in many K–12 classrooms. Although more directly incorporating creativity in the curriculum will require a sustained and collaborative effort on the part of educators and creativity researchers, it is creativity researchers who, undoubtedly, will have to play a key role in helping move creativity from the margins into the mainstream curriculum. There are a variety of important directions that creativity researchers might take in attempting to attain this goal.

For instance, additional work is needed to explore and clarify the connection between learning and creativity. This is particularly important given that student learning is a core responsibility of teachers. Although a variety of researchers have noted this connection (e.g., Beghetto & Kaufman, 2007; Freund & Holling, 2008; Guilford, 1950; Plucker, Beghetto, & Dow, 2004; Sawyer et al., 2003), additional elaboration and empirical testing of this connection is needed. Unless educators, policymakers, and the general public can see a clear connection between creativity and learning, barriers to creativity in classrooms will likely continue.

Connecting creativity research to teacher-preparation and teacher-development efforts is another important future direction. Although schools and classrooms have been and will continue to be key sites for creativity research, studies focused on exploring ways to better prepare teachers for supporting creativity in their classrooms are also needed.

Combining research on creativity and teacher development will go a long way in identifying and addressing lingering misconceptions about creativity and problematic practices that teachers have inherited from their own prior schooling experiences. This work will require the development of meaningful collaborations between creativity researchers and teacher educators and increased efforts on the part of creativity researchers to share their findings in venues specifically aimed at teacher educators, educational policymakers, and the general public.

Finally and perhaps most importantly, there is a need for creativity researchers to assist in the development, testing, and implementation of new pedagogical models that simultaneously support the development of creative potential and academic learning. This is not to deny the value or success of existing programs and models, most of which are found in gifted education programs (e.g., Isaksen & Treffinger, 2004; Piirto, 2004; Renzulli & Reis, 1997). Rather, it is a call for the development and testing of additional models – aimed particularly at infusing creativity in the mainstream, K–12 curriculum. Indeed, without multiple models for how teachers might mainstream creativity into their curriculum, it is unlikely that any meaningful transformation in convergent teaching practices will occur. This need is particular acute in high-poverty and culturally diverse school settings that have increasingly adopted extremely narrow (and even scripted) curricula in response to external accountability mandates (McNeil, 2000; Sawyer, 2004).

Future directions for research on creativity in the classroom present a variety of challenges and complexities. However, there are at least as many exciting and important opportunities for creativity researchers to help educators address and replace longstanding barriers to creativity in the classroom.

References

Aljughaiman, A., & Mowrer-Reynolds, E. (2005). Teachers' conceptions of creativity and creative students. *Journal of Creative Behavior*, 39, 17–34.

Amabile, T. M. (1996). *Creativity in context: Update to the social psychology of creativity*. Boulder, CO: Westview.

Bandura, A. (1997). *Self-efficacy: The exercise of control*. New York: Freeman.

Beghetto, R. A. (2005a). Does assessment kill student creativity? *The Educational Forum*, 69, 254–263.

Beghetto, R. A. (2005b). Pre-service teachers' self-judgments of test taking. *Journal of Educational Research*, 95, 376–380.

Beghetto, R. A. (2006a). Creative justice? The relationship between prospective teachers' prior schooling experiences and perceived importance of promoting student creativity. *Journal of Creative Behavior*, 40, 149–162.

Beghetto, R. A. (2006b). Creative self-efficacy: Correlates in middle and secondary students. *Creativity Research Journal*, 18, 447–457.

Beghetto, R. A. (2007a). Ideational code-switching: Walking the talk about supporting student creativity in the classroom. *Roeper Review*, 29, 265–270.

Beghetto, R. A. (2007b). Does creativity have a place in classroom discussions? Prospective teachers' response preferences. *Thinking Skills and Creativity*, 2, 1–9.

Beghetto, R. A. (2007c). Prospective teachers' beliefs about students' goal orientations: A carry-over effect of prior schooling experiences? *Social Psychology of Education*, 10, 171–191.

Beghetto, R. A. (2009a). In search of the unexpected: Finding creativity in the micromoments of the classroom. *Psychology of Aesthetics, Creativity, & the Arts*, 3, 2–5.

Beghetto, R. A. (2009b). Correlates of intellectual risk taking in elementary school science. *Journal of Research in Science Teaching*, 46, 210–223.

Beghetto, R. A., & Kaufman, J. C. (2007). Toward a broader conception of creativity: A case for mini-c creativity. *Psychology of Aesthetics, Creativity, and the Arts*, 1, 73–79.

Beghetto, R. A., & Kaufman, J. C. (2009). Intellectual estuaries: Connecting learning and creativity in programs of advanced academics. *Journal of Advanced Academics*, 20, 296–324.

Beghetto, R. A., Kaufman, J. C., & Baxter, J. (2010). *Exploring the link between students' and teachers' perceptions of creativity in elementary science and math*. Manuscript in preparation.

Beghetto, R. A., & Plucker, J. A. (2006). The relationship among schooling, learning, and creativity: "All roads lead to creativity" or "You can't get there from here?" In J. C. Kaufman & J. Baer (Eds). *Creativity and reason in cognitive development* (pp. 316–332). Cambridge: Cambridge University Press.

Borko, H., & Putnam, R. (1996). Learning to teach. In R. Calfee & D. Berliner (Eds.), *Handbook of educational psychology* (pp. 69–87). New York: Macmillan.

Byrnes, J. P. (1998). *The nature and development of decision-making: A self-regulation model*. Hillsdale, NJ: Erlbaum.

Calderhead, J., & Robson, M. (1991). Images of teaching: Student teachers' early conceptions of classroom practice. *Teaching and Teacher Education*, 7, 1–8.

Callahan, C. M., & Miller, E. M. (2005). A child-responsive model of giftedness. In R. J. Sternberg & J. E. Davidson (Eds.), *Conceptions of giftedness* (2nd ed., pp. 38–50). Cambridge: Cambridge University Press.

Cazden, C. B. (2001). *Classroom discourse: The language of teaching and learning* (2nd ed.). Portsmouth, NH: Heinemann.

Chan, D. W., & Chan, L. (1999). Implicit theories of creativity: Teachers' perception of student characteristics in Hong Kong. *Creativity Research Journal*, 12, 185–195.

Claxton, A. F., Pannells, T. C., & Rhoads, P. A. (2005). Developmental trends in the creativity of school-age children. *Creativity Research Journal*, 17, 327–335.

Clifford, M. M. (1991). Risk taking: Theoretical, empirical, and educational considerations. *Educational Psychologist*, 26, 263–297.

Clifford, M. M., & Chou, F. (1991). Effects of payoff and task context on academic risk taking. *Journal of Educational Psychology*, 83, 499–507.

Cohen, L. M. (1989). A continuum of adaptive creative behaviors. *Creativity Research Journal*, 2, 169–183.

Collins, M. A., & Amabile, T. M. (1999). Motivation and creativity. In R. J. Sternberg (Ed.), *Handbook of creativity* (pp. 297–312). Cambridge: Cambridge University Press.

Craft, A. (2005). *Creativity in schools: Tensions and dilemmas*. London: Routledge

Craft, A. (2007). Possibility thinking in the early years and primary classroom. In A. G. Tan (Ed.), *Creativity: A handbook for teachers*. Singapore: World Scientific.

Craft, A. (in press). Possibility thinking and wise creativity: Educational futures in England. In R. A. Beghetto & J. C. Kaufman (Eds.), *Nurturing creativity in the classroom*. Cambridge: Cambridge University Press.

Craft, A., Gardner, H., & Claxton, G. (2008). *Creativity, wisdom and trusteeship: Exploring the role of education*. Thousand Oaks, CA: Corwin Press.

Cramond, B. (1994). We can trust creativity tests. *Educational Leadership*, 52, 70–71.

Crutchfield, R. (1962). Conformity and creative thinking. In H. Gruber, G. Terrel, & M. Wertheimer (Eds.), *Contemporary approaches to creative thinking* (pp. 120–140). New York: Atherton.

Csikszentmihalyi, M. (1988). The dangers of originality: Creativity and the artistic process.

In M. M. Gedo (Ed.), *Psychoanalytic perspectives on art* (pp. 213–224). Hillsdale, NJ: The Analytic Press.

Csikszentmihalyi, M. (1996). *Creativity: Flow and the psychology of discovery and invention.* New York: HarperCollins.

Csikszentmihalyi, M. (1998). Reflections on the field. *Roeper Review, 21,* 80–81.

Cuban, L. (1993). *How teachers taught: Constancy and change in American classrooms 1890–1990* (2nd ed.). New York: Teachers College Press.

Darling-Hammond, L., & Rustique-Forrester, E. (2005). The consequences of student testing for teaching and teacher quality. *Yearbook of the National Society for the Study of Education, 104,* 289–319.

Dawson, V. L. (1997). In search of the Wild Bohemian: Challenges in the identification of the creatively gifted. *Roeper Review, 19,* 148–152.

Dunning, D., Health, C., & Suls, J. M. (2004). Flawed self-assessment: Implications for health, education, and the workplace. *Psychological Science in the Public Interest, 5,* 69–106.

Dweck, C. S. (1999). *Self-Theories: Their role in motivation, personality and development.* Philadelphia: Taylor & Francis.

Eisenberger, R., & Cameron, J. (1998). Reward, intrinsic interest, and creativity: New findings. *American Psychologist, 53,* 676–679.

Eisenberger, R., & Shanock, L. (2003). Rewards, intrinsic motivation, and creativity: A case study of conceptual and methodological isolation. *Creativity Research Journal, 15,* 121–130.

Eisner, E. W. (2002). *The arts and the creation of mind.* New Haven, CT: Yale University Press.

Feist, G. J. (1998). A meta-analysis of personality in scientific and artistic creativity. *Personality and Social Psychology Review, 2,* 290–309.

Freund, P. A., & Holling, H. (2008). Creativity in the classroom: A multilevel analysis investigating the impact of creativity and reasoning on GPA. *Creativity Research Journal, 20,* 309–318.

Florida, R. (2004). *The rise of the creative class: And how it's transforming work, leisure, community and everyday life.* New York: Basic Books.

Ford, D. Y., & Grantham, T. C. Providing access for culturally diverse gifted students: From deficit to dynamic thinking. *Theory into Practice, 42,* 217–225.

Gerrard, L. E., Poteat, G. M., & Ironsmith, M. (1996). Promoting children's creativity: Effects of competition, self-esteem, and immunization. *Creativity Research Journal, 9,* 339–346.

Goodlad, J. L. (2004). *A place called school: Prospects for the future.* New York: McGraw-Hill.

Grigorenko, E. L., Jarvin, L., Tan, M., & Sternberg, R. J. (2008). Something new in the garden: Assessing creativity in academic domains. *Psychology Science Quarterly, 50,* 295–307.

Guilford, J. P. (1950). Creativity. *American Psychologist, 5,* 444–454.

Halpern, D. F. (in press). Creativity in college classrooms. In R. A. Beghetto & J. C. Kaufman (Eds.), *Nurturing creativity in the classroom.* Cambridge: Cambridge University Press.

Harter, S. (1978). Pleasure derived from challenge and the effects of receiving grades on children's difficulty level choices. *Child Development, 49,* 788–799.

Hennessey, B. A., Amabile, T. M., & Martinage, M. (1989). Immunizing children against the negative effects of reward. *Contemporary Educational Psychology, 14,* 212–227.

Hennessey, B. A., & Zbikowski, S. M. (1993). Immunizing children against the negative effects of reward: A further examination of intrinsic motivation training techniques. *Creativity Research Journal, 6,* 297–307.

Hunsaker, S. L., & Callahan, C. M. (1995). Creativity and giftedness: Published instrument uses and abuses. *Gifted Child Quarterly, 39,* 110–114.

Ingersoll, R. M. (2003). *Who controls teachers' work? Power and accountability in America's schools.* Cambridge, MA: Harvard University Press.

Isaksen, S. G., & Treffinger, D. J. (2004). Celebrating 50 years of reflective practice: Versions of creative problem solving. *Journal of Creative Behavior, 38* (2), 75–101.

Kaufman, J. C., & Beghetto, R. A. (2009). Beyond big and little: The four C model of creativity. *Review of General Psychology, 13,* 1–12.

Kaufman, J. C., Plucker, J. A., & Baer, J. (2008). *Essentials of creativity assessment.* New York: Wiley.

Kaufman, J. C., & Sternberg, R. J. (Eds.). (2006). *The international handbook of creativity.* Cambridge: Cambridge University Press.

Kennedy, M. (2005). *Inside teaching: How classroom life undermines reform.* Cambridge, MA: Harvard University Press.

Krampe, R. Th., & Ericsson, K. A. (1996). Maintaining excellence: Deliberate practice and elite performance in young and older pianists.

Journal of Experimental Psychology: General, 125, 331–359.

Lortie, D. (1975). *Schoolteacher: A sociological study.* Chicago: University of Chicago Press.

Marland, S. P. (1972). *Education of the gifted and talented: Report to the Congress of the United States by the U.S. Commissioner of Education.* Washington, DC: Department of Health, Education and Welfare.

McNeil, L. M. (2000). *Contradictions of school reform: Educational costs of standardized testing.* New York: Routledge.

Mehan, H. (1979). *Learning lessons: Social organization in the classroom.* Cambridge, MA: Harvard University Press.

No Child Left Behind Act of 2001, *Pub. 1, No.* 107–110, 115 Stat. 1425 (2002).

Oakes, J., & Lipton, M. (2007). *Teaching to change the world* (3rd ed.). Boston: McGraw.

O'Quin, K., & Besemer, S. P. (1989). The development, reliability, and validity of the revised Creative Product Semantic Scale. *Creativity Research Journal,* 2, 267–278.

Pajares, M. F. (1992). Teachers' beliefs and educational research: Cleaning up a messing construct. *Review of Educational Research,* 62, 307–332.

Piirto, J. (2004). *Understanding creativity.* Scottsdale, AZ: Great Potential Press.

Plucker, J., Beghetto, R. A., & Dow, G. (2004). Why isn't creativity more important to educational psychologists? Potential, pitfalls, and future directions in creativity research. *Educational Psychologist,* 39, 83–96.

Plucker, J. A. & Dow, G. T. (in press). Attitude change as the precursor to creativity enhancement. In R. A. Beghetto & J. C. Kaufman (Eds.), *Nurturing creativity in the classroom.* Cambridge: Cambridge University Press.

Renzulli, J. S. (2005). The three-ring conception of giftedness: A developmental model for promoting creative productivity. In R. J. Sternberg & J. E. Davidson (Eds.). *Conceptions of Giftedness* (2nd ed., pp. 217–245). Cambridge: Cambridge University Press.

Renzulli, J. S., & Reis, S. M. (1997). *The schoolwide enrichment model: A how-to guide for educational excellence* (2nd ed.). Mansfield Center, CT: Creative Learning Press.

Renzulli, J. S., Smith, L. H., White, A. J., Callahan, C. M., & Hartman, R. K. (1976). *Scales for rating the behavioral characteristics of superior students.* Mansfield Center, CT: Creative Learning Press.

Richardson, V. (2003). Preservice teachers' beliefs. In J. Raths & A. C. McAninch (Eds.), *Teacher beliefs and classroom performance: The impact of teacher education* (pp. 1–22). Greenwich, CT: Information Age Publishing.

Rimm, S. B. (1980). *Group inventory for finding creative talent (GIFT).* Waterton, WI: Educational Assessment Service.

Runco, M. A. (2003). Creativity, cognition, and their educational implications. In J. C. Houtz (Ed.), *The educational psychology of creativity* (pp. 25–56). Cresskill, NJ: Hampton Press.

Runco, M. A. (2004). Creativity. *Annual Review of Psychology,* 55, 657–687.

Runco, M. A. (2005). Motivation, competence, and creativity. In A. Elliott & C. Dweck (Eds.), *Handbook of achievement motivation and competence* (pp. 609–623). New York: Guilford.

Runco, M. A. (2007). *Creativity. Theories and themes: Research, development, and practice.* Burlington, MA: Elsevier Academic Press.

Runco, M. A., Johnson, D. J., & Bear, P. K. (1993). Parents' and teachers' implicit theories of children's creativity. *Child Study Journal,* 23, 91–113.

Sawyer, R. K. (2004). Creative teaching: Collaborative discussion as disciplined improvisation. *Educational Researcher,* 33, 12–20.

Sawyer, R. K., John-Steiner, V., Moran, S., Sternberg, R., Feldman, D. H., Csikszentmihalyi, M., et al. (2003). *Creativity and development.* New York: Oxford University Press.

Scott, C. L. (1999). Teachers' biases toward creative children. *Creativity Research Journal,* 12, 321–337.

Sirotnik, K. A. (1983). What you see is what you get: Consistency, persistency, and mediocrity in classrooms. *Harvard Educational Review,* 53, 16–31.

Sternberg, R. J. (2004). Four alternative futures for education in the United States: It's our choice. *School Psychology Review,* 33, 67–77.

Stein, M. I. (1953). Creativity and culture. *The Journal of Psychology,* 36, 311–322.

Sternberg, R. J., & Grigorenko, E. L. (2007). *Teaching for successful intelligence* (2nd ed.). Thousand Oaks, CA: Corwin.

Stokes, P. D. (2006). *Creativity from constraints: The psychology of breakthrough.* New York: Springer.

Tan, A. G. (Ed.). (2007). *Creativity: A handbook for teachers.* Singapore: World Scientific.

Tannenbaum, A. (1986). Giftedness: A psychosocial approach. In R. J. Sternberg & J. Davidson (Eds.), *Conceptions of giftedness* (pp. 21–52). New York: Cambridge University Press.

Thomas, N. G., & Burke, L. E. (1981). Effects of school environments on the development of young children's creativity. *Child Development*, 52, 1153–1162.

Tierney, P., & Farmer, S. M. (2002). Creative self-efficacy: Its potential antecedents and relationship to creative performance. *Academy of Management Journal*, 45, 1137–1148.

Tighe, E., Picariello, M. L., & Amabile, T. M. (2003). Environmental influences on motivation and creativity in the classroom. In J. C. Houtz (Ed.), *The educational psychology of creativity* (pp. 199–222). Cresskill, NJ: Hampton Press.

Torrance, E. P. (1959). Current research on the nature of creative talent. *Journal of Counseling Psychology*, 6, 309–316.

Torrance, E. P. (1963). The creative personality and the ideal pupil. *Teachers College Record*, 65, 220–226.

Torrance, E. P. (1968). A longitudinal examination of the fourth grade slump in creativity. *Gifted Child Quarterly*, 12, 195–199.

Torrance, E. P. (1970). *Encouraging creativity in the classroom.* Dubuque, IA: William C. Brown Company.

Torrance, E. P. (1998). *The Torrance tests of creative thinking: Norms-technical manual.* Bensenville, IL: Scholastic Testing Service.

Torrance, E. P., & Gupta, R. K. (1964). *Programmed experiences in creative thinking. Final report on Title VII Project to the U. S. Office of Education.* Minneapolis: University of Minnesota.

U.S. Department of Education. (1993). *National excellence: A case for developing America's talent.* Washington, DC: Author.

Vygotsky, L. S. (2004). Imagination and creativity in childhood (M. E. Sharpe, Inc., Trans.). *Journal of Russian and East European Psychology*, 42, 7–97. (Original work published 1967)

Wallach, M. A., & Kogan, N. (1965). *Modes of thinking in young children.* New York: Holt, Rinehart, & Winston.

Wells, G. & Claxton, G. (Eds.). (2002). *Learning for life in the 21st century.* Malden, MA: Blackwell.

Westby, E. L., & Dawson, V. L. (1995). Creativity: Asset or burden in the classroom. *Creativity Research Journal*, 8, 1–10.

Section IV

Conclusion

CHAPTER 24

Constraints on Creativity

Obvious and Not So Obvious

Robert J. Sternberg and James C. Kaufman

In this chapter, we conclude the handbook with an attempt to analyze the chapters of the book in order to understand a consensual conception of the constraints that exist on creativity. This book is about not only what creativity is, but also about why it occurs and does not occur. With regard to the latter in particular, what prevents people, processes, and products from being labeled "creative"? In a conventional assessment of intelligence, things are considerably easier: One counts "right" answers. But what is a "right" answer with regard to creativity, or even, what makes a product creative at all? Usually, what is creative is a matter of consensual assessment (Amabile, 1996; see also Plucker & Makel, Chapter 3, this volume). We consider questions such as these, as well as possible answers, in this chapter.

Definitional Constraints

The definition of creativity immediately implies constraints, as we will see.

Definition

Students of creativity agree on the main aspects of a definition of creativity. There are two main aspects. The first is novelty: Creative work is original and somehow distinctive with respect to the work with which it is compared. The second aspect is variously called quality. These ideas refer to the judgment of some reference group that the work is not merely novel, but also good, or perhaps even useful, according to some reference group. For example, one could draw random lines on a piece of paper and correctly point out that the configuration of lines is literally unique: In all likelihood, no one has ever before created quite the same pattern of lines. At the same time, the set of lines is likely not to pass the test of quality or usefulness, because they fail to evoke in judges a feeling that they are aesthetically pleasing as well as distinctive.

Many years ago, on a television show called *All in the Family*, an episode introduced the main character, Archie Bunker, in possession of a remote-control doorbell ringer that someone had invented. One could ring a person's doorbell from one's automobile so as not to have to ring it upon reaching the door. The contraption was novel but it was not useful: People would come to the door of their house, find no one is there, and then shut the door in exasperation.

The difficulty of judging just what is creative, by definition, arises in part from the notion that creativity represents an "appropriate solution to a problem or response to a situation" (Moran & Gardner, Chapter 4, this volume). What is appropriate is a judgment call, and may vary across time, space, persons, and situational constraints. Lowering taxes may be viewed by some people at some times as a creative solution to stimulating the economy; it may conversely be viewed by other people at the same or different time as a foolhardy way to increase national debt.

Kozbelt, Beghetto, and Runco (Chapter 2, this volume) capture some of the notion that constraints inhere in creativity when they state that "the claim usually worded 'moderation in all things' applies to many aspects of creativity." Their point is that, by definition, more is not necessarily better when it comes to creativity.

In a sense, we have evolved to be creative (Gabora & Kaufman, Chapter 15, this volume). Those organisms that could not adapt to the progressive novelties of the ever-changing environment have been extinguished in the course of evolution, leaving over those who are evolved in order to function in a creative way that enables them to adapt as environments change, at least to a certain degree. Evolution thus forms a constraint on creativity, in the sense that insufficiently creative organisms die out over evolutionary time.

The definitional constraint has the interesting implication that creativity is not and cannot be simply about sitting around, brainstorming, and coming up with wildly imaginative ideas. There are always constraints on creativity in the real world. The most creative people are those who can be very original and yet work within the constraints of the construct. Those who are imaginative but whose ideas are useless become frustrated dreamers. Those who have useful ideas that are not imaginative become, whether in name or in deed, technicians.

Creativity has a property that is not true of all psychological constructs – it exists in the interaction of the stimulus and the beholder. A maker may view his or her work as creative, but if there is not an audience that sees it that way, the maker aside, then the work is not considered creative. Moreover, what is creative to one audience may be seditious or even treasonous to another. This interaction places a constraint that one would not see, say, in an intelligence test. If one is asked the meaning of the English word "ambiguous," the meaning of the word will be, at least to a first order of approximation, the same in the years 1900, 2000, and 2001. But an ambiguous drawing by (for example) Jackson Pollock might be viewed as creative today, but might not have been in times before such abstract modern art was valued. In the classical period of David, for example, such work might have been viewed as not creative at all.

Even at a given time, people may argue over whether work is creative. The senior author remembers, as an adolescent, seeing an artwork at the New York Museum of Modern Art entitled *White on White*. The artwork was a patch of white on top of a white background. As the author recalls, several people were standing around the artwork ridiculing it. The curator may have had the last word as to which artworks were exhibited in the museum, but he or she was not the last word on whether the work was creative. And that's precisely the point. In the judgment of creativity, there is nothing like $1 + 1 = 2$. There is no last word.

This discussion implies that creativity inheres, in part, in work – in products. As Cropley and Cropley (Chapter 16, this volume) point out, there is a road to be traveled from simply talking about creativity or the potential for creativity to real, functionally creative products. What has changed the world is not merely the potential for creativity, but creativity as manifested in functional products. A constraint on creative products, however, is that there are many environmental factors that can make it more or less difficult to translate creative ideas into functionally creative products.

We sometimes think of the judgment of work as creative as being like an absorbing Markov state – once a work is judged creativity, even if belatedly, it will always be so adjudged. But the constraints do not work this way at all. Consider Jean-Louis-Ernest Meissonier, the French painter whose work was presented to Napoleon III and displayed in prominent exhibitions. Founder of the Salon style of painting, with its great attention to detail, he represented an alternate approach to the work of such impressionists as Manet (King, 2006). Meissonier's work is still known today (indeed, a quick Google search turns up 212,000 hits), yet Manet has become legendary (in comparison, Manet's name gets nearly 4 million hits) and Meissonier has not. When the senior author was in college, he studied diverse theories of learning and of personality, to each of which several books were devoted. Few of these grand theories are taught today, except perhaps in history and systems courses.

Constraints on the Locus of Creativity

Wherein resides creativity? Creativity, it seems, can be in the person, the process, the product, or the place.

The Person

As you have learned from this volume, people are typically adjudged as creative through their work. But the constraints on this process of judgment remain shrouded in some ambiguity. Is one judged by one's most creative work or works, the average creative expression of one's work, the least creative of one's works, or some combination heuristic that perhaps may vary between or even within persons.

For example, the widely acknowledged cocreator of the theory of evolution, Alfred Russel Wallace, had many ideas that now seem strange, such as spiritualism, or the belief in the nonmaterial origin of higher mental skills. He is much less well known today than Darwin. Is his lower placement in the pantheon of creative greats due to his less valued ideas bringing down the judgment, to his lesser role in publicizing the theory of evolution, to his lesser development of the theory, or what? It is not always easy to say. Merton (1979) has pointed out that, in science, there are many doubles – codiscoveries made at roughly the same time. But the codiscoverers often do not receive the same amount of credit.

Some educators and researchers are content to judge creativity through a test such as one of divergent thinking (see Runco, Chapter 22, this volume). But such tests are used primarily as predictors of creative performance rather than as creative of it (see Plucker & Makel, Chapter 3, this volume). That is, the level of creativity they entail is generally not viewed as sufficient or as sufficiently relevant societally for it to form a basis for labeling someone as truly creative.

Person constraints are hard to interpret. Does a modest or poor score on a test such as the Torrance Tests of Creative Thinking imply that a person cannot be creative, say, as a musician? Does it even imply that the person cannot be creative in any domain whatsoever? Creativity is as much attitudinal as it is cognitive, and so one does not necessarily wish to say someone cannot be creative on the basis of limited data. Indeed, strong intrinsic motivation to be creative (see Hennessey, Chapter 18, this volume) may help a person overcome cognitive constraints.

Creativity within a person is a complex interaction involving not only ability, but also personality factors as well. As Feist (Chapter 6, this volume) points out, personality places constraints on creativity. A person could have a great deal of creative ability – that is, the ability to think in novel ways – but if he or she is not willing to take a risk, or to defy conventions, or to fight for ideas that others might scoff at, that creative ability may remain latent and never see the light of day.

Most research on creativity looks at the person within the range of normal functioning. But as Silvia and J. Kaufman (Chapter 20, this volume) point out, there are associations between creativity and certain forms of mental illness. For example, according to Silvia and J. Kaufman, writers show a higher-than-expected rate of affective disorders, such as depression and bipolar disorder. But one would scarcely want to become depressed to become creative, especially because the nature of the causal link is not well established. At the same time, there is a chance that treating various disorders, such as attention-deficit hyperactivity disorder, may result in the world's missing out on creative contributions that otherwise might have been made.

Intelligence also places constraints on creativity. Many investigators have argued that there is a threshold effect – that up to an IQ of roughly 120, there is a correlation between IQ and creativity, but over that level, the correlation disappears (Barron, 1961; MacKinnon, 1961; see Kim, Cramond, & VanTassel-Baska, Chapter 21, this volume). As Kim and colleagues point out, it is not at all clear that the threshold theory is empirically supportable. But what is clear is that at low levels of IQ, creativity becomes more difficult, if only because part of creativity is not only coming up with ideas, but analytically evaluating whether the ideas are good ones.

The Process

Luthiers – makers of stringed instruments – are engaged in a noble but, so far, frustrating pursuit. How do you make a violin or other stringed instrument that sounds like a Stradivarius or like the stringed instruments of any of the other great makers, such as Montagna or Amati. The pursuit is interesting because these makers lived so long ago and yet their craft has proven elusive. Stradivarius, for example, lived from 1644 to 1737, and yet, more than 270 years later, luthiers cannot replicate what he did.

Stokes (2005) argued that components of the creative process (such as differing tasks, goals, subjects, functions, materials, and styles) are inherently constraining. Similarly, Howard Gardner and his colleagues (Connell, Sheridan, & Gardner, 2003; Keinänen & Gardner, 2004; Keinänen, Sheridan, & Gardner, 2006) argue for vertical and horizontal orientations toward creativity. Vertical orientations have restrictive constraints (such as in preparing sushi); horizontal orientations have very few constraints (such as tossing different leftovers together to create a new taste).

The mental process most associated with creative thinking is almost certainly divergent thinking (Runco, Chapter 22, this volume), which refers roughly to open-ended generation of ideas in response to some kind of task or stimulus. Divergent thinking is probably the aspect of creativity that is most readily measured. But it probably does not encompass all of what laypeople and scientists alike mean by creative thinking.

Not only are particular processes important, but also how they are directed. For example, Martindale (1999) noted that people are more creative when they are able to defocus their attention, where "defocused attention refers to the ability to consider numerous elements simultaneously, rather than limiting attention to only a few elements" (A. Kaufman, Kornilov, Briston, Tan, & Grigorenko, Chapter 11, this volume). In most cases, we are told to concentrate on what we are working on. This is a case where it is useful not always to concentrate too much!

These considerations, however, are more focused on everyday-type creativity (such as cooking – see Richards, Chapter 10, this volume). Everyday creativity is the kind we all need in our daily lives. Might there be other elements when the entire field is considered? The replication of the luthiers would seem to be the least creative of creative processes (Sternberg, 1999; Sternberg, Kaufman, & Pretz, 2002). Yet even the most creative of instrument makers have not been able to replicate Stradivarius. Are these luthiers really so uncreative that they cannot reach even the most trivial level of creativity?

What the Stradivarius paradox makes clear is that the locus of creativity is not always immediately obvious. In this case, the creativity is in finding the means to do what was done many years before. Is the secret of the sound in the wood, in the varnish, in the design of the frame, or where? No one knows for sure.

Three processes seem to be especially important in creative insights (Sternberg & Davidson, 1983):

1. *Selective encoding.* Selective encoding involves sifting out relevant information from irrelevant information. Significant problems generally present us with large amounts of information, only some of which is relevant to problem solution. For example, the facts of a legal case are usually both numerous and confusing: An insightful lawyer must figure out which of the myriad facts are relevant to principles of law. Similarly, a doctor or a psychotherapist must sift out those facts that are relevant for diagnosis or treatment. Perhaps the occupation that most directly must employ selective encoding is that of the detective: In trying to figure out who has perpetrated a crime, the detective must figure out what the relevant facts are. Failure to do so may result in the detective's following up on false leads, or in having no leads to follow up on at all.

2. *Selective combination.* Selective combination involves combining what might originally seem to be isolated pieces of information into a unified whole that may or may not resemble its parts. For example, the lawyer must know how the relevant facts of a case fit together to make (or break) the case. A doctor or psychotherapist must be able to figure out how to combine information about various isolated symptoms to identify a given medical (or psychological) syndrome. A detective, having collected the facts that seem relevant to the case, must determine how they fit together to point at the guilty party rather than at anyone else.

3. *Selective comparison.* Selective comparison involves relating newly acquired information to old information that you already have. Problem solving by analogy, for example, is an instance of selective comparison: The solver realizes that new information is similar to old information in certain ways (and dissimilar from it in other ways) and uses this information better to understand the new information. For example, an insightful lawyer will relate a current case to past legal precedents; choosing the right precedent is absolutely essential. A doctor or psychotherapist relates the current set of symptoms to previous case histories in his or her own or in others' past experiences. Again, choosing the right precedents is essential. A detective may have been involved in or know about a similar case where the same method was used to commit a crime. Drawing an analogy to the past case may be helpful to the detective both in understanding the nature of the crime and in figuring out who did it.

The Product

One of the most hotly debated issues around constraints is whether creativity is domain specific or domain general. This issue has been at times debated with not only heat, but fury. But more and more (Baer, Chapter 17, this volume; Sternberg, 2005), researchers are realizing that the question of whether creativity is domain specific or domain general in the kinds of products people can produce is improperly posed. Creativity has aspects that are both. For example, people may have the capability to be creative in many domains, but then the knowledge they acquire leads them in one direction or another (Simonton, Chapter 9, this volume).

We have argued (Sternberg, Kaufman, & Pretz, 2002) that there are eight types of creative products. They may be viewed as different kinds of propulsions within a conceptual space:

1. *Replication.* As with the luthiers, the contribution is an attempt to show that the field is in the right place. The propulsion keeps the field where it is rather than moving it. This type of creativity is represented by stationary motion, as of a wheel that is moving but staying in place.

2. *Redefinition.* The contribution is an attempt to redefine where the field is. The current status of the field thus is seen from different points of view. The propulsion leads to circular motion, such that the creative work leads back to where the field is, but as viewed in a different way.

3. *Forward Incrementation.* The contribution is an attempt to move the field forward in the direction it already is going. The propulsion leads to forward motion.

4. *Advance Forward Incrementation.* The contribution is an attempt to move the field forward in the direction it is already going, but by moving beyond where others are ready for it to go. The propulsion leads to forward motion that is accelerated beyond the expected rate of forward progression.

5. *Redirection.* The contribution is an attempt to redirect the field from where it is toward a different direction. The propulsion thus leads to motion in a direction that diverges from the way the field is currently moving.

6. *Reconstruction/Redirection.* The contribution is an attempt to move the field back to where it once was (a reconstruction of the past) so that it may move onward from that point, but in a direction different from the one it took from that point onward. The propulsion thus leads to motion that is backward and then redirective.

7. *Reinitiation.* The contribution is an attempt to move the field to a different, as-yet-unreached starting point and then to move from that point. The propulsion is thus from a new starting point in a direction that is different from that the field previously has pursued.

8. *Synthesis.* The contribution is an attempt to meld together or otherwise synthesize different existing paradigms and merge them into a new one. Thus the future direction represents a new combination of already existing vectors.

We have argued that the kind of creativity that is most widely accepted is forward incrementation, which moves a field forward while threatening almost no one.

In the world many of us imagine when we first start thinking about creativity and its role in society, the more creative a contribution is, the more it is welcomed. In fact, though, the opposite is often the case. Creative contributions defy the crowd (Sternberg & Lubart, 1995) and hence are discouraged, sometimes actively. The more creative a contribution is, the more likely it is to engender resentment and opposition.

A curiosity of creativity is that the fact that one is oneself creative in no way guarantees that one's reaction to others who are creative will be positive. Indeed, one may have struggled to gain acceptance for one's ideas in the face of opposition and then oppose others who do the same. Why might creative people become oppositional to creativity in others?

First, they may feel that they worked hard to get where they are, and they do not want to see their work overturned by upstarts who are still green behind the ears and don't know the "score." Second, they may come to believe that they and only they have the truth and that others who don't see things their way are foolish. Third, they may come to have a vested interest in their ideas – for example, in terms of professional or even financial rewards – and not wish to lose the fruits of their labor. Fourth, they may be "legislative" in their own thinking style (Sternberg, 1997) but not legislative in the thinking style they encourage in others. That is, they may view creativity as appropriate for them but not for others. Finally, they may not even realize that, when they judge the work of others in their field, they value it in part by dint of its support of their own work. Indeed, authors of articles for journals learn that if they wish to gain acceptance for their articles, they would do well to cite favorably anyone who is likely to be a peer-reviewer of their work.

Time Constraints on Creativity

Secular Time

A popular view on leadership is a contingency view, according to which a leader's success depends in large part on the match of that leader's style of leadership to the style that is suitable for the constituency he or she is to lead. Similarly, what is creative for one time or place may not be creative for another.

Norman Rockwell, an American painter, made his reputation with wonderfully romanticized and nostalgic paintings of mid-twentieth-century life in the United States. For many years, he was responsible for the covers of a magazine, the *Saturday Evening Post*. Would his artistic work have had the same success had he been born in a time of lesser nostalgia, or in a time that offered a different kind of human landscape to paint? What if he had been working today and was expected to use computerized imaging techniques? If someone had the idea today to paint in an impressionistic way, and that idea was original to him or her – the individual was unfamiliar with the Impressionists – the idea might be creative to him or her and yet not be adjudged by society as creative because many artists earlier in time had the same idea. Would that person have come up with some other creative idea that would be more creative for the times? Maybe and maybe not.

If one looks at the creative greats in any field of endeavor, one is simultaneously not looking at much larger numbers of individuals who never quite made it into the pantheon of the greats of an era. These individuals might have had comparable skills but ones that did not fit as well to the times

in which they lived. Even within the stars, there are the supernovas – the Mozarts and the Shakespeares – who dwarf the "merely" eminent (Kaufman & Beghetto, 2009).

Time of Life

Simonton (1997) has shown how individuals in different careers have different career trajectories, with their most creative work occurring at various points in their careers. Some professions, such as poetry and physics, peak young, around age 25. Other careers, such as historians, can peak several decades later. It may be in part that there is some kind of developmental creative process in which people can reach creative heights early in some fields (such as those requiring strong problem-solving skills and insight) and require more time to develop prowess in other fields.

Contextual Constraints on Creativity

Contextual constraints can be random (e.g., Emanuel Feuerstein, one of the most creative cellists of all times, lost his life early in a botched medical operation) or systemic (e.g., the same Emanuel Feuerstein grew up in a family that valued music and gave him opportunities to develop his cello-playing skills, although not so many opportunities as they gave to his violinist brother, who flamed out as an adult). But even systemic constraints are not always so easy to get a grasp on. As Sawyer (Chapter 19, this volume) notes, "Many such systems are *chaotic*, highly nonlinear and essentially impossible to explain and predict from mechanisms and laws." The constraints on creativity, therefore, are often difficult to put into a formula. That is probably part of what makes creativity always at least a bit unpredictable. Both opportunities and losses of opportunities have a great effect on what people can contribute (Gladwell, 2008).

Contextual constraints, although called as such, really depend on the interaction of the person with his or her present and past contexts. In the case of the senior author of this chapter, for example, he has almost always done his most creative work in trying to understand areas of human functioning that have posed particular challenges for him. Locher (Chapter 7, this volume) states that "there is a long history of interest, which continues to this day, in the psychological connection between an artist's personal history and his/her resulting motives for creating an artwork, as well as its content and style." This connection applies not just to artists, but to other kinds of creative individuals as well, who draw from their life experience in their attempts to understand the world.

The effect of life experience may start quite early. As Simonton (Chapter 9, this volume) put it, creative individuals can be "deflected toward divergent domains." In theory, they might have expressed their creativity in a number of different domains. But perhaps as a result of parental channeling, or peer pressure, or financial pressure, or their own internal urgings, they are pushed one way or another. They then become creative in the domain toward which they have been deflected.

As noted by Puccio and Cabra (Chapter 8, this volume), people often do not operate only in an individual context, but rather in a larger, organizational context. That organizational context can have a substantial effect on their displayed creativity. Some organizations promote, whereas others severely constrain, creative behavior.

Not only organizations, but society and culture can constrain culture. As Lubart (Chapter 14, this volume) points out, various cultures can have somewhat different conceptions of what it means to be creative and can evaluate creativity in different ways. A person who is creative in one cultural context will not necessarily be in another. There are stark differences in the numbers (as well as kinds) of creative contributions from different cultures. Some people who might have been highly creative if born into one cultural environment may not be if born into another.

Different cultures emphasize different things. For example, in a culture that does not support music, musical creativity will not have the opportunity to develop. Russ (Chapter 12, this volume) points out the importance of play for the development of creativity. Cultures that do not reward or that actually discourage play may find lesser development of creativity. Ironically, society in the contemporary United States places increasingly greater emphasis on academic programs for young children and increasingly less emphasis on play. It is possible that these respective emphases will have deleterious effects on the development of creativity in children.

The pressure for students to achieve has increased over time, in part because international comparisons of students' school achievement has made it more apparent where schools are better succeeding and where they are not, but also in part because the knowledge economies that have evolved around the world have placed a greater premium on education than was the case in the past. At the same time, some of the knowledge that schools teach can become out of date more rapidly than ever before, simply because new knowledge is being created faster than ever before. In some fields, especially the sciences and technology, new knowledge supersedes old knowledge at a lightning pace. So creativity needs to be an important part of education, even though often it is not (Beghetto, Chapter 23, this volume; Smith & Smith, Chapter 13, this volume).

Knowledge can both help and hinder creativity (Sternberg & Lubart, 1995). As Ward and Kolomyts (Chapter 5, this volume) point out, knowledge places a major constraint on creativity. You can't go beyond what is known if you don't know what is known. But as Sternberg and Lubart, among others, have pointed out, knowledge can also lead to entrenchment or crystallization so that it becomes increasingly difficult to see things in novel ways.

The greater emphasis on advanced forms of knowledge in the modern world, which leads to ever-more-rapid knowledge creation, has created something of a paradox. The more important knowledge becomes, the faster that knowledge becomes outdated. So the greater the pressure to acquire new knowledge, the shorter will be the half-life of the knowledge that one has acquired. As a result, the knowledge base acquired in schooling will not be adequate for a person's lifetime or even, likely, the first half of that person's career. As editors, we have both seen the effects in our own lives. The senior editor, for example, received a doctorate in 1975 in psychology, and few of the research findings that formed the core of his doctoral education then are even much cited today. The junior editor was one of the first generations to take advantage of such now commonplace tools as research journal databases.

The virtually inescapable conclusion from these facts is that academic knowledge and skills as taught at a given secular time in history will be inadequate to meet the needs of a rapidly changing world, and as many of the authors of chapters point out, creativity, and more generally, skill in coping with novel environments, is more important than ever. Indeed, at different times, creativity has also been viewed in different ways (Runco & Albert, Chapter 1, this volume). Yet there is general agreement that schools around the world, today as in the past, on average, do little to develop creativity. Indeed, the greater the emphasis is on high-stakes assessment, the less is the emphasis on creativity.

This consensus among the contributors to this handbook is not based on facts that are particularly obscure. The question then is why creativity is not afforded more importance in schools, which are the main socializing agents of children in our society. There are probably several reasons (see also Beghetto, Chapter 23, this volume).

First, as noted in the *Handbook*, conventional standardized tests do not value creativity and, at best, are indifferent to it and, at worst, are discouraging of it. Teacher-made tests typically are no different. When the senior author was in college, the professor teaching his introductory psychology course utilized both multiple-choice and essay examinations. The author made the

mistake of thinking that the essays were the opportunity for creative thinking. On the contrary, after the tests, the professor passed out a list of the points he expected one to make in each essay. Thus, the essay tests were actually unstructured recall tests, where the student had to second-guess what the professor had in mind. Even in writing sections of standardized tests, computer-based scoring typically yields intercorrelations of the computer-based assessments with human raters that are at least as high as the intercorrelations of human raters with each other. It would be conceivable to devise scoring programs that sought out creativity, but that is not what these programs do. On the contrary, the elements of writing that are valued are formulaic and, if anything, antithetical to creativity in writing.

It might not matter much what tests measure were it not the case that teachers teach to tests, whether their own or standardized ones, so the more tests emphasize basic knowledge and skills and the less they emphasize creativity, the more teaching will be orthogonal or antithetical to the development of creative thinking.

Second, it is much easier to teach for rote recall or even for basic comprehension and analysis than it is to teach for creative thinking. Teachers generally have not been trained in a way that develops their pedagogical skills in teaching for creative thinking. As a result, if they are to teach and assess for creative thinking, they are largely on their own in finding methods. Teaching for creativity takes additional time, and time is often something that teachers have relatively little of.

Third, although it might seem to those who have bothered to read or write for this volume that creativity is important in schooling, it might be much less obvious to others. They might believe that there just is not time to teach for creative thinking. But more likely, perhaps, they believe that creativity is a superordinate skill one masters only *after* one has acquired a knowledge base and learned to think critically about it. In Bloom's taxonomy, for example, creative thinking, which occurs under synthesis, is at the fifth of six hierarchical levels. Below it are knowledge, understanding, application, and analysis. There is no empirical evidence that strongly supports the taxonomy, but there are few teachers who do not learn it, and many use it. Teachers may believe that creativity is simply too "high-falutin" for the students they teach. Similarly, creative students may be seen as rebellious, difficult, and overly time consuming. A related view is that creativity is something that might be relevant in teaching gifted students but is not something that is relevant for more typical students. On this view, creativity is a part of giftedness, and those who are not gifted simply do not have it.

Fourth is the reward system that is in place for teachers. Teachers may be rewarded if students' test scores go up. They are less likely to be rewarded for teaching in ways that encourage creativity. Indeed, such teaching may be viewed by administrators as well as by parents as wasting student time that could be more productively spent in instruction that increases test scores.

Fifth and finally is sheer inertia. When things have been done a certain way for a long time, it is difficult to get people to change what they do. Teaching for creativity would, in most schools, be a novelty, and with all the other novelties competing for attention, this one may not win out. It is easier to do things the way they have always been done before.

Negative Mechanisms for Constraining Creativity

There are a number of mechanisms in place in virtually any society that tend to constrain creativity.

At one extreme is societal acceptance, within a domain, of only one ideology. This ideology could be political, as in the case of countries that have only one viable political party; if there are others, they exist only if they are allowed and often more for show than for anything else. But the ideology also could be scientific, artistic, educational, or of anything else. For example,

in the days of behaviorism, it was difficult to get accepted into a prestigious scientific journal a psychological article that made reference to internal states, especially if the states were of consciousness, which became practically a taboo word. When there is just one prevailing ideology, it tends to stamp out others, and indeed, has probably stayed the sole prevailing ideology in part because of its success in stamping out creative competitors.

At the other extreme, an anarchic system also may discourage creativity because those who prevail are those who have the most power within the constraints of the system, and there is no guarantee that the most powerful person or group will be the most creative. Creativity and brute force do not necessarily go together. Or those who are most powerful may be creative, but not necessarily in ways that will move the society forward.

One would expect that the form of government that most would promote creativity is a democracy, and this may well be true, but there is no guarantee that even a democracy will promote creativity. Where the majority rules, creativity may actually be squelched. To the extent that creative people make others uncomfortable, being creative may actually result in one's being rejected by any voting procedure. Langlois and Roggman (1990) report that people found that the most beautiful faces were those that were actually the most average. The greater number of different faces that were averaged to form a computer composite, the more attractive the averaged face was. Similarly, the individual may be viewed as most socially desirable who best represents the consensus of a group rather than a creative departure from its prevailing ideology. Being creative requires some amount of deviating from the norm.

Many people find, in terms of the propulsion theory described above, that the ideas that are most rewarded are small forward incrementations – ideas that move an existing state of affairs forward, but not by too much. If an idea is viewed as too radical, it is likely to be rejected. In a way, democratic society is set up so that majority rule will not favor departures from existing practice that are too radical, unless existing practice is seen as so inadequate that bold new steps are needed. For example, as president, Barack Obama has an unusual situation in that the economic situation of the country is so bad that people may be willing to go along with changes that, in a better economy, they would not risk.

Often, when products are evaluated, there are several judges (see Plucker and Makel, Chapter 3, this volume). Using a mean rating of these several judges is at heart a fairly conservative procedure that also places constraints on creativity. Here is why.

Consider as an example the funding of grant proposals, regardless of field of endeavor. The more creative an idea is, the more likely it is to arouse opposition. Moreover, if the selection ratio for funding is very low – that is, few grant proposals can be funded – then the likelihood is that highly creative proposals will do even worse. For one thing, funding agencies will be more reluctant to take risks. For another, if even one evaluator has a negative view of a proposal, then that evaluator will bring down the mean, and it may be that, with strict funding constraints, even one negative review will be enough to knock a grant proposal out of the competition.

The same principle applies in the case of admissions situations. One way to increase the creativity of a society is to admit more creative people into competitive schools, whether they be private schools, colleges, graduate programs, or professional programs. But if the selection ratio is very low, then schools will be reluctant to take risks, and safe candidates who do not upset any members of a selection committee are more likely to be selected. The same principle applies to hiring for jobs. So in intensely competitive situations, whatever their nature, creative or offbeat applicants may be rejected because they are perceived as involving risks that the selecting or hiring institution does not feel it has to take.

An oddity is, then, that the more an institution needs creative ideas, the less it may be willing to risk them. Consider a corporate situation, such as that of the Detroit automakers over the past 25 years. Two of three automakers went into bankruptcy proceedings. To the person on the street, it is somewhat hard to understand how this could be. The companies had 25 years or so to catch up with German and Japanese automobile manufacturers who came to lead the pack in terms of design, technology, marketing, and sales. How could they lose the opportunity to catch up, with so much time on their hands?

The same principle that applies to grant proposals or college applicants applies to businesses or other organizations. As they begin to feel pressure, they need more and more to take a risk. But at the same time, their margin for risk narrows. A risk that might be acceptable when an organization has a large cash or even reputational cushion may seem less acceptable when even a small loss on the risk can mean bankruptcy and ruin. So, as the organization needs more and more to take a creative risk, it becomes less and less willing to do so.

The senior author once gave an invited address at a manufacturing company that had fallen on hard times. The company's management realized it needed creatively to innovate, and asked the author to speak on creative innovation, which he did. After he spoke, the company's CEO got up and spoke. He thanked the speaker for his talk, and then reassured the audience that, in these perilous times, the company was not going to be cowed and was going to do a much better job of what it had been doing before, assuring success. The company went bankrupt not long afterward.

In the investment theory of creativity (Sternberg & Lubart, 1995), creativity is viewed as, in large part, an attitude toward life: Creative people defy the crowd by buying low and selling high in the world of ideas. We have seen that there are external constraints on buying low and selling high – on being creative. But there are also internal constraints that begin within the individual.

Internal Constraints on Creativity

Suppose one takes a risk, and does something creative. In most instances, one will generate opposition, especially in the short term. The question is how much time one has to show that the creative innovation will pay off in the long-term. Often, the time frame is short, especially in the case of individuals or organizations that have to produce quarterly or even annual reports. People usually want gains now, not later. If they make short-term gains, they may not care much about long-term strategy. If they are taking short-term losses, they may not give a creative idea time to show what potentially it could yield.

Historically, four out of five professionally managed stock mutual funds have done worse than the S&P 500 average. So why pay money to have a fund professionally managed? Many people have answered this question by buying into index funds that simply track the S&P 500 – they do not seek to do better than the market average. Others invest in the professionally managed funds, and may be so eager for gains that they do not even bother to ask whether the gains they are exhibiting are the result of a creative strategy that defies the crowd – the information already built into stock prices – or rather is a result of a creative fraud. That Bernard Madoff could get away as long as he did with the financial chicanery in which he engaged shows the great extent to which people will go not to ask questions.

When one does behave creatively and engender opposition, one has to decide whether to succumb to the pressures to get back with whatever the existing program is. Many people who go too creative end up paying for it by losing their jobs. They depart from the organizational norm and are viewed as a threat to the stability of the organization. To those who fire them, these individuals are not viewed as creative, but rather as dangers to the organization's well-being. So people learn on jobs, as they often do in school, that creativity comes with a price tag.

This depiction of events may make it sound as though the constraints on creativity are unfair and counterproductive. Often they are. But not always, and that is part of the problem. They may be perfectly reasonable in some instances. To pick an extreme example: A researcher believes that as a result of his great creativity, he has discovered a way to prevent burns when skin is exposed to fire. He is confident that the ointment he has invented will essentially make a person burn-proof. He tries out the ointment on himself and burns to death.

There are times when the risk-reward ratio of a creative idea is simply too great and it is foolish to pursue the idea. The anti-burn ointment is an example, but of course there are many others. The United States has the Federal Drug Administration (FDA) to ensure that creative ideas for new medications do not result in people's being gravely injured or even dying as the result of unexpected side effects of newly proposed medications. When there have been failures, they often have been dramatic, as in the case of Fen-Phen, a diet pill that led to heart-valve damage, or more recently, Vioxx, an anti-inflammatory associated with cardiovascular damage. Rezulin, an anti-diabetes drug, was pulled off the market when its side effects were found to be more negative than the good that it was believed to produce for diabetics.

The unanswered question is just what level of risk-reward ratio is high enough to suppress what may appear to be a highly creative idea. People with chronic ailments who are close to death may be willing to take chances that are far greater than those that normally would be taken by those with only minor acute illnesses. Yet no society can have a set of rules that is completely flexible with regard to risks and rewards. The ratio may be set somewhere in a middle that characterizes relatively few people, so that those with minor problems are allowed too much risk and those with major problems too little.

The issue of risk-reward ratio pervades all creativity, perhaps posing the most serious constraint. It applies at all levels.

Individuals may decide against creativity, merely because it exposes them to risk that they deem unacceptable. Why risk your job when you can do it a little less creatively or perhaps a lot less so, and retain it? Why risk your grades in classrooms when, by taking fewer creative risks, you are likely to please teachers more, not less?

Societies send to their children all kinds of signals about how constrained creativity is within the society, without even realizing it. The senior author has consulted several times in a society that, overtly, rewards creativity. Indeed, he has been hired to work with various agencies to enhance the creativity of students within that society. But at the same time, the messages children (and adults) receive through tacit communications are that risks must be taken within very narrowly defined domains. The risk of criticizing the government, even verbally, is profound and likely will result in civil or even criminal action that will put a person out of commission for many years to come. When the tacit signals conflict with the explicit ones, people are likely to follow the tacit ones, as people respond more to what others do rather than what they say. Actions do indeed speak louder than words.

Risk is not the only internal constraint on creativity. There are others, and what makes them so effective is that the individual is usually not even aware that they exist. Most of these constraints involve both skills and attitudes. The attitude is relevant in determining whether one even tries to release oneself from the constraint. The skill is relevant in determining one's effectiveness in releasing oneself from the constraint. Our goal here is not to list all possible internal constraints but merely to make the point that such internal constraints are at least as powerful as external constraints in reducing levels of potential creativity.

A first constraint is in one's willingness and ability to redefine existing problems in new terms. Some creative work is done because an individual sees things that others see, but in a new way. Alexander Fleming's discovery of penicillin, for example, depended on his seeing bacteria-destroying mold in a Petri dish not merely as a spoiled culture, but as a useful culture for showing that the mold from which penicillin is derived (penicillium) is useful for its antibacterial properties. Monet saw the same scenes that others saw, but he was able to recreate them in an Impressionistic way that formed one basis for an entire movement in art. When Paul Gauguin did not find in Tahiti the scenes he had imagined he would find, he recreated the landscape he viewed so as to include what he had hoped to see. That is, he redefined the problem of his painting as not what he saw but rather what he had hoped he would see!

A second constraint is in one's willingness to be critical of one's own creative work. When one looks at great works of art using modern ultraviolet fluorescence technology, one often sees layers representing discarded ideas beneath the layers of paint that comprise the final painting. The artists realized that the painting was not quite what they wanted and they painted over what they had done. Similarly, notebooks of authors often show that their final writings are somewhat different from what they had originally planned. In science, scientists often have to go through many revisions before an article is accepted for publication. If they do not find the flaws in their own work, external referees very likely will.

A third constraint is in one's willingness to overcome the obstacles that typically block creative work. Creative ideas often do not sell themselves – it is up to the creator or others representing the creator to overcome these obstacles. Thus we end up with cases such as Vincent Van Gogh, whose creativity was not appreciated during his lifetime, or Ignaz Semmelweis, the medical doctor whose advice to other doctors to wash their hands to reduce sepsis was treated with ridicule and resulted, ultimately, in his being institutionalized (and later dying of sepsis in the institution to which he was committed).

A fourth constraint is in the entrenchment that accompanies developing expertise. Once one gets used to looking at things in a certain way, it can become increasingly difficult to see them in another way.

In effect, one becomes a prisoner of one's own expertise. Arguably, an example could be drawn from one of the founding fathers of the creativity movement, J. P. Guilford, one of the great psychologists of his era. Guilford proposed early in his career a cube model for human abilities. The number of abilities in the cube kept increasing until it eventually reached 180. Because the cube was set up with orthogonal dimensions, it became increasingly hard to argue for the orthogonality of all 120, then 150, and then 180 dimensions, but Guilford nevertheless tried to make such an argument. A fifth constraint is motivational. Research suggests that creative people are generally those who are doing what they love to do – they are intrinsically motivated (Hennessey, Chapter 18, this volume). But people often choose vocations or other activities not because the activities represent what they want to do but rather for other reasons – money, fame, social pressure, availability of routes to success, or even basic survival. So one may be constrained by one's own choices, whether limited by society or by one's own set of values.

Resource Constraints on Creativity

In a society that forbids music – there are any number of fundamentalist societies of this kind today – a child will have little or no opportunity to develop creativity in this area, no matter how potentially musical the child is. In a preliterate society, one never discovers whether one of its members will be a creative writer. The opportunity to be creative simply never arises. Similarly, many of today's discoveries in science and engineering would not have been possible without the computing facilities that are available at the present time. If the resources are not there, the discovery or invention cannot be realized.

We probably tend, as societies, to underestimate the importance of resource constraints. The senior author once did some work with collaborators in a city in north-

ern India, Lucknow. As is the case in many countries, including the United States, children who grow up in slums may barely have an opportunity to get any education at all. They may in fact develop high levels of creativity in survival skills, but this is not the kind of creativity that will be remembered historically. It may be an example of little-c rather than Big-C creativity. Of course, for those who are acutely or chronically short of funds, creativity may be directed toward the "dark side," for example, to illegally acquiring resources in creative ways. The shortage of funds need not be objective. Bernard Madoff, one of the great swindlers of modern times, had enough money to live a comfortable life, but it was never enough.

Ironically, the child who grows up with many privileges may have much less opportunity to develop her or his creativity than the child growing up in the slums. If everything is done for the child, and the child has little opportunity to show initiative, then whatever latent potentials there are for creative work may be suppressed because there is no need to develop these potentials. Or the potentials may be directed in destructive ways, such as terrorism (Cropley, Kaufman, & Cropley, 2008).

Task Constraints on Creativity

Someone may have the potential for creativity but simply not have the chance to execute tasks that allow much creativity. For example, a welder on an assembly line may be expected to do a perfect weld – there is no real room for creativity. On the contrary, each weld is supposed to be exactly the same and entirely uncreative. And this may be one of many cases in which creativity is actually not desirable.

Higher level cognitive tasks also do not necessarily encourage or even allow creativity. When taking a multiple-choice test, students are creative only at their peril. When the senior author was a college freshman, his first tests were essay tests; he mistakenly thought that the professor therefore wished the students to be creative in answering the essay questions. In fact, he had 10 points in mind that he wanted students to make on each essay, and one's score was the number of points one made out of the 10 that the professor wished the student to make.

In organizational settings, tasks are often highly constrained. One is allowed to be creative, but only within those fairly tight constraints. For example, if one is fund-raising for an organization, the targets for one's efforts and the particular causes for which one is expected to raise money may be quite constrained. For example, a limited number of wealthy individuals or corporations provide the majority of donations. It will be unhelpful if one is too creative in soliciting people with no disposable income. One's creativity may be allowed only in how one raises the money from given individuals or organizations, and even here, there may be constraints in what one is allowed to say to raise the funds.

Conclusion

In this chapter, we have sought to discuss some of the constraints that exist on creativity. These constraints can originate with the definition of creativity itself – work can be creative only if it is both novel and useful in some way. Other constraints are internal to the person or external to the society. The two kinds of constraints interact: Someone who is constantly beaten down as a result of being creative may give up and simply decide not to be creative again.

Constraints do not necessarily harm creative potential – indeed, they are built into the construct of creativity itself. Many consider the haiku to be an ultimate creative expression precisely because only a handful of words is allowed. What makes a person or product creative is the flair of originality constrained by usefulness, and the benefit of usefulness constrained by originality.

References

Amabile, T. M. (1996). *Creativity in context: Update to the social psychology of creativity.* Boulder, CO: Westview.

Barron, F. (1961). Creative vision and expression in writing and painting. In D. W. MacKinnon (Ed.), *The creative person* (pp. 237–251). Berkeley: Institute of Personality Assessment Research, University of California.

Connell, M. W., Sheridan, K., & Gardner, H. (2003). On abilities and domains. In R. Sternberg (Ed.), *Psychology of abilities, competencies and expertise* (pp. 126–155). New York: Cambridge University Press.

Cropley, D. H., Kaufman, J. C., & Cropley, A. J. (2008). Malevolent creativity: A functional model of creativity in terrorism and crime. *Creativity Research Journal, 20,* 105–115.

Gladwell, M. (2008). *Outliers.* New York: Little, Brown.

Kaufman, J. C., & Beghetto, R. A. (2009). Beyond big and little: The Four C Model of creativity. *Review of General Psychology, 13,* 1–12.

Keinänen, M., & Gardner, H. (2004). Vertical and horizontal mentoring for creativity. In R. J. Sternberg, E. L. Grigorenko, J. L. Singer (Eds.), *Creativity: From potential to realization* (pp. 169–193). Washington, DC: American Psychological Association.

Keinänen, M., Sheridan, K., & Gardner, H. (2006). Opening up creativity: The lenses of axis and focus. In J. C. Kaufman & J. Baer (Eds.), *Creativity and reason in cognitive development* (pp. 202–218). New York: Cambridge University Press.

King, R. (2006). *The Judgment of Paris.* New York: Walker & Company.

Langlois, J. H., & Roggman, L. A. (1990). Attractive faces are only average. *Psychological Science, 1,* 115–121.

MacKinnon, D. W. (1961). Creativity in architects. In D. W. MacKinnon (Ed.), *The creative person* (pp. 291–320). Berkeley: Institute of Personality Assessment Research, University of California.

Martindale, C. (1999). Biological basis of creativity. In R. J. Sternberg (Ed.), *Handbook of creativity* (pp. 137–152). Cambridge, UK: Cambridge University Press.

Merton, R. K. (1979). *The sociology of science.* Chicago: University of Chicago Press.

Simonton, D. K. (1997). Creative productivity: A predictive and explanatory model of career trajectories and landmarks. *Psychological Review*, 104, 66–89.

Sternberg, R. J. (1997). *Thinking styles.* New York: Cambridge University Press.

Sternberg, R. J. (1999). A propulsion model of types of creative contributions. *Review of General Psychology*, 3, 83–100.

Sternberg, R. J. (2005). The domain generality versus domain specificity debate: How should it be posed? In J. C. Kaufman & J. Baer (Eds.), *Creativity across domains: Faces of the muse* (pp. 299–306). Hillsdale, NJ: Erlbaum.

Sternberg, R. J., & Davidson, J. E. (1983). Insight in the gifted. *Educational Psychologist*, 18, 51–57.

Sternberg, R. J., Kaufman, J. C., & Pretz, J. E. (2002). *The creativity conundrum: A propulsion model of kinds of creative contributions.* New York: Psychology Press.

Sternberg, R. J., & Lubart, T. I. (1995). *Defying the crowd: Cultivating creativity in a culture of conformity.* New York: Free Press.

Stokes, P. D. (2005). *Creativity from constraints: The psychology of breakthrough.* New York: Springer.

Index

creativity, 147
Institute of Personality Assessment and
    Research, 387
intelligence, 192
    creativity, 425
    fluid intelligence and creativity, 401
    GDP, 397
    genotype, 398
intelligence quotient
    heritability and SES, 398
    socioeconomic status (SES), 396
intelligence tests
    measuring creativity, 400
intrinsic motivation, 122, 343
    curiosity, 343
    evaluation, 356
    flow, 351
    principle of creativity, 351
intuition, 200
investment theory of creativity, 477
IPAR. *See also* Institute of Personality
    Assessment and Research
IQ
    creativity, 470

Jamison, Kay, 387

Kinney, Dennis, 190
knowledge, 422
Kozbelt, Aaron, 133
Kroeber, Alfred
    Configuration of Culture Growth, 175

lack of specificity, 369
latent inhibition, 225
lateral thinking, 160
LCS. *See also* Lifetime Creativity Scales
leader behaviors
    creativity, 164
leadership, 163
Lifetime Creativity Scales, 190, 191
    fluency, 191
    peak creativity, 191
    vocational and avocational, 191
little-c, 23, 193, 233
    self-expression, 82
Ludwig, Arnold, 387, 388

Mad-genius controversy, 415
Mad-genius stereotype, 383, 384
making artwork, 132
malevolant creativity, 415
Martindale, Colin
    Theory of creative cognition, 222
McNeil, Linda

standardization mandates, 452
meaningfulness, 206
Mednick, Sara, 415
Meta-analysis, 391
metabolism of the new, 206
metacognitive processes, 32
meta-representational thought, 283
mimetic mode, 281
mindlessness, 414
mini-c, 24, 193, 258
model of the creative personality, 114
    brain plasticity, 117
    clinical traits, 123
    cognitive personality traits, 120
    genetic explanations of personality, 115
    Motivational traits, 122
    Social traits of personality, 121
moderation
    pluralism, 20
motivation, 150, 325
    effects of reward, 346
Multicultural experiences and creativity,
    274
Murray, Charles
    Human Accomplishment, 175

national culture, 151
natural selection, 288
negative moods, 356
Nettle, Daniel, 387
neural basis. *See* Bogen, Joseph
neuroaesthetics, 140
    brain activation, 141
    functional magnetic resonance imaging,
    141
neurons, 285
niches, 288
No Child Left Behind, 252
nonreductive individualism, 372
novelty, 467

Ocean, Humphrey, 135, 141
organizational creativity, 145
    models, 148
organizational culture, 155
original genius vs. talent, 8
originality, 206

Pandora's Box, 195
Pennebaker study, 195
perception among art students vs. non-artists
    Kozbelt, Aaron, 133
perceptual processes during art making
    eyetracker, 135
person, 149